Related Books of In

Patterns of Information Management

By Mandy Chessell and Harald C. Smith

ISBN: 978-0-13-315550-1

Use Best Practice Patterns to Understand and Architect Manageable, Efficient Information Supply Chains That Help You Leverage All Your Data and Knowledge

Building on the analogy of a supply chain, Mandy Chessell and Harald Smith explain how information can be transformed, enriched, reconciled, redistributed, and utilized in even the most complex environments. Through a realistic, end-to-end case study, they help you blend overlapping information management, SOA, and BPM technologies that are often viewed as competitive.

Using this book's patterns, you can integrate all levels of your architecture—from holistic, enterprise, system-level views down to low-level design elements. You can fully address key non-functional requirements such as the amount, quality, and pace of incoming data. Above all, you can create an IT landscape that is coherent, interconnected, efficient, effective, and manageable.

The Business of IT
How to Improve Service and Lower Costs

By Robert Ryan and Tim Raducha-Grace

ISBN: 978-0-13-700061-6

Drive More Business Value from IT...and Bridge the Gap Between IT and Business Leadership

IT organizations have achieved outstanding technological maturity, but many have been slower to adopt world-class business practices. This book provides IT and business executives with methods to achieve greater business discipline throughout IT, collaborate more effectively, sharpen focus on the customer, and drive greater value from IT investment. Drawing on their experience consulting with leading IT organizations, Robert Ryan and Tim Raducha-Grace help IT leaders make sense of alternative ways to improve IT service and lower cost, including ITIL, IT financial management, balanced scorecards, and business cases. You'll learn how to choose the best approaches to improve IT business practices for your environment and use these practices to improve service quality, reduce costs, and drive top-line revenue growth.

Related Books of Interest

The Art of Enterprise Information Architecture

A Systems-Based Approach for Unlocking Business Insight

By Mario Godinez, Eberhard Hechler, Klaus Koenig, Steve Lockwood, Martin Oberhofer, and Michael Schroeck
ISBN: 978-0-13-703571-7

Architecture for the Intelligent Enterprise: Powerful New Ways to Maximize the Real-Time Value of Information

Tomorrow's winning "Intelligent Enterprises" will bring together far more diverse sources of data, analyze it in more powerful ways, and deliver immediate insight to decision-makers throughout the organization. Today, however, most companies fail to apply the information they already have, while struggling with the complexity and costs of their existing information environments.

In this book, a team of IBM's leading information management experts guide you on a journey that will take you from where you are today toward becoming an "Intelligent Enterprise."

The New Era of Enterprise Business Intelligence:

Using Analytics to Achieve a Global Competitive Advantage

By Mike Biere
ISBN: 978-0-13-707542-3

A Complete Blueprint for Maximizing the Value of Business Intelligence in the Enterprise

The typical enterprise recognizes the immense potential of business intelligence (BI) and its impact upon many facets within the organization—but it's not easy to transform BI's potential into real business value. Top BI expert Mike Biere presents a complete blueprint for creating winning BI strategies and infrastructure and systematically maximizing the value of information throughout the enterprise.

This product-independent guide brings together start-to-finish guidance and practical checklists for every senior IT executive, planner, strategist, implementer, and the actual business users themselves.

 Listen to the author's podcast at:
ibmpressbooks.com/podcasts

Related Books of Interest

Mining the Talk
Unlocking the Business Value in Unstructured Information

Spangler, Kreulen

ISBN: 978-0-13-233953-7

Decision Management Systems
A Practical Guide to Using Business Rules and Predictive Analytics

Taylor

ISBN: 978-0-13-288438-9

Enterprise Master Data Management
An SOA Approach to Managing Core Information

By Allen Dreibelbis, Eberhard Hechler, Ivan Milman, Martin Oberhofer, Paul Van Run, and Dan Wolfson

ISBN: 978-0-13-236625-0

The Only Complete Technical Primer for MDM Planners, Architects, and Implementers

Enterprise Master Data Management provides an authoritative, vendor-independent MDM technical reference for practitioners: architects, technical analysts, consultants, solution designers, and senior IT decision makers. Written by the IBM® data management innovators who are pioneering MDM, this book systematically introduces MDM's key concepts and technical themes, explains its business case, and illuminates how it interrelates with and enables SOA.

Drawing on their experience with cutting-edge projects, the authors introduce MDM patterns, blueprints, solutions, and best practices published nowhere else—everything you need to establish a consistent, manageable set of master data, and use it for competitive advantage.

IBM Cognos Business Intelligence v10
The Complete Guide

Gautam

ISBN: 978-0-13-272472-2

IBM Cognos 10 Report Studio
Practical Examples

Draskovic, Johnson

ISBN: 978-0-13-265675-7

Data Integration Blueprint and Modeling
Techniques for a Scalable and Sustainable Architecture

Giordano

ISBN: 978-0-13-708493-7

Praise for
Getting Started with Data Science

"A coauthor and I once wrote that data scientists held 'the sexiest job of the 21st century.' This was not because of their inherent sex appeal, but because of their scarcity and value to organizations. This book may reduce the scarcity of data scientists, but it will certainly increase their value. It teaches many things, but most importantly it teaches how to tell a story with data."

—Thomas H. Davenport, Distinguished Professor, Babson College;
Research Fellow, MIT; author of *Competing on Analytics* and *Big Data @ Work*

"We have produced more data in the last two years than all of human history combined. Whether you are in business, government, academia, or journalism, the future belongs to those who can analyze these data intelligently. This book is a superb introduction to data analytics, a must-read for anyone contemplating how to integrate big data into their everyday decision making."

—Professor Atif Mian, Theodore A. Wells '29 Professor of Economics and
Public Affairs, Princeton University;
Director of the Julis-Rabinowitz Center for Public Policy and Finance
at the Woodrow Wilson School; author of the best-selling book *The House of Debt*

"The power of data, evidence, and analytics in improving decision-making for individuals, businesses, and governments is well known and well documented. However, there is a huge gap in the availability of material for those who should use data, evidence, and analytics but do not know how. This fascinating book plugs this gap, and I highly recommend it to those who know this field and those who want to learn."

—Munir A. Sheikh, Ph.D., Former Chief Statistician of Canada;
Distinguished Fellow and Adjunct Professor at Queen's University

"*Getting Started with Data Science* (*GSDS*) is unlike any other book on data science you might have come across. While most books on the subject treat data science as a collection of techniques that lead to a string of insights, Murtaza shows how the application of data science leads to uncovering of coherent stories about reality. *GSDC* is a hands-on book that makes data science come alive."

—Chuck Chakrapani, Ph.D., President, Leger Analytics

"This book addresses the key challenge facing data science today, that of bridging the gap between analytics and business value. Too many writers dive immediately into the details of specific statistical methods or technologies, without focusing on this bigger picture. In contrast, Haider identifies the central role of narrative in delivering real value from big data.

"The successful data scientist has the ability to translate between business goals and statistical approaches, identify appropriate deliverables, and communicate them in a compelling and comprehensible way that drives meaningful action. To paraphrase Tukey, 'Far better an approximate answer to the right question, than an exact answer to a wrong one.' Haider's book never loses sight of this central tenet and uses many real-world examples to guide the reader through the broad range of skills, techniques, and tools needed to succeed in practical data-science.

"Highly recommended to anyone looking to get started or broaden their skillset in this fast-growing field."

—Dr. Patrick Surry, Chief Data Scientist, www.Hopper.com

Getting Started with Data Science

Making Sense of Data with Analytics

Murtaza Haider

IBM Press: Pearson plc
Boston • Columbus • Indianapolis • New York • San Francisco
Amsterdam • Cape Town • Dubai • London • Madrid • Milan • Munich
Paris • Montreal • Toronto • Delhi • Mexico City • Sao Paulo • Sidney
Hong Kong • Seoul • Singapore • Taipei • Tokyo

ibmpressbooks.com

Note to U.S. Government Users: Documentation related to restricted right. Use, duplication, or disclosure is subject to restrictions set forth in GSA ADP Schedule Contract with IBM Corporation.

IBM Press Program Managers: Steven M. Stansel, Natalie Troia
Cover design: IBM Corporation

Associate Publisher: Dave Dusthimer
Marketing Manager: Stephane Nakib
Executive Editor: Mary Beth Ray
Publicist: Heather Fox
Editorial Assistant: Vanessa Evans
Development Editor: Box Twelve Communications
Managing Editor: Kristy Hart
Cover Designer: Alan Clements
Senior Project Editor: Lori Lyons
Copy Editor: Paula Lowell
Senior Indexer: Cheryl Lenser
Senior Compositor: Gloria Schurick
Proofreader: Kathy Ruiz
Manufacturing Buyer: Dan Uhrig

Published by Pearson plc

Publishing as IBM Press

For information about buying this title in bulk quantities, or for special sales opportunities (which may include electronic versions; custom cover designs; and content particular to your business, training goals, marketing focus, or branding interests), please contact our corporate sales department at corpsales@pearsoned.com or (800) 382-3419.

For government sales inquiries, please contact governmentsales@pearsoned.com.

For questions about sales outside the U.S., please contact international@pearsoned.com.

This book is dedicated to my parents, Lily and Ajaz

Contents-at-a-Glance

Contents

Chapter 9 Categorically Speaking About Categorical Data 349

Chapter 10 Spatial Data Analytics 415

Preface

It was arguably the largest trading floor in Canada. Yet when it came to data and analytics, parts of the trading floor were still stuck in the digital Stone Age.

It was the mid-nineties, and I was a new immigrant in Toronto trying to find my place in a new town. I had to my credit a civil engineering degree and two years of experience as a newspaper reporter. The Fixed Income Derivatives desk at BMO Nesbitt Burns, a Toronto-based investment brokerage, was searching for a data analyst. I was good in Excel and proficient in engineering-grade Calculus. I applied for the job and landed it.

I was intimidated, to say the least, on the very first day I walked onto the sprawling trading floor. Right in the heart of downtown Toronto, a vast floor with thousands of computer screens, specialized telephone panels, huge fax machines, and men dressed in expensive suits with a telephone set in each hand, were busy buying and selling stocks, bonds, derivatives, and other financial products.

I walked over to the Derivatives desk where a small group of youngish traders greeted me with the least bit of hospitality and lots of disinterest. I was supposed to work for them.

My job was to determine the commission owed to Nesbitt Burns by other brokerages for the trades executed by the Derivatives traders. Before Futures, Options, and other securities are traded, the brokerages representing buyers and sellers draw up contracts to set commissions for the trade. Thus, for every executed trade, the agents representing buyers and sellers receive their agreed upon commissions. The Derivatives desk had fallen behind in invoicing other brokerages for their commission. My job was to analyze the trading data and determine how much other brokerages owed to Nesbitt Burns.

I was introduced to the person responsible for the task. She had been struggling with the volume of trades, so I was hired to assist her. Because she was not trained in statistics or analytics, she did what a layperson would have done with the task.

She received daily trades data in a text file that she re-keyed in Excel. This was the most time-consuming and redundant step in the process. The data identified other brokerages, the number of trades executed, and the respective commission for each block of trades executed. After she had entered the data from the printouts of the digital text files, she would then sort the data by brokerages and use Excel's **Subtotal** command to determine the daily commissions owed by other brokerages. She would tabulate the entire month in roughly 30 different Excel files, and then add the owed commissions using her large accounting calculator. Finally, she would type up the invoice for each brokerage in Microsoft® Word.

I knew right away that with her methodology, we would never be able to catch up. I also knew that this could be done much faster. Therefore, I got on with the task.

I first determined that the text files containing raw data were in fixed width format that allowed me to import them directly into Excel using the `Import` Function. Once I perfected the automated importing, I asked my superiors to include a month's worth of trading data in each text file. They were able to oblige.

This improved the most time-consuming part of the process. Right there, I had eliminated the need to re-key the data. As soon as I received the text file carrying a month's worth of trade data, I would import it into Microsoft Excel.

With data imported in a spreadsheet, I was ready to analyze it. I did not sort data and then obtain subtotals for each brokerage. Instead, I used Pivot Tables, which were part of the Excel's Data Analysis toolpack. Within seconds, I had a table ready with a brokerage-by-brokerage breakdown of amounts owed. The task that took weeks in the past took me less than 10 minutes to accomplish.

I was elated. Using analytics, I had solved a problem that troubled workers at one of the most sophisticated workplaces in Canada. At the same time, I realized the other big problem I was about to create for myself. If I were to advise my employers of the breakthrough, they might have no need for me anymore. Using analytics, I had effectively made my job redundant.

I came up with a plan and shared it with one of the traders, David Barkway—who, unfortunately, died later on September 11, 2001, at the World Trade Center.[1] He was there to meet with bond traders at Cantor Fitzgerald. David was the scholarly looking, well-mannered person on the Derivatives Desk who had helped me with the project. I shared with him my breakthrough. He advised me to renegotiate my contract to include the additional responsibilities to recover the amounts. I took his advice and was fortunate to have a renegotiated contract.

Within weeks, I had switched to Microsoft Access and automated the entire task, including data import, analysis, and invoice generation. I would then fax invoices to my counterparts at other brokerages. I successfully recovered substantial amounts for Nesbitt Burns. A year later, I quit and started graduate studies at the University of Toronto.

Why I Wrote This Book

The day I left Nesbitt Burns, I knew that one day I would write a book on analytics. I did not realize then it would take me 19 years to write the book. Since Nesbitt, I have completed consulting assignments for numerous public and private sector agencies. In every consulting assignment, I walked away with the same realization that a little bit of improvement in data savviness would significantly improve the profitability of these firms.

---

1. Haider, M. (2011, September 11). "They killed my husband." Retrieved September 13, 2015, from http://www.dawn.com/2011/09/11/they-killed-my-husband-for-no-good-reason/

In 2005, I helped establish the Geographic Information Systems (GIS) Laboratory for the Federal Bureau of Statistics in Pakistan. The United Nations Population Fund supported the project. Imagine a national statistical agency not having the digital maps of its census geography. As a result, the agency could not perform any spatial analysis on the Census data that cost hundreds of millions of dollars to collect. With analytics, the Bureau could help improve government planning.

A few years later, I analyzed hundreds of thousands of customer complaints filed with Canada's largest public transit agency, the Toronto Transit Commission (TTC). Using analytics, I discovered that the Commission received much more customer complaints on days with inclement weather than it did otherwise. This allowed TTC to forewarn its employees and plan for customer care on days with heavy rains, snowfalls, or high-speed winds.

Similarly, I analyzed the failure rates for water pumps for a firm who had just acquired the business. The client was concerned about the higher than expected failure rates of the pumps. My analysis revealed that failure rates were higher than what was disclosed at the time the business was acquired. It allowed the firm to renegotiate the terms with the former seller to recuperate the existing and expected future losses.

Repeatedly I reached the same conclusion: If these businesses had invested in analytics, they would have determined the answers to problems they encountered. As a result, they would have adapted their business strategies in light of the insights drawn from analytics.

Over the past 15 years, we have seen tremendous advancements in data collection, data storage, and analytic capabilities. Businesses and governments now routinely analyze large amounts of data to improve evidence-based decision-making. Examples include designing more effective medicines or developing better economic policies. If analytics and data science were important 20 years ago, they are now the distinguishing factor for successful firms who increasingly compete on analytics.[2]

I am neither the first nor the only person to realize the importance of analytics. Chelsea Clinton, the daughter of former President Bill Clinton and Secretary Hillary Clinton, the 2016 presidential candidate, is also acutely aware of the importance of analytics for the success of businesses, firms, and not-for-profit organizations. At present, Chelsea Clinton is the vice chair of the Clinton Foundation, a U.S.-based NGO focused on improving global health.

She once revealed that the most important thing she learned in her graduate studies was statistics.[3] Ms. Clinton obtained a master's degree in public health from Columbia Mailman School of Public Health. Of all the training she received in the graduate program at the University, Ms. Clinton identified statistics (analytics) as the one that had the most utility for her. She credited statistical analysis software (Stata) for helping her to "absorb information more quickly and mentally sift through and catalog it."

2. Davenport, T. H., & Harris, J. G. (2007). *Competing on Analytics: The New Science of Winning* (1 edition). Harvard Business Review Press.

3. Feldscher, K. (2015, April 14). Chelsea Clinton, TOMS founder Blake Mycoskie share insights on global health leadership | News | Harvard T.H. Chan School of Public Health. Retrieved September 13, 2015, from http://www.hsph.harvard.edu/news/features/chelsea-clinton-toms-founder-blake-mycoskie-share-insights-on-global-health-leadership/.

You may note that Ms. Clinton is neither a statistician nor is she aspiring to be a data scientist. Still, she believes that as a global leader in public health, she is able to perform better because of her proficiency in analytics and statistical analysis. Put simply, data science and analytics make Chelsea Clinton efficient and successful at her job where she is tasked to improve global health.

Who Should Read This Book?

While the world is awash with large volumes of data, inexpensive computing power, and vast amounts of digital storage, the skilled workforce capable of analyzing data and interpreting it is in short supply. A 2011 McKinsey Global Institute report suggests that "the United States alone faces a shortage of 140,000 to 190,000 people with analytical expertise and 1.5 million managers and analysts with the skills to understand and make decisions based on the analysis of big data."[4]

Getting Started with Data Science (GSDS)is a purpose-written book targeted at those professionals who are tasked with analytics, but do not have the comfort level needed to be proficient in data-driven analytics. GSDS appeals to those students who are frustrated with the impractical nature of the prescribed textbooks and are looking for an affordable text to serve as a long-term reference. GSDS embraces the 24/7 streaming of data and is structured for those users who have access to data and software of their choice, but do not know what methods to use, how to interpret the results, and most importantly, how to communicate findings as reports and presentations in print or online.

GSDS is a resource for millions employed in knowledge-driven industries where workers are increasingly expected to facilitate smart decision-making using up-to-date information that often takes the form of continuously updating data.

At the same time, the learning-by-doing approach in the book is equally suited for independent study by senior undergraduate and graduate students who are expected to conduct independent research for their coursework or dissertations.

About the Book

Getting Started with Data Science (*GSDS*) is an applied text on analytics written for professionals like Chelsea Clinton who either perform or manage analytics for small and large corporations. The text is equally appealing to those who would like to develop skills in analytics to pursue a career as a data analyst (statistician), which Google's chief economist, Hal Varian, calls the new sexiest job.[5]

---

4. http://www.mckinsey.com/features/big_data

5. Lohr, S. (2009, August 5). For Today's Graduate, Just One Word: Statistics. *The New York Times*. Retrieved from http://www.nytimes.com/2009/08/06/technology/06stats.html.

GSDS is uniquely poised to meet the needs for hands-on training in analytics. The existing texts have missed the largest segment of the analytics market by focusing on the extremes in the industry. Some books are too high-level as they extol the virtues of adopting analytics with no hands-on training to experience the art and craft of data analytics. On the other hand, are the textbooks in statistics or econometrics written for senior undergraduate or graduate students? These textbooks require extensive basic knowledge and understanding of the subject matter. Furthermore, the textbooks are written for the academic audience, designed to fit a four-month semester. This structured approach may serve the academic needs of students, but it fails to meet the immediate needs of working professionals who have to learn and deliver results while being on the job full-time.

The Book's Three Key Ingredients: Narrative, Graphs, and Tables

Most books on statistics and analytics are often written by academics for students and, at times, display a disconnect with the needs of the industry. Unlike academic research, industry research delivers reports that often have only three key ingredients: namely summary tabulations, insightful graphics, and the narrative. A review of the reports produced by the industry leaders, such as PricewaterhouseCoopers, Deloitte, and large commercial banks, revealed that most used simple analytics—i.e., summary tabulations and insightful graphics to present data-driven findings. Industry reports seldom highlighted advanced statistical models or other similar techniques. Instead, they focused on creative prose that told stories from data.

GSDS appreciates the fact that most working analysts will not be required to generate reports with advanced statistical methods, but instead will be expected to summarize data in tables and charts (graphics) and wrap these up in convincing narratives. Thus, *GSDS* extensively uses graphs and tables to summarize findings, which then help weave a compelling and intriguing narrative.

The Story Telling Differentiator

This book is as much about storytelling as it is about analytics. I believe that a data scientist is a person who uses data and analytics to find solutions to problems, and then uses the findings to tell the most convincing and compelling story. Most books on analytics are tool or method focused. They are either written to demonstrate the analytics features of one or more software, or are written to highlight the capabilities of discipline-specific methods, such as data mining, statistics, and econometrics. Seldom a book attempts to teach the reader the art and craft of turning data into insightful narratives.

I believe that unless a data scientist is willing to tell the story, she will remain in a back office job where others will use her analytics and findings to build the narrative and receive praise, and in time, promotions. Storytelling is, in fact, the final and most important stage of analytics. Therefore, successful communication of findings to stakeholders is as important as conducting robust analytics.

Understanding Analytics in a 24/7 World

GSDS is written for the world awash with data where the focus is on how to turn data into insights. The chapter on data focuses on data availability in the public and private sectors. With FRED, Quandl, development banks, municipalities, and governments embracing the open data paradigm, opportunities to perform innovative analytics on current and often real-time data are plenty. The book expects readers to be keen to work with real-world data.

The book is organized to meet the needs of applied analysts. Instead of subjecting them to hundreds of initial pages on irrelevant background material, such as scarcely used statistical distributions, *GSDS* exposes the readers to tools they need to turn data into insights.

Furthermore, each chapter focuses on one or more research questions and incrementally builds upon the concepts, repeating worked-out examples to illustrate key concepts. For instance, the chapter on modeling binary choices introduces binary logit and probit models. However, the chapter repeatedly demonstrates the most commonly used tools in analytics: summary tables and graphics.

The book demonstrates all concepts for the most commonly used analytics software, namely R, Stata, SPSS®, and SAS. While each chapter demonstrates one, or at times two, software, the book's accompanying website (www.ibmpressbooks.com/title/9780133991024) carries additional, detailed documentation on how to perform the same analysis in other software. This ensures that the reader has the choice to work with her preferred analytics platform.

The book relies on publically available market research survey data from several sources, including PEW Research Center. The PEW global data sets offer survey data on 24 countries, including the U.S. (http://www.pewglobal.org/). The data sets offer information on a variety of topics, ranging from the use of social media and the Internet to opinions about terrorism. I use Pew data and other similar global data sets, which would be appealing to readers in the U.S. and other countries.

A Quick Walkthrough of the Book

Chapter 1, "The Bazaar of Storytellers," establishes the basic definitions of what data science is and who is a data scientist. It may surprise you to know that individuals and corporations are battling over who is a data scientist. My definition is rather simple and straightforward. If you analyze data to find solutions to problems and are able to tell a compelling story from your findings, you are a data scientist. I also introduce in Chapter 1 the contents of the book in some detail. I conclude the first chapter by answering questions about data science as a career.

Chapter 2, "Data in the 24/7 Connected World," serves as an introduction to the brave new world of data. It is astonishing to realize that until recently we complained about the lack of sufficient data. Now we face data deluge. The Internet of (every) things and wearable and ubiquitous computing have turned human beings into data generation machines. The second chapter thus provides a bird's eye view of the data world. I identify sources of propriety and open data. I also offer an introduction to big data, an innovation that has taken the business world by storm.

I, however, warn about the typical pitfall of focusing only on the size and not the other equally relevant attributes of the data we collectively generate today. The coverage of big data is rather brief in this chapter. However, I point the reader to a 2015 paper I co-wrote on big data in the *International Journal of Information Management*, which provides a critical review of the hype around big data.[6] Lastly, I introduce readers to survey-based data.

Chapter 3, "The Deliverable," focuses on the differentiator: storytelling. I do not consider data science to be just about big or small data, algorithms, coding, or engineering. The strength of data science lies in the power of the narrative. I first explain the systematic process one may adopt for analytics. Later, I present several examples of writings (copies of my syndicated published blogs) to illustrate how you can tell stories with data and analytics.

Chapter 4, "Serving Tables," incrementally evolves the discussion on generating summary tables from very basic tables to rather advanced, multidimensional tables. I highlight the need for effective communication with tabular summaries by urging data scientists to avoid ambiguous labeling and improper formatting.

Chapter 5, "Graphic Details," introduces readers to a systematic way of generating illustrative graphics. Graphics are uniquely suited to present the interplay between several variables to help communicate the complex interdependencies that often characterize the socioeconomic questions posed to data scientists. Using real-world data sets, including the data on *Titanic*'s survivors, I illustrate how one can generate self-explaining and visually pleasing graphics. I also demonstrate how graphics help tease out complex, and at times latent, relationships between various phenomena.

Chapter 6, "Hypothetically Speaking," formally introduces readers to hypothesis testing using the standard statistical methods, such as `t-tests` and correlation analysis. Often we are interested in determining whether the differences we observe in data are real or merely a matter of chance. The chapter first introduces the very fundamental building blocks of statistical thought, probability distributions, and then gradually builds on the discussion by demonstrating hypothesis testing.

All else being equal is the focus of Chapter 7, "Why Tall Parents Don't Have Even Taller Children." Using regression analysis, I demonstrate that only after controlling for other relevant factors, we are able to isolate the influence of the variable of interest on the phenomenon we analyze. Chapter 7 begins by remembering Sir Frances Galton's pioneering work that introduced regression models as a tool for scientific inquiry. I use examples from housing markets, consumer spending on food and alcohol, and the relationship between teaching evaluations and instructors' looks to illustrate regression models.

Chapter 8, "To Be or Not to Be," introduces the tools to analyze binary or dichotomous variables. I first demonstrate that ordinary least squares (OLS) regression models are not ideally suited to analyze binary dependent variables. I then introduce two alternatives: logit and probit

---

6. Gandomi, A. and Haider, M. (2015). Beyond the hype: Big data concepts, methods, and analytics. *International Journal of Information Management*, *35*(2), 137–144.

models. I also demonstrate the use of grouped logit models using sample Census data on public transit ridership in and around New York City. I explain interpreting logit and probit models using marginal effects and graphics.

Chapter 9, "Categorically Speaking About Categorical Data," begins with a brief refresher on binary logit models. I then introduce multinomial variables, which are categorical variables with more than two categories. The bulk of the discussion focusses on how to analyze multinomial variables. A key feature of Chapter 9 is the use of multiple data sets to estimate a variety of models. Finally, I illustrate how to estimate conditional logit models that use the attributes of choice and the characteristics of the decision-maker as explanatory variables.

Chapter 10, "Spatial Data Analytics," addresses the oft-neglected aspect of data science: spatial analytics. The emergence of Geographic Information Systems (GIS) has enabled spatial analytics to explore the spatial interdependencies in data. The marriage between the GIS software and demographic/spatial data has improved to market research and data science practice. I illustrate how sophisticated algorithms and tools packaged in affordable or freeware GIS software can add spatial analytical capabilities to a data scientist's portfolio.

Chapter 11, "Doing Serious Time with Time Series," presents a detailed discussion of the theory and application of time series analysis. The chapter first introduces the types of time series data and its distinctive features, which are the trend, seasonality, autocorrelation, lead, and lags. The chapter shows how one can adopt the OLS regression model to work with time series data. I then introduce the advanced time series modeling techniques and their applications to forecasting housing markets in Canada and the U.S.

The final Chapter 12, "Data Mining for Gold," serves as an introduction to the rich and rapidly evolving field of data mining. The topics covered are a very small subset of techniques and models being used for data mining purposes. The intent is to give readers a taste of some commonly used data mining techniques. I believe that over the next few years, data-mining algorithms are likely to experience a revolution. The availability of large data sets, inexpensive data storage capabilities, and advances in computing platforms are all set to change the way we go about data analysis and data mining.

Acknowledgments

With aging parents in Pakistan and a young family in North America, I, like millions of other immigrants, struggle to balance parts of my life that are spread across oceans. Immigrants might be CEOs, academics, doctors, and engineers; to a varying degree, they all struggle to take care of those who once took care of them. My circumstances are therefore not unique.

This book is a few months behind schedule. I have been flying across the Atlantic to assist my siblings and their spouses who have been the primary caregivers for my parents. This has also allowed me the opportunity to be near my mother, who has had the most profound impact on my aspirations and dreams. She died in August 2015 after battling illnesses with courage and dignity. Exactly a month later, my father also passed away.

Raising a child is a challenge irrespective of place and circumstances. Hilary Clinton reminds us that "it takes a village." But raising a physically disabled child in an impoverished country with poor health care poses extraordinary challenges. My mother, though, was relentless to beat the odds to ensure that I grew up a confident and productive member of society, irrespective of my abilities and disabilities.

I was born in 1969. A birth trauma severely affected my right arm and hand. My parents tried for years to reverse the damage, but in vain. Back then, the medical technology and expertise in Pakistan was inadequate. As a result, I grew up with only one functional arm.

My mother decided that she would not let this setback change her plans for me. She had the good fortune of being an educated woman. She was a professor of literature, a writer, and a poet. She, like my father, was also a fearless individual. As an academic, she ensured that I inherited her love for Persian and Urdu poetry.

My mother was born in the British India. A British nurse, who attended her birth, called her Lily. That became her nickname, which soon became her primary identity.

Lily grew up in one of the most conservative parts of this world, and yet she tirelessly pursued higher education and dedicated her life to spreading it. She was among the pioneers who founded several institutions of higher learning to educate young women in Pakistan's most conservative Frontier province.

This book and I owe a mountain of debt to her. She instilled in me a sense of duty to others. She wanted me to dream, write, and lead. I did that and more because she enabled me to look beyond my disabilities.

My father, Ajaz, is the other person from whom I have not just inherited genes, but also great values. Like my mother, he was also a professor of literature. I inherited his love for books and the respect for the published word. My father was an incorruptible man who cherished how little he needed rather than what material wealth he possessed. He ensured that my siblings and I inherit his sense of fairness and social justice.

It was a privilege just to know them, and my good fortune to have them as my loving parents.

Along the way, hundreds, if not thousands, of individuals, including teachers, neighbors, colleagues, mentors, and friends, have made remarkable contributions to my intellectual growth. I am indebted to all and would like to acknowledge those who influenced this book.

I came formally to statistics rather late in my academic life. My formal introduction to statistical analysis happened at the graduate school when I took a course in engineering probability and statistics with Professor Ezra Hauer, an expert in traffic safety at the University of Toronto.[7]

It did not take Professor Hauer long to realize that I was struggling in his course. He brought a set of VHS tapes on introductory statistics for me. He ensured that I watched the videos and other reading material he selected for me. I most certainly would have failed his course if it were not for his dedicated efforts to help me learn statistics.

Several other academics at the University of Toronto were also instrumental in developing my interest in analytics. Professor Eric Miller introduced me to discrete choice models. Professors Ferko Csillag (late) and Carl Amrhein introduced me to spatial analytics and Geographic Information Systems (GIS). Professor Richard DiFrancesco helped me with input-output models.

I worked on the book during a sabbatical leave from Ryerson University. I am grateful to Ryerson University for providing me with the opportunity to concentrate on the book. Several individuals at Ryerson University have influenced my thoughts and approach to analytics. Professor Maurice Yeates, the former Dean of graduate studies, and Professor Ken Jones, former Dean of the Ted Rogers School of Management, have mentored me over the past 15 years in spatial statistical analysis. I served briefly as their graduate research assistant during doctoral studies. Later, as their colleague at Ryerson University, I continued to benefit from their insights.

I had the privilege of working along Dr. Chuck Chakrapani at Ryerson University. Chuck was a senior research fellow at Ryerson. Currently, he is the President of Leger Analytics, a leading market research firm in Canada. Chuck is a prolific writer and the author of several bestselling texts on market research. I benefited from dozens of conversations with him on statistical methods.

I am also grateful to Kevin Manuel, who is a data librarian at Ryerson University. Kevin has been a strong supporter of my analytics efforts at Ryerson University.

I have been fortunate to receive generous support from the analytics industry. Dr. Howard Slavin and Jim Lam of Caliper Corporation ensured that I always had enough licenses for GIS software to learn and teach spatial analytics. Later, colleagues at Pitney Bowes, makers of Map-Info and other customer analytics software, donated significant data and software to support my

7. Huer, E. (2015). *The Art of Regression Modeling in Road Safety*. Springer.

research and teaching. Dr. Mark Smith, who earlier managed Pitney Bowes' Portrait Miner, Dr. Robert Cordery, Dr. John Merola, Ali Tahmasebi, and Hal Hopson are some of the amazing colleagues at Pitney Bowes who have supported and influenced my work on spatial analytics.

I am also grateful to Professor Luc Anselin and his team for creating several tools to undertake spatial analytics. I have illustrated applications of Geoda for spatial analytics in Chapter 10. I have greatly benefitted from Professor Anselin's training workshops in spatial analytics, which he conducted at the University of Michigan in Ann Arbor.

I am indebted to numerous authors whose works have inspired me over the years. In econometrics, I am grateful to Professors Damodar Gujarati, Jeffery Wooldridge, and William Greene for their excellent texts that I have relied on over the past 20 years.

I have used R extensively in the book. R is a collective effort of thousands of volunteers. I owe them tons of gratitude. Some I would like to mention. I am grateful to Professor John Fox of McMaster University for creating R Commander, an intuitive GUI for R. The amazing contribution to graphics in R by Deepyan Sarkar (Lattice package) and Hadley Wickham (ggplot2, dplyr, and several other packages) is also recognized. Other authors of texts on R and statistical modeling, who are too numerous to list, are collectively acknowledged for helping me understand analytics.

I had the pleasure of working with several editors for this book. Professor Amar Anwar at the Cape Breton University and Professor Sumeet Gulati at the University of British Columbia (UBC) have been great friends. Along with Alastair Fraser of the UBC, Sumeet and Amar went over the draft and suggested many improvements. I am grateful for their diligence and support.

I am also grateful to Rita Swaya, Liam Donaldson, and Ioana Moca for their help with editing.

Several colleagues at IBM® have been instrumental in getting this book published. Raul Chong and Leon Katsnelson of IBM Canada were the first two IBM colleagues who championed the idea for this book. They introduced me to Susan Visser and Steven Stansel at IBM Publishing, who then introduced me to colleagues at Pearson North America. I am grateful to colleagues at IBM and Pearson who shared my enthusiasm for this book and favorably reviewed the book proposal.

Mary Beth Ray, Executive Editor at Pearson, guided me through the complex task of authoring a book. She has been a great support during the writing and editing phases. Chris Cleveland and Lori Lyons at Pearson North America also provided abundant help with technical matters and editing.

Jeff Riley, Paula A. Lowell, Lori Lyons, and Kathy Ruiz have combed through this book. Once they go through a chapter, I receive it back with thousands of big and small edits. I have learned much about editing and publishing by merely responding to their edits. Their attention to detail and commitment to quality has helped improve this book.

I would like to express my gratitude to Antoine Haroun, CIO at Mohawk College, who has been a steadfast friend over the past two decades and a strong supporter of this book. He kept cheering me on to ensure that I complete the manuscript. Also, I am profoundly grateful to my brothers and their families for attending to our parents, providing me the opportunity to work on this book.

Over the past year, my family has made numerous sacrifices to ensure that this book becomes a reality. My wife, Sophia, has sacrificed the most to help me get this book completed. She brings the sharp eye and the no-nonsense approach of a banker to my ideas. To see an example, you might want to skip to the section on the "Department of Obvious Conclusions" in Chapter 7. Sophia remains the foremost editor and critic of my writings and the original source of numerous ideas I have articulated. Our sons, Mikael (7) and Massem (5), saw me type through many afternoons and evenings. I even smuggled my work on family vacations. I am not proud of it.

Without my family's support and love, I would not have been able to follow my passions in life: analytics and writing.

About the Author

Murtaza Haider, Ph.D., is an Associate Professor at the Ted Rogers School of Management, Ryerson University, and the Director of a consulting firm Regionomics Inc. He is also a visiting research fellow at the Munk School of Global Affairs at the University of Toronto (2014-15). In addition, he is a senior research affiliate with the Canadian Network for Research on Terrorism, Security, and Society, and an adjunct professor of engineering at McGill University.

Haider specializes in applying analytics and statistical methods to find solutions for socio-economic challenges. His research interests include analytics; data science; housing market dynamics; infrastructure, transportation, and urban planning; and human development in North America and South Asia. He is an avid blogger/data journalist and writes weekly for the *Dawn* newspaper and occasionally for the *Huffington Post*.

Haider holds a Masters in transport engineering and planning and a Ph.D. in Urban Systems Analysis from the University of Toronto.

CHAPTER 1

The Bazaar of Storytellers

Don't thank God it's Friday, especially if you happen to be in Pakistan or in the troubled parts of the Middle East. For Muslims, Friday is supposed to be a day of rest and atonement. In Pakistan, though, it is anything but. Friday is the preferred day for suicide bombers to attack others in markets, mosques, and streets. Statistically speaking, the odds of one dying in a suicide bomb blast are much higher on Friday than on any other day.

As I write these words on September 18, 2015, a Friday, Taliban militants have stormed a Pakistan Air Force base in Badaber, a suburb of Peshawar, which is a fabled town in the northwest of Pakistan. The attack left 20 civilians and officers dead. Also killed were the 13 militants.[1]

The Badaber Air Force Base used to be the epicenter of the CIA's war against the Soviet Union in Afghanistan. You can catch a glimpse of the staged Badaber airbase in Steven Spielberg's spy thriller, *Bridge of Spies*. You may also recall Tom Hanks playing Congressman Charlie Wilson in the 2007 movie *Charlie Wilson's War*, which told the story of the CIA's covert (it was an open secret) war against the Soviet Army in Afghanistan.[2] By 1988, the CIA and other American agencies, such as the USAID, left the region after the Soviets retreated from Afghanistan. Nevertheless, the war in Afghanistan continued and transformed into a civil war, which now threatens the State and society in both Afghanistan and Pakistan. For curious minds interested in knowing why the Islamic militancy has taken such hold in South and West Asia, they might want to watch the last five minutes of *Charlie Wilson's War*.

The September 18 attack in Badaber by the Taliban militants is similar to other previous attacks on civil and military establishments. Oftentimes such attacks take place on a Friday, which as you know by now is the day of communal prayers in Islam. For militants, Friday is preferred for two reasons. The mosques on Friday are filled to capacity for the early afternoon prayers. The militants want to get the biggest bang for their "bang" and afternoon prayers on Friday look like the ideal time. At the same time, and despite the elevated risks on Friday, the security is routinely lax because even the police personnel are busy kneeling with the other believers!

I first discovered the elevated risk for Fridays in 2011 while analyzing the security data for Pakistan. I obtained data on terrorism in Pakistan from the South Asia Terrorism Portal.[3]

The 2010 terrorism incidents in Pakistan revealed a clear trend. The odds of suicide bombings were significantly higher for Friday than on any other weekday. "In 2010 alone, 43 percent of the 1,547 victims of bomb blasts were killed on a Friday. In Balochistan and Punjab, Fridays accounted for almost 60 percent of all bomb blast-related deaths."[4]

The targeted Friday bombings have returned in 2015. Almost 40% of the fatalities from suicide bombings occurred on a Friday (see Figure 1.1). Thanks to data science and analytics, we are able to identify elevated risks and the order in what otherwise appears to be chaos. I relied on very simple tools to expose the trends in militancy that plagues Pakistan today. It involved importing unstructured data from a website and turning into a database. After the data were transformed in a structured format, I extracted the date for each attack, and tabulated the number of deaths and injured. I cleaned the data set and applied pivot tables to obtain a breakdown of incidents by year, month, and day of the week. In the end, I generated a graphic to highlight the key finding: Don't thank God it's Friday.

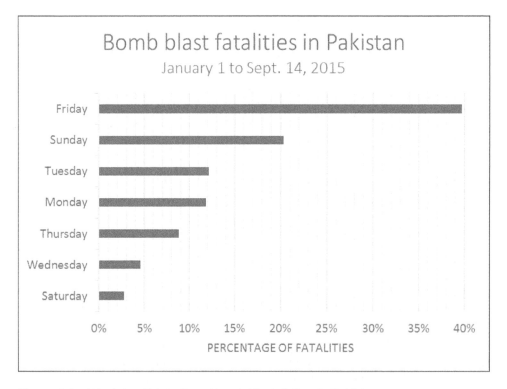

Figure 1.1   Weekday distribution of bomb blast victims in Pakistan

This book extolls the virtues of narratives supported by data-driven analytics. In a world awash with data, sophisticated algorithms, inexpensive storage and computing capabilities, analytics have emerged as the defining characteristics of smart firms and governments. The notion of "competing on analytics" is now well understood and appreciated.[5]

Data science will not be the exclusive dominion of computer scientists/engineers and statisticians. Millions trained or schooled in other disciplines will embrace data science and analytics to contribute to evidence-based planning in their respective fields. As millions will make the transition to data science, they will have to start somewhere. This book intends to be their first step on the path to becoming an established data scientist.

I believe data science and analytics are as much about storytelling as they are about algorithms. The ability to build a strong narrative from your empirical findings and then communicating it to the stakeholders will distinguish accomplished data scientists from those who would prefer to remain confined to coding and number crunching. This book makes a concerted effort to establish data science as an emerging field where data, analytics, and narrative blend to give life to stories that will help devise winning strategies in business, government, and not-for-profit sectors.

Even when I was a young child, I had an inkling that storytelling would play some part in my life. It was hard to miss those clues. For starters, my ancestral home in Peshawar was located in the Kissa Khawani Bazaar, which literally means the Bazaar of Storytellers. A labyrinth of small streets—some so narrow that if you were to stretch your arms wide, you could touch walls on either side—culminated in the grand bazaar.

Even before my ancestors arrived in Peshawar, there were no storytellers left in the Kissa Khawani Bazaar, which had morphed into an intense place of commerce with hundreds of matchbox-sized shops that prompted Peshawar's former British Commissioner, Herbert Edwardes, to proclaim it the "Piccadilly of Central Asia."

Although it's no Bazaar of Storytellers, this book is full of stories based on the findings from simple and advanced analytics. This chapter does the following:

- Establishes the point that data science and data scientists will be in greater demand in the future than they already are. The demand for data scientists is unlikely to be met by the number of graduates being produced by the institutes of higher learning. Thus, switching to data science will be a prudent career move for those looking for new challenges at their work.

- Introduces readers to the distinguishing theme of this book: storytelling with analytics. I offer further details about the book's structure and my approach to teaching data science.

- Addresses the controversies about data science and answers the question: who is, or is not, a data scientist. I also present a brief, yet critical, review of big data. This book is not infatuated with data sizes; instead, it focuses on how data is deployed to develop strategies and convincing narratives. Examples highlight how big data might have been mistakenly considered as the panacea for all problems and limitations.

- Provides answers to frequently asked questions about data science. The new and potential converts to data science have questions about what to learn, where to go, and what career options are available to them. I provide answers to these questions so that the readers might find their own path to data science.

Data Science: The Sexiest Job in the 21st Century

In the data-driven world, data scientists have emerged as a hot commodity. The chase is on to find the best talent in data science. Already, experts estimate that millions of jobs in data science might remain vacant for the lack of readily available talent. The global search for skilled data scientists is not merely a search for statisticians or computer scientists. In fact, the firms are searching for well-rounded individuals who possess the subject matter expertise, some experience in software programming and analytics, and exceptional communication skills.

Our digital footprint has expanded rapidly over the past 10 years. The size of the digital universe was roughly 130 billion gigabytes in 1995. By 2020, this number will swell to 40 trillion gigabytes.[6] Companies will compete for hundreds of thousands, if not millions, of new workers needed to navigate the digital world. No wonder the prestigious *Harvard Business Review* called data science "the sexiest job in the 21st century."[7]

A report by the McKinsey Global Institute warns of huge talent shortages for data and analytics. "By 2018, the United States alone could face a shortage of 140,000 to 190,000 people with deep analytical skills as well as 1.5 million managers and analysts with the know-how to use the analysis of big data to make effective decisions."[8]

Because the digital revolution has touched every aspect of our lives, the opportunity to benefit from learning about our behaviors is more so now than ever before. Given the right data, marketers can take sneak peeks into our habit formation. Research in neurology and psychology is revealing how habits and preferences are formed and retailers like Target are out to profit from it. However, the retailers can only do so if they have data scientists working for them. For this reason it is "like an arms race to hire statisticians nowadays," said Andreas Weigend, the former chief scientist at Amazon.com."[9]

There is still the need to convince the C-suite executives of the benefits of data and analytics. It appears that the senior management might be a step or two behind the middle management in being informed of the potential of analytics-driven planning. Professor Peter Fader, who manages at the Customer Analytics Initiative at Wharton, knows that executives reach the C-suite without having to interact with data. He believes that the real change will happen when executives are well-versed in data and analytics.[10]

SAP, a leader in data and analytics, reported from a survey that 92% of the responding firms in its sample experienced a significant increase in their data holdings. At the same time, three-quarters identified the need for new data science skills in their firms. Accenture believes that the demand for data scientists may outstrip supply by 250,000 in 2015 alone. A similar survey of 150 executives by KPMG in 2014 found that 85% of the respondents did not know how to analyze data. "Most organizations are unable to connect the dots because they do not fully understand how data and analytics can transform their business," Alwin Magimay, head of digital and analytics for KPMG UK, said in an interview in May 2015.[11]

Bernard Marr writing for *Forbes* also raises concerns about the insufficient analytics talent. "There just aren't enough people with the required skills to analyze and interpret this information—transforming it from raw numerical (or other) data into actionable insights—the ultimate aim of any Big Data-driven initiative," he wrote.[12] Bernard quotes a survey by Gartner of business leaders of whom more than 50% reported the lack of in-house expertise in data science.

Bernard reported on Walmart, which turned to crowdsourcing for its analytics need. Walmart approached Kaggle to host a competition for analyzing its proprietary data. The retailer provided sales data from a shortlist of stores and asked the competitors to develop better forecasts of sales based on promotion schemes.

Given the shortage of data scientists, the employers are willing to pay top dollars for the talent. Michael Chui, a principal at McKinsey, knows this too well. Data science "has become relevant to every company ... There's a war for this type of talent," he said in an interview.[13] Take Paul Minton, for example. He was making $20,000 serving tables at a restaurant. He had majored in math at college. Mr. Minton took a three-month programming course that changed everything. He made over $100,000 in 2014 as a data scientist for a web startup in San Francisco. "Six figures, right off the bat ... To me, it was astonishing," said Mr. Minton.[14]

Could Mr. Minton be exceptionally fortunate, or are such high salaries the norm? Luck had little to do with it; the *New York Times* reported $100,000 as the average base salary of a software engineer and $112,000 for data scientists.

Given that the huge demand for data scientists is unlikely to be met by universities and colleges, alternatives are popping up all over the place. In the United States, one such private enterprise is Galvanize. Its data science course runs for 12 weeks and Galvanize claims the median salary of its graduates to be $115,000.[15] Numerous other initiatives, including MOOCs, are adding data science courses in a hurry.

Realizing the demand sooner than other universities, North Carolina University launched a Master's in Analytics degree in 2007. Michael Rappa, director of the Institute for Advanced Analytics informed, the *New York Times* that each one of the 84 graduates of the class of 2012 received a job offer. Those without experience on average earned $89,000 and the experienced graduate netted more than $100,000.[16]

In 2014, I taught an MBA course in data science and analytics. It was an elective course with a small class of approximately 12 students. One student in particular, whose undergraduate degree was in nursing, was enthralled by the subject and made extra effort to follow the course and learn to code in R. He obtained a management internship at a Toronto hospital, which a few months later matured into a fulltime job offer. The jubilant former student sent me an email. Here is what he wrote:

> I just got a job as a Senior Decision Support Consultant at Trillium Health Partners for a six-figure salary! And the secret was data-mining!
>
> I never gave up on learning R! I was able to create multiple projects using ML and NLP working in my previous job ... And what I have done stunned the employer, and they gave me the job two days after I showed them my codes.
>
> I just want to say thank you for introducing me to this wonderfully fruitful and interesting field.

Isn't it wonderful when it really works!

Storytelling at Google and Walmart

The key differentiator of this book is the concerted focus on turning data-driven insights into powerful narratives or stories that would grab the attention of all stakeholders and compel them to listen. This is not to say that statistical analysis and programming are not important. They indeed are. However, these are certainly not sufficient for a successful data scientist. Without storytelling abilities, you might be a computer scientist or a statistician, but not a data scientist.

Tom Davenport, a best-selling author of books on analytics, believes in telling stories with data. In a recent posting, he lists five reasons to explain why analytics-based stories are important and four reasons why so many organizations either do it badly or not at all.

I reproduce verbatim his five reasons for why storytelling is paramount:[17]

1. Stories have always been effective tools to transmit human experience; those that involve data and analysis are just relatively recent versions of them. Narrative is the way we simplify and make sense of a complex world. It supplies context, insight, interpretation—all the things that make data meaningful and analytics more relevant and interesting.

2. With analytics, your goal is normally to change how someone makes a decision or takes an action. You're attempting to persuade, inspire trust, and lead change with these powerful tools. No matter how impressive your analysis is, or how high-quality your data, you're not going to compel change unless the stakeholders for your work understand what you have done. That may require a visual story or a narrative one, but it does require a story.

3. Most people can't understand the details of analytics, but they do want evidence of analysis and data. Stories that incorporate data and analytics are more convincing than those based on anecdotes or personal experience. Perhaps the most compelling stories of all are those that combine data and analytics, and a point of view or example that involves real people and organizations.

4. Data preparation and analysis often take time, but we need shorthand representations of those activities for those who are spectators or beneficiaries of them. It would be time-consuming and boring to share all the details of a quantitative analysis with stakeholders. Analysts need to find a way to deliver the salient findings from an analysis in a brief, snappy way. Stories fit the bill.

5. As with other types of stories, there are only a few basic types; couching our analytical activities in stories can help to standardize communications about them and spread results. It has been argued that there are only seven basic plots in all of literature. I once argued that there are ten types of analytical stories. Regardless of the number, if an organization is clear on the different types of stories that can be told with data and analytics, it makes it more likely that analysts will explore different types over time. Most importantly, the story repertoire should go well beyond basic "here's what happened" reporting stories.

Mr. Davenport believes that most quantitative analysts are poor storytellers to begin with. They are introverts, more comfortable with machines and numbers than with humans. They are not taught storytelling at schools and are encouraged to focus even more on empirical disciplines. Some analysts might consider storytelling less worthy of a task than coding. Developing and telling a good story takes time, which the analysts may not be willing to spare.

Storytelling is equally important to the biggest big data firm in the world. "Google has a very data-led culture. But we care just as much about the storytelling..." said Lorraine Twohill, who served as Google's senior vice president of global marketing in 2014.[18] Twohill believes "getting the storytelling right—and having the substance and the authenticity in the storytelling—is as respected internally as [is] the return and the impact."

In fact, Ms. Twohill sees storytelling gaining even more importance in the world of sophisticated tools. She is concerned that the data science world is too narrowly focused on "data" and "science," and overlooking the primary objective of the entire exercise: storytelling. She warns, "if you fail on the messaging and storytelling, all that those tools will get you are a lot of bad impressions." I couldn't have said it any better myself.

If the world's largest big data company is singing praise of storytelling, so is the world's largest retailer. Mandar Thakur is a senior recruiter for IT talent at Walmart. His job is to hunt for data science talent to meet the growing needs of Walmart, which has used analytics and logistics as its competitive advantage. "The Kaggle competition created a buzz about Walmart and our analytics organization. People always knew that Walmart generates and has a lot of data, but the best part was that this let people see how we are using it strategically," Mr. Thakur told *Forbes* in 2015 (Marr, 2015).

He also believes communication and storytelling are key to data scientist's success. Again, it does not mean that analytics and algorithms don't matter. Certainly, data science competency is a must as Mr. Thakur puts it: "we need people who are absolute data geeks: people who love data, and can slice it, dice it and make it do what they want it to do." He sees communication and presentation skills as the great differentiator. "...[T]here is one very important aspect we look for, which perhaps differentiates a data analyst from other technologists. It exponentially improves their career prospects if they can match this technical, data-geek knowledge with great communication and presentation skills," said Mr. Thakur.

And if you're still not convinced about the importance of storytelling for a data scientist, let us consult America's chief data scientist, D.J. Patil. Yes, this position does exist and is held by Dr. D.J. Patil, at the White House Office of Science and Technology Policy.[19] Dr. Patil told the *Guardian* newspaper in 2012 that a "data scientist is that unique blend of skills that can both unlock the insights of data and tell a fantastic story via the data."[20] Ain't I glad to see storytelling being mentioned by Dr. Patil as a key characteristic of data science?

I find it quite surprising that even when the world's largest big data firm and the world's largest retailer define data science in terms of storytelling capabilities, we still see the data science discourse burdened with the jargon of algorithms, methods, and tools.

In summary, I am not arguing that programming and statistical analysis are redundant. In fact, I echo Davenport and Patil (2012) who define the ability to code as data scientist's "most basic, universal skill." However, as the programming languages evolve to a state where they will become increasingly convenient to learn programming, the focus will shift to data scientists' ability to communicate. "More enduring will be the need for data scientists to communicate in language that all their stakeholders understand—and to demonstrate the special skills involved in storytelling with data, whether verbally, visually, or—ideally—both," wrote Davenport and Patil (2012).

Getting Started with Data Science

Let me formally introduce you to this book. Imagine a three-way cross between *Freakonomics*, *Statistics For Dummies*, and a stats software manual, and you will get *Getting Started with Data Science* (GSDS). This book offers hands-on training in analytics and is targeted at the two million managers and analysts expected to be proficient users of analytics with big data problems.[21] The secondary audience for GSDS is the 1.2 million undergraduate students in business and management programs, 260,000 MBA students, and 173,000 graduate students in research-oriented master's degrees enrolled in the faculties of business and management.[22] The tertiary audience for this book is the community of data-oriented practitioners and researchers who would like to do more than just basic tabulations in their applied work.

The success of *Freakonomics* and Malcolm Gladwell's several excellent books offer pertinent insights. First, the success of the pop-economics texts reveals an appetite for non-fiction that introduces economics and management concepts to the general reader. Second, readers can relate to even the advanced economics concepts, provided the narrative is powerful and is within the grasp of the average reader. Third, in the age of iPads and iPhones, the printed book still matters.

GSDS is the survival manual for researchers, students, and knowledge workers who have been given the mandate to turn data into gold, but they lack the adequate training in analytics to harness the benefits of data and computing power of their firms. GSDS offers the applied utility of a software manual, but adopts a storytelling, lucid style where stories are woven with data.

Do We Need Another Book on Analytics?

A short answer to the question is yes. This is not to suggest that quality texts do not already exist. The real issue is that most books on statistics and econometrics are often written for students and not practitioners. This also frustrates Hadley Wickham, an uber data scientist and a professor who is revolutionizing data science with his innovations programmed in R.[23] He believes that the emergence of data science as a field suggests "a colossal failure of statistics." Dr. Wickham warns about the "total disconnect between what people need to actually understand data and what was being taught."

Similar frustration is expressed by the MIT economist and author Joshua Angrist, and Jorn-Steffen Pischke, who is a professor at the London School of Economics. Angrist and Pischke are authors of *Mastering 'Metrics*, which offers a fresh take on problem solving analytics.[24]

In an essay for the World Economic Forum, Angrist and Pischke wonder aloud about "what's the use of econometrics...at least as currently taught?" The same way the academic statistics has lost touch with real-life applications, econometrics in academic settings has also become an inert exercise in parameter estimation with no real connection to the real world. "It's both remarkable and regrettable, therefore, that econometrics classes continue to transmit an abstract body of knowledge that's largely irrelevant for economic policy analysis, business problems, and even for much of the econometric research undertaken by scholars," wrote Angrist and Pischke.[25]

This criticism of the out-of-touch econometrics is not new. The authors cite earlier work by Becker and Greene (2001) who have been equally critical of the way econometrics has been taught to undergraduate students at universities. Becker and Greene observed that econometrics text focused primarily on "presenting and explaining theory and technical details with secondary attention given to applications, which are often manufactured to fit the procedure at hand." [26]

The applications, Becker and Greene argued, "are rarely based on events reported in financial newspapers, business magazines or scholarly journals in economics."

No one can accuse GSDS of the same crime. This book is filled with hands-on examples of the challenges faced by businesses, governments, and societies. The rise of radical Islam in South and West Asia, income inequality in Toronto, teaching evaluations in Texas, commuting times in New York, and religiosity and extramarital affairs are all examples that make GSDS resonate with what is current and critical today.

As I mentioned earlier, in a world awash with data, abundant and ubiquitous computing power, and state-of-the-art algorithms for analytics, a new scarce commodity has emerged: analysts and data scientists. Despite the ready availability of inexpensive tools and data, businesses continue to struggle to turn their data into insights. The challenge is to hire new talent in analytics and to train and repurpose the existing workforce in analytics. This is easier said than done due to less-than-desirable analytics proficiency in the existing workforce and lack of analytics training opportunities in the higher education sector, which is trying to play catch-up with the recent advances in computing, big data, and analytics. Until this occurs, the demand for advanced users of analytics is likely to remain unmet.

Most books on analytics are written for university coursework and are thus not suited for industry professionals. In fact, there is no shortage of excellent books on the theory behind statistics, econometrics, and research methods. There is, however, one major problem: These books are geared to academic settings where the authors are trying to teach skills that they would like to see in their students, some of whom they need to employ as research assistants. These books, therefore, do not appreciate the constraints faced by industry professionals interested in learning about applied analytics who may not have the luxury to spend a semester or a year acquiring basic skills.

The following are some of the unique features of this book.

Repeat, Repeat, Repeat, and Simplify

Often books on analytics and statistics do not repeat discussion on methods and techniques. Most topics are illustrated just once and it is assumed that the reader will grasp the concept by following just one illustration. This is a big assumption on the part of most authors because this approach fails to appreciate how humans learn; they learn by repeating the task until they get it right. Just watch an infant learn a new word.

Professor Deb Roy, an Associate Professor at MIT, proved this point with his newborn son as he recorded every living moment of his son's life since his birth.[27] Dr. Roy recorded the "birth of a word," a feat never accomplished before. Two important insights emerged from the process. First, the child made tremendous effort to learn a new word by constantly repeating the word over weeks, if not months. The child's effort demonstrates the key aspect of learning: repetition, until you get it right.

The second key finding about learning a new word was about the child's caregivers, who simplified their complex language to a structure that was conducive for the child to learn the new word. Every time the child added a new word to his vocabulary, the caregivers, without consciously being aware of their own transformation, modified their language structure and put more effort in enunciating the key word, such as water, until the child learned the word.

Learning analytics, I believe, is no different from learning a new language, and hence analytics should be learned and taught the same way. The text should repeat the key concepts several times so that the learner has adequate opportunity to grasp the new concept. In addition, the concepts should be taught without jargon, using simple language and powerful imagery with the intent to meet the learner halfway at his or her level.

GSDS embraces these key learning principles and repeats the key techniques, tabulations, graphs, and simple statistical analysis numerous times in the text using examples and imageries to which most readers can relate. The goal is to assist adult learners, who are professionals in their own right, in developing skills in analytics so that they may be more productive to their organizations.

Thus, GSDS aims to serve the learning needs of millions of workers who have some basic understanding and knowledge of data and analytics, but are interested in taking leadership roles in the fast-evolving landscape of analytics. GSDS's hands-on approach will empower those who have done some work in analytics, but have the desire to learn more to pursue senior-level opportunities.

Chapters' Structure and Features

Chapters 1, 2, and 3 establish the foundation for the book. A book on data science cannot be complete without a detailed discussion of what data is, its types, and where can one find it.[28] Chapter 2 serves this purpose. My decision to devote a complete chapter to data should be indicative of how important it is to get data "right."

Chapter 3 reinforces the primary message in this book about using data to build strong narratives. I illustrate this by sharing several examples of storytelling using data and analytics. The remaining chapters offer hands-on training in analytics and adopt the following structure.

Chapters 4 and higher are structured to tell one or more stories. Chapter 4, for instance, tells the story of the rise of Brazil and its adoption of the Internet in communication technologies. Chapter 5 tells the stories of the *Titanic,* and how teaching evaluations might be influenced by instructors' looks. Chapter 7 starts with a discussion of smoking and its adverse impacts on society. The underlying theme throughout these chapters is that analytic methods, algorithms, and statistical tools are discussed not in an abstract way, but in a proper socioeconomic context so that you might be able to see how the story is being told.

Chapters 4 and higher first introduce the problems needing answers. I then advance some hypotheses to test using the tools and methods introduced in the chapter. For each method, I first explain the problem to solve, what tools are needed, what the desired answers are, and in the end, what story to tell.

Data is centric to data science and also to this book. I provide ready access to data sets in the chapters so that you could follow and repeat the analysis presented in this book. Most chapters use more than one data set to illustrate concepts and tell stories from analytics. Even in chapters that are focused on advanced statistical and analytics methods, I start with simple tabulations and generate graphics to provide the intuitive foundations for advanced analytics work. For Chapters 4 and higher, I repeat this strategy to ensure that you can get a hang of why simple tools and insightful graphics are equally as important as advanced analytical tools.

Each chapter works its way from simple analytic tools to advanced methods to find answers to the questions I pose earlier in the chapter. In most cases, the final sections test the hypothesis stated earlier in the chapter. In some chapters, I illustrate how to tell a story by reproducing the analytics-driven blogs/essays I have published earlier to answer questions that concern our society.

I have made a deliberate effort to find interesting puzzles to solve using the analytics. I chose data sets for relevance and their nuance value to keep you interested in the subject. Using data, this book addresses several interesting questions. Following is a brief sample of questions I have answered using data and analytics.

- Are religious individuals more or less likely to have extramarital affairs?
- Do attractive professors get better teaching evaluations?
- What motivates one to start smoking?
- What determines housing prices more: lot size or the number of bedrooms?
- How do teenagers and older people differ in the way they use social media?
- Who is more likely to use online dating services?
- Why do some people purchase iPhones and others Blackberries?
- Does the presence of children influence a family's spending on alcohol?

Analytics Software Used

Unlike most texts in statistics and analytics, which settle on one or the other software, GSDS illustrates all concepts and procedures using the most frequently used analytics software, namely R, SPSS, Stata, and SAS.

The very purpose of using multiple platforms for GSDS is to make it attractive to readers who might have invested in learning a particular software in the past, and who would like to continue using the same platform in the future.

I have demonstrated mostly Stata and R in the textbook. Some chapters demonstrate analytics with SPSS. I have not demonstrated the same statistical concepts for the four software in the book. This has helped me to keep this book limited to a manageable size. However, this should not deter the reader who might not find her favorite software illustrated in the book. The book is accompanied with a live website (www.ibmpressbooks.com/title/9780133991024) that offers hundreds of additional pages and software codes to illustrate every method from the book in R, SPSS, Stata, and SAS. In fact, I encourage readers to develop the same resources in other excellent software, such as Eviews, LimDep, and Python, and share with me so that I may make them available on the book's website. Of course, we will respect your intellectual property and credit your effort.

The website offers the following resources to assist the applied reader for a hands-on experience in R, SPSS, Stata, and SAS. The files are sorted by chapters.

- The data sets in proprietary format for the four computing platforms
- Individual script files (codes) for each software
- A PDF file showing the output from each software

With these resources at hand, the reader can repeat the analysis illustrated in the book in the computing platform of their choice.

What Makes Someone a Data Scientist?

Now that you know what is in the book, it is time to put down some definitions. Despite their ubiquitous use, consensus evades the notions of big data and data science. The question, "who is a data scientist?" is very much alive and being contested by individuals, some of whom are merely interested in protecting their discipline or academic turfs. In this section, I attempt to address these controversies and explain why a narrowly construed definition of either big data or data science will result in excluding hundreds of thousands of individuals who have recently turned to the emerging field.

"Everybody loves a data scientist," wrote Simon Rogers (2012) in the *Guardian*. Mr. Rogers also traced the newfound love for number crunching to a quote by Google's Hal Varian, who declared that "the sexy job in the next ten years will be statisticians."

Whereas Hal Varian named statisticians sexy, it is widely believed that what he really meant were data scientists. This raises several important questions:

- What is data science?
- How does it differ from statistics?
- What makes someone a data scientist?

In the times of big data, a question as simple as, "What is data science?" can result in many answers. In some cases, the diversity of opinion on these answers borders on hostility.

I define *data scientist* as someone who finds solutions to problems by analyzing big or small data using appropriate tools and then tells stories to communicate her findings to the relevant stakeholders. I do not use the data size as a restrictive clause. A data below a certain arbitrary threshold does not make one less of a data scientist. Nor is my definition of a data scientist restricted to particular analytic tools, such as machine learning. As long as one has a curious mind, fluency in analytics, and the ability to communicate the findings, I consider the person a data scientist.

I define *data science* as something that data scientists do. Years ago, as an engineering student at the University of Toronto I was stuck with the question: What is engineering? I wrote my master's thesis on forecasting housing prices and my doctoral dissertation on forecasting homebuilders' choices related to what they build, when they build, and where they build new housing. In the civil engineering department, others were working on designing buildings, bridges, tunnels, and worrying about the stability of slopes. My work, and that of my supervisor, was not your traditional garden-variety engineering. Obviously, I was repeatedly asked by others whether my research was indeed engineering.

When I shared these concerns with my doctoral supervisor, Professor Eric Miller, he had a laugh. Dr. Miller spent a lifetime researching urban land use and transportation, and had earlier earned a doctorate from MIT. "Engineering is what engineers do," he responded. Over the next 17 years, I realized the wisdom in his statement. You first become an engineer by obtaining a degree and then registering with the local professional body that regulates the engineering profession. Now you are an engineer. You can dig tunnels; write software codes; design components of an iPhone or a supersonic jet. You are an engineer. And when you are leading the global response to financial crisis in your role as the chief economist of the International Monetary Fund (IMF), as Dr. Raghuram Rajan did, you are an engineer.

Professor Raghuram Rajan did his first degree in electrical engineering from the Indian Institute of Technology. He pursued economics in graduate studies, later became a professor at a prestigious university, and eventually landed at the IMF. He is currently serving as the 23rd Governor of the Reserve Bank of India. Could someone argue that his intellectual prowess is rooted only in his training as an economist and that the fundamentals he learned as an engineering student played no role in developing his problem-solving abilities?

Professor Rajan is an engineer. So are Xi Jinping, the President of the People's Republic of China, and Alexis Tsipras, the Greek Prime Minister who is forcing the world to rethink the fundamentals of global economics. They might not be designing new circuitry, distillation equipment, or bridges, but they are helping build better societies and economies and there can be no better definition of engineering and engineers—that is, individuals dedicated to building better economies and societies.

So briefly, I would argue that data science is what data scientists do.

Others have much different definitions. In September 2015, a co-panelist at a meetup organized by BigDataUniversity.com in Toronto confined data science to machine learning. There you have it. If you are not using the black boxes that make up machine learning, as per some experts in the field, you are not a data scientist. Even if you were to discover the cure to a disease threatening the lives of millions, turf-protecting colleagues will exclude you from the data science club.

Dr. Vincent Granville (2014), an author on data science, offers certain thresholds to meet to be a data scientist.[29] On pages 8 and 9 in *Developing Analytic Talent* Dr. Granville describes the new data science professor as a non-tenured instructor at a non-traditional university, who publishes research results in online blogs, does not waste time writing grants, works from home, and earns more money than the traditional tenured professors. Suffice it to say that the thriving academic community of data scientists might disagree with Dr. Granville.

Dr. Granville uses restrictions on data size and methods to define what data science is. He defines a data scientist as one who can "easily process a 50-million-row data set in a couple of hours," and who distrusts (statistical) models. He distinguishes data science from statistics. Yet he lists algebra, calculus, and training in probability and statistics as necessary background "to understand data science" (page 4).

Some believe that big data is merely about crossing a certain threshold on data size or the number of observations, or is about the use of a particular tool, such as Hadoop. Such arbitrary thresholds on data size are problematic because with innovation, even regular computers and off-the-shelf software have begun to manipulate very large data sets. Stata, a commonly used software by data scientists and statisticians, announced that one could now process between 2 billion to 24.4 billion rows using its desktop solutions. If Hadoop is the password to the big data club, Stata's ability to process 24.4 billion rows, under certain limitations, has just gatecrashed that big data party.[30]

It is important to realize that one who tries to set arbitrary thresholds to exclude others is likely to run into inconsistencies. The goal should be to define data science in a more exclusive, discipline- and platform-independent, size-free context where data-centric problem solving and the ability to weave strong narratives take center stage.

Given the controversy, I would rather consult others to see how they describe a data scientist. Why don't we again consult the Chief Data Scientist of the United States? Recall Dr. Patil told the *Guardian* newspaper in 2012 that a "data scientist is that unique blend of skills that can both unlock the insights of data and tell a fantastic story via the data." What is admirable about Dr. Patil's definition is that it is inclusive of individuals of various academic backgrounds and training, and does not restrict the definition of a data scientist to a particular tool or subject it to a certain arbitrary minimum threshold of data size.

The other key ingredient for a successful data scientist is a behavioral trait: curiosity. A data scientist has to be one with a very curious mind, willing to spend significant time and effort to explore her hunches. In journalism, the editors call it having the nose for news. Not all reporters know where the news lies. Only those who have the nose for news get the story. Curiosity is equally important for data scientists as it is for journalists.

Rachel Schutt is the Chief Data Scientist at News Corp. She teaches a data science course at Columbia University. She is also the author of an excellent book, *Doing Data Science*. In an interview with the *New York Times*, Dr. Schutt defined a data scientist as someone who is part computer scientist, part software engineer, and part statistician (Miller, 2013). But that's the definition of an average data scientist. "The best," she contended, "tend to be really curious people, thinkers who ask good questions and are O.K. dealing with unstructured situations and trying to find structure in them."

Existential Angst of a Data Scientist

Statisticians, wrote Rob Hyndman, "seem to go through regular periods of existential crisis as they worry about other groups of people who do data analysis."[31] Rob Hyndman is no ordinary statistician. He is a professor of econometrics and business statistics at Monash University in Australia. He is also the author of highly regarded texts on time series forecasting (http://robjhyndman.com/publications/). In addition, he is the lead programmer for several packages in R including the one on time series forecasting (http://robjhyndman.com/publications/software/). In a blog posted in December 2014, Professor Hyndman addresses the question: "Am I a data scientist?"

He explains how statisticians are concerned that individuals in other disciplines—he mentions computer science, and I would add those in the faculty of engineering—are actively engaged in analyzing data. Shouldn't statisticians be the only ones working with data? After all, their entire training is focused on how best to analyze data.

Unlike some statisticians, Professor Hyndman is not worried about others stepping onto his academic turf. In fact, he is welcoming of those who have embraced analytics. He wrote:

> The different perspectives are all about inclusiveness. If we treat statistics as a narrow discipline, fitting models to data, and studying the properties of those models, then statistics is in trouble. But if we treat what we do as a broad discipline involving data analysis and understanding uncertainty, then the future is incredibly bright.

I find parallels between my definition of data science, which is data science is something that data scientists do, and that of Professor Hyndman. "I am a data scientist because I do data analysis, and I do research on the methodology of data analysis," he wrote. He explains that he brings statistical theory and modelling to the data science table; others might approach data science with equally valuable skills attained in different disciplines, including but not limited to, computer science. He urges that we must adopt a team perspective on data science. I wholeheartedly agree.

Professor Hyndman gives examples from the medical profession. We are used to going to general practitioners for common ailments. However, when we deal with serious health challenges that may affect a particular part of our physiology, we turn to specialists; for example, cardiologists, nephrologists, and neurosurgeons. We understand and appreciate that it is beyond the capacity of a single individual to have all the expertise needed to deal with the entire rubric of health-related complexities one may face. Thus, there is no one doctor who specializes in cardiology, nephrology, and neurosurgery. The odds of finding such specialist are more remote than finding a unicorn.

Data Scientists: Rarer Than Unicorns

If you believe a data scientist is one who excels in computer programming, statistics, and econometrics, possesses the subject matter expertise, and is an exceptional storyteller, then you must realize that you are in fact describing the equivalent of a unicorn. Jeanne Harris, the co-author of *Competing on Analytics*, and Ray Eitel-Porter, Managing Director of Accenture Analytics in the UK, know too well about the scarcity of talent when it comes to data scientists. Writing in the *Guardian*, they explained the frustration of executives who believe that finding the perfect data scientist was perhaps as rare as finding a unicorn.[32]

Describing the perfect data scientist as a unicorn is quite common now, even though many still might not understand the extent of expertise required in a variety of disciplines that makes one a unicorn. In fact, in September 2015, I spoke at a data science meet-up, which was sponsored by IBM. When one of my co-panelists asked those present in the audience to raise their hands if they considered themselves statisticians, a couple of people raised their hands from a crowd of about hundred people. What I found surprising was that no fewer than five individuals raised their hands when we asked unicorns to identify themselves. Obviously, we all think very highly of our own limited skills.

I trace the origin of the term *unicorn* to describe a perfect data scientist to Steve Geringer, who is a U.S.-based machine-learning consultant.[33] Mr. Geringer, in a blog in January 2014, presented a Venn diagram to highlight the diversity of skills required in a good data scientist (Figure 1.2). He depicts data science as an all-encompassing discipline that brings under its tent the diverse fields of computer science, math and statistics, and subject matter expertise.

Figure 1.2 presents a rather consensus definition of data science in that it is not merely confined to a particular discipline, but in fact lies at the intersection of several disciplines, which contribute to our abilities to collect, store, and analyze data. What is interesting in Figure 1.2 is the depiction of subsets of data science, which emerge at the intersection of two or more disciplines. For instance, an individual who specializes in computer science and has a profound understanding of statistical theory is the one involved with machine learning. An individual who specializes in computer science and possesses subject matter expertise in a particular discipline, for instance, health sciences, is engaged in the traditional trade of software development. Similarly, an individual with fluency in mathematics and statistics combined with the subject matter expertise is the one engaged in traditional research. An example of traditional researchers is epidemiologists, who have profound understanding of the science of disease and are fluent in statistical analysis.

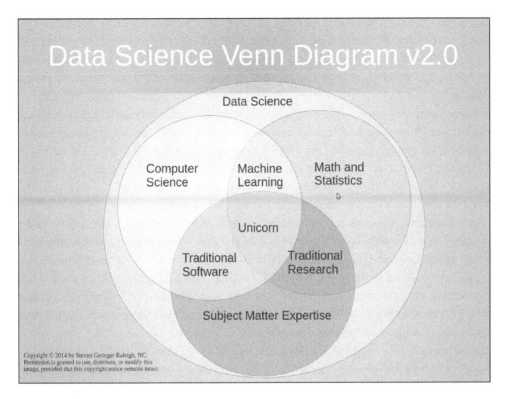

Figure 1.2   Making of a data scientist in a Venn diagram

The magic really happens when we combine the three diverse set of skills—that is, computer science, statistical analysis, and subject matter expertise. The fusion of these three skills give birth to unicorns. Rob Hyndman, D. J. Patil (Davenport and Patil, 2012), Nate Silver (FiveThirtyEight.com), and Hadley Wickham (Kopf, 2015) are all unicorns.

Beyond the Big Data Hype

Big data makes only a guest appearance in this book. Today, even those who cannot differentiate between standard deviation and standard error are singing praise of big data and the promise it holds. I must confess I have not yet drank the Kool-Aid. This is not to argue that I am in denial of big data. Quite the contrary. I am, like thousands of others who have worked with large data sets over the past several decades, know that big data is a relative term, and is more of a moving target, and that it has always been around. What has changed today is the exquisite marketing around big data by the likes of IBM, SAS, and others in the analytics world, which has created mass awareness of what data can do for businesses, governments, and other entities.

The slick marketing has done a great favor to data science. It has converted the skeptics by millions. It is no secret that most university graduates leave with an awkward feeling about their statistics courses. Some describe it as an invasive, yet unavoidable, medical examination that left their minds and bodies a little sore. Only in the geek-dominated domains of computer science, economics, engineering, and statistics does one find individuals enthralled about data and statistical analysis. The sustained marketing campaign about big data analytics, which IBM and others have run across the globe in publications of high repute since 2012, has made big data a household name.

The downside of this enthusiastic embrace of big data is the misconception that big data did not exist before. This would be a false conclusion. In fact, big data has always been around. Even with the smallest storage capacity, any large data set that exceeded the storage capacity was big data. Given the massive increase in capacity to hold and manipulate data in the past decade, one could see that what was big data yesterday is not big data today, and will certainly not be regarded big data tomorrow—hence the notion of big data being a moving target.

Dr. Amir Gandomi, who was a postdoctoral fellow with me at Ryerson University, and I ended up writing the paper on the hype around big data and took upon ourselves to describe various definitions of big data and the analytics deployed to analyze structured and unstructured data sets.[34] Our primary assertion in the paper was the following: When it comes to big data, it's not the size that matters, but how you use it. "Size is the first, and at times, the only dimension that leaps out at the mention of big data. This paper attempts to offer a broader definition of big data that captures its other unique and defining characteristics," we wrote.

Because open access is available for our paper on big data, I decided not to repeat the discussion in this book, but instead encourage readers to consult the *Journal* directly. Thus, you may find big data playing only a minor role in this book. You will also notice that almost all data sets used in this book are small-sized data. I expect the critics to have a field day with this feature of the book. Why on earth would someone use small data at a time when the world is awash with big data?

The answer is simple. It is quite likely that by the time you review this book, the definition of big data would have evolved. More importantly, this book is intended to be the very first step on one's journey to becoming a data scientist. The fundamental concepts explained in this book are not affected by the size of data. Thus, small-sized data sets are likely to be less intimidating for those who are embarking on this new brave journey of data science, and the same concepts that apply to small-sized data could readily be applied to big data.

Big Data: Beyond Cheerleading

Big data coverage in academic and popular press is ubiquitous, but often it ends up telling the following three stories. These include how big data helped Google predict flu trends faster than the government, how UPS saved millions of miles with advanced algorithms, and how the retailer Target became aware of a teenager's pregnancy before her father did. If one were to take off the cheerleading uniform and the blinders, one would realize that neither big data nor advanced analytics were behind these so-called big data miracles.

Let me begin with Google's flu trends. Writing in the *New York Times*, Gary Marcus and Ernest Davis explained the big problems with big data.[35] They described how in 2009 Google claimed to have a better understanding of flu trends than the Centers for Disease Control and

Prevention. Google relied on flu-related searches and was able to pick up on the incidence of flu across the United States. As of late, Google's flu trends is making more bad predictions than good ones. In fact, a 2014 paper in the journal *Science* revealed that Google's algorithm was predicting twice as many visits to doctors for influenza-like illnesses.[36] The authors attributed the erroneous Google forecasts to "big data hubris" and algorithm dynamics in social media, which change over time and make it difficult to generate consistent results. "'Big data hubris,'" they explained, "is the often implicit assumption that big data are a substitute for, rather than a supplement to, traditional data collection and analysis."

Big Data Hubris

Another example of big data hubris dates back to 1936 when Alfred Landon, a Republican, was contesting the American presidential elections against F.D. Roosevelt. Long before the word *big data* was coined, a publication decided to engage in a big data exercise of their time. Tim Harford explains the story in the *New York Times*.[37] The *Literary Digest*, a respected publication, decided to survey 10 million individuals, which constituted one-fourth of the electorate, about their choice of the presidential candidate. The *Digest* compiled 2.4 million responses received in the mail and claimed that Alfred Landon would win by a landslide. It predicted Landon would receive 55% of the vote, whereas Roosevelt would receive 41%.

On election day, F.D. Roosevelt won by a landslide by securing 61% of the votes. His Republican opponent could muster only 37% of the votes. While the *Literary Digest* was busy compiling 2.4 million responses, George Gallup, a pollster, conducted a small survey of a few thousand voters and forecasted Roosevelt's victory by a comfortable margin. "Mr. Gallup understood something that the *Literary Digest* did not. When it comes to data, size isn't everything," wrote Mr. Harford.

What happened was that the *Literary Digest* posed the right question to the wrong (unrepresented) sample, probably the elites who subscribed to their publication. The elite favored Landon, which was captured by the *Digest* in the survey. However, a much smaller, yet representative of the electorate, sample of 3,000 individuals, polled by Mr. Gallup revealed the true intent of the electorate, which favored President Roosevelt.

I must point out that regardless of how sophisticated a method or technique is, human error and hubris can cause major embarrassment for those involved in forecasting. A few years later, Mr. Gallup made the wrong prediction in the 1948 presidential elections when he forecasted that Republican Thomas Dewey would defeat Harry Truman.

Gallup blamed the error on the decision to stop polling weeks before the November 2 elections. During that period, Harry Truman was busy crisscrossing the nation campaigning on a platform of civil rights. Millions attended Truman's speeches and became convinced of his ideals. The other limiting factor was that polling was often done using telephones, which were more common among Dewey's voters than those of Truman's.

Decades later, we again saw pollsters and news media forecast victory for yet another Republican candidate (George W. Bush), whereas the final vote count was much less definitive.

Leading by Miles

United Parcel Service (UPS) is a global leader in logistics and express delivery services. Its fleet of thousands of trucks, boats, and airplanes helps make deliveries all across the globe. UPS made big news with big data when it ceremoniously announced that by using big data and advanced analytics, its logistics experts were able to shave off millions of miles from its vehicles' itineraries. This meant millions of dollars in savings.

In an interview with *Bloomberg Business*, David Barnes, Chief Information Officer for UPS claimed that they "were using big data to drive smarter."[38]

Although the CIO at UPS believes they are harnessing the power of big data, the team that implemented those advanced algorithms was not convinced whether it was indeed big data that delivered the dividends. Jack Levis is the UPS Senior Director of Process Management. He avoids the term *big data*. His view is that UPS has been working with terabytes of data delivering millions of packages since the early '90s, which was long before the term *big data* became popular. To Mr. Lewis, "Big data is a 'how'; it's not the 'what.' The 'what' is big insight and big impact, and if you do that through big data, great."[39]

UPS indeed was able to have a significant impact on its operations by deploying advanced algorithms to reduce the number of miles traveled by its fleet of nearly 100,000 vehicles. Engineers at UPS have been working on finding innovative solution for the "traveling salesman problem," which refers to minimizing the total transportation effort for an individual or a fleet of vehicles by devising cost-minimizing routes. They "reduced 85 million miles driven a year. That's 8.5 million gallons of fuel that we're not buying and 85,000 metric tons of CO_2 not going in the atmosphere." Although these are substantial improvements in business operations, they certainly are not a result of unique algorithms. See, I know a thing or two about routing algorithms. I have spent a considerable time implementing such algorithms since the mid-nineties. I worked with a software, TransCAD, which is designed to build large and complex models to forecast travel times and traffic volumes on a street network. I developed one such model for the greater Montréal area when I taught in the faculty of engineering at McGill University. The model predicted travel times and volumes on 135,000 bidirectional links that comprised Montreal's regional street network.[40]

Off-the-shelf software like TransCAD and EMME/2 offered the functionality to minimize travel times/distance/cost for a fleet operating on a large network long before UPS made the "traveling salesman problem" popular. Just like IBM made big data a media sensation, UPS made route assignment algorithms popular with the popular press.

Predicting Pregnancies, Missing Abortions

The poster child of big data and predictive analytics stories is a long piece in the *New York Times* by Charles Duhigg, who is also the author of an engaging book, *The Power of Habit*. Mr. Duhigg profiles Andre Pole, a data scientist at Target who developed a model that would identify potential pregnant customers by reviewing their past purchases. Based on the analysis of past purchases, Target's researchers observed that a customer purchasing calcium, magnesium, and zinc supplements had a high probability of being in the first 20 weeks of pregnancy. Armed with this insight, the marketing team mailed coupons for other related items to expecting mothers.[41]

This was all fine and dandy until one day a father walked into a Target store in Minneapolis angrily complaining about the coupons for cribs and diapers sent to his teenage daughter. Mr. Duhigg reported the same father calling the store weeks later to apologize primarily because unbeknown to him his daughter was pregnant.

Charles Duhigg's account of big data and predictive analytics making retailers aware of a young woman's pregnancy before her father has created a false image of what data and analytics could accomplish. Harford (2014) explains the obvious pitfalls in such glorified portrayal of analytics. For starters, getting one pregnancy correctly predicted does not say much about the false positives; that is, the number of customers who were incorrectly identified as being pregnant.

Let's assume for a second that predictive analytics empower retailers to be so precise in forecasting that they could predict pregnancies by reviewing customer purchases. Such powerful analytics should contribute to the profitability of retailers and help them minimize losses. The reality, however, is quite different.

I find it quite surprising that Target had the capability to predict a teenager's pregnancy, yet it failed to see its operations being aborted in Canada. In January 2015, Target packed up its operations in Canada and took a $5.4 billion hit on its balance sheet. Target entered the Canadian market with much fanfare in March 2013 and opened 133 stores across Canada. In fewer than two years, the retailer called it quits after struggling to keep its shelves stocked and customers happy. The multibillion-dollar losses also had a human face. Target's 17,000 Canadian employees lost their livelihood.[42]

I believe Target serves as an excellent example of not falling for the hype. Vendors who specialize in big data products will spare no effort to project big data and analytics as the panacea for all our problems. At the same time, journalists and others in their naivety repeat the so-called success stories of big data and analytics without applying a critical lens to them. What happened to Target could happen to any other firm regardless of the size of its databases and the sophistication of its predictive algorithms. Remember, no amount of digital sophistication is a substitute for adequate planning and execution.

What's Beyond This Book?

Is it a good time to be involved in data science and analytics? The discussion presented so far in this chapter offers a clear answer: Yes. In fact, some would argue that it might already be a little too late for some to get involved in this emerging field. I would contend that the sooner you start, the better it is.

In fact, at the St. Luke Elementary School in Mississauga, Ontario, students as young as four are being exposed to the fundamentals of data science. On a recent visit to the school, I was pleasantly surprised to see students, even in junior kindergarten, were being taught to summarize data in graphics. As you will see in Chapter 5 of this book, data visualization is data science's most powerful weapon in communicating your findings. In a very creative way, children were learning to make pictographs, which in statistics are called bar charts (see Figure 1.3).

Young students were asked about how they arrived at school every day. If they arrived by car, they were asked to paste a picture of a car on a chart. If they arrived by bus, they pasted a picture of a bus, and those who walked to school pasted a picture of a young boy walking. The result was a bar chart clearly depicting the frequency distribution of the mode of travel to school for the 27 students enrolled in the kindergarten class.

I have taught statistics and research methods for over 15 years now. I have seen even senior undergraduate students struggling with presenting their information in simple bar charts. If the four-year-olds at St. Luke can generate bar charts of such quality today, imagine their potential 20 years down the road.

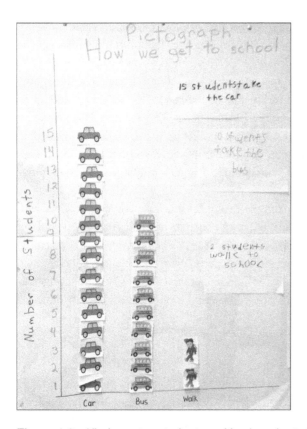

Figure 1.3   Kindergarten students making bar charts in Canada

Source: Photographed by the author on February 19, 2015, at the St. Luke Elementary School in Mississauga, Ontario

Those interested in switching to data science and adopting it as a career would like to know where, and whom, they might turn to for training in data science and analytics. Given the vast interest in data science, it is obvious that universities and colleges will be unable to deal with the demand for training in data science and analytics. In fact, universities and colleges are merely catching up to the demand, and are launching mostly graduate programs in data science. As I write these words in Fall 2015, only a handful of undergraduate degrees in data science have surfaced in North America and Europe. University of San Francisco, for instance, offers an undergraduate major in data science.[43] Similarly, University of Nottingham in the UK offers a BSc in data science.[44] The web portal Data Science 101 offers a partial list of undergraduate programs in data science.[45]

Because this book is primarily targeted at those who have already completed an undergraduate degree, or are in the process of completing one, I am inclined to offer information on programs that are more suitable for such cohorts. Essentially, I believe there are two paths of learning. The first is a structured path where one can pursue further education either full-time or part-time in a graduate program with a focus on data science. Another web portal, datascience.community, offers a comprehensive list of graduate and undergraduate programs majoring in data science and analytics.[46]

At the same time, most colleges and universities offer similar training in their continuing education divisions, which are more suited for those who are already employed and would like to take evening courses to enhance their skills. For individuals who lack discipline, I strongly urge them to pursue the structured route by pursuing further training at a university.

Those who are disciplined enough to follow a curriculum without supervision have a plethora of options available through MOOCs. Specialized platforms dedicated to online learning, such as Coursera and Udacity, are offering free as well as paid courses in a variety of fields including data science and analytics. Julia Stiglitz heads business development at Coursera, which has more than 13 million registered users. She revealed that data science is one of the most popular programs at Coursera. "To satisfy the demand ... means going beyond the traditional walls of higher education," said Ms. Stiglitz.[47]

Numerous universities have also joined the fray by offering free online courses. Some universities offer academic credits for paid versions of the same courses. Increasingly large corporations involved in data science and predictive analytics have also started to offer online training. BigDataUniversity.com is an IBM initiative with the objective to train one million individuals in data science.

Summary

Data science and analytics have taken the world by storm. Newspapers and television broadcasts are filled with praise of big data and analytics. Business executives and government leaders do not get tired of praising big data and how they have embraced it to improve their respective bottom lines. The hype around big data has created the demand for individuals skilled in analytics and data. Stories of six-figure starting salaries for data scientists are feeding the craze.

In this introductory chapter, I set out to explain that data science and analytics will continue to be the rage for the near future. As we are able to capture increasing amounts of data, the need to analyze data and turn it into workable insights is being felt even more. Firms are climbing over each other to compete for the scarcely available talent in data science.

Whereas most of the discourse about data science and analytics is focused on algorithms and data size, I see storytelling as being an integral part of the data science portfolio. I explained that the ability to program and the knowledge of statistical principles remain the core capabilities of data scientists. However, to excel in this field, one must have the ability to turn insights into convincing narratives.

I have also introduced the differentiating features of this book. Each chapter focuses on one or more puzzles, which I solve using data and analytics. Methods are not randomly introduced. Instead, the nature of the question or puzzle dictates the methods I deploy. The book repeats the primary messages so that the reader is able to register them. This book also illustrates statistical methods using a variety of statistical software and products, thus allowing readers to learn using their favorite tool.

I have also presented a detailed discussion on what data science is and who a data scientist is. Apparently, consensus evades on these important definitions. Instead of defining data science as an application of a particular tool, or an exercise involving data of certain size or beyond, I define a data scientist as one who uses data and analytics to find solutions to challenges she or her organization faces, and is able to present her findings in a convincing narrative.

Lastly, I discuss the hype that surrounds big data. I offer a critical review of the claims being made in the popular press about what is achievable by utilizing big data or predictive analytics. Finally, I introduce readers to options to pursue training in data science and analytics in the traditional academic domains as well as MOOCs, which are being offered by dedicated online portals as well as specialized firms, such as IBM and Microsoft.

Endnotes

1. Haider, M. and Akbar, A. (2015, September 18). "Army captain among 20 killed in TTP-claimed attack on PAF camp in Peshawar." Retrieved September 18, 2015, from http://www.dawn.com/news/1207710.

2. Platt, Marc; Kristie Macosko Krieger; and Steven Spielberg (Producers); and Steven Speilberg (Director). (2015). *Bridge of Spies* [Motion Picture]. United States: DreamWorks Studios. Goetzman, G. (Producer) and Nichols, M. (Director). (2007). *Charlie Wilson's War* [Motion Picture]. United States: Universal Pictures.

3. http://www.satp.org/

4. Haider, M. (2011, August 31). "Exploring the fault lines." Retrieved September 18, 2015, from http://www.dawn.com/2011/08/31/exploring-the-fault-lines/.

5. Davenport, T. H. and Harris, J. G. (2007). *Competing on Analytics: The New Science of Winning* (1 edition). Harvard Business Review Press.

6. Miller, C. C. (2013, April 11). "Data Science: The Number of our Lives." *The New York Times*. Retrieved from http://www.nytimes.com/2013/04/14/education/edlife/universities-offer-courses-in-a-hot-new-field-data-science.html.

7. Davenport, T. H. and Patil, D. J. (2012). "Data scientist: the sexiest job of the 21st century." *Harvard Business Review*, *90*(10), 70–6, 128.

8. Manyika, J., Chui, M., Brown, B., Bughin, J., Dobbs, R., Roxburgh, C., and Byers, A. (2011, May). *Big data: The next frontier for innovation, competition, and productivity*. McKinsey Global Institute San Francisco.

9. Duhigg, C. (2012, February 16). "How Companies Learn Your Secrets." *New York Times*. Retrieved from http://www.nytimes.com/2012/02/19/magazine/shopping-habits.html.

10. Murray, S. (2015, May 11). "MBA Careers: Leaders Need Big Data Analytics to Rise to C-Suite." Retrieved September 18, 2015, from http://www.businessbecause.com/news/mba-careers/3248/leaders-need-analytics-to-progress.

11. Ibid.

12. Marr, B. (2015, July 6). "Walmart: The Big Data Skills Crisis and Recruiting Analytics Talent." *Forbes*. Retrieved September 19, 2015, from http://www.forbes.com/sites/bernardmarr/2015/07/06/walmart-the-big-data-skills-crisis-and-recruiting-analytics-talent/.

13. Miller, C. C. "Data Science: The Number of our Lives."

14. Lohr, S. (2015, July 28). "As Tech Booms, Workers Turn to Coding for Career Change." *New York Times*. Retrieved from http://www.nytimes.com/2015/07/29/technology/code-academy-as-career-game-changer.html.

15. "Education at Galvanize—Programming, Data Science, & More." (n.d.). Retrieved September 19, 2015, from http://www.galvanize.com/courses/#.Vfzxt_1VhBe.

16. Miller, C. C. "Data Science: The Number of our Lives."

17. Davenport, T. (2015, February 10). "Why Data Storytelling is So Important, and Why We're So Bad at It." Retrieved September 19, 2015, from http://deloitte.wsj.com/cio/2015/02/10/why-data-storytelling-is-so-important-and-why-were-so-bad-at-it/?mod=wsjrc_hp_deloitte.

18. Gordon, J. and Twohill, L. (2015, February). "How Google breaks through." Retrieved September 19, 2015, from http://www.mckinsey.com/insights/marketing_sales/how_google_breaks_through?cid=other-eml-nsl-mip-mck-oth-1503.

19. D.J. Patil | LinkedIn. (n.d.). Retrieved September 21, 2015, from https://www.linkedin.com/in/dpatil.

20. Rogers, S. (2012, March 2). "What is a data scientist?" *Guardian*.

21. http://www.mckinsey.com/features/big_data

22. http://www.aacsb.edu/dataandresearch/dataglance/enrollment_total.html

23. Kopf, D. (2015, July 24). "Hadley Wickham, the Man Who Revolutionized R." Retrieved September 19, 2015, from http://priceonomics.com/hadley-wickham-the-man-who-revolutionized-r/.

24. Angrist, J. D. and Pischke, J.S. (2014). *Mastering 'Metrics: The Path from Cause to Effect*. Princeton University Press.

25. Angrist, J. and Pischke, J.S. (2015, May 21). "Why econometrics teaching needs an overhaul." Retrieved September 19, 2015, from https://agenda.weforum.org/2015/05/why-econometrics-teaching-needs-an-overhaul/?utm_content=buffer98041&utm_medium=social&utm_source=twitter.com&utm_campaign=buffer.

26. Becker, W. E. and Greene, W. H. (2001). "Teaching Statistics and Econometrics to Undergraduates." *The Journal of Economic Perspectives: A Journal of the American Economic Association*, *15*(4), 169–182.

27. Roy, D. (2011, March). "The birth of a word." Retrieved September 19, 2015, from http://www.ted.com/talks/deb_roy_the_birth_of_a_word.

28. It is unfortunate to lose the distinction between datum, which is singular noun, and data, which is plural noun. Data *are* increasingly used in a singular context and because it has taken off, I surrender on this front and treat data as a singular noun.

29. Granville, V. (2014). *Developing Analytic Talent: Becoming a Data Scientist*. John Wiley & Sons.

30. "More than 2 billion observations." (n.d.). Retrieved September 21, 2015, from http://www.stata.com/new-in-stata/huge-datasets/.

31. Hyndman, R. J. (2014, December 9). "Am I a data scientist?" Retrieved September 21, 2015, from http://robjhyndman.com/hyndsight/am-i-a-data-scientist/.

32. Harris, J. G. and Eitel-Porter, R. (2015, February 12). "Data scientists: As rare as unicorns." *Guardian*.

33. Geringer, S. (2014, January 6). "Steve's Machine Learning Blog: Data Science Venn Diagram v2.0." Retrieved September 21, 2015, from http://www.anlytcs.com/2014/01/data-science-venn-diagram-v20.html.

34. Gandomi, A. and Haider, M. (2015). "Beyond the hype: Big data concepts, methods, and analytics." *International Journal of Information Management*, *35*(2), 137–144. http://dx.doi.org/10.1016/j.ijinfomgt.2014.10.007.

35. Marcus, G. and Davis, E. (2014, April 6). "Eight (No, Nine!) Problems with Big Data." *New York Times*. Retrieved from http://www.nytimes.com/2014/04/07/opinion/eight-no-nine-problems-with-big-data.html.

36. Lazer, D., Kennedy, R., King, G., and Vespignani, A. (2014). "The parable of Google Flu: traps in big data analysis." *Science*, 343 (14 March). Retrieved from http://scholar.harvard.edu/files/gking/files/0314policyforumff.pdf.

37. Harford, T. (2014, March 28). "Big data: are we making a big mistake?" FT.com. Retrieved September 21, 2015, from http://www.ft.com/intl/cms/s/2/21a6e7d8-b479-11e3-a09a-00144-feabdc0.html.

38. Schlangenstein, M. (2013, October 30). "UPS Crunches Data to Make Routes More Efficient, Save Gas." Retrieved September 21, 2015, from http://www.bloomberg.com/news/articles/2013-10-30/ups-uses-big-data-to-make-routes-more-efficient-save-gas.

39. Dix, J. (2014, December 1). "How UPS uses analytics to drive down costs (and no, it doesn't call it big data)." Retrieved September 21, 2015, from http://tinyurl.com/upsbigdata.

40. Spurr, T. and Haider, M. (2005). "Developing a GIS-based detailed traffic simulation model for the Montreal region: Opportunities and challenges." In *Canadian Transport Research Forum Annual Proceedings—Old Foundations, Modern Challenges*. CTRF. Retrieved from http://milute.mcgill.ca/Research/Students/Tim_Spurr/Tim_paper_CTRF.pdf.

41. Duhigg, C. (2012, February 16). "How Companies Learn Your Secrets." *New York Times*. Retrieved from http://www.nytimes.com/2012/02/19/magazine/shopping-habits.html.

42. Ho, B. S. (2015, January 15). "In surprise move, Target exits Canada and takes $5.4 billion loss." Retrieved September 21, 2015, from http://www.reuters.com/article/2015/01/15/us-target-canada-idUSKBN0KO1HR20150115.

43. https://www.usfca.edu/arts-sciences/undergraduate-programs/data-science

44. http://www.nottingham.ac.uk/ugstudy/courses/computerscience/bsc-data-science.aspx

45. http://101.datascience.community/2013/08/21/undergraduate-programs-in-data-science/

46. http://datascience.community/colleges

47. Murray, S. (2015, May 11). "MBA Careers: Leaders Need Big Data Analytics To Rise To C-Suite." Retrieved September 21, 2015, from http://ww.businessbecause.com/news/mba-careers/3248/leaders-need-analytics-to-progress.

Data in the 24/7 Connected World

By the time you are halfway through this paragraph, 2.5 million Facebook users would have exchanged contents online. Google would have received more than 4 million search requests. More than 200 million email messages would have flown over the Internet and some 275,000 tweets would have been heard.[1] Never before in the history of humankind have we been able to generate a living history of ourselves. In the process, we are creating new data of immense size and scope. It is indeed a transformative change to see that within a few decades we have moved from complaining about the lack of data to a data deluge.[2] This makes data analytics even more exciting and indispensable.

At any point in time, the global population of smartphones alone registers billions of data points with their mobile phone carriers. This allows governments and marketers to track subscribers' movements in real time. Advanced analysis of the smart phone data alone can add trillions of dollars of value to global value chains. The advances in wearable computing devices alone will open new avenues for improving the health and wellbeing of the unwell and those at risk.

There is, however, a limiting factor. The data is in plenty and so is the capacity of the analytics infrastructure. What is limited is the expertise to translate analytics into insights. As I highlighted in Chapter 1, "The Bazaar of Storytellers," the McKinsey Global Institute estimates the United States alone will face a "shortage of 140,000 to 190,000 people with analytical expertise and 1.5 million managers and analysts with the skills to understand and make decisions based on the analysis of big data."[3] Imagine the shortfall for managers who could not turn small data into insights. A hint: The expertise to analyze small data is even scarcer than that for big data.

This chapter introduces readers to the wide world of data. Of course, I am not claiming an exhaustive coverage of the topic. Instead, the goal is to offer a taste of what the landscape looks like for a world awash with data. I focus on topics that cover the more emerging domains, such as open data and big data. Although I refer those readers interested in a detailed discussion of big data to Gandomi and Haider (2015),[4] I briefly comment on big data in this chapter. This book makes the case that when it comes to data, size does not matter; it is how you use it. Even more crucial is the ability to make data sing with stories that capture the imagination of readers.

I begin the discussion with the open data movement that has made data sets freely available to the public by public and private sector entities.

The Liberated Data: The Open Data

One cannot discuss open data without mentioning Hans Rosling, the promoter-in-chief for data and analytics.[5] Dr. Rosling is a Swedish medical doctor whose passionate and animated presentations about analytics spiced up the dialogue on data-driven analytics. He manages Gapminder, a not-for-profit agency that promotes the use of data and statistics to achieve global development and the United Nation's Millennium Development Goals.

Gapminder provides videos through its website, which is an amazing resource to learn about data and analytics applied to human development. It is universally acknowledged that learning statistics and analytics has been no different than having one's teeth pulled. What makes Hans Rosling different is his ability to communicate complex ideas clearly and advocate for the use of statistical analysis in achieving goals for human development. His passion about data and analytics oozes out of the media listed on his website.

His particular focus on open data has been instrumental in convincing large public sector and other organizations to release data to be used for research and analysis. He has been able to convince the likes of the World Bank to release its information to the public. His team has created innovative software for dynamic data display, which is available on the Gapminder website.

Open data refers to the idea that the liberation of all sorts of data whose subsequent use by a larger community will result in the benefit of the human race. Other similar movements advocating for free access to software (open source), and publications and other media (open content) work on the same principle. A widely held belief in the development community is that free data assists in making informed decisions about human development. In the case of developing countries, open data allows one to determine what competing ideologies and policies are more likely to alleviate poverty.

Responding to the call for open data, government institutions and commercial enterprises released data to be used by interested parties. Web-based data archiving and disbursement made data liberation convenient. Gapminder and other groups like it took data liberation to another level by making data visualization and analytics available through the Internet. The two sites www.Data.gov and www.Data.gov.uk are examples of web-based data dissemination platforms of the U.S. and the UK central governments, respectively. Another source of research-related data is the Dataverse Project (www.dataverse.org), which is "dedicated to sharing, archiving, and citing research data."

Later in this chapter, I discuss other public and private sources of data that are freely available, or are available for non-commercial uses.

The Caged Data

It follows that because there is liberated or open data, there is also caged or proprietary data. Governments, businesses, and others hold on to the vast majority of data that exists today. Most of such data sets will never be made public because they are as valuable to enterprise profitability as any other resource. In fact, Microsoft calls data the new natural resource, equally powerful and profitable as other natural resources, such as forests, petroleum, or land.

The ready availability of data and our ability to analyze it in real time and in large quantities makes it an important factor of productivity that gives enterprises a competitive edge. Consider, for instance, the battle between search engines where Google is the industry leader. It has in fact been so successful that the brand has become a verb. We do not just search online for information, we "Google" it. However, that was not always the case as I recall from the early days working with AltaVista, Yahoo!, and many other search engines.[6] The most prominent today are Google, Microsoft's Bing, and Yahoo!. Their proprietary algorithms are the most guarded secrets of the modern-day businesses and they are guarded the way Coca-Cola has been guarding its secret formula!

Equally important in the search engine business model is the information they archive, which in fact transforms into one of the world's biggest sources of "big data." Any time you run a search on Google, you may not realize that the answers queued up on your screen in a fraction of a second have been extracted from data sets that are so large that the traditional metrics of defining size are no longer sufficient. Those humongous data sets make Google a huge success and give it the edge over its competitors. Google knows more about what is being archived digitally in the world today than anyone else.

It is hard to imagine, at least for the near future, that Google or others will put the very data sets that define their competitive edge in public domains. It may happen sometime down the road when open data would help individual businesses more than their practice to hold on to these resources. But until then, businesses, governments, and other organizations will keep their data under lock and key.

Because most data will remain proprietary, it does create an opportunity for data analysts. Instead of analytics becoming a domain of the specialized few firms, the need for analytics skills will be felt by all those who have stockpiled data. This is perhaps the reason why the McKinsey Global Institute thinks that the U.S. alone will experience a severe shortage of analytics professionals.[7] As the understanding of the potential for data and analytics is realized, firms will rush to retain analytics talent. From a career perspective, it will be prudent for recent graduates and the already employed, who would like to experience a sharp ascent in their careers, to develop meaningful skills in analytics to be prepared for an analytics-driven, brave new corporate world.

Big Data Is Big News

One of the biggest business stories of the past few years has been that of big data. Academics, businesses, governments, and journalists have all bought into big data nirvana lock, stock, and barrel. Journalists cannot stop writing enough stories about it, and viewers cannot watch enough coverage of the same. They all seem to be convinced: Big data is the panacea for all our ills and challenges. While some may be skeptical of the potential of big data, most have set their critical thinking aside and have willingly jumped on to the big data bandwagon.

It is hard to imagine that as recently as 2010, big data was not on the horizon. There was hardly any mention of the phenomena in the academic literature. Similarly, the news media was equally silent. This all, however, changed in 2011 when the coverage of big data took off in a dramatic fashion. According to the Factiva database of news media, more than 5,000 new stories were reported worldwide in the English news media in 2011. The media frenzy peaked in 2014 with more than 60,500 news reports in the English press (see Figure 2.1). During January 2006 and December 2014, no fewer than 136,300 news reports were filed in the popular press of which an overwhelming majority appeared after 2010 (source: Factiva). In comparison, between January 1982 and December 2005 only 1,916 stories mentioned big data.

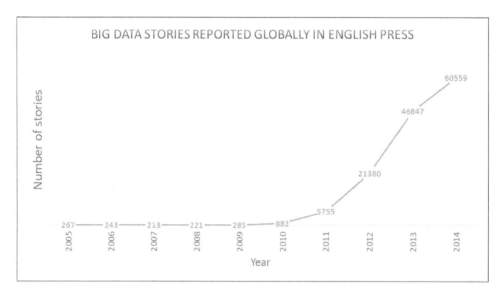

Figure 2.1   Coverage of big data in the English news media

The big question about the mass coverage of big data is what prompted it. What was behind media's fixation with the concept? Journalists, given their predominantly social science academic backgrounds, are not generally empirically inclined and hence their infatuation with data and algorithms merits curiosity. I contend that the media frenzy about big data was generated single-handedly by IBM, who ran a global ad campaign about big data, analytics, and smart decision-making. Numerous newspapers, magazines, and other publications of repute carried the ad campaign. Within months, the editorial followed the advertorial.

The IBM advertisements about big data are more successful in creating not only brand awareness, but also product awareness, than the Super Bowl ads. IBM, in the process, created a new niche, which many other software and hardware providers would benefit from. I analyzed 43,700 news reports filed between January 2006 and May 2013 to determine the top businesses referenced in the news coverage of big data.

That IBM was the most cited corporation in those new stories (1,836 news items) came as no surprise (see Figure 2.2). The second most cited business was EMC Corporation, which is a U.S.-based multinational that offers data storage, information security, visualization, cloud-based analytics, and other similar services. In 2013, EMC's revenue was in excess of $23 billion. In comparison, IBM in 2014 reported $92.8 billion in revenue.

The list of most cited businesses in big data stories is in fact the Who's Who of computing. Oracle Corporation, Hewlett-Packard, SAP, Google, Microsoft, Terra data, Intel, and Amazon were the other most cited companies. Whereas IBM invented the niche, its competitors and others also benefited from it, and collectively they all grew the big data pie globally.

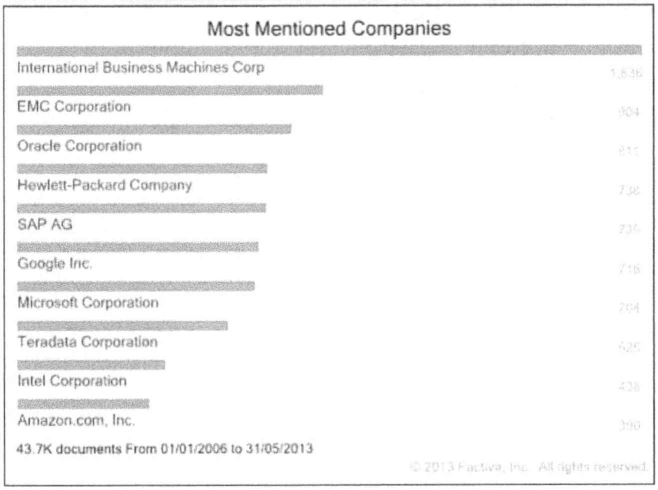

Most Mentioned Companies

International Business Machines Corp	1,836
EMC Corporation	904
Oracle Corporation	811
Hewlett-Packard Company	758
SAP AG	735
Google Inc.	718
Microsoft Corporation	704
Teradata Corporation	626
Intel Corporation	438
Amazon.com, Inc.	390

43.7K documents From 01/01/2006 to 31/05/2013

Figure 2.2   Most cited businesses referenced in big data news coverage

The most cited businesses in big data news coverage belong to the computing sector in general. However, news coverage also mentions business sectors other than computing, such as telecommunications, banking and credit, health care, and wireless telephony.

It's Not the Size of Big Data; It's What You Do with It

I caution against the infatuation with the size of big data and the misplaced faith in its limitless abilities to offer solutions.[8] To generate meaningful insights from big data, it has to be reduced to small data. After it is summarized, all big data reduces to small, or very small, data. A summary table generated from data comprising a few trillion observations is essentially what one needs to draw inferences and devise strategies. The summary table is, for all intents and purposes, small data. After it is summarized in a table or a graph, data becomes easier to comprehend. We can see patterns and trends and devise strategies to develop our competitive advantage. In its raw form, big data is too complex and abstract to develop insights.

Equally important is the fact that big data is a moving target. What may be considered big today may not be big tomorrow given the technological advances of the time. Today, even laptops are being shipped with hard drives of 1 TB or more. My first Toshiba laptop in the early '90s boasted a hard drive with 40 MB in storage capacity. What is important to realize is that any data is big data if its storage, manipulation, and analysis is beyond the capacity of the resources available to an entity.

As the need to store even larger data sets is felt even more, firms will have to decide whether to build analytic and data storage capacities in-house, or to outsource these tasks to businesses that specialize in cloud computing and storage. Those firms that have heavily invested in developing storage capacities are now ahead of the pack in offering cloud-based computing and data storage to other businesses. Most readers will recognize Amazon.com as an online retailer. However, the investments made by Amazon in cloud computing and storage allows it to be one of the leading providers of cloud data storage and analytics.

I believe that the future of computing will be cloud based where individuals and corporations will store and analyze their data online. At the same time, software will be available as a service rather than a product. In such circumstances, most analytics will take place in clouds such that the analysts will send commands for execution to the cloud and will receive output locally. Therefore, the size will become irrelevant because running the same analysis on small or big data will be no different.

The most important and significant point to realize is that what we do with data is more important than its size, or frequency, or complexity. We will not be limited by our ability to store or analyze data, but by our inability to interpret the empirical findings and devise strategies as a result. Therefore, I repeat the thesis statement: When it comes to big data, it is not the size that matters, but how we use it.

Free Data as in Free Lunch

From data starvation to data deluge, the shift was immediate and massive in magnitude. Those who saw value in liberating data and making it easier for the rest of us to access and use it have facilitated the new dawn of the age of data. These entities have made huge strides in making the data freely available to a wide variety of interests.

Here I review three entities that serve as examples of how data liberation, archiving, and dissemination have evolved in the recent past. I have selected one entity each from the institutional, private, and public sectors.

FRED

If you are an analyst interested in macroeconomics, you better befriend FRED, which is one of the richest sources of time series data on economic indicators that focuses primarily on the U.S., but also covers other jurisdictions. The Federal Reserve Bank of St. Louis maintains FRED, short for the Federal Reserve Economic Data.[9] When accessed in October 2015, FRED listed 291,000 up-to-date economic time series from 80 different sources. FRED makes it convenient to search, download, graph, and track economic data.

Who uses FRED? I believe FRED has a huge fan and user base. Readers of the uber economist and commentator (data scientist), Paul Krugman, will note his frequent use of the FRED graphs in his blog with the *New York Times* (see Figure 2.3). The FRED data provides ready access to economic time series and the built-in charting abilities allow one to illustrate the main argument.

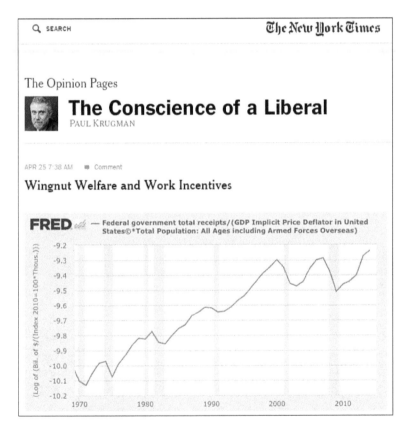

Figure 2.3   Paul Krugman routinely illustrates his points using charts drawn with FRED data

Source: Wingnut Welfare and Work Incentives. (2015, April 25). *The New York Times*. Retrieved from http://krugman.blogs.nytimes.com/2015/04/25/wingnut-welfare-and-work-incentives/

To Rent or Not to Rent: That Is the Question

A recent blog by FRED researchers illustrates the use of FRED data and charting abilities. The blog addresses a question many first-time homebuyers ask: Should they continue to rent or enter the home ownership market? The answer is not that straightforward because it depends on the individual circumstances of the decision-maker. Still, some empirical evidence could help with the decision-making. For instance, one would like to know whether the rents have increased faster over time than the imputed rents (owners' equivalent rent of primary residence). FRED can help answer such riddles.

Figure 2.4 charts out the annual inflation in housing rents paid by the renters and the equivalent rents the homeowners paid. Starting in the late eighties, we can see that the home ownership costs experienced a higher year-over-year increase than the rents did. This trend lasted until the late nineties when the rents increased at a faster rate. We see a decline in Consumer Price Index (CPI) for rents and imputed rents during and immediately after the great recession in 2007–08. The latest numbers suggest that the rents have been increasing at a faster rate than the ownership costs. If one is inclined to avoid higher inflation rates for rents, one may choose to switch to the ownership side, assuming all other factors remain the same.

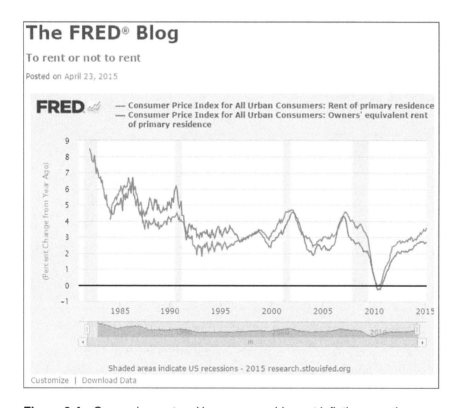

Figure 2.4   Comparing rent and home ownership cost inflation over time

Source: To rent or not to rent I FRED Blog. (2015, April 23). Retrieved October 29, 2015, from https://fredblog.stlouisfed.org/2015/04/to-rent-or-not-to-rent/

Figure 2.4 at the bottom shows a link to Download data that has been used to generate the graphic. The data are downloaded in a Microsoft Excel-ready format that could be subjected to further analysis. Statistical software, such as Stata and R, have customized commands that import data directly from the FRED database. Stata supports a command, `freduse`, which imports data from the FRED repository.[10] Similarly, the `quantmod` package in R offers the opportunity to import data directly into R.[11]

Has Fun Become More Expensive in Turkey?

Most time series available from FRED are focused on the U.S., but you can still access numerous interesting international data sets. Let us for instance try to compare Turkey with the others in Europe. Turkey, because of its unique location, literally hangs between Europe and Asia. Europeans often question how European Turkey is. Most comparisons are about the economic performance or socioeconomic values. The FRED blog has an interesting take on this. It compares how *fun* is priced in Turkey, Ireland, and Europe.

FRED researchers charted the change in price of games, toys, and hobbies in the 27 European Union countries (in aggregate), and national prices in Turkey and Ireland. Figure 2.5 illustrates quite clearly that the prices for fun activities and commodities have stayed rather stable in the European Union since 2006. In fact, in Ireland we see a decline in prices relative to 2006. Turkey, however, presents a completely different picture. Fun has become very expensive in Turkey as the price of toys, games, and hobbies have skyrocketed since 2012. This leads to another interesting question: Why has fun become so expensive so quickly in Turkey? Is it merely a result of a disequilibrium in demand and supply, or is it because a hardline, radical government is taxing fun aggressively to put it out of the reach of the masses? I leave it to you to explore the answer to this riddle.

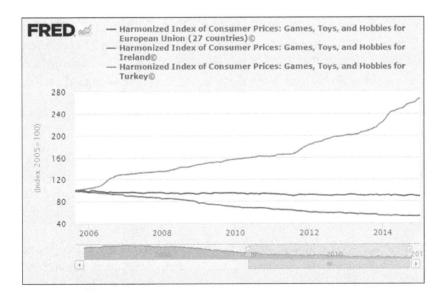

Figure 2.5 Consumer prices of games, toys, and hobbies in Turkey, Ireland, and Europe

Source: The price of fun I FRED Blog. (2015, April 1). Retrieved October 29, 2015, from https://fredblog.stlouisfed.org/2015/04/the-price-of-fun/

Quandl

Imagine a Wikipedia for data. If one existed it would look like Quandl, a Toronto-based startup that wants to serve data to the world.[12] Its goal is to help you find and use data, easily. I have known Quandl's founder, Tamer Kamel, for some time. His vision is extraordinary and his enthusiasm is contagious. He is very much a younger version of Hans Rosling, the Swedish public health advocate of big data and analytics. Mr. Kamel wants his portal to be the world's window to data.

Quandl is fast becoming one of the biggest repositories of data. At present, it is similar to FRED because most available data sets are economic time series. However, Quandl aims to be much more than a disburser of time series data.

As the data gets bigger, getting lost in the data portals becomes easier. What one needs is a guided tour of the facilities. Quandl provides a guided tour by archiving data in categories, in several curated data collections. For instance, for those interested in housing data, a curated housing data collection is available at https://www.quandl.com/c/housing. A search for San Francisco housing data results in a web page offering several housing-related data sets for San Francisco. Under home prices overview, select price per square foot to plot the data (see Figure 2.6). The graphing engine right away draws the line chart, which shows that the price per square foot increased from $200 before 1998 to over $700 post-2014. The impact of the Great Recession can be seen in the same figure where the price per square foot stopped increasing around 2006. The price per square foot remained flat until 2008 and declined from 2008 to 2012. The signs of housing market recovery are obvious as of 2012 when the price per square foot started to climb again.

You can also try searching for oil prices. Under commodities, search for WTI Crude. The resulting graphic shows that the price of crude oil remained stable around $20 per barrel from the late '80s to 2000.[13] Starting in 2002, the price for crude steadily climbed from $20 per barrel to more than one $40 per barrel in 2008. The graphic, not shown here, also illustrates a sudden decline in crude oil price in 2008 again because of the Great Recession. The subsequent decline in prices in 2014 is also highlighted in the graphic.

U.S. Census Bureau and Other National Statistical Agencies

National data sets are usually maintained by agencies sponsored by the central or federal governments. Often, more than one agency is involved. In the United States, the U.S. Census Bureau maintains a variety of data sets including information about demographics and economy.[14] In Canada, federally mandated Statistics Canada is responsible for collecting, disseminating, and reporting data.[15]

The national statistical agencies maintain national-level accounts, which are collected using standard definitions and procedures so that the data may be shared with other national and international agencies. The national agencies make a large number of data sets available for free. The type and scope of available data differs by agency. Some national agencies make almost all data publicly available, whereas others offer a complicated set of licensing arrangements for data disbursement.

Figure 2.6 Price per square foot for housing

Search-Based Internet Data

Since 2011, big data has captivated the imagination of academics, businesses, governments, and others. Analytics and big data are being projected as the promised solutions for all planning and strategy problems. Because *big* is the most commonly recognized attribute of big data, many walk away with the impression that big data is about large-sized data. Nothing could be farther from the truth. Size is just one element of big data. Another key attribute of big data is the speed at which it is being created. Thus, big data is as much about high velocity as it is about high volume.

The emergence of information and communication technologies has enabled the creation of new data at a rapid pace. The estimated 2 billion smartphones by 2016 will register their location every few seconds with the service providers and generate petabytes of data every day.[16]

Another miracle of the Internet age is digital search engines. Every day, Google processes billions of searches, which collectively exceed a trillion searches executed each year.[17] While users are searching the Internet, they also are generating tons of digital data that is visible to search engine operators. At times, Google is able to discover trends faster than those responsible for early detection are. Google Flu Trends is one such use of search engine data that allowed Google to identify flu-related epidemics faster than the health authorities in the U.S. Google Flu Trends used the search data to estimate the spread of flu across the globe.[18] In 2008, Google researchers highlighted their flu forecasting capabilities in *Nature*.[19]

Since 2008, the enthusiasm about forecasting events in the future using Google's search data has subsided a bit after limitations of the Internet-based searches became obvious.[20] It turned out that the same algorithms that had predicted flu trends correctly earlier missed their marks in the later years. The reality is that there is no shortcut to good research and appropriate collection of data. Internet-based data, which is often derived from the searches conducted by the users, is collected passively, and thus carries very little marginal costs associated with data collection. Despite the low cost, Internet-based data must not be considered a substitute for purpose-driven, quality data collection.

With the aforementioned caveat in mind, I present in this section examples of search-based Internet data that may prove helpful in generating insights. Thus, I briefly describe Google Trends and Google Correlate.

Google Trends

Google Trends allows users to run searches on searches.[21] Of the trillions of searches run every year, Google Trends lifts the cover off those searches to determine what captivated the imagination of the Internet users. In 2014, the most searched individuals included media personalities like Jennifer Lawrence, Kim Kardashian, Tracy Morgan, Renee Zellweger, and the late comedian Robin Williams. While these results represent searches conducted around the globe, given the large American population and its ubiquitous use of the Internet, it is quite possible that these results are predominantly from searches conducted in the United States.

When I restrict my query to the Internet searches conducted from within the United States in 2014, I find that almost the same media personalities appeared at the top as the ones did for the data representing global Internet searches. It might be worthwhile to see how interests differ from place to place. For instance, did Internet users in the United Kingdom search for similar personalities? When I restrict data to searches conducted by the Internet users in the United Kingdom, I find that only Kim Kardashian, the American celebrity, made it to the top of the list in the UK. At the same time, the late Robin Williams appears along with Philip Seymour Hoffman under a separate list of departed celebrities. Also, the most frequent search for departed celebrities in the UK in 2014 concerned Peaches Geldof, a British writer and journalist who died at the age of 25.

Indians, on the other hand, are more utilitarian with their Internet searches. Instead of searching predominantly for celebrities, the Internet users in India searched for Indian railways and electronic commerce websites. In Egypt, a nation with its fair share of political turmoil, Internet users most frequently searched information for presidential elections, the soccer World Cup, and the fasting month of Ramadan.

I illustrate the utility of Google Trends with a representative example from market research. Nike and Adidas are two global brands that have dominated the industry for sports-related equipment and apparel. Nike is an American multinational company whereas Adidas is a German-based firm with a global outreach. Adidas started operations in 1949 and was already a well-recognized brand by the time Nike appeared on the horizon in the sixties. There are obvious reasons to assume that the national origin of the two firms will give them home turf advantage over the other in their respective homelands: Adidas in Germany and Nike in the U.S. We can test our assumptions using Google Trends.

I plot the search intensity index for Nike and Adidas for searches conducted in the U.S. and Germany to explore the differences in the interest in each brand among the Internet users. The "search intensity index," my term and not Google's, is primarily an index that normalizes the searches between 0 and 100 to reflect how frequently the Internet users searched for a particular term relative to all other searches conducted in the same time period from the same jurisdiction. Comparing searches for two or more search terms will thus illustrate the relative importance of each term after the searches have been normalized. This approach generates results relative to other search terms and avoids the pitfalls of erroneous comparisons that will, by default, favor searches conducted in places with larger populations and greater Internet penetration.

Figure 2.7 plots the search intensity for Nike and Adidas in the U.S. The line at the top represents Nike and the flat line at the bottom represents Adidas. You can tell from the figure that Nike has been the more popular brand in the U.S. since 2004, when the Google Trends data became available. You can also discern from the figure that Nike expanded its lead over Adidas starting in 2011.

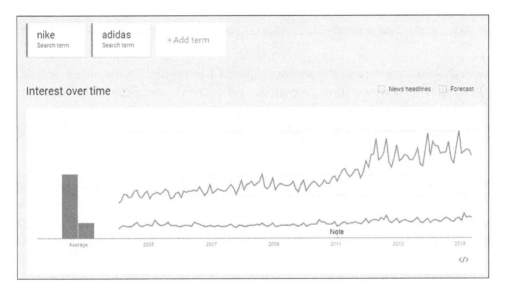

Figure 2.7   Google searches conducted in 2014 in the U.S. for Nike and Adidas

I see better results for Adidas in Germany where Nike does not necessarily enjoy an over-whelming lead over Adidas (see Figure 2.8). I do see Nike turning the tables on Adidas in 2012 by becoming the more frequent subject of searches by the Internet users in Germany. Nike's advance continued in 2013 and the gap with Adidas widened over time. I, however, see a sharper increase in Adidas' popularity in July 2014, which I believe was a result of Adidas capturing the attention of soccer fans during the 2014 soccer World Cup. Despite the short-lived hype for Adi-das, Nike maintained its lead over Adidas in Germany.

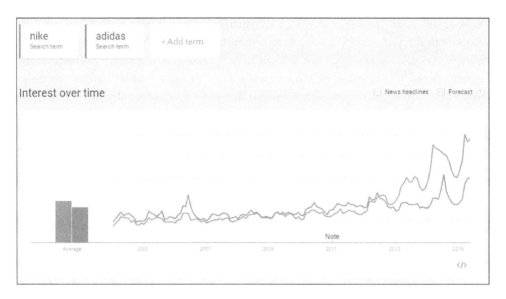

Figure 2.8   Google searches conducted in 2014 in Germany for Nike and Adidas

You can download the data used to generate Figure 2.7 and Figure 2.8 for further analysis. Each row in the data set corresponds to a month and the columns correspond to the respective search terms. You can import the data set into econometric software for further analysis using the time series forecasting algorithms.

Google Correlate

Correlation is simply not the same as causation. However, to ignore correlation altogether would be throwing out the baby with the bathwater. Google Correlate puts the power of correlation at your fingertips.[22] Let's say we are interested in determining what terms correlate the most with Nike. We want to know what other search terms carry a similar digital signature recorded by Google. For instance, Nike may be interested in determining what other brands are being searched by prospective consumers who are also interested in Nike.

A search for correlations for Nike reveals that the term most correlated with the search for Nike is "mens running" (see Figure 2.9). The strength of the correlation is captured by a correlation coefficient of 0.95. Figure 2.9 shows that the search for Nike and for "mens running" peak at the same time over time.

I repeat the analysis for Adidas and find that a misspelled version of the brand (adida) enjoys the highest correlation with Adidas (see Figure 2.10). Note the reported correlation between Adidas and adida is for the Google searches conducted in the U.S. Can one assume that other English-speaking countries are equally like to misspell Adidas? Repeating the analysis for searches conducted in Canada, reveals that Nike enjoys the highest correlation with Adidas. The second-highest correlation is noted for cleats.

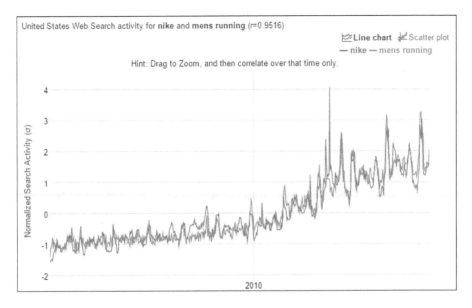

Figure 2.9 Terms most correlated with Nike

You can download the data as a comma-separated file from Google for further analysis. The data are structured such that the terms most correlated are listed in the first row of the data set. The correlation coefficient is reported for each term as a time series such that each row represents the correlation at a particular point in time.

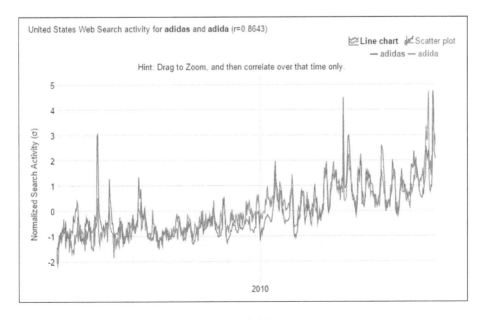

Figure 2.10 Terms most correlated with Adidas

Survey Data

Unlike other animals, we are curious not just about other human beings, but also about what other human beings are thinking. We have formal ways to determine the thoughts and preferences of others. We call them surveys. Political interests, businesses, governments, and others are also interested in determining our preferences. We conduct surveys to determine who is most likely to be the next American president, who likes a particular brand of cereal, and whether our preference for the brand of cereal or a restaurant correlates with the political choices we make.

Most survey research is proprietary, which implies that only those who sponsored the survey will be able to see its findings. There are, however, exceptions to this self-serving approach to information gathering and knowledge creation. The globally recognized market research firm Gallup conducts surveys for clients spread all over the world. The client-sponsored surveys generate proprietary data, which most of the time remains unavailable to researchers and others. Over time, Gallup and other similar market research firms release some of their data sets whose further analysis might be in the public interest.

I begin the discussion about individual or household surveys with an introduction of data sets available from Pew Research Centre.

PEW Surveys

Pew Research Centre (Pew) is a "nonpartisan fact tank that informs the public about the issues, attitudes, and trends shaping America and the world."[23] Pew conducts several surveys every year and generates tremendous insights about the changing world and especially the evolving trends in the United States. What distinguishes Pew from other similar entities is its exceptional efforts to make its data publicly available.

Pew's research and advocacy interests include American politics, media and news, social trends, religious trends, penetration of the Internet and technology in our lives, Hispanics in the United States, and global trends. Pew conducts numerous surveys every year to understand how norms, behaviors, and preferences are evolving over time. It produces several publications over the course of the year on these subjects, and releases the primary data for most surveys within one or two years of collecting the data.

I believe that Pew serves as an excellent starting point for budding data scientists to learn about survey data and gain hands-on experience in analyzing household and individual level data. Apart from releasing the data sets, Pew also releases additional, yet necessary, documents—namely the survey questionnaire and data dictionary. Without survey questionnaire and data dictionary, analyzing data collected by others becomes increasingly difficult.

Often the response to a particular question depends to some extent on the wording of the questionnaire. At times, even the sequencing of questions can influence the answers of subsequent questions. A detailed review of the survey questionnaire allows data analysts to understand the latent considerations that might influence the way data could be interpreted.

Equally important is the data dictionary, which is essentially documentation about each variable in the data set. For instance, in a survey about satisfaction with one's career, the variable capturing the individual's response about job satisfaction may record answers of those who were employed when surveyed by the employer. Asking the same question to the unemployed makes little sense. At the same time, asking the question about employment status first before asking about satisfaction with employment also makes sense. These and related issues are explained in data dictionary so that the analyst can appreciate the limitations in the data set and draw reasonable inferences.

ICPSR

The Inter-University Consortium for Political and Social Research (ICPSR) is yet another invaluable repository of social science survey data. In its own words, "ICPSR advances and expands social and behavioral research, acting as a global leader in data stewardship and providing rich data resources and responsive educational opportunities for present and future generations."[24] More than 700 universities and similar institutions are members of the consortium, which holds approximately 500,000 data sets. The data sets include information on education, aging, criminal justice, substance abuse, terrorism, and other related fields. The consortium was established in 1962.

In addition to acting as a repository for social science data sets, the consortium also runs a summer school in quantitative methods. Leading social scientists specializing in empirical research conduct training in statistical methods for short-term courses during summer. If your educational institution is a member of the consortium, you can readily download data sets of interest from the consortium's website.

Summary

There has never been a better time to be a data scientist. Not only do you have access to state-of-the-art open-source software to conduct analytics, but also access to a whole host of data sets made available by not-for-profit organizations, businesses, and governments. The ready availability of data, open-source software, and inexpensive computing power has made it possible for individuals to be proficient data scientists even if they are not associated with big firms or academic institutions. This democratization of analytics will help the world explore solutions for pressing problems such as income inequality in developed countries; poverty and disease in low-income countries; and cures for illnesses that affect all irrespective of their financial well-being.

This chapter serves as an introduction to the brave new world of data and analytics. It is astonishing to see that we were complaining of the scarcity of data only a few years ago. Now we face data deluge. The Internet of (every) Things and "wearable computing" have turned human beings into data-generating machines. Our smartphones alone generate a treasure trove of data about our lives: the places we visit, the people we communicate with, and events we tweet about are all being archived in real time.

This chapter provides a bird's eye view of the data world. The open data movement has liberated proprietary data sets, which had spent too much time under lock and key. That prevented many from using these data sets for devising innovative solutions for economic prosperity and human development. This chapter serves as an introduction to big data, an innovation that has taken the business world by storm, but also warns about the typical pitfall of focusing only on the size and not the other equally relevant attributes of the data we collectively generate today.

The coverage of big data is rather brief in this chapter. However, I point the reader to a 2015 paper I co-wrote on big data in the *International Journal of Information Management*, which provides a critical review of the hype around big data.[25] The paper remained the most downloaded paper for the *Journal* until the writing of this chapter. The paper is open access; hence, you should have ready access to it via the Internet.

The freemium model of time series data sets on economy and business are in vogue. Various resources, such as FRED and Quandl, offer users ready and free access to time series data useful for strategic and evidence-based decision-making.

Lastly, this chapter introduced readers to survey-based data. The Pew Research Center is a phenomenal resource for excellent survey data, which is indispensable for data scientists interested in analyzing surveys and polls.

As I have said earlier, this is the best time to be a data scientist. So get ready and start practicing the art of data science.

Endnotes

1. http://aci.info/2014/07/12/the-data-explosion-in-2014-minute-by-minute-infographic/

2. Ryder, B. (2010). Technology: The data deluge. *Economist.*

3. McKinsey Global Institute. (2011). *Big data: The next frontier for innovation, competition, and productivity.*

4. Gandomi, A. and Haider, M. (2015). "Beyond the hype: Big data concepts, methods, and analytics." *International Journal of Information Management, 35*(2), 137–144.

5. Wikipedia contributors. (2015, February 7). *Hans Rosling. Wikipedia, The Free Encyclopedia.* Retrieved April 21, 2015, from http://en.wikipedia.org/w/index.php?title=Hans_Rosling&oldid=646014220.

6. Sullivan, D. (2003). "Where are they now? Search engines we've known and loved." *SearchEngineWatch. Com, 4.* Retrieved from http://searchenginewatch.com/sew/study/2064954/where-are-they-now-search-engines-weve-known-loved.

7. Manyika, J., Chui, M., Brown, B., Bughin, J., Dobbs, R., Roxburgh, C., McKinney Global Institute (2011). *Big data: The next frontier for innovation, competition, and productivity.*

8. Gandomi, A. and Haider, M. (2015). "Beyond the hype: Big data concepts, methods, and analytics." *International Journal of Information Management, 35*(2), 137–144.

9. http://research.stlouisfed.org/fred2/

10. http://www.stata-journal.com/article.html?article=st0110

11. http://www.quantmod.com/documentation/getSymbols.FRED.html

12. https://www.quandl.com/

13. https://www.quandl.com/data/DOE/RWTC-WTI-Crude-Oil-Spot-Price-Cushing-OK-FOB

14. http://www.census.gov/

15. http://www.statcan.gc.ca/start-debut-eng.html

16. http://www.emarketer.com/Article/2-Billion-Consumers-Worldwide-Smartphones-by-2016/1011694

17.1http://www.internetlivestats.com/google-search-statistics/

18.1https://www.google.org/flutrends/about/how.html

19. http://www.nature.com/nature/journal/v457/n7232/full/nature07634.html

20. Salzberg, S. (2014, March 23). "Why Google Flu Is A Failure." Retrieved May 11, 2015, from http://www.forbes.com/sites/stevensalzberg/2014/03/23/why-google-flu-is-a-failure/.

21. www.google.com/trends

22. https://www.google.com/trends/correlate

23. http://www.pewresearch.org/about/

24. https://www.icpsr.umich.edu/icpsrweb/landing.jsp

25. Gandomi, A. and Haider, M. (2015). "Beyond the hype: Big data concepts, methods, and analytics." *International Journal of Information Management*, *35*(2), 137–144.

CHAPTER 3

The Deliverable

What makes one a data scientist? If you were to read any other book on the subject, it is likely to speak of someone who specializes in data collection, storage, and manipulation. Some even argue if data science were really a "science." Others might focus on computer engineering while arguing that the engineering aspect of data management overrides the science aspects of it and vice versa. Others would define data science to be all about software and coding. Some would focus on the size of data and others would focus on what to do with the data. Some would say data science is all about forecasting and predictive analytics, others would contend that it has more to do with data mining. Seldom will you find anyone stress the importance of the narrative.

This book differs from the others because it focuses on the narrative derived from data and analysis. The final deliverable, I argue, is not merely a deck of PowerPoint slides with tables and graphics. The final deliverable is the narrative or the story that the data scientist tells from the insights presented as graphs and tables. A data scientist, I contend, should be as concerned with the narrative as with data and analytics.

The earliest mention of the phrase *data science* in the news media is that of the firm Mohawk Data Science Corp. in the *New York Times* in April 1969. The company was one of the pioneers in digitizing documents. It was founded in 1964. Initially, it introduced magnetic tapes to replace punch cards for data storage and transmission.[1] As for *data scientist*, the first mention I find is in the *News Gazette* in Champaign, Illinois. The November 2000 story in fact announces the wedding plans for Jeanette Sanders, who was then employed as a data scientist with Pfizer Pharmaceuticals in Groton, Connecticut.

Interestingly, the roots of the terms *data science* and *data scientist* take us back to a paper by Bryce and others (2001) who were of the view that the term *data scientist* might be more appropriate than *statistician* for the computer and data-centric role of statisticians. Writing in the *American Statistician*,[2] they observed: "The terms 'data scientist' or 'data specialist' were suggested as perhaps more accurate descriptions of what should be desired in an undergraduate statistics degree."

Regardless of the origins of the term, some still question whether data science is really "a science." It is quite likely that the term *data science* evolved in the traditional disciplines, such as statistics and computer science. Bryce and others (2001) offer an insight into the thinking of those structuring the undergraduate curricula in statistics in the early 2000s as they married data and computer science to come up with data science. The debate about how different data science is from traditional statistics will continue for some time.

My definition is radically different from others who view data scientists in the narrow context of algorithms and software code. I believe a data scientist is a storyteller who weaves narrative from bits and bytes, thus presenting a comprehensive argument to support the evidence-based strategic planning, which is essential in a data-rich world equally awash with analytics.

I am not alone in thinking of data scientist as a storyteller. Tom Davenport, a thought leader in data and analytics, explains why storytelling is important for data scientists.[3] He observes that despite the "compelling reasons for the importance of stories, most quantitative analysts are not very good at creating or telling them. The implications of this are profound—it means analytical initiatives don't have the impact on decisions and actions they should. It means time and money spent on acquiring and managing data and analyzing it are effectively wasted."

Ignoring the importance of narrative restricts the role of a data scientist to that of a computer scientist or an engineer who cherishes the opportunity to improve computing by devising improved algorithms. A data scientist, I argue, is more than just that. By having the control over, and fluency in, developing the narrative, a data scientist ensures the intermediate fruits of her labor, that is the analytics, are nurtured into a final deliverable that serves the decision-making needs of the stakeholders.

By being a storyteller, a data scientist has a better chance of being at the forefront of decision-making. Having one's byline on the final deliverable further ensures that one gets credit for one's hard work. An analyst might toil through the inhospitable terrain of raw data sets, clean the data, conduct analyses, and summarize results as graphs and tables. Yet the analyst hands over the fruits of her labor to a colleague or a superior who builds a narrative from the findings and presents it to the stakeholders to be the subject of all praise and glory. A preferred approach is for the analyst to complete the task by offering the final deliverable complete with the narrative, rather than a litany of tables and graphs.

Hal Varian, Google's chief economist, believes that careers in data analytics will be the most coveted in the near future. Dr. Varian is not referring to computer scientists or statisticians per se. I believe he is referring to those who will effectively turn data into insights. As governments and businesses are able to archive larger amounts of data, the need to turn data into insights will be felt evermore. This will not necessarily generate demand for those who will create new algorithms. Instead, it will increasingly generate demand for those who will apply the existing algorithms to extract insights from data.

Tim O'Reilly is the founder of O'Reilly Media. Mr. O'Reilly devised a list of the seven top data scientists and ranked Larry Page, the founder of Google (Alphabet, as of late), at the top. There is no doubt that Mr. Page has a much larger impact on computing and analytics than anyone else could have. Google has effectively transformed the way we search for and analyze information. However, Mr. Page's contributions are more in line with that of a brilliant computer scientist. Larry Page earned a bachelor's of science in computer engineering and a master's in computer science. Computer science was in Larry Page's genes. His father, Dr. Carl Vincent Page Sr., was a professor of computer science at Michigan State University. It is not hard to imagine that the future incarnations of Larry Pages are also likely to come from a computer science background.

In a 2011 report, the McKinsey Global Institute claimed that the "United States alone faces a shortage of 140,000 to 190,000 people with deep analytical skills as well as 1.5 million managers and analysts to analyze big data and make decisions based on their findings." I believe that technological innovations would make size irrelevant to analytics. This has happened numerous times in the past. The advances in computer engineering and computer science, the work done by the likes of Google, will make it possible for others to deploy analytics on "large" data sets with success and little effort. Consider running searches on Google. You are already playing with big data when you run a query on Google. The challenge in analytics is to staff the enterprise with data-savvy analysts and managers who can deploy the available tools and algorithms for knowledge and insight generation.

I believe that Larry Page is one of the most influential computer scientists of our time. I also believe that a world awash with data will require even more data scientists, and not necessarily computer scientists, who can turn existing data and other resources into actionable insights and strategies. What data scientists need is not necessarily a background in computer science with advanced programming skills in C, Spark, Hadoop, Java™, or Python, but a passion for analytics, a curious mind, and the ability to tell a data-driven story.

In this chapter, I focus on the deliverable. The final step in analytics involves communicating the findings to the intended audiences. The communication might take the form of summary tables, figures, and other similar products, which must be complemented with a narrative. I believe that a good data scientist builds a comprehensive road map before she embarks on the journey. What questions need to be answered, what resources are available, and what stories need to be told are the questions a data scientist asks about the final deliverable before embarking on analytics.

This chapter is organized as follows. First, I define the ingredients and requirements of the final deliverable. Second, I explain how to search for background information. Third, I define the tools needed to generate the deliverable. Finally, I reproduce in this chapter standalone research briefs I have published earlier as syndicated blogs. The research briefs serve as examples of how data scientists can use data and analytics to tell compelling stories. Each research note is a standalone piece of varying length between 750 to 2,000 words and uses data to weave the narrative. The briefs discuss a broad range of topics related to human and urban development in Canada, the United States, and South Asia. These pieces were published by the *Dawn* newspaper in Pakistan, *Global News* in Canada, and the *Huffington Post*.

The Final Deliverable

The ultimate purpose of analytics is to communicate findings to the concerned who might use these insights to formulate policy or strategy. Analytics summarize findings in tables and plots. The data scientist should then use the insights to build the narrative to communicate the findings. In academia, the final deliverable is in the form of essays and reports. Such deliverables are usually 1,000 to 7,000 words in length.

In consulting and business, the final deliverable takes on several forms. It can be a small document of fewer than 1,500 words illustrated with tables and plots, or it could be a comprehensive document comprising several hundred pages. Large consulting firms, such as McKinsey[4] and Deloitte,[5] routinely generate analytics-driven reports to communicate their findings and, in the process, establish their expertise in specific knowledge domains.

Let's review the *United States Economic Forecast*, a publication by the Deloitte University Press.[6] This document serves as a good example for a deliverable that builds narrative from data and analytics. The 24-page report focuses on the state of the U.S. economy as observed in December 2014. The report opens with a "grabber" highlighting the fact that contrary to popular perception, the economic and job growth has been quite robust in the United States. The report is not merely a statement of facts. In fact, it is a carefully crafted report that cites Voltaire and follows a distinct theme. The report focuses on the "good news" about the U.S. economy. These include the increased investment in manufacturing equipment in the U.S. and the likelihood of higher consumer consumption resulting from lower oil prices.

The Deloitte report uses time series plots to illustrate trends in markets.[7] The GDP growth chart shows how the economy contracted during the Great Recession and has rebounded since then. The graphic presents four likely scenarios for the future. Another plot shows the changes in consumer spending. The accompanying narrative focuses on income inequality in the U.S. and refers to Thomas Pikkety's book on the same.[8] The Deloitte report mentions many consumers did not experience an increase in their real incomes over the years, while they still maintained their level of spending. Other graphics focused on housing, business and government sectors, international trade, labor and financial markets, and prices. The appendix carries four tables documenting data for the four scenarios discussed in the report.

Deloitte's *United States Economic Forecast* serves the very purpose that its authors intended. The report uses data and analytics to generate the likely economic scenarios. It builds a powerful narrative in support of the thesis statement that the U.S. economy is doing much better than what most would like to believe. At the same time, the report shows Deloitte to be a competent firm capable of analyzing economic data and prescribing strategies to cope with the economic challenges.

Now consider if we were to exclude the narrative from this report and presented the findings as a deck of PowerPoint slides with eight graphics and four tables. The PowerPoint slides would have failed to communicate the message that the authors carefully crafted in the report citing Pikketty and Voltaire. I consider the Deloitte's report a good example of storytelling with data and encourage you to read the report to decide for yourself whether the deliverable would have been equally powerful without the narrative.

Now let us work backward from the Deloitte report. Before the authors started their analysis, they must have discussed the scope of the final deliverable. They would have deliberated the key message of the report and then looked for the data and analytics they needed to make their case. The initial planning and conceptualizing of the final deliverable is therefore extremely important for producing a compelling document. Embarking on analytics, without due consideration to the final deliverable, is likely to result in a poor-quality document where the analytics and narrative would struggle to blend.

I would like you to focus on the following considerations before embarking on analytics.

What Is the Research Question?

The key to good analytics is to understand the research question. All analytics are conducted to gain insights into a research question. A better understanding of the research question ensures that the subsequent actions are likely to bear fruit. It is also important to recognize that advanced analytics are not a panacea for a poorly structured research question.

For example, assume that you are the senior director for human resources at a large firm. You have been asked to review a grievance filed by women workers who contend that the firm pays them less than what it pays men. Your goal is to investigate whether a gender bias exists in compensation.

Over the years, and almost all across the world, women are known to earn, on average, less than men. Several factors contributed to the wage gap between men and women. The choice for employment sectors, labor market preferences for certain skills, and the difference in qualifications are some of the reasons cited for the wage gap.[9] Labor market studies suggest that the wage gap between men and women has narrowed. Many socially responsible businesses are committed to eliminating the structural barriers and biases that promote such gaps. Yet much more work still needs to be done.

Earlier research has helped identify wage gaps and their determinants. As an analyst, you might be asked to run a basic query on the average compensation for each department broken down by gender. This would be appropriate to answer the question: Does compensation differ for men and women employees in the firm? If your goal is to investigate allegations of gender bias, your research question should be more nuanced than what you have selected.

Gender bias in this particular case implies that women employees are paid less for doing the same job when no difference exists in experience, education, productivity, and other attributes of the work done by men and women. The research question thus has to account for relevant attributes. A more appropriate research question is stated as follows: Given the same education, experience, and productivity levels, does the firm compensate women less than men? You might want to include other considerations, such as whether the firm promotes women to leadership positions as frequently as it promotes men. You might also want to explore the race dimension to see whether the gender bias is more pronounced for racialized women.

What Answers Are Needed?

After you have refined the research question, you need to think about the answers or solutions that you will have to present to the stakeholders. Think not merely about the format of the final report, but also about the content in the answers you will present. Building on the gender bias example, the executives might want your report to offer robust evidence that either refutes or confirms the allegations. Let us assume that your analysis reached a rather fuzzy conclusion that suggested the gender bias might have taken place in some circumstances but not in others. The bias might be apparent in compensation, but the differences are not statistically significant, a concept I later introduce in Chapter 6, "Hypothetically Speaking."

You need to know in advance whether the executives at the firm would be satisfied with an answer that falls short of being a smoking gun. If you are expected to produce a robust response, then you must choose those methods and data that will help you reach a conclusive answer. In fact, you must always select the most appropriate and robust methods to answer the questions. However, you must also be cognizant of the deadlines. If the right method will take months to collect and analyze data, and your deadline is a week from today, you must find appropriate alternatives to provide an answer that might have limitations, but could guide, and provide the motivation for, further investigations. The analytics should inform and guide the narrative and not the other way around. Remember, integrity is the most important attribute of a data scientist.

At the same time, you should think of the format in which the answer must be presented to the executives. If they are expecting a report, you should be prepared to draft a formal report. If they are expecting a PowerPoint presentation, then you should produce one that will help you convey your findings.

How Have Others Researched the Same Question in the Past?

After you have sharpened your research question, you might want to see how others in the past have researched the same or similar question. In academia, this stage is referred to as a *literature review*. In business, this is called *background research*. Consider the gender bias example I discussed earlier. You should consult the academic and professional literature to see how others have explored the same question in the past. This enables you to benefit from the experience of other researchers.

Sources of Information

Google Scholar is arguably the best place to begin your search for related research. Unlike other indexes, discussed later in the chapter, Google Scholar archives publications from academic and other sources. In addition, Google Scholar searches the entire text of the publication and not just its abstract and title. Google Scholar reported 208,000 items when I searched for gender bias and wages.[10] I refined the search term by enclosing *gender bias* in quotes. This reduced the search to 21,200 records, still an unrealistically large number of publications to review. One can select the apparently more relevant publications that are usually listed first by Google Scholar. Otherwise, one can restrict the search to the title of the publication to get a shorter list of publications. A search for gender bias and wages restricted to the title of publications returned only six documents.

Academics have an "unfair" advantage over others in searching for information. Most universities subscribe to custom indexes that archive information by topic. Such services are prohibitively expensive to subscribe to for small firms, and even more so for individual researchers. However, there is hope. Often public libraries subscribe to some of the commonly used indexes. Otherwise, you might want to subscribe to the library at your former alma mater, which will allow you to access, even remotely, the digital resources subscribed to by the university. Remember, universities often offer discounted subscriptions to alums. Also, try the library at your local university for a guest membership.

Assuming that you have secured access to resources commonly found at an institute of higher learning, you will have a rich choice of resources to play with. I want to recommend a few key resources that can help your life as a data scientist. I restrict the discussion to resources more relevant to business and social sciences. If you work in engineering, law, or medicine, you might have to explore other domain-specific resources.

In business and social science research, news coverage of events offers great insights. The events could be socio-political, economic, or environmental. The news reports record history in real time. For instance, the news coverage of an oil spill would carry details about the saga as it unfolds, how different actors involved in the containment react, and what methods or techniques are used for containment.

Factiva and LexisNexis are the two most powerful tools to search the entire text of newspapers and other news media from across the world, with some limitations. Whereas Factiva covers only news, the Lexis part of LexisNexis searches through legal documents and judgments.

The biggest limitation for these indexes is language. Most newspapers covered by Factiva and LexisNexis are published in English. If you are researching political outcomes in the Middle East, then the word on the street, the wall chalking, and the most relevant commentary will be in Arabic. Neither Factiva nor LexisNexis will be of much help in knowing what the buzz is in Arabic. However, if you can be content with the coverage in the English press, Factiva and LexisNexis are your best options.

Using Factiva, for instance, you can search for a combination of words in the title, lead paragraph, or the entire text of the news item. You can restrict your search to publications of a particular type, jurisdiction, or an individual source. Factiva also offers unique news pages focused on specific topics where it aggregates recent relevant coverage of the same topic.

I am aware of several good tools to search the academic press. There is still no good source to search the publicly available but privately generated research. Banks, consulting firms, government agencies, and non-governmental organizations (NGOs) generate hundreds of thousands of reports each year. Unless you know of a publication or individually research the available archive online on the respective websites, you are not likely to stumble upon such reports by default. At present, Google Scholar is the best source for materials published in non-academic outlets.

Whereas all indexes permit searching for relevant publications and access to abstracts, some indexes offer access to the entire text of the publication. A good place to start is ProQuest Digital Library, which also offers access to the entire text whenever it is available. Other relevant indexes include Web of Science, EconLit, and Springer Link. Web of Science offers a unique feature that permits sorting results by the times a publication has been cited by others. This is in addition to sorting papers by publication date and relevance.

ProQuest Digital Dissertations is another excellent resource for academic research. Master's theses and doctoral dissertations contain many more details than what is ultimately published in journal publications resulting from graduate student research. Dissertations often include copies of survey instruments that the authors developed for their research. If you need to collect new data, I believe that adapting a survey instrument for your project is far more efficient than developing one from scratch. You can modify the survey to meet your needs by collaborating with the researcher who devised the original survey instrument.

I have presented here only a small subset of resources. Searching for information using digital resources is evolving rapidly. It is quite likely that by the time this book hits the shelves, other players might have surfaced offering search capabilities across academic, non-academic, and emerging blogospheres. We are fortunate to be living in a time when solutions are emerging at a rate faster than the problems we encounter.

Finders Keepers

In a digital world where information is ubiquitous and without interruption, storing relevant information as we stumble across it is a challenge. Even when we search formally for information, the volume of information is so large that archiving research-related information for future retrieval is becoming increasingly difficult. Recall that when I ran a search for gender bias and wages, Google Scholar returned 21,200 records. Let us assume that after browsing through the first few pages, we determined that at least 22 publications were of interest to us. One option is to type the list of references. Obviously, this exercise will be time-consuming and at the same time will be redundant primarily because we are going to retype the already archived references. In an ideal world, we should be able to select the key references of interest from a search engine or index, which should populate our custom database of relevant information.

Fortunately, several freeware and commercial software programs are available for exactly this purpose. The Paperpile service enables you to generate and maintain bibliographies, and import records from Google Scholar and other web-based environments.[11] EndNote and Reference Manager dominate the commercially available software market for generating and maintaining bibliographies. Several freeware options are also available, including Zotero, which I would encourage you to consider.

Using Zotero

To see how Zotero or similar software works, you can set up a free account with Zotero. You have the option to work with the browser version that will maintain your references in the cloud, or you can download a desktop version as well. Google Chrome also offers a plug-in for Zotero.

After setting up the account and installing the plug-in into Google Chrome, suppose I conduct a search for "gender bias" (in quotation marks) and "wages" using Google Scholar. I found 21,200 publications that matched my query. The plug-in adds an additional folder symbol on the right side of the web address field. After Google displays the search results, I can click on the folder symbol, which opens another dialog box enabling me to select the references of interest by clicking on them. Clicking OK saves those references in my personal database. I can choose to include accompanying abstracts, and even the PDF versions of those publications that are readily available for download.

After the chosen references are archived in the database, I can search and retrieve them later and even generate automatic bibliographies without ever needing to type the references. As an example, I have included four references from the ones generated by the search command. I logged in to my account at www.zotero.org to locate the recently added references. I selected the APA style to generate the following bibliography. The entire process from search to bibliography took 20 seconds. I have numbered the references, which is not the norm for the APA style:

1. Borooah, V. K. (2004). Gender bias among children in India in their diet and immunization against disease. *Social Science & Medicine*, *58*(9), 1719–1731. Retrieved from www.sciencedirect.com/science/article/pii/S0277953603003423

2. Estevez-Abe, M. (2005). Gender bias in skills and social policies: the varieties of capitalism perspective on sex segregation. *Social Politics: International Studies in Gender, State & Society*, *12*(2), 180–215. Retrieved from sp.oxfordjournals.org/content/12/2/180.short

3. Hultin, M. and Szulkin, R. (1999). Wages and unequal access to organizational power: An empirical test of gender discrimination. *Administrative Science Quarterly*, *44*(3), 453–472. Retrieved from asq.sagepub.com/content/44/3/453.short

4. Kim, M. (1989). Gender bias in compensation structures: a case study of its historical basis and persistence. *Journal of Social Issues*, *45*(4), 39–49. Retrieved from onlinelibrary.wiley.com/doi/10.1111/j.1540-4560.1989.tb02358.x/full

The Need for a Bigger Shoe Box

The ubiquitous nature of the Internet is such that if one is not talking or speaking, one is busy browsing the Internet. A long list of Net-enabled devices, including smartphones, tablets, and even some TVs, compete with the way we have browsed the Internet in the past—that is, laptops and desktops. The constant flow of information implies that a large enough shoebox is needed to house all the brief and long notes that you scribble and the important emails you want to archive, or ensure that the news story you just read is saved with complete text. Evernote is the shoebox[12] you are looking for. It is freely available with some restrictions or for a nominal monthly subscription, which costs less per month than an expensive cold beverage at the local Starbucks.

I have more than 3,000 notes archived in over three dozen notebooks. I can click and save the entire text in the web browser to Evernote. I can even email notes to my Evernote account to be stored in specific notebooks. In addition, and most important of all, my data is updated on my smart phone, tablet, and laptop in real time. If I am on the move, I am moving with my shoebox.

What Information Do You Need to Answer the Question?

A review of relevant research will put you in a better position to determine what information you need to answer the research questions. To explore the gender bias in wages, for instance, we not only need the details on total compensation received by each employee, but also details such as employees' sex, age, experience, education, job classification, and some measure of productivity, to name a few. Let us assume that the firm did not maintain detailed records on employees. This would seriously limit the analyst's ability to answer the question about gender bias. Remember that no amount of technical savviness can be a substitute for little or poor information.

If we realize that the information required to answer the research question is not readily available, we need to determine whether we can collect the information internally or ask an external agency to collect it for us. Consider, for instance, that the company interested in determining the gender bias had collected information about the highest degree obtained by the employees when they first joined the firm. However, the firm's internal database was not subsequently updated for any subsequent improvement in education of the employees. Over the course of their careers, employees could have gone back to school for part-time graduate studies or diplomas. This is akin to an investment in their respective human capital.

Without this information, the gender bias analysis will be based on dated information on the employees' education attainment. One way of dealing with this limitation is for the firm to conduct an internal survey, asking the employees to report any additional training, courses, or degrees they might have completed since they started working. With this additional information on education attainment in hand, you can analyze how investment in human capital by the employees might impact their wages. You can also determine the difference between men and women in pursuing higher or technical education opportunities subsequent to their employment with the firm.

At times, the ideal information needed for the analysis might take too long or cost too much to obtain. In such circumstances, the analyst has to make a decision. One option is to postpone the analysis until all relevant information is available. This might not be a viable option because executives need answers and they need them fast. The other option is to adopt a satisficing approach where you proceed with the analysis with what you have and conclude while you adequately state the limitations in your work.

What Analytical Techniques/Methods Do You Need?

It is important to know in advance what methods or techniques to use for the analysis. This has an impact on the type of data you need for the analysis. Consider our gender bias example where we need to determine whether a gender bias in wages or compensation exists when men and women with similar education, experience, and productivity are employed to do the same job. Given that analysts are expected to hold constant other factors while investigating the impact of gender, it appears that a regression-type model is better suited to answer the research question.[13] If I were asked only to compare the difference in average wages for men and women, I would have opted for a t-$test$.[14] I demonstrate the use of t-$test$ and regression analysis in Chapter 6.

The Narrative

The narrative gives life to numbers. Suspended in columns and rows, numbers in tables seldom speak to the reader. The narrative is always what calls attention to the gems latent in tables. After sitting through thousands of presentations over the years, I cannot recall a single incidence when a presenter showed a table onscreen and it made sense without the presenter explaining what was depicted in the table. Numbers slowly start to make sense as the speaker explains what they represent and imply.

The same goes for publications. One needs to read the accompanying text to make sense of the information summarized in tables. I must admit that some exceptionally talented researchers are capable of generating self-explanatory tables. However, they are in a minority. Most analysts have yet to master the art of generating tables that can convey the information without relying on accompanying text.

I believe that even when the tables and charts are well-illustrated, the need for powerful narrative never diminishes. Narrative adds color to facts. It allows you to contextualize the findings. The choice of verbs and metaphors allow you to leave your distinct mark on the findings.

One way to appreciate the power of strong narrative is to compare the coverage of a big event in a local and a national newspaper. Newspapers with a large national subscriber base, such as the *New York Times* in the U.S. and the *Guardian* in the UK have the distinct privilege of working with some of the finest writers and editors. Local newspapers, given their limited resources, are often unable to retain the best talent. Still, they cover the same international or national events. Global thought leaders, who have mastered the craft of creative thinking and writing, contribute opinion pieces to national newspapers. You might want to compare commentary on the same issue from a national and local newspaper to see how the quality of narrative makes all the difference even when the subject matter and facts presented are the same.

I would like to share names of the writers I have admired over the years for their ability to communicate ideas with powerful narrative. From the *New York Times*, I recommend Maureen Dowd, David Brooks, Nicolas Kristoff, and Roger Cohen.

Paul Krugman is a professor of economics, a Nobel Laureate, and a blogger and columnist with the *New York Times*. I think he serves a much better example of a data scientist for the readers of this book. Professor Krugman illustrates his writings with numbers and graphics (krugman.blogs.nytimes.com/). Writing about the French economy, Mr. Krugman shares a time series plot of the yield on French 10-year bonds. While challenging Eugene Fama and others from the "Chicago School" on public sector spending, he graphs the theoretical relationships between variables of interest. Often, Professor Krugman uses data and charts from FRED (Federal Reserve Economic Data) in his blogs. I believe Professor Krugman is the ultimate data scientist because he dances with bold ideas, flirts with numbers, and romances the expression.

Another good source of data-driven narrative are the data blogs set up by leading newspapers. The one I recommend is from the *Guardian*.[15] The *Guardian* has in fact taken data and visualization to a new level. The newspaper even offers courses in data visualizations.[16] A blog in December 2014 discussed the soaring rates of imprisonment in Australia. The narrative was supported by customizable graphics showing differences across states and territories.[17]

The Report Structure

Before starting the analysis, think about the structure of the report. Will it be a brief report of five or fewer pages, or will it be a longer document running more than 100 pages in length? The structure of the report depends on the length of the document. A brief report is more to the point and presents a summary of key findings. A detailed report incrementally builds the argument and contains details about other relevant works, research methodology, data sources, and intermediate findings along with the main results.

I have reviewed reports by leading consultants including Deloitte and McKinsey. I found that the length of the reports varied depending largely on the purpose of the report. Brief reports were drafted as commentaries on current trends and developments that attracted public or media attention. Detailed and comprehensive reports offered a critical review of the subject matter with extensive data analysis and commentary. Often, detailed reports collected new data or interviewed industry experts to answer the research questions.

Even if you expect the report to be brief, sporting five or fewer pages, I recommend that the deliverable follow a prescribed format including the cover page, table of contents, executive summary, detailed contents, acknowledgements, references, and appendices (if needed).

I often find the cover page to be missing in documents. It is not the inexperience of undergraduate students that is reflected in submissions that usually miss the cover page. In fact, doctoral candidates also require an explicit reminder to include an informative cover page. I hasten to mention that the business world sleuths are hardly any better. Just search the Internet for reports and you will find plenty of reports from reputed firms that are missing the cover page.

At a minimum, the *cover page* should include the title of the report, names of authors, their affiliations, and contacts, name of the institutional publisher (if any), and the date of publication. I have seen numerous reports missing the date of publication, making it impossible to cite them without the year and month of publication. Also, from a business point of view, authors should make it easier for the reader to reach out to them. Having contact details at the front makes the task easier.

A *table of contents (ToC)* is like a map needed for a trip never taken before. You need to have a sense of the journey before embarking on it. A map provides a visual proxy for the actual travel with details about the landmarks that you will pass by in your trip. The ToC with main headings and lists of tables and figures offers a glimpse of what lies ahead in the document. Never shy away from including a ToC, especially if your document, excluding cover page, table of contents, and references, is five or more pages in length.

Even for a short document, I recommend an *abstract* or an *executive summary*. Nothing is more powerful than explaining the crux of your arguments in three paragraphs or less. Of course, for larger documents running a few hundred pages, the executive summary could be longer.

An *introductory* section is always helpful in setting up the problem for the reader who might be new to the topic and who might need to be gently introduced to the subject matter before being immersed in intricate details. A good follow-up to the introductory section is a review of available relevant research on the subject matter. The length of the *literature review* section depends upon how contested the subject matter is. In instances where the vast majority of researchers have concluded in one direction, the literature review could be brief with citations for only the most influential authors on the subject. On the other hand, if the arguments are more nuanced with caveats aplenty, then you must cite the relevant research to offer the adequate context before you embark on your analysis. You might use literature review to highlight gaps in the existing knowledge, which your analysis will try to fill. This is where you formally introduce your research questions and hypothesis.

In the *methodology* section, you introduce the research methods and data sources you used for the analysis. If you have collected new data, explain the data collection exercise in some detail. You will refer to the literature review to bolster your choice for variables, data, and methods and how they will help you answer your research questions.

The *results* section is where you present your empirical findings. Starting with descriptive statistics (see Chapter 4, "Serving Tables") and illustrative graphics (see Chapter 5, "Graphic Details" for plots and Chapter 10, "Spatial Data Analytics" for maps), you will move toward formally testing your hypothesis (see Chapter 6, "Hypothetically Speaking"). In case you need to run statistical models, you might turn to regression models (see Chapter 7, "Why Tall Parents Don't Have Even Taller Children") or categorical analysis (see Chapters 8, "To Be or Not to Be" and 9, "Categorically Speaking About Categorical Data"). If you are working with time series data, you can turn to Chapter 11, "Doing Serious Time with Time Series." You can also report results from other empirical techniques that fall under the general rubric of data mining (see Chapter 12, "Data Mining for Gold"). Note that many reports in the business sector present results in a more palatable fashion by holding back the statistical details and relying on illustrative graphics to summarize the results.

The *results* section is followed by the *discussion* section, where you craft your main arguments by building on the results you have presented earlier. The *discussion* section is where you rely on the power of narrative to enable numbers to communicate your thesis to your readers. You refer the reader to the research question and the knowledge gaps you identified earlier. You highlight how your findings provide the ultimate missing piece to the puzzle.

Of course, not all analytics return a smoking gun. At times, more frequently than I would like to acknowledge, the results provide only a partial answer to the question and that, too, with a long list of caveats.

In the *conclusion* section, you generalize your specific findings and take on a rather marketing approach to promote your findings so that the reader does not remain stuck in the caveats that you have voluntarily outlined earlier. You might also identify future possible developments in research and applications that could result from your research.

What remains is housekeeping, including a list of *references*, the *acknowledgement* section (acknowledging the support of those who have enabled your work is always good), and *appendices*, if needed.

Have You Done Your Job as a Writer?

As a data scientist, you are expected to do a thorough analysis with the appropriate data, deploying the appropriate tools. As a writer, you are responsible for communicating your findings to the readers. *Transport Policy*, a leading research publication in transportation planning, offers a checklist for authors interested in publishing with the journal. The checklist is a series of questions authors are expected to consider before submitting their manuscript to the journal. I believe the checklist is useful for budding data scientists and, therefore, I have reproduced it verbatim for their benefit.

1. Have you told readers, at the outset, what they might gain by reading your paper?
2. Have you made the aim of your work clear?
3. Have you explained the significance of your contribution?
4. Have you set your work in the appropriate context by giving sufficient background (including a complete set of relevant references) to your work?
5. Have you addressed the question of practicality and usefulness?
6. Have you identified future developments that might result from your work?
7. Have you structured your paper in a clear and logical fashion?

Building Narratives with Data

Talking about the deliverable is one thing, seeing it is another. In this section, I reproduce brief reports (averaging around 1,000 words), which are based on data and analytics to reinforce the key message. In fall 2011, I started writing a weekly blog for a newspaper in Pakistan, the *Dawn*. The syndicated blog focused on socio-economic and security challenges that continue to stall growth and development of a 180-million strong nation. Given the digital format of the blogs, I included tables and figures in my writings that are showcased every Wednesday on the newspapers' website, www.dawn.com. Later, I started writing for the *Huffington Post* and a Canadian news channel, Global TV. The approach, though, remained the same across the three channels: I searched for data and generated tables and figures to illustrate my arguments.

In this section, I reproduce slightly modified versions of some blogs to serve as an example for deliverables that data scientists and analysts are expected to produce. Recall the key message that I repeat in this book: It is not for the lack of analytics or algorithms that data are not effectively turned into insights. Instead, it is the lack of the ability to communicate the findings from analytics to the larger audience, which is not fluent in analytics, that prevents data- and evidence-driven decision-making. A data scientist therefore is the lynchpin that connects raw

data to insights. The analytics-driven reports in blog format presented next illustrate how t
data and analytics to communicate the key message.

Here are the key features that are common in the blogs presented:

1. Though the strength of the argument relies on the power of the narrative, graphics and tables bolster the key message.

2. Although the tables and figures are simple and easy to comprehend, which they should be for effective communication, the analytics used to generate them might be more involved and comprehensive.

3. You do not need to generate all analytics by yourself. A good data scientist should have the nose to go after processed insights generated by the larger fraternity. Remember, the goal is not to reinvent the wheel!

The blogs presented here are organized along four key themes that intersect with various dimensions of human development challenges, including urban transport and housing, human development in South Asia, and the trials and tribulations of immigrant workers. I begin, though, with the familiar discourse on big data.

"Big Data, Big Analytics, Big Opportunity"

Metrics	Details
Date published	July 25, 2012
Word count	1980
URL	www.dawn.com/news/737165/big-data-big-analytics-big-opportunity

The world today is awash with data. Corporations, governments, and individuals are busy generating petabytes of data on culture, economy, environment, religion, and society. While data has become abundant and ubiquitous, data analysts needed to turn raw data into knowledge are in fact in short supply.

With big data comes the big opportunity for the educated middleclass in the developing world where an army of data scientists can be trained to support the offshoring of analytics from the western countries where such needs are unlikely to be filled from the locally available talent.

The McKinsey Global Institute in a 2011 report revealed that the United States alone faces a shortage of almost 200,000 data analysts.[18] The American economy requires an additional 1.5 million managers proficient in decision-making based on insights gained from the analysis of large data sets. Even when Hal Varian,[19] Google's famed chief economist, profoundly proclaimed that "the real sexy job in 2010s is to be a statistician," there were not many takers for the opportunity in the West where students pursuing degrees in statistics, engineering, and other empirical fields are small in number and are often visa students from abroad.

A recent report by Statistics Canada revealed that two-thirds of those who graduated with a PhD in engineering from a Canadian University in 2005 spoke neither English nor French as

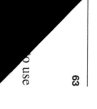

four out of 10 PhD graduates in computers, mathematics, and physical
… estern language as mother tongue. In addition, more than 60 percent of
… re visible minorities, suggesting that the supply chain of highly quali-
… Canada, and largely in North America, is already linked to the talent
… gypt, India, Iran, and Pakistan.

… lata and the scarcity of analysts present a unique opportunity for devel-
… ve an abundant supply of highly numerate youth who could be trained
and mobilized en masse to write a new chapter in modern-day offshoring. This would require a
serious rethink for the thought leaders in developing countries who have not taxed their imagina-
tions beyond dreaming up policies to create sweatshops where youth would undersell their skills
and see their potential wilt away while creating undergarments for consumers in the west. The
fate of the youth in developing countries need not be restricted to stitching underwear or making
cold calls from offshored call-centers in order for them to be part of the global value chains.[20]
Instead, they can be trained as skilled number crunchers who would add value to the otherwise
worthless data for businesses, big and small.

A Multi-Billion Dollar Industry

The past decade has witnessed a major evolution of some very large manufacturing firms known
in the past mostly for hardware engineering that are now transforming into service-oriented firms
to provide business analytics. Take IBM, for example, which specialized as a computer hardware
company producing servers, desktop computers, laptops, and other supporting infrastructure.
That was the IBM of yesteryears. Today, IBM is a global leader in analytics. IBM has divested
from several hardware initiatives, such as manufacturing laptops, and has instead spent billions
in acquisitions to build its analytic credentials. For instance, IBM has acquired SPSS for over a
billion dollars to capture the retail side of the Business Analytics market.[21] For large commercial
ventures, IBM acquired Cognos® to offer full service analytics. The aggressive acquisitions continue to date.

In 2011 alone, the software market for business analytics was worth over $30 billion.[22]
Oracle ($6.1bn), SAP ($4.6 bn), IBM ($4.4 bn), and Microsoft and SAS each with $3.3 bn in
sales led the market. It is estimated that the sale of business analytics software alone will hit
$50 billion by 2016. Dan Vesset of IDC, a company known for gauging industry trends, aptly
noted that business analytics had "crossed the chasm into the mainstream mass market" and the
"demand for business analytics solutions is exposing the previously minor issue of the shortage
of highly skilled IT and analytics staff."

In addition to the bundled software and service sales offered by the likes of Oracle and
IBM, business analytics services in the consulting domain generated additional several billion
dollars worldwide. While the large firms command the lion's share in the analytics market, the
billions left as crumbs by the industry leaders are still a large enough prize for the startups and
small-sized firms to take the analytics plunge.

Several Billion Reasons to Hop on the Analytics Bandwagon

While the IBMs of the world are focused largely on large corporations, the analytics needs for small and medium-sized enterprises (SMEs) are unlikely to be met by IBM, Oracle, or other large players. Cost is the most important determinant. SMEs prefer to have analytics done on the cheap while the overheads of the large analytics firms run into millions of dollars thus pricing them out of the SME market. With offshoring comes the access to affordable talent in developing countries who can bid for smaller contracts and beat the competition in the West on price, and over time on quality as well.

The trick therefore, is to exist along the large enterprises by not competing against them. Realizing that business analytics is not a market, but an amalgamation of several types of markets focused on delivering value-added services involving data capture, data warehousing, data cleaning, data mining, and data analysis, developing countries can carve out a niche for themselves by focusing exclusively on contracts that large firms will not bid for because of their intrinsic large overheads.

Leaving the fight for top dollars in analytics to the top dogs, a cottage industry in analytics could be developed in the developing countries that might strive to serve the analytics need of SMEs. Take the example of the Toronto Transit Commission (TTC), Canada's largest public transit agency with annual revenues exceeding a billion dollars. When TTC needed to have a mid-sized database of almost a half-million commuter complaints analyzed, it turned to Ryerson University, rather than a large analytics firm.[23] TTC's decision to work with Ryerson University was motivated by two considerations. First is the cost. As a public sector university, Ryerson believes strongly in serving the community and thus offered the services gratis. The second reason is quality. Ryerson University, like most similar institutions of higher learning, excels in analytics where several faculty members work at the cutting edge of analytics and are more than willing to apply their skills to real-life problems.

Why Now?

The timing had never been better to engage in analytics on a very large scale. The innovations in Information and Communication Technology (ICT) and the ready availability of the most advanced analytics software as freeware allows entrepreneurs in developing countries to compete worldwide. The Internet makes it possible to be part of global marketplaces with negligible costs. With cyber marketplaces such as Kijiji and Craigslist, individuals can become proprietors offering services worldwide.

Using the freely available Google Sites, one can have a business website online immediately at no cost. Google Docs, another free service from Google, allows one to have a free web server to share documents with collaborators or the rest of the world. Other free services, such as Google Trends, allow individual researchers to generate data on business and social trends without needing subscriptions for services that cost millions. For instance, Figure 3.1 has been generated using Google Trends showing daily visits to the websites of leading analytics firms. Without free access to such services, access to the data used to generate the same graph would carry a huge price tag.

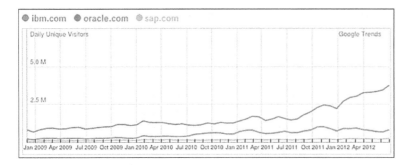

Figure 3.1   Internet traffic to websites of leading analytics firms

Similarly, another free service from Google allows one to determine, for instance, which cities registered the highest number of search requests for a search term, such as *business analytics*. It appears that four of the top six cities where analytics are most popular [July 2012] are located in India, which is evident from Figure 3.2 where search intensity is mapped on a normalized index of 0 to 100.

1. Bangalore (India)	100
2. Singapore (Singapore)	78
3. Chennai (India)	49
4. Mumbai (India)	34
5. New Delhi (India)	28
6. New York (USA)	12

Figure 3.2   Cities with highest number of searches for big data

The other big development of the recent times is freeware that is leveling the playing field between the analytics' haves and have-nots. In analytics, one of the most sophisticated computing platforms is R,[24] which is freely available. Developers worldwide are busy developing the R platform, which now offers over 6,000 packages for analyzing data. From econometrics to operations research, R is fast becoming the lingua franca for computing. R has evolved from being popular just among the computing geeks to having its praise sung by the *New York Times*.[25]

R has also made some new friends, especially Paul Butler,[26] a Canadian undergraduate student who became a worldwide sensation (at least among the geek fraternity) by mapping the geography of Facebook. While being an intern at Facebook, Paul analyzed petabytes of data to plot how friendships were registered in Facebook. His map (see Figure 3.3) became an instant hit worldwide and has been reproduced in publications thousands of times. You might be wondering what computing platform Paul used to generate the map. Wonder no more, the answer is R.

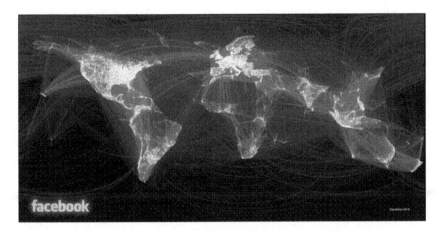

Figure 3.3 Facebook friendship networks mapped across the globe

R is fast becoming the preferred computing platform for data scientists worldwide (see Figure 3.4). For decades, the data analysis market was ruled by the likes of SAS, SPSS, Stata, and other similar players. R has taken over the imagination of data analysts as of late who are fast converging to R. In fact, most innovations in statistics are first coded in R so that the algorithms become freely available immediately to all.

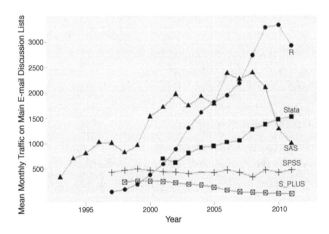

Figure 3.4 R gaining popularity over other statistical software

Source: r4stats.com/articles/popularity/

Another advantage of using R is that training materials are widely available on the Internet, including videos on YouTube.[27]

Where to Next

The private sector has to take the lead for business analytics to take root in emerging economies. The governments could also have a small role in regulation. However, the analytics revolution has to take place not because of the public sector, but in spite of it. Even public sector universities in developing countries cannot be entrusted with the task where senior university administrators do not warm up to innovative ideas unless they involve a junket in Europe or North America. At the same time, the faculty in public sector universities in developing countries is often unwilling to try new technologies.

The private sector in developing countries might want to launch first an industry group that takes upon the task of certifying firms and individuals interested in analytics for quality, reliability, and ethical and professional competencies. This will help build confidence around national brands. Without such certification, foreign clients will be apprehensive to share their proprietary data with overseas firms.

The private sector will also have to take the lead in training a professional workforce in analytics. Several companies train their employees in the latest technology and then market their skills to clients. The training houses would therefore also double as consulting practices where the best graduates might be retained as consultants.

Small virtual marketplaces could be set up in large cities where clients can put requests for proposals and pre-screened, qualified bidders can compete for contracts. The national self-regulating body might be responsible for screening qualified bidders from its vendor-of-record database, which it would make available to clients globally through the Internet.

Large analytics firms believe the analytics market will hit hundreds of billions in revenue in the next decade. The abundant talent in developing countries can be polished into a skilled workforce to tap into the analytics market to channel some revenue to developing countries while creating gainful employment opportunities for the educated youth who have been reduced to making cold calls from offshored call centers.

Urban Transport and Housing Challenges

In addition to death and taxes, traffic congestion is the third inescapable fact of life for those who live in large cities. The following pieces analyze the challenges faced by road warriors and those who struggle to tap into the prohibitively expensive urban housing markets in the developed world.

"You Don't Hate Your Commute, You Hate Your Job!"

Metrics	Details
Date published	May 24, 2014
Word count	850
URL	www.huffingtonpost.ca/murtaza-haider/hate-commuting_b_5381757.html

You don't hate your commute, it's your job. A Statistics Canada survey revealed that workers who disliked their jobs were much more likely to hate their commutes than those who liked their jobs. Our hatred of the morning commute might be driven by our unsatisfactory jobs.

The General Social Survey in 2005, and later in 2010, quizzed thousands of Canadians about their satisfaction with various aspects of their lives, including commuting. At least 64 percent of workers who greatly disliked their jobs were displeased with their commutes.[28] On the other hand, only 10 percent of those who greatly liked their jobs reported disliking their commutes.

Extensive surveys of workers in Canada have revealed that our love-hate relationship with daily commutes is much more nuanced than what we had believed it to be. Furthermore, public transit riders, who spend 63 percent more time commuting to work than those who commute by car, dislike commuting even more, even when they commute for shorter distances than commuters by car do. Lastly, commuters who face frequent congestion, and not necessarily longer commutes in terms of distance or duration, report much higher levels of stress than others. These findings suggest that the urban transport planning discourse should move beyond the diatribe on commute times and instead focus on ways of making commutes more predictable rather than shorter.

Martin Turcotte,[29] a senior analyst with Statistics Canada, has produced several insightful reports on commutes to work in Canada, relying on two separate waves of the General Social Survey. Mr. Turcotte is one of the first few researchers who pointed out the longer commutes by public transit relative to those by car. His findings about public transit's tardiness, which most transit enthusiasts hate to acknowledge, have largely been ignored by those active in planning circles and municipal politics. Instead, an ad nauseam campaign against excessive commute times, wrongly attributed to cars, has ensued.

The dissatisfaction with work seems to be playing into the dislike of commuting. Mr. Turcotte used mathematical models to show that even when one controls for trip length and duration, those who disliked their jobs were much more likely to hate their commutes. It appears that our inherent dissatisfaction with present employment is manifesting in more ways than we might acknowledge. The anticipation of working with colleagues one despises or a supervisor one hates is contributing to one's lack of satisfaction with the daily commute (see Figure 3.5).

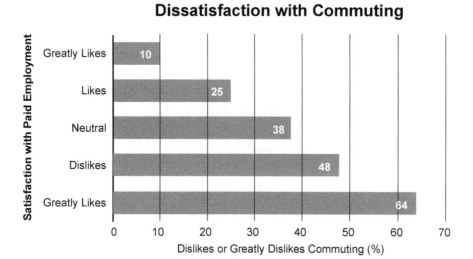

Figure 3.5   The interplay between dislike for commuting and paid employment

Source: Martin Turcotte. Statistics Canada. Catalogue No. 11-088.

A key finding of the 2005 survey is that city slickers hated their commutes more than those who lived in small or mid-sized towns. This requires one to acknowledge the common sense explanations for why people hate commuting. The survey revealed that those who either commuted for longer durations or greater distances hated their commutes more than those who commuted for shorter durations or distances. At the same time, those who faced frequent congestion, and not necessarily longer commutes, hated their commutes even more.

The mobility dialogue in North America remains hyperbolic. The discourse in Canada's largest city region of over 6 million, Toronto, is even more animated and exaggerated. The media has caught on to the notion that Toronto has the longest commute times in Canada, while ignoring the fact that Toronto is also the largest labor market in Canada. In fact, the sizes of regional labor markets explain the difference in average commute times across Canada. At the same time, most Torontonians might not know that commuters in other large cities are even more contemptuous of their daily commutes. The survey revealed that Toronto commuters were the least likely of the six large Canadian cities to hate their commutes (see Figure 3.6).

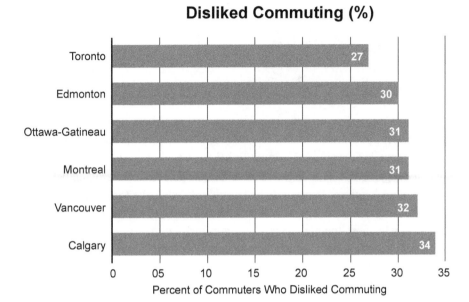

Figure 3.6   Who hates commuting the most?

Source: Martin Turcotte. Statistics Canada. Catalogue No. 11-088.

These findings should help contextualize transport planning discourse in Canada. Our focus should be on what we can change and improve rather than on what is beyond our abilities to influence. Transport planners cannot improve the employment satisfaction for millions of commuters, nor can they devise an urban transit system that will deliver shorter average travel times than cars. Therefore, the focus should be on making commutes bearable and predictable. This might cost much less than the expensive interventions we hear being proposed.

A transport network performance system that informs commuters in real time on their smart phones about accidents, breakdowns, congestion, and delays can be operationalized at a fraction of cost than building new freeways or subways. Consider that in the United States, smartphones, based on their location on the transport network, are delivered real-time Amber alerts about possible kidnappings of minors. Extend the system to include real-time alerts for the entire urban transport network and deliver it to commuters based on their real-time location. This will help commuters plan and execute their commutes better and will reduce their dissatisfaction with commuting.

Communication and information technology to improve commuting has been in existence for years. What has been missing is imagination and the drive to achieve the possible.

"Are Torontonians Spending Too Much Time Commuting?"

Metrics	Details
Date published	May 07, 2014
Word count	750
URL	www.huffingtonpost.ca/murtaza-haider/toronto-commute-times_b_5280934.html

Toronto's long commute times have become a constant refrain dominating the public discourse. Many believe that the commute times are excessive. However, if the laws of physics and common sense were to prevail, Toronto's 33-minute one-way commutes make perfect sense.

Commuting and congestion in Toronto have long been a source of concern and debate. As early as in July 1948, the *Globe* and *Mail* published stories of gridlocked downtown Toronto, calling it the "suffering acres." The recent discourse, however, is prejudiced against Toronto's average commute times, which are the highest in Canada. Remedial measures to shorten Toronto's long commutes are being proposed, whereas commuters (mostly drivers) and transport planners are being criticized for creating rather than solving the problem.

The simple fact that commute times increase with the size of the underlying labor force has been ignored altogether in the ongoing debate. Also overlooked is the fact Toronto's long average commute times are partially due to the slower commutes of many public transit riders. In fact, the size of the labor force, transit ridership, and the presence of satellite commuter towns (for example, Oshawa) explain Toronto's long commute times (see Figure 3.7). The focus should not necessarily be on reducing commute times, but instead on improving the quality of commutes and the reliability of their duration.

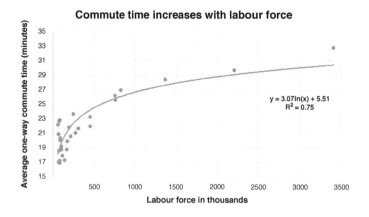

Figure 3.7   Commute times increase with the labor force size

Source: National Household Survey, 2011

Toronto Census Metropolitan Area (CMA) is the largest urban center in Canada, with over 3.5 million workers comprising its labor force. These workers and their jobs cannot be contained in a smaller space, such as London, Ontario, which boasts an average commute time of 21 minutes for a small labor force of 268,000 workers. Whereas Toronto's labor force is 13 times larger, its average commute time is only 1.6 times greater than that of London. In fact, Toronto's labor force is 54 percent larger than that of Montreal, Canada's second largest employment hub. Still, the commute times in Toronto are merely 10 percent larger than that of Montreal.

Toronto's success with public transit is another reason for its large commute times. Almost one in four work trips in Toronto CMA is made by public transit. The 2011 National Household Survey revealed that trips made by public transit were 81 percent longer than those by private car. This means that one in four trips in Toronto is made using a slower mode of travel (see Figure 3.8). Given our stated planning priority to move more commuters off cars and on to public transit, average commute times are likely to increase, and not decrease.

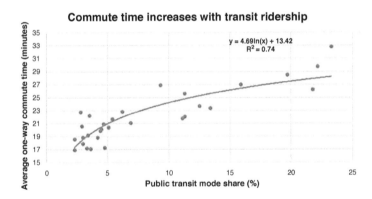

Figure 3.8 Commute times increase with transit use

Source: National Household Survey, 2011.

But how bad is it to have an average commute time of 33 minutes? Is Toronto's average commute time anomalously larger than that of other comparable metropolitan areas in Canada? The average commute time in Montreal of 30 minutes and that in Vancouver of 28 minutes, with significantly smaller respective labor forces, suggest that Toronto's commute time is certainly not anomalous or an outlier.

In fact, simple statistical techniques applied to the commute time data for the 33 large CMAs in Canada revealed that the size of the labor force, the presence of satellite towns in the catchment of the large urban centers, and the public transit share explained 85 percent of the variance in commuting times across Canada. The analysis revealed that average commute times increased by a minute for every 2.7 percent increase in public transit ridership, after I controlled for the size of the labor force and the presence of satellite towns (see Figure 3.9).

Variable	A
Lab Force −15 Plus, Thousands	0.0018 *
Near Large Urban	8.0378 ***
Transit Mode Split	0.3705 ***
Constant	18.0254 ***
N	33
r2_a	0.8504

legend: * p<0.05; ** p<0.01; *** p<0.001

Figure 3.9   Commute times are explained by labor force size and transit market share

Joel Garreau, in his seminal text, *Edge City*,[30] observed that throughout human history, and irrespective of transport technology, the longest desirable commute has been no more than 45 minutes. Toronto, or any other city in Canada, has not reached that critical threshold to become a historical anomaly. The fact that average commute times have approached 30 minutes in large urban centres in Canada is merely an artifact of the size of labor markets.

The debate in Canada should focus not on reducing commute times in large urban centers, which will be akin to setting an impossible goal. Instead, the focus should be on improving the quality of commutes, and more importantly, on making commute times more predictable. It is not the duration of commutes that stresses commuters more, but rather the unpredictability of their commute quality and duration.

"Will the Roof Collapse on Canada's Housing Market?"

Metrics	Details
Date published	July 31, 2014
Word count	800
URL	www.huffingtonpost.ca/murtaza-haider/canada-housing-market_b_5638452.html

The word on the (Bay) street, and in the news media, is that of an overdue "correction" in Canada's housing markets. Some analysts sound more alarming than others do and liken Canada's housing market to that in Ireland. Others sound more calming and speak of a "soft landing."

Households and investors worry that if the concerns of an inflated housing market were true, would it lead to a drastic collapse? Is the roof about to cave in?

A look at the long-term trends suggests that Canada might experience a "correction." However, a housing market collapse similar to the one experienced by Ireland or the United States is unlikely to occur. Furthermore, Canada's housing markets are largely swayed by a small number of relatively large markets in Greater Vancouver, Calgary, and Toronto. If there were to be a correction, it is most likely to be confined to those urban markets that have experienced above average gains in the past few years.

In a recent comment in the *Globe* and *Mail*,[31] Tara Perkins compares Canada's housing market to that of Ireland. A line in a 2007 report about Ireland's housing market gave her the chills. It read: "Most available evidence would now appear to suggest that the housing market appears to be on the way to achieving a soft landing." The real estate collapse in Ireland concerns Tara because she hears similar muted warnings of a soft landing for Canada.

The warnings might be similar, but that is where the similarities end. A look at the long-term trends in house price appreciation between the two housing markets reveals how different they are as one compares the Consumer Price Index (CPI) for housing for Canada and Ireland (see Figure 3.10). One simply cannot miss the spike in shelter costs in Ireland that began in early 2006 and lasted until the fall of 2008, returning a record 61 percent increase over a 34-month period. In comparison, the Canadian CPI for housing does not depict any sudden spikes, and instead suggests a gradual appreciation in shelter costs.

Figure 3.10 Housing price trends in Canada and Ireland

Source: Federal Reserve Bank of St. Louis

In the eight months following October 2008, the CPI for shelter in Ireland dropped from 143.4 to 93.3 (35 percent decline) causing havoc in the housing and other markets. Even a long-term review of Canadian housing markets do not reveal either a sudden exuberance-driven spike or a hungover crash in property markets like the one seen in Ireland.

The concern about Canadian housing markets is largely driven by the higher rates of house price appreciation in Canada's large urban markets, such as Toronto, Vancouver, and Calgary. In the early eighties, the average housing prices in local housing markets were similar in magnitude to that of the overall Canadian average (see Figure 3.11). Afterward, however, local markets started to experience greater price appreciation over the Canadian average. Toronto and

Vancouver took off in the mid-eighties, while Calgary broke away from the national average in 2005. Whereas Toronto experienced a sluggish housing price appreciation in the nineties, Vancouver continued to appreciate at faster rates, picking up even more steam starting in 2002.

Figure 3.11   Housing price trends in Canadian cities

Source: Canadian Real Estate Association

Another important factor to consider, which was also highlighted by Ms. Perkins in the *Globe*, is the record low mortgage rates that facilitate borrowing larger amounts for real estate acquisitions. Figure 3.12 confirms this fact. Since the early eighties, I see a gradual decline in mortgage rates along with a sustained increase in shelter costs.

A sudden increase in mortgage rates could prevent a large number of households from servicing their mortgages. At the same time, we see an unprecedented increase in the household debt-to-GDP ratio for Canada, suggesting that Canadian households might have overborrowed and would feel the pinch if debt servicing becomes expensive. These are serious and legitimate concerns.

The other concern is about how much of the household debt is made up of the mortgage debt. If the housing prices collapse, which some economists have warned, what will it do to the *loan-to-value* ratios and default rates in Canada?

Given that we expect the population in Canada's large urban centres to continue to increase by millions, mostly sustained by immigration, we are, to some extent, immune from the drying up of local housing demand. This suggests that as long as urban Canada is the preferred destination of immigrants from South and Southeast Asia, workers and capital will continue to flow to fuel Canadian housing markets. This is, however, more relevant to the markets in the short run.

Figure 3.12   Shelter costs and mortgage rates in Canada

Source: CANSIM

In the long run, we will all be dead, and that is all we know for certain. In the meanwhile, it never hurts to keep your debt (housing or otherwise) in check.

Human Development in South Asia

The following pieces focus on the human and economic development challenges in South Asia, mostly Pakistan. I begin by favorably reviewing the progress made by Bangladesh in food security since its painful independence from Pakistan in 1971.

"Bangladesh: No Longer the 'Hungry' Man of South Asia"

Metrics	Details
Date published	October 23, 2013
Word count	700
URL	www.dawn.com/news/1051282

In less than a quarter century, Bangladesh has outperformed Pakistan in reducing hunger and malnourishment. From trailing Pakistan in hunger reduction in 1990, Bangladesh has sped ahead of Pakistan and even India by halving hunger statistics.

The recently released Global Hunger Index (GHI) by the International Food Policy Research Institute reveals that hunger has improved globally since 1990.[32] However, South Asia and sub-Saharan Africa are home to the worst forms of hunger. Estimates by the Food and

Agriculture Organization suggest that no fewer than 870 million people go hungry across the globe.

The pejorative reference to the starving, naked Bangalis (Bhookay, Nungay Bengali) is still part of the Pakistani lexicon. The West Pakistan's establishment thought not much of Bangladesh (before separation from Pakistan, Bangladesh was referred to as East Pakistan) when it separated after a bloody war that left hundreds of thousands of Bangladeshis and others dead. Fast forward to 2013 and a new picture emerges where Pakistan struggles to feed its people while Bangladesh gallops ahead in human development. One wonders why Pakistan, which was once thought to have so much promise, has become the sick (and hungry) man of South Asia.

The GHI explains how countries have performed over the past two decades in fighting hunger and disease. The report reveals the early gains made by South Asia in the 1990s to fight hunger and malnutrition. It was the same time when sub-Saharan Africa trailed far behind South Asia in human development. However, since 2000 sub-Saharan Africa has picked up pace and in 2013 it has on average performed better on hunger than the countries in South Asia.

Despite the slow growth in South Asia, Bangladesh is one of the top 10 countries that have made the most progress in reducing hunger since 1990 (see Figure 3.13). The Bangladeshi success with reducing hunger deserves a closer look to determine if this has resulted from sound planning or is merely a result of happenstance. Given that Bangladesh has beaten not just Pakistan, but also India, Nepal, and Sri Lanka in the pace at which it reduced hunger, the success is likely a result of good planning and execution.

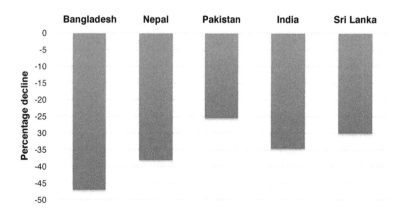

Figure 3.13   Reduction in Global Hunger Index

Source: International Food and Policy Research Institute. (2013). *2013 Global hunger index: The challenge of hunger: Building resilience to achieve food and nutrition security.*

The GHI is computed by averaging three indicators: prevalence of undernourishment in the population, prevalence of underweight children under five years, and under-five mortality rate (see Figure 3.14). The latest data reveals that compared to Pakistan, Bangladesh has lower prevalence of undernourishment in population and under-five mortality rate. However, Pakistan has slightly lower prevalence of underweight children under five years old.

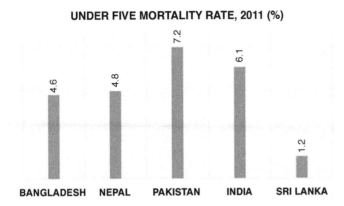

UNDER FIVE MORTALITY RATE, 2011 (%)

Figure 3.14 Under-five mortality rate comparison

Source: International Food and Policy Research Institute. (2013). *2013 Global hunger index: The challenge of hunger: Building resilience to achieve food and nutrition security.*

Research in northwestern Bangladesh suggests that hunger impacts are rather seasonal.[33] During times of low crop yields, food prices rise and result in lower accessibility to sufficient nutrition. The researchers found that the most food insecure are the perpetual poor. A combination of safety nets, set up by the government, and the use of micro-credit help the poor to manage food supply during lean periods.

Apart from safety nets, the improvement in hunger reduction is a result of several commitments and policies. The federal budget in Bangladesh has a dedicated provision for nutrition. Article 15 of the Bangladeshi constitution instructs the State to provide citizens with the necessities of life, including food. The Bangladeshi government in 2012 committed to food security "for all people of the country at all times." The Bangladesh Integrated Nutrition Project (BINP) improved the nutritional outcomes as of 1995. Later in 2002, the National Nutrition Program was launched. Also included in the effort were Expanded Programme on Immunisation and vitamin A supplementation.

The preceding are some examples of how strategic planning resulted in faster reduction of hunger in Bangladesh. Despite the earlier-stated successes, 17 percent of the population in Bangladesh (25 million) continue to suffer from hunger. In fact, 41 percent of the under-five children are likely to be stunted and another 16 percent of under-five children are likely to be "wasted." These numbers show that Bangladesh still has a long way to go in providing food security to its people.

Given that South Asian countries now lag behind sub-Saharan Africa in hunger reduction, it might be prudent for South Asian heads of state to join hands in collaborative efforts to feed the hungry. They might want to learn from the best practices in Bangladesh and elsewhere to protect the food insecure among them.

"Keeping Pakistan's High Fertility in Check"

Metrics	Details
Date published	August 28, 2013
Word count	880
URL	www.dawn.com/news/1038948

While contraceptives do help with family planning, what really helps is preventing women from marrying very young.

A survey in Pakistan revealed that women under 19 years of age at marriage were much more likely to give birth to five or more children than those who were at least 19 years old at marriage. The same survey also revealed that a visit by family planning staff did not have a significant impact on reducing fertility rates. Instead, women who watched family planning commercials on TV were much less likely to have very large families.

Being the sixth most populous nation in the world, Pakistanis are also exposed to disease, violence, and natural disasters, which increase the odds of losing children to accidents or disease. At the same time, many consider the use of contraceptives to be un-Islamic. In addition, the preference for a male offspring is also widespread. As a result, women in Pakistan give birth more frequently than the women in developed economies do. The immediate task for the State is to ensure that the rate of decline in the fertility rate observed over the past two decades continues. At the same time, the governments in Pakistan should learn from Bangladesh, which has made significant progress in stemming the population tide (see Figure 3.15).

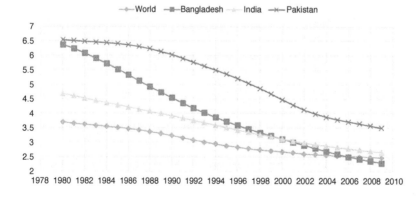

Figure 3.15   Fertility rates (births per woman)

Source: The World Bank (2013)

Getting down to two children per family might seem an elusive target; however, Pakistanis have made huge dents in the alarmingly high fertility rates, despite the widespread opposition to family planning. Since 1988, the fertility rate in Pakistan has declined from 6.2 births per woman to 3.5 in 2009. In a country where the religious and other conservatives oppose all forms of family planning, a decline of 44 percent in fertility rate is nothing short of a miracle.

A recent paper explores the impact of family planning programs in Pakistan.[34] The paper uses data from the 2006–07 Pakistan Demographic and Health Survey, which interviewed 10,023 ever-married women between the ages of 15 and 49 years. The survey revealed that only 30 percent of women used contraceptives in Pakistan. The paper in its current draft has several shortcomings, yet it still offers several insights into what contributes to high fertility and highlights the effective strategies to check high fertility in Pakistan.

The survey revealed that the use of contraceptives did not have any significant impact for women who had given birth to six or more children. While 24 percent of women who did not use any contraceptives reported six or more births, 37 percent of those who used contraceptives reported six or more births. At the same time, 27 percent of women who were not visited by the family planning staff reported six or more births compared with 22 percent of women who had a visit with the family planning staff.

Meanwhile, demographic and socio-economic factors reported strong correlation with the fertility outcomes. Women who were at least 19 years old at marriage were much less likely to have four or more births than those who were younger at the time of marriage. Similarly, those who gave birth before they turned 19 were much more likely to have four or more births.

Education also reported strong correlation with fertility outcomes. Consider that 58 percent of illiterate women reported four or more births compared to 21 percent of those who were highly educated. Similarly, 60 percent of the women married to illiterate men reported four or more births compared to 39 percent of the women married to highly educated men. The survey revealed that literacy among women mattered more for reducing fertility rates than literacy among their husbands.

The underlying variable that defines literacy and the prevalence of contraceptives in Pakistan is the economic status of the households. The survey revealed that 32 percent of women from poor households reported six or more births compared to 21 percent of those who were from affluent households.

The preceding results suggest that family planning efforts in Pakistan are likely to succeed if the focus is on educating young women. Educated young women are likely to get married later and have fewer children. This is also supported by a comprehensive study by the World Bank in which Andaleeb Alam and others observed that cash transfer programs in Punjab to support female education resulted in a nine percentage point increase in female enrollment.[35] At the same time, the authors found that those girls who participated in the program delayed their marriage and had fewer births by the time they turned 19.

"In fact, women in Punjab with middle and high school education have around 1.8 fewer children than those with lower than middle school education by the end of their reproductive life.

Simple extrapolations also indicate that the 1.4 year delay in marriage of beneficiaries associated with the program could lead to 0.4 fewer births by the end of their childbearing years."

The religious fundamentalists in Pakistan will continue to oppose family planning programs. They cannot, however, oppose the education of young women. The results presented here suggest that high fertility rates could be checked effectively by improving young women's access to education. At the same time, educated mothers are the best resource for raising an educated nation.

The Big Move

Economic migrants and globalization of trade and services are some of the defining characteristics of economic development that have taken place in the past few decades. Millions of economic migrants left their homelands in pursuit of better economic prospects abroad. Those who landed at Google or other similar successful IT firms wrote a new chapter in wealth generation. Many others, though, never got an opportunity to prove their skills. In fact, new immigrants defined the face of poverty in many large cities in North America and Europe. The material presented here offers an account of the rewards reaped and challenges faced by the new immigrants in their adopted homelands.

"Pakistani Canadians: Falling Below the Poverty Line"

Metrics	Details
Date published	May 16, 2012
Word count	900
URL	www.dawn.com/news/718842/pakistani-canadians-falling-below-the-poverty-line

Pakistan-born immigrants are the new face of poverty in urban Canada. The Canadian census revealed that 44 percent of Pakistan-born immigrants fell below the poverty line, making them the second most poverty-prone group of immigrants in Canada.

While they might project an aura of opulence during their visits back home, their life in Canada, however, is often full of struggle and frustration. Numerous Pakistani trained engineers, doctors, and PhDs drive cabs or work as security guards in large cities. In fact, one in three taxi-drivers in Canada was born in either India or Pakistan.[36] Several other immigrant professionals are unemployed, thus becoming a burden on Canadian taxpayers.

The Census data for income for 2005 revealed that Pakistan-born immigrants reported the second highest incidence for the low-income cut-off, a proxy for poverty in Canada. In comparison, only 18 percent of the India-born immigrants belonged to a low-income economic family. Immigrants born in the United Kingdom, Portugal, Italy, and Germany reported the lower incidence of poverty in Canada (see Figure 3.16).

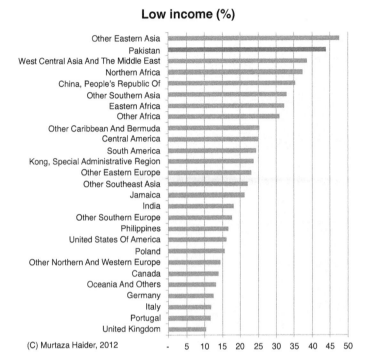

Low income (%)

(C) Murtaza Haider, 2012

Figure 3.16   Percentage of low-income households by country of origin

Source: 2006 Public Use Microdata File, Statistics Canada

Unlike in the Middle East where the Arab governments do not allow assimilation of migrant workers, the Canadian government, and the society, largely does not create systematic barriers that might limit the immigrants' ability to succeed and assimilate. This is not to suggest that immigrants face no hurdles in Canada. They in fact do. For instance, foreign-trained doctors cannot practice medicine without completing further training in Canada. The shorter duration of medical training in Pakistan necessitates the additional certification for doctors. Engineering graduates from Pakistan, however, face no such barrier because the engineering curriculum and the duration of training in Pakistan are similar to that in Canada.

Despite the opportunities (and constraints), Pakistani-Canadians have not prospered as much as immigrants from other countries have. In 2005, wages earned by Pakistan-born immigrants were on average 70 percent of the wages earned by those born in Canada (see Figure 3.17). In comparison, wages earned by the India-born immigrants were 86 percent of the wages earned by Canadians. At the same time, immigrants born in America earned 20 percent more in wages than those born in Canada. Similarly, UK-born immigrants also reported on average higher wages than that of Canadian-born.

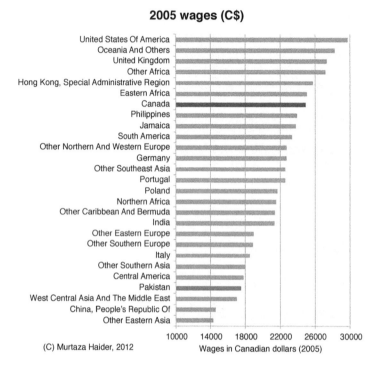

2005 wages (C$)

(C) Murtaza Haider, 2012

Figure 3.17   Wages earned by immigrants and others

Source: 2006 Public Use Microdata File, Statistics Canada

Because of lower wages, the Pakistan-born immigrants reported one of the lowest home-ownership rates. Only 55 percent of Pakistan-born immigrants owned their homes. In comparison, 75 percent of the India-born immigrants owned their homes. At the same time, while only 12 percent of the India- and Philippines-born immigrants had never been part of the workforce, 22 percent of the Pakistan-born immigrants in Canada reported never being in the workforce.

The difference in wages, home-ownership rates, and employment rates between immigrants from India and Pakistan extend beyond the economic spheres. Pakistan-born immigrants live in relatively large-sized families. Whereas only 13 percent of India-born immigrants lived in households of five persons or more, 44 percent of the Pakistan-born immigrants lived in households with five or more people.

Given similar cultural endowments, education, and language skills, it is important to explore why Pakistan-born immigrants in Canada have lagged behind their Indian counterparts. The Indian diaspora is much larger and has been established in Canada for a longer period, which has allowed immigrants from India to develop and benefit from the social networks required to establish in new employment markets.

The limited success of (mostly Asian and African) immigrants in the economic spheres and their modest assimilation in the mainstream Canadian culture has prompted the right-wing groups to launch campaigns against immigration to Canada. While opponents of immigration are mostly naïve and their recommendations to reduce immigration border on lunacy, given Canada's demographic deficit, the fact remains that huge changes in the Canadian immigration policies are already taking place.[37] In Saskatchewan,[38] for instance, the provincial government in May 2012 changed the law that now prohibits immigrants from sponsoring their extended family members unless they secure a "high skill" job offer before arrival.

Since 2001, Pakistan has lost the most in its share of supplying immigrants to Canada.[39] Pakistan was the third largest source of immigrants to Canada in 2001 supplying 6.1 percent of the total immigrants. However, by 2010 Pakistan's share of immigrants declined by 71 percent. Pakistan is no longer even in the top 10 sources of immigrants for Canada. At the same time, the Philippines experienced a 153 percent increase in its share of immigrants making it the biggest source of immigrants to Canada in 2010.

While there is no shortage of skilled applicants from Pakistan, it is hard to establish the precise reason for the declining number of emigrants from Pakistan. It could be that the dismal performance of Pakistan-based immigrants might have prompted the government to reduce the intake from Pakistan. It might also be true that the exponential increase in violence and militancy in Pakistan might have made the task of verifying credentials difficult.

Over the next 50 years, Canada will need millions more immigrants. The current and future lower fertility rates in Canada suggest that immigration is the only possible way of securing sufficient workers to sustain economic growth. Given the lackluster performance of Pakistani emigrants in Canada, it is unlikely that aspirants from Pakistan will get a chance to benefit from Canada's demographic deficit.

"Dollars and Sense of American Desis"

Metrics	Details
Date published	May 23, 2012
Word count	1500
URL	www.dawn.com/news/720712/dollars-and-sense-of-american-desis

American immigrants born in India outdo others in achieving economic success. Pakistan-born immigrants, while trailing behind Indians, also do better than the native-born Americans do.

The estimates reported in the 2010 American Community Survey revealed that the median salaried household income of India-born immigrants was around $94,700. In comparison, the median household income of native-born Americans was estimated at $51,750. Unlike the Pakistan-born immigrants in Canada, who lagged behind others in economic prosperity, Pakistani emigrants in America are relatively better off with their median household incomes 18 percent higher than that of the native-born Americans.

The American Community Survey for 2010 reveals that among the South Asians living in the U.S., India-born immigrants are far ahead of Pakistanis, Bangladeshis, and Afghanis (see Figure 3.18). Even when compared with immigrants from Egypt, a country known for supplying highly educated immigrants, Indian emigrants report exceptionally higher indicators of economic progress.

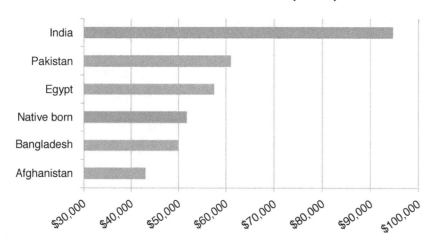

Median household income (2010$)

Figure 3.18   Median household income of immigrants and others in the U.S. (2010)

Source: American Community Survey, 2010

India-born immigrants also reported one of the lowest poverty rates at 4 percent (see Figure 3.19). On the other hand, Afghanistan-born immigrants reported the highest poverty rate where one in five Afghan immigrants was deemed below the poverty line in the U.S. Although Pakistan-born immigrants reported higher median household incomes than the native-born Americans did, surprisingly 14 percent of the Pakistan-born immigrants were below the poverty line compared to only 9.4 percent of the native-born Americans.

Another indicator of financial distress is the percentage of household income spent on gross rent. Households spending 30 percent or more of household income on rent are considered financially distressed. Among households who live in rental units, 57 percent of the immigrants from Pakistan, Bangladesh, and Egypt spent more than 30 percent of the household income on rent compared to only 24 percent of immigrants from India.

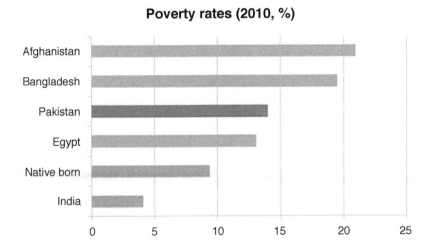

Poverty rates (2010, %)

Figure 3.19   Incidence of poverty among immigrants and others in the U.S. (2010)

Source: American Community Survey, 2010

These poverty statistics raise several questions. For instance, despite having similar South Asian heritage, Pakistan-born immigrants report a 2.4-times higher rate of poverty than their Indian counterparts do. Furthermore, poverty among younger cohorts (18 years old or younger) is even worse among immigrants from Pakistan than from India. At the same time, almost 50 percent of under-18 Afghan immigrants are reportedly below the poverty line in the U.S. These statistics necessitate the need to explore the reasons behind the economic disparities among the immigrants from South Asia.

Let us undertake a socio-economic comparison of South Asians living in the U.S. I have restricted the reporting to immigrants originating from India, Pakistan, Bangladesh, and Afghanistan. This is done because India, Pakistan, Bangladesh, and to some extent Afghanistan have more in common in culture and recent history than other countries in South Asia. I have thrown in Egypt for good measure to serve as a control for immigrants from another Muslim-majority country with a different cultural background.

The purpose of this comparative review is to determine the reasons behind the success of India-born immigrants in the U.S. Could it be that the immigrants from India had luck on their side, or could it be that Indian immigrants possessed the necessary ingredients to succeed in the highly competitive labor market in the U.S.? More importantly, one needs to explore why immigrants from Pakistan and Bangladesh lag behind those from India in achieving the same levels of economic success.

Sizing the South Asians

With approximately 1.8 million individuals, India-born immigrants form the largest cohort among South Asians in the U.S. The American Community Survey (ACS) in 2010 estimated Pakistan-born immigrants at 300,000, Bangladesh-born immigrants at 153,000, and Afghanistan-born immigrants at 60,000. Egypt-born immigrants totaled 133,000. Immigrants from India were approximately five times the size of Pakistan-born immigrants. The relatively large size of Indian immigrants leads to larger social networks, which are helpful in seeking better employment and social prospects.

Despite their large population base, most India-born immigrants in the U.S. are recent arrivals. Whereas 47 percent of the India-born immigrants arrived in the U.S. after 2000, only 36 percent of the Pakistan-born immigrants arrived after 2000 (see Figure 3.20). This suggests that the economic success of immigrants from India is driven by the recent arrivals. Relatively speaking, immigrants from Afghanistan have enjoyed the longest tenure in the U.S. of the South Asian immigrants. Notice that although 42 percent of Afghan emigrants arrived in the U.S. before 1980, only 25 percent of the Indian emigrants accomplished the same.

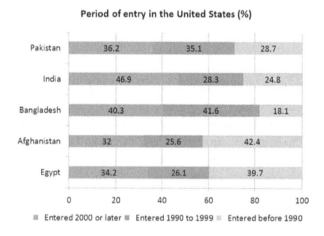

Figure 3.20   Waves of immigration

Source: American Community Survey, 2010

Pakistanis Have Larger Families

With 4.3 persons per household, immigrants from Pakistan and Afghanistan reported significantly larger family sizes. In comparison, the native-born population reported an average household size of 2.6 persons whereas the size of India-born immigrant households was around 3.5 persons. The difference between immigrants from India and other South Asians is more pronounced when one looks at the per capita earnings. Owing to their smaller household size, immigrants from India reported significantly higher per capita incomes than other immigrants and even native-born Americans. For instance, Bangladesh-born immigrants reported 50% less in median per capita income than those from India. Moreover, although immigrants from Pakistan reported higher household incomes than the immigrants from Egypt, the larger household size of Pakistan-born immigrants brought their per capita incomes lower than that of the Egyptians.

Larger household size results in overcrowding, especially among low-income households, who often live in rental units. The average household size of rental households from Pakistan was 33 percent larger than the same for Indian emigrants in the U.S. Fifteen percent of the households from Pakistan were found to have more than one occupant on average per room compared to only 6 percent of those from India.

Women in the Labor Force

A key source of distinction between the immigrants from India and other South Asians is the higher participation of Indian women in the labor force. A much higher integration of women in the labor force is one of the reasons why immigrants from India have fared much better than others in the United States. Consider that only 42 percent of the women from Pakistan were active in the U.S. labor force compared to 57 percent of women emigrants from India. In fact, women from Pakistan reported one of the lowest labor force participation rates in the U.S., falling behind women from Egypt, Afghanistan, and Bangladesh.

Education Matters the Most

It should come as no surprise that emigrants from India are one of the most educated cohort in the United States. Almost 42 percent of the adult Indian emigrants had a graduate (master's) or a professional degree. In comparison, only 10 percent of the native-born adults reported a graduate or professional degree. Approximately 23 percent of adult immigrants from Egypt and Pakistan reported the same.

The correlation between higher education attainment and higher median household incomes is explicitly presented in Figure 3.21. India-born immigrants with professional degrees also reported significantly higher incomes than other immigrants and native-born Americans. Immigrants from Afghanistan, with one of the lowest incidence of professional degrees, reported the lowest median household incomes.

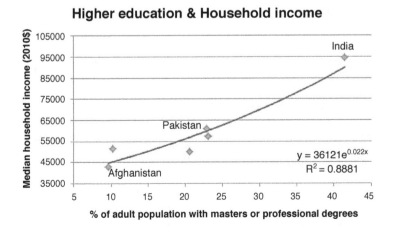

Figure 3.21   Correlation between higher incomes and higher education

Source: American Community Survey, 2010

The gender divide is again instrumental between immigrants from India and other immigrants. Whereas 70 percent of India-born female adults held a bachelor's degree or higher, only 46 percent of adult females born in Pakistan reported the same. At the same time, only 28 percent of the native-born female adults in the U.S. reported completing university education.

Better Education Better Careers

The education attainment levels among adult immigrants largely determine their career choices. University education resulting in professional or graduate degrees allows immigrants to qualify for well-paying jobs in the U.S. Immigrants from India have been able to use their high-quality education to make inroads into the high-paying employment markets. One is therefore hardly surprised to see that of the adult employed population, 70 percent immigrants from India are working in occupations focusing on management, business, science, and arts. In comparison, only 44 percent of immigrants from Pakistan and 33 percent of immigrants from Bangladesh are employed in similar occupations.

What We Have Learned

"Give me your tired, your poor, Your huddled masses yearning to breathe free, The wretched refuse of your teeming shore. Send these, the homeless, tempest-tost to me, I lift my lamp beside the golden door!"

In 1883, Emma Lazarus asked for the tired, the poor, and the wretched refuse. India instead sent her very best to the United States. Instead of the huddled masses, graduates from the Indian Institutes of Technology and Management landed in thousands at the American shores. These immigrants were products of a sophisticated higher education system whose foundations were laid by the first Indian Prime Minister, Pandit Nehru, in the early fifties.

In the rest of South Asia, especially in Pakistan and Bangladesh, education has never been a national priority. The results of such conflicting priorities are obvious. Graduates from Indian universities are outdoing others in competitive labor markets at home and abroad.

"The Grass Appears Greener to Would-Be Canadian Immigrants"

Metrics	Details
Date published	July 3, 2013
Word count	750
URL	www.dawn.com/news/1022553

Canada should have gotten it right by now. A 146-year old country of immigrants should know how to integrate new immigrants. The recent census data, however, suggests that not to be the case.

While Canadians celebrated the 146th birthday of their country, many recent immigrants, however, had little to celebrate in their adopted homeland where their unemployment rate was 75 percent higher than that of the native-born Canadians.

Details from the 2011 National Household Survey (NHS) on labor outcomes paint a dismal picture for many immigrant groups, especially those considered a visible minority, a term referring to the people who visibly do not belong to the majority race at a place. For the would-be South Asian emigrants, the grass appears greener in Canada.

The labor force statistics from the NHS reveal the uneven geography of employment outcomes for various ethnic groups. More than one in four working-age Arabs, who migrated to Canada between 2006 and 2011, was unemployed (see Figure 3.22). During the same time-period, one in seven South Asian immigrants was also unemployed.

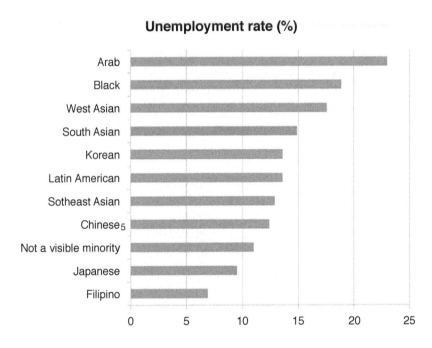

Figure 3.22   Unemployment rates for visible minorities in Canada (2010)

Source: Statistics Canada. National Household Survey, 2011.

The recent immigrants are most likely to experience adverse labor market outcomes, such as un- or under-employment. This is primarily a result of moving to a new place where one does not have social networks, one is unfamiliar with the system, and one's professional credentials are either not recognized at all or are not recognized fast enough for one to have a career in one's chosen field. The result of these limitations is that recent immigrants end up working odd jobs, trying to make ends meet. Eventually, they should be able to address these limitations and improve their employment prospects. For South Asian emigrants, this happens to be the case in Canada.

The unemployment rate of recent immigrants from South Asia, that is, those who arrived between 2006 and 2011, was 14.9 percent in 2011. The same for those who arrived between 2001 and 2005 was lower at 10.9 percent. Similarly, for South Asians who landed in the 90s, the unemployment rate was even lower at 9.2 percent. As for those who arrived in the 80s, the unemployment rate was 6.8 percent. Finally, for those who arrived before 1981, it was 5.9 percent.

These figures offer proof for the assimilation effect in labor market outcomes for immigrants. The longer the immigrants stay in the adopted homeland, the more knowledgeable they become of the rules and customs, and are more likely to succeed in the labor markets.

Despite the assimilation effect, immigrants classified as visible minorities continue to have larger unemployment rates than non-visible minority migrants. While 5.9 percent of the South Asian emigrants who arrived in Canada before 1981 were unemployed, only 5.1 percent of the non-visible minority immigrants (who arrived before 1981) were unemployed.

According to the NHS, the unemployment rates of immigrants also vary across Canada. The worst employment markets for South Asian emigrants were in Quebec. In Montreal, Quebec's largest city, the unemployment rate for South Asian emigrants was 14.6 percent. On the other hand, the most favorable employment markets for South Asians were in the oil rich Alberta province. In Edmonton, Alberta's second most populous city, the unemployment rate for South Asian emigrants was much lower at 5.9 percent in 2011. Similarly, the unemployment rate for Arab emigrants was over 16 percent in Quebec and around 9.5 percent in Alberta.

Education plays a role in securing better employment prospects. Highly educated immigrants with an earned doctorate or master's degree had an unemployment rate of 5.2 percent and 7.2 percent, respectively. However, the unemployment rates for similarly educated non-immigrants in Canada were significantly lower. The unemployment rate for non-immigrants with an earned doctorate degree was merely 2.9 percent, suggesting that highly educated immigrants, such as PhDs, had a 79 percent higher unemployment rate than non-immigrants with similar credentials. Even worse, one in 10 recent immigrants who arrived in Canada between 2006 and 2011 and had an earned doctorate degree was unemployed.

Although the immigrants are able to improve their lot over time in their adopted homelands, the initial years of struggle are always painful. Secondly, immigrants are seldom able to plug the wage gap with the native-born, irrespective of their education and skills.

It is never an easy decision to begin with. However, as professionals chart out plans to migrate to foreign lands, they should know that the grass always appears greener on the other side of the fenced border!

"Bordered Without Doctors"

Metrics	Details
Date published	August 24, 2012
Word count	850
URL	www.dawn.com/news/744190/pakistani-americans-bordered-without-doctors

Despite thousands of distinguished doctors of Pakistani origin practicing in the U.S., Pakistani Americans are among the most deprived of healthcare services. Almost one in four Pakistanis is uninsured and thus enjoys no or limited access to the American healthcare system.

The data from the U.S. Census Bureau reveals that 23 percent of the 409,000 Pakistanis in the U.S. were uninsured in 2009, making Pakistanis the most uninsured cohort of all Asians in the U.S. Although the number of Pakistanis has doubled in the U.S. between 2001 and 2010, their per capita incomes continue to trail behind Indians and other immigrants from Asian countries, which keep a large cohort of Pakistanis uninsured in the U.S.

Immigrants from Pakistan are not alone in the healthcare wasteland in the U.S. Also performing poorly in healthcare accessibility are immigrants from Bangladesh, Korea, and Cambodia. India-born immigrants fare much better (see Figure 3.23). The percent of uninsured Indians in the U.S. is half of that of Pakistanis.

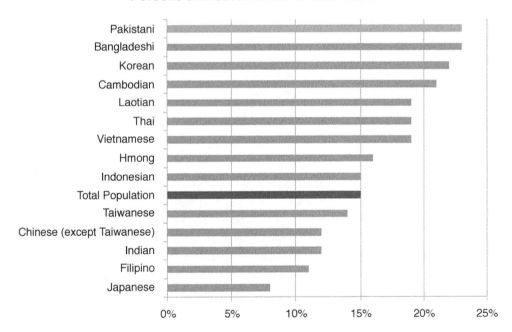

Percent Uninsured in the United States

Figure 3.23 Uninsured American immigrants by place of origin

Source: A Community of Contrasts: Asian Americans in the United States (2011)

A report by the Asian American Center for Advancing Justice explores the uneven landscape of success and deprivation among South Asians in the U.S.[40] Although the American establishment selectively cites Asians as a successful example of the American melting pot, the reality, however, is quite nuanced. Unlike the *softwared* immigrants from Bangalore, whose economic success in the U.S. enjoys bipartisan acclaim, the plight of Bangladeshis or Hmongs in the U.S., who experience significantly more poverty than other immigrants, has largely been ignored.

Access to affordable healthcare has been a major policy hurdle for the U.S. where, unlike Canada, Australia, and most of Western Europe, universal healthcare does not exist. This implies that individuals have to purchase healthcare at market prices from vendors or purchase health insurance instead. The gainfully employed in the U.S. do not share this concern since their employers insure them and their families. However, for a sizeable low-income cohort of approximately 45 million Americans who are uninsured, the healthcare costs can be financially crippling.

A brief visit to a hospital in the U.S. for a few routine tests and an overnight stay can easily run into tens of thousands of dollars. Many, if not most, of the 45 million low-income uninsured Americans cannot afford even a single night's stay in the hospital. Thus, the uninsured either forgo medical treatment or consult doctors only when it is necessary, which ultimately results in inferior health outcomes for the uninsured in America than the insured.

The free market enterprise in healthcare in the U.S. has created a system whose costs can no longer be borne by the society. The wage bill of healthcare professionals, mostly doctors, and the profits demanded by the pharmaceuticals and HMOs has left 45 million without adequate healthcare in one of the most resource-rich countries in the world.

Realizing the challenges faced by uninsured Americans, President Barack Obama has remained determined to extend the healthcare coverage to the 45 million uninsured Americans. The Obama Health Care Reform promises affordable healthcare for all by regulating the healthcare marketplace.[41]

One would have hoped to see universal support for universal healthcare in the U.S. What can be so wrong in extending the healthcare protection to 45 million uninsured in the U.S.? The reality, however, is quite different in the U.S. where the Obama Healthcare Reform has become a bone of contention between the Democrats (proponents) and the Republicans, who believe that the U.S. government and businesses cannot afford to pay the healthcare costs of their fellow (low-income 45 million) citizens. The Republicans challenged the proposed healthcare reforms in the U.S. Supreme Court, which decided in favor of President Obama's plan and in the process diluted the plan as well. The equally split verdict between the Supreme Court judges (four judges voted to keep the plan while another four found the plan unconstitutional) needed Chief Justice John G. Roberts Jr.'s vote to break the tie. Fortunately, for President Obama, the Chief Justice favored the President's plan.

While Americans have continued to debate and agonize over the merits of their healthcare system, the fact remains that theirs is one of the most expensive healthcare systems, even among the developed economies (see Figure 3.24).[42] The U.S. spends 18 percent of its GDP on health, which is 50 percent more than that of Germany. Canadians also enjoy universal healthcare and spend only 11 percent of their GDP on health.

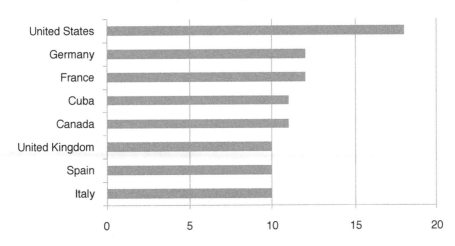

Figure 3.24   Health spending levels in developed economies

Source: WHO (Data obtained from *Guardian*)[43]

A large number of Pakistanis are also included in the 45 million uninsured in the U.S. It is rather odd to see the 10,000-plus Pakistan-born influential and vocal physicians in the U.S. on one side and on the other the 100,000 Pakistanis with no access to healthcare who are ultimately left at the mercy of charities.

Although the Pakistan-born physicians in the U.S. continue to play a role in lobbying the U.S. government on its foreign policy, they might also want to consider expanding their efforts to extend healthcare to thousands of uninsured Pakistani-Americans who have been bordered without doctors.

Summary

Imagine the joy the dancing daffodils brought to William Wordsworth, one of the greatest poets of the English language. As he walked through the countryside, he spotted golden daffodils dancing in the breeze. He couldn't resist the splendor. He wrote:

Beside the lake, beneath the trees,

Fluttering and dancing in the breeze.

Continuous as the stars that shine

And twinkle on the Milky Way,

They stretch'd in never-ending line

Along the margin of a bay

Wordsworth even guesses their number, 10,000 flowers. But what is memorable is not the number of flowers, but the way he describes how the daffodils move and bring joy to his heart.

Ten thousand saw I at a glance,

Tossing their heads in sprightly dance.

The poem, "Daffodils," circa 1804, is my favorite example of mixing the power of narrative with numbers to paint a picture that will forever remain embedded in the reader's mind. I am not suggesting here that you consider inserting poetry in your reports. Instead, I want you to be open to creative thinking and powerful expression. The narrative detailing numbers need not be dry. As Wordsworth shows us in "Daffodils" wagering a guess about the number of flowers allows him to suggest they were in plenty. However, the real story was in the way the breeze and flowers joined in a "sprightly dance."

In this chapter I have detailed the thesis statement about data science. I do not consider data science to be exclusively about big or small data, algorithms, coding, or engineering. I believe data science is about telling stories with data. The strength of data science lies in the power of the narrative.

There is no dearth of statisticians, computer scientists and engineers, and software developers. In fact, the tech bubble bust a decade earlier revealed that we might have graduated too many computer scientists. Still, the leading management consultants forecast a shortage of millions of workers who can put data to good use. I believe the real scarcity is of those who not only can analyze data, but who also could weave powerful data-driven narratives, illustrating their arguments with expressive graphics and tables.

This chapter focused on the deliverable; that is, a report or a presentation that constituted the final step in analytics. Too often the focus of data science texts is on the technical aspects focusing on statistics or programming. Seldom have such texts highlighted the need for storytelling with data. This book differs from others on data science by focusing on the deliverable and encouraging the reader to become a storyteller who uses numbers to capture the imagination of her readers.

Endnotes

1. Virgil Johnson personality sketch; Role as Mohawk Data Sciences Corp pres discussed. (1969, April 20). *The New York Times*, p. 3.

2. Bryce, G. R., Gould, R., Notz, W. I., and Peck, R. L. (2001). "Curriculum Guidelines for Bachelor of Science Degrees in Statistical Science." *The American Statistician*, 55(1), 7–13.

3. Davenport, T. (2015, January 22). "Why Data Storytelling Is So Important, and Why We're So Bad at It." Retrieved September 19, 2015, from http://deloitte.wsj.com/cio/2015/02/10/why-data-storytelling-is-so-important-and-why-were-so-bad-at-it/?mod=wsjrc_hp_deloitte.

4. www.mckinsey.com/

5. www.deloitte.com/

6. tinyurl.com/deloitte-us-2014

7. We illustrate time series plots in Chapter 11.

8. Piketty, T. (2014). *Capital in the Twenty-First Century*. Translated by Arthur Goldhammer. Harvard University Press. Cambridge, MA.

9. Blau, F. D. and Kahn, L. M. (n.d.). "Gender differences in pay." *The Journal of Economic Perspectives: A Journal of the American Economic Association, 14*(4), 75–99.

10. We conducted our searches on January 5, 2015. Your results for the same search might differ because of the ever-expanding corpus of Google Scholar.

11. paperpile.com

12. https://evernote.com/

13. See Chapter 7 for regression models.

14. See Chapter 6 for t-tests.

15. www.theguardian.com/data

16. www.theguardian.com/guardian-masterclasses/digital

17. www.theguardian.com/news/datablog/2014/dec/12/jail-rates-soar-in-states-and-territories-statistics-show

18. www.mckinsey.com/features/big_data

19. zomobo.net/play.php?id=D4FQsYTbLoI

20. www.flixster.com/movie/outsourced/

21. www-01.ibm.com/software/analytics/spss/

22. www.information-age.com/channels/information-management/perspectives-and-trends/2112153/analytics-software-market-hits-and3630-billion.thtml

23. www.ttc.ca/News/2012/June/0613_ryerson_ttc.jsp

24. cran.r-project.org/

25. www.nytimes.com/2009/01/07/technology/business-computing/07program.html?_r=1&pagewanted=all

26. www.facebook.com/notes/facebook-engineering/visualizing-friendships/469716398919

27. www.youtube.com/watch?v=sT7GzZsf3Hg&feature=channel&list=UL

28. www.statcan.gc.ca/pub/11-008-x/2006004/pdf/9516-eng.pdf

29. www.statcan.gc.ca/pub/11-008-x/2011002/article/11531-eng.pdf

30. www.amazon.ca/Edge-City-Life-New-Frontier/dp/0385424345

31. www.theglobeandmail.com/report-on-business/economy/housing/canada-better-served-learning-from-the-housing-crash-in-ireland/article19815811/

32. www.ifpri.org/publication/2013-global-hunger-index-0

33. www.tandfonline.com/doi/abs/10.1080/00220388.2012.720369#.UmdZd_ljtTo

34. papers.ssrn.com/sol3/papers.cfm?abstract_id=2172547

35. elibrary.worldbank.org/content/workingpaper/10.1596/1813-9450-5669

36. www.theglobeandmail.com/news/opinions/editorials/overqualified-immigrants-really-are-driving-taxis-in-canada/article2429356/

37. www.theglobeandmail.com/news/national/time-to-lead/rethinking-immigration-the-case-for-the-400000-solution/article2421322/

38. www.leaderpost.com/business/Protesters+outside+Regina+Legislature+immigration+rule+changes+betrayal/6626818/story.html

39. www.cic.gc.ca/english/resources/statistics/facts2010/permanent/10.asp

40. www.advancingjustice.org/pdf/Community_of_Contrast.pdf

41. www.standupforhealthcare.org/learn-more/quick-facts/12-reasons-to-support-health-care?gclid=CP7Y1NK__bECFRERNAod9BQAlQ

42. www.guardian.co.uk/news/datablog/2012/jun/30/healthcare-spending-world-country

43. www.guardian.co.uk/news/datablog/2012/jun/30/healthcare-spending-world-country

Serving Tables

As I have emphasized throughout this book, a report or a deliverable comprises three neces-
sary ingredients, namely graphics, tables, and a narrative. This chapter focuses on generating
tables. I illustrate the fundamentals of what you should present in tables. Even more importantly,
I explain how you should format and present tables. I reinforce the key lessons illustrated in this
chapter throughout the book.

I find it quite strange that most books on statistics and analytics do not dedicate space to the
fundamentals of summarizing data in tables. Such books are full of tables. However, these books
assume that their readers already know how to generate the tables and, more importantly, format
them adequately to serve as effective tools for communicating findings to their intended audiences. However, based on my experience with the research generated by students and colleagues,
I conclude that most tables either fail completely or partially to communicate the findings to the
intended audience. Recall how many times you have seen some summary statistics reported for
the variable "gender" in a table, forcing you to spend extra time trying to figure out whether gender refers to male or female.

Most off-the-shelf software programs, including SPSS, Stata, R, and SAS readily generate
tables that summarize data and present it in a variety of formats. Despite their user-friendliness
and flexibility, their outputs are seldom ready to be copied and pasted into your finished deliverable. Ill-formatted tables with dubious variable names and column headings make their way into
documents, adding to the readers' anguish, rather than facilitating comprehension.

This chapter is about generating tables to summarize data such that the tables become an
essential tool for your storytelling. Each table in the document should serve a specific purpose
in building the narrative. Only include a table if it is absolutely necessary. If you can replace the
table with a figure, use the figure instead. If you can eliminate the table without any loss of information, then you must exclude it.

I illustrate these concepts with two stories: One explores the use of digital technologies
and social media in the rising economic power, Brazil. There is more than soccer and beaches to

Brazil. The second story is about the widely (and rather erroneously held) held belief that "beauty pays"; that is, attractive individuals get higher pay, better grades in school, and better service in restaurants, and so on.

In the first story, I review the use of the Internet and social media in Brazil. Not so long ago, the news media, investment bankers, and others had gone gaga over the emerging economies of Brazil, Russia, India, and China (also referred to with the acronym *BRIC*). The hype was created in a 2004 report by Goldman Sachs that listed the four economies as the emerging powerhouses. Since then, South Africa has been added to the group and the new acronym is BRICS. In addition, the hype of yesteryears about these emerging economies and their envious double-digit growth has also dissipated much. The double-digit growth rates are no longer achievable even by China or India.

I analyze data from Brazil to see whether it has eventually emerged as a powerhouse by reviewing the prevalence of the Internet and social media there. I use data from a survey by the Pew Research Center to paint a picture of the consumer adoption of digital media.

The second story is about beauty and the beast. Do you believe or suspect that your attractive colleagues are being paid more? Or if you are a student, have you noticed, perhaps, that the more attractive students in your class might be getting more breaks or even better grades? I am interested in determining the answer to the question: Does beauty pay? Using data from the University of Texas, I try to determine whether professors' looks are instrumental in getting higher or lower teaching evaluations from students. An excellent exposé of this topic is presented in the book, *Beauty Pays* by Professor Daniel Hamermesh, who has generously made his Texas University data set available for further analysis.

2014: The Year of Soccer and Brazil

The year 2014 will be remembered for many reasons, some good, and others bad. The good brings us to the 2014 soccer world cup in Brazil where the "beautiful game," which is called football outside of Canada and the United States, is not only a part of the culture, but a defining aspect of it. Seeing Brazil lose in the semi-finals was devastating for Brazilians, who had their eyes set on the finals. Despite the loss, Brazil proved to be an excellent host where the game was played and celebrated inside stadia and on the streets.

Brazil came to prominence after a well-crafted report from Goldman Sachs coined the BRIC acronym, and with it, illustrated a new market for potential and growth.[1] With the newfound attention came the expectations for above-average growth and socioeconomic development.

At the same time, the advances in Communication and Information Technologies (CIT) served both as an indicator of economic development and as an input to economic productivity and development. I use data from the 2010 Pew Global Attitudes Survey to determine how many inroads CITs have made in Brazil.

The Pew data is an excellent resource for applied comparative research in socioeconomics. The 2010 survey interviewed a representative sample comprising 25,000 individuals from 20 countries about a variety of topics including economics, the environment, politics, and the like. In this chapter, I extract data for Brazil and focus on the adoption of the Internet and social media.

I am interested in determining whether the hype around Brazil as being a member of the BRIC economies is matched by the adoption and penetration of social media to the level one would expect in a modern or rapidly modernizing economy. We have observed across several countries that economic development has been accompanied by a significant improvement in CITs. I am neither arguing causation nor suggesting that either economic development increases CITs, or the other way around; I am merely referring to correlation between economic development and the increase in CIT use. See Figure 4.1.

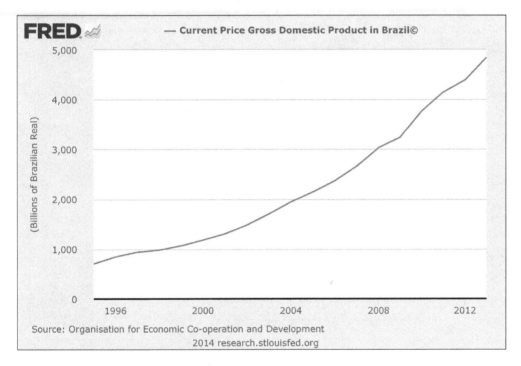

Figure 4.1   Current price GDP in Brazil

The Pew data is from 2010, which is recent enough to allow for comparisons between economic development and CITs to be made. I commented about Pew data sets in Chapter 2, "Data in the 24/7 Connected World," as an excellent source of survey data sets that are available for free. I extracted data for Brazil and restricted the data set to a select few variables. The data set is downloadable from the book's website, via the link under Chapter 4.[2] The data set contains 1,000 observations and includes variables listed in Table 4.1.

Table 4.1   Description of Variables in the Pew Data Set on Brazil

Variable	Description
country	Country of residence of the respondent
satisfied	Is the respondent satisfied with country's direction and development
Internet	Does the respondent use the Internet?
email	Does the respondent use email?
cell	Does the respondent use cell phones?
social	Does the respondent use social media?
gender	Gender of the respondent
age	Age of the respondent
education	Educational attainment
income	Annual income reported by the respondent
ethnicity	Ethnicity of the respondent
pol.party	Political affiliation
weight	Sampling weight
new.cell	Revised variable for cellphone use
new.email	Revised variable for email
new.Internet	Revised variable for Internet use
new.social	Revised variable for social media
new.satis	Revised variable for satisfaction with the country
new.inc	Revised variable for respondent's income
new.age	Revised variable for respondent's age

I illustrate the concepts using R in the text. I also reproduce some key results for Stata in the concluding section of this chapter. The book's website, under Chapter 4, provides scripts to generate similar output, as the one presented with R in the text, for Stata, SAS, and SPSS.

You can directly download the data set in R using the script provided here.

```
setInternet2(TRUE) # solution for https files
download.file("https://sites.google.com/site/
econometriks/docs/brazil.RData", "brazil2.RData")
```

At the same time, the R script can load the data set from the working directory and lists the variables included in the data set.

```
load("brazil2.Rdata")
names(brazil)
```

I will illustrate R packages **htmlTable**, **xtable**, and **RMarkdown** to generate the output. You can open the accompanying **RMarkdown** script, also available for download from the book's website, directly in **RStudio** (a GUI for R) to generate all outputs presented in this section.

I begin by determining the percentage of the Brazilian population that uses the Internet. I tabulate the `Internet` variable. Note that the command generates the output as an html file that you can readily load into Microsoft Excel or Microsoft Word to manipulate tabular data for presentation. Also, note that the `Internet` variable is a categorical variable suited for frequency distributions, rather than for calculations of the mean or standard deviation.

```
tab<-cbind("Internet"=table(brazil$Internet))
htmlTable(tab, rowlabel = "User status")
```

Table 4.2 shows that out of 1,000 respondents, only 358 reported using the Internet and at the same time, another four blessed souls were unsure if they had used the Internet. I recommend treating such data with care. In this particular case, I cannot think of a reason for being unsure of one's use of the Internet. I would treat these four responses with suspicion and convert the *do not knows* into missing values.

Table 4.2   Tabulation on the Use of the Internet

User status	Internet
yes	358
no	638
don't know	4
refused	0

Let's look at the distribution for the other variables of interest. I use the R script to tabulate the responses for `Internet`, `email`, `cellphone`, and `social media`. Table 4.3 shows the tabulating of responses for several categorical variables.

```
tab<-sapply(brazil[,3:6],function(x) table(x))
htmlTable(tab, cgroup = c("Internet & digital media users"),
  n.cgroup = c(4), rowlabel = "User status")
```

Table 4.3   Tabulating Responses for Several Categorical Variables

	Internet & Digital Media Users			
User status	Internet	email	cell	social media
yes	358	296	675	265
no	638	702	324	97
don't know	4	2	1	0
refused	0	0	0	0

Again, I recommend converting the *don't know* responses into missing values. Also, note for social media that the tabulation has already excluded those observations that originally reported missing values. The total number of responses for social media is 362. What about the remaining 1000–362=638 responses? The 638 responses are missing because the question for the use of `social media` was not asked of those 638 respondents who earlier reported not using the Internet. Thus, the 362 respondents included 358 respondents who said yes to using the Internet and the 4 who did not know whether they had used the Internet.

Using Percentages Is Better Than Using Raw Numbers

Table 4.3 reports the responses in raw numbers. However, communicating results in percentages is often more effective. Let's therefore transform Table 4.3 into percentages, using the following code.

```
tab<-(cbind("Internet"=table(brazil$Internet),
            "email"=table(brazil$email),
            "social media"=table(brazil$social),
            "cell"=table(brazil$cell) ))
tab1<- addmargins((prop.table(tab,2)*100),1)
htmlTable(txtRound(tab1,1), cgroup = c("Internet & digital media
  users"), n.cgroup = c(4), rowlabel = "User status")
```

Table 4.4 shows that 35.8% of the respondents reported using the Internet and 63.8% did not use the Internet. The remaining 0.4% were not sure of their use of the Internet. The other two variables, `email` and `cell`, are interpreted the same way. The use of social media has to be interpreted with care. Just by looking at the reported numbers, I might be tempted to report that 73.2% of respondents reported using social media. However, this is not true. Because I know that the question about social media was asked only of those respondents who reported using the Internet, I therefore have to interpret the results accordingly. The correct description of the result is as follows: Of those who reported using the Internet, 73.2% also reported using social media.

Table 4.4 Tabulating Responses for Several Categorical Variables Using Percentages

User status	Internet & digital media users			
	Internet	email	social media	cell
yes	35.8	29.6	73.2	67.5
no	63.8	70.2	26.8	32.4
don't know	0.4	0.2	0	0.1
refused	0	0	0	0
Sum	100	100	100	100

Also note that each column in the table adds up to 100%. This is quite different from summing up the rows in Table 4.4. You must ensure that you are summing up the right way (either by columns or by rows) to make the inferences you intended.

There remains a minor problem with Table 4.4. I report results with decimal points. We have to ask ourselves, is it necessary to use decimal points in reporting percentages? Situations where valid and statistically significant statistics end up below one percent warrant the use of decimal points. Otherwise, you can reduce the number of digits after the decimal point to 1, or in this particular case, eliminate them altogether. Table 4.5 reports the revised results and the R code used to generate the output. Note that **txtRound(tab1,0)** is the code used to restrict responses to integer format.

```
tab<-sapply(brazil[,3:6],function(x) table(x))
tab1<- addmargins((prop.table(tab,2)*100),1)
htmlTable(txtRound(tab1,0), cgroup = c("Internet & digital media
users"), n.cgroup = c(4), rowlabel = "User status")
```

As shown in Table 4.5, 36% of the respondents reported using the Internet. The "*don't knows*" have been reduced to 0% because after I round 0.4%, it reduces to 0%. I would argue that this change results in no loss of information, but provides us with added ease and effectiveness of communication.

Table 4.5 Presenting Results as Integers

User status	Internet & digital media users			
	Internet	email	cell	social media
yes	36	30	68	73
no	64	70	32	27
don't know	0	0	0	0
refused	0	0	0	0
Sum	100	100	100	100

Data Cleaning

Let us now clean the observations and eliminate respondents categorized as *do not know* and *refused to answer*. Note that I have not restricted the use of decimals so that you can appreciate the small change in responses. Table 4.6 presents the data after cleaning up the variables.

```
tab<-(cbind("Internet"=table(brazil$new.Internet),
      "email"=table(brazil$new.email),
      "social media"=table(brazil$new.social),
      "cell"=table(brazil$new.cell)
      ))
tab1<- addmargins((prop.table(tab,2)*100),1)
htmlTable(txtRound(tab1,1),
 cgroup = c("Internet & digital media users"),
 n.cgroup = c(4), rowlabel = "User status")
```

Table 4.6   Presenting Data After Cleaning Up the Variables

User status	Internet & digital media users			
	Internet	email	social media	cell
no	64.1	70.3	26.8	32.4
yes	35.9	29.7	73.2	67.6
Sum	100	100	100	100

Weighted Data

Most survey data is weighted so that we can develop estimates for the population using the responses from the surveyed sample. The sampling methods assign a weight to each respondent. The weights are used to ensure that the sampled survey is representative of the underlying population. The weights are ultimately derived from how we have defined our sampling frame.

For instance, we might want to determine the response to a proposed user fee for students at a university. Assume that 80% of the students at the university are enrolled in the undergraduate programs and the remaining 20% in the graduate programs. Also, assume that we do a random survey of both graduate and undergraduate students but interview the same number of students from graduate and undergraduate groups. We can see that each graduate student in our sample should be weighted less than the undergraduate students in the sample to reflect the 80-20 split in the underlying student populations. The sampling frame and weights are thus devised to ensure that the weighted statistics are reflective of the underlying population and not just the sampled cohorts.

If I calculate statistics without incorporating weights, we will make correct inferences about the sampled cohorts, but not about the underlying larger population. Let me illustrate this with a simple calculation to compute the average GDP per capita for the United States and China. China's GDP per capita for 2012 was US$6,091. In comparison, the per capita American GDP was US$51,749 for 2012. The average per capita GDP for the two countries can be calculated as follows:

$$\frac{51749 + 6091}{2} = 28920 \text{ Equation 4.1}$$

However, there is a huge problem. The average GDP per capita of US$28,920 for the United States and China disregards the huge difference in their respective populations. The 1,351 million people living in China and 314 million living in the U.S. suggest that the difference in their respective populations should not be ignored. Thus, we need to calculate the weighted mean, which is given by the following equation:

$$mean_{weighted} = \frac{\Sigma\left(w_i x_i\right)}{\Sigma w_i} \text{ Equation 4.2}$$

Where w_i represents the weight, which is population in our case, and x_i represents the GDP per capita.

$$GDPPC_{weighted} = \frac{1351*6091 + 314*51749}{1351 + 314} = 14701.5 \text{ Equation 4.3}$$

The weighted GDP per capita of US$14701.5 is almost half of the initially calculated average per capita GDP of US$28,920. The weighted statistics reflect the fact that a larger Chinese population with a lower per capita GOP results in a much smaller average GDP per capita for the two countries. The unweighted statistics implicitly assign a weight of 1 for both China and the U.S., which I illustrate in the following equation:

$$GDP_{weighted} = \frac{1*6091 + 1*51749}{1 + 1} = 28920 \text{ Equation 4.4}$$

The Pew data for Brazil comes from a survey where each respondent is assigned a weight based on the sampling frame. Instead of counting each observation, the weighted frequency distribution is simply the sum of the weights for each category. Thus, for the Internet use, I can sum the weights for all respondents who said yes to using the Internet and the same for those who said no:

```
tab1<-(cbind("Internet"=xtabs(weight ~ new.Internet),
             "email"=xtabs(weight~new.email),
             "social media"=xtabs(weight~new.social),
             "cell"=xtabs(weight~new.cell)
             ))
htmlTable(txtRound(tab1,0),
 cgroup = c("Internet & digital media users"),
 n.cgroup = c(4), rowlabel = "User status")
```

If one were to compare Table 4.7 with the unweighted results, one would see very large differences in the outputs. The unweighted tabulations showed 358 respondents using the Internet, whereas the weighted tabulations show 428 respondents using the Internet. This data set reveals that not using weights might lead to significantly different conclusions about the population. The unweighted tabulations are representative of the sample, and the weighted tabulations are representative of the underlying population.

Table 4.7   Tabulations of Categorical Variables with Weighted Data

	Internet & digital media users			
User status	`Internet`	`email`	`social media`	`cell`
no	570	640	105	271
yes	428	359	328	728

One can generate percentages with the weighted data. Note that the R code uses the **sapply** function, which is much more economical, to generate the basic tabulation. The results are produced in Table 4.8.

```
tab1<-sapply(brazil[,14:17],function(x,y)
 xtabs(y ~ x), y=brazil[,13])
tab3<- txtRound(addmargins((prop.table(tab1,2)*100),1),0)
htmlTable(tab3, rowlabel = "User status")
```

Table 4.8   Tabulations of Weighted Data Using Percentages

User status	`new.cell`	`new.email`	`new.Internet`	`new.social`
no	27	64	57	24
yes	73	36	43	76
Sum	100	100	100	100

Again, if you compare the output from the weighted data in Table 4.8 with the respective table earlier, you can see the significant differences in the two outputs.

Cross Tabulations

So far, I have tabulated variables across one dimension. We might have to explore data across two or more dimensions. For instance, is the Internet use in Brazil the same among men and women? Let us tabulate the percentage of the Internet use among men and women. The Pew data set contains information on 503 men and 497 women. A cross tabulation between gender and use of the Internet using weighted data is presented in the following R code. Table 4.9 presents the cross tabulation between gender and use of the Internet.

```
tab1<-cbind("Gender"=xtabs(weight ~ gender+new.Internet))
tab2<-txtRound(tab1, 0)
htmlTable(tab2, cgroup = c("Internet users"), n.cgroup = c(2),
          rgroup=c("Gender"), n.rgroup=c(2))
```

Table 4.9 Cross-Tabulating Gender and the Internet

	Internet users	
Gender	**no**	**yes**
male	274	229
female	296	199

The raw numbers are hard to interpret. A better approach is to determine the percentages rather than the raw numbers. Table 4.10 shows cross-tabulations of weighted data using percentages.

```
tab3<-addmargins((prop.table(tab1,1)*100),2)
tab4<-txtRound(tab3,1)
htmlTable(tab4, cgroup = c("Internet users"),
 n.cgroup = c(3), rowlabel = "Gender")
```

Table 4.10 Cross-Tabulations of Weighted Data Using Percentages

	Internet users		
Gender	**no**	**yes**	**Sum**
male	54.5	45.5	100
female	59.9	40.1	100

Note that 45.5% of men and 40.1% of women use the Internet. While a greater percentage of men than women use the Internet, we still need to ascertain whether these differences are statistically significant. I address this question later in Chapter 6, "Hypothetically Speaking." However, for now, I repeat this process for other cross tabulations.

As shown in Table 4.10, men use the Internet with greater frequency than women. But what about education? Can we assume that those who are highly educated use the Internet more often? The answer to this question can be obtained by a cross-tabulation between education and the use of the Internet. Note that I have not reproduced cross-tabulation on the raw data, but instead I show the percentages in Table 4.11.

```
tab1<-cbind("Education"=xtabs(weight ~ education+new.Internet))
tab2<-txtRound(addmargins((prop.table(tab1,1)*100),2),1)
htmlTable(tab2, cgroup = c("Internet users"), n.cgroup = c(3),
          rowlabel = "Education attainment")
```

Table 4.11   Cross-Tabulation of Education and Internet with Weighted Data Using Percentages

Education attainment	Internet users		
	no	yes	Sum
no formal education	100	0	100
incomplete primary school	96.8	3.2	100
complete primary school	91	9	100
incomplete secondary school	74	26	100
complete secondary school	55.8	44.2	100
incomplete tertiary school	40.6	59.4	100
complete tertiary school	36.4	63.6	100
incomplete university	13	87	100
complete university	9.3	90.7	100
don't know			
refused			

Table 4.11 demonstrates that the use of the Internet increases with education. Whereas 100% of the respondents with no formal education reported not using the Internet, almost 91% of those who completed a university education reported using the Internet. Thus, I can conclude that the use of the Internet increases with education.

Education might, in fact, be a proxy for income. Highly educated individuals are likely to earn higher income, and thus are able to afford the costs associated with accessing the Internet. I test this assumption in another cross tabulation. I have suppressed the raw data and report only the percentages in Table 4.12.

```
tab1<-cbind("income"=xtabs(weight ~ income+new.Internet))
tab2<-txtRound(addmargins((prop.table(tab1,1)*100),2),1)
htmlTable(tab2, cgroup = c("Internet users"), n.cgroup = c(3),
          rowlabel = "Income level")
```

Table 4.12   Cross-Tabulation of Income and Internet with Weighted Data Using Percentages

	Internet users		
Income level	**no**	**yes**	**Sum**
up to 200	83.8	16.2	100
from 201 to 400	73	27	100
from 401 to 600	81	19	100
from 601 to 1,000	66	34	100
from 1,001 to 1,400	56.5	43.5	100
from 1,401 to 2,000	42.4	57.6	100
from 2,001 to 3,000	26	74	100
from 3,001 to 4,000	30.4	69.6	100
from 4,001 to 6,000	18.6	81.4	100
from 6,001 to 10,000	6.7	93.3	100
from 10,001 to 15,000	0	100	100
over 15,000	0	100	100
don't know	53.6	46.4	100
refused	37.4	62.6	100

The income data is reported in Brazilian currency, Real. Note that the table provides clear evidence for the association between an increase in the use of the Internet and an increase in income. Similarly, I cross-tabulate the relationship between age and the use of the Internet. I assume that younger cohorts will exhibit lower use of the Internet because of their lower earning potential. Similarly, I assume that older cohorts would use the Internet more often because they can afford to access the Internet. Table 4.13 shows cross-tabulation between age and Internet with weighted data using percentages.

```
tab1<-cbind("age"=xtabs(weight ~ new.age+new.Internet))
tab2<-txtRound(addmargins((prop.table(tab1,1)*100),2),1)
htmlTable(tab2, cgroup = c("Internet users"), n.cgroup = c(3),
          rowlabel = "Age cohorts")
```

Table 4.13   Cross-Tabulation of Age and Internet with Weighted Data Using Percentages

Age cohorts	Internet users		
	no	yes	Sum
middle aged	60.7	39.3	100
seniors	85	15	100
young adults	47.5	52.5	100
youth	28.8	71.2	100

Table 4.13 clearly contradicts my hypothesis. The youth are by far more likely to use the Internet than older cohorts are. The table shows that 71% of the youth reported using the Internet compared to 15% of seniors and 52% of middle-aged cohorts.

Note that Table 4.13 is not sorted in a logical way. The rows are neither sorted chronologically for age nor in order of the number of "yes" responses. I address this limitation by sorting the table in Microsoft Word using the sort option available when formatting the table. Also note that R, Stata, and other software applications provide programing tools to control the output format, including how to sort the resulting tabulation. Table 4.14 shows cross-tabulation of age and Internet after sorting responses.

Table 4.14   Cross-Tabulation of Age and Internet After Sorting Responses

Age cohorts	Internet users		
	no	yes	Sum
youth	28.8	71.2	100
young adults	47.5	52.5	100
middle aged	60.7	39.3	100
seniors	85	15	100

Table 4.14 is sorted on the "yes" column. The youth report the highest use of the Internet, followed by young adults, the middle aged, and seniors. The reader can get these visual clues without having to struggle with the table. Remember, our primary goal is to communicate and present the information to the reader in a way that requires the least amount of effort to grasp the concept. Sorting the columns in a logical fashion makes readers' lives a little easier.

Going Beyond the Basics in Tables

In advanced analytics, often the final step in the applied research involves estimating a statistical or econometric model whose results are presented in a tabular format. Figure 4.2 shows the formatted output from statistical models. The later chapters on statistical modeling explain how to estimate these models.

I present two versions of the model that attempts to determine what factors influence the use of the Internet in Brazil. Remember I have survey data; I first estimate the model using non-weighted data; in the second step, I estimate the model with weighted data.

Table 4.15 and the accompanying R code presents the output for the non-weighted model.

```
GLM.1 <- glm(new.Internet ~ gender + new.age + new.cell + new.inc,
family=binomial(logit), data=brazil)
logit1<-xtable(summary(GLM.1))
print(logit1, type="html")
```

Table 4.15 Modelling Internet Use in Brazil Using Logit Models with Unweighted Data

	Estimate	Std. Error	z value	Pr(>|z|)
(Intercept)	0.0940	0.3513	0.27	0.7892
genderfemale	-0.2467	0.1738	-1.42	0.1559
new.ageseniors	-1.4793	0.2529	-5.85	0.0000
new.ageyoung adults	0.5988	0.2209	2.71	0.0067
new.ageyouth	1.6487	0.2541	6.49	0.0000
new.cellyes	1.6515	0.2411	6.85	0.0000
new.inclow	-2.9382	0.3186	-9.22	0.0000
new.incmedium	-1.9228	0.2736	-7.03	0.0000

Table 4.16 and the accompanying R code presents the output for the weighted model.

```
GLM.2 <- glm(new.Internet ~ gender + new.age + new.cell + new.inc,
family=binomial(logit),    weights=weight, data=brazil)
logit2<-xtable(summary(GLM.2))
print(logit2, type="html")
```

Table 4.16 Modelling Internet Use in Brazil Using Logit Models with Weighted Data

	Estimate	Std. Error	z value	Pr(>|z|)
(Intercept)	0.1594	0.3373	0.47	0.6364
genderfemale	-0.1748	0.1645	-1.06	0.2878
new.ageseniors	-1.3409	0.2627	-5.11	0.0000
new.ageyoung adults	0.5527	0.2067	2.67	0.0075
new.ageyouth	1.5403	0.2244	6.86	0.0000
new.cellyes	1.6031	0.2288	7.01	0.0000
new.inclow	-2.9232	0.3101	-9.43	0.0000
new.incmedium	-1.9146	0.2696	-7.10	0.0000

Figure 4.2 presents the two models in a single table. This particular format of the table is typical of how statistical results are presented in academic and professional publications. The purpose of presenting these tables is to demonstrate the utility of tables in summarizing the results from advanced statistical methods. Whether it is a simple tabulation or summary of an econometric model, tables remain a quintessential tool in presenting the findings. I will elaborate on these models later when I discuss regression models in the book.

```
GLM.1 <- glm(new.Internet ~ gender + new.age + new.cell + new.inc,
family=binomial(logit), data=brazil)
GLM.2 <- glm(new.Internet ~ gender + new.age + new.cell + new.inc,
family=binomial(logit),    weights=weight, data=brazil)
stargazer(GLM.1, GLM.2, type="html", dep.var.labels=c("Internet use
(unweighted data), Internet use (weighted data)"),
covariate.labels=c("Female", "seniors","young adults", "youth", "own
cell phone", "low income hhld", "medium income hhld"))
```

	Dependent variable:	
	Internet use (unweighted data), Internet use (weighted data)	
	(1)	(2)
Female	−0.247	−0.175
	(0.174)	(0.164)
Seniors	−1.479***	−1.341***
	(0.253)	(0.263)
Young Adults	0.599***	0.553***
	0.221)	(0.207)
Youth	1.649***	1.540***
	(0.254)	(0.224)
Own Cell Phone	1.652***	1.603***
	(0.241)	(0.229)
Low Income hhld	−2.938***	−2.923***
	(0.319)	(0.310)
Medium Income hhld	−1.923**	−1.915***
	(0.274)	(0.270)
Constant	0.094	0.159
	(0.351)	(0.337)
Observations	928	928
Log Likelihood	−411.062	−439.018
Akaike Inf. Crit.	838.125	894.035
Note:		$p<0.1$; ** $p<0.05$; *** $p<0.01$

Figure 4.2   Formatted output in publication-ready format

Seeing Whether Beauty Pays

Do attractive people earn more? Many among us would believe this to be true. A plethora of anecdotal evidence suggests that attractive individuals do get better service at restaurants, airports, and at work. However, is there any truth to the fact that looks contribute to better economic welfare? You might have felt that the reason your colleague got the promotion instead of you was your colleague's better looks, but was that in fact the reason?

Daniel S. Hamermesh is a professor of economics at the University of Texas. Over the years, he has researched how "beauty" plays a role in determining socioeconomic outcomes, such as promotions or higher wages at work, or better grades at school. Professor Hamermesh's book, *Beauty Pays*, is an excellent treatise of how beauty affects human behavior as it relates to economic and other outcomes. It is a must-read for data scientists who are interested in determining how human beings make decisions.

I hope that the readers of this book have either studied at a university or are currently enrolled at a university. I need the readers to rely on their university experience to understand the story I would like to tell here. Recall your university days when you got a B- for an assignment, but your fellow course mate received an A. Let us assume that you both worked together on the assignment and there was only a marginal difference in quality between the two assignments that would have explained, perhaps, a grade of B- for you and a B for your fellow student. Now let us throw beauty in the equation. Your fellow student was better looking and you believe her or his good looks were instrumental in why the teacher or the teaching assistant gave him or her a better grade.

Despite this widely held belief that attractive students get better grades, or they are failed less than the others, the empirical evidence is either lacking or suffers from several methodological shortcomings. Here we flip the question and ask whether attractive professors receive better teaching evaluations from students than others do.

If you have attended college/university, you might recall completing course evaluation surveys in which you rated the instructors on their teaching effectiveness. As a student, you were asked to rate the instructor on several attributes on a scale ranging from 1 to 5 or 1 to 7, or some variant of these. Let me throw beauty into the equation and ask you to answer the question: Do attractive instructors receive higher teaching evaluations?

For those who came of age in the dotcom era, instructors' looks were influential in selecting the instructor and the course. After the word-of-mouth, the most commonly used tool these days to select an elective course, is the professor's ranking on the website http://www.ratemyprofessors.com/ where students rank professors on helpfulness, clarity, easiness, and yes, looks. Attractive professors receive a chili pepper for their hot looks. In fact, the website maintains a list of the hottest professors. Professor David B. Daniel of the James Madison University in 2013 was ranked the hottest academic in the United States.[3]

Given that the universities collect data on teaching evaluations, an opportunity exists to answer the aforementioned question, provided we are able to develop an objective measure of attractiveness for instructors and then complement the instructor evaluation data with their scores on looks. Thanks to Professor Hamermesh, we can attempt to answer this question.

In a widely acclaimed study, Professor Hamermesh used the teaching evaluation data for 493 courses involving 94 instructors from the University of Texas to determine whether the teaching evaluations were influenced by a professor's looks. Professor Hamermesh used a panel of students to rank each professor on their looks by providing them with photographs of the instructors. He then aggregated the responses from the panel and converted them into a normalized attractiveness index to study how instructors' looks affected teaching evaluations (Hamermesh and Parker, 2003).[4] Professor Hamermesh has generously made available the data that I use extensively in this chapter and elsewhere in the book to demonstrate the intricacies of data analysis.

Before I proceed, I recommend you also read a critique of the Hamermesh study by Andrew Christopher Edmunds in order to understand the limitations in measuring hard-to-measure phenomena. Remember, unlike measuring height or weight, measurements on beauty can be highly subjective.[5]

We are interested in the question:

Do instructors' looks affect the teaching evaluations they receive from the students?

If you have read the Hamermesh and Parker (2003) paper, you will notice that I have cast a narrower question than Professor Hamermesh did. He linked beauty with teaching productivity. I believe that teaching evaluations measured students' subjective appreciation of the course and the instructor, and might not necessarily translate into "teaching productivity." Furthermore, I must point out the inherent disconnect in the Hamermesh study between the beauty rank and teaching evaluation. A separate group of students ranked instructors on looks from those who actually took and evaluated the courses. The panel of students ranking instructors on looks might have a distinct taste in beauty, which could have been inherently different from that of the students who attended the course and evaluated the instructors.

Data Set

The data set used here is available from the book's website at www.ibmpressbooks.com/title/ 9780133991024. Also available are the codes to reproduce results presented in this chapter. I illustrate the results in R within the text. However, the book's website reproduces the code and results in Stata, SPSS, and SAS.

The R version of the data set includes the variables that provide information about the instructors and courses. Instructor attributes include age, beauty score, minority status, gender, native competency in English, tenure status, and a variable uniquely identifying each professor. Course-related attributes include teaching evaluation score, course credits, course division, number of students completing the teaching evaluation survey, and the number of students enrolled in the course.

The variables can also be characterized by type; that is, continuous variables and categorical variables. R refers to categorical variables as *factors*. Gender is a categorical variable, describing gender in two distinct categories, male and female, whereas age is a continuous variable. Table 4.17 shows the description of relevant variables in the teaching evaluations data set.

Table 4.17   Description of Relevant Variables in the Teaching Evaluations Data Set

Variable	Description
beauty	Rating of the instructor's physical appearance by a panel of six students, averaged across the six panelists, transformed to have a mean of zero.
eval	Course overall teaching evaluation score, on a scale of 1 (very unsatisfactory) to 5 (excellent).
minority	Factor variable. Does the instructor belong to a minority (non-Caucasian)?
age	The professor's age.
gender	Factor indicating instructor's gender (male/female).
native	Factor variable. Is the instructor a native English speaker?
tenure	Factor variable. Is the instructor on tenure track?
credits	Factor variable. Is the course a single-credit elective (for example, yoga, aerobics, dance)?
division	Factor variable. Is the course an upper or lower division course? (Lower division courses are mainly large freshman and sophomore courses.)
students	Number of students who participated in the evaluation.
allstudents	Number of students enrolled in the course.
prof	Factor variable indicating instructor identifier.

What Determines Teaching Evaluations?

Teaching evaluations largely depend on how satisfied students are with the course and the instructor. The instructor's ability to communicate, willingness to help, and competency in the subject matter are some of the factors that influence teaching evaluations. At the same time, student's course-related workload and difficulty of the subject matter also influence teaching evaluations. Instructor's looks might or might not have a bearing on teaching evaluations.

Let us begin by calculating descriptive statistics for the continuous variables in the data set. Note that I am relying on the **describe** and **describeBy** commands from the **psych** package in R. You must install the **psych** package before you can use these commands. Also, remember that I have used the **RMarkdown** and **xtable** packages in **RStudio** to generate and document statistical outputs.

Basic descriptive statistics include measures of central tendency, that is, mean, median, and mode, and dispersion, such as variance and standard deviation. In addition, one can include other measures, such as the minimum and maximum values for the data set. Table 4.18 shows the descriptive statistics for main variables.

```
tab<-xtable(describe(cbind(age, beauty, eval, students, allstudents),
                     skew=F, ranges=T))
print(tab, type="html")
```

Table 4.18 Descriptive Statistics for Main Variables

	vars	n	mean	sd	median	trimmed	mad	min	max	range	se
age	1	463.00	48.37	9.80	48.00	48.35	11.86	29.00	73.00	44.00	0.46
beauty	2	463.00	0.00	0.79	-0.07	-0.05	0.87	-1.45	1.97	3.42	0.04
eval	3	463.00	4.00	0.55	4.00	4.03	0.59	2.10	5.00	2.90	0.03
students	4	463.00	36.62	45.02	23.00	27.54	14.83	5.00	380.00	375.00	2.09
allstudents	5	463.00	55.18	75.07	29.00	38.66	19.27	8.00	581.00	573.00	3.49

The first row in Table 4.18 lists the statistics computed by the command. The first column lists the name of the variables. Second column, vars, identifies each variable with a unique integer. The number of observations (463) is listed under n. The average age, listed under mean, is 48.37 years. The standard deviation for age, listed under sd, is 9.80. The median age is 48.0 years. The column trimmed reports the mean for the trimmed version of the variable, which excludes a certain number of the smallest and largest values for the underlying variables. Mean absolute deviation, listed under mad, is 11.86. The minimum age for the instructors (listed under the column min) is 29 years and the maximum age (listed under max) is 73 years. The difference between the maximum and minimum ages (reported under range) is 44 years. The standard error of the mean age (reported under se) is 0.46. All other variables are explained in the same fashion.

There is a reason why I used age to interpret the table. I will now tell you that even though the computations for age are done properly, still these results are erroneous for age and beauty in Table 4.18. At the same time, the statistics reported for eval (teaching evaluation score), students, and allstudents are correct.

The discrepancy exists because of the distinct nature of the data set. Note that there are 463 observations (rows) in the data set, one corresponding to each course. However, numerous professors have taught more than one course, which implies that the reported average age in Table 4.18 is influenced by the multiple appearances of the same age of those instructors who have taught multiple courses. This results in erroneous results. The correct approach is to isolate the records that identify each instructor and prevent any duplication of records by instructor. I use the R code to subset the data by keeping only unique records. Table 4.19 shows descriptive statistics for instructor-specific variables.

```
profs <- subset(TeachingRatings, !duplicated(TeachingRatings$prof))
attach(profs)
tab <- xtable(describe(cbind(age, beauty), skew=F, ranges=F))
print(tab, type="html")
```

Table 4.19   Descriptive Statistics for Instructor-Specific Variables

	vars	n	mean	sd	se
age	1	94.00	47.55	10.26	1.06
beauty	2	94.00	0.09	0.83	0.09

Table 4.19 now reports statistics for the 94 instructors without duplication. Note that the average age is now slightly lower, at 47.55 years. The mean value for beauty remains close to zero. Also, note that I have produced results with two decimal points. One should, however, report decimals only when it is absolutely required. There is no need to use decimal points for integers. One can modify the syntax to customize the format for individual columns, which I illustrate later in the book. However, you can copy these results first to a spreadsheet, for example, Microsoft Excel, to make necessary, small changes to the tables' format and then paste them to a word processor.

I will now evaluate how teaching evaluations might differ as a result of certain attributes of the instructor or the course. Let us first look at the difference in teaching evaluations by gender. I have no reason to believe that teaching evaluations might be different for male and female instructors. I used the **describeBy** command in the **psych** package to generate Table 4.20.

```
tab <- xtable(describeBy(eval, gender, mat=T, skew=F, ranges=T))
print(tab, type="html")
```

Table 4.20   Descriptive Statistics by Categories Using the psych Package

	item	group1	vars	n	mean	sd	median	trimmed	mad	min	max	range	se
11	1	male	1.00	268.00	4.07	0.56	4.15	4.10	0.52	2.10	5.00	2.90	0.03
12	2	female	1.00	195.00	3.90	0.54	3.90	3.92	0.59	2.30	4.90	2.60	0.04

Table 4.20 suggests that men received slightly higher teaching evaluations than women did. Are these differences statistically significant? I can test the significance of this difference by using either the T-test or a regression model. However, I revisit this question later in Chapter 6, where I introduce methods to test hypotheses.

University professors are often categorized by tenure. Tenured professors are guaranteed job security with some limitations. They are senior instructors who receive tenure as recognition for their excellence in research and teaching. Untenured instructors are contractual employees whose jobs can be terminated at the conclusion of their contracts, or they can be removed from service with cause.

One can argue that job security might make tenured professors too comfortable in their jobs and hence they might not invest as much effort in teaching as the professors who are on tenure track or contract. Others might argue that tenured professors are experienced instructors who bring a wealth of experience to the classroom that students would value. Table 4.21 explores the veracity of these arguments.

```
tab<-cbind("Teaching Evaluations"=tapply(eval, tenure, mean))
htmlTable(txtRound(tab,2),rowlabel = "Tenure status")
```

Table 4.21   Average of Teaching Evaluations by Tenure Status

Tenure status	Teaching Evaluations
no	4.13
yes	3.96

Note that non-tenured professors enjoyed higher teaching evaluations than their counterparts did. Also, note that I have used the built-in command in R, **tapply**, to calculate mean evaluation scores by tenure.

I would now like to add another dimension to the tabulations; that is, gender. Specifically, how do teaching evaluations differ by gender and tenure? That is, do teaching evaluations for male tenured professors differ from those of the female tenured professors? The answer can be obtained by obtaining four different means, one for each combination of gender and tenure status. Table 4.22 shows an average of teaching evaluations by tenure status and gender.

```
tab<-cbind("Teaching Evaluation"=tapply(eval,
list(tenure, gender), mean))
htmlTable(txtRound(tab,2),
          cgroup = c("Gender"), n.cgroup = c(2),
          rowlabel = "Tenure Status")
```

Table 4.22   Average of Teaching Evaluations by Tenure Status and Gender

	Gender	
Tenure Status	**male**	**female**
no	4.40	3.86
yes	3.99	3.92

Note that tenure status in Table 4.22 is listed in the first column as a variable taking values as either yes or no, and gender is listed in the second row as male or female. One can see that the highest teaching evaluations are recorded for untenured male instructors and the lowest correspond to untenured female professors. Tenured female instructors received higher teaching evaluations than untenured female instructors did.

There are ways to get additional statistics for a two-way distribution of the data, In R, I can write a custom function and use it with the aggregate command. Table 4.23 offers three summary statistics (number of observations, mean, and standard deviation) for a combination of gender and tenure status attributes. The system-generated column headings (for example, `eval.sd`) identify the statistics being computed on the variable. Thus, `eval.sd` stands for standard deviation of the `eval` variable.

```
f <- function(x) c(obs=length(x), mean=mean(x), sd=sd(x))
tres<-as.matrix(aggregate(eval ~ gender+tenure, FUN=c("f")))
htmlTable(txtRound(tres,0,excl.cols = c(1,2,4,5)))
```

Table 4.23   Summary Statistics on Teaching Evaluations by Tenure Status and Gender

gender	tenure	eval.obs	eval.mean	eval.sd
male	no	52	4.3961538	0.5048632
female	no	50	3.8600000	0.4733726
male	yes	216	3.9902778	0.5405836
female	yes	145	3.9151724	0.5604228

Note that the mean values reported in the last two tables are the same. The difference is the additional statistics being reported in Table 4.23. I have revised the column names in Table 4.24 to make them appear in a more standard fashion.

```
colnames(tres)[3:5]<-c("n", "mean", "std. dev.")
htmlTable(txtRound(tres,0,excl.cols = c(1,2,4,5)))
```

Table 4.24   Summary Statistics on Teaching Evaluations by Tenure Status and Gender with Improved Labels

gender	tenure	n	mean	std. dev.
male	no	52	4.3961538	0.5048632
female	no	50	3.8600000	0.4733726
male	yes	216	3.9902778	0.5405836
female	yes	145	3.9151724	0.5604228

I can add a third dimension and see how teaching evaluation differed by tenure, gender, and the instructor's minority status. The results are presented in Table 4.25.

```
f <- function(x) c(obs=length(x), mean=mean(x), sd=sd(x))
tres<-as.matrix(aggregate(eval ~ gender+tenure+minority, FUN=c("f")))
colnames(tres)[4:6]<-c("n", "mean", "std. dev.")
htmlTable(txtRound(tres,0,excl.cols = c(1,2,3,5,6)))
```

Table 4.25 Summary Statistics on Teaching Evaluations by Tenure/Minority Status and Gender

gender	tenure	minority	n	mean	std. dev.
male	no	no	42	4.3047619	0.5174762
female	no	no	50	3.8600000	0.4733726
male	yes	no	198	4.0156566	0.5394181
female	yes	no	109	3.9743119	0.5644407
male	no	yes	10	4.7800000	0.1475730
male	yes	yes	18	3.7111111	0.4837220
female	yes	yes	36	3.7361111	0.5150050

It turns out that the untenured male instructors belonging to a minority group received the highest average teaching evaluation, at 4.78, whereas the lowest average teaching evaluation was recorded for tenured male professors with minority status. Also, note that there were no records corresponding to untenured minority female instructors.

Now let us consider the situation in which we need to determine summary statistics by gender, but for two or more variables. See the R code that generated Table 4.26, which shows summary statistics for beauty and evaluations by gender.

```
f <- function(x) c(obs=length(x), mean=mean(x), sd=sd(x))
tres<-t(as.matrix(aggregate(cbind(eval, beauty) ~ gender,
 FUN=c("f"))))
rownames(tres)[2:7]<-c("n", "mean", "std. dev.", "n", "mean",
 "std. dev.")
htmlTable(txtRound(tres,0, excl.rows = c(3,4,6,7)),
         rgroup=c("","evaluation score","beauty score"),
         n.rgroup = c(1,3,3))
```

Table 4.26   Summary Statistics for Beauty and Evaluations by Gender

gender	male	female
evaluation score		
n	268	195
mean	4.0690299	3.9010256
std. dev.	0.5566518	0.5388026
beauty score		
n	268	195
mean	-0.08448224	0.11610907
std. dev.	0.75712993	0.81780964

Table 4.26 shows the average evaluation score for the 268 male-taught courses in the sample is 4.07. The average evaluation for the 195 female-taught courses is 3.90. The average beauty score (normalized) is –0.08 for male instructors and 0.12 for female instructors.

Does Beauty Affect Teaching Evaluations?

We have not yet attempted to answer the very question that piqued our interest. We would like to know whether good-looking instructors receive higher teaching evaluations than others do. A simple statistic to compute to answer this question is the Pearson Correlation Coefficient. We can rephrase our question as follows: Are teaching evaluations and instructors' looks correlated? The answer is presented in Table 4.27.

```
myvars<- c("eval", "beauty", "age", "students", "allstudents")
x <- TeachingRatings[myvars]
tab <-xtable(cor(x), digits=3)
print(tab, type="html")
```

Table 4.27   Correlation Between Beauty and Other Variables

	eval	beauty	age	students	allstudents
eval	1.000	0.189	-0.052	0.035	-0.001
beauty	0.189	1.000	-0.298	0.131	0.100
age	-0.052	-0.298	1.000	-0.030	-0.013
students	0.035	0.131	-0.030	1.000	0.972
allstudents	-0.001	0.100	-0.013	0.972	1.000

I note the positive correlation of 0.189 between beauty and teaching evaluation. This suggests that instructors' looks are positively correlated with their teaching evaluations. This is, however, not conclusive evidence for the fact that looks were influential in getting the instructors higher teaching evaluations. Remember, correlation does not imply causation. The best way to determine the impact of looks on teaching evaluations is to estimate a regression-type model in which we can control for other relevant determinants of teaching evaluations. We can then see whether in the presence of other explanatory variables, beauty still returns a positive and statistical significant correlation with teaching evaluations.

Putting It All on (in) a Table

Most reports and publications impose a limit on the number of tables you can include in a deliverable. This requires analysts to be sensitive to space limitations and thus design tables that can amalgamate results from several commands. This concept is best illustrated in a table from a paper written by Professor Hamermesh and Amy Parker. The paper was finally published in *Economics of Education Review* in 2005.[6] The table from an earlier version of the same paper is reproduced in Figure 4.3.

Variable	All	Lower Division	Upper Division
Course Evaluation	4.022 (0.525)	4.060 (0.563)	3.993 (0.493)
Instructor Evaluation	4.217 (0.540)	4.243 (0.609)	4.196 (0.481)
Number of Students	55.18 (75.07)	76.50 (109.29)	44.24 (45.54)
Percent Evaluating	74.43	73.52	74.89
Female	0.359	0.300	0.405
Minority	0.099	0.110	0.090
Non-Native English	0.037	0.007	0.060
Tenure Track	0.851	0.828	0.869
Lower Division	0.339	--------	--------
Number of Courses	463	157	306
Number of Faculty	94	42	79

Means with standard deviations in parentheses. All statistics except for those describing the number of students, the percent evaluating the instructor and the lower-upper division distinction are weighted by number of students completing the course evaluation forms.

Figure 4.3 Summary statistics table reproduced from the Hamermesh and Parker paper

Source: http://www.nber.org/papers/w9853.pdf

The table reports summary statistics for several variables, which are listed in the first column. The second column reports the statistics for all observations. The third and fourth columns report statistics for courses in lower and upper divisions, respectively.

There are several ways to generate this table. The conventional way is to estimate or calculate the statistics and then copy and paste them in MS Excel or MS Word. The other option could be to generate the entire table in the statistical software. This might be a little more involved than the first option, but this approach is preferred because it eliminates the need to copy and paste, which is often a frequent cause of unintended statistical errors. Fortunately, statistical software such as R and Stata allow us to generate these custom tables within the native programming environment. I illustrate this with R.

Reproducing Hamermesh's Table in R

Before I begin, I would like you to recall the discussion on weighted means and standard deviation. The table being reproduced reports weighted statistics for several variables. Though weighted mean statistics can be computed readily from base R, a function for weighted standard deviation is not yet available in the base R. Fortunately in R, we have the freedom to define custom functions. I first write the custom function for weighted standard deviation. I call the new function *my.wsd*.

```
my.wsd<-  function(w, x, wx, n)  sqrt(sum(w*(x-wx)^2)/((n-1)*sum(w)/n))
```

Let us begin by generating the statistics for all courses. We can then use the same code to reproduce statistics for the subsamples corresponding to upper and lower divisions, respectively. The first variable in the table in Figure 4.3 is course evaluation, which is labeled as `eval` in the R data set. A weighted mean for `eval` is reported in Figure 4.3. The mean is weighted by the number of students who answered the teaching evaluation questionnaire. Results have been weighted by the number of students responding to the questionnaire to ensure that courses where only a small number of students who responded do not skew the results.

Because the weighted mean function is available with base R, I use the R code to compute the weighted mean.

```
attach(TeachingRatings)
wm.course <-weighted.mean(eval,students); wm.course
```

The results are now stored in a scalar, `wm.course`. Using the newly created weighted standard deviation function, I calculate the weighted standard deviation and store the results in a scalar, `wsd.course`.

```
wsd.course<-my.wsd(students,eval, wm.course, length(eval)) ; wsd.course
```

I do not have data on the second variable, `Instructor Evaluation` from Figure 4.3, so I will skip it. The next variable is number of students registered in the course. I do not need to determine a weighted mean or standard deviation for this variable.

```
m.studs <- mean(allstudents); sd.studs <-sd(allstudents); m.studs
```

The next variable is the percentage of the students who responded to the teaching evaluation questionnaire. I need to generate this variable on the fly because it does not exist in the data set. This can be calculated as follows:

$$Percent_{responding} = \frac{students_{responding}}{students_{enrolled}} * 100 \quad \textbf{Equation 4.5}$$

The R code to generate the variable and to calculate its mean highlights this change.

```
TeachingRatings$p.eval <- students/allstudents*100
m.peval <-mean(p.eval)
```

I do not report the mean for the next variable, `Female`, because it is a categorical variable. The variable is labelled `gender` in the data set. I need to tabulate this variable and, in fact, generate a weighted tabulation using the number of students who responded to the questionnaire as weights. I store the results in an entity labeled `tabgen`.

```
tabgen<-xtabs(students~gender)/sum(students)
```

The result from the previous tabulation includes statistics for males (reported first) and females (reported second). Note that we are interested in reporting the percentage of female instructors, listed in the second column. I will therefore have to reference only the second element in the last tabulation by typing `tabgen[2]` to isolate the answer for female instructors.

I repeat the same for the variables `minority`, `native`, and `tenure`. The R code generates three additional variables and the results are stored in appropriately named matrices.

```
tabmin<-xtabs(students~minority)/sum(students)
tabeng<-xtabs(students~native)/sum(students)
tabten<-xtabs(students~tenure)/sum(students)
```

The variable `Lower Division` requires unweighted tabulation; hence I use the simple R code to calculate the courses categorized as lower division.

```
tabdiv<-table(division)/sum(table(division))
```

I need to list the number of courses, which is generated using the **length** function.

```
courses <- length(eval)
```

The last variable requires us to enumerate the instructors. Because numerous instructors taught more than one course, the number of instructors is likely to be less than the total number of courses. In R, I relied on the **unique** function to identify unique instructors and then computed the total number of instructors.

```
faculty <- length(unique(prof))
```

So far, I have obtained all relevant statistics and have stored them in appropriate scalars, tables, or matrices. The next step is to amalgamate these in one column. This is done using the **rbind** function in R.

```
all.res<- rbind(wm.course, wsd.course, m.studs, sd.studs, m.peval,
female=tabgen[2], minority=tabmin[2], 'native english' =tabeng[2],
tenure = tabten[2],  "lower division" = tabdiv[2], courses, faculty)
colnames(all.res) <- "all courses"; all.res
```

I have stored the results in a column called `all.res` and then named the column `all courses`.

Later, I subset the data to isolate the upper and lower division courses and generate two additional columns reporting the same summary statistics, one each for lower and upper division courses.

```
lower <- subset(TeachingRatings, subset=division =="lower")
attach(lower)
upper <- subset(TeachingRatings, subset=division =="upper")
attach(upper)
```

After the statistics are calculated for each division and stored in a column, the results could thus be amalgamated into one single table. Table 4.28 shows the table reproduced from Professor Hamermesh's paper.

```
tab <-xtable(cbind(all.res, lower.res, upper.res), digits=3)
print(tab, type="html")
```

Table 4.28   Reproducing the Table from Professor Hamermesh's Paper

	all courses	lower division	upper division
wm.course	4.022	4.060	3.993
wsd.course	0.525	0.563	0.492
m.studs	55.177	76.503	44.235
sd.studs	75.073	109.287	45.541
m.peval	74.428	73.523	74.892
female	0.359	0.300	0.405
minority	0.099	0.110	0.090
native english	0.037	0.007	0.060
tenure	0.851	0.828	0.869
lower division	0.339	1.000	0.000
courses	463.000	157.000	306.000
faculty	94.000	42.000	79.000

You might want to compare the results you have obtained here with the ones listed in the original paper that I have reproduced in Figure 4.3.

The next section of this chapter presents similar results generated by Stata. Note that the results were originally generated in an html file that was loaded into Microsoft Word. The book's website presents the code that can be run automatically to generate the results in a software program of your choice.

Generating Output with Stata

This section reproduces in Stata some of the tables I generated earlier using R. I have kept the description and discussion to a minimum primarily because I have explained the concepts and rationale for these tabulations in the earlier sections. The intent here is to illustrate the use of Stata commands to generate similar outputs. I restrict the examples to the beauty and teaching evaluations data.

The book website offers a detailed reproduction of the tables from this chapter in Stata, SPSS, and SAS.

You can download data from the book's website from files listed under Chapter 4.

Summary Statistics Using Built-In Stata

I use a user-written routing **htsummary** to generate the output and set up the html file to receive the output. Note that the user-written command has to be first installed before you can use it. You can install the command by typing the following code in Stata's command window.

```
findit htsummary
```

The command opens a help page from which you can install the command and its accompanying helpfiles.

Using Descriptive Statistics

```
* Using htsummary, non-weighted data
htopen using ht_beauty, replace
htput <h1> Chapter 4 </h1>
htput <h2> Beauty example </h2>
htput Murtaza Haider, September 02, 2014. Using Beauty Pays as the
example.
htclose
```

Figure 4.4 shows summary statistics using Stata's built-in commands.

```
htopen using ht_beauty, append
htput <h3> With Summary Statistics using builtin Stata </h3>
htlog summarize age beauty eval students allstudents
htclose
```

```
    Variable |   Obs       Mean   Std. Dev.        Min        Max
-------------+--------------------------------------------------
         Age |   463   48.36501   9.802742         29         73
      Beauty |   463   6.27e-08   .7886477  -1.450494  -1.970023
        Eval |   463   3.998272   .5548656        2.1          5
    Students |   463   36.62419   45.01848          5        380
 Allstudents |   463   55.17711    75.0728          8        581
```

Figure 4.4   Standard output generated by Stata

Descriptive Statistics on Continuous Variables

I generate summary statistics for instructor-specific attributes using all observations. Table 4.29 shows summary statistics generated using **htsummary**.

```
htopen using ht_beauty, append
htput <h3> Descriptive statistics on continuous variables </h3>
htsummary age, format(%8.2f) head
htsummary age,  median
```

```
htsummary beauty, format(%8.2f)
htsummary eval, format(%8.2f)
htsummary students, format(%8.2f)
htsummary allstudents, format(%8.2f) close
htlog sum age beauty if nprofs == 1
htclose
```

Table 4.29 Summary Statistics Generated Using `htsummary`

Variable	Summary statistics
prof's age[1]	48.37 (9.80) [463]
prof's age[2]	48 (15) [463]
prof's beauty score[1]	0.00 (0.79) [463]
evaluation score[1]	4.00 (0.55) [463]
students responded[1]	36.62 (45.02) [463]
students enrolled in class[1]	55.18 (75.07) [463]

1: Arithmetic Mean (SD) [n]
2: Median (IQR) [n]

Note that Table 4.29, under the column *Summary statistics*, presents a composite output because it amalgamates the mean, standard deviation, and the number of observations in a single cell. When I ask for the median, the algorithm reports the median inter-quartile range and the number of observations in the same cell.

The last chunk of code also provides the command to generate summary statistics for the variables `age` and `beauty` for instructors. Note that I include only one observation for each instructor to prevent multiple observations per instructor from biasing our summary statistics. The results are presented in Figure 4.5, which demonstrates results in Stata native format.

```
Variable │ Obs     Mean   Std. Dev.        Min        Max
─────────┼────────────────────────────────────────────────
     Age │  94  47.55319  10.25651         29         73
  Beauty │  94  .0883492   .8275058  -1.450494   1.970023
```

Figure 4.5 Restricting to instructor-specific observations for age and beauty

Descriptive Statistics by Categorical Variables

Now I illustrate several features to generate descriptive statistics in Stata.

```
htopen using ht_beauty, append
htput <h3> Descriptive statistics by categorical variables </h3>
```

```
htsummary eval gender, format(%8.2f) head close
htsummary eval tenure, format(%8.2f) head close
htsummary gender tenure, freq head close
htlog table gender tenure, contents(mean eval sd eval freq )
htlog table gender tenure, contents(mean eval sd eval freq )
by(minority)
htclose
```

First, I generate summary statistics for teaching evaluation scores by gender in Table 4.30.

Table 4.30   Descriptive Statistics for Teaching Evaluation by Gender Using `htsummary`

| Variable | gender | | |
	female	male	Total
evaluation score[1]	3.90 (0.54) [195]	4.07 (0.56) [268]	4.00 (0.55) [463]

1: Arithmetic Mean (SD) [n]

Second, I generate summary statistics for teaching evaluation scores by tenure status. The results are presented in Table 4.31.

Table 4.31   Descriptive Statistics for Teaching Evaluation by Tenure Using `htsummary`

| Variable | tenured | | |
	no	yes	Total
evaluation score[1]	4.13 (0.56) [102]	3.96 (0.55) [361]	4.00 (0.55) [463]

1: Arithmetic Mean (SD) [n]

Third, I generate a cross-tabulation between gender and tenure status. The results are presented in Table 4.32.

Table 4.32   Descriptive Statistics for Teaching Evaluation by Gender Using `htsummary`

| Variable | | tenured | | |
		no	yes	Total
gender[1]	female	50 (49%)	145 (40%)	195 (42%)
	male	52 (51%)	216 (60%)	268 (58%)

1: n (column percentage)

The remaining two commands in the last chunk of code present the output in native Stata format. The output presents the mean and standard deviation for evaluations for each combination of gender and tenure status. For instance, the mean evaluation for male tenured instructors was 3.99 and 4.39 for non-tenured male instructors. The standard deviation for evaluations for female untenured instructors is 0.473. The results are presented in Figure 4.6.

```
-------------------------------
        |     Tenured
 Gender |     No         Yes
--------+----------------------
 Female |     3.86      3.915172
        |  -4733726    -.5604228
        |      50         145
        |
   Male |  4.396154    3.990278
        |  .5048633     .5405836
        |      52         216
-------------------------------
```

Figure 4.6 Summary statistics for evaluation by gender and tenure

I take the additional step by adding another dimension. What if we want to determine the mean for teaching evaluations for minority instructors who are female and tenured? I added this dimension in the syntax, which generated Figure 4.7.

```
---------------------------
Minority |
and      |     Tenured
Gender   |     No       Yes
---------+-----------------
No       |
  Female |    3.86    3.974312
         | .4733726   .5644407
         |    50        109
         |
    Male |  4.304762  4.015656
         | .5174762   .5394181
         |    42        198
---------+-----------------
Yes      |
  Female |            3.736111
         |             .515005
         |                36
         |
    Male |    4.78    3.711111
         | .147573    .4837219
         |    10         18
---------------------------
```

Figure 4.7 Summary statistics for evaluation by minority, gender, and tenure

Note that the output is divided into two sections and four quadrants. The first section is for non-minority instructors and the second is for minority instructors. Within each section, the output is further disaggregated for each combination of gender and tenure. Note that because there were no untenured female minority instructors, the respective quadrant is empty.

Weighted Statistics

An accompanying command to `htsummary` is `htsvysummary`, which at the time of writing was available only from the individual who had coded the command. `htsvysummary` can generate summary statistics for weighted data. The Stata code using `htsvysummary` produces the weighted mean and standard deviation for teaching evaluations for upper and lower division courses, as well as for the total responses. Table 4.33 shows descriptive statistics for teaching evaluation by course level using weighted data.

```
htopen using ht_beauty, append
htput <h3> Weighted statistics </h3>
* Setting up survey data
/* declare survey design */
svyset, clear
svyset  [iw=students]
* Summary stats
htsvysummary eval upper, format(%8.3f) head close
htclose
```

Table 4.33   Descriptive Statistics for Teaching Evaluation by Course Level Using Weighted Data

	upper division		
Variable	**lower**	**upper**	**Total**
evaluation score[1]	4.060 (0.496) [7393]	3.993 (0.533) [9564]	4.022 (0.525) [16957]

1: Arithmetic Mean (SD) [n]

Correlation Matrix

The `htsummary` command can store almost any output in native Stata format. For instance, in the Stata code, I use the `cor` command to generate the correlation matrix.

```
* Correlation
htopen using ht_beauty, append
htput <h3> Correlation matrix </h3>
htlog cor eval beauty age students allstudents
htclose
```

Figure 4.8 shows that the teaching evaluation and beauty score are positively correlated (0.18). I leave the discussion on the statistical significance of these relationships for a later chapter.

```
           |   Eval    Beauty      Age  Students  Allstu~s
-----------+--------------------------------------------------
      Eval |  1.0000
    Beauty |  0.1890    1.0000
       Age | -0.0517   -0.2979   1.0000
  Students |  0.0355    0.1306  -0.0305   1.0000
Allstudents | -0.0012    0.0996  -0.0126   0.9721   1.0000
```

Figure 4.8   Correlation matrix in Stata-native format

Reproducing the Results for the Hamermesh and Parker Paper

Finally, I reproduce results for the same table from the Hamermesh and Parker paper.

```
htopen using ht_beauty, append
htput <h3> Hamermesh paper </h3>

.
htsvysummary eval upper, format(%8.3f) head
htsummary allstudents upper, format(%8.3f)
htsummary p_eval upper , format (%8.3f)
htsvysummary female upper, freq
htsvysummary minority upper, freq
htsvysummary native upper, freq
htsvysummary tenure upper, freq
htsummary nprofs upper, freq
htsummary nprofs2 upper, freq  close
htclose
```

Table 4.34 is generated entirely by the last chunk of code. Again, I reiterate the need to use the syntax for generating the table so that we can avoid the perils associated with copying and pasting. Furthermore, we can alter the table by altering the code, without having to generate an output, store it, copy it, paste it, and reformat it.

Table 4.34   Reproducing the Table from Hamermesh and Parker Study Using Stata

Variable		upper division		
		lower	upper	Total
evaluation score[1]		4.060 (0.496) [7393]	3.993 (0.533) [9564]	4.022 (0.525) [16957]
students enrolled in class[1]		76.503 (109.287) [157]	44.235 (45.541) [306]	55.177 (75.073) [463]
percent responded[1]		73.523 (18.589) [157]	74.892 (15.746) [306]	74.428 (16.756) [463]
female[2]	male	5172 (70%)	5691 (60%)	10863 (64%)
	female	2221 (30%)	3873 (40%)	6094 (36%)

minority[2]	no	6583 (89%)	8700 (91%)	15283 (90%)
	yes	810 (11%)	864 (9%)	1674 (10%)
native speaker of English[2]	no	50 (1%)	570 (6%)	620 (4%)
	yes	7343 (99%)	8994 (94%)	16337 (96%)
tenured[2]	no	1271 (17%)	1256 (13%)	2527 (15%)
	yes	6122 (83%)	8308 (87%)	14430 (85%)
faculty members (total)[2]	unique	30 (100%)	64 (100%)	94 (100%)
faculty members (divisional)[2]	unique	42 (100%)	79 (100%)	121 (100%)

1: Arithmetic Mean (SD) [n]
2: n (column percentage)

Statistical Analysis Using Custom Tables

Lastly, I illustrate the flexibility of using syntax to produce customized tables. The code generates an html file whose output is controlled by the code. Such a code is extremely useful in generating tabulations that need to be reproduced regularly over time with new data. Table 4.35 shows customized tabulations using Stata.

```
htopen using ht_beauty, append
htput <h1> Statistical Analysis using custom tables </h1>
htput <table border=1>
htput <tr>
htput <th>Variable</th>
htput <th>Mean</th>
htput <th>SD</th>
htput <th>Min</th>
htput <th>Max</th>
htput </tr>
foreach var of varlist eval beauty female upper nprofs nprofs2 {
local lab: var lab 'var'
summarize 'var'
local mean: display %8.2f r(mean)
local sd: display %8.2f r(sd)
local min: display %8.0f r(min)
local max: display %8.0f r(max)
htput <tr align=right>
htput <td>'lab'</td>
htput <td>'mean' </td>
```

```
htput <td>'sd' </td>
htput <td>'min' </td>
htput <td>'max' </td>
htput </tr>
}
htput </table>
htclose
```

Table 4.35 Customized tabulations using Stata

Variable	Mean	SD	Min	Max
evaluation score	4.00	0.55	2	5
prof's beauty score	0.00	0.79	-1	2
female	0.42	0.49	0	1
upper division	0.66	0.47	0	1
faculty members (total)	1.00	0.00	1	1
faculty members (divisional)	1.00	0.00	1	1

The resulting table presents mean, standard deviation, minimum, and maximum values for the selected variables. I am at liberty to pick any other variable or summary statistics of our choice to be included in customized tabulations.

Summary

Thinking about tables, and more importantly their comparison with graphics, reminds us of Daniel Kahneman, who is one of the most prominent thinkers of our time. Professor Kahneman received a Nobel for his research in decision-making, which he conducted earlier in collaboration with another giant in the field, Amos Tversky. Professor Kahneman provides an accessible discourse of his findings in the bestselling book, *Thinking Fast and Slow*.

Professor Kahneman introduces two systems in mind, namely System 1 and System 2. I argue that charts and graphics engage System 1 whereas tables engage System 2.

Professor Kahneman believes System 1 "operates automatically and quickly, with little or no effort and no sense of voluntary control." When one sees a bar chart and other similar graphs, one can readily make a judgment about which bar is taller than the rest. This conclusion takes place rather involuntarily. Such conclusions are based on System 1 in our minds. Still, the bar chart offers no clues regarding the exact difference in magnitude between the tallest bar and the one less than that.

System 2, Professor Kahneman explains, "allocates attention to the effortful mental activities that demand it, including complex computations." A table, I argue, engages System 2 because while reviewing the information in tables one uses slightly more brainpower to determine the difference in magnitudes in more specific terms. Thus, it might take longer to draw conclusions from tables than it might with graphics; the added advantage is the specificity one gains from the tabular representation of data.

Despite the tremendous progress in the visual display of data and the emergence of info-graphics, tabular display of summary statistics continues to be a part and parcel of academic and professional publications. Some have argued, although erroneously, that the advances in data visualization will make tables obsolete. I humbly disagree and contend that tables provide a unique opportunity to present a succinct view of the underlying data with a certain degree of precision that is not possible with graphics.

Consider a graphic representing the electoral outcome of an election contested by several political parties. One can eyeball the graphic to determine the vote share of the leading and other parties. However, if the graphic does not mention the exact vote share in a closely contested election, one might not be able to speak of the results with some degree of certainty.

On the other hand, a table would have listed the vote share for each party in specific terms. The precision and the ability to present a multitude of statistics in a single table are the reasons behind the longevity of tables.

In this chapter, I have incrementally evolved the discussion on generating summary tables from very basic tables to rather advanced, multidimensional tables. At times, data presented in tables correspond to different variables measured at different scales. For instance, income may be recorded in dollars and age in years. The average value for age is usually much smaller than the average value for annual income. Whereas a table can document this information without any special interventions, presenting the same in a graphic requires the use of multiple axes and customized scaling. Adding a third or more dimensions will make the graph even more complex if the multiple dimensions record information on multiple scales.

This chapter highlighted the need for effective communication with tabular summaries by urging data scientists to avoid ambiguous labeling and improper formatting. Using gender instead of male or female as a column heading will only confuse the reader. Similarly, adding unnecessary multiple digits after the decimal point contributes only confusion and not clarity to the message being delivered.

Tables, with illustrative graphics, which I discuss in Chapter 5, "Graphic Details," will continue to be the two primary elements that supplement data scientists' data-driven narrative. It is, therefore, incumbent upon data scientists to master the art of generating tables and graphics that are self-explaining and appealing to the reader.

Endnotes

1. The acronym is attributed to Jim O'Neill in a 2001 Goldman Sachs paper entitled "Building Better Global Economic BRICs."

2. https://sites.google.com/site/econometriks/3-chapters/4-serving-tables

3. Read more on Professor Daniel's achievements at www.timesdispatch.com/news/state-regional/jmu-has-hottest-professor/article_3a6476fc-60cb-5cfa-ae34-69b51f8ea966.html.

4. The study is available at www.nber.org/papers/w9853.

5. See comments on https://www.essex.ac.uk/sociology/documents/pdf/ug_journal/vol2/2009SC203_AndrewEdmunds.pdf.

6. Hamermesh, D. and Partker, A. "Beauty in the Classroom: Instructors' Pulchritude and Putative Pedagogical Productivity." *Economics of Education Review*, August 2005, v. 24, iss. 4, pp. 369–76.

CHAPTER 5

Graphic Details

It was indeed an epic movie based on an epic story. Titanic, *directed by the Canadian director James Cameron, was released in December 1997.* Titanic *became one of the most profitable movies in the history of movie making.*

For those who have watched *Titanic*, the image of Leonardo DiCaprio and Kate Winslet standing at the ship's hull with their arms stretched wide will remain forever etched in their memories. The movie portrayed the story of two passengers, Rose DeWitt Bukater (Kate Winslet), an aristocrat, and Jack Dawson (Leonardo DiCaprio), a struggling artist. The class hierarchy that was characteristic of the society in Europe manifested in the very literal sense on the *Titanic* as it sailed from South Hampton in England for New York City. The ship hosted passengers in first, second, and third class.

The movie focused on the short-lasting romance between Rose, a passenger in the first class, and Jack, a passenger travelling in the third class of the ship. The *RMS Titanic* sank on April 15, 1912. The tragedy has captivated the imagination of writers, moviemakers, and others. The masses have never been able to overcome their morbid fascination with the life and the death of the celebrity. The *Titanic* fits the bill for such fascination. The ship carried 2,224 passengers on her maiden voyage. Of those, 1,500 perished with the *Titanic*.

The data about those who died and others who survived the sinking offers a glimpse of the class structure of that time, which was prevalent even on the *Titanic*. A disproportionately large number of men died in the accident. At the same time, a disproportionately large number of the third-class passengers perished. In fact, women and children traveling on the upper deck survived the shipwreck in greater proportion than did those who traveled in second and third classes.

There is a reason for such disproportionate outcome in survival rates. The ship carried two very different classes of passengers comprising the aristocratic elite from England and Europe, and the poor emigrants from Great Britain, Ireland, and Scandinavia. Their destination was the same; however, their fateful ends differed.

The rich travelled in the first class with all the luxuries and entitlements, and the poor were condemned to the dark and windowless quarters in the third class. When it became a question of survival, the rich prevailed over the rest.

The *Titanic* carried far fewer rescue boats than needed. In fact, the lifeboats could carry only 1,178 passengers whereas the ship carried 2,224 passengers. When it became obvious that not every passenger could be saved, those who were launching the lifeboats adopted a "women and children first" policy. However, rich women and children survived in greater proportions than did poor women and children.

This chapter uses three data sets to demonstrate the communication power of illustrative graphics:

- I take advantage of the teaching ratings data from the University of Texas. (I discussed the data in some detail in Chapter 4, "Serving Tables," on tabulations.)

- I use a data set based on the *Titanic* to illustrate multifaceted bar charts.

- Finally, I introduce a data set on commute times and their determinants for New York City. I show that increasing population densities can help increase the share of trips made on public transit, but at the same time, it could worsen region-wide commute times.

Telling Stories with Figures

I tell the story of life and death on the *Titanic* in Figure 5.1. The figure presents a plot of those who survived and those who did not. In fact, the figure offers much more details. It reveals how the survival rates differed by the three passenger classes; that is, the first class hosting the aristocrats, the second class, and the third class passengers who were predominantly poor. The figure also presents the breakdown between male and female passengers. In addition, the survival rates are marked separately for children and adults. I present in this chapter the R-code used to generate the figures.

```
barchart(Class ~ Freq | Sex + Age, data = as.data.frame(Titanic),
         groups = Survived, stack = TRUE, layout = c(4, 1),
         auto.key = list(title = "Survived", columns = 2),
         par.settings = standard.theme(color = F),
         scales = list(x = "free"))
```

Briefly, Figure 5.1 presents a consolidated picture of what I have explained in the previous paragraphs about the class structure and its influence on how the passengers traveled and died on the *Titanic*. You will notice four panels in the figure where the first panel represents the data for male children, the second for female children, the third for adult males, and the fourth for adult females. Those who survived are represented by a lighter shade of gray and those who did not are represented by a darker shade.

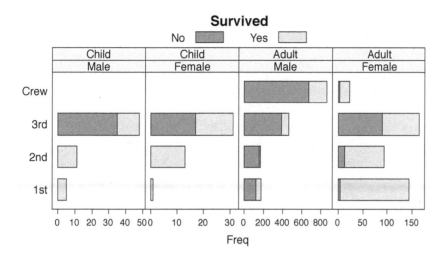

Figure 5.1   Survival stats for the *Titanic* differentiated by age, gender, and travel class

A quick glance of Figure 5.1 reveals that almost all children travelling in the first or the second class, either male or female, survived. However, not all children travelling in the third class were equally fortunate. In addition, male children travelling in the third class died in greater proportion than the female children in the same class did. Specifically, three-fourths of the male children travelling in third class perished. On the other hand, slightly more than 50 percent of the female children died in the third class.

Figure 5.1 explicitly portrays the lower odds of survival for the male passengers. Most male crewmembers died on the *Titanic*. However, we see that most female crewmembers survived the shipwreck. An overwhelming majority of adult males travelling in the third class died. In comparison, slightly more than 50 percent of the female passengers travelling in the third class died. Most of the first-class male passengers died and almost all adult males in the second class died as well. However, most female passengers in first class and an overwhelming majority of female passengers in second class survived the shipwreck.

Figure 5.1 offers an example of how to present results as graphics. I told the story of how people travelled, died, and survived on the *Titanic*. I present the same information differentiated by the travelling class, the gender, and the age structure of passengers in one simple graphic.

I have advocated throughout this book that summary statistics should be presented as illustrative graphics and tables. Furthermore, graphics should be preferred over tables because human beings process graphical information faster than even well-formatted tabular data.

Data Types

You can categorize data into two broad categories: continuous variables, such as housing prices, and categorical variables, such as gender. The type of graphic drawn for two or more variables largely depends on the type of variables. Here are some general suggestions.

If two variables are continuous, you can present the relationship as a scatter plot. If two or more variables are categorical, you can use bar charts. You can plot summary statistics as bar charts or dot plots for continuous variables being categorized by categorical variables.

You will notice that I have excluded line charts from the discussion here. This is because I illustrate in detail the use of line graphs later in Chapter 11, which focuses on time series forecasting. Also, note that all graphics have been deliberately generated in grayscale.

I have reproduced the R code used in generating the graphics in this book. If you use SAS, SPSS, or Stata, you can download the command syntax, data sets, and resulting output from the book's website at www.ibmpressbooks.com/title/9780133991024. Note that R has a very powerful graphic engine that allows for extensive customization of the elements in a graphic. Other software might be limited in their abilities to generate exactly the same graphic as you see in the text.

Teaching Ratings

I demonstrate the use of illustrative graphics by returning to the discussion on instructors' looks and their teaching ratings. You might recall from Chapter 4 how I used tabulations to analyze a data set from the University of Texas to explore the relationship between the teaching evaluation score and the appearance of the instructor. Professor Hamermesh and his co-author collected data on 400-plus courses taught by 98 instructors from the University of Texas. They obtained the average teaching evaluation scores recorded by students in the teaching evaluation surveys. The authors also constituted a panel of students who reviewed photographs of instructors and ranked them on their looks. The authors normalized the beauty score such that the average normalized beauty score returned a mean zero and variance of one.

Obviously, the teaching evaluation score relies much on an instructor's ability to communicate with students, in addition to having a sound understanding of the subject matter. Regrettably, I do not have information on these two important determinants of teaching effectiveness. The data set, however, offers insights about other possible determinants of teaching evaluation, including the instructor's gender, tenure status, English language fluency, and the minority status. In addition, the data offers course-specific variables, such as upper- or lower-level course, students enrolled in the course, and course credits.

I present a scatter plot (and the R script) between the two variables of interest, namely beauty and teaching evaluation score (see Figure 5.2). Notice that beauty is the variable on the x-axis. In the plain Cartesian system, the x-axis is called *abscissa*, and the y-axis is called *ordinate*. It is common practice to use "x-axis" and "y-axis" to refer to the axes in charts. Notice also that beauty score has been transformed to fall between –2 and +2. At the same time, the teaching evaluation score ranges from 2 to 5.

```
xyplot(eval ~ beauty, data = TeachingRatings)
```

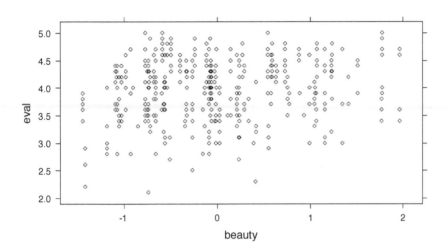

Figure 5.2 Scatter plot of teaching evaluations and the normalized beauty score

Notice that both the beauty and teaching evaluation scores are continuous variables. Even though the values are bracketed in a narrow range from 2 to 5 for evaluation score and from –2 to +2 for beauty score, still we consider both variables continuous because each variable may assume any value in the ranges stated earlier.

You will notice the following shortcoming in Figure 5.2. The axis labels are not necessarily illustrative. Most software, as is the case with R and Stata, automatically report the variable name corresponding to the data plotted in the figure. For Figure 5.2, beauty and evaluation scores are the variables of interest. However, you should use descriptive labels that can assist the reader in understanding the relationships illustrated in figures.

I address the labeling shortcomings in Figure 5.3. Note that x-axis label reads "normalized beauty score" and the y-axis label reads "teaching evaluation score." The reader can now easily ascertain that the plot represents values for beauty and teaching evaluation scores. I prefer Figure 5.3 with illustrative axis labels to Figure 5.2 with generic variable labels.

```
xyplot(eval ~ beauty, data = TeachingRatings,
       xlab = "normalized beauty score",
       ylab= "teaching evaluation score")
```

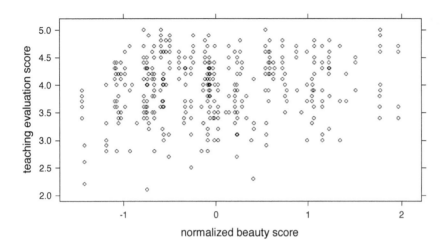

Figure 5.3   Improved labels for the scatter plot between teaching and beauty scores

The scatter plot in Figure 5.3 does not suggest a trend. We are unable to determine whether the beauty score and teaching evaluation score have a positive or negative correlation. You can explore further by trying to fit a regression (or a best fit) line to the data set. I explain the regression concepts later in the book; however, at this stage, it is sufficient to say that I will plot a line that will attempt to capture the underlying relationship in the data set.

Figure 5.4 builds on Figure 5.3 by adding the best-fit line to the data set. We see that there is an upward trend between the normalized beauty score and the teaching evaluation score when beauty score ranges between –1 to 0. However, the slope of the curve tapers off around 0 only to increase later for higher values of the beauty score. Notice also that the black line drawn on top of black circles is not easily distinguishable.

```
xyplot(eval ~ beauty, data = TeachingRatings,
       type = c("p", "g", "smooth"),
       xlab = "normalized beauty score",
       ylab= "teaching evaluation score")
```

I would like to refine the figure to accentuate the appearance of best-fit line. Figure 5.5 improves the appearance of the best-fit line by implementing two changes. First, I have changed the appearance of dots by filling them with gray color. Second, I have made the best-fit line thicker than the one in Figure 5.4.

```
xyplot(eval ~ beauty, data = TeachingRatings,
       type = c("p", "g", "smooth"), pch=16, lwd=2,
       col.symbol = "dark grey",
       xlab = "normalized beauty score",
       ylab= "teaching evaluation score")
```

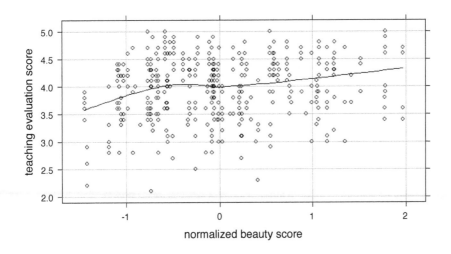

Figure 5.4   Scatter plot with best-fit line

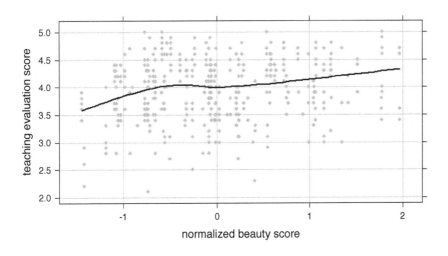

Figure 5.5   Improved coloring for the scatter plot with best-fit line

By implementing these two changes, you can see that the best-fit line is more obvious and easily recognizable on top of the gray-colored dots that represent the scatter between teaching evaluation and normalized beauty scores. In summary, we can spot, with the help of a best-fit line, an upward trend between the normalized beauty score and the teaching evaluation score.

I generate a scatter plot between instructors' age and the teaching evaluation score in Figure 5.6 to determine the relationship, if any, between the instructors' age and teaching evaluation scores. I also generate a best-fit line along with the scatter plot.

```
xyplot(eval ~ age, data = TeachingRatings,
        type = c("p", "g", "smooth"), pch=16, lwd=2,
        col.symbol = "dark grey", xlab = "age in years",
        ylab= "teaching evaluation score")
```

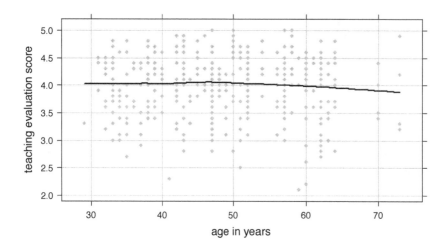

Figure 5.6   Scatter plot of teaching evaluation score and instructor's age

Figure 5.6 reveals that the best-fit line is essentially horizontal, suggesting no meaningful relationship between instructor's age and teaching evaluation score.

Figure 5.7 presents tabulation for a categorical variable; that is, the visible minority status of instructors as a bar chart. Figure 5.7 presents two bars: One is labeled as "yes", and the other "no". At the same time, we see that the bar labelled *no* extends beyond the maximum value identified on the y-axis.

```
plot(TeachingRatings$minority)
```

A reader, unfamiliar with the context, will not be able to determine what is being depicted in Figure 5.7. The "no" and "yes" labels are meaningless without an illustrative label for the x-axis. At the same time, the y-axis should be extended so that it covers the entire range of values depicted by the bar labeled "no".

Figure 5.8 addresses the concerns for the y-axis.

```
plot(TeachingRatings$minority,ylim=c(0,500))
```

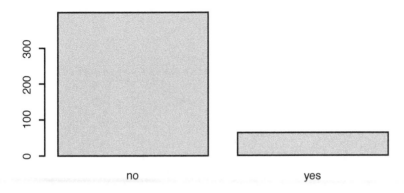

Figure 5.7 Graphical depiction of the minority status

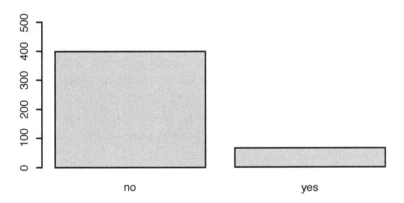

Figure 5.8 Corrected ordinate for the graphical depiction of the minority status

Notice now that the bar labeled "no" now falls within the value plotted on the y-axis. However, we still do not know by just looking at the figure what is being depicted as no or yes on the x-axis.

Figure 5.9 addresses the two concerns I have highlighted about Figure 5.7.

```
plot(TeachingRatings$minority,ylim=c(0,500),
    xlab="minority status", ylab="number of courses")
```

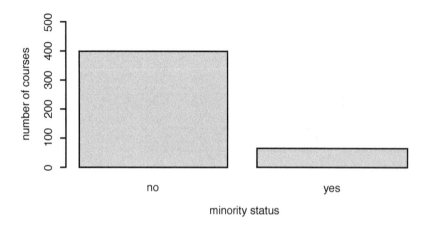

Figure 5.9   Appropriately labelled depiction of the minority status

Notice that the label for x-axis adequately informs that we present a breakdown for the minority status of the instructors. At the same time, the values depicted on the y-axis refer to the number of courses being taught by the instructors. We can deduce by reviewing Figure 5.9 that most courses are taught by non-minority instructors.

Notice that the bars presented in Figure 5.9 are in the shape of columns. I can present the same information by rotating the bars by 90 degrees. I illustrate this by presenting the breakdown of courses taught by gender (see Figure 5.10).

```
plot(TeachingRatings$gender,horiz=TRUE, xlim=c(0,300),
     ylab="gender", xlab="number of courses")
```

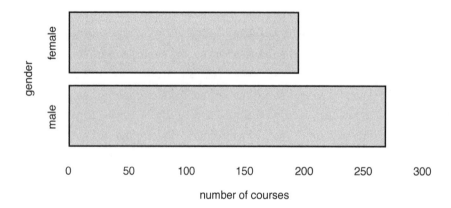

Figure 5.10   Breakdown of courses by gender

Notice that the two bars are plotted horizontally showing that the male instructors teach more courses than the female instructors do. We can conveniently infer this from Figure 5.10 because of the illustrative labels for the x-axis, which represents the number of courses taught, and y-axis, which presents the breakdown of gender for male and female instructors.

Graphics are even more powerful when we present multiple variables in one image. For instance, Figure 5.11 presents a cross tabulation between two categorical variables, namely gender and tenure. In a tabular format, a cross-tabulation between two variables is presented as a two-by-two matrix.

```
xtab<-table(x$tenure,x$gender)
barplot(xtab, ylim=c(0,300),    legend=rownames(xtab),
        xlab= "gender", ylab= "number of courses")
```

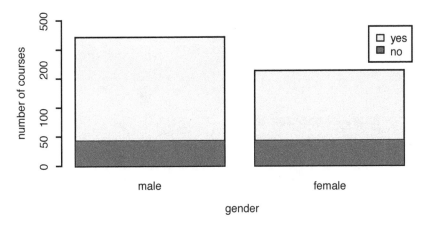

Figure 5.11   Breakdown of courses by gender and tenure

Figure 5.11 presents the same two-by-two matrix in a graphical format. We can tell from the x-axis that the two bars represent the gender and we can tell from the y-axis that the height of the bars represents the number of courses. We also note that each bar has two distinct colors. From the legend placed in the top-right corner, we see that the darker shade represents "no" and the lighter shade represents "yes". Knowing that we have plotted gender and tenure, we can infer that the yes and no refer to the tenure status of the instructors. Thus, by reviewing the information in Figure 5.11, we can conclude that tenured faculty members teach the overwhelming majority of courses. We infer this by looking at the larger light gray shaded parts of the bars representing male and female instructors.

There are two obvious shortcomings in Figure 5.11. First is that the legend in the top-right corner refers to the tenure status as "yes" and "no". This information is automatically generated from the data labels for the minority variable. Because the labels identified tenured professors as "yes" and non-tenured professors as "no", the plotting command automatically generates the same labels for the corresponding data in the figure. While these labels are useful, they are certainly not illustrative. The information value of this figure will improve if we were to replace "yes" with "tenured" and "no" with "non-tenured" in the legend.

The other limitation of this graph is the way it represents the breakdown between male and female instructors for their respective tenure status. A quick review of Figure 5.11 suggests that the number of courses taught by non-tenured instructors is almost the same for both male and female instructors. That is, the dark-shaded areas for the two bars representing male and female instructors are of almost equal height. This equivalency is misleading.

Even though untenured male and female instructors taught a similar absolute number of courses, relatively speaking, untenured female instructors taught a larger proportion of courses taught by female instructors than the same for their male counterparts. I address these shortcomings by plotting the respective percentage of courses across the two dimensions of gender and tenure in Figure 5.12.

```
x<-TeachingRatings
plot(x$gender, x$tenure, main="Share of courses taught", ylab="tenure
status", xlab="gender")
```

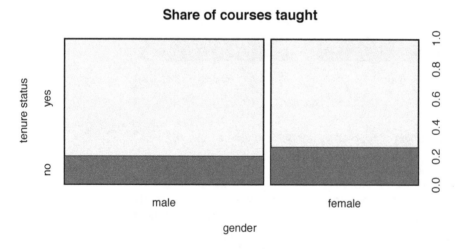

Figure 5.12   Proportionate breakdown of courses by gender and tenure

Note that the x-axis in Figure 5.12 represents gender and y-axis represents the tenure status of instructors. Also, note that width of the bars is proportionate to the courses taught by male and female instructors, respectively. Given that male instructors taught more courses than the female instructors, the width of the bar representing male instructors is proportionately wider than that of the bar representing female instructors. At the same time, the darker shaded portion of the bars representing non-tenured instructors for both male and female instructors illustrates that untenured female instructors taught a larger proportion of the courses taught by the female instructors than the untenured males did as a fraction of the courses taught by male instructors.

Histograms are widely used to determine the distribution of continuous variables. Histograms can help you determine outliers and the central tendency in a data set. Figure 5.13 presents the histogram for the normalized beauty scores. The figure reveals that most instructors received a score between –1 and 0, and only a small number of instructors received beauty scores in the range of 1 and 2. The y-axis presents the percentage of observations that fell in each category for the beauty score.

```
histogram(x$beauty)
```

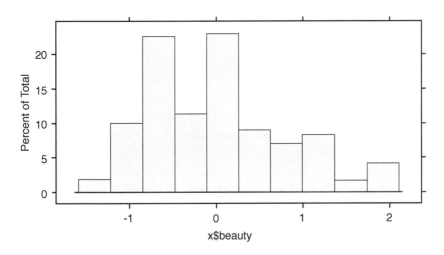

Figure 5.13   Histogram of beauty score

I can identify at least two limitations in this graph. First, the bars are lightly shaded and they may not print well on paper. Thus, a darker shade of gray will be helpful. At the same time, the label for x-axis, which is automatically generated, is not very illustrative. This can be addressed by replacing it with a more descriptive label.

```
histogram(x$beauty, nint=15,
          xlab="normalized beauty score", col=c("dark grey"))
```

Figure 5.14 addresses the aforementioned limitations.

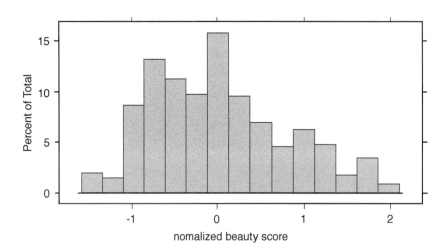

Figure 5.14   Fine-tuned histogram of beauty score

Notice that the x-axis label appropriately identifies the data as normalized beauty score whereas the y-axis continues to represent the percentage of observations corresponding to each segment of the beauty score. You will also notice that I have added additional bars to segment the beauty score compared to the ones shown in Figure 5.13. By selecting a larger number of bars, I have obtained a better distribution of data than the one in Figure 5.13.

I present a slightly different histogram for beauty score in Figure 5.15. Notice that compared to Figure 5.14, the histogram in Figure 5.15 is narrower and taller. At the same time, the information presented in Figure 5.15 appears to have a more 'normally' distributed shape than the one in Figure 5.14.

```
histogram(x$beauty, nint=15, aspect=2,
         xlab="normalized beauty score", col=c("dark grey"))
```

Figure 5.15 differs in its layout because of a different aspect ratio. Figure 5.14 presents the same information in a rectangular format where the width is greater than the height of the figure. Because Figure 5.14 is wider, we visually deduce a different conclusion than what we are able to deduce from Figure 5.15. Notice that other than aspect ratio, everything else is the same between the two figures including the color and the number of the bars. Why is it that we see different trends in the two figures?

The answer to this question perhaps lies in how we process visual signals. Because the rectangular depiction in Figure 5.15 is characterized by taller bars, we visualize a more central tendency in the normalized beauty score in Figure 5.15 than we do in Figure 5.14.

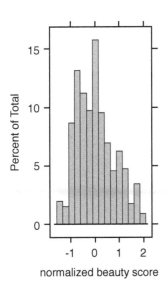

Figure 5.15 Histogram of beauty score with height greater than width

Figure 5.16 illustrates dot plots. As of late, this particular graphic has gained significant importance and is seen in business publications, such as the *Economist*. It is a powerful technique to present information on several variables, both continuous and categorical, in one comprehensive figure.

```
dotplot(variety ~ yield|year*site,
        scales=list(y = list(cex=.7)), xlab = "Barley yield (bushels/acre)",
data=barley)
```

I illustrate this technique by using the historical data on barley growth. The barley data set has been used and analyzed by the giants of statistical thought, including Ronald Fisher and others. W. Cleveland in his book *Visualizing Data*, which was published in 1993, explains the Barley data set, which essentially measures the barley yields observed in 1931 and 1932 at different sites in Minnesota. Several varieties of barley were grown at each site. Subsequent yields were recorded for each type of barley grown at each site. Figure 5.16 presents the multi-facet data in one coherent graphic. The x-axis represents the yield and the y-axis represents the 10 distinct varieties of barley. The 12 panels collectively represent the yield for the years 1931 and 1932 for each of the six locations. For instance, the panel at the top left of the figure represents the yields for 1932 recorded at Waseca and the panel on the top right represents the yield for Waseca in 1931. The y-axes for the top-left and top-right panels represent the 10 varieties of barley.

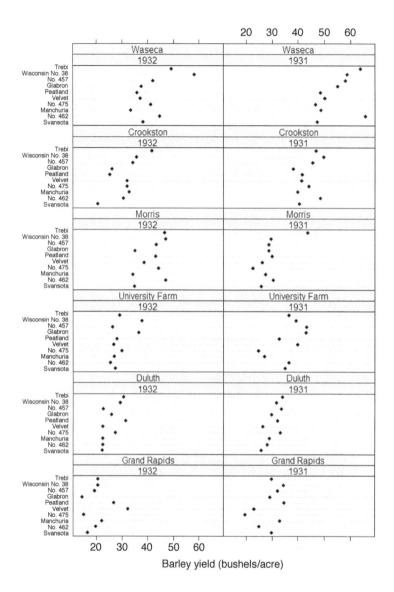

Figure 5.16   A dot plot of Barley yields, farm location, and year of harvest

A review of the information presented in Figure 5.16 suggests that the yields recorded in 1932 differed by location where on average we saw higher yields for Waseca and lower yields for the different variety of barley for Grand Rapids. We see similar trends for the six different locations for the yields recorded in 1931.

Figure 5.17 essentially presents the same information as the one presented in Figure 5.16. However, Figure 5.17 is more compact and it uses symbol typology to summarize the information. Notice that instead of 12 panels in Figure 5.16, I now present the same information in only 6 panels in Figure 5.17. The main difference is that for each location, the information for the two years, that is, 1931 and 1932, is presented in one panel such that the symbols are differentiated by the harvest year.

```
dotplot(variety ~ yield |site,
        panel=panel.superpose, groups=factor(year),
        xlab = "Barley yield (bushels/acre)",
        cex=1, auto.key=T, scales=list(y = list(cex=.7)),
        data=barley)
```

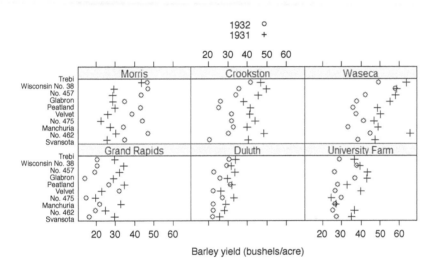

Figure 5.17   A compact dot plot of barley yields, farm location, and year of harvest

As was the case in Figure 5.16, the x-axis in Figure 5.17 represents yield and the y-axis represents the variety of barley variety. Notice that I have included a legend with the figure, which shows that the circle represents the data from 1932 and the plus sign represents the data from 1931. By looking at the information in Figure 5.17, we conclude that the highest yields were observed for Waseca for 1931 and the lowest yields were observed for Grand Rapids for year 1932. I believe that Figure 5.17, given its compact nature, is more informative and easy to comprehend than Figure 5.16.

I represent the same information again in Figure 5.18 with a slight difference.

```
dotplot(site ~ yield |variety,
        panel=panel.superpose, groups=factor(year),
        xlab = "Barley yield (bushels/acre)",
        cex=1, auto.key=T, scales=list(y = list(cex=.7)),
layout=c(2,5,1), data=barley)
```

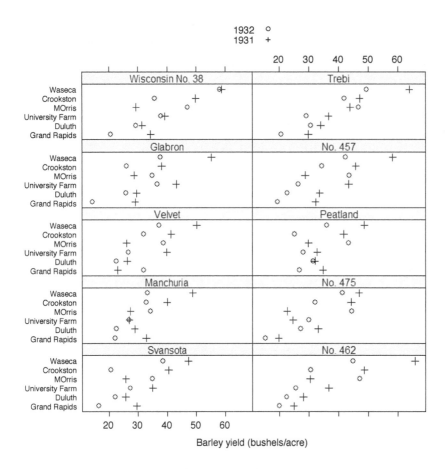

Figure 5.18   Transposed dot plot of barley yields, farm location, and year of harvest

The x-axis continues to represent the yield. However, the y-axis now represents the locations. Recall that in the previous two figures, the y-axis represented the variety of barley. Notice further that there are 10 panels in this figure representing the 10 varieties of barley. I have used the same symbols to represent the two harvest years; that is, 1931 and 1932. You can identify the highest and the lowest yields rather quickly by reversing the axes.

Graphics are also very useful in presenting summary statistics. It is customary to present summary statistics as tables. I recommend using graphs rather than tables to present summary statistics. Consider, for instance, the teaching evaluation scores for instructors differentiated by their minority status. I illustrate the difference using a box plot in Figure 5.19.

```
plot(TeachingRatings$minority, TeachingRatings$eval,
    xlab="minority status", ylab="teaching evaluation score")
```

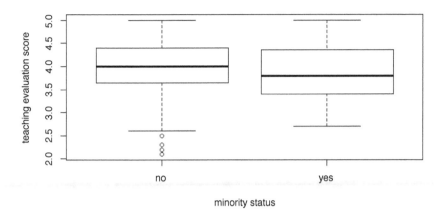

Figure 5.19   Box plot for teaching scores, differentiated by instructor's minority status

The box plot presents several statistical measures in a very compact format. The figure shows two boxes (rectangles) and lines extending from each box. The x-axis controls for the minority status such that one box and the associated lines represent the statistics for non-minority instructors and the other one represents the same for minority instructors. The y-axis represents the teaching evaluation scores.

The dark line in the middle of the box represents the median for teaching scores whereas the outer bound of the box represents the interquartile range, which represents the observations bounded by the first quartile and the third quartile. The lines extending outward from the boxes appear as whiskers, and hence the alternate name for such graphics is the box-and-whisker plot. The whiskers represent the outer fences, which are 1.5 times the interquartile range for the inner fence and 3 times the interquartile range for the outer fence. Similarly, notice the dots at the bottom for non-minority instructors, which suggest the presence of outliers. The definition for outliers in a box-and-whisker plot is data that lies 3 times outside the interquartile range.

The mosaic plot is another interesting way to present data. However, mosaic plots are unique to the R environment. Consider a cross tabulation between gender and tenure. In tabular format, the output will be a two-by-two matrix where gender will have two categories, male and female, and tenure status will be represented as tenured and non-tenured. The mosaic plot in Figure 5.20 is yet another way to represent a two-by-two or a higher dimension matrix.

```
mosaicplot( ~ TeachingRatings$tenure +TeachingRatings$gender,
           main=" Tenure status and gender differences in the number
           of courses taught",
           xlab="tenure status", ylab="gender", cex=1)
```

Tenure status and gender differences in the number of courses taught

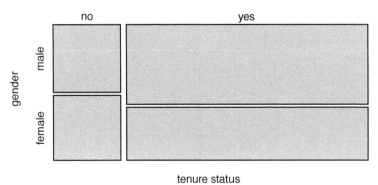

Figure 5.20   Mosaic plot for instructor's gender and tenure

The tenure status is plotted on the x-axis and gender is plotted on the y-axis. The width of the bars on the x-axis is indicative of the frequency of courses taught by tenured versus non-tenured instructors. The wider bar for "yes" suggests that more courses are taught by tenured instructors than by non-tenured instructors. The height of bars represents gender. One could see that tenured male instructors teach more courses.

Simple averages can also be presented as figures. For instance, I present the average number of students enrolled in the course for male and female instructors in Figure 5.21. The figure illustrates that male instructors on average teach larger classes than female instructors.

```
barplot(tapply(x$allstudents, x$gender,mean), ylim =c(0,70),
        ylab="No. of students enrolled", xlab = "instructor's gender")
```

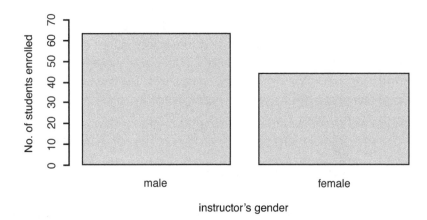

Figure 5.21   Bar chart representing enrolled students for male and female instructors

I prefer graphics to present summary statistics for multidimensional data. For instance, if you were to determine the average age of instructors differentiated by their tenure status and gender, you can easily accomplish this using the bar chart. Consider Figure 5.22 where I have plotted the average age on the y-axis and the x-axis presents data differentiated by tenure and gender.

```
xtab<-tapply(x$age, list(x$gender,x$tenure), mean)
barplot(xtab, legend=rownames(xtab),
        beside=T, ylim=c(0,60),
        xlab="tenure status", ylab="average age")
```

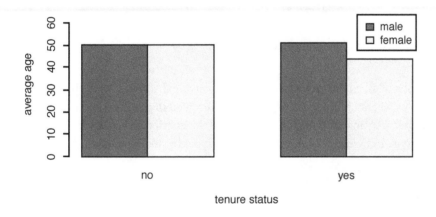

Figure 5.22   Average age of instructors differentiated by tenure status and gender

The tenure status is labelled as "yes" and "no" on the x-axis and the color of the bars controls for gender. We can see from the figure that the average age for male and female instructors is almost the same for non-tenured professors. However, the average age of tenured males is higher than that of tenured females.

You can use the box-and-whisker plot to present the same data on gender and instructors' age. Figure 5.23 shows that the median age of male instructors is higher than the median age of female instructors. At the same time, the figure plots the interquartile range for both male and female instructors.

```
plot(x$gender, x$age,
     xlab="gender", ylab="instructor's age")
```

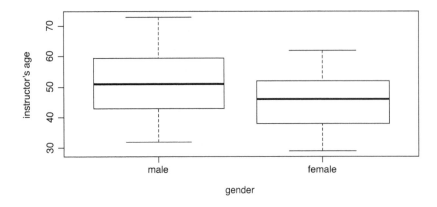

Figure 5.23   Box-and-whisker plot for average age of instructors by gender

One of the strengths of R, Stata, and other advanced statistical software is their ability to produce complex graphics where continuous variables are presented in groups, which are identified by categorical variables. In an earlier figure, I illustrated the distribution of teaching evaluation score using histograms. In Figure 5.24, I reproduce the figure by adding another dimension.

```
histogram(~ x$eval | x$gender, nint=15,
          xlab="teaching evaluation score",
          col=c("dark grey"))
```

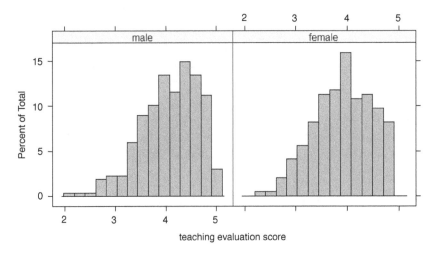

Figure 5.24   Histograms for teaching evaluation scores differentiated by gender

I have plotted in Figure 5.24 separate histograms for males and females. We notice now that compared to female instructors, male instructors have many more observations above the average value of 4 for teaching evaluation scores.

As I suggested earlier, well-illustrated figures can represent information along several dimensions. For instance, if you are interested in visualizing the differences in teaching evaluation scores for males and females and for tenured and untenured professors, you can generate a "conditional" graphic. Consider Figure 5.25 where I present histograms for teaching evaluation scores for female and male instructors who are further differentiated by their tenure status.

```
histogram(~ x$eval | x$gender * x$tenure, nint=15,
          xlab="teaching evaluation score", col=c("dark grey"))
```

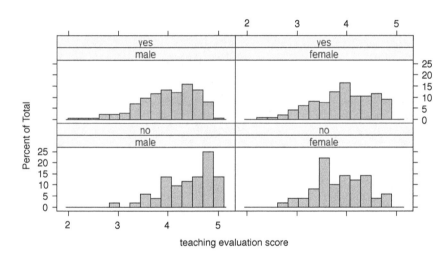

Figure 5.25 Histogram of teaching evaluation differentiated by gender and tenure

We see four panels in Figure 5.25. The x-axis represents teaching evaluation scores and the y-axis represents the percentage of observations falling within each category of teaching evaluation scores.

Each panel represents a unique combination of gender and tenure status. For instance, the panel on the top left represents the histogram for the distribution of teaching evaluation scores for male tenured instructors. The panel on the top right presents the histogram for tenured female instructors. The histograms at the bottom represent the histograms for male and female untenured instructors.

A comparison of the two panels on the left for male instructors reveals that the distribution of teaching evaluation scores is different for tenured male instructors than for untenured male instructors. Similarly, we see that the teaching evaluation scores for male untenured instructors are higher than the same for non-tenured female instructors.

Figure 5.25 suffers for an obvious limitation. The tenure status is labeled as "yes" or "no". A more informative labeling regime could be "tenured" and "non-tenured". I addressed this limitation in Figure 5.26, which essentially presents the same information as in Figure 5.25; however, the primary difference between the two is the use of informative labels for the tenure status.

```
x$tenure2 <- factor(x$tenure,
                    levels = c("no", "yes"),
                    labels =c("non-tenured", "tenured"))
histogram(~ x$eval | x$gender * x$tenure2, nint=15,
          xlab="teaching evaluation score",
          col=c("dark grey"))
```

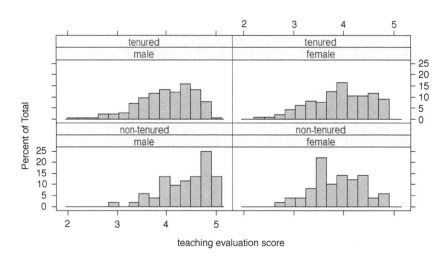

Figure 5.26   Adequately labelled histogram of teaching evaluation differentiated by gender and tenure

If you were to focus on any panel, such as the one in the bottom left in Figure 5.26, it clearly identifies the histogram for the non-tenured male instructors. The obvious advantage of using adequate labels in a figure is the ease with which the user obtains information from the graphic.

Figure 5.25 and Figure 5.26 illustrate the usefulness of illustrative labels. It is preferred to use correct labels in the data set so that the graphing algorithms can feed off the metadata in generating figures. Therefore, generation of illustrative graphics to communicate the story requires you to generate a properly labeled and well-documented data set. On the same note, I return to Figure 5.1 where I presented the distribution of survival rates differentiated by gender, age, and class for passengers on the *RMS Titanic*. Figure 5.27 differs from Figure 5.1 in one small aspect; that is, I have corrected the label for the x-axis by replacing "freq," a dubious label, with "passengers."

```
barchart(Class ~ Freq | Sex + Age, data = as.data.frame(Titanic),
         groups = Survived, stack = TRUE, layout = c(4, 1),
         auto.key = list(title = "Survived", columns = 2),
         par.settings = standard.theme(color = FALSE),
         xlab="Passengers",
         scales = list(x = "free"))
```

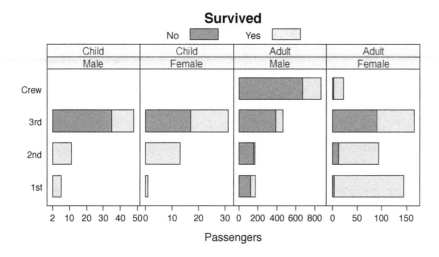

Figure 5.27   Corrected labels for the *Titanic* survival data

It is beyond the scope of this text to illustrate all possible ways to present analytics as graphics. Instead, my intent is to introduce the realm of possibilities for illustrative graphics for both methods and style. For instance, you can make further cosmetic changes to Figure 5.27 to alter its appearance. Figure 5.28 differs from Figure 5.27 in only one aspect: The bars in Figure 5.28 do not have a solid border. Just by removing the border, Figure 5.28 presents a different look.

```
fig.2<-barchart(Class ~ Freq | Sex + Age, data = as.data.frame(Titanic),
                groups = Survived, stack = TRUE, layout = c(4, 1),
                auto.key = list(title = "Survived", columns = 2),
                par.settings = standard.theme(color = FALSE),
                xlab="Passengers",
                scales = list(x = "free"))

update(fig.2,
       panel = function(..., border) {
         panel.barchart(..., border = "transparent") })
```

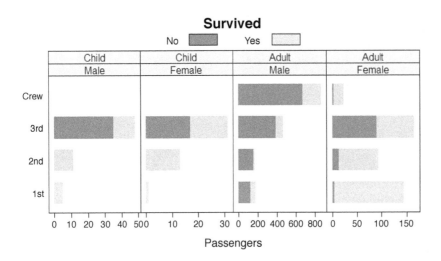

Figure 5.28   Transparent border for bars in the *Titanic* data set

Moving further, I report a graphic depiction of a cross tabulation between upper- and lower-division courses taught by instructors who are further differentiated by their tenure status. Consider Figure 5.29, where the x-axis represents the number of courses and the y-axis identifies male and female instructors. The four panels present the four bar charts representing the combination of the level of courses and tenure status of instructors.

```
tab1 <- table(x$gender, x$tenure2, x$division); tab1
tab2 <- as.data.frame.table(tab1); tab2
barchart(Var1 ~ Freq | Var2 + Var3, data=tab2, col=c("dark grey"),
         xlab="number of courses")
```

Again, Figure 5.29 is an example of presenting three dimensions of data in one illustrative graphic. I differentiate the number of courses by gender, course level, and the tenure status of instructors in a single figure, which illustrates that tenured faculty members teach most upper division courses. I readily deduce this information from the bottom-right panel, which is properly labeled as *upper* for course level and *tenured* for instructors' tenure status.

Recall that my primary interest in the teaching evaluation scores has been to determine whether the students' perception of the instructors' appearance or looks affects teaching scores. I present a scatter plot between the normalized beauty score and the teaching evaluation score in Figure 5.30.

```
xyplot(eval ~ beauty|gender, data = TeachingRatings,
       type = c("p", "g", "smooth"), pch=16, lwd=2,
 col.symbol = "dark grey", xlab = "normalized beauty score",
       ylab= "teaching evaluation score")
```

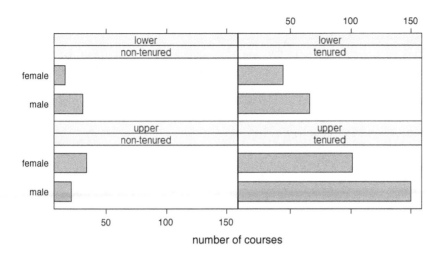

Figure 5.29 Graphic depiction of a cross tabulation of course level and tenure status

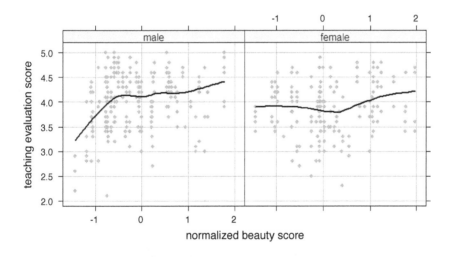

Figure 5.30 Scatter plot between teaching and beauty scores for males and females

I have differentiated the data by gender and presented two separate scatter plots along with the best-fit lines to visualize how the relationship between looks and evaluation scores differs for male and female instructors. The left panel presents the results for male instructors. I see a positive relationship between beauty and teaching evaluation scores for the lower values of beauty scores for male instructors. The slope of this relationship flattens for male instructors as the beauty scores approach 0. On the other hand, the relationship for female instructors shows that the slope is initially a downward sloping best-fit line between beauty score and teaching evaluation score. I observe a positive relationship between beauty score and evaluation score for female instructors only when beauty scores exceed 0.

You may add another variable to the mix to see how gender and tenure affect the relationship between beauty and teaching scores. Consider Figure 5.31 where I present four scatter plots between beauty and teaching evaluation scores for four different combinations of gender and tenure status.

```
xyplot(eval ~ beauty|gender+tenure2, data = x,
       type = c("p", "g", "smooth"), pch=16, lwd=2,
       col.symbol = "dark grey",
       xlab = "normalized beauty score",
       ylab= "teaching evaluation score")
```

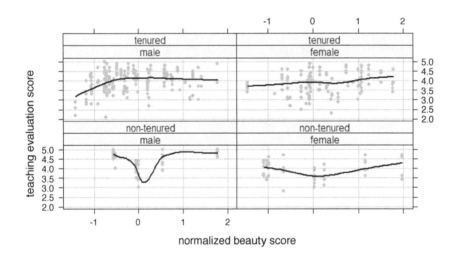

Figure 5.31   Scatter plot between teaching and beauty scores differentiated by gender and tenure

You can see that the relationship between beauty scores and teaching evaluation scores for male or female instructors differs between tenured and untenured faculty members. Figure 5.31 offers a good example of plotting multiple variables to act as controls on correlations between two variables.

The Congested Lives in Big Cities

I demonstrate illustrative graphics further with an example of traffic congestion in large cities. If you happen to live in Chicago, New York, or San Francisco, your mobility is constrained by congested arterials and overcrowded public transit vehicles. The reality is that traffic congestion in large and prosperous cities, regardless of their location, is as real and unavoidable as taxes. In fact, in places like Mumbai, a city of 15-plus million persons, you might be able to beat taxes, but not traffic.

Congestion costs billions of dollars in lost productivity. In Toronto, Canada's largest city of 5.5 million people, annual congestion-related costs are estimated at $11 billion (Canadian).[1] Urban planners, transport professionals, and municipal and state officials are increasingly concerned about the increase in traffic congestion resulting from an increase in population, automobile ownership, and the resulting auto-based commuting.

Urban scholars have identified several determinants of traffic congestion. They believe that the low-density residential suburban development in North America, especially after the Second World War, has been instrumental in promoting automobile-dependent lifestyles. At the same time, urban scholars believe that the construction of freeways further facilitated the automobile-based commuting in North America.

Some researchers, such as Newman and Kenworthy (1991),[2] believe that returning to high-density residential developments will result in greater use of public transit, lesser reliance on automobile-based commuting, and reduced fuel consumption. The urban planning literature boasts numerous studies that advocate for higher residential densities, which researchers believe are a prerequisite for operating successful public transit. The researchers further believe that an increase in public transit use will likely result in a reduction in automobile-based commuting, which they think is a prerequisite for mitigating traffic congestion in North American cities.

The purpose of this discussion is not to have an academic debate about the merits of higher population densities and public transit. Instead, the purpose is to test the assumptions commonly found in the narrative around traffic congestion and its proposed solutions.

I believe that the discourse regarding traffic congestion, public transit, and population densities suffers from several logical and methodological inconsistencies. For instance, population densities are an outcome of complex economic processes. It is difficult, and at times impossible, to alter population densities by merely formulating policies. High-density residential or commercial developments occur only at places where land values exceed certain thresholds. Stated otherwise, high-density developments seldom take place at locations where land values are relatively lower. The high-rise construction seen in Manhattan offers proof in support of this argument. The scarcity of land in Manhattan has contributed to high-rise construction where builders over the past few centuries have tried to optimize their land use by building vertical communities.

I am also concerned that a shift to a higher public transit use will not necessarily reduce congestion or commute times. In fact, I argue that such a shift from a fast-moving mode, that is, private automobile, to a slow moving mode, that is, public transit, will increase commute times in large cities in North America. While transit-based commuting has a much lower environmental footprint than commuting by car, still public transit commuting is much slower than by car. Therefore, if one is concerned about the costs of congestion, a shift to public transit will worsen congestion costs (imputed from the increase in commute times) in urban centers.

The preceding discussion is in need of evidence. I believe that data on commuting, automobile ownership, and population densities will help us develop a better picture of the nuanced arguments I have made in the preceding paragraphs.

I use data from the 2000 U.S. Census on commuting at the neighborhood level for New York City. The data set comprises more than 5,100 neighborhoods (census tracts) covering the New York Census Metropolitan Statistical Area. The average population in a neighborhood is around 4,000 persons. The neighborhood-level population density in mapped in Figure 5.32, which shows that the highest density neighborhoods are mostly located in Manhattan, or neighborhoods in other boroughs located closer to Manhattan. Neighborhood-level densities decline with distance from Manhattan. I conduct a graphical analysis of this data to determine the scope of relationship between commuting times and their determinants.

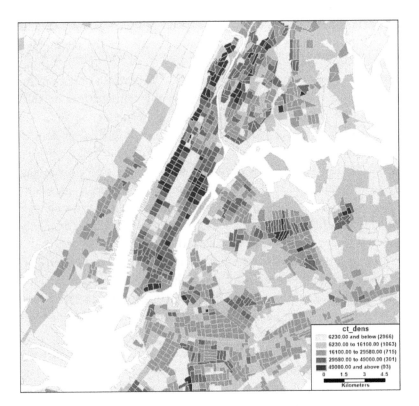

Figure 5.32   Map of New York

I deploy graphical analysis to test certain assumptions that have dominated the public, and to some extent the academic, discourse on population densities and their impact on public transit and commuting times. In particular, I am interested in the following questions:

- What is the relationship between population density and public transit use?

- How are commute times related to public transit use at the neighborhood level?

- What role, if any, does poverty play in public transit use and commute times?
- Do neighborhoods dominated by racial minorities and/or low-income households report longer commute times than others?

I will generate a series of plots to answer these questions.

Figure 5.33 presents a scatter plot between percentage of transit commutes and median commute times recorded at the neighborhood level.

```
scatterplot(m.commtime~p.transit | f.m.hhinc, reg.line=lm,
        smooth=TRUE,
        xlab="percent of transit commutes",
        ylab="median commute time",
        spread=TRUE, boxplots='xy',
        span=0.5, by.groups=TRUE,  data=NY)
```

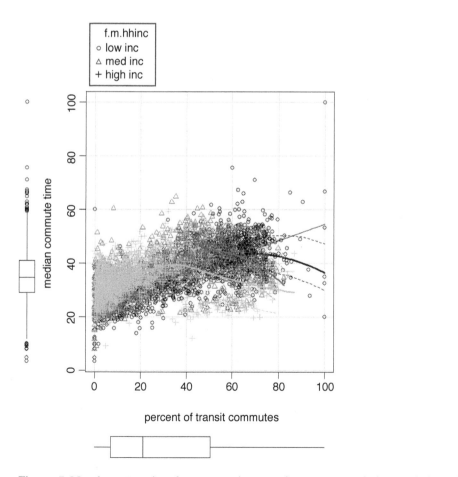

Figure 5.33 A scatter plot of commute times and percentage of trips made by public transit

I have also characterized each neighborhood as low-, medium-, or high-income. The legend informs the income categories. I have also superimposed box plots for the percentage of transit trips and median commute times. Also plotted are the locally weighted regression lines (best-fit lines, for short) and confidence intervals.

Figure 5.33 is rich in information. However, it is quite complex to comprehend. The clutter of 5,000+ symbols, one representing each neighborhood, conveys the overall impression that median commute times increase with the increase in public transit commutes. However, the obvious clutter in the figure prevents you from appreciating the nuanced details that remain hidden. Furthermore, because we know that population densities decline with distance from Manhattan, we are inadvertently assuming that the relationship between public transit usage and commute times does not change over space. You can address these limitations by replotting the same data in a more illustrative manner.

I first segment the neighborhoods into six distinct categories based on their distance from downtown Manhattan (see Table 5.1). The neighborhoods are thus labelled as nearest, nearer, medium near, medium far, farther, and farthest from downtown Manhattan. The neighborhoods located nearest to downtown Manhattan are on average 6.5-km away, whereas neighborhoods located farthest from downtown Manhattan are on average 97-km away.

I have already categorized neighborhoods as low-income, medium-income, and high-income neighborhoods. I draw six individual scatter plots for the percent of trips made by public transit and median commute times by accounting for the distance of the neighborhood from downtown Manhattan. I control for neighborhood income level by color-coding the symbols in each scatter plot.

Table 5.1   Distance Thresholds for the Six Neighborhood Categories

Distance from Manhattan CBD (km)	Mean	Min	Max
Nearest	6.59	0.28	10.04
Nearer	12.63	10.05	15.55
Medium near	18.70	15.57	22.40
Medium far	30.01	22.44	40.16
Farther	54.28	40.17	71.36
Farthest	97.35	71.79	179.80

Figure 5.34 presents the revised graphic with six panels. The panel at the bottom left presents the neighborhoods that are located nearest to downtown Manhattan. I see a positive correlation between public transit use and commute times. Even for the neighborhoods that are closest

to Manhattan, which is served by fast-moving subways on dedicated right-of-way, I see that commute times, on average, are higher for the neighborhoods with higher transit use. The positive correlation between the two variables persists for neighborhoods that are nearer, medium near, medium far, or farther from downtown Manhattan. I see the correlation weakens for only those neighborhoods that are located farthest from downtown Manhattan.

```
key.variety <- list(space = "top", text = list(levels(NY$f.m.hhinc)),
 border=TRUE, columns=4, points = list(pch=16, col=c(gray(0:3/3))))

xyplot(m.commtime ~ p.transit | f.d.cbd, outer=TRUE, layout=c(2, 3),
   groups=f.m.hhinc, type="p", pch=16, col.symbol = c(gray(0:3/ 3)),
   key = key.variety, par.settings = standard.theme(color = FALSE),
   scales=list(x=list(relation='free'), y=list(relation='free')),
   xlab="percent of transit commutes", ylab= "median commute time (min)",
data=NY)
```

If you were to focus on the color of circles, which control for the neighborhood income level, you will see that low-income neighborhoods report the highest public transit use and the longest commute times. This is true even for neighborhoods located near downtown Manhattan. It is only for the neighborhoods located very far from downtown Manhattan, that is neighborhoods in New Jersey and in other boroughs or beyond, that you see relatively higher commute times for high-income neighborhoods than those for low-income neighborhoods.

Recall that Figure 5.32 demonstrated that population densities declined with distance from Manhattan. Urban planning literature argues that low-density neighborhoods are known for chronically long commutes. I test this assumption by plotting box-and-whisker plots for median commute times for neighborhoods with respect to downtown Manhattan. Figure 5.35 illustrates that median commute times are the lowest for neighborhoods located farthest from downtown Manhattan.

I believe that Figure 5.35 offers some evidence against the conventional wisdom as it relates to population densities and commute times. The figure illustrates that neighborhoods nearer to downtown Manhattan (categorized as highest-density neighborhoods, see Figure 5.32) experience the longest commute times. At the same time, those who live farther away from the downtown in lower-density neighborhoods enjoy lower commute times than those who live nearer or the nearest to downtown. It is quite possible that those who live in outer suburbs in New York City perhaps work in other suburban locations and their suburb-to-suburb commutes are shorter than suburb-to-urban center commutes.

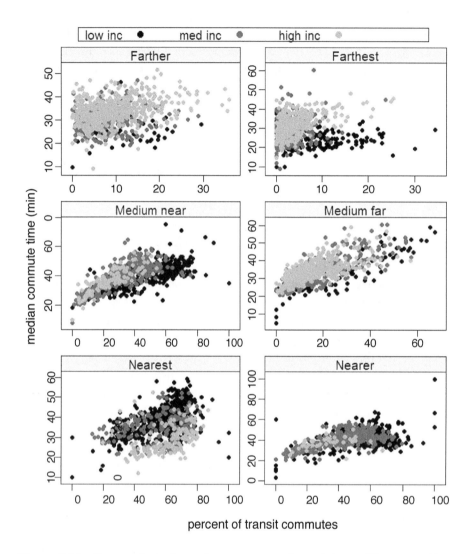

Figure 5.34   Scatter plots of transit commutes and travel times differentiated by distance from downtown Manhattan and income levels

The fundamental argument I present here is the following. The urban planning literature suggests that higher density neighborhoods within the same city will have lower commute times than the suburban, lower-density neighborhoods. Several papers argue that the suburbanites have a longer commute than the urbanites. That may be true in terms of distance, but not in terms of commute times. I show for New York City that the argument does not hold where the suburban, low-density neighborhoods report lower commute times than the centrally located high-density neighborhoods.

```
plot(NY$f.d.cbd, NY$m.commtime,
    xlab="distance from downtown Manhattan",
    ylab="median commute time (min)")
```

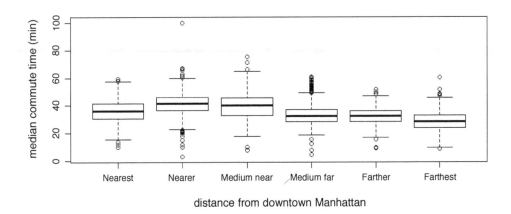

Figure 5.35 A box plot of median commute times by distance from Manhattan

Also, in Figure 5.39, I explicitly demonstrate that as the neighborhood (census tract) level density increases, so do the commute times.

It is important to note that any discussion on commuting and commute times in North America cannot take place without an explicit recognition of the role played by income and race. It is well known that low-income households and visible minorities, that is, racialized groups, are more likely to commute by public transit because of the income constraints. These groups choose public transit as the preferred mode not for its performance, but because they cannot afford commuting by private automobile. I also find that the median commute time for New York City and the surrounding areas is the highest for low-income neighborhoods and the lowest for high-income neighborhoods (see Figure 5.36).

```
barplot(tapply(NY$m.commtime, NY$f.m.hhinc,mean,na.rm=T),
        ylim=c(0,45),
        ylab= "median commute time (min)",
        xlab="household income categories")
```

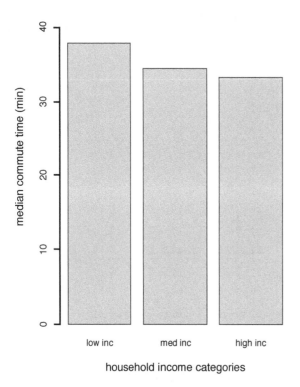

Figure 5.36   Median commute times for neighborhoods differentiated by income

Furthermore, I believe that the relationship between income and commute times is rather complex and is defined, to some extent, by the location of neighborhoods. I present median commute times for neighborhoods differentiated by both income levels and their distance from downtown Manhattan in Figure 5.37.

```
barplot(tapply(NY$m.commtime, list(NY$f.m.hhinc,
  NY$f.d.cbd),mean,na.rm=T), horiz=T, beside=T,
  xlim=c(0,55), legend=T,
  ylab= "distance from downtown Manhattan",
  xlab="median commute time (min)")
```

Note that the median commute times are higher for low-income neighborhoods located nearest to downtown Manhattan. The same is true for neighborhoods located near or medium near to downtown Manhattan. However, as you focus on neighborhoods located in the outer suburbs or the ones located even farther away from downtown Manhattan, the relationship between commute time and income levels reverses. The remotely located neighborhoods in the outer suburbs or beyond report higher commute times for the high-income neighborhoods and lower commute times for the low-income neighborhoods.

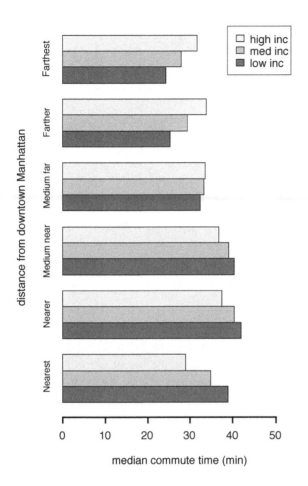

Figure 5.37   Median commute times differentiated by distance and neighborhood income level

I find strong evidence for the argument that high-density neighborhoods report higher public transit use. I find this relationship to hold even when I control for the neighborhood income level (see Figure 5.38).

```
xyplot(p.transit ~ ct.dens|f.m.hhinc, data = NY,
       type = c("p", "g", "smooth"), pch=16,         lwd=2, col.symbol =
       "dark grey",
       lab = "census tract density (person/ sq. km.)",
       xlim=c(0,20000),
       ylab= "percent of transit commutes")
```

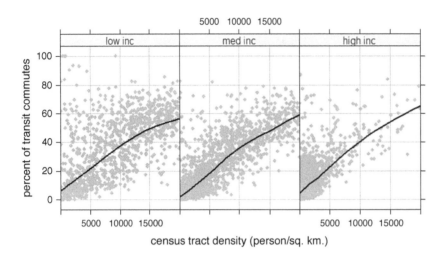

Figure 5.38   Scatter plot between population density and transit use

At the same time, I find evidence for longer commute times for high-density neighborhoods (see Figure 5.39). Often the conversation about density does not extend beyond highlighting its positive correlation with public transit use. Increasing public transit use is a desirable public policy objective that benefits from higher population densities. However, the fact that high-density neighborhoods also report longer commute times has largely been ignored in the discourse on sustainable transportation.

```
xyplot(m.commtime ~ ct.dens|f.m.hhinc, data = NY,
       type = c("p", "g", "smooth"), pch=16, lwd=2,
       col.symbol = "dark grey",
       xlab = "census tract density (persons/ sq. km.)",
       xlim=c(0,20000),
       ylab= "median commute time (min)")
```

Why should households, who prefer to minimize commute times, choose to live in neighborhoods where commuting by public transit will result in relatively slower commutes is a question urban and transport planners must consider.

Much of what transpires in socioeconomic spheres in the urban United States is still influenced by race, poverty, and the lack of opportunity for the marginalized groups. In an egalitarian society, racial or other minorities should not be disproportionately exposed to poverty. Much progress has to take place before we reach a stage where race and other factors become irrelevant in the socioeconomic development.

In the following figures, I plot the commute times against various racial concentrations at the neighborhood level, while I also control for income. I find that irrespective of the neighborhood's income level, commute times increase with the concentration of African Americans in a neighborhood. In fact, the discrepancy is felt the strongest for higher concentration of African Americans in high-income neighborhoods (see Figure 5.40).

```
xyplot(m.commtime ~ p.black|f.m.hhinc, data = NY,
       type = c("p", "g", "smooth"), pch=16, lwd=2,
       col.symbol = "dark grey",
       xlab = "African Americans (%)",
       ylab= "median commute time (min)")
```

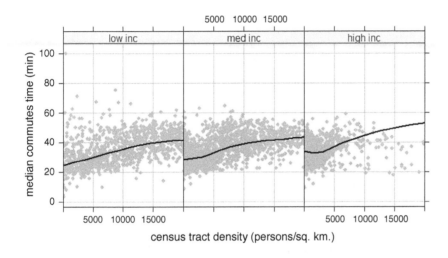

Figure 5.39   Scatter plot between population density and commute times

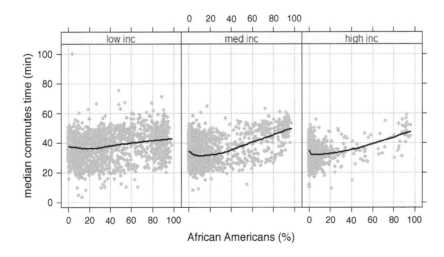

Figure 5.40   Scatter plot of commute times and concentration of African Americans in a neighborhood

In comparison, I do not observe any relationship between commute times and the concentration of individuals of Hispanic origin at the neighborhood level (see Figure 5.41). This holds for all income levels.

```
xyplot(m.commtime ~ p.hispanic|f.m.hhinc, data = NY,
       type = c("p", "g", "smooth"), pch=16, lwd=2,
       col.symbol = "dark grey",
       xlab = "Hispanics (%)", ylab= "median commute time (min)")
```

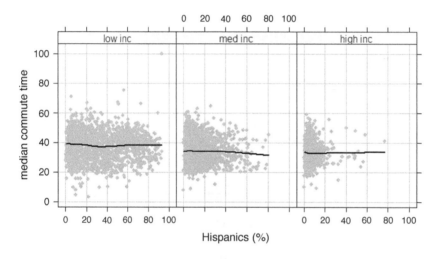

Figure 5.41   Scatter plot of commute times and concentration of Hispanics in a neighborhood

I observe three distinct relationships between commute times and the concentration of individuals of Asian origin at the neighborhood level (see Figure 5.42). For low-income neighborhoods, I observe a nonlinear trend where commute times initially increase with the increase in the concentration of individuals of Asian heritage and then decline for higher concentrations. However, for medium-income and high-income neighborhoods, I observe a positive correlation between commute times and the concentration of individuals of Asian heritage at the neighborhood level.

```
xyplot(m.commtime ~ p.asian|f.m.hhinc, data = NY,
       type = c("p", "g", "smooth"), pch=16, lwd=2,
       col.symbol = "dark grey",
       xlab = "Asians (%)", ylab= "median commute time (min)")
```

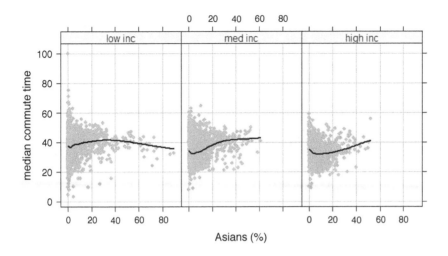

Figure 5.42 Scatter plot of commute times and concentration of Asians in a neighborhood

Unlike the racial minorities, the concentration of Whites in a neighborhood is negatively correlated with commute times (see Figure 5.43). This suggests that an increase in the concentration of Whites at the neighborhood level is correlated with a decline in commute times. I, however, observe an increase in commute times for high-income neighborhoods where Whites constitute 80% or more of the neighborhood population.

```
xyplot(m.commtime ~ p.white|f.m.hhinc, data = NY,
       type = c("p", "g", "smooth"), pch=16, lwd=2,
       col.symbol = "dark grey",
       xlab = "White population (%)",
       ylab= "median commute time (min)")
```

Race is primarily a proxy for income in the relationships you have observed in the preceding figures. Because the neighborhoods predominantly inhabited by racial minorities are relatively low-income neighborhoods, we observe an increase in commute times with the increase in the concentration of racial minorities at the neighborhood level.

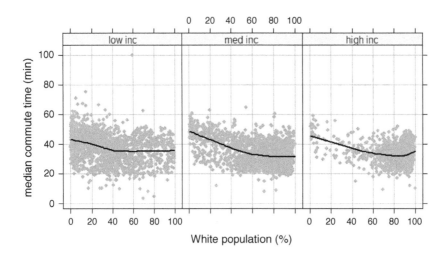

Figure 5.43   Scatter plot of commute times and concentration of Whites in a neighborhood

    I plot the concentration of low-income households and commute times while I characterize each neighborhood as low-, mid-, and high-income (see Figure 5.44). Again, I see three distinct relationships defined by the type of neighborhood. First, I observe that in low-income neighborhoods, commute times increase with the concentration of low-income households. However, when the concentration of low-income households exceeds 20 percent of the local population, I do not observe any further increase in commute times.

```
xyplot(m.commtime ~ p.poverty|f.m.hhinc, data = NY, xlim=c(0,60),
       type = c("p", "g", "smooth"), pch=16, lwd=2,
       col.symbol = "dark grey",
       xlab = "low-income households (%)",
       ylab= "median commute time (min)")
```

    I observe a similar relationship for mid-income neighborhoods with the difference that commute times decline for mid-income neighborhoods where low-income households constitute more than 20% of the local population.

    Interestingly for high-income neighborhoods, I observe a negative correlation between the concentration of low-income households and commute times.

    Certain demographic attributes at the household level, such as presence of young children, influence the travel behavior of individuals. Given that households with similar attributes cluster in space, such household-level attributes influence the overall travel behavior manifested at the neighborhood level.

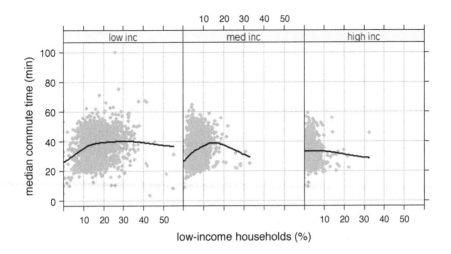

Figure 5.44 Scatter plot of commute times and concentration of low-income households in a neighborhood

In Figure 5.45, I present a scatter plot between the concentration of single mothers and median commute times at the neighborhood level. I see an increase in commute times when single mother households constitute at least 20 percent (low-income neighborhoods) and 10 percent (mid-income neighborhoods) of the local population. I do not observe a similar relationship for high-income neighborhoods.

```
xyplot(m.commtime ~ p.singmom| f.m.hhinc, data = NY,
       scales = list(x = "free"),
       type = c("p", "g", "smooth"), pch=16, lwd=2,
       col.symbol = "dark grey",
       xlab = "single mothers (%)", ylab="median commute time (min)")
```

Lastly, I present a plot between households with children and neighborhood commute times (see Figure 5.46).

```
xyplot(m.commtime ~ p.children|f.m.hhinc, data = NY,
       type = c("p", "g", "smooth"), pch=16, lwd=2,
       col.symbol = "dark grey",
       xlab = "households with children (%)",
       ylab= "median commute time (min)")
```

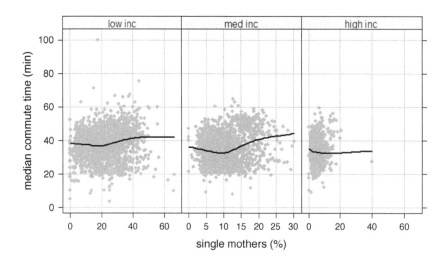

Figure 5.45   Scatter plot of commute times and concentration of single mothers in a neighborhood

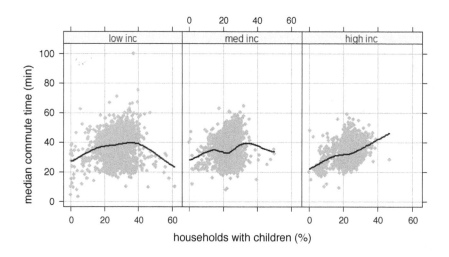

Figure 5.46   Scatter plot of commute times and households with children in a neighborhood

I observe three different relationships for the three types of neighborhoods defined by income levels. The median commute times initially increase with the increase in the proportion of households with children. However, when households with children constitute 40% or more of the low-income neighborhoods, I see a decline in median commute times. I observe a largely positive correlation between the presence of children and commute times for mid- and high-income households.

Summary

This chapter introduces data scientists to the art of creating illustrative graphics and then telling stories with them. I used the *Titanic* as the metaphor to tell a story of how people lived and died in a class-conscious society.

Graphics are uniquely suited to present the interplay between several variables to help communicate the complex interdependencies that often characterize the questions posed to data scientists. The short-lived class-based society on the *Titanic* can be described either in a few thousand words or with one illustrative graphic. I believe graphics are a powerful medium to tell stories, even that of the *Titanic*.

I have used a systematic approach to build the graphics by first drawing a bare-bones image and then adding components to make the graphic more illustrative. Using the Teaching Evaluations data, I illustrated how you can plot multidimensional data, including descriptive statistics, as graphics to explore the determinants of teaching evaluations.

It is hard to imagine that a simple question about neighborhood commute times could be analyzed in so many different ways. In the final section, I have illustrated how graphics help tease out the complex, and at times latent, relationships between various interlinked determinants of travel behavior and commute times. I used graphics to illustrate the fact that while high population densities correlate with high public transit use, high transit use in fact is correlated with higher commute times. The very purpose of using the density and commute times example is to demonstrate how you can argue your case with the help of graphics, which also includes maps.

If you are interested in learning more about representing data with illustrative maps, I encourage you to skip to Chapter 10, "Spatial Data Analytics," which illustrates the use of thematic maps to analyze geo-spatial data. Maps, like other plots, are powerful tools that enable data scientists to visualize and analyze data.

Endnotes

1. http://www.cdhowe.org/pdf/Commentary_385.pdf
2. Newman, P. W. G. and Kenworthy, J. K. (1991). "Transport and urban form in thirty-two of the world's principal cities." *Transport Reviews*, *11*(3), 249–272.

CHAPTER 6

Hypothetically Speaking

The Great Recession in 2008 wiped clean the savings portfolios of hundreds of millions in North America and Europe. Before the recession, people like columnist Margaret Wente, who were fast approaching retirement, had a 10-year plan. But then a "black swan pooped all over it."[1]

Nassim Nicholas Taleb, a New York-based professor of finance and a former finance practitioner, used the black swan analogy in his book of the same title to explain how past events are limited in forecasting the future.[2] He mentions the surprise of the European settlers when they first arrived in Western Australia and spotted a black swan. Until then, Europeans believed all swans to be white. However, a single sighting of a black swan changed that conclusion forever. This is why Professor Taleb uses the black swan metaphor to highlight the importance of extremely rare events, which the data about the past might not be able to forecast. The same phenomenon is referred to as the "fat tails" of probability distributions that explain the odds of the occurrence of rare events.

The fat tails of probability distributions resulted in trillions of dollars of financial losses during the 2007–08 financial crisis. In a world where almost nothing looks and feels normal, the empirical analysis is rooted in a statistical model commonly referred as the Normal distribution. Because of the ease it affords, the Normal distribution and its variants serve as the backbone of statistical analysis in engineering, economics, finance, medicine, and social sciences. Most readers of this book are likely to be familiar with the bell-shaped symmetrical curve that stars in every text on statistics and econometrics.

Simply stated, the Normal distribution assigns a probability to a particular outcome from a range of possible outcomes. For instance, when meteorologists advise of a 30% chance of rainfall, they are relying on a statistical model to forecast the likelihood of rain based on past data. Such models are usually good in forecasting the likelihood of events that have occurred more frequently in the past. For instance, the models usually perform well in forecasting the likelihood of a small change in a stock market's value. However, the models fail miserably in forecasting large swings in the stock market value. The rarer an event, the poorer will be the model's ability to forecast its likelihood to occur. This phenomenon is referred to as the fat tail where the model assigns a very low, sometimes infinitely low, possibility of an event to occur. However, in the real world, such extreme events occur more frequently.

In *Financial Risk Forecasting*, Professor Jon Danielsson illustrates fat tails using the Great Recession as an example.[3] He focuses on the S&P 500 index returns, which are often assumed to follow Normal distribution. He illustrates that during 1929 and 2009, the biggest one-day drop in S&P 500 returns was 23% in 1987. If returns were indeed Normally distributed, the probability of such an extreme crash would be 2.23×10^{-97} Professor Danielsson explains that the model predicts such an extreme crash to occur only once in 10^{95} years. Here lies the problem. The earth is believed to be roughly 10^7 years old and the universe is believed to be 10^{13} years old. Professor Danielsson explains that if we were to believe in Normal distribution, the 1987 single day-crash of 23% would happen in "once out of every 12 universes."

The reality is that the extreme fluctuations in stock markets occur much more frequently than what the models based on Normal distribution suggest. Still, it continues to serve as the backbone of empirical work in finance and other disciplines.

With these caveats, I introduce the concepts discussed in this chapter. Most empirical research is concerned with comparisons of outcomes for different circumstances or groups. For instance, we are interested in determining whether male instructors receive higher teaching evaluations than female instructors. Such analysis falls under the umbrella of hypothesis testing, which happens to be the focus of this chapter.

I begin by introducing the very basic concepts of random numbers and probability distributions. I use the example of rolling two dice to introduce the fundamental concepts of probability distribution functions. I then proceed to a formal introduction of Normal and t-distributions, which are commonly used for statistical models. Finally, I explore hypothesis testing for the comparison of means and correlations.

I use data for high-performing basketball players to compare their career performances using statistical models. I also use the teaching evaluations data, which I have introduced in earlier chapters, to compare means for two or more groups.

Random Numbers and Probability Distributions

Hypothesis testing has a lot to do with probability distributions. Two such distributions, known as the normal or Gaussian distribution and the t-distribution, are frequently used. I restrict the discussion about probability distributions to these frequently used distributions.

Probability is a measure between zero and one of the likelihood that an event might occur. An event could be the likelihood of a stock market falling below or rising above a certain threshold. You are familiar with the weather forecast that often describes the likelihood of rainfall in terms of probability or chance. Thus, you often hear the meteorologists explain that the likelihood of rainfall is, for instance, 45%. Thus, 0.45 is the probability that the event, rainfall, might occur.

The subjective definitions of probability might be expressed as the probability of one's favorite team winning the World Series or the probability that a particular stock market will fall by 10% in a given time period. Probability is also described as outcomes of experiments. For instance, if one were to flip a fair coin, the outcome of head or tail can be explained in probabilities. Similarly, the quality control division of a manufacturing firm often defines the probability of a defective product as the number of defective units produced for a certain predetermined production level.

I explain here some basic rules about probability calculations. The probability associated with any outcome or event must fall in the zero and one (0–1) interval. The probability of all possible outcomes must equate to one.

Tied with probability is the concept of randomness. A random variable is a numerical description of the outcome of an experiment. Random variables could be discrete or continuous. Discrete random variables assume a finite or infinite countable number of outcomes. For instance, the imperfections on a car that passes through the assembly line or the number of incorrectly filled orders at a grocery store are examples of random variables.

A continuous random variable could assume any real value possible within some limited range. For instance, if a factory produces and ships cereal in boxes, the average weight of a cereal box will be a continuous random variable. In finance, the daily return of a stock is a continuous variable.

Let us build on the definition of probability and random variables to describe probability distributions. A probability distribution is essentially a theoretical model depicting the possible values a random variable may assume along with the probability of occurrence. We can define probability distributions for both discrete and continuous random variables.

Consider the stock for Apple computers for the period covering January 2011 and December 2013. During this time, the average daily returns equaled 0.000706 with a standard deviation of 0.01774. I have plotted a histogram of daily return for the Apple stock and I have overlaid a normal distribution curve on top of the histogram shown in Figure 6.1. The bars in the histogram depict the actual distribution of the data and the theoretical probability distribution is depicted by the curve. I can see from the figure that the daily returns equaled zero or close to zero more frequently than depicted by the Normal distribution. Also, note that some negative daily returns were unusually large in magnitude, which are reflected by the values to the very left of the histogram beyond –0.05. I can conclude that while the Normal distribution curve assigns very low probability to very large negative values, the actual data set suggests that despite the low theoretical probability, such values have realized more frequently.

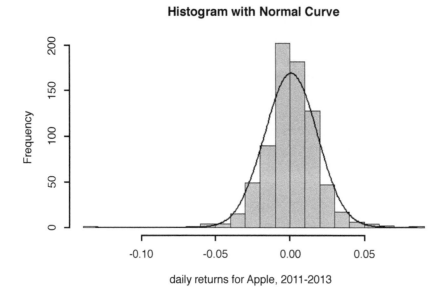

Figure 6.1   Histogram of daily Apple returns with a normal curve

Casino Royale: Roll the Dice

I illustrate the probability function of a discrete variable using the example of rolling two fair dice. A die has six faces, so rolling two dice can assume one of the 36 discrete outcomes, because each die can assume one of the six outcomes in a roll. Hence rolling two dice together will return one out of 36 outcomes. Also, note that if one (1) comes up on each die, the outcome will be 1 + 1 = 2, and the probability associated with this outcome is one out of thirty-six (1/36) because no other combination of the two dice will return two (2). On the other hand, I can obtain three (3) with the roll of two dice by having either of the two dice assume one and the other assuming two and vice versa. Thus, the probability of an outcome of three with a roll of two dice is 2 out of 36 (2/36).

The 36 possible outcomes obtained from rolling two dice are illustrated in Figure 6.2.

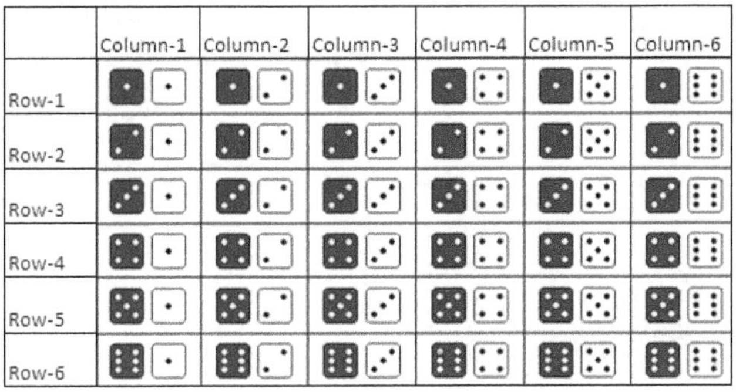

Figure 6.2   All possible outcomes of rolling two dice

Source: http://www.edcollins.com/backgammon/diceprob.htm

Based on the possible outcomes of rolling two dice, I can generate the probability density function. I present the outcomes and the respective probabilities in the Probability column in Table 6.1.

Table 6.1   Probability Calculations for Rolling Two Dice

Sum of Two Dice, x	f(x)	Probability	F(x)	Prob <=x	Prob > x
2	1/36	0.028	1/36	0.028	0.972
3	2/36	0.056	3/36	0.083	0.917
4	3/36	0.083	6/36	0.167	0.833
5	4/36	0.111	10/36	0.278	0.722
6	5/36	0.139	15/36	0.417	0.583
7	6/36	0.167	21/36	0.583	0.417
8	5/36	0.139	26/36	0.722	0.278
9	4/36	0.111	30/36	0.833	0.167
10	3/36	0.083	33/36	0.917	0.083
11	2/36	0.056	35/36	0.972	0.028
12	1/36	0.028	1	1	0

The cumulative probability function F(x) specifies the probability that the random variable will be less than or equal to some value x. For the two dice example, the probability of obtaining five with a roll of two dice is 4/36. Similarly, the cumulative probability of 10/36 is the probability that the random variable will be either five or less (Table 6.1).

Figure 6.3 offers a vivid depiction of probability density functions. Remember that the probability to obtain a certain value for rolling two dice is the ratio of the number of ways that particular value can be obtained and the total number of possible outcomes for rolling two dice (36). The highest probable outcome of rolling two dice is 7, which is $\frac{6}{36} = .167$

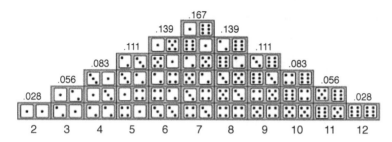

Total number of states: 36

Figure 6.3   Histogram of the outcomes of rolling two dice

Source: http://hyperphysics.phy-astr.gsu.edu/hbase/math/dice.html

I have plotted the probability density function and the cumulative distribution function of the discrete random variable representing the roll of two dice in Figure 6.4 and Figure 6.5. Notice again that the probability of obtaining seven as the sum of rolling two dice is the highest and the probability of obtaining 2 or 12 are the lowest. Probability density function is a continuous function that describes the probability of outcomes for the random variable X. A histogram of a random variable approximates the shape of the underlying density function.

Figure 6.5 depicts an important concept that I will rely on this chapter. The figure shows the probability of finding a particular value or less from rolling two dice, also known as the cumulative distribution function. For instance, the probability of obtaining four (4) or less from rolling two dice is 0.167. Stated otherwise, the probability of obtaining a value greater than four (4) from rolling two dice is 0.833.

Recall Figure 6.1, which depicted the histogram of the daily returns for Apple stock. The shape of the histogram approximated the shape of underlying density function.

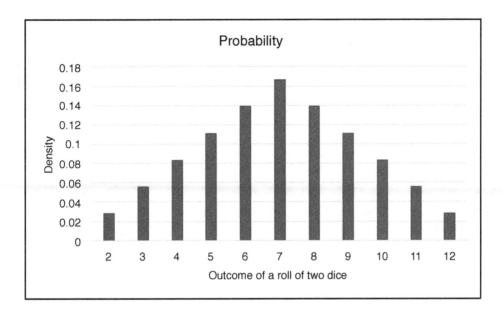

Figure 6.4 Histogram of the outcomes for rolling two dice

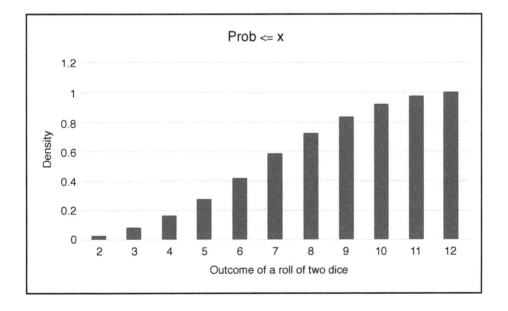

Figure 6.5 Probability distribution function for rolling two dice

Normal Distribution

The Normal distribution is one of the most commonly referred to distributions in statistical analysis and even in everyday conversations. A large body of academic and scholarly work rests on the fundamental assumption that the underlying data follows a Normal distribution that generates a bell-shaped curve. Mathematically, Normal distribution is expressed as shown in Equation 6.1:

$$f(x, \mu, \sigma) = \frac{1}{\sigma\sqrt{2*pi}} e^{-\frac{(x-\mu)^2}{2\sigma^2}} \quad \textbf{Equation 6.1}$$

Where x is a random variable, μ is the mean and σ is the standard deviation. The standard normal curve refers to 0 mean and constant variance; that is, $\sigma = 1$ and is represented mathematically as shown in Equation 6.2:

$$f(x, 0,1) = \frac{1}{\sqrt{2*pi}} e^{-\frac{(x)^2}{2}} \quad \textbf{Equation 6.2}$$

I generate a regular sequence of numbers (x) between –4 and 4. I can transform x as per Equation 6.2 into y. The plot in Figure 6.6 presents the standard normal curve or the probability density function, which plots the random variable x on the x-axis and density (y) on the y-axis.

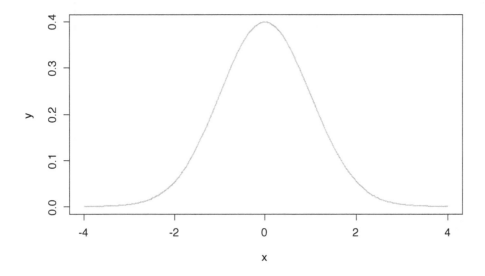

Figure 6.6   The bell-shaped Normal distribution curve

The Student Who Taught Everyone Else

The other commonly used distribution is the Student's t-distribution, which was specified by William Sealy Gosset. He published a paper in Biometrika in 1908 under the pseudonym, Student. Gosset worked for the Guinness Brewery in Durbin, Ireland, where he worked with small samples of barley.

Mr. Gosset is the unsung hero of statistics. He published his work under a pseudonym because of the restrictions from his employer. Apart from his published work, his other contributions to statistical analysis are equally significant. The *Cult of Statistical Significance*, a must read for anyone interested in data science, chronicles Mr. Gosset's work and how other influential statisticians of the time, namely Ronald Fisher and Egon Pearson, by way of their academic bona fides ended up being more influential than the equally deserving Mr. Gosset.

The t-distribution refers to a family of distributions that deal with the mean of a normally distributed population with small sample sizes and unknown population standard deviation. The Normal distribution describes the mean for a population, whereas the t-distribution describes the mean of samples drawn from the population. The t-distribution for each sample could be different and the t-distribution resembles the normal distribution for large sample sizes.

In Figure 6.7, I plot t-distributions for various sample sizes, also known as the degrees of freedom, along with the normal distribution. Note that the t-distribution with a sample size of 30 resembles the normal distribution the most.

Over the years, 30 has emerged as the preferred threshold for a large enough sample that may prompt one to revert to the Normal distribution. Many researchers, though, question the suitability of 30 as the threshold. In the world of big data, 30 obviously seems awfully small.

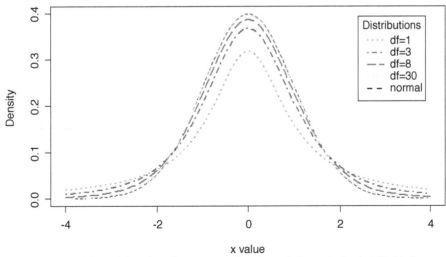

Adapted from http://www.statmethonds.net/advgraphs/probability.html

Figure 6.7 Probability distribution curves for normal and t-distributions for different sample sizes

Statistical Distributions in Action

I now illustrate some applied concepts related to the Normal distribution. Assuming that the data are "normally" distributed, I can in fact determine the likelihood of an event. For instance, consider the Teaching Ratings data, which I have discussed in detail in Chapters 4 and 5. The data set contains details on course evaluations for 463 courses and the attributes of the instructors. Professor Hamermesh and his co-author wanted to determine whether the subjective measure of an instructor's appearance influenced his or her teaching evaluation score.

The descriptive statistics for some variables in the data set are presented in Table 6.2. I also report the R code in this chapter used to generate the output. The following code launches two R packages: xtable and psych. It commits the data file to R's dedicated reference memory and then runs summary statistics, which are formatted and produced using the RMarkdown extensions.

```
### download data from the course's website
library(xtable)
library(psych)
attach(TeachingRatings)
tab <- xtable(describe(cbind(eval, age, beauty, students, allstudents),
                   skew=F, ranges=F), digits=3)
rownames(tab)<- c("teaching evaluation score", "instructor's age",
            "beauty score", "students responding to survey","students
            registered in course")
print(tab, type="html")
```

Table 6.2   Summary Statistics for Teaching Evaluation Data

	vars	n	mean	sd	se
teaching evaluation score	1	463	3.998	0.554	0.026
instructor's age	2	463	48.365	9.803	0.456
beauty score	3	463	0.000	0.789	0.037
students responding to survey	4	463	36.624	45.018	2.092
students registered in course	5	463	55.177	75.073	3.489

Table 6.2 demonstrates that the average course evaluation (non-weighted mean) was 3.998 and the standard deviation (SD) was 0.554. I also report descriptive statistics for other variables in the table and plot the histogram for the teaching evaluation score to visualize the distribution (see Figure 6.8). I see that the teaching evaluation scores peak around 4.0 with a relatively larger spread on the right, suggesting more frequent occurrence of higher than average teaching evaluation scores than lower teaching evaluation scores.

```
histogram(TeachingRatings$eval, nint=15, aspect=2,
          xlab="teaching evaluation score", col=c("dark grey"))
```

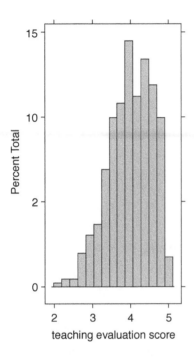

Figure 6.8   Histogram of teaching evaluation scores

I can plot a Normal density function based on descriptive statistics for the evaluation data. If I were to assume that the teaching evaluation scores were normally distributed, I only need the mean and standard deviation to plot the Normal density curve. The resulting plot is presented in Figure 6.9.

Unlike the histogram presented in Figure 6.8, the theoretical distribution in Figure 6.9 is more symmetrical, suggesting that the theoretical distributions are neater and symmetrical, whereas the real-world data is "messier."

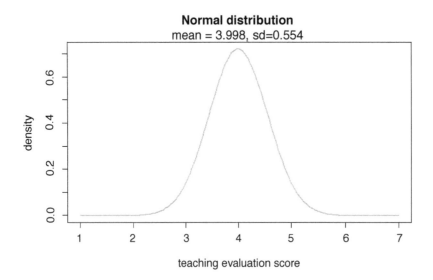

Figure 6.9   Normal distribution curve with mean=3.998, and sd=0.554

Z-Transformation

A related and important concept is the z-transformation of a variable. One can transform a variable such that its transformed version returns a mean of 0 and a standard deviation of 1. I use the formula in Equation 6.3 for z-transformation:

$$z = \frac{x - \mu}{\sigma}$$ **Equation 6.3**

The preceding equation showcases x as the raw data, μ as the mean and σ as the standard deviation. For example, if an instructor received a course evaluation of 4.5, the z-transformation can be calculated as follows:

$$z = \frac{4.5 - 3.998}{.554} = 0.906$$

I can create a new variable by standardizing the variable `eval` and plot a histogram of the standardized variable. The mean of the standardized variable is almost 0 and the standard deviation equals 1 (see Figure 6.10).

```
z.eval<-as.matrix((TeachingRatings$eval-3.998)/.554)
histogram(z.eval, nint=15, aspect=2,
   xlab=" normalized teaching evaluation score", col=c("dark grey"))
```

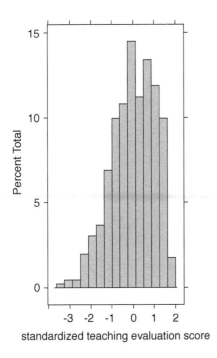

Figure 6.10 Histogram of standardized teaching evaluation score

The z-transformed data is useful in determining the probability of an event being larger or smaller than a certain threshold. For instance, assuming that the teaching evaluations are normally distributed, I can determine the probability of an instructor receiving a teaching evaluation greater or lower than a particular value. I explain this concept in the following section.

Probability of Getting a High or Low Course Evaluation

Let us assume that the variable `eval` is Normally distributed. I can determine the probability of obtaining the evaluation higher or lower than a certain threshold. For instance, let us determine the probability of an instructor receiving a course evaluation of higher than 4.5 when the mean evaluation is 3.998 and the standard deviation (SD) is 0.554. All statistical software, including spreadsheets such as Microsoft Excel, provide built-in formulae to compute these probabilities. See the following R code.

```
pnorm(c(4.5), mean=3.998, sd=0.554, lower.tail=FALSE)
```

R readily computes 0.1824, or simply 18.24%. This suggests that the probability of obtaining a course evaluation of higher than 4.5 is 18.24%.

Another way of conceptualizing the probability of obtaining a teaching evaluation of higher than 4.5 is to see it illustrated in a plot (see Figure 6.11). Notice that the area under the curve to the right of the value 4.5 is shaded gray, which represents the probability of receiving a teaching evaluation score of higher than 4.5.

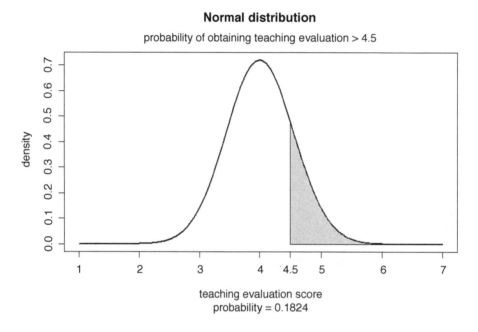

Figure 6.11   Probability of obtaining a teaching evaluation score of greater than 4.5

The gray-shaded part of the area represents 18.24% of the area under the curve. The area under the normal distribution curve is assumed as one, or in percentage terms, 100%. This is analogous to a histogram and represents the collective probability of all possible values attained by a variable. Thus, the probability of obtaining a course evaluation of greater than or equal to 4.5 (the area shaded in gray) is 0.1824. The probability of obtaining a teaching evaluation of less than or equal to 4.5 will be $1 - 0.1824 = 0.8176$ or 81.76%, which is shaded gray in Figure 6.12.

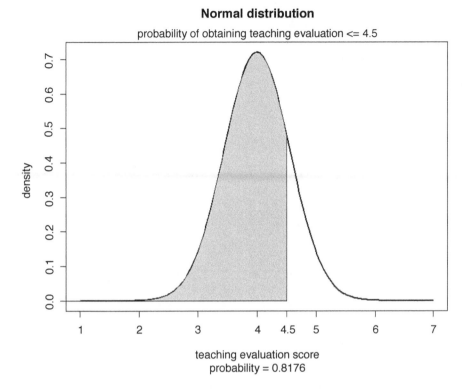

Figure 6.12   Probability of obtaining a teaching evaluation score of less than 4.5

Probabilities with Standard Normal Table

Now let us repeat the same calculations using a calculator and the probability tables. I first standardize the raw data to determine the probability of a teaching evaluation score of higher than 4.5. I have demonstrated earlier the calculations to standardize 4.5, which equals 0.906.

The next step is to determine the probability value (p-value) from the probability table in Figure 6.13. Notice that the p-values listed in the table are for probability of less than or equal to a certain value, which is referred to as the left tail of the distribution. I need to subtract the p-value from 1 to obtain the probability value for greater than the selected value. The table expresses z-scores up to two decimal points.

From the calculations, you see that z approximates to 0.91, for a teaching evaluation score of 4.5. I search for the p-value corresponding to Z = 0.91 in Figure 6.13. I locate 0.9 in the first column and then locate 0.01 in the first row. The p-value reported in the cell at the intersection of the aforementioned row and column is 0.8186 or 81.86% (also highlighted in the table with a box). Notice that this is the probability of getting a course evaluation of 4.5 or less. Notice also that this value is almost the same as reported in the value listed in the figure generated by R. Slight differences are due to rounding.

Probability Content from -oo to Z

Z	0.00	0.01	0.02	0.03	0.04	0.05	0.06	0.07	0.08	0.09
0.0	0.5000	0.5040	0.5080	0.5120	0.5160	0.5199	0.5239	0.5279	0.5319	0.5359
0.1	0.5398	0.5438	0.5478	0.5517	0.5557	0.5596	0.5636	0.5675	0.5714	0.5753
0.2	0.5793	0.5832	0.5871	0.5910	0.5948	0.5987	0.6026	0.6064	0.6103	0.6141
0.3	0.6179	0.6217	0.6255	0.6293	0.6331	0.6368	0.6406	0.6443	0.6480	0.6517
0.4	0.6554	0.6591	0.6628	0.6664	0.6700	0.6736	0.6772	0.6808	0.6844	0.6879
0.5	0.6915	0.6950	0.6985	0.7019	0.7054	0.7088	0.7123	0.7157	0.7190	0.7224
0.6	0.7257	0.7291	0.7324	0.7357	0.7389	0.7422	0.7454	0.7486	0.7517	0.7549
0.7	0.7580	0.7611	0.7642	0.7673	0.7704	0.7734	0.7764	0.7794	0.7823	0.7852
0.8	0.7881	0.7910	0.7939	0.7967	0.7995	0.8023	0.8051	0.8078	0.8106	0.8133
0.9	0.8159	0.8186	0.8212	0.8238	0.8264	0.8289	0.8315	0.8340	0.8365	0.8389
1.0	0.8413	0.8438	0.8461	0.8485	0.8508	0.8531	0.8554	0.8577	0.8599	0.8621
1.1	0.8643	0.8665	0.8686	0.8708	0.8729	0.8749	0.8770	0.8790	0.8810	0.8830
1.2	0.8849	0.8869	0.8888	0.8907	0.8925	0.8944	0.8962	0.8980	0.8997	0.9015
1.3	0.9032	0.9049	0.9066	0.9082	0.9099	0.9115	0.9131	0.9147	0.9162	0.9177
1.4	0.9192	0.9207	0.9222	0.9236	0.9251	0.9265	0.9279	0.9292	0.9306	0.9319
1.5	0.9332	0.9345	0.9357	0.9370	0.9382	0.9394	0.9406	0.9418	0.9429	0.9441
1.6	0.9452	0.9463	0.9474	0.9484	0.9495	0.9505	0.9515	0.9525	0.9535	0.9545
1.7	0.9554	0.9564	0.9573	0.9582	0.9591	0.9599	0.9608	0.9616	0.9625	0.9633
1.8	0.9641	0.9649	0.9656	0.9664	0.9671	0.9678	0.9686	0.9693	0.9699	0.9706
1.9	0.9713	0.9719	0.9726	0.9732	0.9738	0.9744	0.9750	0.9756	0.9761	0.9767
2.0	0.9772	0.9778	0.9783	0.9788	0.9793	0.9798	0.9803	0.9808	0.9812	0.9817
2.1	0.9821	0.9826	0.9830	0.9834	0.9838	0.9842	0.9846	0.9850	0.9854	0.9857
2.2	0.9861	0.9864	0.9868	0.9871	0.9875	0.9878	0.9881	0.9884	0.9887	0.9890
2.3	0.9893	0.9896	0.9898	0.9901	0.9904	0.9906	0.9909	0.9911	0.9913	0.9916
2.4	0.9918	0.9920	0.9922	0.9925	0.9927	0.9929	0.9931	0.9932	0.9934	0.9936
2.5	0.9938	0.9940	0.9941	0.9943	0.9945	0.9946	0.9948	0.9949	0.9951	0.9952
2.6	0.9953	0.9955	0.9956	0.9957	0.9959	0.9960	0.9961	0.9962	0.9963	0.9964
2.7	0.9965	0.9966	0.9967	0.9968	0.9969	0.9970	0.9971	0.9972	0.9973	0.9974
2.8	0.9974	0.9975	0.9976	0.9977	0.9977	0.9978	0.9979	0.9979	0.9980	0.9981
2.9	0.9981	0.9982	0.9982	0.9983	0.9984	0.9984	0.9985	0.9985	0.9986	0.9986
3.0	0.9987	0.9987	0.9987	0.9988	0.9988	0.9989	0.9989	0.9989	0.9990	0.9990

Figure 6.13   Normal distribution table

Source: http://www.math.unb.ca/~knight/utility/NormTble.htm

To obtain the probability of receiving a course evaluation of higher than 4.5, I simply subtract 0.8186 from 1; I have $1 - 0.8186 = 0.1814$ or 18.14%.

Let us now try to determine the probability of receiving a course evaluation between 3.5 and 4.2. I first need to standardize both scores. Here are the calculations.

Remember that:

$$z = \frac{x - \mu}{\sigma}$$

Thus,

$$z = \frac{4.2 - 3.998}{.554} = 0.36$$

$$z = \frac{3.5 - 3.998}{.554} = -0.89$$

From the Standard Normal Table you need to search for two values: one for Z = 0.36 and the other for Z = –0.89. The difference between the corresponding p-values will give the probability for course evaluations falling between 3.5 and 4.2. The calculations are straightforward for 4.2. The standardized value (z-score) is 0.36, which is highlighted in the table where the corresponding row and column intersect to return a p-value of 0.64 or 64%. This implies that the probability of receiving a course evaluation of 4.2 or less is 64%.

The z-transformation for 3.5 returns a negative z-score of –0.899. I again use Figure 6.13 to first locate 0.8 in the first column and then 0.09 in the first row and search for the corresponding p-value that is located at the intersection of the two. The resulting value is 0.8133. However, this is the p-value that corresponds to a z-score of +0.899. The p-value corresponding to a z-score of –0.899 is 1-p-value, which happens to be 1–0.8133 = 0.18 or 18%, which suggests that the probability of obtaining a course evaluation of 3.5 or less is 18%. The results are presented in Table 6.3.

Table 6.3 Standardizing Teaching Evaluation Scores

Raw Data	Z-transformed	P-value ≤ Z
4.2	0.362	0.64 or 64%
3.5	–0.899	1–0.8133 = 0.186 or 18.6%

I still have not found the answer to the question regarding the probability of obtaining a course evaluation of greater than 3.5 and less than or equal to 4.2. To illustrate the concept consider Figure 6.14. The shaded area represents the probability of obtaining a teaching evaluation between 3.5 and 4.2. From Table 6.3, I see that the probability of a teaching evaluation of 4.2 or less is 0.64 and for a teaching evaluation of 3.5 or lower is 0.186, so the difference between the two will have our answer.

Mathematically:

$$0.64 - 0.18 = 0.46$$

Thus, 46% is the probability of obtaining a course evaluation of greater than 3.5 and 4.2 or lower. It is marked by the unshaded area in Figure 6.14.

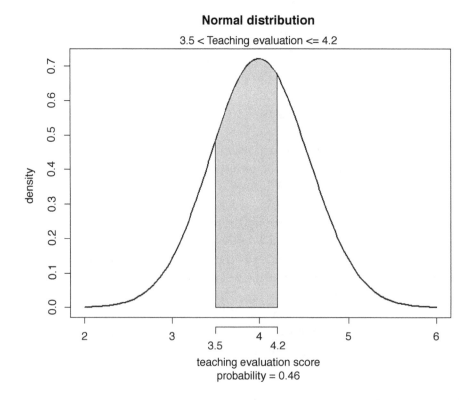

Figure 6.14   Probability of obtaining teaching evaluation score of greater than 3.5 and 4.2 or less

The probability can be readily obtained in statistical software, such as R and Stata.
R code:

```
1-(pnorm(c(4.2, 3.5), mean = 3.998, sd = .554, lower.tail=F))
or
pnorm(.362)-pnorm(-.899)
```

Stata code:

```
di 1-(1-normal(.362) + normal(-.899))
```

Hypothetically Yours

Most empirical analysis involves comparison of two or more statistics. Data scientists and analysts are often asked to compare costs, revenues, and other similar metrics related to socioeconomic outcomes. Often, this is accomplished by setting up and testing hypotheses. The purpose of the analysis is to determine whether the difference in values between two or more entities or outcomes is a result of chance or whether fundamental and statistically significant differences are at play. I explain this in the following section.

Consistently Better or Happenstance

Nate Silver, the former blogger for the *New York Times* and founder of fivethirtyeight.com has been at the forefront of popularizing data-driven analytics. His blogs are followed by hundreds of thousands readers. He is also credited with popularizing the use of data and analytics in sports. The same trend was highlighted in the movie *Moneyball*, in which a baseball coach with a data-savvy assistant puts together a team of otherwise regular players who were more likely to win as a team. The coach and his assistant, instead of relying on the traditional criterion, based their decisions on data. They were, therefore, able to put together a winning team.

Let me illustrate hypothesis testing using basketball as an example. Michael Jordan is one of the greatest basketball players. He was a consistently high scorer throughout his career. In fact, he averaged 30.12 points per game in his career, which is the highest for any basketball player in the NBA.[4] He spent most of his professional career playing for the Chicago Bulls. Jordan was inducted into the Hall of Fame in 2009. In his first professional season in 1984–85, Jordan scored on average 28.2 points per game. He recorded his highest seasonal average of 37.1 points per game in the 1986–87 season. His lowest seasonal average of 20 points per game was observed toward the end of his career in the 2002–03 season.

Another basketball giant is Wilt Chamberlain, who is one of basketball's first superstars and is known for his skill, conspicuous consumption, and womanizing. With 30.07 points on average per game, Chamberlain is a close second to Michael Jordan for the highest average points scored per game. Whereas Michael Jordan's debut was in 1984, Chamberlain began his professional career with the NBA in 1959 and was inducted into the Hall of Fame in 1979.

Just like Michael Jordan, who scored the highest average points per game in his third professional season, Chamberlain also scored an average of 50.4 points per game in 1961–6, his third season. Again, just like Michael Jordan, Chamberlain's average dropped at the tail end of his career when he scored 13.2 points per game on average in 1972–73.

Jordan's 30.12 points per game on average and Chamberlain's 30.06 points per game on average are very close. Notice that I am referring here to average points per game weighted by the number of games played in each season. A simple average computed from the average of points per game per season will return slightly different results.

While both Jordan and Chamberlain report very similar career averages, there are, however, significant differences in the consistency of their performance throughout their careers.

Instead of the averages, if we compare standard deviations, we see that Jordan with a standard deviation of 4.76 points is much more consistent in his performance than Chamberlain was with a standard deviation of 10.59 points per game. If we were to assume that these numbers are normally distributed, I can plot the Normal curves for their performance. Note in Figure 6.15 that Michael Jordan's performance returns a sharper curve (colored in black), whereas Chamberlain's curve (colored in gray) is flatter and spread wide. We can see that Jordan's score is mostly in the 20 to 40 points per game range, whereas Chamberlain's performance is spread over a much wider interval.

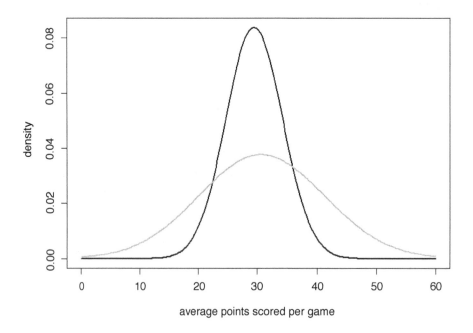

Figure 6.15   Normal distribution curves for Michael Jordan and Wilt Chamberlain

Mean and Not So Mean Differences

I use statistics to compare the consistency of scoring between two basketball giants. The comparison of means (averages) comes in three flavors. First, you can assume that the mean points per game scored by both Jordan and Chamberlain are the same. That is, the difference between the mean scores of the two basketball legends is zero. This becomes our null hypothesis. Let μ_j represent the average points per game scored by Jordan and μ_c represent the average points per game scored by Chamberlain. My null hypothesis, denoted by H_0, is expressed as follows:

$H_0: \mu_j = \mu_c$

The alternative hypothesis, denoted as H_a, is as follows:

$H_a: \mu_j \neq \mu_c$; their average scores are different.

Now let us work with a different null hypothesis and assume that Michael Jordan, on average, scored higher than Wilt Chamberlain did. Mathematically:

$H_0: \mu_j > \mu_c$

The alternative hypothesis will state that Jordan's average is lower than that of Chamberlain's, $H_a: \mu_j < \mu_c$. Finally, I can restate our null hypothesis to assume that Michael Jordan, on average, scored lower than Wilt Chamberlain did. Mathematically:

$H_0: \mu_j < \mu_c$

The alternative hypothesis in the third case will be as follows:

$H_a: \mu_j > \mu_c$; Jordan's average is higher than that of Chamberlain's.

I can test the hypothesis using a t-test, which I will explain later in the chapter.

Another less common test is known as the z-test, which is based on the normal distribution. Suppose a basketball team is interested in acquiring a new player who has scored on average 14 points per game. The existing team's average score has been 12.5 points per game with a standard deviation of 2.8 points per game. The team's manager wants to know whether the new player is indeed a better performer than the existing team. The manager can use the z-test to find the answer to this riddle. I explain the z-test in the following section.

Handling Rejections

After I state the null and alternative hypotheses, I conduct the z- or the t-test to compare the difference in means. I calculate a value for the test and compare it against the respective critical value. If the calculated value is greater than the critical value, I can reject the null hypothesis. Otherwise, I fail to reject the null hypothesis.

Another way to make the call on the hypothesis tests is to see whether the calculated value falls in the rejection region of the probability distribution function. The fundamental principal here is to determine, given the distribution, how likely it is to get a value as extreme as the one we observed. More often than not, we use the 95% threshold. We would like to determine whether the likelihood of obtaining the observed value for the test is less than 5% for a 95% confidence level. If the calculated value for the z- or the t-test falls in the region that covers the 5% of the distribution, which we know as the rejection region, we reject the null hypothesis. I illustrate the regions for normal and t-distributions in the following sections.

Normal Distribution

Recall from the last section that the alternative hypothesis comes in three flavors: The difference in means is not equal to 0, the difference is greater than 0, and the difference is less than 0. We have three rejection regions to deal with the three scenarios.

Let us begin with the scenario where the alternative hypothesis is that the mean difference is not equal to 0. We are not certain whether it is greater or less than zero. We call this the *two-tailed test*. We will define a rejection region in both tails (left and right) of the normal distribution. Remember, we only consider 5% of the area under the normal curve to define the rejection region. For a two-tailed test, we divide 5% into two halves and define rejection regions covering 2.5% under the curve in each tail, which together sum up to 5%. See the two-tailed test illustrated in Figure 6.16.

Recall that the area under the normal density plot is 1. The gray-shaded area in each tail identifies the rejection region. Taken together, the gray area in the left (2.5% of the area) and in the right (2.5% of the area) constitute the 5% rejection region. If the absolute value of the z-test is greater than the absolute value of 1.96, we can safely reject the null hypothesis that the difference in means is zero and conclude that the two average values are significantly different.

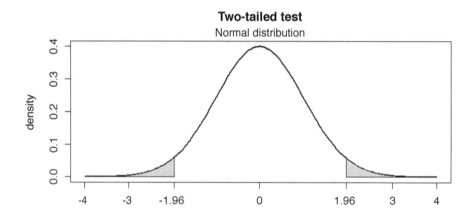

Figure 6.16   Two-tailed test using Normal distribution

Let us now consider a scenario where we believe that the difference in means is less than zero. In the Michael Jordan–Wilt Chamberlain example, we are testing the following alternative hypothesis:

$H_a:\mu_j < \mu_c$; Jordan's average is lower than that of Chamberlain's.

In this particular case, I will only define the rejection region in the left tail (the gray-shaded area) of the distribution. If the calculated z-test value is less than −1.64, for example, −1.8, we will know that it falls in the rejection region (see Figure 6.17) and we will reject the null hypothesis that the difference in means is greater than zero. The test is also called one-tailed test.

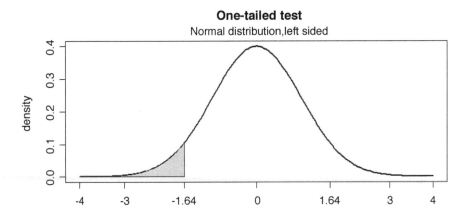

Figure 6.17   One-tailed test (left-tail)

Along the same lines, let us now consider a scenario where we believe that the difference in means is greater than zero. In the Michael Jordan–Wilt Chamberlain example, we are testing the following alternative hypothesis:

$H_a{:}\mu_j > \mu_c$; Jordan's average is higher than that of Chamberlain's.

In this particular case, I will only define the rejection region (the gray-shaded area) in the right tail of the distribution. If the calculated z-test value is greater than 1.64, for example, 1.8, we will know that it falls in the rejection region (see Figure 6.18) and we will reject the null hypothesis that the difference in means is less than zero.

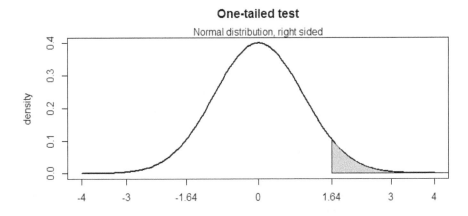

Figure 6.18   One-tailed test (right-tail)

t-distribution

Unlike the `z-test`, most comparison of means tests are performed using the t-distribution, which is preferred because it is more sensitive to small sample sizes. For large sample sizes, the t-distribution approximates the normal distribution. Those interested in this relationship should explore the *central limit theorem*. For the readers of this text, suffice it to say that for large sample sizes, the distribution looks and feels like the normal distribution, a phenomenon I have already illustrated in Figure 6.7.

I have chosen not to illustrate the rejection regions for the t-distribution, because they look the same as the ones I have illustrated for the normal distribution for sample sizes of say 200 or greater. Instead, I define the critical t-values.

As the number of observations increases, the critical t-values approach the ones we obtain from the `z-test`. For a left tail (mean is less than zero) test with 30 degrees of freedom, the critical value for a `t-test` at 5% level is −1.69. However, for a large sample with 400 degrees of freedom, the critical value is −1.648, which comes close to −1.64 for the normal distribution. Thus, one can see from Figure 6.19 that the critical values for t-distribution approaches the ones for normal distribution for larger samples. I, of course, would like to avoid the controversy for now on what constitutes as a large sample.

Critical values for t (lower tail)

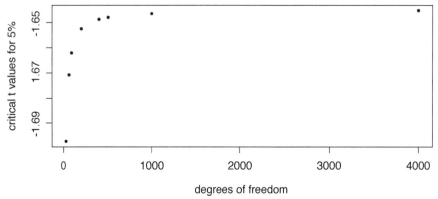

Figure 6.19   Critical t-values for left-tail test for various sample sizes

General Rules Regarding Significance

Another way of testing the hypothesis is to use the probability values associated with the `z-` or the `t-test`. Consider the general rules listed in Table 6.4 for testing statistical significance.

Table 6.4 Rules of Thumb for Hypothesis Testing

Type of Test	z or t Statistics*	Expected p-value	Decision
Two-tailed test	The absolute value of the calculated z or t statistics is greater than 1.96	Less than 0.05	Reject the null hypothesis
One-tailed test	The absolute value of the calculated z or t statistics is greater than 1.64	Less than 0.05	Reject the null hypothesis

* With large samples only for t statistics

Note that for t-tests, the 1.96 threshold works with large samples. For smaller samples, the critical t-value will be larger and depend upon the degrees of freedom (the sample size).

The Mean and Kind Differences

We are often concerned with comparing two or more outcomes. For instance, we might be interested in comparing sales from one franchise location with the rest. Statistically, we might have four conditions when we are concerned with comparing the difference in means between groups. These are

1. Comparing the sample mean to a population mean when the population standard deviation is known

2. Comparing the sample mean to a population mean when the population standard deviation is not known

3. Comparing the means of two independent samples with unequal variances

4. Comparing the means of two independent samples with equal variances

I discuss each of the four scenarios with examples in the following sections.

Comparing a Sample Mean When the Population SD Is Known

I continue to work with the basketball example. Numerous basketball legends are known for their high-scoring performance. The two in the lead are Wilt Chamberlain and Michael Jordan. However, there appears to be a huge difference between the two leading contenders and others. LeBron James, who is third in the NBA rankings for career average points per game at 27.5, is very much behind Jordan and Chamberlain, and is marginally better than Elgin Baylor at 27.36 (see Figure 6.20).

Average points scored per game

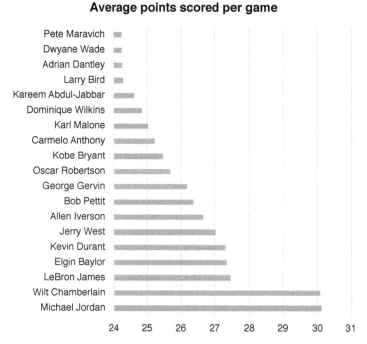

Figure 6.20   Average points scored per game for the leading NBA players

Source: http://www.basketball-reference.com/leaders/pts_per_g_career.html

Many believe that the hefty salaries of celebrity athletes reflect their exceptional performance. In basketball, scoring high points is one of the criteria, among others, that determines a player's worth. There is some truth to it. During 2013–14, Kobe Bryant of the LA Lakers earned more than $30 million. However, he was not the highest scorer in the team (see Figure 6.21). The basketball example provides us the backdrop to conduct the comparison of means test.

Lakers: are they earning their keep?

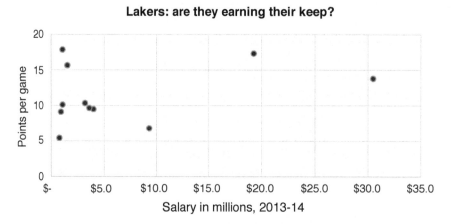

Figure 6.21   Lakers: Are they earning their keep?

The Basketball Tryouts

Let us assume that a professional basketball team wants to compare its performance with that of players in a regional league. The pros are known to have a historic mean of 12 points per game with a standard deviation of 5.5. A group of 36 regional players recorded on average 10.7 points per game. The pro coach would like to know whether his professional team scores on average are different from that of the regional players. I will use the two-tailed test from a normal distribution to determine whether the difference is statistically different. I start by calculating the z-value as shown in Equation 6.4:

$$z = \frac{\bar{x} - \mu}{\dfrac{\sigma}{\sqrt{n}}}$$ **Equation 6.4**

The specs are as follows:

Average points per player for the regional players: 10.7 ($\bar{x}$)

Std. Dev of the population: 5.5 (σ)

Average points per game scored by pros: 12 (μ)

Our null hypothesis: $H_0: \mu = 12$

Alternative hypothesis: $H_a: \mu \neq 12$

$$z = \frac{10.7 - 12}{\dfrac{5.5}{\sqrt{36}}} = -1.42$$

For a two-tailed test at the 5% level, each tail represents 2.5% of the area under the curve. The critical value for the z-test at the 95% level is ±1.96. Because the absolute value for −1.42 is lower than the absolute value for −1.96, I fail to reject the null hypothesis that the difference in means is zero and conclude that statistically speaking, 10.7 is not much different from the pros' average of 12 points scored per game.

Figure 6.22 presents the z-test graphically. Note that −1.42 does not fall in the gray-shaded area, which constitutes the rejection region. Thus, I cannot reject the null hypothesis that the mean difference is equal to 0.

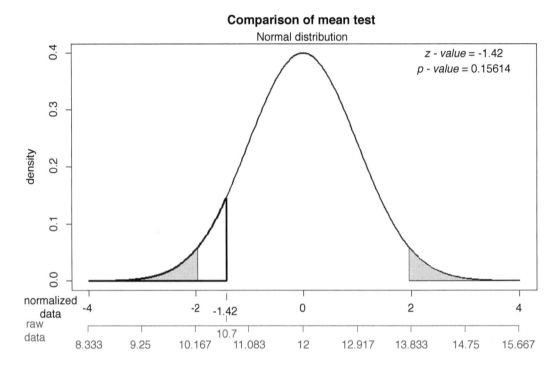

Figure 6.22   Two-tailed test for basketball tryouts

All statistical software and spreadsheets can calculate the p-value associated with the observed mean. In this example using a two-tailed test, the p-value associated with the average score of 10.7 points per game is 0.156, if the mean of the distribution is 12 and the standard error of the mean is $\frac{5.5}{\sqrt{36}} = 0.912$

Left Tail Between the Legs

A university basketball team might become a victim of austerity measures. Forced to reduce the budget deficit, the university is considering cutting off underperforming academic and nonacademic programs. The basketball team has not done well as of late. Hence, it has been included in the list of programs to be terminated.

The coach, however, feels that the newly restructured team has the potential to rise to the top of the league and that the bad days are behind them. Disbanding the team now would be a mistake. The coach convinces the university's vice president of finance to have the team evaluated by a panel of independent coaches to rank the team on a scale of 1 to 10. It was agreed that if the team received the average score of 7 or higher, the team may be allowed to stay for another year, at which time the decision will be revisited.

A panel of 20 independent coaches was assembled to evaluate the team's performance. After reviewing the team's performance, the panel's average score equaled 6.5 with a standard deviation of 1.5. The VP of finance now has to make a decision. Should the team stay or be disbanded?

The VP of finance asked a data analyst in her staff to review the stats and assist her with the decision. She was of the view that the average score of 6.5 was too close to 7, and that she wanted to be sure that there was a statistically significant difference that would prompt her to disband the basketball team.

The analyst decided to conduct a one-sample mean test to determine whether the average score received was 7 or higher.

The null hypothesis: $H_0: = \mu \geq 7$.
The alternative hypothesis: $H_a: = \mu < 7$.

$$z = \frac{6.5 - 7}{\frac{1.5}{\sqrt{20}}} = -1.491$$

Based on the test, the analyst observed that the `z-value` of -1.49 does not fall in the rejection region. Thus, he failed to reject the null hypothesis, which stated that the average score received was 7 or higher. The VP of finance, after reviewing the findings, decided not to cut funding to the team because, statistically speaking, the average ranking of the basketball team was not different from the threshold of 7.

The test is graphically illustrated in Figure 6.23.

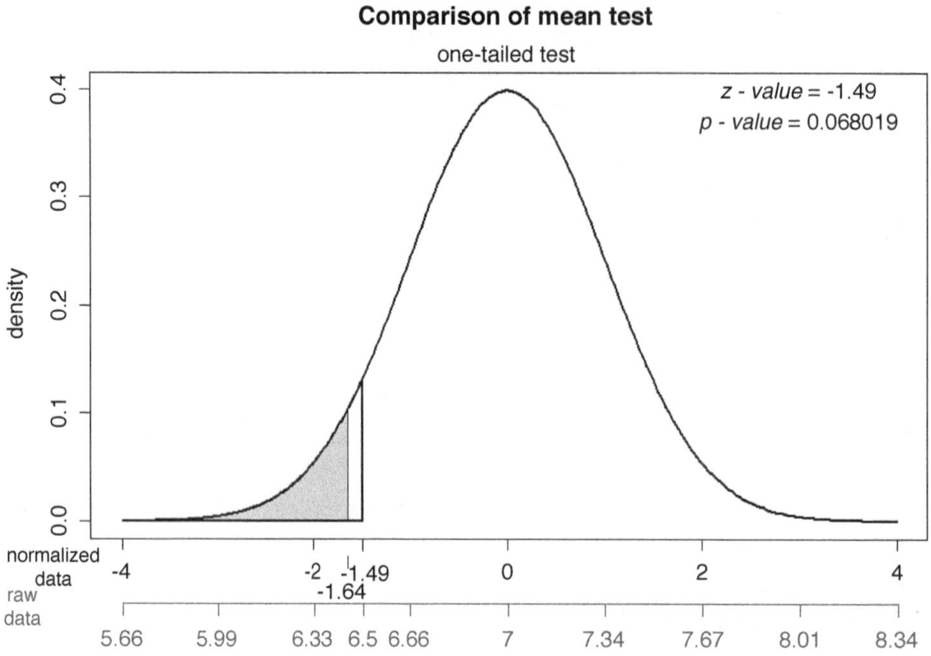

Figure 6.23   Basketball tryouts, left-tail test

Lastly, consider hotdog vendors outside a basketball arena where the local NBA franchise plays. It has been known that when the local team was not winning, the vendors would sell on average 500 hotdogs per game with a standard deviation of 50. Assume now that the home team has been enjoying a winning streak for the last five games that is accompanied with an average sale of 550 hotdogs. The vendors would like to determine whether they are indeed experiencing higher sales. The hypothesis is stated as follows:

The null hypothesis: H_0: $\mu \leq 500$
Alternative hypothesis: H_a: $\mu > 500$
The z-value is calculated as follows:

$$z = \frac{550 - 500}{\left(\dfrac{50}{\sqrt{5}}\right)} = 2.24$$

I see that the z-value for the test is 2.24 and the corresponding p-value is 0.0127, which is less than 0.05. I can therefore reject the null hypothesis and conclude that there has been a statistically significant increase in hotdog sales.

Given that I only had five observations, it would have been prudent to use the t-distribution instead, which is more suited to small samples. The test is illustrated in Figure 6.24.

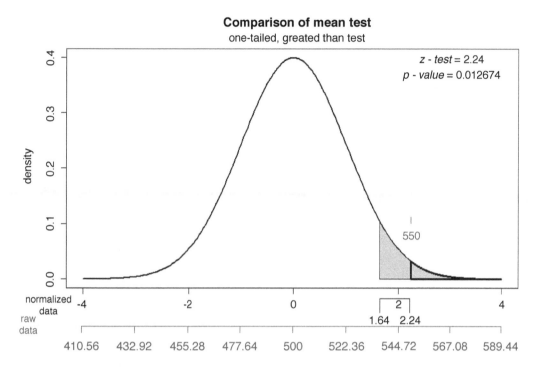

Figure 6.24   Hotdog sales

Comparing Means with Unknown Population SD

We use the t-distribution in instances where we do not have access to population standard deviation. The test statistic is shown in Equation 6.5:

$$t = \frac{\bar{x} - \mu}{\dfrac{s}{\sqrt{n}}}$$

Equation 6.5

Note that σ (population standard deviation) has been replaced by s(sample standard deviation).

Consider the case where a large franchise wants to determine the performance of a newly opened store. The franchise surveyed a sample of 35 existing stores and found that the average weekly sales were $166,000 with a standard deviation of $25,000. The new store on average reported a weekly sale of $170,000. The managers behind the launch of the new store are of the view that the new store represents the new approach to retailing, which is the reason why the new store sales are higher than the existing store. Despite their claim of effectively reinventing the science of retailing, the veteran managers maintain that the new store is reporting slightly higher sales because of the novelty factor, which they believe will soon wear off. In addition, they think that statistically speaking, the new store sales are no different from the sample of existing 35 stores.

The question, therefore, is to determine whether the new store sale figures are different from the sales at the existing stores. Because the franchise surveyed 35 of its numerous stores, we do not know the standard deviation of sales in the entire population of stores. Thus, I will rely on t-distribution, and not Normal distribution.

Average sales per week for the 35 stores: $166,000 ($\mu$)

Std. Dev of the weekly sales: $25,000 ($s$)

Average sales reported by the new store: $170,000 ($\bar{x}$)

Our null hypothesis: H_0: $\mu = 166000$

Alternative hypothesis: H_a: $\mu \neq 166000$

Because we are not making an assumption about the sales in the new store being higher or lower than the average sales in the existing stores, we are using a two-tailed test. The purpose is to test the hypothesis that the new stores sales are different from that of the existing store sales. Mathematically:

$$t = \frac{170000 - 166000}{\dfrac{25000}{\sqrt{35}}} = 0.947$$

The estimated value of the `t-statistics` is 0.947. Figure 6.25 shows a graphical representation of the test.

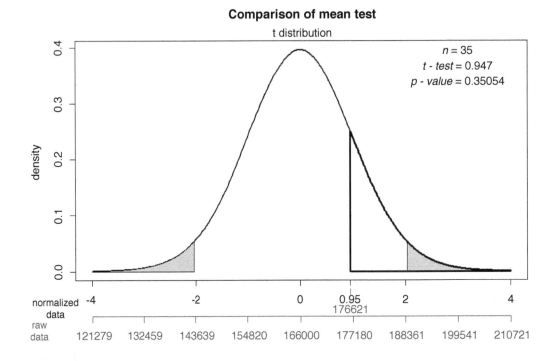

Figure 6.25   Retail sales and hypothesis testing

We see that the new store sales do not fall in the rejection region (shaded gray). Furthermore, the `p-value` for the test is 0.35, which is much higher than the threshold value of 0.05. We therefore fail to reject the null hypothesis and conclude that the new store sales are similar to the ones reported for the 35 sample stores. Thus, the new store manager may not have reinvented the science of retailing.

Comparing Two Means with Unequal Variances

In most applied cases of statistical analysis, we compare the means for two or more groups in a sample. The underlying assumption in this case is that the two means are the same and thus the difference in means equals 0. We can conduct the test assuming the two groups might or might not have equal variances.

I illustrate this concept using data for teaching evaluations and the students' perceptions of instructors' appearance. Recall that the data covers information on course evaluations along with course and instructor characteristics for 463 courses for the academic years 2000–2002 at the University of Texas at Austin.

You are encouraged to download the data from the book's website. A breakdown of male and female instructors' teaching evaluation scores is presented in Table 6.5.

```
t.mean<-tapply(x$eval,x$gender, mean)
t.sd<- tapply(x$eval,x$gender, sd)
round(cbind(mean=t.mean, std. dev.=t.sd),2)
```

Table 6.5 Teaching Evaluation for Male and Female Instructors

	mean	std.dev.
Male	4.07	0.56
Female	3.90	0.54

We notice that the teaching evaluations of male instructors are slightly higher than that of the female instructors. We would like to know whether this difference is statistically significant. Hypothesis:

$$H_0: x_1 = x_2$$
$$H_a: x_1 \neq x_2$$

I conduct the test to determine the significance in the difference in average values for a particular characteristic of two independent groups, as shown in Equation 6.6.

$$t = \frac{x_1 - x_2}{\sqrt{\frac{s_1^2}{n_1} + \frac{s_2^2}{n_2}}}$$

Equation 6.6

The shape of the t-distribution depends on the degrees of freedom, which according to Satterthwaite (1946)[5] are calculated as shown in Equation 6.7:

$$dof = \frac{\left(\dfrac{s_1^2}{n_1} + \dfrac{s_2^2}{n_2}\right)^2}{\dfrac{\left(\dfrac{s_1^2}{n_1}\right)^2}{n_1 - 1} + \dfrac{\left(\dfrac{s_2^2}{n_2}\right)^2}{n_2 - 1}}$$

Equation 6.7

Substituting the values in the equation, I have the following:

$s_1 = .56$

$s_2 = .54$

$n_1 = 268$

$n_2 = 195$

$x_1 = 4.07$

$x_2 = 3.90$

Subscript 1 represents statistics for males, and subscript 2 represents statistics for females. The results are as follows: $dof = 426$ and $t = 3.27$. The output from R is presented in Figure 6.26.

```
> t.test(eval~gender, alternative='two', conf.level=.95,
+        var.equal=FALSE, data=TeachingRatings)

        Welch Two Sample t-test

data:  eval by gender
t = 3.2667, df = 425.756, p-value = 0.001176
alternative hypothesis: true difference in means is not equal to 0
95 percent confidence interval:
 0.06691754 0.26909088
sample estimates:
  mean in group male mean in group female
          4.069030               3.901026


> pt(c(3.267), df=425.76, lower.tail=FALSE)*2
[1] 0.001174933
```

Figure 6.26   Output of a t-test in R

Figure 6.27 shows the graphical output:

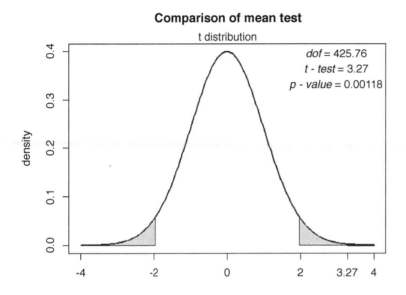

Figure 6.27   Graphical depiction of a two-tailed `t-test` for teaching evaluations

I obtain a `t-value` of 3.27, which falls in the rejection region. I also notice that the `p-value` for the test is 0.0018, which suggests rejecting the null hypothesis and conclude that the difference in teaching evaluation between male and female instructors is statistically significant at the 95% level.

Conducting a One-Tailed Test

The previous example tested the hypothesis that the average teaching evaluation for males and females was not the same. Now, I adopt a more directional approach and test whether the teaching evaluations for males were higher than that of the females: H_a: $x_1 > x_2$.

Given that it is a one-sided test, the only thing that changes from the last iteration is that the rejection region is located only on the right side (see Figure 6.28). The t-value and the associated degrees of freedom remain the same. What changes is the `p-value`, because the rejection region, representing 5% of the area under the curve, lies to only the right side of the distribution. The probability value will account for the possibility of getting a `t-value` of 3.27 or higher, which is different from the two-tailed test where I calculated the `p-value` of obtaining a `t-value` of either lower than –3.27 or greater than 3.27.

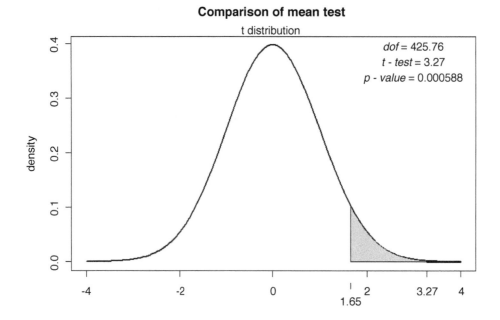

Figure 6.28   Teaching evaluations, right-tailed test

The resulting `p-value` is 0.00058, which is a lot less than 0.05, our chosen threshold to reject the null hypothesis. I thus reject the null and conclude that male instructors indeed receive on average higher teaching evaluations than female instructors do.

Figure 6.29 shows the output from R for a one-tailed test.

```
> t.test(eval~gender, alternative='greater', conf.level=.95,
+          var.equal=FALSE, data=TeachingRatings)

          Welch Two Sample t-test

data:  eval by gender
t = 3.2667, df = 425.756, p-value = 0.000588
alternative hypothesis: true difference in means is greater than 0
95 percent confidence interval:
 0.0832263         Inf
sample estimates:
  mean in group male mean in group female
            4.069030             3.901026



> pt(c(3.267), df=425.76, lower.tail=FALSE)
[1] 0.0005874666
```

Figure 6.29   R output for teaching evaluations, right-tailed test

Comparing Two Means with Equal Variances

When the population variance is assumed to be equal between the two groups, the sample variances are pooled to obtain an estimate of σ. Use Equation 6.8 to get the standard deviation of the sampling distribution of the means:

$$sdev = \sqrt{\frac{vpool * (n_1 + n_2)}{n_1 * n_2}}$$

Equation 6.8

Equation 6.9 provides the pooled estimate of variance:

$$vpool = \frac{s_1^2 (n_1 - 1) + s_2^2 (n_2 - 1)}{n_1 + n_2 - 2}$$

Equation 6.9

Get the test statistics via Equation 6.10:

$$t = \frac{x_1 - x_2}{sdev}$$

Equation 6.10

I use the same example of teaching evaluations to determine the difference between the evaluation scores of male and female instructors assuming equal variances. The calculations are reported as follows:

$$vpool = \frac{.557^2 (268 - 1) + .539^2 (195 - 1)}{268 + 195 - 2} = .302$$

$$sdev = \sqrt{\frac{.302 (268 + 195)}{268 * 195}} = .052$$

$$t = \frac{4.069 - 3.901}{.052} = 3.250$$

The degrees of freedom for equal variances are given by $dof = n_1 + n_2 - 2$.
Figure 6.30 shows the R output:

```
        Two Sample t-test

data:  eval by gender
t = 3.2499, df = 461, p-value = 0.001239
alternative hypothesis: true difference in means is not equal to 0
95 percent confidence interval:
 0.06641797 0.26959045
sample estimates:
  mean in group male mean in group female |
            4.069030              3.901026
```

Figure 6.30   R output for equal variances, two-tailed test

Figure 6.31 presents the graphical display.

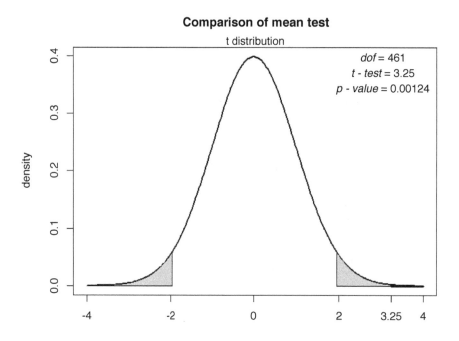

Figure 6.31   Graphical output for equal variances, two-tailed test

Note that the results are similar to what I obtained earlier for the test conducted assuming unequal variances. The t-value is 3.25 and the associated p-value is 0.00124. I reject the null hypothesis and conclude that the average teaching evaluations for males are different from that of the females. These results are statistically significant at the 95% (even 99%) level.

I can repeat the analysis with a one-tailed test to determine whether the teaching evaluations for males are statistically higher than that for females. I report the R output in Figure 6.32. The associated p-value for the one-tailed test is 0.0006194, which suggests rejecting the null hypothesis and conclude that the teaching evaluations for males are greater than that of the females.

```
          Two Sample t-test

data:  eval by gender
t = 3.2499, df = 461, p-value = 0.0006194
alternative hypothesis: true difference in means is greater than 0
95 percent confidence interval:
 0.08280296          Inf
sample estimates:
  mean in group male mean in group female
            4.069030             3.901026


> pt(c(3.2498), df=461, lower.tail=FALSE)
[1] 0.0006196742
```

Figure 6.32   R output for equal variances, right-tailed test

Figure 6.33 shows the graphical display.

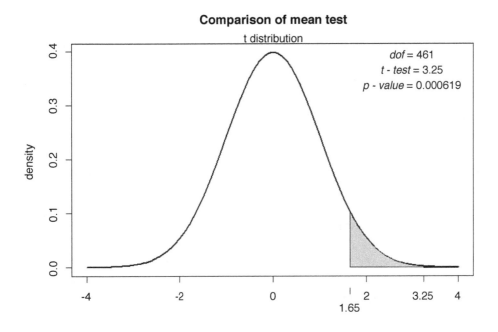

Figure 6.33   Graphical output for equal variances, right-tailed test

Worked-Out Examples of Hypothesis Testing

The best way of mastering a new concept is to practice the concept with more examples. Here I present additional worked-out examples of the `t-test`. I encourage you to repeat the analysis presented in these examples with a handheld calculator to get a real feel of the concepts.

Best Buy–Apple Store Comparison

Assuming unequal variances, let us see whether the average daily sales between fictional versions of a Best Buy (BB) outlet and an Apple Store (AS) are statistically different. Here are some cooked up numbers.

- **BB:** Average daily sales $110,000, SD $5000, sales observed for 65 days
- **AS:** Average sales $125,000, SD $15,000, sales observed for 45 days

Recall that we conduct a `t-test` to determine the significance in the difference in means for a particular characteristic of two independent groups. Equation 6.6 presents the `t-test` formula for **unequal variances**.

Subscript 1 represents statistics for Best Buy, and subscript 2 represents statistics for the Apple Store. The shape of the t-distribution depends on the degrees of freedom, which was presented earlier in Equation 6.7.

The *dof* are needed to determine the probability of obtaining a t-value as extreme as the one calculated here. When I plug in the numbers in the equations, I obtain the following results:

t = –6.46

dof = 50.82

The absolute `t-stat` value of –6.4 is significantly greater than the absolute value for +/–1.96, suggesting that the Best Buy outlet and the Apple Store sales are significantly different (using a two-tailed test) for large samples at the 95% confidence level. Let us obtain the critical value for the t-test that is commensurate with the appropriate sample size.

If I were to consult the t-table for *dof* = 50, (the closest value to 50.8) the largest t-value reported is 3.496, which is less than the one I have obtained (–6.46). Note that I refer here to the absolute value of –6.46. The corresponding probability value from the t-table for a two-tailed test for the maximum reported `t-test` of 3.496 is 0.001 (see the highlighted values in the image from the t-table in Figure 6.34). Thus, I can conclude that the probability of finding such an⌐ extreme t-value is less than 0.001% (two-tailed test).

I would now like to test whether Best Buy Store sales are lower than that of the Apple Stores. A one-tailed test will help us determine whether the average sales at the fictional versions of BestBuy are lower than at the Apple Store. The probability to obtain a t-value of –6.46 or higher is 0.0005% (see Figure 6.34). This suggests that the fictional BestBuy average daily sales are significantly lower than that of the Apple Store.

A `p-value` of less than 0.05 leads us to reject the null hypothesis that $x_1 > x_2$ and conclude that the Best Buy sales are lower than that of the Apple Store at the 95% confidence level.

44	1.301	1.666	2.015	2.414	2.692	3.286	3.526	44
46	1.300	1.679	2.013	2.410	2.687	3.277	3.515	46
48	1.299	1.677	2.011	2.407	2.682	3.269	3.505	48
50	1.299	1.676	2.009	2.403	2.678	3.261	3.496	50
55	1.297	1.673	2.004	2.396	2.668	3.245	3.476	55
60	1.296	1.671	2.000	2.390	2.660	3.232	3.460	60
65	1.295	1.669	1.997	2.385	2.654	3.220	3.447	65
70	1.294	1.667	1.994	2.381	2.648	3.211	3.435	70
80	1.292	1.664	1.990	2.374	2.639	3.195	3.416	80
100	1.290	1.660	1.984	2.364	2.626	3.174	3.390	100
150	1.287	1.655	1.976	2.351	2.609	3.145	3.357	150
200	1.286	1.653	1.972	2.345	2.601	3.131	3.340	200

Two Tails	0.20	0.10	0.05	0.02	0.01	0.002	0.001
One Tail	0.10	0.05	0.025	0.01	0.005	0.001	0.0005
Tail Probabilities							

Figure 6.34   T-distribution table

Assuming Equal Variances

I repeat the preceding example now assuming equal variances. Equation 6.8 provides the standard deviation of the sampling distribution of the means. Equation 6.9 describes the pooled estimate of variance, whereas Equation 6.10 describes the test statistics.

Here is the R code:

```
vpool= (s1^2*(n1-1)+s2^2*(n2-1))/(n1+n2-2);
sdev = sqrt(vpool*(n1+n2)/(n1*n2))
t = (x1-x2)/sdev ;
dof= n1+n2-2
t =   -7.495849
dof =108
vpool =   106481481
sdev = 2001.108
```

Notice that when I assume equal variances, I get an even stronger t-value of –7.49, which is again much larger than the absolute value for 1.96. Hence, I can conclude both for one- and two-tailed tests that Best Buy sales (assumed values) on average are lower than that of the average daily (fictional) sales for the Apple Store.

The closest value on the t-table for 108 (*dof*) is 100. The highest value reported along the 100 *dof* row is 3.390, which is lower than the absolute value of –7.49, which I estimated from the test. This suggests that the probability for a two-tailed test will be even smaller than 0.001 and for a one-tailed test will be less than 0.0005, allowing us to reject the null hypothesis.

Comparing Sales from an Urban and Suburban Retailer

A franchise operates stores in urban and suburban locations. The managers of two stores are competing for promotion. The manager at the suburban store is liked by all while the manager in the downtown location has a reputation of being a hot-head. The stores' weekly sales data over a 50-week period are as follows:

Downtown Store	Suburban Store
Average weekly sales = $800,000	Average weekly sales = $780,000
std dev = $100,000	std dev = $30,000
$n_1 = 50$	$n_2 = 50$

Hypothesis:
$H_0: x_1 = x_2$
$H_a: x_1 \neq x_2$
Assuming unequal variances:

$$t = \frac{20000}{\sqrt{\dfrac{100000^2}{50} + \dfrac{30000^2}{50}}}$$

The calculations return t = 1.35 and the *dof* = 57.75. The p-value for the test from the t-distribution table is approximately equal to 0.15. I therefore fail to reject the null hypothesis and conclude that both stores on average generate the same revenue. Thus, the manager of the suburban store, who happens to be a nice person but appears to be selling $20,000 per week less in sales, could also be considered for promotion because the t-test revealed that the difference in sales was not statistically significant. Also remember that t = 1.35 should have made the conclusion easier because the calculated t-value is less than 1.96 for a two-tailed test.

Exercises for Comparison of Means

Using the teaching ratings data, answer the following questions:

1. Determine the mean and standard deviation for course evaluations for minority and non-minority instructors. Determine whether the instructors belonging to minority groups are more or less likely to obtain a course evaluation of 4.1 or higher.

2. Determine the mean and standard deviation for course evaluations for upper- and lower-level courses. Determine whether the probability of obtaining a below-average course evaluation is higher for lower-level courses. Use 3.999 as the average course evaluation.

3. Determine whether tenured professors receive above-average course evaluations.

Regression for Hypothesis Testing

So far, I have relied on the traditional tools for hypothesis testing that are prescribed in texts for statistical analysis and data science. I would argue that regression analysis, which I explain in detail in Chapter 7, "Why Tall Parents Don't Have Even Taller Children," could also be used to compare means of two or more groups. I favor regression analysis over other techniques primarily because of the simplicity in its application, which is a desired feature for most data scientists.

Let us focus on the teaching ratings example where we determine whether the average teaching evaluation differed for males and females. I have noted earlier that the average teaching evaluation for female instructors was 3.90 and for males 4.07.

Assuming equal variances, I conducted a t-test and concluded that a statistically significant difference in teaching evaluations existed for males and females (see Figure 6.35).

```
> t2 <- t.test(eval~gender,var.equal = TRUE, data=x); t2

 Two Sample t-test

data:  eval by gender
t = 3.2499, df = 461, p-value = 0.001239
alternative hypothesis: true difference in means is not equal to 0
95 percent confidence interval:
 0.06641797 0.26959045
sample estimates:
  mean in group male mean in group female
            4.069030              3.901026
```

Figure 6.35 Equal variances two-tailed t-test to determine gender-based differences in teaching evaluations

The p-value of 0.0012 suggests that I can reject the null hypothesis of equal means and conclude that the average teaching evaluations between male and female instructors differ. Now let us attempt the same problem using a regression model. Figure 6.36 presents the output from the regression model.

Note that the column tvalue under Coefficients reports 3.25 for the row labelled as gen-2male. This statistic is identical to the t-value obtained in the traditional t-test assuming equal variances. Furthermore, the column labelled Pr(>|t|) reports 0.00124 as the p-value for gen2male, which is again identical to the p-value reported in the t-test. Thus, we can see that when we assume equal variances, a regression model generates identical results.

```
> summary(lm(eval~gen2, data=x))

Call:
lm(formula = eval ~ gen2, data = x)

Residuals:
    Min      1Q   Median      3Q     Max
-1.96903 -0.36903  0.03097  0.43097  0.99897

Coefficients:
            Estimate Std. Error t value Pr(>|t|)
(Intercept)  3.90103    0.03933   99.19  < 2e-16 ***
gen2male     0.16800    0.05169    3.25  0.00124 **
---
Signif. codes:  0 '***' 0.001 '**' 0.01 '*' 0.05 '.' 0.1 ' ' 1

Residual standard error: 0.5492 on 461 degrees of freedom
Multiple R-squared:  0.0224, Adjusted R-squared:  0.02028
F-statistic: 10.56 on 1 and 461 DF,  p-value: 0.001239
```

Figure 6.36 Regression model output for gender differences in teaching evaluations

The real benefit of the regression model emerges when we compare the means for more than two groups. t-tests are restricted to comparison of two groups. Regression models are useful when the null hypothesis states that the average values are the same for multiple groups.

To illustrate this point, I have categorized the age variable into a factor variable with three categories namely young, mid-age, and old. I would like to know whether a statistically significant difference exists between the teaching evaluation scores for young, mid-age, and old instructors. Again, I estimate a simple regression model (see Figure 6.37) to test the hypothesis. Figure 6.37 shows the results, and the R code follows.

```
x$f.age <- cut(x$age, breaks = 3)
x$f.age <- factor(x$f.age,labels=c("young", "mid age", "old"))
cbind(mean.eval=tapply(x$eval,
x$f.age,mean),observations=table(x$f.age))
plot(x$age,x$eval,pch=20)
summary(lm(eval~f.age, data=x))
```

```
> summary(lm(eval~f.age, data=x))

Call:
lm(formula = eval ~ f.age, data = x)

Residuals:
     Min      1Q  Median      3Q     Max
-1.78125 -0.38125  0.01875  0.46396  1.01875

Coefficients:
             Estimate Std. Error t value Pr(>|t|)
(Intercept)   4.00435    0.04361  91.831   <2e-16 ***
f.agemid age  0.03169    0.05727   0.553    0.580
f.ageold     -0.12310    0.07568  -1.626    0.105
---
Signif. codes:  0 '***' 0.001 '**' 0.01 '*' 0.05 '.' 0.1 ' ' 1

Residual standard error: 0.5533 on 460 degrees of freedom
Multiple R-squared:  0.00997,  Adjusted R-squared:  0.005665
F-statistic: 2.316 on 2 and 460 DF,  p-value: 0.09981
```

Figure 6.37 Regression model output for teaching evaluations based on age differences

I see that the values reported under the column labelled Pr(>|t|) in Figure 6.37 for the two categories of age; namely *f.age mid age* and *f.age old* are greater than .05. I therefore fail to reject the null hypothesis and conclude that average teaching evaluations do not differ by age in our sample.

Note that mid-age and old-age are represented in the model, whereas the category young is missing from the model. In regression models, when factor variables are used as explanatory variables, one arbitrarily chosen category, in this case young, is omitted from the output, and is used as the base against which other categories are compared.

The purpose here is not to explain the intricacies of regression models. Instead, my intent is to indicate a possible use of regression models for hypothesis testing. I do, however, explain the workings of regression models in Chapter 7.

Analysis of Variance

Analysis of variance, ANOVA, is the prescribed method of comparing means across groups of three or more. The null hypothesis in this case states that the average values do not differ across the groups. The alternative hypothesis states that at least one mean value is different from the rest.

I use the F-test for ANOVA. If the probability (p-value) associated with the F-test is greater than the threshold value, which is usually .05 for the 95% confidence level, we fail to reject the null hypothesis. In instances where the probability value for the F-test is less than .05, we reject the null hypothesis. In such instances, we conclude that at least one mean value differs from the rest.

I will repeat the comparison of means for the three age groups using the ANOVA test. The R code and the resulting output (see Figure 6.38) follow.

```
> summary(aov(eval~f.age, data=x))
             Df Sum Sq Mean Sq F value Pr(>F)
f.age         2   1.42  0.7090   2.316 0.0998 .
Residuals   460 140.82  0.3061
---
Signif. codes:  0 '***' 0.001 '**' 0.01 '*' 0.05 '.' 0.1 ' ' 1
```

Figure 6.38   ANOVA output for influence of age on teaching evaluations

Note that the value reported under Pr(>F) is 0.0998, which is greater than 0.05. Thus, we fail to reject the null hypothesis and conclude that the teaching evaluations do not differ by age groups.

Let us test the average teaching evaluations for a discretized variable for beauty, which in raw form is a continuous variable. I convert the continuous variable into three categories namely: low beauty, average looking, and good looking. The R code and the resulting output (see Figure 6.39) follow.

```
x$f.beauty<-cut(x$beauty, breaks=3)
x$f.beauty<-factor(x$f.beauty, labels=c("low beauty", "average
            looking", "good looking"))
cbind(mean.eval=tapply(x$eval,x$f.beauty,mean),
            observations=table(x$f.beauty))
summary(aov(eval~f.beauty, data=x))
```

```
             Df Sum Sq Mean Sq F value Pr(>F)
f.beauty      2    2.2  1.1013   3.618 0.0276 *
Residuals   460 140.0  0.3044
---
Signif. codes:  0 '***' 0.001 '**' 0.01 '*' 0.05 '.' 0.1 ' ' 1
```

Figure 6.39   ANOVA output for influence of beauty on teaching evaluations

The probability value associated with the F-test is 0.0276, which is less than .05, our threshold value. I therefore reject the null hypothesis and conclude that teaching evaluations differ by students' perception of instructors' appearance.

Significantly Correlated

Often we are interested in determining the independence between two categorical variables. Let us revisit the teaching ratings data. The university administration might be interested to know whether the instructor's gender is independent of the tenure status. This is of interest because in the presence of a gender bias, we might find that a larger proportion of women (or men) have not been granted tenure. A chi-square test of independence can help us with this challenge.

The null hypothesis (H_0) states that the two categorical variables are statistically independent, whereas the alternative hypothesis (H_a) states that the two categorical variables are statistically dependent. The test statistics is expressed shown in Equation 6.11.

$$\chi^2 = \Sigma(\frac{\left(f_o - f_e\right)^2}{f_e} \quad \textbf{Equation 6.11}$$

Where f_o is the observed frequency, and f_e is the expected frequency. We reject the null hypothesis if the p-value is less than the threshold for rejection ($1-\alpha$) and the degrees of freedom.

Let us test the independence assumption between gender and tenure in the teaching ratings data set. My null hypothesis states that the two variables are statistically independent. I run the test in R and report the results in Figure 6.40. Because the p-value of 0.1098 is greater than 0.05, I fail to reject the null hypothesis that the two variables are independent and conclude that a systematic association *does* exist between gender and tenure.

```
> t1<-table(x$gender,x$tenure);t1

          no yes
  male    52 216
  female  50 145
> round(prop.table(t1,1)*100,2)

            no    yes
  male    19.40 80.60
  female  25.64 74.36
> chisq.test(t1, correct=F)

 Pearson's Chi-squared test

data:  t1
X-squared = 2.5571, df = 1, p-value = 0.1098
```

Figure 6.40   Pearson's chi-squared test to determine association between gender and tenure status of instructors

We can easily reproduce the results in a spreadsheet or statistics software. The f_e in the formula is calculated as follows:

1. Determine the row and column totals for the contingency table (t1 in the last example: see the following code)

2. Determine the sum of all observations in the contingency table

3. Multiply the respective row and column totals and divide them by the sum of all observations to obtain f_e.

The R code required to replicate the programmed output follows.

```
t1<-table(x$gender,x$tenure);t1
round(prop.table(t1,1)*100,2)
r1<-margin.table(t1, 1)  #  (summed over rows)
c1<-margin.table(t1, 2)  #  (summed over columns)
r1;c1
e1<-r1%*%t(c1)/sum(t1);e1
t2<-(t1-e1)^2/e1;t2;sum(t2)
qchisq(.95, df = 1)
1-pchisq(sum(t2),(length(r1)-1)*(length(c1)-1))
```

Summary

Let me hypothesize in the concluding section of this chapter that you are now at least familiar with the statistical concepts about testing assumptions and hypotheses. The process of stating one's assumptions and then using statistical methods to test them is at the core of statistical analysis. I would like to conclude this section with a warning or two about the limitations of statistical analysis. As budding data scientists, you may naively assume that the techniques you have learned can be applied to all problems. Such a conclusion would be erroneous.

Recall the story of European settlers who spotted a black swan in Western Australia that immediately contradicted their belief that all swans were white. The settlers could have treated the black swan as an outlier, a data point that is very different from the rest of the observations. They could have ignored this one observation. But that would have been a mistake, because in this particular case, a black swan challenged the existing knowledge base.

Let me explain this with an example of when an outlier/s might be ignored. Assume you are working with the housing sales data where the average sale price in the neighborhood is around $450,000. However, you may have a couple or more housing units in the same data set that sold for more than two million dollars each. Given the nature of the housing stock in the neighborhood, you might conclude that a very small number of housing units in the area are much larger in size than the rest of the housing stock and hence have transacted for a larger amount. Because you are interested in forecasting the average price of an average house in the neighborhood, you might declare the very expensive transactions as outliers and exclude those from the analysis.

Now let us assume that you were (in a previous life) Charles Darwin's assistant and assigned the task to document the colors of swans found on the planet. As you landed in Western Australia with the rest of the settlers, you also spotted a black swan. Would you have treated the black swan as an outlier? The answer is emphatically no. Just one out of ordinary outcome or observation that could not be foreseen based on our prior body of knowledge is not an outlier, but the most important observation to ponder in detail.

Similarly, I would like to draw your attention again to Professor Jon Danielsson's estimation that an S&P 500 single-day decline of 23% in 1987 would happen once out of every 12 universes. We know that financial market meltdowns of similar proportions happen at a more rapid frequency than the statistical models would allow us to believe. Our continued reliance on the Gaussian distribution, which we refer to as the Normal distribution, erroneously lead us to believe that natural phenomenon can be approximated using the Normal distribution. This erroneous assumption is behind our poor risk perception of natural disasters and overconfidence in financial markets.

I submit that a data scientist is not one who believes the use of algorithms and statistical methods will provide him or her with "the" answer. Instead, I believe a data scientist is one who is fully cognizant of one's innate inability in predicting the future. A data scientist is one who appreciates the analytics will deliver an informed possible view of the future out of many other possible incarnations. A data scientist is one who never becomes a victim of compound ignorance; that is, the state when one is ignorant of one's own ignorance.

Endnotes

1. Wente, M. (2008, November 22). "A black swan comes home to roost." *The Globe and Mail.* Retrieved from http:// www.theglobeandmail.com/news/national/a-black-swan-comes-home-to-roost/article 716947/.

2. Taleb, N. N. (2007). *The Black Swan: The Impact of the Highly Improbable*. Random House Publishing Group.

3. Danielsson, J. (2011). *Financial Risk Forecasting: The Theory and Practice of Forecasting Market Risk with Implementation in R and Matlab.* John Wiley & Sons.

4. http://www.basketball-reference.com/leaders/pts_per_g_career.html

5. Satterthwaite, F. E. (1946), "An Approximate Distribution of Estimates of Variance Components." *Biometrics Bulletin* 2: 110–114.

CHAPTER 7

Why Tall Parents Don't Have Even Taller Children

You might have noticed that taller parents often have tall children who are not necessarily taller than their parents—and that's a good thing. This is not to suggest that children born to tall parents are not necessarily taller than the rest. That may be the case, but they are not necessarily taller than their own "tall" parents. Why I think this to be a good thing requires a simple mental simulation. Imagine if every successive generation born to tall parents were taller than their parents, in a matter of couple of millennia, human beings would become uncomfortably tall for their own good, requiring even bigger furniture, cars, and planes.

Sir Frances Galton in 1886 studied the same question and landed upon a statistical technique we today know as *regression models*. This chapter explores the workings of regression models, which have become the workhorse of statistical analysis. In almost all empirical pursuits of research, either in the academic or professional fields, the use of regression models, or their variants, is ubiquitous. In medical science, regression models are being used to develop more effective medicines, improve the methods for operations, and optimize resources for small and large hospitals. In the business world, regression models are at the forefront of analyzing consumer behavior, firm productivity, and competitiveness of public- and private-sector entities.

I would like to introduce regression models by narrating a story about my Master's thesis. I believe that this story can help explain the utility of regression models.

The Department of Obvious Conclusions

In 1999, I finished my Masters' research on developing hedonic price models for residential real estate properties.[1] It took me three years to complete the project involving 500,000 real estate transactions. As I was getting ready for the defense, my wife generously offered to drive me to the university. While we were on our way, she asked, "Tell me, what have you found in your research?" I was delighted to be finally asked to explain what I have been up to for the past three years. "Well, I have been studying the determinants of housing prices. I have found that larger homes sell for more than smaller homes," I told my wife with a triumphant look on my face as I held the draft of the thesis in my hands.

We were approaching the on-ramp for a highway. As soon as I finished the sentence, my wife suddenly turned the car to the shoulder, and applied brakes. As the car stopped, she turned to me and said: "I can't believe that they are giving you a Master's degree for finding just that. I could have told you that larger homes sell for more than smaller homes."

At that very moment, I felt like a professor who taught at the department of obvious conclusions. How can I blame her for being shocked that what is commonly known about housing prices will earn me a Master's degree from a university of high repute.

I requested my wife to resume driving so that I could take the next ten minutes to explain her the intricacies of my research. She gave me five minutes instead, thinking this may not require even that. I settled for five and spent the next minute collecting my thoughts. I explained to her that my research has not just found the correlation between housing prices and the size of housing units, but I have also discovered the magnitude of those relationships. For instance, I found that *all else being equal*, a term that I explain later in this chapter, an additional washroom adds more to the housing price than an additional bedroom. Stated otherwise, the marginal increase in the price of a house is higher for an additional washroom than for an additional bedroom. I found later that the real estate brokers in Toronto indeed appreciated this finding.

I also explained to my wife that proximity to transport infrastructure, such as subways, resulted in higher housing prices. For instance, houses situated closer to subways sold for more than did those situated farther away. However, houses near freeways or highways sold for less than others did. Similarly, I also discovered that proximity to large shopping centers had a nonlinear impact on housing prices. Houses located very close (less than 2.5 km) to the shopping centers sold for less than the rest. However, houses located *closer* (less than 5 km, but more than 2.5 km) to the shopping center sold for more than did those located farther away. I also found that the housing values in Toronto declined with distance from downtown.

As I explained my contributions to the study of housing markets, I noticed that my wife was mildly impressed. The likely reason for her lukewarm reception was that my findings confirmed what we already knew from our everyday experience. However, the real value added by the research rested in quantifying the magnitude of those relationships.

Why Regress?

A whole host of questions could be put to regression analysis. Some examples of questions that regression (hedonic) models could address include:

- How much more can a house sell for an additional bedroom?
- What is the impact of lot size on housing price?
- Do homes with brick exterior sell for less than homes with stone exterior?
- How much does a finished basement contribute to the price of a housing unit?
- Do houses located near high-voltage power lines sell for more or less than the rest?

In this chapter, I begin by covering the history of regression models, and reviewing the initial studies done using this method. I introduce Sir Frances Galton, who studied the correlation between parents' heights and that of their children. His study led to the very term *regression to the mean*. I briefly mention Carl Friedrich Gauss, the mathematician who devised the *least square* method, which has been widely used to estimate simple regression models.

However, I focus in detail on the concept of *all else being equal*. What sets regression models apart from almost all other statistical methods is that the regression models allow us to control for the impact of other factors while we study and analyze the impact of a particular factor.

Let us illustrate this with an example involving wage, education, and experience. It is safe to assume that additional years of schooling will result in higher wages. However, it may also be true that years of experience are also influential in determining one's wage. In a regression model, we include both years of schooling and years of experience as explanatory variables to determine their impact on wages. A regression model enables us to account for the impact of years of schooling by controlling for years of experience. Similarly, we can determine the impact of years of experience on wages by holding years of education constant.

Housing price data plays a big role in this chapter. I use it to illustrate basic regression modeling techniques. Furthermore, I also use housing price data to demonstrate how to interpret the output from regression models.

The housing price data has only 88 observations. Because I have produced this book on data science in the age of big data, you may wonder why I use such a small data set.

As I have said earlier, when it comes to big data, *it is not the size that matters, but how you use it*. I believe that the small-sized data set of housing prices allows new learners to focus more on how to estimate, and more importantly, how to interpret the output from regression models than on the logistics of dealing with a large data set. My purpose of using the housing data is to illustrate the concept of *all else being equal*. Because the data set contains the necessary variables needed to illustrate not only regression, but also the main principle behind regression (all else being equal), I am pleased with my choice of the small data set.

Using the housing price data, I want to test the hypothesis that large-sized homes sell for higher prices. I have three proxies for size in the data set, namely the number of bedrooms, square footage of the lot, and square footage of the built-up space. I will explore what proxy of housing size is a more significant determinant of housing prices.

I also revisit the discussion on beauty and its socioeconomic outcomes. Recall the earlier discussion in Chapter 4, "Serving Tables," about how instructors' looks might influence their teaching evaluations. Simply put, do attractive instructors receive higher teaching evaluations from students? When I last discussed this topic, I conducted a series of tabulations and `t-tests` to explore bivariate relationships. This chapter takes the discussion to a new level involving multiple variables.

I now ask more nuanced questions. Does an instructor's appearance and looks affect his or her teaching evaluations even when I hold other factors constant? The discussion in this chapter focuses on those "other factors." For instance, if I were to hold gender, tenure status, proficiency in English language, visible minority status, and other attributes constant, would I still observe the impact of instructors' looks on teaching evaluations? Hence, when I say *all else being equal*, I imply that I am controlling for other possible factors (in addition to the instructors' looks) that could influence teaching evaluations.

Lastly, I analyze household expenditure data to determine what influences households' spending on food and alcohol. This particular example allows one to appreciate how certain attributes affect consumption decisions. For instance, I would like to see whether the presence of children influences households' spending on food. I also estimate a separate model to determine whether children's presence in a household influences spending on alcohol.

Introducing Regression Models

I started this chapter with the discussion about tall parents often having tall children. That is, "[t] all couples almost always beget tall progeny."[2] Again, if one looks at the average height of individuals across the globe, one sees that populations in certain countries are taller than in others. For instance, the average height for men in North America, especially those of European descent, is higher than the average height of men in East Asia. Such observations are certainly not new. In fact, the link between the parents' height and that of their children resulted in the first manifestation of the regression model. In 1886, Sir Frances Galton published a paper in the *Journal of the Anthropological Institute of Great Britain and Ireland* on the very same topic. In his paper, which he titled "Regression towards Mediocrity in Hereditary Stature" he observed the following:

> The average regression of the offspring is a constant fraction of their respective mid-parental
>
> deviations... So if its parents are each two inches taller than the averages from men and women,
>
> on average, the child will be shorter than its parents by some factors.

His research is of great interest because it highlights a profound observation about human genetics. Sir Frances Galton noted that if parents were on average taller than the relative population, their children would on average be shorter than their parents. Stated otherwise, children of very tall parents will be shorter and not taller than their parents.

Imagine for a second if the reverse were true. That is, the children born to taller parents ended up being taller than their own tall parents. The average height of the population would therefore increase in every successive generation. A few generations later, human beings would be slightly taller than their ancestors would be. If this were to continue for a few millennia, we would have much taller human beings than before. By having this tendency to regress to the mean height, which Sir Frances Galton called the regression towards mediocrity, we observe that unusually tall parents give birth to children who grow up to be shorter than their parents, thus keeping the height of the human race in check.

This is not to say that the average height of human beings has remained the same over centuries. In fact, the opposite is true. Over the past 150 years, the average height of humans in the industrialized countries has increased by approximately 10 centimeters (Hadhazy, 2015). The

Dutch however "stand head and shoulders above all others." The Dutch men or women today on average are 19 centimeters taller than their mid-nineteenth century counterparts.

The study of intergenerational height gains by Sir Frances Galton led to the birth of the regression models, which have become the workhorse of modern-day empirical research. While it is true that Sir Frances Galton first observed the concept of regression towards the mean, however, the mathematical formulation of the regression models was devised earlier by a brilliant mathematician, Carl Friedrich Gauss. The German mathematician devised the ordinary least squares (OLS) method in 1795. I discuss the OLS method in detail in the following sections.

Both Galton and Gauss have numerous accomplishments to their credit. While Sir Frances Galton is a well-known name in eugenics, his half-cousin, Charles Darwin, is known much more widely. In fact, it is believed that Sir Frances Galton discussed his research with Charles Darwin, who reportedly pushed him toward regression.

Gauss, on the other hand, is a celebrated mathematician. In fact, all texts in mathematics pay tribute to the genius of Gauss. However, one of his most commonly known and widely used discoveries is not directly attributed to him. The widely used normal distribution is in fact the Gaussian distribution, which he formulated.

All Else Being Equal

A fundamental concept in understanding regression analysis relates to *all else being equal*. Specifically, we want to isolate the impact of a particular factor on a behavior or phenomenon of interest while we control for other relevant factors. Consider wages as an example. One can argue that the years of schooling affect wages such that those with more years of schooling are likely to earn higher wages than those with fewer years of schooling. In fact, if one were to plot years of schooling and wages, one would observe a positive correlation between schooling and wages.

However, several other factors could be instrumental in determining one's wages. For instance, gender could also be a determinant. Regrettably, we see gender discrimination in wages where for doing the same job, men earn more than women do. At the same time, we may observe that people with similar years of schooling earn different wages because of the difference in years of experience. Consider two employees, both with undergraduate degrees in business, with one earning much higher wages than the other does. It may turn out that the one with higher wages has far more experience the other employee.

We may also observe that even when gender and the years of schooling and experience are the same, two individual workers may still earn very different wages. For instance, two women workers, both with a master's degree and five years of experience in their respective fields, may earn significantly different wages because one may have a graduate degree in arts while the other may have earned an MBA.

The *all else being equal* property of the regression models allows us to isolate the effect of one particular influence by controlling the impact of others. Earlier, we were interested in determining the impact of years of schooling on wages. I can use a regression model to control for gender, experience, and types of education or specialization to isolate the impact of years of schooling on wages. If I were to consider only two variables in isolation, that is, wages and years of schooling, I would have then ignored the impact of other factors that may be significant determinants of wages.

Regression models are therefore the right tool to conduct analysis with multiple variables. Such models allow one to control for a variety of factors on the variable or behavior of interest.

What Questions Can We Pose to Regression Models?

It is important to think of the questions that one can put to regression models. A better way to understand the regression modelling process is to think through the process of answering questions and riddles of interest. Because we will think systematically through the research question, an appropriate analytical framework will emerge from the process, which we then can subject to a regression model for empirical testing.

Let us first think of the difference in spending habits of men and women. For marketing professionals, several interesting questions may emerge from this line of inquiry. For instance, do women spend more on clothing than men do? One can compute average spending on clothing for men and women to answer this question. One can also think more holistically by entertaining other factors that could be influential in spending on clothing. For instance, one can refine the question by including the marital status to determine whether unmarried women spend more on clothes than married women do. Similarly, along with marriage, the presence of children in the household could also be a factor in spending decisions. One can pose the revised question as follows: Do married women with children spend less on clothing than married women without children do? Alternatively, do married women with children spend less on clothing than unmarried women do? Alternatively, do married women with children spend less on clothing than married men with children do?

Another way of thinking about the regression models is to consider the purchase of big-ticket items, such as cars and refrigerators. In 2008, the American economy in particular, and the global economy in general, experienced one of the worst recessions in decades. The economic slowdown in 2008 is commonly referred to as the Great Recession. Related to the Great Recession, one can explore whether households postpone purchase of expensive items during recession. One can further refine this question by asking whether low-income households postpone buying expensive goods or big-ticket items during recession. The reason for this qualifier is that recessions perhaps affect the discretionary spending of low-income households more so than it does that of the high-income households. Additionally, if we include the presence of young children, we can further refine the question and ask whether households with young children postpone buying expensive goods during recessions more so than households without children do. The presence of children in the household would affect discretionary spending because children's expenses during recessions occur regardless, prompting households to cut discretionary spending.

Another example is that of couples postponing child rearing to later years in their lives. Demographers have advised that the average age of women at the birth of their first child has increased over the past few decades (Mathews and Hamilton, 2009).[3] Demographers attribute this change to a large number of women opting for careers, which has delayed household formation, marriage or common law partnerships, and eventually the birth of children. However, asking this question in isolation would not do it justice. One has to account for other factors. For instance, one must consider whether both individuals in a relationship have demanding careers or otherwise. It may be true in some instances that only one of the two individuals has a demanding career that may not influence their decision to have children at a later stage in their lives.

Additionally, recall the discussion from Chapter 4 about instructors' perceived attractiveness by students and its impact on their teaching evaluations. I presented a series of tabulations that showed how teaching evaluations differed, not just for the looks, but also by gender, visible minority status, fluency in English, and other related attributes of the instructor. A regression model is better suited to isolate the impact of an instructor's perceived attractiveness on his or her teaching evaluation, while I control for other possible determinants of teaching evaluation including gender, English-language fluency, visible minority status, and the like.

If Suburbs Make Us Fat, They Must Also Make Us Pregnant

One can obtain partial answers to questions by relying on correlation analysis, which I briefly introduced in Chapter 6, "Hypothetically Speaking." For instance, consider that researchers have found a positive correlation between obesity and suburban living (Vandegrift and Yoked, 2004).[4] Similarly, we also observe a positive correlation between fertility and suburban living, which suggests that suburban women are more likely to have children than those who live in or near downtowns.[5,6] Another example is that of poverty and fertility rates. Research has shown that low-income economies report higher fertility rates than high-income economies do.[7] Stated otherwise, households in low-income countries are likely to have higher fertility than those living in high-income countries. What we must not forget is that these are all examples of correlations between two phenomenon observed without any consideration for other factors that might be at play.

As I have stated earlier, one can use correlation analysis to test the relationship between the aforementioned phenomena. However, one is likely to obtain a partial picture from the correlation analysis. Take the example of obesity and suburban living where a statistical test using correlation will confirm the relationship. However, one may not know the impact of age and income that might have confounded the relationship between obesity and suburban living.

Age and affordable housing likely influence the positive correlation between suburban living and higher fertility rates for women. We know from demographic data that in most North American cities younger cohorts are more likely to live in, or near, downtowns. Younger individuals, even when in committed relationships, often wait to have children later in their lives. Thus, younger couples live in smaller housing units because their shelter space requirements are less than that of the households with children.

From the above, we find that households with children require more space than those without children. Because suburban real estate is cheaper than one in or near downtowns (think

Manhattan or Chicago), households with children or those who are expecting to have children relocate to suburbs in search of cheaper housing. This is partially the reason for why we observe a difference in fertility rates for urban and suburban women. As a result, we might find that affordable housing has more to do with higher fertility observed in suburbs than anything else does.

As individuals become older and have children, they require more shelter space. These households relocate to suburbs in search of affordable housing. At the same time, as one ages, the metabolism slows down. Additionally, one faces significantly more pressures for time, which result in less discretionary time. In other words, as individuals become older, their metabolism slows down and they have less time to do exercise. If you put all this together, you can see that even when a positive correlation exists between obesity and suburban living, it is explained by other factors, which are aging, slower metabolism, and less time available for exercise.

The obesity question informs us that correlation between two variables can offer only a partial answer. For a complete answer, we have to use a regression (or other multivariate) analysis to account for other relevant factors.

Holding Other Factors Constant

As I pointed out earlier, the strength of regression analysis lies in its ability to isolate the impact of one factor while we control for the impact of others. We call this *all else being equal*.

To understand this phrase, let us revisit the question about factors affecting women's spending on clothing. One can think of several factors that could influence spending on clothing. Consider age, for instance, where younger women employed in the labor force may spend more on clothing if they are more responsive to the latest fashion trends. At the same time, women with established careers would have much more discretionary spending power than women who are just beginning their careers, and hence they may outspend the younger women for clothing. All else being equal, women earning higher incomes are more likely to spend more on clothing than others would. At the same time, the type of career may also influence women's spending on clothing. Certain professions require one to maintain a professional look and may require higher spending on clothing and appearance.

Married women might also have access to their spouse's income, which would further enhance their ability to spend on clothing. Conversely, they might have to support their spouses, which may leave less to spend on their own clothing. In addition, personal taste can also influence spending on clothing. For instance, women who prefer designer brands spend more on clothing.

Thus, if we are interested in determining what influences women's spending on clothing, we have to account for the outlined factors. I admit that the factors mentioned do not constitute an exhaustive list of influences on clothing-related spending. The purpose is to illustrate the fact that mere correlation between two variables of interest—that is, spending on clothing and gender—may not be sufficient to paint a complete picture. We use regression analysis to overcome the limitations of bivariate analytical techniques, such as the correlation analysis.

All else being equal enables us to isolate one particular factor by holding the influences of others constant. I offer one final example to illustrate this point. You may have heard that houses near public transit facilities (metro or subway stations) sell for more than the rest. However, we may find that in addition to proximity to subway stations, such houses could be different in structural type, quality of construction, and size, which would affect housing prices. Proximity to public transit may only partially explain the difference in housing prices. All else being equal implies that when holding other factors constant, we can determine the impact of the proximity to subway station on housing prices.

Do Tall Workers Earn More Than the Rest? Not When All Else Is Equal

I share findings from a study on workers' height and wages to reinforce all else being equal. Do you believe taller workers earn more than the rest? A quick answer is they do. Studies of workers' earnings and their respective heights have revealed that taller workers earn more than their shorter colleagues do. How did these studies reach this conclusion? They used regression models, much the same way Sir Frances Galton did in 1886 to determine the relationship between parents' heights and that of their children. Similarly, Professor Hamermesh and his undergraduate student Amy Parker also used regression models to conclude that good-looking instructors receive higher teaching evaluations. Maybe students learn more from good-looking instructors!

Schick and Steckel (2015) undertook a systematic study of earnings and height and concluded that "[t]aller workers receive a substantial wage premium."[8] In plain English, they observed that taller individuals earn more than others do. But this is not all they found. They also observed that when they controlled for other factors—that is, all else being equal—they found little if any evidence in support for height's impact on earnings.

Consider the relationship between earnings and individual's height. If we ignore other factors that influence an individual's earning potential, we will erroneously conclude that the mere correlation between height and earnings perhaps implies causation. Schick and Steckel (2015), however, demonstrate that such a conclusion will be false. They identified other cognitive and noncognitive determinants of earnings in addition to height.

They used a longitudinal data set in which all children born in the week of March 3, 1958 in Britain were tracked over time and were subsequently interviewed at ages 7, 11, 16, 23, 33, and 42. The final sample was much smaller than the starting sample in 1958, primarily because of the difficulty in keeping track of individuals over the long run.

The individuals were tested for scholastic aptitude (math and reading skills) and behavioral traits (extrovert, introvert, restless, and so on) during school years. Later surveys tested the adult respondents for problem-solving skills as well as for other proxies for motivation, such as pessimistic or optimistic outlook on life.

Using regression models, Schick and Steckel (2015) found that in the absence of other controls, height was a statistically significant determinant of earnings, suggesting taller workers earned more than shorter workers. However, the effect of height as an explanatory variable reduced when other controls were introduced in the model. Height remained a statistically significant determinant of earnings even when individual's experience, region of residence, ethnicity, father's socio-economic standing, and parents' involvement and interest in the child's education were controlled for in the model. But it all changed when workers' math and reading scores, recorded at age 11, and problem-solving skills, recorded at age 33, were added to the model. Suddenly, with the inclusion of cognitive abilities, height became a statistically insignificant determinant of earnings. When non-cognitive measures—such as emotional stability and extraversion assessments made at ages 11, 16, 23, and 33—were included in the model, height remained a statistically insignificant determinant of earnings. In addition, the magnitude of the coefficient for height decreased, approaching almost zero.

Spuriously Correlated

Even when we find statistically significant correlation between two variables, it may turn out that the two variables might be completely unrelated. Consider the case of ice cream sales and drownings. One may find a statistically significant and positive correlation between drownings and the sale of ice cream. Can one assume that drownings are caused by ice cream sales? As a result, would one impose a restriction on ice cream sales to reduce deaths by drownings?

The preceding example depicts spurious correlation between two rather unrelated variables. During summer season, hot weather leads to higher ice cream sales. At the same time, people head to pools, lakes, rivers, and beaches for swimming. As more people swim, the odds of drowning increase. Hence, the positive correlation between ice cream sales and drownings has no causal linkage, except that both ice cream sales and drowning are influenced by hot weather.

While one acknowledges the utility of correlation analysis, spurious correlations and the presence of confounding or mitigating factors warn that correlation is not the same as causation, and hence, one has to undertake more involved and systematic analysis to determine the relationships between behaviors. Regression analysis is more apt for such analysis.

Another point to remember regarding spurious correlation is that this challenge will become pronounced with big data. Very large data sets by default will show some statistically significant correlations among rather unrelated variables. An example of spurious correlation could be found in Varian (2014) where Google Correlate finds high correlation between new homes sold in the U.S. and oldies lyrics.

Hal Varian, Google's chief economist, while talking about Google Trend data, speaks of the emerging challenges posed by large-sized data and spurious correlation. He warns: "The challenge is that there are billions of queries so it is hard to determine exactly which queries are the most predictive for a particular purpose. Google Trends classifies the queries into categories, which helps a little, but even then we have hundreds of categories as possible predictors so that overfitting and spurious correlation are a serious concern."[9]

A Step-By-Step Approach to Regression

Before I get to regression modeling, or any other empirical analytical technique, I need to have a well-defined question and a sound theoretical model. Recall the example of wage and gender bias discussed earlier under "All Else Being Equal." I demonstrated how the research question was refined and a theoretical underpinning of the model was developed by considering factors other than gender that could influence an individual worker's wage.

In Chapter 3, "The Deliverable," I presented a detailed discussion of what considerations should precede any empirical analysis. I argued for the following:

1. Develop a well-defined research question.

2. Determine in advance what answers are needed.

3. Review research by others to determine what methodologies have been tested and what answers are already known.

4. Identify what information (data) is needed to answer the research question.

5. Determine what analytical methods, for example, regression, are most suited for the analysis.

6. Determine the format and structure of the expected final deliverable (report, essay, and so on).

I must insist that no amount of statistical sophistication can compensate for a poorly construed research question or an ill-devised theoretical model. After you have a sound theoretical model, you can adopt the following systematic approach to regression modeling.

Figure 7.1 shows a step-by-step approach to conduct regression analysis. I argue that the regression analysis comes at the end of a process that involves several other significant and intermediary steps. The first step involves having access to data. If you have not collected or acquired the data, the analytic process then begins with data collection.

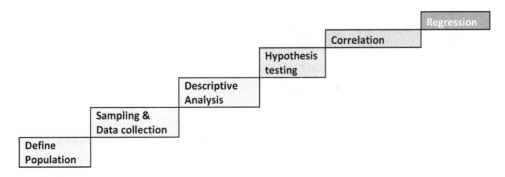

Figure 7.1   Step-by-step approach to regression analysis

You must first define the population that needs to be analyzed. For instance, if a school board is interested in determining the factors influencing the dropout rates from schools in the district, the population for that project will include all schools in the district. The next step is to sample the population. One can conduct a random sample, a stratified random sample, or other advanced sampling procedures, which are beyond the scope of this text. Refer to Batterham and Greg (2005) for further readings on determining sample sizes for your work.[10]

After you have identified a representative sample, you must design, test, and execute a survey questionnaire, either in print or online. What follows is collecting responses and properly coding them in a database. After the database is ready, it is subjected to analytics, including regression modeling.

This book assumes you already have access to data. I therefore do not cover material on data collection and survey design. After the data is ready to be analyzed, you proceed with descriptive analysis. In this step, you generate tabulations, cross tabulations, and charts to summarize data. The purpose of descriptive analysis is to get appreciation for the data set, so that when you estimate models or conduct hypothesis testing, you possess an intuitive sense of what lies in the data.

Recall the earlier discussion in Chapters 4 and 5 about teaching evaluations. The tabulations in Chapter 4 and graphics in Chapter 5 offer examples of descriptive analysis.

Jumping straight to regression modelling could result in errors that may not become obvious to the analyst. Consider the case where age is coded in years and is recorded as 25, 26, and so on. A common practice is to code missing data as 99 in the data set. Thus, respondents who truly are 99 years old and those with missing data for age will all be coded 99. If one were to compute the average age, and assuming there are lots of missing data coded as 99, one will end up with an erroneous estimate of average age. A histogram of the age variable would have highlighted this anomaly by highlighting the unusually large number of respondents aged 99 during the descriptive analysis.

The next steps involve hypothesis testing and correlation analysis in a bivariate or univariate environment. I covered this in Chapter 6. Recall that tabulations in Chapter 4 showed a slight difference in the teaching ratings for male and female instructors. We may be interested in determining whether the difference in teaching evaluations was statistically significant on its own; that is, when we do not consider other relevant factors. I demonstrated how one could use a t-test to determine the statistical significance in average teaching evaluations between male and female instructors.

Finally, you estimate a regression model after conducting descriptive analyses, hypothesis testing, and have already developed some insights about the data. Given the ease with which regression models are estimated using off-the-shelf software, the tendency among many data scientists and researchers is to jump straight to the regression, skipping the necessary intermediary steps, such as hypothesis testing and descriptive analysis. Skipping the intermediary steps is akin to practicing bad data science.

You may wonder why I promote hypothesis testing using t-tests or other tests in a chapter on regression analysis. First, I must point out that regression modeling is also a formal way of conducting hypothesis testing. What differentiates regression from other bivariate tests is that regression models can simultaneously analyze more variables than just two or three. The reason I want you to still conduct hypothesis tests, as illustrated in Chapter 6, is to have the necessary ingredients in hand as you prepare the final deliverable—the report or an essay. I explain the reasons in the following paragraph.

Let us assume you are commissioned to analyze any potential gender bias in wages at a large organization. You are expected to deliver a report that will document your findings. The report will lay out the problem statement in the introduction. In the descriptive analysis section, you will refer to the wage differences that you may have observed between male and female employees. As part of the natural flow in the report, you will then entertain the question if the observed wage difference is statistically significant or otherwise. If the wage difference between males and females is not statistically significant, you may even decide to conclude your report with no further analysis. But, if the wage difference is statistically significant, which a `t-test` would have shown, you will then decide to proceed further with the analysis to explore the determinants of wage differences. Regression model could be the next step. However, the initial hypothesis testing using `t-tests` will provide the justification to proceed further with the analysis.

Learning to Speak Regression

Regression models use specific terms to describe the processes. To be proficient in regression analysis, we need to know the unique terms and be comfortable with their usage. The variable of interest, the one being analyzed, is called the *dependent variable*, which is usually denoted by Y. Other variables that explain the phenomenon or behavior of interest are called the explanatory variables or the *independent variables*, which are usually denoted by X. Earlier, I spoke of wage being defined by years of schooling. In this example, wage is the dependent variable or the response variable. Education attainment, measured in years of schooling, serves as the explanatory variable or the independent variable. Wage is also referred to as *regressand* and education is referred to as the *regressor*.

We often explain regression models by describing the relationship between the dependent variable and the explanatory variable/s. For wage and education, I describe the relationship as follows: Wage is a function of education. In simple terms, I am saying that wage is determined by years of schooling. If I was to represent the dependent variable (wage) as y and the explanatory variable (years of schooling) as x, I will say that y is a function of x.

There will be times when a dependent variable, such as wage, is being informed by more than one explanatory variable. In such circumstances, I would say that y is a function of x_1 and x_2. Mathematically, we use the notation shown in Equation 7.1:

$$y = f(x_1, x_2) \quad \textbf{Equation 7.1}$$

Equation 7.1 suggests that the dependent variable y is informed by not one but two variables.

In the early days, regression models often used only a single variable as an explanatory variable. Lack of data and limited computing power made estimating large and complex models difficult or impossible. Because we now experience a data deluge, the abundance of data allows us to use not one or two, but several variables.

In the instance where we use only two explanatory variables x_1 and x_2, we can represent this as a statistical relationship, as shown in Equation 7.2.

$$y = \beta_0 + \beta_1 x_1 + \beta_2 x_2 + \varepsilon \quad \textbf{Equation 7.2}$$

y in Equation 7.2 is the dependent variable, and x_1 and x_2 are the explanatory variables.

Notice in Equation 7.2 the other entities that need explaining. β_1 relates to x_1 and it defines the relationship between x_1, which is an explanatory variable, and the dependent variable y while I control for the other explanatory variable, x_2. Similarly, β_2 accounts for the relationship between x_2, the second explanatory variable, and y, the dependent variable, while I control for the first explanatory variable, x_1.

β_0 is the conditional mean or the mean value of y when both x_1 and x_2 are set to 0. Recall the example of education and wages: If y is wage, x_1 is the years of schooling, and x_2 is the years of experience, then β_0 will represent the average wage of workers with zero years of schooling and no experience.

ε is the error term, which accounts for the residuals or what is not explained by the regression model. Let us assume that I have estimated a regression model using education and experience as the explanatory variables. Using the same model, I forecast the wages of individuals based on the years of schooling and years of experience. I then determine the difference between the actual value and forecasted values for wages. The difference between the two is called the *error term* or *residuals*.

I must mention that the regression model being explained here is often referred to as linear regression. This implies that the regression model will generate a straight (linear) "best-fit" line to approximate the relationship between the dependent and explanatory variables. Other more advanced regression models, not discussed in Chapter 7, are quite capable of capturing the inherently non-linear relationships.

The Math Behind Regression

The relation between variables can be described either as a *functional relationship* or a *statistical relationship*. I restrict the conversation here to a bivariate scenario where one variable is the dependent variable (y) and the other is the explanatory variable (x). A functional relationship between two variables is represented as a mathematical formula and is of the form shown in Equation 7.3:

$$y = f(x) \quad \textbf{Equation 7.3}$$

I would interpret the preceding as y is a function of x, implying that y is explained by x.

Therefore, an example could be $y = 2x$, which suggests that when x increases by 1, y increases by 2. I plot the relationship in Figure 7.2.

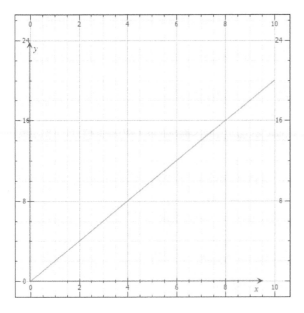

Figure 7.2 Example of a functional relationship

Unlike a functional relationship, a statistical relationship is not a perfect one that would result in a straight line where the entire observed points lie on the line. Usually, observations in a statistical relationship do not fall directly on the line approximating the relationship. This is because a statistical relationship approximates a functional relationship. Also, whereas a functional relationship may return a clean straight line, a statistical relationship may not be as smooth as a functional relationship. I illustrate this in Figure 7.3, which shows that the observed points scatter around the straight line that approximates the relationship. In this particular case, I have plotted the relationship between housing prices (Y) and the built-up area in square feet (X). Equation 7.4 shows the hypothesized relationship:

$$Price = f(Area) \quad \textbf{Equation 7.4}$$

A regression line is very much like the line in Figure 7.3, which captures the statistical relationship between two variables. We can see that larger homes sell for higher price. The scattering of points around the line represents the variations in the dependent variable. We can see in Figure 7.3 that most points do not fall exactly on the regression line.

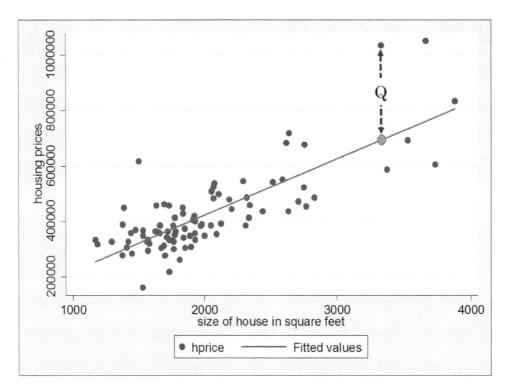

Figure 7.3   A scatter plot of housing prices and sizes with a regression line

The regression model attempts to minimize the deviation (difference) between the actual observation and its corresponding location on the regression line. I have identified the deviation for one particular observation in Figure 7.3 and labeled it as Q. The process to generate a regression line that minimizes the sum of all such possible deviations is called the *ordinary least squares method*, which I will explain in a bit.

You have a choice at this stage in the chapter. You can proceed to the next section to learn about the guts of the regression models. However, if math was not your favorite subject in high school, I offer an alternative and encourage you to skip to the section, "Regression in Action." For those who like to learn by doing and not be burdened by math, skipping to the aforementioned section is a good choice. Others are welcome to join us to learn about the math behind regression analysis in the following section.

Ordinary Least Squares Method

Let us consider a regression model with one explanatory variable. The dependent variable (y) is the housing price and the explanatory variable is square footage of the built-up area (x). The model is expressed as shown in Equation 7.5:

$$y_i = \beta_0 + \beta_1 x_i + \varepsilon_i \quad \textbf{Equation 7.5}$$

y_i represents the dependent variable for the ith observation; that is, a particular house in the data set. y_1 is therefore the price of the first housing unit in the data set. x_i stands for the explanatory variable in the ith observation. x_1 is therefore the square footage of the built-up area of the first housing unit in the data set. Table 7.1 presents the first 10 observations from a sample data set of housing prices.

Table 7.1 A Sample of 10 Observations from a Dataset of Housing Prices

Observation	Price ($)	Size (sft)
1	435000	2438
2	536500	2076
3	276950	1374
4	282750	1448
5	540850	2514
6	676098	2754
7	482125	2067
8	456750	1731
9	298700	1767
10	348000	1890

β_1 is the estimated parameter or the slope of the regression line. It represents the relationship between the explanatory variable (x), that is, square footage, and the housing prices. β_1 informs us of the impact of a change in square footage on housing prices. β_0 is the intercept of the regression line. It is also referred to as the *constant*. Theoretically speaking, it is the *conditional mean* of the dependent variable. It is the average value conditional upon the explanatory variables. In the housing example, β_0 represents the mean housing price conditional upon square footage of the built-up area. Mathematically, it is the mean price of housing when the built-up area equals 0, which effectively implies that β_0 represents the value of an empty lot with zero square footage for built-up space.

ε_i is the random error term for the ith observation. It is also referred to as the residual and represents the difference between the actual price for a housing unit and the estimated price from a regression model. It is represented as Q in Figure 7.3. The regression model requires us to minimize the error term, or to have its expected value as 0. Mathematically, I represent the expected mean as $E\{\varepsilon_i\} = 0$.

Another property of the regression model requires the error term to have constant variance. This implies that the variance of the error term does not increase or decrease in a systematic manner. This property is called *homoscedasticity*, which I discuss later in this chapter.

Mathematically, constant variance is expressed as $\sigma^2\{\varepsilon_i\} = \sigma^2$, suggesting that variance does not change with observations.

Regression models require that individual observations are not correlated. In the housing example, I would like the price of one housing unit to be independent of another unit. In a regression model, such assumption implies that the error terms are not correlated. Mathematically, the covariance between ε_i and ε_j is expected to be 0; that is, $\sigma\{\varepsilon_i,\varepsilon_j\} = 0$ for all $i, j; i \neq j$. In simple terms, I have stated that the residuals are not correlated.

The model in Equation 7.5 is called a *simple* (only one predictor) *linear in the parameters* (because no parameter appears as an exponent or is multiplied or divided by another parameter), *and linear in predictor variable* (the explanatory variable appears only in the first power) regression model. It is also referred to as the *first-order model*.

Because the expected value of the random error term is zero ($E\{\varepsilon_i\} = 0$), mathematically I can derive the model as shown in Equation 7.6:

$$E\{y_i\} = E\{\beta_0 + \beta_1 x_i + \varepsilon_i\}$$
$$= E\{\beta_0 + \beta_1 x_i\} + E\{\varepsilon_i\} \qquad \textbf{Equation 7.6}$$
$$= E\{\beta_0 + \beta_1 x_i\} + 0 = \beta_0 + \beta_1 x_i$$
$$E\{y_i\} = \beta_0 + \beta_1 x_i$$

For the housing price example, Equation 7.7 shows the estimated regression equation.

$$y = 16246 + 203x \quad \textbf{Equation 7.7}$$

The β_0 equals \$16,246 in Equation 7.7. This is the value of a house with zero square footage of built-up space. Essentially, I am referring to the price of an empty lot. β_1 in Equation 7.7 equals \$203. This implies that the price per square foot is \$203. Thus, the price of a house with 1500 square feet in built space is estimated as follows:

$$y = 16246 + 203 * 1500 = 320746$$

Let us now see how the model is derived. We are interested in the deviation of y_i from its expected value obtained from the model, as shown in Equation 7.8.

$$y_i - E(y_i) = y_i - (\beta_0 + \beta_1 x_i) \quad \textbf{Equation 7.8}$$

We consider the sum of n such squared deviations, where n is the number of observations in the data set. We are squaring the deviations because some deviation will be positive and others negative. Squaring the deviations guarantees a positive value. Consider Equation 7.9:

$$Q = \sum_{i=1}^{n}(y_i - (\beta_0 + \beta_1 x_i))^2 \quad \textbf{Equation 7.9}$$

The least squares method returns the estimates for β_0 and β_1 as b_0 and b_1 that minimize Q. Therefore, in Equation 7.10, $\bar{x}$ and $\bar{y}$ are the respective means of x and y:

$$b_1 = \frac{\sum (x_i - \bar{x})(y_i - \bar{y})}{\sum (x_i - \bar{x})^2}$$

Equation 7.10

$$b_0 = \bar{y} - b_1 \bar{x}$$

Estimating Parameters by Hand

Let us consider a simple example of two variables x and y. I estimate the regression parameters b_0 and b_1 by hand and present the calculations in Table 7.2. The mean for x is 42.4 and for y is 13.9. The third column in the table presents the difference between x_i and the mean value for x. The fourth column does the same for y. The other column headings are self-explanatory.

Table 7.2 Regression Model Calculations for a Simple Example

y	x	$x_i - \bar{x}$	$y_i - \bar{y}$	$(x_i - \bar{x}) * (y_i - \bar{y})$	$(x_i - \bar{x})^2$
12	35	−7.4	−1.9	14.06	54.76
14	48	5.6	0.1	0.56	31.36
18	54	11.6	4.1	47.56	134.56
8	22	−20.4	−5.9	120.36	416.16
19	66	23.6	5.1	120.36	556.96
15	45	2.6	1.1	2.86	6.76
7	18	−24.4	−6.9	168.36	595.36
16	48	5.6	2.1	11.76	31.36
19	55	12.6	5.1	64.26	158.76
11	33	−9.4	−2.9	27.26	88.36
				$\Sigma(x_1 - \bar{x}) * \Sigma(y_i - \bar{y})$ = 577.4	$\Sigma(x_1 - \bar{x})^2$ = 2074.4

Thus,

$$b_1 = \frac{577.4}{2074.4} = 0.27835$$

$$b_0 = 13.9 - .27835 * 42.4 = 2.0980$$

The estimated regression equation is expressed as shown in Equation 7.11:

$$\hat{y} = b_0 + b_1 x = 2.098 + 0.279x \quad \textbf{Equation 7.11}$$

$\hat{y}$ is the value of the dependent variable predicted by the regression model for a given value of x.

Residuals (Error Terms) and Their Properties

The ith residual is the difference between the observed value y_i and the corresponding value predicted by the model, $\hat{y}_i$. The estimated value for the first observation in Table 7.3 is expressed as follows:

$$\hat{y} = 2.098 + 0.279 * 35 = 11.84$$

The residual is the difference between the estimated value and the actual observation, given by:

$$\varepsilon_1 = y_1 - \hat{y}_1 = 12 - 11.84 = 0.16$$

Table 7.3 shows the calculations for the rest of the data.

Table 7.3   Calculations for Residuals and Forecasted Values

y	$\hat{y}$	Residuals	Residuals^2
12	11.840	0.160	0.026
14	15.459	−1.459	2.128
18	17.129	0.871	0.759
8	8.222	−0.222	0.049
19	20.469	−1.469	2.158
15	14.624	0.376	0.142
7	7.108	−0.108	0.012
16	15.459	0.541	0.293
19	17.407	1.593	2.537
11	11.284	−0.284	0.080

The error term (residuals) obtained from a regression model has the following properties:

- Sum of all residuals equals 0; that is, $\sum_{i=1}^{n} e_i = 0$.

- The sum of squared residuals, $\sum_{i=1}^{n} e_i^2$, is the minimum for the regression line. This implies that no other line will minimize the sum of squared residuals than the regression line.

- The sum of observed values equals the sum of the fitted values; that is, $\sum_{i=1}^{n} y_i = \sum_{i=1}^{n} \hat{y}_i$.

- The sum of the weighted residuals is zero; that is, $\sum_{i=1}^{n} x_i e_i = 0$ and $\sum_{i=1}^{n} \hat{y}_i e_i = 0$.

Is the Model Worth Anything?

The purpose of the regression analysis is not only to find the relationship between two or more variables, but also to determine whether the relationships are statistically significant. The statistical tests are based on the comparison between the predicted values and the observed values in the data set. Put simply, the analysis of the goodness of fit is primarily an analysis of the residuals.

In the end, we would like to say how good our model is. A commonly used proxy for the goodness of fit is the coefficient of determination. The following discussion leads to estimating the coefficient of determination.

Errors Squared

Let me first introduce the term *Sum of Squared Errors* (SSE), which is the sum of the squared residuals. Mathematically, SSE is represented as shown in Equation 7.12:

$$SSE = \sum_{i=1}^{n} (y_i - \hat{y}_i)^2 = \sum_{i=1}^{n} e_i^2 \quad \textbf{Equation 7.12}$$

The SSE is used to determine the *Mean Squared Error* (MSE). I divide the SSE with the degrees of freedom (DOF) to determine MSE. In the preceding example, I have lost two DOF. The MSE is expressed as shown in Equation 7.13:

$$MSE = \frac{SSE}{n-2} = \frac{\sum_{i=1}^{n} (y_i - \hat{y}_i)^2}{n-2}$$

$$= \frac{\sum_{i=1}^{n} e_i^2}{n-2}$$

$$= \frac{8.183}{10-2} = 1.023 \quad \textbf{Equation 7.13}$$

The model fit can be expressed as the *Standard Error* of the model, which is calculated by taking the square root of the MSE.

Coefficient of Determination r^2

The purpose of a statistical model is to capture or at least approximate the dynamics of the underlying data. We are interested in explaining the variance in the dependent variable, which is a proxy for how well the model fits to data. The coefficient of determination (r^2) is the most commonly used measure of the goodness of fit. It involves two entities, the Sum of Squared Errors, which I already explained, and the *Total Sum of Squares* (SSTO), which is the sum of squared differences between the dependent variables and its mean $SSTO = \sum_{i=1}^{n}(y_i - \bar{y})^2$. Mathematically, the coefficient of determination is computed as shown in Equation 7.14:

$$r^2 = 1 - \frac{SSE}{SSTO} = 1 - \frac{\sum_{i=1}^{n}(y_i - \hat{y}_i)^2}{\sum_{i=1}^{n}(y_i - \bar{y})^2} \qquad \textbf{Equation 7.14}$$

The r^2 for our worked-out example is computed as follows:

$$r^2 = 1 - \frac{8.183}{168.9} = 0.95155$$

I interpret the goodness of fit for our model as follows: The model explains 95% variance in the data. r^2 is bounded by 0 and 1 with higher values suggesting a better fit.

Numerous texts in statistics have mentioned several arbitrary thresholds for r^2. Some have gone as far as to suggest that an r^2 of less than 0.5 suggests a poor fit. Some have suggested that r^2 should be higher than 0.7 for a model to be considered a good fit. It is increasingly important to realize for data scientists, especially those who work with behavioral data, that there is absolutely no foundation for insisting on such arbitrary thresholds. The decision-making processes of human beings are very complex and it is naïve to expect a statistical model to explain 80 to 90% variance in human behavior.

One should always consult existing literature to see examples of model fits. In microeconomics, the model fits often range from 0.1 to 0.5. It is extremely rare to see a model with an r^2 of 0.9 in models related to human behavior. At the same time, in engineering studies involving measurements on materials, one finds significantly higher values for r^2.

Are the Relationships Statistically Significant?

After estimating a regression model, you would like to know whether the estimated coefficients bear any statistical significance. You need to undertake hypothesis testing to see whether the outcome of the model is an artifact of chance or it reflects a sound relationship. I will build on the discussion on hypothesis testing covered in Chapter 6. The fundamental concepts remain the same as in Chapter 6.

Recall Equation 7.7 from the housing price example in which I estimated values for b_0 and b_1. I found that housing price increases by \$203 for a square foot increase in the built-up area and that the land value equaled \$16,246. How would we know whether these estimates are statistically significant? Fortunately, we can conduct a `t-test` to determine the statistical significance of the estimated parameter.

Assume that the true value of an estimated parameter is zero, but we have obtained a different value from the regression model. We set the null hypothesis to state that the value of the estimated parameter is zero. The alternative hypothesis states that the true value does not equal zero. Equation 7.15 shows this mathematically:

$$H_0 : \beta_1 = 0$$

Equation 7.15

$$H_a : \beta_1 \neq 0$$

If $\beta_1 = 0$, it implies that there exists no linear relationship between the dependent and the explanatory variables. Let us first estimate the variance ($s^2\{b_1\}$) of the sampling distribution of b_1, which is an estimate of β_1. Continuing with our worked-out example, we can obtain the *standard error of the estimate* $s\{b_1\}$ as follows:

$$s^2\{b_1\} = \frac{MSE}{\sum (x_i - \bar{x})^2} = \frac{1.023}{2074.4} = 4.9315 * 10^{-4}$$

$$s\{b_1\} = \sqrt[2]{4.9315 * 10^{-4}} = 2.2207 * 10^{-2}$$

Statistical theory informs us that the point estimator $s^2\{b_1\}$ is an unbiased estimator of $\sigma^2\{b_1\}$. The square root of $s^2\{b_1\}$ will give us the point estimator of $\sigma\{b_1\}$. I can then use t-statistic to test the hypothesis:

$$t^* = \frac{b_1}{s\{b_1\}} = \frac{.2783}{.0222} = 12.536$$

After I have obtained the t-statistic, I can use the following decision rules to test the hypothesis. You will notice that these tests are similar to the tests I conducted in Chapter 6.

Remember, our null hypothesis states that the estimated coefficient is equal to zero and that there is no relationship between the dependent and explanatory variables. I will conclude the null to be true if the calculated value for the test is less than the critical value obtained from the t-distribution for the relevant degrees of freedom. Equation 7.16 shows that, mathematically, for a two-tailed test:

$$\text{Conclude } H_0 \text{ if } |t^*| \leq \left(1 - \frac{\alpha}{2}; n - k\right)$$

Equation 7.16

$$\text{Conclude } H_a \text{ if } |t^*| > \left(1 - \frac{\alpha}{2}; n - k\right)$$

α is the level of significance, n is the number of observations, and k is the lost degrees of freedom. For a 95% level of significance, 10 observations, and 2 lost degrees of freedom, the critical value from t-distribution is

$$\text{For } n = 10; k = 2; \alpha = 0.05, \ t_{critical}\left(1 - \frac{.05}{2}; 10 - 2\right) = 2.306$$

Because 12.536 > 2.306, I conclude H_a and reject the null hypothesis of no statistical significant relationship between the dependent and the explanatory variable. Note that I cannot conclude that we accept the alternative hypothesis. The way statistical tests are structured, we can either reject or fail to reject the null hypothesis. However, we may never accept or reject the alternative hypothesis.

For large samples, and again there are no fixed thresholds for how large a sample should be to be considered statistically large, the critical value for the t-test is 1.96.

Inferences Concerning β_0

In statistical analyses, discussing the statistical significance of the constant term (β_0) is rather uncommon. This is primarily because in most applications the constant term does not contribute to the interpretation of the model. Still, I discuss this here so that the topic is covered in full and this chapter serves as a basic reference.

Equation 7.17 presents the mathematical formulation to conduct statistical tests for significance of the constant term.

$$s^2\{b_0\} = MSE\left[\frac{1}{n} + \frac{\overline{x^2}}{\sum(x_i - \overline{x})^2}\right] \qquad \textbf{Equation 7.17}$$

For our worked-out example, we have:

$$s^2\{b_0\} = 1.023\left(\frac{1}{10} + \frac{42.4^2}{2074.4}\right) = 0.98887$$

$$s\{b_0\} = \sqrt[2]{s^2\{b_0\}} = \sqrt[2]{0.98887} = 0.99442$$

$$t^* = \frac{b_0}{s\{b_0\}} = \frac{2.09}{.99442} = 2.1$$

Should the Model Receive an F?

Let us now test the hypothesis that the coefficients of all variables in the regression model, except the intercept, are jointly 0. That is, taken together the variables included in the model have no predictive value. When the probability value of F-statistics is very small, we can reject the null hypothesis that the set of right-hand side variables has no predictive utility. An F-test is conducted as follows:

$$F = \frac{SSR/1}{SSE/(n-2)} = \frac{\sum_{i=1}^{n}(\hat{y}_i - \overline{y})^2/1}{\sum_{i=1}^{n}(y_i - \hat{y}_i)^2/(n-2)} = \frac{160.7/1}{8.183/8} = 157.1$$

where SSR is the sum of squares due to regression and SSE is the sum of squared errors. In our worked-out example with only one explanatory variable, we are testing the hypothesis:

$$H_0: \beta_1 = 0$$
$$H_a: \beta_1 \neq 0$$

In multiple linear regression, when we have more than one explanatory variable, we test the null hypothesis that all estimated coefficients are equal to 0. The decision rule is stated as shown in Equation 7.18:

$$\text{Conclude } H_0 \text{ if } |F^*| \leq \left(1 - \frac{\alpha}{2}; 1, n - 2\right)$$

Equation 7.18

$$\text{Conclude } H_a \text{ if } |F^*| > \left(1 - \frac{\alpha}{2}; 1, n - 2\right)$$

For $n = 10$, $\alpha = .05$, $F(.95; 1,8) = 5.32$. Because $157.1 > 5.32$, I reject the null hypothesis. Again, remember in this particular case, I only had one explanatory variable in the model.

Regression in Action

Let us now test-drive some regression models. Because some readers may have opted to skip through the technical details to see how models are estimated, I believe it will help to repeat the important criteria for model fit. The following items are important in reading the output from a regression model:

- **R-squared** (r^2): The overall fit of the model is determined by R-squared or the adjusted R-squared. Its value varies between 0 and 1. When comparing models, a higher R-squared means a better fit.

- **P-value**: The p-value is the probability associated with a statistical test. Usually, we use 95% level as our benchmark. Hence, we conclude a statistically significant finding when the p-value associated with a test is less than 0.05.

- **F-test**: When the p-value associated with the F-test is less than 0.05, we conclude that taken together the explanatory variables in the regression model are collectively different from 0.

- **T-statistic**: This evaluates the significance of an individual coefficient corresponding to a variable. If the t-test for a variable is greater than the critical value from the t-distribution (usually 1.96 for a two-tailed test; see Chapter 6 for details), we conclude that there exists a statistically significant relationship between the dependent and explanatory variable. Also, we can rely on the p-value, also reported in the regression output, for the corresponding t-test. If the p-value is less than 0.05, we can conclude a statistically significant relationship between the dependent and explanatory variables.

I begin with a small data set about the determinants of housing sales.

This Just In: Bigger Homes Sell for More

I start with an example of the determinants of housing prices that might establish my bona fides as a professor who teaches in the "department of obvious conclusions." I am interested in determining the answer to the question: Do large homes sell for more?

The dependent variable is housing prices. The explanatory variables include the number of bedrooms, lot size, square footage of the built-up area, and a categorical variable that controls for the architectural style of the residential unit (see Table 7.4). The data set comprises 88 observations.

Table 7.4   Variables Included in the Housing Dataset

Variable	Description
hprice	housing price
bdrms	number of bedrooms
lotsize	size of lot in square feet
sqrft	size of house in square feet
colonial	=1 if home is colonial style
lprice	log(price)
llotsize	log(lot size)
lsqrft	log(square feet)
lnrooms	log(bed rooms)

In this chapter, I report the Stata code used to generate the output. The code for other software is available from the book's website under Chapter 7.

I present basic summary statistics in Table 7.5. The following Stata code highlights the use of a user-written command, **outreg2**.[11] It is a powerful command to generate tabular outputs. Roy Wada is the programmer behind **outreg2**. You can type **findit outreg2** within Stata to install it.

```
outreg2 using 88h_1.doc , label sum(log)  ///
eqkeep(mean sd min max)  replace
```

The advantage of using outreg2 is that it generates tables directly as Word documents, thus eliminating the need for cumbersome copying and pasting that requires painful formatting adjustments.

Table 7.5   Descriptive Statistics of Housing Data

Variables	mean	sd	min	max
assessed value, $1000s	315.7	95.31	198.7	708.6
number of bedrooms	3.568	0.841	2	7
size of lot in square feet	9,020	10,174	1,000	92,681
size of house in square feet	2,014	577.2	1,171	3,880
=1 if home is colonial style	0.693	0.464	0	1
log(price)	12.91	0.304	11.99	13.87
log(assessed value)	5.718	0.262	5.292	6.563
log(lotsize)	8.905	0.544	6.908	11.44
log(sqrft)	7.573	0.259	7.066	8.264
Square of beds	13.43	6.873	4	49
Log of bedrooms	1.246	0.227	0.693	1.946
House price	425,642	148,934	160,950	1.051e+06

Let us have a look at the numbers reported in Table 7.5. The average house price is $425,642 with a standard deviation of $148,934. The average number of bedrooms is 3.6. The average lot size is 9,020 square feet. Right away, we notice that there is something odd about the average lot size. Usually in the U.S. and Canada, the average lot size varies between 3,000 to 6,000 square feet. The reported lot size is unusually large in the data. This becomes even more suspicious when I compare the average lot size with the average built-up space, which is 2,014 square feet.

We can learn more about the lot size by plotting a histogram. The histogram in Figure 7.4 reveals that a very small number of very large properties (lot size over 80,000 sft) are skewing the data set. We need to make a call here regarding how representative these properties are with respect to the sample. Should we declare these observations as outliers and conduct the analysis after excluding them? I leave the answer to this question to you. The following Stata command generates a histogram of lot sizes.

```
hist lotsize, bin(10) percent
```

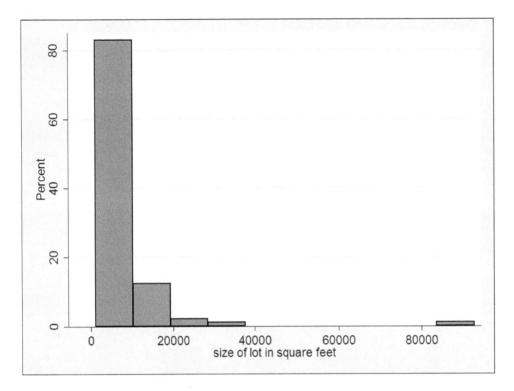

Figure 7.4   Histogram of lot size

Sample Regression Output in Stata

I would like to estimate housing price as a function of bedrooms, lot size, square footage of the built-up area, and colonial-style home. The resulting output is presented in Figure 7.5. The output is similar to the one generated by other software, such as R, SAS, and SPSS. The output is organized in three components. The one on the top left presents the analysis of variance and summarizes the values for SSE ($6.25 * 10^{11}$), SSTO ($1.93 * 10^{12}$), MSE ($7.53 * 10^{9}$), and degrees of freedom (df).

The component on the top right summarizes the overall goodness of fit statistics. It advises us that the data set comprises 88 observations. The F-statistics equal to 43.25 and the associated probability is less than 0.0001. Recall the earlier discussion regarding the F-statistics and hypothesis testing using the F distribution (Equation 7.18). The probability of getting an F-test value higher than what I have obtained in Figure 7.5 (43.25) is less than 0.05, therefore I reject the null hypothesis that collectively the coefficients in the model effectively equal to 0.

The coefficient of determination (Equation 7.14) or r^2 is represented as R-squared in Figure 7.5. The goodness-of-fit of the model (R-squared) is .676, which suggests that the model explains 67.6% variance in housing prices. I would consider it an excellent fit for the model. The additional statistic is the adjusted R-squared, which discounts the R-squared for the additional explanatory variables used in the model. The adjusted R-squared is more conservative than the R-squared because it penalizes the R-squared for using additional explanatory variables.

The following Stata code regresses the housing price on bedrooms, lot size, square footage of the built-up space, and a binary variable indicating the colonial style of the structure.

```
reg hprice bdrms lotsize sqrft colonial
```

Source	SS	df	MS			
Model	1.3041e+12	4	3.2603e+11			
Residual	6.2565e+11	83	7.5380e+09			
Total	1.9298e+12	87	2.2181e+10			

```
Number of obs =     88
F( 4,  83)    = 43.25
Prob > F      = 0.0000
R-squared     = 0.6758
Adj R-squared = 0.6602
Root MSE      = 86822
```

hprice	Coef.	Std. Err.	t	P>|t|	[95% Conf. Interval]	
bdrms	15956.22	13797.13	1.16	0.251	-11485.71	43398.16
lotsize	3.009957	.931844	3.23	0.002	1.156557	4.863357
sqrft	180.1443	19.34047	9.31	0.000	141.6769	218.6118
colonial	19887.54	21224.03	0.94	0.351	-22326.21	62101.29
_cons	-34983.47	42925.01	-0.81	0.417	-120359.6	50392.65

Figure 7.5 Regression model output from Stata software

The section at the bottom of Figure 7.5 reports the estimated coefficients and tests for their statistical significance. The coefficients for bedrooms (bdrms) is 15956.22. I illustrated how to estimate the coefficients in a simple regression model in Equation 7.10. This suggests that each additional bedroom adds $15,956 to the price of the house, all else being equal. Here all else being equal implies that if the built-up area, lot size, and the style of the house are kept constant, one additional bedroom will contribute $15,956 to the price. The next column reports standard errors for each estimated coefficient, which is used to conduct the test for statistical significance (t-test). I would like to refer you to the earlier discussion about calculating standard errors of coefficients and t-statistics that followed Equation 7.15.

The calculated value for the t-test is obtained by dividing the coefficient by its standard error. For the variable bdrms, I have:

$$t = \frac{15956.22}{13797.13} = 1.16$$

Because the calculated value of the t-test is less than the one corresponding to $\alpha = 0.95$, that is, 1.99, I fail to reject the null hypothesis that the coefficient for bdrms is equal to 0. The remaining coefficients are interpreted the same way. I see that the lot size and the built-up area are statistically significant determinants of house price because the calculated value of the `t-test` is greater than the one obtained by the theoretical t distribution.

Reporting Style Matters

It is rather odd that most books on statistics report regression results formatted the same way as the output from a software. However, academic papers and professional reports seldom report regression results the way they are reported in Figure 7.5. Often, the preferred format for reporting regression results includes reporting of the estimated coefficients, their standard errors in parentheses, and asterisks indicating the goodness of fit for each parameter. Some overall goodness of fit, such as the `R-squared` and number of observations are also reported at the bottom of the table.

This book reports the results formatted the way they should be reported in a publication. Table 7.6 presents the output for the same model discussed earlier but formatted for publication.

Table 7.6   Regression Output Formatted for Publication

Variables	(1) House price
number of bedrooms	15,956
	(13,797)
size of lot in square feet	3.010***
	(0.932)
size of house in square feet	180.1***
	(19.34)
=1 if home is colonial style	19,888
	(21,224)
Constant	−34,983
	(42,925)
Observations	88
R squared	0.676

Standard errors in parentheses

*** p<0.01, ** p<0.05, * p<0.1

Housing Prices: Do Bigger Homes Sell for More?

I use the housing prices to explain the mechanics of regression. Let us begin with a simple model, which models housing price as a function of the number of bedrooms. I do not include other explanatory variables in the model. Furthermore, I treat the bedroom variable as a continuous variable in the first model and as a categorical variable in the second model. When a variable is introduced in the model as a categorical variable, the model estimates a separate coefficient for each level of the variable except one, which it treats as the base case.

Let us first see how housing prices differ by the number of bedrooms by calculating mean housing price for each level of bedroom variable. You can see in Table 7.7 that there are no homes in the data set with one bedroom. The average price for a two-bedroom house is $364,413. It increases to $379,870 for a three-bedroom house. The difference in price for a two-bedroom and a three-bedroom house is $15,557. Note that there are only four units in the data set with two bedrooms and one unit each with six and seven bedrooms.

Table 7.7   House Price by Number of Bedrooms

number of bedrooms	House price
2	364313 (57641) [4]
3	379870 (79965) [42]
4	413487 (112656) [33]
5	751105 (234667) [7]
6	449500 (.) [1]
7	692375 (.) [1]
Total	425642 (148934) [88]

Arithmetic Mean (SD) [n]

Continuous Versus Categorical Explanatory Variables

Now let us estimate two regression models with housing price as the dependent variable and the number of bedrooms treated first as a continuous variable and then as a categorical variable. Results are reported in Table 7.8. The first model reports the results for bedrooms being a continuous variable. The model suggests that the price of a housing unit increases by $89,936 for each additional bedroom. There are no other variables in the model; hence, I cannot use the phrase *all else being equal*. The constant (β_0) is $104,735, which is the price of the empty lot or a house with zero bedrooms. The model explains 25.8% variance in housing prices.

Table 7.8   Regression Model of Housing Prices as a Function of Bedrooms

Variables	(1) hprice	(2) hprice
3.bdrms		15,557
		(58,035)
4.bdrms		49,175
		(58,720)

Variables	(1) hprice	(2) hprice
5.bdrms		386,793***
		(69,516)
6.bdrms		85,188
		(124,001)
7.bdrms		328,063***
		(124,001)
bdrms	89,936***	
	(16,440)	
Constant	104,735*	364,312***
	(60,252)	(55,455)
Observations	88	88
R-squared	0.258	0.477

Standard errors in parentheses

*** p<0.01, ** p<0.05, * p<0.1

The second model carries significantly more coefficients. Note that there is no coefficient reported for two-bedrooms, which serves as the base case and in fact its value is reported by the constant in the model, which is $364,312. Given that the only other information in the model is the number of bedrooms treated as a categorical variable, the constant represents the base case, which is the average price for a house with two bedrooms.

Compare the value for Constant in the model labeled 2 in Table 7.8 and the average price of a house with two bedrooms reported in Table 7.7. The numbers are identical except for the rounding. Model 2 reports the coefficient for a three-bedroom house to be $15,557. It suggests that all else being equal, a three-bedroom house will sell for $15,557 more than the base case, which is a two-bedroom house. Again, compare the results with Table 7.7 and you will notice that the price difference between a two- and three-bedroom house is indeed $15,557. Thus, when no other variable is included in the model, a regression model with a categorical variable effectively reports the average or mean values. In the presence of other explanatory variables, the reported coefficients are conditional upon other factors in the model being held constant.

Notice that Table 7.8 carries additional information in the footnote. It advises us that the table reports standard errors for each coefficient in parentheses. It also provides us with a key to interpret the statistical significance of each variable. If the coefficient is missing an asterisk, it is not statistically significant at the 90% level. A single asterisk identifies statistical significance at 90% level. Two asterisks suggest statistical significance at 95% level; that is, corresponding to a test of 1.96 or better. Three asterisks suggest even higher statistical significance.

Building a Housing Model Brick-by-Brick

When we have several explanatory variables, a better approach is to introduce each new variable in the model either individually or as a group. Because of the ease of estimating models using the modern statistical software, one may be tempted to simply dump all possible explanatory variables in the model and then cherry-pick to select a subset of explanatory variables in a revised model. This approach reflects bad data science. The choice of explanatory variables must be dictated by theory and not by the model or parameter fit. For this very reason, I do not cover the step-wise modeling approaches in the text, which are essentially tools designed for those who have no fundamental understanding of the problem they are analyzing, but are willing to accept any answer that a heuristic will generate.

I believe that the price of a house is influenced by its size. I have three proxies for size; namely the number of bedrooms, the built-up area, and the lot size. I also believe that architectural style of the house could be a determinant of its price. With this theory in hand, I estimate five separate models and report them in Table 7.9.

I first estimate a simple regression model to regress housing prices on the number of bedrooms. The results are reported in Model 1 in Table 7.9. The model estimates that each additional bedroom will fetch an additional $89,936. The coefficient for bedrooms is statistically significant and the model explains 25.8% variance in housing prices (R-squared).

In Model 2, I introduce square footage of the lot as an explanatory variable in addition to the number of bedrooms. I know from experience that under normal circumstances, adding a bedroom does not change the square footage of the lot. Hence, I do not expect the coefficient for bedroom to change drastically between Models 1 and 2. The model suggests that each additional square foot in lot size will add $4.14 to the price, if the number of bedrooms is held constant. Similarly, each additional bedroom will add $83,104 to the price, if the lot size remains constant.

Model 3 presents an amazing illustration of all else being equal where I regress the housing prices as a function of number of bedrooms and the square footage of the built-up area of the house. Note now that each additional bedroom fetches far less and the coefficient is statistically insignificant. Each additional bedroom will increase the price of the house by $22,037 holding the built-up area constant. However, given that the coefficient for bedrooms is statistically insignificant, I fail to reject the null hypothesis that bedrooms have no impact on housing prices. How is that possible?

The answer to this riddle lies in all else being equal. Our model states that the number of bedrooms has no impact on housing prices when I keep the built-up area constant. If adding a new bedroom does not add more built space, we would have effectively either bisected a room or converted another room to a bedroom. In both circumstances, the actual built space for a unit does not change with the addition of a bedroom. In such circumstances, when the built-up space does not change, the addition of a bedroom is rather meaningless from the price perspective.

Model 3 suggests that each additional square foot of built space will fetch $186.2, while I keep the number of bedrooms constant. The coefficient for built space is statistically significant. Also note that the R-squared jumps from 25.8% in Model 1 to 63.2% in Model 3 suggesting that the square footage of the built-up space is a very strong predictor.

I reintroduce the square footage of the lot size in the model along with the number of bedrooms and the built-up space. Again, I find the number of bedrooms to be statistically insignificant in Model 4, whereas the other two variables are statistically significant. The model fit improves slightly to 67.2%.

Lastly, I introduce Colonial to the model and find that in the presence of the proxies for size, Colonial returns a statistically insignificant coefficient.

The following Stata code generates the output reported in Table 7.9.

```
reg hprice bdrms
outreg2 using 88h_4.doc, label replace
reg hprice bdrms lotsize
outreg2 using 88h_4.doc, label append
reg hprice bdrms sqrft
outreg2 using 88h_4.doc, label append
reg hprice bdrms lotsize sqrft
outreg2 using 88h_4.doc, label append
reg hprice bdrms lotsize sqrft colonial
outreg2 using 88h_4.doc, label append
```

Table 7.9   An Incremental Approach to Building a Model

Variables	(1) House price	(2) House price	(3) House price	(4) House price	(5) House price
number of bedrooms	89,936***	83,104***	22,037	20,086	15,956
	(16,440)	(15,783)	(13,751)	(13,065)	(13,797)
size of lot in square feet		4.144***		2.998***	3.010***
		(1.305)		(0.931)	(0.932)
size of house in square feet			186.2***	178.0***	180.1***
			(20.05)	(19.19)	(19.34)
=1 if home is colonial style					19,888
					(21,224)
Constant	104,735*	91,730	-28,007	-31,567	-34,983
	(60,252)	(57,448)	(45,018)	(42,739)	(42,925)
Observations	88	88	88	88	88
R squared	0.258	0.337	0.632	0.672	0.676

Standard errors in parentheses

*** p<0.01, ** p<0.05, * p<0.1

Don't Throw Out the Baby or the Bath Water

Model 5 in Table 7.9 includes four variables, namely bedrooms, lot size, built space, and Colonial. Bedrooms and Colonial are statistically insignificant, while the other two are statistically significant. Why should not we remove the statistically insignificant coefficients? After all the two variables do not contribute to the model fit. Some would argue that we should remove the statistically insignificant coefficients. I urge strongly against it. If the theoretical model requires a variable to be included, then it should be included, regardless of its statistical significance.

Logs, Levels, Non-Linearities, and Interpretation

The functional form of a model influences its interpretation. Jeffery Wooldridge in *Introductory Econometrics* mentions the four basic combinations of variable types in a regression model and their interpretation.[12] Consider that we can introduce a variable either in its raw form as level or as log transformed. In business and economics, the relationship between two variables is explained as elasticity: that is, the percentage change in one variable with respect to a percentage change in other. This is easily achieved in regression by (natural) log-transforming the dependent and the explanatory variables before regressing them. The five functional forms, including four from Wooldridge, are listed in Table 7.10.

Table 7.10 Variable Transformation and Interpretation in Regression Models

Model Type	Dependent Variable	Explanatory Variable	Interpretation of the Coefficient
Level-level	y	x	$$\Delta y = \beta_1 \Delta x$$ A unit change in x results in a unit change in y. Models presented in Table 7.9 follow this formulation.
Log-log	$Log(y)$	$Log(x)$	$$\%\Delta y = \beta_1 \%\Delta x$$ A percentage change in x results in a percent change in y. This is the classic definition of elasticity.
Log-level	$Log(y)$	x	$$\%\Delta y = (100\beta_1)\Delta x$$ A unit change in x results in a percentage change in y. This formulation is used when the explanatory variable is categorical and the dependent variable is in level or raw format.
Level-log	y	$Log(x)$	$$\Delta y = (\beta_1/100)\%\Delta x$$ A percent change in x results in a unit change in y. This formulation is not used often.

Model Type	Dependent Variable	Explanatory Variable	Interpretation of the Coefficient
Level-Squared	y	x and x^2	$$y = \beta_0 + \beta_1 x + \beta_2 x^2$$ $$\Delta y = -\frac{\beta_1}{2\beta_2} \Delta x$$ This formulation is used to capture nonlinearities. For instance, if wage is modeled as a function of age and age^2, the model will capture the slowing of wage increases with old age.

These concepts are illustrated in Table 7.11, which presents three model formulations. Model 1 presents the elasticity model where I have log transformed the dependent and the explanatory variables. The estimated coefficient is interpreted as elasticity; that is, a percentage change in the built space increases housing price by 0.87%. The second model uses colonial as the explanatory variable while the dependent variable is log-transformed housing price. The estimated coefficient for Colonial homes is 0.118. I multiply the coefficient by 100 to conclude that the Colonial-styled houses sell for 11.8% higher than otherwise. Model 3 attempts to capture the non-linearities in the data set. The positive coefficient for the variable, square of beds, suggests that housing prices are higher for very large homes.

I would like to explain the need for variable transformation. Consider a wage model where the only explanatory variable is experience. The model suggests that the hourly wage rate increases with experience in a particular industry. Let us assume that the minimum wage is $7 and is earned by those without any experience. Let us also assume that on average the wage rate increases by $2 for every additional year of experience. Thus, our model suggests that someone with two years of experience will earn $7 + 2 * 2 = 11$ dollars. And someone with 40 years of experience will earn $87 per hour.

I also know that someone with 40 years of experience will be older. If we are speaking of workers in the manufacturing sector, the experienced old age workers may not be in very high demand. It may turn out that after some point in time, additional experience may not result in higher wages, which may taper off or start declining after some time. This non-linear relationship is common in many sectors and behaviors and can be modeled using a quadratic formulation.

Let us now consider the same wage equation, but this time I account for the fact that wages will not continue to climb with experience. The revised wage (quadratic) equation is as follows.

$$wage = 7 + 2 * experience - .03 * experience^2$$

I plot this relationship in Figure 7.6. I can see that the wage continues to increase with experience up to 33 years in our hypothesized model. After that, any further experience in experience results in a decline in wages.

The regression models are quite capable of capturing such non-linearities. All we need to do is to include the squared term of any variable that we think enjoys a quadratic relationship with the dependent variable. I report the Stata code used to generate the output in Table 7.11.

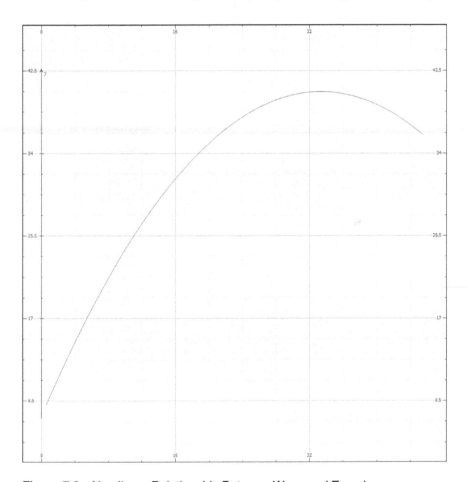

Figure 7.6   Non-linear Relationship Between Wage and Experience

```
reg lprice lsqrft
outreg2 using 88h_5.doc, label replace
reg lprice colonial
outreg2 using 88h_5.doc, label append
reg lprice bdrms bedsq
outreg2 using 88h_5.doc, label append
```

Table 7.11   Model Formulations

Variables	(1) log(price)	(2) log(price)	(3) log(price)
log(sqrft)	0.873***		
	(0.0846)		
=1 if home is colonial style		0.118*	
		(0.0694)	
number of bdrms			-0.0356
			(0.186)
Square of beds			0.0253
			(0.0228)
Constant	-0.975	5.551***	5.421***
	(0.641)	(0.0578)	(0.369)
Observations	88	88	88
R squared	0.553	0.033	0.226

Standard errors in parentheses

*** p<0.01, ** p<0.05, * p<0.1

Does Beauty Pay? Ask the Students

Mirror mirror on the wall, who is the smartest professor of all?

In this section, I present a systematic analysis of the determinants of teaching evaluation scores recorded at the University of Texas. The primary purpose of the analysis is to determine whether teaching evaluation scores are influenced by an instructor's looks. My underlying hypothesis is that attractive instructors receive higher teaching evaluations from students, even when I hold other factors, which could influence teaching evaluations, constant.

Table 7.12 lists the variables and their descriptions in the data set. I have worked with the same data set in Chapters 4, 5, and 6. The teaching evaluations are recorded on a scale of 1 to 5, where 5 represents the highest teaching evaluation. I believe that teaching evaluations are a reflection of the instructor's ability to communicate concepts to students. A successful instructor would therefore require at least two attributes. First, the instructor has to be knowledgeable of the subject. Second, the instructor should possess good communication skills. Unfortunately, these two important determinants of teaching evaluations are not recorded in the data set. I do have other proxies for factors that may influence one's teaching effectiveness.

Table 7.12 List of Variables in the Teaching Evaluation Data Set

Variable	Variable Description
age	age of instructor in years
beauty	normalized score of instructor's appearance
eval	teaching evaluation score (1 to 5)
students	number of students who completed evaluations
allstudents	total students enrolled in the class
prof	unique id for instructor
female	female
single_credit	single credit
minority_inst	minority instructor
upper	upper division
english_speaker	native English speaker
tenured	tenured professor
weight	ratio of students who completed the evaluation

I outline some of the assumptions here. I believe that the native English speakers would have an advantage in communicating in English over other instructors whose first language is not English. The language proficiency, or the lack of it, could serve as a determinant of teaching effectiveness. I also believe that upper-level courses are usually harder in content and therefore instructors who teach advanced courses may receive lower teaching evaluation primarily because of the advanced contents and the complexity of the subject matter.

Another proxy for advanced courses is the number of credits attached to the course. Single credit courses are normally offered in the early years and their content is usually of introductory nature. I hypothesize that instructors teaching introductory courses will receive higher teaching evaluations because of the ease in learning facilitated by the simplicity of the contents.

Research-oriented instructors at a university are often tenured, which guarantees them job security so that they may pursue and publish their research without the fear of losing their job. Tenured professors are thus senior academics with years of teaching and research experience. Tenure is the fundamental tenant of academic freedom that distinguishes universities from community colleges or schools. One can argue that tenured professors, given their vast teaching experience, are likely to receive higher teaching evaluations. On the other hand, one can also argue that since the tenured professors have job guarantee, they may not necessarily put as much effort in teaching as the untenured instructors would.

I also hypothesize that the visible minority status of an instructor may play a role in their teaching evaluations. In North America, universities have, in the recent past, opened their doors to non-Caucasian academics. Students usually are not exposed to visible minority instructors. Faculty members in certain disciplines, such as engineering, often include a large number of visible minority professors who are often recent immigrants. However, in other disciplines, such as humanities and letters, visible minority instructors are not that common.

I hypothesize that visible minority instructors would focus more on their teaching because of their smaller numbers in academia and their desire to prove themselves. Based on this assumption, I believe that visible minority instructors would receive higher teaching evaluations because of their willingness to prove themselves in academia.

Gender has been a source of controversy in academia for a very long time. Women instructors have been paid less than their male counterparts have, even when their performance has been similar, if not better, than their male colleagues. Similarly, few women have been installed in academic leadership roles. Given these systematic differences between men and women instructors, I believe that gender might play some role in teaching evaluations. However, I do not know in advance whether gender should have a positive or a negative influence on teaching evaluations.

Armed with these assumptions and hypotheses, I move ahead to test them using regression analysis. I estimate a series of models moving from a simpler to more complex specifications. I report model results in Table 7.13.

The first model in Table 7.13 regresses teaching evaluations as a function of instructors' gender. The negative and statistically significant coefficient for female instructors in Model 1 suggests that female instructors receive lower teaching evaluations than their male counterparts do. I cannot use *all else being equal* here because there is no other explanatory variable used in the model.

The second model introduces two other instructor-specific variables in addition to gender. I notice that teaching evaluations for minority instructors are negative. However, this coefficient is not statistically significant. I also notice a positive and statistically significant coefficient for native speakers of English language. Female continues to be a statistically significant and negative coefficient in the second model. This implies that even when I hold minority status and English proficiency constant, female instructors receive lower teaching evaluations than their male counterparts do.

In the third model, I introduce three additional variables to the model in addition to the ones reported earlier in Model 2 (Table 7.13). I find that the instructors' tenure status and upper division courses report negative coefficients. However, both variables returned statistically insignificant coefficients. I find higher teaching evaluations for single credit courses, which are introductory courses and the coefficient is statistically significant. Female and minority status of an instructor continued to be negative and statistically significant predictors, all else being equal.

In Model 4, I introduce instructors' appearance as an explanatory variable in the model in addition to the variables reported in Model 3. I note that instructors' looks are positively correlated with the teaching evaluations, all else being equal. The coefficient for instructors' appearance is statistically significant and positive even when I hold gender, minority status, English proficiency, tenure status, and attributes of courses constant in the model.

I also notice an increase in the model fit when I include more variables to explain teaching evaluations. Model 4 explains 15.6% variance in teaching evaluations.

I report here the Stata code and the resulting Table 7.13.

```
reg eval female
outreg2 using teaching.doc, label replace
reg eval female minority_inst english_speaker
outreg2 using teaching.doc, label append
reg eval female minority_inst english_speaker tenured upper
single_credit
outreg2 using teaching.doc, label append
reg eval female minority_inst english_speaker tenured upper
single_credit beauty
outreg2 using teaching.doc, label append
```

Table 7.13   Do Teaching Evaluations Depend Upon Instructor's Looks?

Variable	(1) teaching evaluation score (1 to 5)	(2) teaching evaluation score (1 to 5)	(3) teaching evaluation score (1 to 5)	(4) teaching evaluation score (1 to 5)
female	−0.168***	−0.165***	−0.148***	−0.178***
	(0.0517)	(0.0516)	(0.0507)	(0.0496)
minority instructor		−0.0328	−0.142*	−0.158**
		(0.0772)	(0.0792)	(0.0769)
native English speaker		0.314***	0.230**	0.236**
		(0.111)	(0.111)	(0.107)
tenured professor			−0.0689	−0.0562
			(0.0634)	(0.0616)
upper division			−0.0284	−0.00913
			(0.0560)	(0.0545)
single credit			0.535***	0.603***
			(0.119)	(0.117)

Variable	(1) teaching evaluation score (1 to 5)	(2) teaching evaluation score (1 to 5)	(3) teaching evaluation score (1 to 5)	(4) teaching evaluation score (1 to 5)
normalized score of instructor's appearance				0.165***
				(0.0308)
Constant	4.069***	3.777***	3.905***	3.888***
	(0.0335)	(0.112)	(0.136)	(0.133)
Observations	463	463	463	463
R squared	0.022	0.043	0.103	0.156

Standard errors in parentheses

*** p<0.01, ** p<0.05, * p<0.1

Survey Data, Weights, and Independence of Observations

Sample data, such as the one reported for teaching evaluations, often require two additional considerations, which must be accounted for in the regression models. First, not every observation in the survey data carries the same influence. Their relative importance, or weight, depends upon the sampling frame. Some observations would carry more weight than others.

In addition, not all observations may be treated as independent observations in a sample data set. For instance, the same respondent might record more than one observation in the data set, which would require you to account for the fact that multiple observations from the same respondent cannot be treated as independent observations. I explain these concerns and how to deal with them in the following paragraphs.

The results reported earlier are subject to certain possible biases. For instance, what if higher teaching evaluations are reported for small-sized classes and vice versa? In addition, it may turn out that a small number of students responding to a teaching evaluation questionnaire in a large class may bias the evaluation scores.

We need to account for students' response rate in the model. One way to do this is to use the response rate as *weights* in the model. Thus, courses in which a higher proportion of students responded to the teaching evaluation questionnaire would get a higher weight in the model. Furthermore, courses with lower response rates will not be able to influence or bias teaching evaluations.

The other thing to consider is that teaching evaluations are recorded for courses, and not necessarily for instructors. In our data set, several instructors have taught more than one course. Hence, I have multiple observations for several instructors. One can argue that teaching evaluations recorded for courses taught by the same professor could not be treated as independent observations.

In this section, I account for both biases. Table 7.14 reports three models. Model 1 is the same as Model 4 in Table 7.13. I refer to this as the unweighted model. I have repeated the output to facilitate comparison between the weighted and the unweighted model. Model 2 in Table 7.14 presents the results for the weighted model where I have used response rate as weights.

A comparison between the weighted and unweighted model reveals that parameter estimates and standard errors differ between the two models. However, the differences are relatively small in magnitude. More importantly, the direction of the relationship and the statistical significance of the estimated parameters have not changed between the weighted and unweighted models. In addition, the overall model fit, depicted by the `R-squared`, suggests that both models explained approximately 16% variance in teaching evaluations.

Model 3 in Table 7.14 accounts for the limitation that not all observations are independent of each other. Because numerous instructors have taught more than one course, I need to account for such clustering in the data set. A convenient way to address this limitation is to use robust standard errors. The revised model specification affects only the standard errors and not the estimated parameters. If I were not to account for such clustering, non-robust standard errors could be smaller than the robust standard errors, which could erroneously make some coefficients statistically significant. The use of robust standard errors accounts for such false positives.

Notice the output in Model 3 in Table 7.14. I have used student response rates as weights in the model. At the same time, I have used robust standard errors by accounting for the clustered nature of the data set. You will notice that the estimated coefficients do not differ between Models 2 and 3. However, standard errors are different between the two models.

The most profound impact of using robust standard errors is seen for the variable that controls for English proficiency. The coefficient for native English speaker is statistically significant in Model 2. However using robust standard errors makes this coefficient statistically insignificant in Model 3. Thus, if I were to rely on Model 3, I would say that English proficiency is not a statistically significant predictor of teaching evaluation, all else being equal.

I present here the Stata code and the resulting output in Table 7.14.

```
reg eval female minority_inst english_speaker tenured upper
single_credit beauty
outreg2 using teach_2.doc, label ctitle(un-weighted model) replace
reg eval female minority_inst english_speaker tenured upper
single_credit beauty [aw=weight]
outreg2 using teach_2.doc, label ctitle(weighted model)  append
reg eval female minority_inst english_speaker tenured upper
single_credit beauty [aw=weight], vce(cluster prof)
outreg2 using teach_2.doc, label ctitle(weighted model, clustered
standard errors)  append
```

Table 7.14   Robust Estimates of Teaching Evaluations Weighted by Student Response Rate

Variables	(1) Unweighted model	(2) Weighted Model	(3) Weighted Model Clustered Standard Errors
female	−0.178***	−0.184***	−0.184**
	(0.0496)	(0.0491)	(0.0800)
minority instructor	−0.158**	−0.171**	−0.171*
	(0.0769)	(0.0749)	(0.0958)
native English speaker	0.236**	0.212**	0.212
	(0.107)	(0.107)	(0.137)
tenured professor	−0.0562	−0.0509	−0.0509
	(0.0616)	(0.0613)	(0.0976)
upper division	−0.00913	−0.0614	−0.0614
	(0.0545)	(0.0554)	(0.0856)
single credit	0.603***	0.539***	0.539***
	(0.117)	(0.113)	(0.157)
normalized score of instructor's appearance	0.165***	0.153***	0.153***
	(0.0308)	(0.0306)	(0.0454)
Constant	3.888***	3.974***	3.974***
	(0.133)	(0.132)	(0.186)
Observations	463	463	463
R squared	0.156	0.157	0.157

Standard errors in parentheses

*** p<0.01, ** p<0.05, * p<0.1

I posed earlier the question whether the instructors' looks affected their teaching evaluations. I now have the answer. Yes they do. Even when I control for language proficiency, gender, tenure, and minority status, and proxies for courses' rigor, looks still mattered. All else being equal, instructors deemed good-looking by the students received higher teaching evaluations than did the rest. I feel doomed but knowledgeable. I now know the reason for not receiving the top teaching evaluations!

You will notice slight differences between the numbers reported in Table 7.14 and the ones in the paper (in Table 3) published by Hamermesh and Parker (2005).[13] I have used identical data sets, but have obtained slightly different results. The reason for the difference is how I weighted the model. Hamermesh and Parker used the number of students responding to the teaching evaluation questionnaire as weights. I instead used the percentage of students registered in a course who responded to the teaching survey as weights—hence the difference.

I would like you to change the weighting variable to the number of students who responded to the questionnaire in the weighted model with clustered standard errors. You will notice the resulting model returns exactly the same output as reported by Hamermesh and Parker in Table 3 of their paper.

What Determines Household Spending on Alcohol and Food

Finally, I illustrate regression models using a data set of household spending on food and alcohol. The recipient of the 2015 Nobel Prize in Economics, Professor Angus Deaton, was in fact recognized for his efforts to improve understanding of income and consumption at the individual level. The data set captures the spending of 1,000 Canadian households, which you can download from the book's website. Table 7.15 lists the variables included with this data set.

Table 7.15 Variables Depicting Household Spending on Food, Alcohol, and Transport

Variable	Variable label
adults	adults in household
alcoh	weekly expenditure on alcohol
food	weekly expenditure on food
kids	children in household
trport	weekly expenditure on transportation
income	weekly income
hhld	households members
nokids	no children (binary variable)

I am interested in determining the answers to the following questions.

- Do households with children spend less on alcohol?
- Do high-income households spend more on alcohol than others do?
- Do high-income households spend more on alcohol, even when they have children?
- What is the impact of an additional child on food expenditure?

Impact of Demographics and Income on Alcohol Expenditure

Let us begin with the basic analysis. The first step is to obtain descriptive statistics. Table 7.16 presents the descriptive statistics. The following is the Stata code to generate Table 7.16.

```
outreg2 using hhld_1.doc , label sum(log)  ///
eqkeep(mean sd min max)  replace
```

Table 7.16   Descriptive Statistics on Household Spending on Food, Alcohol, and Transport

Variables	(1) mean	(2) sd	(3) min	(4) max
adults in household	1.954	0.593	1	3
weekly expenditure on alcohol	30.66	38.00	0.250	762.7
weekly expenditure on food	97.26	52.99	20.02	605.1
children in household	0.822	1.064	0	4
weekly expenditure on transportation	79.41	90.91	0.0300	600.9
weekly income	662.6	407.2	41	4,437
households members	2.776	1.268	1	6
no children	0.560	0.497	0	1

The data set contains information on 1,000 households from Canada. The average number of adults is 1.95 persons per household. The minimum number of adults is 1 and the maximum is 3. There are 0.8 children per household with a minimum of 0 and a maximum of 4 children. In total, the average number of persons per household is 2.78 with a minimum of 1 and a maximum of 6 persons.

On average, households spend $30.7 dollars per week on alcohol and $97.3 per week on food. The average weekly household income is $663.

I would like to determine the impact of the presence of children on spending on alcohol. I tabulate the change in weekly alcohol spending for the number of children in the household. I have hypothesized that households with children would have to spend significant amounts on goods and services related to children. This would leave less discretionary income for alcohol consumption.

Table 7.17 suggests that the weekly expenditure on alcohol in fact declines with the increase in the number of children. I also note that a large number of households in the data set (560 out of 1,000) do not have children living with them.

Table 7.17   Alcohol Spending and Presence of Children

Children in Household	Mean	N
0	32.3	560
1	28.67	158
2	30.73	192
3	23.68	80
4	25.2	10
Total	30.66	1,000

A Theoretical Model of Spending on Alcohol

I assume that weekly spending on alcohol is dependent on the number of adults in the household. I also assume that households with children will spend less on alcohol because such households would have to incur other children-related expenses. I can describe the theoretical model as follows:

If y is the dependent variable, that is, weekly expenditure on alcohol and x_1 represents adults, x_2 represents children, and x_3 represents household income, then the model can be written as:

$$Y = f(x_1, x_2, x_3)$$

The preceding implies that y is a function of x_1, x_2, and x_3. The regression model is expressed as follows:

$$Y = \beta_0 + \beta_1 x_1 + \beta_2 x_2 + \beta_3 x_3 + \varepsilon$$

The *betas* in the preceding equation are the regression coefficients that explain the relationship between weekly alcohol expenditure and the explanatory variables. *Epsilon* is the error term that accounts for what has not been captured by the model.

Table 7.18 presents the results of the regression models estimated using Stata software. I report results for four separate models. Model 1 regresses weekly alcohol spending on the number of adults in the household. Model 2 regresses weekly alcohol spending on adults and households' weekly income. Model 3 regresses weekly alcohol spending on adults, household's weekly income, and the number of children in the household. Model 4 is the same as Model 3 except that it is estimated for the subset of households with children.

```
reg alcoh adults
outreg2 using alcoh-1.doc, label ctitle(alcohol,) replace
reg alcoh adults income
outreg2 using alcoh-1.doc, label ctitle(alcohol,) append
reg alcoh adults income kids
outreg2 using alcoh-1.doc, label ctitle(alcohol,) append
reg alcoh adults income kids if kids>0
outreg2 using alcoh-1.doc, label ctitle(alcohol, households with no
children) append
```

Table 7.18 Regression Model of Household Spending on Alcohol

Variables	(1) alcohol	(2) alcohol	(3) alcohol	(4) alcohol households with children
adults in household	7.775***	4.640**	4.799**	7.064
	(2.012)	(2.195)	(2.189)	(4.537)

Variables	(1) alcohol	(2) alcohol	(3) alcohol	(4) alcohol households with children
weekly income		0.0111***	0.0124***	0.00607
		(0.00320)	(0.00323)	(0.00537)
children in household			-3.045***	-1.182
			(1.132)	(2.646)
Constant	15.47***	14.24***	15.55***	11.68
	(4.108)	(4.101)	(4.117)	(10.84)
Observations	1,000	1,000	1,000	440
R squared	0.015	0.026	0.034	0.014

Standard errors in parentheses

*** p<0.01, ** p<0.05, * p<0.1

Here is the equation for Model 1, which uses one explanatory variable; that is, adults.

$$y = 15.47 + 7.78 * adults + \varepsilon$$

The model suggests that the base weekly expenditure on alcohol is $15.47. Afterward, each additional household member results in $7.78 of additional weekly alcohol spending. The impact of income is captured in Model 2. The revised model is expressed as follows:

$$y = 14.24 + 4.63 * adults + 0.011 * income + \varepsilon$$

This implies that a dollar increase in weekly income results in $.011 increase in weekly alcohol spending, whereas an additional household member results in an additional $4.63/week in alcohol spending. Notice the decline in the coefficient's value for weekly spending resulting from each additional adult from $7.78 in the model without income to $4.63 in the model with income.

I can see the utility of regression analysis in Model 2 in Table 7.18, which allows us to state that if income is controlled, each additional household member will result in an additional $4.64 in weekly alcohol spending. Without controlling for the impact of income, the magnitude of the impact of each adult on alcohol spending was twice as much at $7.78. Again, this property of regression models is called *all else being equal*. I also note that both income and adults return statistically significant coefficients.

Now I add another variable, the number of children, to the model and see the impact of the children on alcohol spending. The estimated model (Model 3 in Table 7.18) is reported as follows:

$$y = 15.5 + 4.79 * adults + .012 * income - 3.04 * children + \varepsilon$$

The preceding equation suggests that the base weekly expenditure on alcohol is $15.5. Afterwards, each additional household member results in $4.79 of additional alcohol spending. The income variable suggests that each additional dollar results in an additional $0.012 spent on alcohol per week. As for children, I find that each additional child results in $3.04 less in weekly alcohol spending. Hence, for a household with two children, the weekly spending on alcohol declines by $6.08 (2 × 3.04).

Another way of looking at the impact of children is to re-estimate the model only for households with children; that is, I exclude households with no children. The results of the revised model are reported in Model 4 in Table 7.18.

I notice that the impact of the presence of children is lower (–$1.18) than what I observed in Model 3. In addition, the coefficient is statistically insignificant such that I can no longer conclude that for households with children, having additional children will result in lower spending on alcohol.

It may turn out that there is a *non-linear relationship* between the number of children and weekly spending on alcohol (see Figure 7.7). I can test this hypothesis by converting the children variable from being a continuous variable to a factor or categorical variables. I do the same for the number of adults and re-estimate the model.

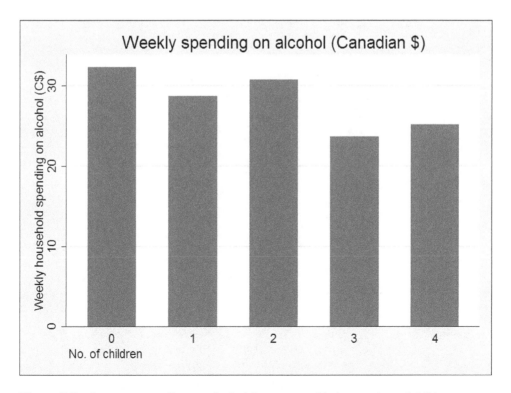

Figure 7.7   Average spending on alcohol decreases with the number of children

The underlying assumption for this approach states that the impact of an increase in the number of adults from 1 to 2 persons is different from the one resulting in an increase from 2 to 3 persons. Table 7.19 reports the results of the revised model estimated using Stata. Also reported is the Stata code to generate the results.

```
reg alcoh income i.adults i.kids
outreg2 using alcoh-2.doc, label ctitle(alcohol) replace
```

Table 7.19   Revised Formulation for Spending on Alcohol

Variables	(1) alcohol
weekly income	0.0123***
	(0.00325)
adults in household = 2	3.974
	(3.263)
adults in household = 3	10.29**
	(4.433)
children in household = 1	−6.162*
	(3.418)
children in household = 2	−5.020
	(3.275)
children in household = 3	−10.29**
	(4.559)
children in household = 4	−6.610
	(11.97)
Constant	21.19***
	(2.939)
Observations	1,000
R squared	0.035

Standard errors in parentheses

*** p<0.01, ** p<0.05, * p<0.1

Notice that a household with two adults spends $3.97 more than the one with one adult, whereas a household with three adults spends $10.3 more than the one-adult household does. The later variable is also statistically significant. Also observe that households with one child spend $6.2 less on alcohol than a household with no children, all else being equal. The estimated coefficient is statistically significant. Households with three children spend $10.3 less on alcohol than households without children, all else being equal. Again, this variable is statistically significant. At the same time, the model returned insignificant coefficients for households with two and four children.

What Influences Household Spending on Food?

I extend the analysis to weekly spending on food. Again, my primary variable of interest is the presence of children in a household and its effect on food spending. I see that average weekly spending on food increases with the number of children in a household (see Table 7.20). Note that I have used `tabout`,[14] a user written command in Stata, which you need to install before using it.

```
tabout kids  using table10.doc, ///
c(mean food) f(2c) sum layout(rb) h3(nil)  npos(both) style(tab) append
```

Table 7.20 Weekly Spending on Food and the Number of Children in a Household

Children in Household	Mean (food)	N
0	82.67	560
1	107.12	158
2	120.92	192
3	120.55	80
4	118.51	10
Total	97.26	1,000

I assume that weekly spending on food is dependent on number of adults in the household and that households with children will spend more on food. The estimated model is identical in specification as the one estimated earlier for weekly spending on alcohol.

Table 7.21 presents the results of the regression models estimated using Stata software. I report results for four different model specifications. Model 1 regresses weekly food spending on the number of adults in the household. Model 2 regresses weekly food spending on adults and households' weekly income. Model 3 regresses weekly food spending on adults, household's weekly income, and the number of children in the household. Model 4 is the same as model 3 except that it is estimated for a subset of households with children.

```
reg food adults
outreg2 using food-1.doc, label ctitle(food,) replace
reg food adults income
outreg2 using food-1.doc, label ctitle(food,) append
reg food adults income kids
outreg2 using food-1.doc, label ctitle(food,) append
reg food adults income kids if kids>0
outreg2 using food-1.doc, label ctitle(food, households with no
children) append
```

Table 7.21   Regression Models to Capture Weekly Spending on Food

Variables	(1) food	(2) food	(3) food	(4) food households with children
adults in household	34.73***	20.33***	19.76***	18.18***
	(2.604)	(2.635)	(2.552)	(5.101)
weekly income		0.0510***	0.0462***	0.0432***
		(0.00384)	(0.00376)	(0.00604)
children in household			10.86***	7.823***
			(1.319)	(2.975)
Constant	29.41***	23.76***	19.09***	31.25**
	(5.317)	(4.923)	(4.800)	(12.19)
Observations	1,000	1,000	1,000	440
R-squared	0.151	0.279	0.325	0.185

Standard errors in parentheses

*** p<0.01, ** p<0.05, * p<0.1

Let us write the equation from the preceding output in which we have used only one explanatory variable: adults.

$$y = 29.4 + 34.73 * adults + \varepsilon$$

The model suggests that the base weekly expenditure on food is $29.4. Afterwards, each additional adult household member results in $34.73 of additional weekly food spending. The impact of `income` on spending on food is captured in Model 2, which is expressed in the following equation:

$$y = 23.7 + 20.3 * adults + .05 * income + \varepsilon$$

The model suggests that a dollar increase in weekly income results in $.05 increase in weekly food spending, whereas an additional adult household member results in an extra $20.3/week in food spending. Notice that when `income` is included in the model, the coefficient for `adults` declines from $34.73 to $20.3. Model 2 states that if we control for income, each additional household member will result in an additional $20.3 in weekly food spending. When we control for the impact of income, the magnitude of the impact of each adult on food spending declines by 40%. Both coefficients in the second model are statistically significant.

Model 3 in Table 7.21 reports the results for the specification with three regressors, namely weekly household income, adults, and the children in households. The resulting three coefficients are all statistically significant and positive. The model can be rewritten as follows:

$$y = 19.1 + 19.76 * adults + .05 * income + 10.86 * kids + \varepsilon$$

Model 3 suggests that the base weekly expenditure on food is $19.1. Afterward, each additional adult results in $19.76 of additional food spending. The income variable suggests that each additional dollar in income results in $0.05 more spent on food per week. As for children, each additional child results in $10.9 more in weekly food spending. Hence, for two children the weekly spending increases by $21.8 (2 × 10.9).

Another way of looking at the impact of children is to re-estimate Model 3 only for households with children; that is, I exclude households without children. The results of the revised model are presented in Model 4. We see a large decline in the model fit (R-squared). However, we do not observe a large difference in the estimated coefficients or their statistical significance.

Lastly, I re-estimate the model by creating a dummy variable for each level of adults and children to isolate their impact on weekly food spending. The underlying assumption here is that the weekly spending on food will increase at a different rate when the number of children increases from 1 to 2 than it would when the number of children increases from 2 to 3. I hypothesize that the increase in food spending does not have a linear relationship with the increase in the number of children in the household. Table 7.22 presents the results estimated in Stata for the revised specification. Also reported is the Stata code used to generate Table 7.22.

```
reg food income i.adults i.kids
outreg2 using food-2.doc, label ctitle(food) replace
```

Table 7.22   Revised Formulation with Dummy Variables for Adults and Children

Variables	(1) food
weekly income	0.0460***
	(0.00378)
adults in household = 2	19.84***
	(3.804)
adults in household = 3	38.67***
	(5.166)
children in household = 1	14.61***
	(3.983)
children in household = 2	23.99***
	(3.817)
children in household = 3	30.13***
	(5.314)
children in household = 4	37.00***
	(13.95)
Constant	38.35***
	(3.425)
Observations	1,000
R squared	0.326

Standard errors in parentheses

*** p<0.01, ** p<0.05, * p<0.1

The regression model presented in Table 7.22 suggests that all else being equal, the household's food expenditure increases with the number of children. For instance, a household with one child will spend $14.6 more than a household with no child will spend. Similarly, a household with four children will spend $37.07 more than the household with no children.

A comparison between the results presented in Table 7.19 and Table 7.22 is important to understand how regression models could be helpful in developing a better understanding of the behaviors we study. Note that the weekly spending on alcohol declines with the increase in the number of children. However, the weekly spending on food increases with the increase in the number of children.

Even more interesting is the comparison of the overall model fit such that the alcohol model explains only 3.5% of the variance in alcohol spending, whereas the other model explains

32.6% of the variance in a household's weekly food spending. This suggests that the explanatory variables used in the models are more suited to explain spending on food than on alcohol.

Advanced Topics

The regression models, though very powerful tools, are vulnerable to mis-specifications and violations of the assumptions that make them work. The applied statisticians, data scientists, and analysts sometimes forget, or worse, are ignorant of the conditions under which the regression models could be applied. Any good introductory text in econometrics, such as the ones by Peter Kennedy, Damodar Gujarati, and Jeffrey Wooldridge, offer detailed discussions on the conditions necessary for regression models to work.[15]

I would like to point our readers to two very important considerations that any applied analyst using regression models should know. First is the assumption about constant variance of error terms, a condition known as *homoskedasticity*. The other is rather a limiting condition known as *multicollinearity*, which happens when two or more explanatory variables are highly correlated. Ignoring these limitations may lead us to draw erroneous conclusions.

Homoskedasticity

Regression models assume that the variance of the error term ($\in$), conditional upon the explanatory variables, is constant. This assumption about constant variance is called homoskedasticity. The violation of this assumption is called *heteroskedasticity*, which implies that the variance of the error term changes systematically for various segments in the population.

A good example of heteroskedasticity is to consider a model where I regress food spending on income. Given that higher income is likely to be associated with higher spending on food, it is quite possible that the residuals' variance may increase in magnitude with income, suggesting heteroskedasticity. Similarly, in a model where I regress savings on income, if the variance of the error term increases with income, heteroskedasticity might be present in the model.

Heteroskedasticity does not bias the coefficients, but it affects the standard errors of the coefficients, which affects inferential statistics. If heteroskedasticity returns lower standard errors for coefficients, we may erroneously conclude statistically significant relationships where none existed. Several tests have been devised to test the presence of heteroskedasticity. If heteroskedasticity is present, some remedial measures are available, which I will discuss in the following paragraphs.

The most commonly used to test for heteroskedasticity is the Breusch-Pagan (BP) test. Following are the steps involved in conducting the BP test.

1. Estimate an ordinary least squares regression model.

2. Generate residuals from the model. Square residuals for each observation.

3. With squared residuals as the dependent variable, run an ordinary least squares regression model using the same explanatory variables.

4. Conduct an `F-test` on the revised model.

5. If the `p-value` of the `F-test` is lower than the threshold, we reject the null hypothesis of constant variance or homoskedasticity.

Let us test for heteroskedasticity using the housing price example. I regress the housing price on lot size, square footage of the built-up area, and the number of bedrooms. I generate the residuals from the model and obtain squared residuals. Lastly, I re-estimate the model with the squared residuals as the dependent variable. The results, obtained in Stata, are presented in Table 7.23 (along with the Stata code) that also lists the `F-test` and the associated `p-value`. Under Model 2, the `p-value` for the `F-test` is 0.002, which recommends that I reject the null hypothesis of constant variance and conclude the presence of heteroskedasticity.

```
reg price lotsize sqrft bdrms
outreg2 using bp-1.doc, label ctitle(BP test,original model) ///
adds(F-test, e(F),  Prob>F, e(p), Adj R-sqrd, e(r2_a)) replace
estat hettest

predict _res1, residuals
gen _res2= _res1^2
twoway (scatter _res1 ) , scheme(s2mono)

reg _res2 lotsize sqrft bdrms
outreg2 using bp-1.doc, label ctitle(BP test,res-squared model) ///
adds(F-test, e(F),  Prob>F, e(p), Adj R-sqrd, e(r2_a)) append
```

Table 7.23 Results for Breusch-Pagan (BP) Test

Variables	(1) BP Test Original Model	(2) BP Test Res-Squared Model
size of lot in square feet	2.998***	423,698***
	(0.931)	(149,297)
size of house in square feet	178.0***	3.555e+06
	(19.19)	(3.078e+06)
number of bedrooms	20,086	2.190e+09
	(13,065)	(2.095e+09)
Constant	−31,567	−1.161e+10*
	(42,739)	(6.853e+09)
Observations	88	88
R squared	0.672	0.160

Variables	(1) BP Test Original Model	(2) BP Test Res-Squared Model
F-test	57.46	5.339
Prob>F	0	0.00205
Adj R-sqrd	0.661	0.130

Standard errors in parentheses

*** p<0.01, ** p<0.05, * p<0.1

Now that I have concluded the presence of heteroskedasticity, I need to find a solution. In most instances, taking the natural log of the variables solves the problem. I repeat the analysis by first regressing the log of price on the log-transformed versions of the same three explanatory variables. After estimating the model, I generate residuals from the model and then square the residuals. Lastly, I re-estimate the model with the squared residuals as the dependent variable and the log-transformed versions of the three explanatory variables. I review the F-test to see if I can reject the null hypothesis.

The results for the revised log-transformed model are presented in Table 7.24. Also listed is the Stata code used to generate the table.

The p-value for the F-test is 0.183, suggesting that I cannot reject the null hypothesis of constant variance and therefore I conclude homoskedasticity.

```
reg lprice llotsize lsqrft lnrooms
outreg2 using bp-2.doc, label ctitle(BP test,log-transformed model) ///
adds(F-test, e(F),  Prob>F, e(p), Adj R-sqrd, e(r2_a)) replace
estat hettest

predict _res1a, residuals
gen _res2a= _res1a^2

reg _res2a llotsize lsqrft lnrooms
outreg2 using bp-2.doc, label ctitle(BP test,res-squared model)  ///
adds(F-test, e(F),  Prob>F, e(p), Adj R-sqrd, e(r2_a)) append
```

Table 7.24 Log-Transformed Version of the Housing Prices Models

Variables	(1) BP Test Log-Transformed Model	(2) BR Test Res-Squared Model
log(lotsize)	0.170***	–0.00508
	(0.0385)	(0.0150)

Variables	(1) BP Test Log-Transformed Model	(2) BR Test Res-Squared Model
log(sqrft)	0.717***	–0.0673*
	(0.0935)	(0.0364)
Log of bedrooms	0.0992	0.0700*
	(0.102)	(0.0397)
Constant	–1.429**	0.501**
	(0.640)	(0.249)
Observations	88	88
R squared	0.639	0.056
F-test	49.64	1.654
Prob>F	0	0.183
Adj R-sqrd	0.626	0.0220

Standard errors in parentheses

*** p<0.01, ** p<0.05, * p<0.1

Because the presence of heteroskedasticity affects the standard errors associated with the estimated parameters, one can also try to address this by fixing the standard errors in the model specification. Statistical software, including Stata, offers the option to report "robust" standard errors, which are robust to the heteroskedasticity present in standard errors. The term "robust" holds a special meaning in statistical analysis. Robustness implies that even in the presence of heteroskedasticity, which affects standard errors, the robust estimator will return standard errors that are immune to the impact of heteroskedasticity.

In Stata, one can ask for robust standard errors by including *vce(robust)* in the model specification. The formal name for the robust standard error estimator is Huber/White/sandwich estimator.

I present the same model with regular and robust standard errors in Table 7.25. I note that the coefficients for the two models are identical. However, the standard errors, and hence the statistical significance, are different between the two models. The coefficient for lot size is statistically significant in the model with regular standard errors. However, it is statistically insignificant, and indistinguishable from 0, for the model reporting robust standard errors.

This implies that if we were not to use robust standard errors, we would have concluded lot size to be a statistically significant predictor. If we were to base our decisions strictly on statistical theory, I would conclude that lot size is not a strong predictor of housing prices. But I know that not to be the case. Lot size matters greatly in determining housing prices. It is for this reason I recommend including variables that make sense theoretically.

```
reg hprice lotsize sqrft bdrms
outreg2 using bp-3.doc, label ctitle(dep_var: house price, regular
standard errors) ///
adds(F-test, e(F),  Prob>F, e(p), Adj R-sqrd, e(r2_a)) replace

reg hprice lotsize sqrft bdrms, vce(robust)
outreg2 using bp-3.doc, label ctitle(dep_var: house price, robust
standard errors) ///
adds(F-test, e(F),  Prob>F, e(p), Adj R-sqrd, e(r2_a)) append
```

Table 7.25 Comparing Regular Standard Errors with Robust Standard Errors

Variables	(1) dep_var: House Price Regular Standard Errors	(2) dep_var: House Price Robust Standard Errors
size of lot in square feet	2.998***	2.998
	(0.931)	(1.815)
size of house in square feet	178.0***	178.0***
	(19.19)	(25.70)
number of bedrooms	20,086	20,086
	(13,065)	(12,294)
Constant	−31,567	−31,567
	(42,739)	(53,850)
Observations	88	88
R squared	0.672	0.672
F-test	57.46	23.72
Prob>F	0	0
Adj R-sqrd	0.661	0.661

Standard errors in parentheses

*** p<0.01, ** p<0.05, * p<0.1

Multicollinearity

Multicollinearity arises when strong correlation exists between some explanatory variables. This happens when more than one explanatory variable in the model measures the same phenomenon. Multicollinearity has puzzled data scientists for years. It is hard to define and its impact is not that straightforward to measure. I would like to mention multicollinearity here because its presence effectively changes the magnitude of variables. In extreme cases, multicollinearity can even reverse the sign of an estimated coefficient or strip the coefficient of its statistical significance.

I illustrate multicollinearity with an example. I regress housing prices on the number of bedrooms, square footage of the built-up area, and lot size in square feet. I enter these variables one-by-one in three regression models. Economic theory tells us that the price of a house is, to a large extent, determined by its size. I have therefore used three proxies for size as regressors. Table 7.26 presents the results of the model estimated in Stata. Also reported with the table is the Stata code used to generate it.

Model 1 in Table 7.26 suggests that each additional bedroom adds $89,936 to housing value. When I add built-up area to the model, the number of bedrooms become statistically insignificant. Model 2 in Table 7.26 suggests that the number of bedrooms do not affect housing values (that is, bedrooms are not statistically significant), when I control for the built-up area. The model fit jumps from 25% (R-squared) to 62.3%. When I add the third variable, that is, lot size, the number of bedrooms continues to be statistically insignificant.

It appears that in the presence of built-up space, the number of bedrooms do not help explain variations in housing prices. This is rather counterintuitive. Two homes with same lot size and built-up area can sell for different prices based on the difference in the number of bedrooms. The architectural design and style allows variety to support a different number of bedrooms, even when the built-up space is the same. This phenomenon is more pronounced in the condominium markets where units may have the same overall square footage, but the number of bedrooms differs based on the layout of the unit. To argue that the unit size is sufficient in explaining prices is a troubling argument.

Could this be a result of multicollinearity? The number of bedrooms and built-up space report a very high correlation (0.53, $p < 0.0001$). It is quite possible that the number of bedrooms lost its statistical significance because of high positive correlation with built-up space.

```
reg hprice bdrms
outreg2 using multi-1.doc, label ctitle(beds) ///
adds(F-test, e(F),  Prob>F, e(p), Adj R-sqrd, e(r2_a)) replace

reg hprice bdrms sqrft
outreg2 using multi-1.doc, label ctitle(beds + sqrft) ///
adds(F-test, e(F),  Prob>F, e(p), Adj R-sqrd, e(r2_a)) append

reg hprice bdrms sqrft lotsize
outreg2 using multi-1.doc, label ctitle(beds + sqrft +lotsize) ///
adds(F-test, e(F),  Prob>F, e(p), Adj R-sqrd, e(r2_a)) append

pwcorr hprice bdrms sqrft lotsize, sig
```

Table 7.26 Regressing Housing Prices to Find Evidence of Multicollinearity

Variables	(1) beds	(2) beds + sqrft	(3) beds + sqrft + lotsize
number of bdrms	89,936***	22,037	20,086
	(16,440)	(13,751)	(13,065)
size of house in square feet		186.2***	178.0***
		(20.05)	(19.19)
size of lot in square feet			2.998***
			(0.931)
Constant	104,735*	−28,007	−31,567
	(60,252)	(45,018)	(42,739)
Observations	88	88	88
R squared	0.258	0.632	0.672
F-test	29.93	72.96	57.46
Prob>F	4.34e-07	0	0
Adj R-sqrd	0.250	0.623	0.661

Standard errors in parentheses

*** $p<0.01$, ** $p<0.05$, * $p<0.1$

Variance Inflation Factors (VIF) are used to test for multicollinearity. If the VIF are above a certain threshold (for example, 5 or 10), one may have to consider dropping one of the correlated variables and re-estimating the model. However, I advise strongly against dropping variables from the model just because of multicollinearity. Our discussion about number of bedrooms and the square footage of a condominium implies that even if the model suggests multicollinearity, we must not drop a statistically insignificant variable from the model, especially when its inclusion in the model is warranted by statistical theory.

If multicollinearity is pervasive in the data set, another option will be to use factor analysis to group highly correlated variables together, and run the regression model using the resulting factors as regressors.

Summary

This chapter started by remembering Sir Frances Galton's pioneering work that introduced regression models as a tool for scientific inquiry. I then introduced the mechanics of regression models for those readers interested in mathematical details. Later, I used examples from housing markets, consumer spending on food and alcohol, and the relationship between teaching evaluations and instructors' looks to illustrate regression models in action.

All else being equal has been the focus of this chapter. I have demonstrated that only when I control for other influences, can I determine an accurate estimate for the influence of another variable on the phenomenon or behavior of interest.

The height-earning example, described earlier in the chapter, reinforces the thesis statement in this chapter; that is, all else being equal, workers' height does not influence their earnings. The regression model helped Schick and Steckel (2015) realize that height was correlated with higher cognitive and non-cognitive skills that reflected favorably in a person's earning potential.

Regression models remain the workhorse of statistical analysis. They will continue to be a prized tool for data scientists who are interested in exploring the complex relationships hidden in large and small data sets.

Endnotes

1. Haider, M. (1999). "Development of Hedonic prices indices for freehold properties in the Greater Toronto Area, application of spatial autoregressive techniques." Retrieved from https://tspace.library.utoronto.ca/handle/1807/12657

2. Hadhazy, A. (2015). "Will humans keep getting taller?" Web published on May 14, 2015. Retrieved July 16, 2015, from http://www.bbc.com/future/story/20150513-will-humans-keep-getting-taller

3. Matthews, T. J. and Hamilton, B. E. (2009). "Delayed childbearing: more women are having their first child later in life." *NCHS Data Brief*, (21) 1–8.

4. Vandegrift, D. and Yoked, T. (2004). "Obesity rates, income, and suburban sprawl: An analysis of US states." *Health & Place*, *10*(3), 221–229.

5. Kulu, H., Boyle, P. J., Andersson, G., and others. (2009). "High suburban fertility: Evidence from four Northern European countries." *Demographic Research*, *21*(31), 915–944.

6. Kulu, H. and Boyle, P. J. (2008). "High Fertility in City Suburbs: Compositional or Contextual Effects?" *European Journal of Population*, *25*(2), 157–174.

7. Repetto, R. (2013). *Economic equality and fertility in developing countries*. Routledge.

8. Schick, A. and Steckel, R. H. (2015). "Height, Human Capital, and Earnings: The Contributions of Cognitive and Noncognitive Ability." *Journal of Human Capital*, *9*(1), 94–115.

9. Varian, H. R. (2014). "Big Data: New Tricks for Econometrics" *The Journal of Economic Perspectives: A Journal of the American Economic Association, 28*(2), 3–27.

10. Batterham, A. M. and Greg, A. (2005). "How big does my sample need to be? A primer on the murky world of sample size estimation." *Physical Therapy in Sport. 6*(3). http://doi.org/10.1016/j.ptsp.2005.05.004

11. http://econpapers.repec.org/software/bocbocode/s456416.htm

12. Wooldridge, J. M. (2012). *Introductory Econometrics: A Modern Approach* (Upper Level Economics Titles) (5th edition). Cengage Learning.

13. Hamermesh, D. S. and Parker, A. (2005). "Beauty in the classroom: Instructors' pulchritude and putative pedagogical productivity." *Economics of Education Review, 24*(4), 369–376.

14. http://www.ianwatson.com.au/stata/tabout_tutorial.pdf

15. *A Guide to Econometrics* by Peter Kennedy. *Econometrics by Example* by Damodar Gujarati. *Introductory Econometrics: A Modern Approach* by Jeffrey Wooldridge.

To Be or Not to Be

To be human is all about making choices. Some choices we cherish, others we regret. But the very freedom to make choices is what we appreciate the most of all the basic human rights. And while we continue to debate about what Shakespeare really meant by "To be or not to be" in a soliloquy in Hamlet, *it indeed became the question that many now seek to answer.*

In statistical analysis, we often analyze choices, both rational and irrational. Why some individuals choose not to study beyond high school while others continue to spend additional years at colleges and universities is one such question that economists, policymakers, and others try to answer. In the financial sector, analysts try to forecast the probability of default for individual borrowers. For analysts, outstanding loans could have only two outcomes. The borrowers may comply with their obligations or default on the loan. These are all examples of binary (that is either/or) choices or outcomes.

This chapter is concerned with analyzing binary outcomes. I therefore illustrate the following methods to analyze binary outcomes:

- Logit models
- Probit models
- Grouped logit models

I illustrate modeling techniques using four software programs, namely SAS, SPSS, Stata, and R. The book's website (www.ibmpressbooks.com/title/9780133991024) offers data and scripts to reproduce the same analysis using R, Stata, SPSS, and SAS. Using real-life data, I articulate the research question, undertake a descriptive analysis of pertinent variables, and lastly, estimate and interpret various formulations of the statistical models. I also present the post-estimation analysis, where output from econometric models is used for inference.

I address the following questions in this chapter:

- How is the dependent variable in binary outcomes different from the ones in ordinary least square regressions?

- What kind of explanatory variables may be used to analyze binary outcomes?

- What statistical methods are appropriate for modeling binary outcomes?

- How do we interpret results from binary outcome models?

To Smoke or Not to Smoke: That Is the Question

Let us consider the decision to smoke to understand how binary choices are made, what the impacts of such choices are, and how we can analyze the determinants of the decision to take up smoking. Each year, smoking-related illnesses account for an estimated 480,000 deaths in the United States.[1] Thus, one in five deaths in the United States is caused by illnesses resulting from cigarette smoking. The smoking-related morbidity burden far exceeds the accumulated deaths caused by HIV, illegal drug use, motor vehicle accidents, suicides, and murders. At the same time, smoking accounts for 90% of all lung cancer deaths among men and 80% of all lung cancer deaths among women.[2]

A whole host of other illnesses and ailments are also associated with cigarette smoking. The economic and social costs make cigarette smoking a serious concern for governments as well as for households who have to care for a loved one fighting an illness caused by cigarette smoking.

The very decision by a youth to take up smoking attracts considerable attention from doctors, other medical professionals, policymakers, sociologists, parents, and other concerned individuals and groups. They are interested in determining the impact of socio-demographic influences on a person's decision to smoke or otherwise. For instance, they would like to know whether age, income, education, or the price of cigarettes affect one's decision to smoke. From a policy perspective, we are interested in the following questions about the possible determinants of cigarette smoking:

1. Do higher cigarettes prices deter cigarette smoking?

2. Do highly educated individuals smoke less than others do?

3. Do high-income individuals smoke more or less than the rest?

4. Is smoking more prevalent among youth than older cohorts?

Consider that in 2004, higher education and income were associated with lower incidence of cigarette smoking in Alabama. Only 19.6% of those with annual income exceeding $35,000 reported smoking. On the other hand, a much higher incidence of smoking (31%) was reported for those living in households earning less than $35,000 annually. Similarly, only 16% of those with higher than grade 12 education in New York reported smoking compared to a much higher 27% of those with less than grade 12 education. In California, 15% of individuals between the ages of 45 and 64 reported smoking cigarettes compared to 18% of individuals between the ages of 18 and 24 years old.

It appears that in California, age may not have a huge impact on the propensity to smoke. However, in Connecticut, 31% of younger cohorts (18 to 24 years old) reported smoking compared with 18% of older cohorts (45 to 64 years old) thus suggesting that age may influence the decision to smoke in some places.

Binary Outcomes

To smoke or not to smoke is an individual choice. Note that the choice has only two alternatives: to smoke or not to smoke. Such a choice is known as a binary choice where an individual may opt between two alternatives. We make several similar choices on a daily basis. Some binary choices are made less frequently than are others. Consider the following examples:

- To call in sick for school or work, or not

- To get married or not

- To work out at a gym or not

- To eat out or prepare your own meal at home

- To attend college or work full-time after completing high school

Apart from choices, there are several other instances where binary outcomes are important concerns for businesses, governments, and the society. Consider, for instance, that banks are concerned about the probability of borrowers defaulting on their obligations. The outcome in this case will again be binary: The borrower may or may not default on the outstanding loan. Similarly, a student writing an exam can either pass or fail the exam; again a binary outcome.

In recent times, analyzing binary outcomes (choices) has attracted significant attention by policymakers, sociologists, economists, and others. The 2000 Nobel Memorial (Sveriges Riksbank) Prize in Economics was awarded to Professor Daniel McFadden for his work on modeling discrete choices.[3] The other recipient in 2000 was Professor James Heckman for developing solutions for self-selection biases in statistical analysis.[4]

Though Professor McFadden was awarded a Nobel in 2000, Robert Duncan Luce, a mathematician and sociologist, was the one who originally framed the choice axiom. He formulated the probability of selecting an alternative from a pool of alternatives. Professor Luce died in 2012.[5]

Binary Dependent Variables

I distinguish between continuous and categorical variables in statistical analysis. Binary or dichotomous variables are a subset of the categorical variables, which deal with situations where the outcome of an experiment or a process can be categorized into a finite number of mutually exclusive classes or categories. For instance, a survey of employment status will record an adult's status as either employed or unemployed. We categorize this as a binary variable. Thus the individual's status can be expressed as a dichotomous variable (1/0) where 1 denotes the outcome of being employed, and 0 denotes the outcome of being unemployed.

Other examples of categorical data include scenarios involving a choice between the make of new automobiles. For instance, automobile executives are interested in learning about the determinants of the consumer choice as it relates to the national make of the automobile. In this case, the choice could again be represented as a dichotomous variable carrying the value '1' if the consumer chooses, for example, an American make, and '0' otherwise. Similarly, if the choice was between American, European, or Japanese car manufacturers, the categorical variable representing the choice would have three categories: 1 (American), 2 (European), and 3 (Japanese). A categorical variable that represents more than two outcomes is called a *multinomial* variable.

The previous examples are those of unordered outcomes where you could have coded American as 2, Japanese as 1, and European as 3. The change in the order does not impact the analysis because the order of alternatives is rather arbitrary. There are, however, scenarios where the ordering of outcomes matters. Consider, for instance, Table 8.1, where households' car ownership is presented.

Table 8.1   Example of an Ordered Categorical Variable

Categories	Description
0	Household without cars
1	Household owning 1 car
2	Household owning 2 cars
3	Household owning 3 cars
4 or more	Household owning 4 or more cars

Such data, where the order of outcomes is not arbitrary, but rather systematic, is called ordered data, which is also a type of categorical data. The categories listed in Table 8.1 are not arbitrary. Instead, the ordering is systematic such that households categorized as 2 own more cars than the households categorized as 1 or 0. In this particular case, I cannot arbitrarily change the order.

The use of a categorical variable as an explanatory variable, such as gender (male versus female), is common in regression models. As an explanatory variable, a categorical variable captures the systematic differences latent in data that cannot be accounted for by other variables. For instance, if there is a systematic difference between the wages of men and women in a particular profession, the gender variable will capture the gender-based wage differences. However, when the dependent variable is categorical, rather than continuous, the use of conventional regression (OLS) techniques is no longer appropriate. The OLS models are therefore modified to account for the categorical dependent variables. Such modified models are called discrete choice, categorical, limited dependent variable, or qualitative response models.

Let's Question the Decision to Smoke or Not

Let us refer to the earlier discussion about the determinants of smoking. I identified at least four key questions that one may be interested in to gain a better understanding of the prevalence of smoking among individuals. These questions are

- Do higher cigarette prices deter cigarette smoking?
- Do highly educated individuals smoke less than others do?
- Do high-income individuals smoke more or less than the rest?
- Is smoking more prevalent among youth than older cohorts?

After I have determined my research questions, I need to transpose research questions into research hypotheses. For instance, the previously mentioned research questions are converted into the following hypotheses:

- **Hypothesis 1:** Individuals faced with higher cigarette prices are less likely to take up smoking.
- **Hypothesis 2:** Highly educated individuals are less likely to take up smoking.
- **Hypothesis 3:** Low-income individuals are more likely to smoke.
- **Hypothesis 4:** Youth are more likely to indulge in smoking.

The aforementioned hypotheses are tied to the following four variables: price, education, income, and age. For each hypothesis, the variable may have more than one expected impact on the probability of smoking. For instance, with an increase in income one may expect an increase in the propensity to smoke because higher income implies that the consumer is not deterred by higher cigarette prices. On the other hand, higher income may imply that the individual's taste preferences may vary where the consumer may prefer higher value goods and services. So smoking may give way to a preference for expensive wines, for instance. Lastly, the income may have no discernible impact on the propensity to smoke because smoking could be seen as a hard-to-break habit and neither lower prices may encourage more cigarette smoking nor higher prices may result in less smoking. Thus, one can map the four explanatory variables around the hypotheses as shown in Table 8.2.

Table 8.2 Mapping Explanatory Variables Around the Four Hypotheses

Variable	Expected Positive Impact	Statistically Not Significant	Expected Negative Impact
Price	None.	Price does not affect cigarette smoking.	Higher prices result in lower propensity to smoke.
Education	Highly educated individuals smoke more than others because of lifestyles associated with higher education, such as writers, editors, and so on.	Education does not affect cigarette smoking.	Highly educated individuals smoke less than others because they are aware of its adverse health impacts.

Variable	Expected Positive Impact	Statistically Not Significant	Expected Negative Impact
Income	High-income individuals smoke more because of high discretionary income.	Income does not affect cigarette smoking.	High-income individuals smoke less because they can afford to indulge in other more expensive substitutes.
Age	Younger cohorts smoke more because of peer pressure.	Age has no impact on cigarette smoking	Older cohorts smoke less because of their concerns about smoking's adverse impact on health.

Smoking Data Set

Because smoking is an individual trait, the data required to answer the research questions has to be individual-based. I have made data available in SAS, SPSS, Stata, and R formats on the book's website at www.ibmpress.com/title/9780133991024.[6]

All versions of the file are titled *smoking* with the appropriate extension indicating the software to be used. I encourage you to download the appropriate format of the smoking data set and repeat the analysis illustrated in the following sections on your own.

The smoking data contains information on a person's age, household income, education, price of a pack of cigarettes and a dichotomous variable that captures the binary outcome of whether the individual is a smoker or otherwise. Note that the data is from 1979 and hence the household income and the price of a pack of cigarettes in cents is much lower than current prices and incomes.

Table 8.3 lists variable names and descriptions. Note that the uploaded versions of data carry additional derived variables that are not reported in Table 8.3.

Table 8.3   List of Base Variables in the Smoking Data Set

Variables	Description
educ	Education in years
age	Age in years
income	Household income in dollars
pcigs79	Price of a pack in cents
ageeduc	Interaction between age and education
smoker	1 if smokes, 0 otherwise

Variables	Description
educincome	Interaction between education and income
qrt_age	4 quantiles of age
inc_10k	Household income/10,000

Exploratory Data Analysis

The first step in analytics always involves exploratory data analysis. Here I determine the central tendencies in the data set. The smoking data contains the variable smoker, which is coded as yes and no (1/0), to indicate whether the individual is a smoker or not. The smoking data contains data from 1,122 individuals.

I illustrate tabular output using the user-written command in Stata, **htsummary**. I favor this command over the Stata's built-in commands because **htsummary** generates tabular outputs conducive for publications.

Table 8.4 illustrates that of the 1,122 adult individuals 427 (38%) reported smoking.

The Stata code is documented in the following lines.

```
htopen using ch8_tables, replace
htsummary smoker, head freq  format(%8.2f) rowtotal close
htsummary educ,  format(%8.1f) head
htsummary age,  format(%8.1f)
htsummary income,  format(%8.0f)
htsummary pcigs79 ,  format(%8.1f)
htsummary smoker,  format(%8.2f) close
htlog sum age income pcigs79 smoker
htsummary educ smoker,  format(%8.1f) head
htsummary age smoker,  format(%8.1f)
htsummary income smoker,  format(%8.0f)
htsummary pcigs79 smoker,  format(%8.1f) close
htclose
```

Table 8.4 A Breakdown of the Smoker Variable

Variable		Summary Statistics
1 if smokes, 0 otherwise[1]	no	695 (62%)
	yes	427 (38%)
	Total	1122 (100%)

1: n (column percentage)

My four hypotheses are concerned with the impact of age, income, education, and the price of cigarettes on the individual's propensity to smoke. Let me first review the descriptive statistics for the four key explanatory variables, which are presented in Table 8.5. The average respondent in the sample is almost 42 years old with approximately 12.2 years of education and average household income of $19,359. The average value for the binary variable smoker is 0.38, which indicates that 38% of the respondents smoke in the sample.

Table 8.5   Descriptive Statistics of Key Variables in the Smoking Data Set

Variable	Summary Statistics
education in years[1]	12.2 (3.3) [1122]
age in years[1]	41.9 (17.1) [1122]
household income in dollars[1]	19359 (9053) [1122]
price of a pack in cents[1]	61.0 (4.9) [1122]
1 if smokes, 0 otherwise[1]	0.38 (0.49) [1122]

1: Arithmetic Mean (SD) [n]

I would first like to determine whether smokers' socio-demographics differ from that of non-smokers. This is achieved by calculating separate averages and standard deviations for smokers and non-smokers, which are presented in Table 8.6.

The average age of a smoker at 38.9 years is lower than that of non-smokers at 43.7 years. However, one observes only a small difference in income and the price of cigarettes between smokers and non-smokers. Smokers, however, appear to have slightly lower level of education than non-smokers do. It appears from Table 8.6 that only age suggests considerable differences between smokers and non-smokers.

Table 8.6   Descriptive Statistics Comparing Smokers with Non-smokers

Variables	1 if Smokes, 0 Otherwise		
	No	Yes	Total
education in years[1]	12.4 (3.5) [695]	11.8 (2.9) [427]	12.2 (3.3) [1122]
age in years[1]	43.7 (18.1) [695]	38.9 (14.7) [427]	41.9 (17.1) [1122]
household income in dollars[1]	19493 (9192) [695]	19142 (8827) [427]	19359 (9053) [1122]
price of a pack in cents[1]	61.2 (4.8) [695]	60.6 (4.9) [427]	61.0 (4.9) [1122]

1: Arithmetic Mean (SD) [n]

Notice that age, income, education, and price of cigarettes are captured as continuous variables. One should try to ensure that all explanatory variables are of similar magnitude. Notice also that while age, education, and price of cigarettes are similar in magnitude, income is not. The difference between minimum and maximum education is 18 and for income the difference is 29,500. Such difference in magnitude limits the way we can interpret the resulting model. Such difficulties in interpretation can be prevented by transforming the variable. I have therefore divided income variable by 10,000 to create a new variable, inc_10k. I will illustrate models with the modified and unmodified versions of the income variable.

What Makes People Smoke: Asking Regression for Answers

I illustrate estimating binary logit/probit models by focusing first on the tried-and-tested OLS regression model, which I explained earlier in Chapter 7, "Why Tall Parents Don't Have Even Taller Children." I use OLS only to take the readers from what they are usually familiar with (the OLS regression model) to the unfamiliar, which are the logit and probit models.

Ordinary Least Squares Regression

Setting aside the concerns regarding the OLS regression, the results are presented in Table 8.7 (Model labeled 1). The model fit, as is evident by the adjusted R-squared of 3.5% (.035), suggests a poor fit. The following equation results from the linear probability model reported in Table 8.7.

$$\Pr(smoker) = 1.18 - .005 * age - .0197 * educ + 7.95 * 10^{-7} * inccome - .00631 * pcigs79 + \varepsilon$$

The estimated coefficients are statistically significant at the 95% level with the exception of household income. The probability of smoking declines with age, education, and the price of cigarettes. Income, as it appears from the model, has no meaningful or statistically significant impact on the probability of smoking.

Notice that the coefficient for income ($7.95*10^{-7}$) is very small. To obtain a meaningful coefficient for income, I replace the income with the modified variable inc_10k. The resulting model is labeled as 2 in Table 8.7 and is presented in an equation as follows.

$$\Pr(smoker) = 1.18 - .005 * age - .0197 * educ + .00795 * inc\_10k - .00631 * pcigs79 + \varepsilon$$

Notice that apart from the coefficient for income, all other coefficients remained the same in the second model (Table 8.7). The revised coefficient for income suggests that the likelihood of smoking increases by .00795 for every $10,000 increase in income. In economic terms, this impact is rather meaningless.

The Stata code is documented in the following lines.

```
reg smoker age educ income pcigs79
outreg2 using tab8-7.doc, replace label cttop(reg_income) adjr2
reg smoker age educ inc_10k pcigs79
outreg2
```

Table 8.7   Comparative OLS Models with income and inc_10k as Explanatory Variables

Variables	(1) reg_income 1 If Smokes 0 Otherwise	(2) reg_inc10k 1 If Smokes 0 Otherwise
age in years	−0.00458***	−0.00458***
	(0.000854)	(0.000854)
education in years	−0.0197***	−0.0197***
	(0.00475)	(0.00475)
household income in dollars	7.95e-07	
	(1.70e-06)	
price of a pack in cents	−0.00631**	−0.00631**
	(0.00294)	(0.00294)
hhld income/10,000		0.00795
		(0.0170)
Constant	1.181***	1.181***
	(0.194)	(0.194)
Observations	1,122	1,122
Adjusted R-squared	0.035	0.035

Standard errors in parentheses

*** $p<0.01$, ** $p<0.05$, * $p<0.1$

You can plot the effects of each estimated coefficient to visualize its impact on the dependent variable, smoker. Notice that as age and education increase, the probability to smoke decreases in Figure 8.1. Notice also the increase in the probability to smoke with an increase in income. However, the wide confidence interval around the regression line for the variable inc_10k suggests lack of statistical significance.

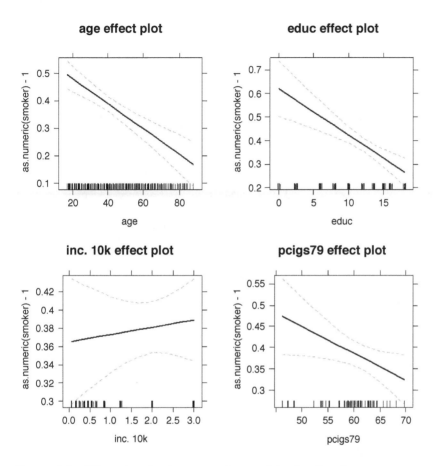

Figure 8.1 Effect plots for the regression model using R software

Stata, R, and other software offer another plot called the *added-variable plot* (AVP) to view the impact of each variable on the dependent variable, while holding the impact of all other variables constant. The AVP reduces the multidimensional, multivariate data back to two dimensions by plotting two entities on x- and y-axes.[7] Also, unlike Figure 8.1, the AVP plots the data points in addition to the linear line that depicts the relationship between the dependent variable and the individual regressor.

I have plotted the AVP for the OLS model (2) presented in Table 8.7. The plots reported in Figure 8.1 and Figure 8.2 suggest that the impact of income on smoking is rather limited compared to the other three explanatory variables.

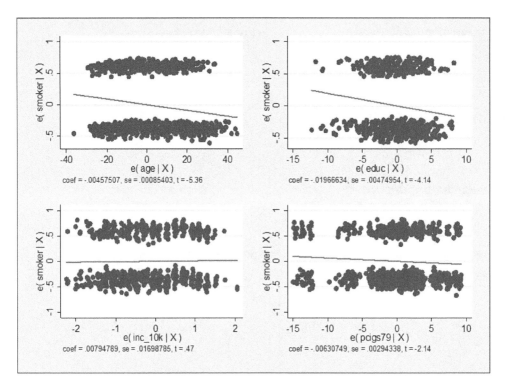

Figure 8.2   Added variable plot for the OLS model generated in Stata

Interpreting Models at the Margins

The slopes of the regression lines shown in Figure 8.2 are the same as the regression coefficients listed in Table 8.7. Let us first interpret the raw coefficients and see how they help us in answering the research questions we posed earlier. For instance, we would like to know whether a higher price of cigarettes deters cigarette smoking. The coefficient for the price of cigarettes suggests that a one-cent increase in the price of cigarettes is correlated with a decline of 0.0063 in smoking.

It appears that the price of cigarettes has almost no impact (in terms of magnitude) on the probability of smoking and thus one may erroneously conclude that higher cigarette prices may not deter cigarette smoking. Such a conclusion will not be sound because one must realize that an increase in the price of cigarettes will not be proposed in cents, but instead, it will be proposed in some percentage terms.

Assume that the price of cigarettes, after being subject to a new tax, increases by 10%. This suggests that the price will increase from the average level of 60.97 to 67.07. Thus, for a 10% increase in price, the probability to smoke is expected to decline from 38.1% to 37.7%. In percentage terms, we can see that a 10% increase in prices is associated with a 10% decline in the probability of smoking. Figure 8.3 presents the decline in smoking (listed on the y-axis) resulting from a change in the price of cigarettes, which is listed in cents on the x-axis.

I should caution that Figure 8.3 is for illustrative purposes only. Often behavioral changes are seen to occur on a small scale around the expected means of the variables.

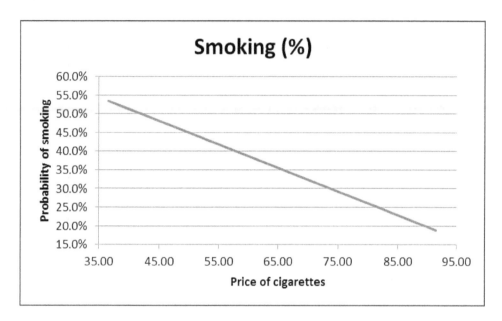

Figure 8.3   Change in smoking levels resulting from changes in cigarette prices

The Logit Model

Before I move on to logit models, let me first revisit the hypotheses I had developed from our research questions about the factors affecting the decision to smoke. These are

- **Hypothesis 1:** Individuals faced with higher cigarette prices are less likely to take up smoking.

- **Hypothesis 2:** Highly educated individuals are less likely to take up smoking.

- **Hypothesis 3:** Low-income individuals are more likely to smoke.

- **Hypothesis 4:** Youth are more likely to indulge in smoking.

I will test these hypotheses using a logit model, which is one of the statistical tools recommended for analyzing dichotomous dependent variables. I use smoking data to illustrate the application of logit models deploying the same set of explanatory variables as the ones used for the OLS regressions.

The binary logit model can be estimated with ease using any statistical analysis/ econometrics software. I will illustrate estimating binary logit using SPSS, Stata, and R. When using Stata, SPSS, or R, one may choose either the command line or the point-and-click convenience of dialog boxes (similar to the one presented in Figure 8.4, which presents the dialog box for a binary logit model in Stata).

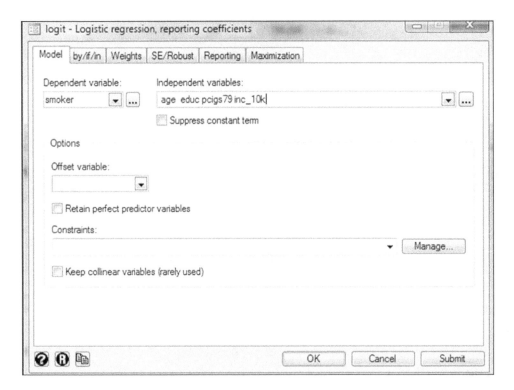

Figure 8.4   Populated dialog box for binary logit model in Stata

The dependent variable is `smoker` (yes/no) and the explanatory variables are age, education, price of cigarettes, and income in tens of thousands of dollars. Table 8.8 reports the syntax for estimating logit models for Stata, R, and SPSS.

You will notice in Table 8.8 that the three software tools differ considerably in syntax. You will also notice that Stata's syntax is the most concise. I prefer Stata's syntax for brevity, simplicity, and for an intuitive, logical structure. Because of these reasons, Stata's code is easy to recall and remains my favorite.

Table 8.8 Binary Logit Commands Syntax in Various Econometrics Software

Software	Command
Stata	`logit smoker age educ inc_10k pcigs79`
R	`glm(smoker ~ age + educ + inc.10k + pcigs79, x = TRUE,` `data = smoking, family = binomial(link = "logit"))`

SPSS	`* Generalized Linear Models.`
	
	 `GENLIN smoker (REFERENCE=FIRST) WITH age educ pcigs79 inc_10k`
	 `  /MODEL age educ pcigs79 inc_10k INTERCEPT=YES`
	 ` DISTRIBUTION=BINOMIAL LINK=LOGIT`
	 `  /CRITERIA METHOD=FISHER(1) SCALE=1 COVB=MODEL`
	 `MAXITERATIONS=100 MAXSTEPHALVING=5`
	 `    PCONVERGE=1E-006(ABSOLUTE) SINGULAR=1E-012`
	 `ANALYSISTYPE=3(WALD) CILEVEL=95 CITYPE=WALD`
	 `    LIKELIHOOD=FULL`
	 `  /MISSING CLASSMISSING=EXCLUDE`
	 `  /PRINT CPS DESCRIPTIVES MODELINFO FIT SUMMARY SOLUTION`
	 `(EXPONENTIATED).`

The logit model output from Stata is presented in Table 8.9. In the following lines, I have also listed the Stata code to illustrate how I transformed the output of the logit model to be publication ready.

```
logit smoker age educ  pcigs79 income
outreg2 using tab8-9.doc, cttop(logit model) replace label  ///
 addstat(Pseudo R-squared, 'e(r2_p)')
```

Table 8.9 Binary Logit Model Output Generated by Stata

Variables	(1) Logit Model 1 If Smokes 0 Otherwise
age in years	−0.0202*** (0.00384)
education in years	−0.0867*** (0.0212)
household income in dollars	3.72e-06 (7.45e-06)

Variables	(1) Logit Model 1 If Smokes 0 Otherwise
price of a pack in cents	–0.0274** (0.0129)
Constant	2.993*** (0.855)
Observations	1,122
Pseudo R-squared	0.0292

Standard errors in parentheses

*** p<0.01, ** p<0.05, * p<0.1

The first thing to notice is that the reported coefficients in the logit model have the same signs as we observed earlier for the OLS regression models in Table 8.7. However, the logit model coefficients appear very different from the coefficients reported in Table 8.7. Notice also that logit model reports a pseudo R-squared of 0.0292.

You may recall from Chapter 7 that we use R-squared to gauge the model fit in OLS regression models. If we were to compare two or more regression models, we will prefer the one with higher R-squared, provided the model offers results that conform to theory.

While individual disciplines, such as engineering, economics, psychology, or political science may have their own benchmarks for R-squared, there are no hard-and-fast rules to accept a model with high R-squared or reject one with a low R-squared.

At the same time, I would like to caution that one should not compare R-squared obtained for an OLS model with a pseudo R-squared for a logit-type model. Over the years, I have observed that logit and other generalized linear models report a lower value for (pseudo) R-squared than an identically specified OLS model. As an illustration, let us compare the adjusted R-squared for the OLS model in Table 8.7 (0.035) with the pseudo R-squared for the logit model in Table 8.9 (0.0292). The OLS model does not offer a "better" fit because it reports a higher value for the adjusted R-squared than the logit model's pseudo R-squared. I caution against such comparisons primarily because the two goodness-of-fit statistics are computed differently.

I advise that you consult the literature in your respective discipline to determine what range of R-squared values represents a good model fit. In economics, for instance, you will seldom see an author singing virtues of a high R-squared of her model. In comparison, engineering studies often boast of the high R-squared values. Remember, a model with high R-squared values offering counterintuitive results may be of little value!

Interpreting Odds in a Logit Model

Interpreting coefficients in a logit model is more involved than it is for regression models. However, there are ways to make interpreting logit models rather easy. If we were to exponentiate the estimated coefficients in a logit model, we would then interpret results as the odds of smoking against not smoking.

A quick discussion about the odds and odds ratio is in order. I have adopted this example from a tutorial available online from the Institute of Digital Research and Education at the University of California in LA.[8] I use a hypothetical example of gender differences in admissions in an engineering school. Let us assume that 7 out of 10 young men who applied were successful in being admitted to the engineering school. The probability of success for men is $7/10 = .7$, and the probability of failure is $3/10 = .3$.

Now, let us assume that only 3 out of 10 young women who applied were successful in being admitted to the engineering school. The probability of success for women is $3/10 = .3$, and the probability of failure is $7/10 = .7$.

Using the probabilities, I can estimates the odds of success for both men and women. The odds of admission for men is the ratio of probability for success over failure. For men, the odds of admission are $.7/.3 = 2.33$ and for women, the odds are $.3/.7 = 0.428$.

In this example, the odds ratio is the ratio of odds for success for men over women, which is calculated as $2.33/.428 = 5.44$. Put simply, the odds of being admitted in an engineering school for men are 5.44 times higher than that for women.

The estimated coefficients in a logit model represent the log of odds ratio. When I exponentiate the coefficients, I convert the log of odds ratio to simply odds ratio. Let us see how this works for the logit model applied to the smoking data set.

Table 8.10 presents the output from two logit models where I have exponentiated the coefficients. Notice that the coefficients in the model labeled 1 correspond to the model that used income as the explanatory variable, whereas the column labeled 2 corresponds to the model where the income variable was divided by 10,000. The asterisks are explained in the footnote. A single asterisk refers to the probability of less than 0.1. Any coefficient without the asterisk is statistically insignificant at $p < .1$. We would look for two asterisks for a 95% level of significance (corresponding to a t-statistics of 1.96 or higher).

The research question required us to determine whether the propensity to smoke declines with age. Let us first review the exponentiated coefficient for age. The exponential of the estimated coefficient for age in Table 8.10 is 0.98 ($e^{-.0202} = \dfrac{1}{e^{0.0202}} = 0.98$)

This implies that when the age increases by a year, the odds for smoking change by 0.98. Sounds mechanical? Yes, indeed. For this reason, using the formula in Equation 8.1, I transform the estimated coefficient to interpret the impact of explanatory variables as a percentage.

$$100 * \left(e^{\beta_k * \delta} - 1 \right) \quad \textbf{Equation 8.1}$$

Substituting for $\delta = 1$ to represent one-year increase in age, we have:

$$100 * \left(e^{-.0202} - 1\right) = -2$$

This implies that when age increases by a year, the odds of smoking against non-smoking decline by 2%, all else being equal. Similarly, for a 10-year increase in age, the odds for smoking decline by 18.29% ($100 * (e^{-.0202*10} - 1) = -18.29\%$). Also, a unit increase in education results in an 8.3% (($100 * (.9169 - 1) = -8.31\%$) decline in the odds of smoking. Lastly, a 10 cent increase in the price of cigarettes results in a 23.9% in the odds of smoking. The coefficient for income is statistically insignificant at 90% level.

The following Stata code generated the output listed in Table 8.10.

```
logit smoker age educ  pcigs79 income
outreg2 using tab8-10.doc, cttop(eform with income) replace label eform
addstat(Pseudo R-squared, 'e(r2_p)')

logit smoker age educ  pcigs79 inc_10k
outreg2 using tab8-10.doc, cttop(eform with inc_10k) append label eform
addstat(Pseudo R-squared, 'e(r2_p)')
```

Table 8.10 Exponentiated Coefficients for Logit Models

Variables	(1) eform with Income 1 If Smokes 0 Otherwise	(2) eform with inc_10k 1 If Smokes 0 Otherwise
1 if smokes, 0 otherwise		
age in years	0.980*** (0.00377)	0.980*** (0.00377)
education in years	0.917*** (0.0194)	0.917*** (0.0194)
price of a pack in cents	0.973** (0.0125)	0.973** (0.0125)
household income in dollars	1.000 (7.45e-06)	
hhld income/10,000		1.038 (0.0773)

Variables	(1) eform with Income 1 If Smokes 0 Otherwise	(2) eform with inc_10k 1 If Smokes 0 Otherwise
Constant	19.94*** (17.05)	19.94*** (17.05)
Observations	1,122	1,122
Pseudo R-squared	0.0292	0.0292

Standard errors in parentheses

*** p<0.01, ** p<0.05, * p<0.1

One can also plot the change in the probability of smoking computed from the logit model against a particular explanatory variable, while holding other explanatory variables constant. Figure 8.5 presents two plots for change in the probability of smoking for a change in the price of cigarettes (left) and the level of education (right). The downward sloping curves in both graphs indicate that the increase in the price of cigarettes and the level of education are associated with a decline in the probability of smoking.

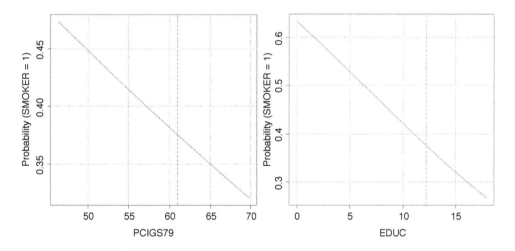

Figure 8.5   Plot of probability of smoking against price and education

Consider the following calculation of the forecasted probability at the mean values of all explanatory variables.

Equation 8.2 shows the logit equation:

$$P = \frac{1}{1 + e^{-Z}}\quad \textbf{Equation 8.2}$$

Where Z is the equation obtained from the logit model. Consider the model presented in Table 8.9. I can write the model as an equation and substitute the average values for each variable to be multiplied with the respective coefficient in the equation. Table 8.5 reports the summary statistics, including averages, for each variable in the model. Table 8.9 reports the coefficient for age to be $-.02017$. The average age of a respondent in our sample, as per Table 8.5, is 41.88 years. I substitute in Equation 8.2 the coefficient and average value for age and other explanatory variables to estimate the probability for smoking at 0.375 or 37.5%.

$$P = \frac{1}{1 + e^{-(\ 2.993 - .02017*41.88 - .087*12.19 + .0372*\ 1.936 - .02739*60.972)}} = 0.375$$

In Equation 8.2, I can substitute alternate values for explanatory variables to estimate corresponding probabilities. Table 8.11 depicts the change in the probability of smoking for different values for the education and age variables. The probability values have been computed in Microsoft Excel using Equation 8.2. Notice the highlighted cell in Table 8.11 corresponds to the average values of age (41.88) and education (12.19) and thus presents the average probability for smoking at 37.5%. Notice also that the probability for smoking for minimum age and grade 5 education is 65%, all else being equal, whereas the probability of smoking for the oldest respondent in the sample with average education is estimated at 19.2%, all else being equal.

Table 8.11   Changes in Smoking Probability for Various Values of Age and Education

		Education			
	37.59%	5	10	12.19	18
Age	17	65.0%	54.6%	49.9%	37.5%
	28	59.8%	49.1%	44.3%	32.5%
	41.88	52.9%	42.1%	37.59%	26.7%
	48	49.8%	39.2%	34.7%	24.3%
	58	44.8%	34.5%	30.3%	20.8%
	68	39.9%	30.1%	26.2%	17.7%
	78	35.2%	26.0%	22.5%	14.9%
	88	30.7%	22.3%	19.2%	12.6%

A user-written package for Stata, **spost**, offers useful post-estimation routines to determine the impact of explanatory variables on the dependent variable.[9] The key commands are **listcoef**, **percent help**, and **prchange**. I have specified the **listcoef** command with two options; that is, help and percent. The help option reports definitions for column headings, whereas the percent option reports the percentage change in odds in Figure 8.6. The column with the % heading reports the percentage change in odds of smoking for a unit change in the explanatory variables.

```
.listcoef, help percent
```

```
logit (N=1122): Percentage change in odds
```

```
  odds of: yes vs no
```

smoker	b	z	p>|z|	%	%StdX	SDofX
age	-0.02017	-5.249	0.000	-2.0	-29.1	17.0812
educ	-0.08674	-4.092	0.000	-8.3	-24.9	3.2959
inc_10k	0.03717	0.499	0.618	3.8	3.4	0.9053
pcigs79	-0.02739	-2.130	0.033	-2.7	-12.4	4.8521

```
      b = raw coefficient
      z = z-score for test of b=0
  p>|z| = p-value for z-test
      % = percent change in odds for unit increase in X
  %StdX = percent change in odds for SD increase in X
  SDofX = standard deviation of x
```

Figure 8.6   Interpreting logit model using the listcoef command in Stata

The results from **prchange** are presented in Figure 8.7. **prchange** is perhaps the most useful tool in determining the effects of explanatory variables on the change in probability for the dependent variable. The command computes the change in probability of the dependent variable in response to a change in the explanatory variable. However, the change in the explanatory variable could take several forms. For instance, if we are interested in determining the change in probability for smoking between the youngest and the oldest respondent in the survey, **prchange** readily estimates the change in probability. For age, the probability to smoke declines from 49.9% for an 18 year old to 19.2% for an 88 year old, all else being equal, resulting in an absolute decline of 30.6%, as is mentioned for the coefficient for age in Figure 8.7.

Similarly, as education varies from minimum to maximum, the resulting absolute change in probability is –0.36. We can see the insignificant impact of income on the probability for smoking from the fact that the net change in the probability for smoking is 0.025 when income variable changes from minimum to maximum value. Similarly, we observe a 15.3% decline in the probability for smoking when the price of cigarettes rises from minimum observed value in the data set to the maximum observed value. The 0–1 column heading is useful for only dichotomous explanatory variables, such as gender.

```
. prchange,help

logit: Changes in Probabilities for smoker

           min->max      0->1     -+1/2     -+sd/2  MargEfct
     age    -0.3067   -0.0049   -0.0047   -0.0806   -0.0047
    educ    -0.3674   -0.0203   -0.0203   -0.0670   -0.0203
 inc_10k     0.0256    0.0086    0.0087    0.0079    0.0087
 pcigs79    -0.1526   -0.0050   -0.0064   -0.0312   -0.0064


             no       yes
Pr(y|x)   0.6242   0.3758


            age      educ   inc_10k  pcigs79
   x=   41.8841   12.1912   1.93592  60.9719
sd_x=   17.0812   3.29595   .905252  4.85213


 Pr(y|x): probability of observing each y for specified x values
Avg|Chg|: average of absolute value of the change across categories
Min->Max: change in predicted probability as x changes from its minimum to
          its maximum
    0->1: change in predicted probability as x changes from 0 to 1
   -+1/2: change in predicted probability as x changes from 1/2 unit below
          base value to 1/2 unit above
  -+sd/2: change in predicted probability as x changes from 1/2 standard
          dev below base to 1/2 standard dev above
MargEfct: the partial derivative of the predicted probability/rate with
          respect to a given independent variable
```

Figure 8.7   Interpreting logit model using the prchange command in Stata

If we were interested in determining the impact of a small change around the mean of an explanatory variable on the probability for smoking, we would consult the probabilities reported under the $-+1/2$ column. For instance, the probability to smoke declines from 38.6% to 36.6% if education changes from 11.69 (average years of education -0.5) to 12.19 (average years of education $+0.5$). Figure 8.7 shows the net difference of 2% decline in the probability of smoking, which corresponds to a unit change in the years of education centered on the mean years of education, while keeping all other explanatory variables constant. Similarly, the $-+sd/2$ column reports the change in probability for ±0.5 standard deviation around the mean of the explanatory variable. The last column, **MargEfct**, reports the partial derivative of the estimated probability with respect to a given explanatory variable, such as income. The **MFX** command in Stata reports marginal effects and elasticities for all explanatory variables used in the model.

Based on the results presented earlier, I can safely conclude the following:

- Higher cigarette prices are associated with lower odds of cigarette smoking.

- An increase in education is associated with lower odds of cigarette smoking.

- Income has no statistically significant impact on the odds of cigarette smoking.

- An increase in age is correlated with lower odds for smoking, thus confirming our hypothesis that odds for smoking are higher for younger cohorts than the rest.

Probit Model

Probit models differ from logit models because unlike logit models, the error terms are assumed to follow Normal distribution. I illustrate the use of R and **R Commander** for estimating and interpreting probit models.[10, 11] I first estimate the probit model using the Generalized Linear Models in R. Later, I illustrate the use of **zelig**, which is an R package that facilitates estimating and simulating econometric models.[12]

One can use either the command line syntax to estimate the binary probit models or use dialog boxes that have been made available with **R Commander**. The command line syntax is very helpful in reproducing and fine-tuning the models, whereas the dialog boxes are useful for those who appreciate the convenience of point-and-click user interfaces.

Figure 8.8 presents the populated dialog box for the probit model in **R Commander**, where the dependent variable (smoker) and the explanatory variables have already been specified in the formula bar. You can also see **binomial** highlighted under the family of distributions (statisticians use "family" to describe the "group" of distributions), and probit selected under the **Link function**.

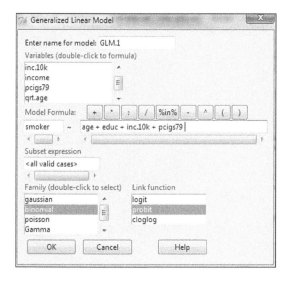

Figure 8.8 Dialog box for probit models in **R Commander**

After you make the choices in the dialog box, **R Commander** generates a script to estimate the probit model. R uses the following convention to specify the model:

```
Dependent variable ~ Explanatory variables
```

Thus `smoker`, being the dependent variable, will appear to the left of the tilde in the formula and the explanatory variables appear to the right. The dialog box shown in Figure 8.8 executes the following script, which one can directly type to estimate the probit model.

```
glm(formula = smoker ~ age + educ + inc.10k + pcigs79,
family = binomial(probit), data = smoking)
```

GLM in the syntax stands for Generalized Linear Models.

Further, notice that the script also identifies the data set being used to estimate the model, which is important because R can work with several data sets at the same time and therefore one must specify the data set in the syntax to ensure that the model is estimated using the correct data set.

After the command is executed, R generates the output presented in Figure 8.9. The output reports the syntax, deviance residuals, the standard model description with coefficients, standard errors, and asterisks to indicate statistical significance and some goodness of fit statistics. Notice the `pseudo R-squared` is not readily reported by R. Instead it reports `AIC` (Akaike Information Criterion).

```
Call:
glm(formula = smoker ~ age + educ + inc.10k + pcigs79, family = binomial(probit),
    data = smoking)

Deviance Residuals:
    Min       1Q    Median       3Q       Max
-1.4392  -0.9872  -0.8035   1.2806   1.8318

Coefficients:
             Estimate Std. Error z value Pr(>|z|)
(Intercept)  1.851707   0.525606   3.523 0.000427 ***
age         -0.012539   0.002341  -5.357 8.47e-08 ***
educ        -0.053713   0.012957  -4.145 3.39e-05 ***
inc.10k      0.021489   0.045853   0.469 0.639312
pcigs79     -0.016871   0.007924  -2.129 0.033242 *
---
Signif. codes:  0 '***' 0.001 '**' 0.01 '*' 0.05 '.' 0.1 ' ' 1

(Dispersion parameter for binomial family taken to be 1)

    Null deviance: 1490.8  on 1121  degrees of freedom
Residual deviance: 1446.9  on 1117  degrees of freedom
AIC: 1456.9

Number of Fisher Scoring iterations: 4
```

Figure 8.9 Probit model output from `R Commander`

The coefficients reported for the probit model are similar to the coefficients estimated earlier from logit and OLS models where the magnitude of coefficients is different while the signs (positive or negative) are consistent across the three models. Age, education, and the price of cigarettes all reported negative coefficients in the three models, whereas income reported a positive, yet statistically insignificant coefficient. We can compare the magnitude and signs of the coefficients obtained from the OLS, logit, and probit models. I estimate the three models using Stata and report the results in Table 8.12 and the Stata code used to generate the results.

```
reg smoker age educ inc_10k pcigs79
outreg2 using tab8-12.doc, replace label cttop(OLS) adjr2

logit smoker age educ  inc_10k pcigs79
outreg2 using tab8-12.doc, cttop(Logit) append label  ///
    addstat(Pseudo R-squared, 'e(r2_p)')

probit smoker age educ  inc_10k pcigs79
outreg2 using tab8-12.doc, cttop(Probit) append label  addstat(Pseudo
R-squared, 'e(r2_p)')
```

Table 8.12 Comparing Estimated Coefficients from the Probit, Logit, and OLS Models

Variables	(1) OLS 1 if smokes 0 otherwise	(2) Logit 1 if smokes 0 otherwise	(3) Probit 1 if smokes 0 otherwise
age in years	−0.00458*** (0.000854)	−0.0202*** (0.00384)	−0.0125*** (0.00236)
education in years	−0.0197*** (0.00475)	−0.0867*** (0.0212)	−0.0537*** (0.0130)
hhld income/10,000	0.00795 (0.0170)	0.0372 (0.0745)	0.0215 (0.0458)
price of a pack in cents	−0.00631** (0.00294)	−0.0274** (0.0129)	−0.0169** (0.00793)
Constant	1.181*** (0.194)	2.993*** (0.855)	1.852*** (0.526)
Observations	1,122	1,122	1,122
Adjusted R-squared	0.035		
Pseudo R-squared		0.0292	0.0295

Standard errors in parentheses

*** p<0.01, ** p<0.05, * p<0.1

Before I interpret the probit model, I would like to state my preference for the choice among the OLS, logit, and probit models. I recommend you disregard OLS as a viable option for binary dependent variables. There are inherent limitations, some discussed earlier in the chapter, that render OLS a poor tool to model a binary dependent variable.

The choice between logit and probit models rests with one's preference for normally distributed errors (in probit's case) or logistic type errors (in logit's case). I prefer logit models over probit because of ease with interpretation. You will see from the following discussion about probit models that interpreting probit models can be tricky and is definitely more involved than interpreting logit models. However, logit models face a unique challenge for the assumption about the "independence of irrelevant alternatives" that arises when the dependent variable has more than two categories. This, of course, is not a concern in the case of binary dependent variables.

Lastly, the estimated coefficients and standard errors of logit and probit models differ by roughly a fraction of 1.6. Logit coefficients and standard errors in Table 8.12 are 1.6 times that of those reported for probit models. The difference in the magnitude of coefficients is largely a function of the assumed variance of the error term (Long and Frees, 2006, p. 139).[13]

Interpreting the Probit Model

Let us interpret the probit model in light of our initial four hypotheses. Briefly, we wanted to determine the impact of age, income, education, and the price of cigarettes on the probability of smoking. The estimated coefficients for probit models cannot be interpreted the same way using the odds ratio as we did earlier with logit models. The best way to interpret the probit model is to first test for statistical significance and later test for the magnitude of the individual coefficients.

Consider that age returns a negative coefficient of –0.0125 for the probit model. I interpret the impact of age as follows:

Older age is associated with a lower probability to smoke $(z = -5.357, p<0.01)$

Where z is similar to the $t\text{-value}$ in OLS and is computed as the ratio of the estimated coefficient and the respective standard error. z is reported in Figure 8.9.

Consider now that the coefficient for income (inc.10k) in Figure 8.9 reports the probability (Pr $(> |z|)$) to be around 0.639. Let us first assume that we had no *apriori* expectation for the sign for this variable. In such a case, we will rely on a two-tailed test for Pr $> |z|$ being 0.639, which is the shaded area in the two tails of the distribution in Figure 8.10. If you were to recall the discussion on hypothesis testing in Chapter 6, "Hypothetically Speaking," we cannot reject the null hypothesis that the estimated coefficient is 0 because the shaded area in Figure 8.10 is not confined to the tail of the distribution marked by –1.96 on the left and 1.96 on the right.

I could also have assumed in advance that higher income is likely to cause lower probability of smoking. This assumption would require us to apply the one-tailed test, which is illustrated in Figure 8.11. Hence even for the one-tailed test, the income variable is statistically insignificant. Here is the Stata code used to generate Figures 8.10 and 8.11.

```
twoway function y=normalden(x), range(-4 4) color(gs3) || ///
function y=normalden(x), range( -4 -.469 ) recast(area) color(gs3) ||
///
```

```
function y=normalden(x), range(.469 4) recast(area) color(gs3) ///
xtitle("{it: z}") ///
ytitle("Density") title("Illustration of hypothesis test") ///
subtitle("-z > Pr > z = 0.639") legend(off) xlabel(-1.96 -.469 0 .469
1.96) scheme(sj)
```

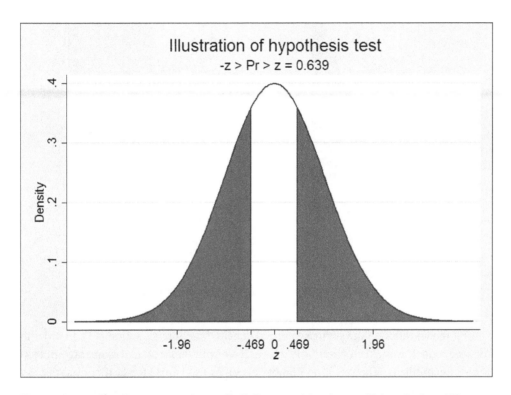

Figure 8.10 Significance test (two-tailed) illustrated for the coefficient for inc_10k

```
twoway function y=normalden(x), range(-4 4) color(gs3) || ///
function y=normalden(x), range(-4 -.469) recast(area) color(gs3) ///
xtitle("{it: z}") ///
ytitle("Density") title("Illustration of hypothesis test") ///
subtitle("Pr < z = 0.320") ///
legend(off) xlabel(-1.64 -.469 0 ) scheme(sj)
```

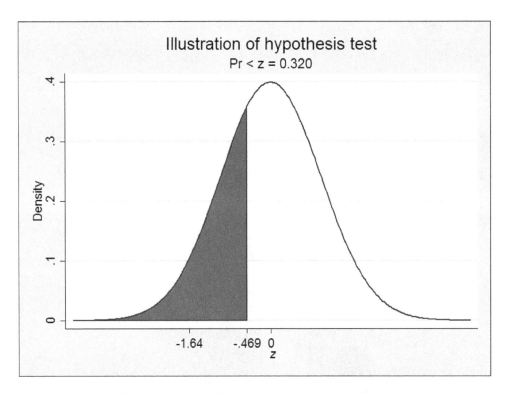

Figure 8.11   Significance test (left-tailed) illustrated for the coefficient for inc_10k

The probit model relies on the standard normal density function (Equation 8.3). In order to forecast from the model, we will first multiply coefficients with their respective average (mean) values and sum the products. The resulting number becomes the x in a standard normal density function (see Equation 8.3). Plugging x in the formula for the cumulative distribution function for normal density returns the probability of smoking using the mean values of explanatory variables.

$$f(x) = \int_{-\infty}^{x} \frac{1}{\sqrt{2 * \pi * \sigma^2}} * e^{\frac{-(x-\mu)^2}{2*\sigma^2}} \quad \textbf{Equation 8.3}$$

I have illustrated these calculations in an Excel spreadsheet (Chapter 8 results.xlsx) in the worksheet labeled probit. The spreadsheet is available from the book's website. The probability estimation is presented in Table 8.13. After multiplying coefficients with the respective average values for each explanatory variable, I obtained the sum-product of –0.3154. Using the standard normal density function in Excel with the *cumulative = True* option, I obtained the probability of `x ≤ -0.3154` to be 37.62%. I used the following built-in Excel function:

`=NORM.S.DIST(-0.3154,TRUE)`

The result is illustrated in Figure 8.12 where the shaded area to the left presents the probability of 37.6%. This implies that for anyone whose characteristics are represented by the average values of the variables in our sample, their probability to smoke is estimated at 37.6%.

Table 8.13 Estimating Probability Using the Probit Model

Smoker	Coef.	Mean	Coef*mean
age in years	–0.013	41.884	–0.5252
education in years	–0.054	12.191	–0.6548
hhld income/10,000	0.021	1.936	0.0416
price of a pack in cents	–0.017	60.972	–1.0287
Constant	1.852	1	1.8517
Z			–0.3154
Probability			37.624%

Here is the Stata code I used to generate Figure 8.12.

```
twoway function y=normalden(x), range(-4 4) color(gs3) || ///
function y=normalden(x), range(-4 -.3154) recast(area) color(gs3) ///
xtitle("{it: z}") ///
ytitle("Density") title("Probability calculations from Probit model")
///
subtitle("Pr < z = 0.3763") ///
legend(off) xlabel(-1.64 -.3154 ) scheme(sj)
```

Based on the model documented in Figure 8.9, I can conclude the following about the hypotheses. Age, education, and price of cigarettes are negatively correlated with the probability of smoking. Income, however, does not have a statistically significant impact on the probability of smoking.

Although determining whether a variable is statistically significant or not is important, it is equally important to determine the magnitude of impact each explanatory variable exerts on the dependent variable; that is, smoking. For this, we can rely on graphic display of effects, determine the marginal effects, or evaluate probability at various key values for explanatory variables.

Let me first illustrate the impact of price of cigarettes on the probability of smoking. I will also add another dimension to the figure to illustrate how different age groups feel price impacts differently. For this, I first discretize the continuous age variable in three mutually exclusive categories: younger, middle-aged, and older cohorts. Using coefficients reported for the model, I hold constant all other explanatory variables, while I change the values for price and age. The resulting plot is illustrated in Figure 8.13. Notice the downward sloping curves for the three cohorts, which illustrate that an increase in the price of cigarettes is correlated with a decline in smoking. Notice for each price point that the probability of smoking is highest for younger cohorts and lowest for the older cohorts. The data used to generate Figure 8.13 is included in the accompanying Excel spreadsheet.

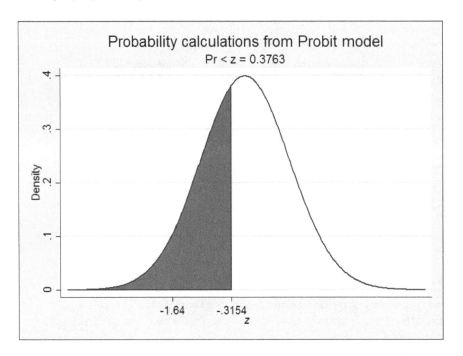

Figure 8.12   Illustration of cumulative probability density function for the probit model

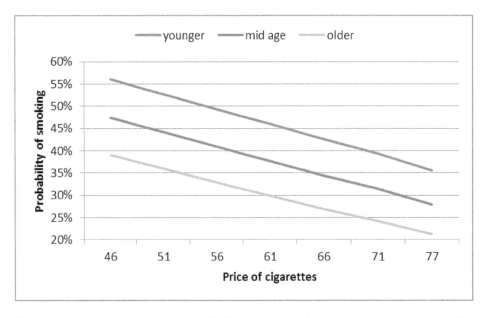

Figure 8.13   Impact of price on probability of smoking for young, mid-aged, and older cohorts

What if we were interested in determining the impact of price on the probability of smoking at two distinct key price points? We can compute the probability of smoking at the mean value for all explanatory variables. Then, we can change the price while keeping other variables at the mean to determine the probability of smoking at a difference price point. Notice that when all variables are held at mean values, the resulting probability to smoke is 37.6%. If one wants to determine the probability of smoking at a higher price point—for example, mean price plus one standard deviation of price (60.96 + 4.85 = 65.81), while holding other variables constant at their mean values—the resulting lower probability is 34.6%. Thus, I interpret the results as follows:

> *One standard deviation increase in the price of cigarettes is associated with 3 percentage point decline in the probability of smoking, all else being equal.*

In relative terms, the decline in the probability to smoke is in fact 8% ($\frac{34.6 - 37.6}{37.6} *100 = -7.9\%$)

Using R, one can readily plot the effect plots for explanatory variables, which are presented in Figure 8.14. Notice the downward-sloping curves for age, education, and price variables. Also plotted are the confidence intervals around the effect line. The confidence interval is smallest near the mean values for the respective variables and expands as one moves away from the mean values. This suggests that the explanatory power of the model is strongest around mean, and lower at the extremes.

Using Zelig for Estimation and Post-Estimation Strategies

R offers user-written packages to perform certain specialized tasks. `Zelig` is one such package that integrates several econometric modeling techniques and provides a uniform wrapper around numerous routines.[14, 15] You will need to install `Zelig` (a freeware) in R before you can use it. After it is installed, you can estimate the probit model using the following syntax:

```
library(Zelig)
z.out1 <- zelig(smoker ~ age + educ + inc.10k + pcigs79, model =
"probit", data = smoking)
summary(z.out1)
```

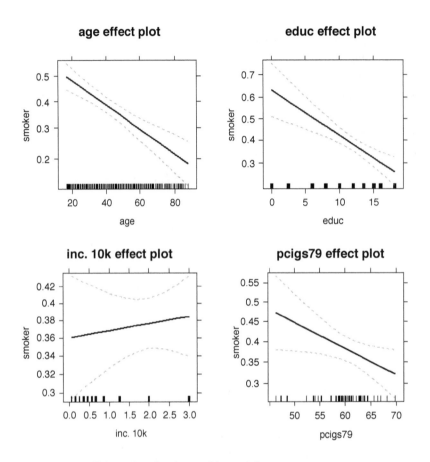

Figure 8.14   Effect plots for the probit models

The output for the `Zelig`-based probit model is the same as the one reported in Figure 8.9. `Zelig` allows one to run simulations based on the estimated model to determine the outcomes for certain specific values of the explanatory variables. For instance, if I run the simulations using the average values for explanatory variables, the distribution of the mean probability to smoke is plotted as part of the standard output from `Zelig` (see Figure 8.15).

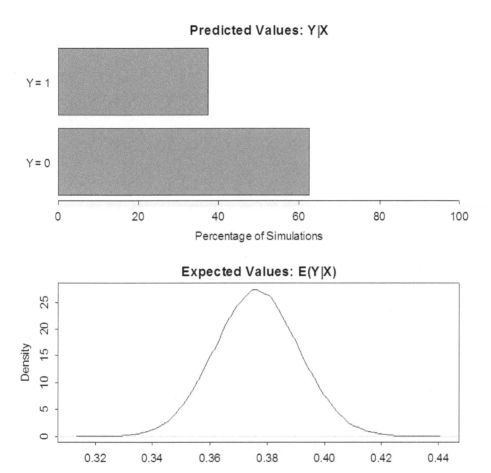

Figure 8.15   Predicted values from the probit model using Zelig

However, the real benefit of **zelig** appears when one is interested in determining the impact of change in an explanatory variable on the outcome reported by the model. Consider that the average price of cigarettes in the model equaled 60.97 cents. What will be the change in the probability to smoke if the price of cigarettes is increased to 77 cents? **zelig** allows one to run such simulations with ease. The output of the simulation is presented in Figure 8.16 where I have highlighted key values of interest. The first set of simulations is run with pcigs79=77 (cents) and the model is labeled as X, whereas the second set of simulations is run with pcigs79=60.97 (cents) and the model is labeled as X1. The predicted value for smoking when pcigs79 is 77 cents is 0.281 or 28.1%. The difference in the probability of smoking between the two price points is simulated to be 9.5%. The risk ratio corresponding to the change in cigarette prices is 1.37, which is the ratio of probability to smoke between the two price scenarios.

```
> summary(s.out2)

  Model: probit
  Number of simulations: 1e+05

Values of X
  (Intercept)      age     educ inc.10k pcigs79
1           1 41.88414 12.19118   1.936      77

Values of X1
  (Intercept)      age     educ  inc.10k  pcigs79
1           1 41.88414 12.19118 1.935918 60.97193

Expected Values: E(Y|X)
     mean         sd      2.5%      97.5%
1 0.280837 0.04444807 0.1990714 0.3722193

Predicted Values: Y|X
        0       1
1 0.71828 0.28172

First Differences in Expected Values: E(Y|X1)-E(Y|X)
        mean         sd       2.5%     97.5%
1 0.09544866 0.04232211 0.008846106 0.1737786

Risk Ratios: P(Y=1|X1)/P(Y=1|X)
     mean        sd     2.5%    97.5%
1 1.372117 0.2151644 1.023852 1.860909
```

Figure 8.16   Simulated results for change in price of cigarettes

R also offers a specialized package (**erer**) to determine marginal effects from probit and other generalized linear models. The package can be downloaded and installed with ease from within R. After the package has been installed, the following commands will generate the output reported in Figure 8.17.

```
library (erer)
ma <- glm(smoker ~ age + educ + inc.10k + pcigs79, x = TRUE,
data = smoking, family = binomial(link = "probit"))
ea <- maBina(w = ma, x.mean = TRUE, rev.dum = TRUE)
ea
```

The same package (**erer**) also allows one to plot the impact of a particular variable on the dependent variable. For instance, if one is interested in plotting the impact of education on the probability to smoke, a mere two line code will generate the plot (see Figure 8.18), which clearly indicates that an increase in education is correlated with a decline in the probability to smoke.

```
edu.1 <- maTrend(q = ea, nam.c="educ")
plot(edu.1)
```

```
[1] "probit"

$f.xb
          [,1]
[1,] 0.3795915

$w

Call:  glm(formula = smoker ~ age + educ + inc.10k + pcigs79, family = binomial(link = "probit"),
    data = smoking, x = TRUE)

Coefficients:
(Intercept)          age         educ       inc.10k       pcigs79
    1.85171     -0.01254     -0.05371       0.02149      -0.01687

Degrees of Freedom: 1121 Total (i.e. Null);   1117 Residual
Null Deviance:      1491
Residual Deviance: 1447  AIC: 1457

$out
            effect error t.value p.value
(Intercept)  0.703 0.200   3.514   0.000
age         -0.005 0.001  -5.363   0.000
educ        -0.020 0.005  -4.148   0.000
inc.10k      0.008 0.017   0.469   0.639
pcigs79     -0.006 0.003  -2.129   0.033
```

Figure 8.17   Marginal effects estimated from the probit model

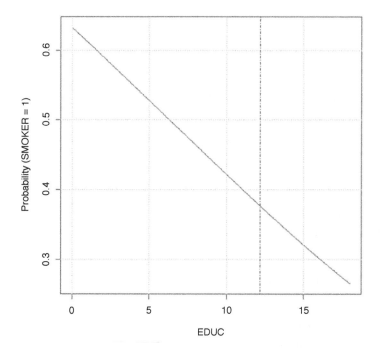

Figure 8.18   Change in the probability to smoke resulting from change in education

Estimating Logit Models for Grouped Data

Logit and probit models are mostly estimated for data obtained from individuals or about individual outcomes. Examples of such data are the decision to smoke, the incidence of a household defaulting on mortgage, or an individual's decision to pursue graduate studies. There are incidences, however, where data are available only as aggregated counts. Consider census data in the U.S. that are often released at an aggregate level such as census tracts (CT). In some circumstances, logit models can be estimated for grouped data using the grouped logit model.

I will illustrate the grouped logit model using an example from the U.S. Census data for the New York (NY) Census Metropolitan Statistical Area (CMSA). I estimate a grouped logit model to determine the transit use for commute (work) trips in the region. I subset the data to include only those Census Tracts whose centroid is no more than 25km from downtown Manhattan. This results in a subset of 2,707 census tracts (observations). The data set contains the variables listed in Table 8.14.

Table 8.14   Grouped Logit Data Set

Variable Name	Description
Id	Unique id
Area	CT area in square kilometers
Tract	Tract number
Name	Tract name
Population	Resident population
hh_autos	Average number of cars per household in the CT
d_cbd	Distance from the central business district, downtown
hh_size	Average number of persons per household
n_trips	Total commute trips reported in CT
n_transit	Total number of public transit trips
n_auto	Total number of auto-based commute trips
n_walk	Total number of commute walk trips
m_commtime	Median commute time reported for the CT

To estimate the grouped logit model of transit use, I require the total number of trips made by residents as well as the number of transit trips reported in each census tract. These two variables would jointly serve as the dependent variables. Explanatory variables used in the model include average number of automobiles per household, average household size, and the distance from the central business district (CBD) for each census tract. Table 8.15 presents descriptive statistics for key variables in the data set. Here is the Stata code used to generate Table 8.15.

```
htopen using ch8_tables, append
htsummary hh_autos,  format(%8.2f) head
htsummary hh_size,  format(%8.2f)
htsummary d_cbd,  format(%8.1f)
htsummary n_trips ,  format(%8.0f)
htsummary n_transit,  format(%8.0f) close
htclose
```

Table 8.15   Descriptive Statistics of Grouped CT-based Data

Variable	Summary Statistics
Average autos per household[1]	0.78 (0.44) [2707]
Average persons per household[1]	2.75 (0.51) [2707]
Distance from CBD[1]	13.4 (5.9) [2707]
Total number of trips[1]	1518 (1073) [2707]
Total transit trips[1]	698 (674) [2707]

1: Arithmetic Mean (SD) [n]

Our hypotheses in this problem are as follows:

1. CTs with a high level of automobile ownership will report lower transit use.

2. CTs inhabited by larger-sized households will report fewer transit trips.

3. CTs located near downtown enjoy higher supply of transit services and therefore will report higher transit use. Thus, the coefficient for distance from CBD should be negative.

Stata offers the weighted least squares method as well as the Maximum Likelihood Estimation method for grouped logit models. The following command in Stata estimates the grouped logit model using the weighted least squares method.

```
glogit n_transit n_trips hh_autos hh_size d_cbd
outreg2 using tab8-16.doc, replace label cttop(Grouped Logit) adjr2
```

Notice in the Stata code that two variables jointly serve as the dependent variable. Our intended dependent variable is the share of trips made by public transit in a given census tract. The share of trips can be obtained by dividing the number of transit trips (n_transit) in a census tract by the number of total trips (n_trips). The syntax for glogit requires us to first list the variable that otherwise should be the numerator of the ratio and then list the variable that should be in the denominator. Following these two variables, I specify the explanatory variables.

Table 8.16 shows the estimated results.

Table 8.16   Grouped Logit Estimation Using Stata

Variables	(1) Grouped Logit n_transit n_trips
Average autos per household	–1.826*** (0.0311)
Average persons per household	0.0959*** (0.0207)
Distance from CBD	–0.00875*** (0.00229)
Constant	1.068*** (0.0521)
Observations	2,688
Adjusted R-squared	0.673

Standard errors in parentheses

*** p<0.01, ** p<0.05, * p<0.1

The model output resembles that of the OLS model. The estimated coefficients are statistically significant. The negative coefficient for the variable hh_autos (average autos per household) suggests that CTs with high automobile ownership will correlate with lower transit use. This is also the case with the variable controlling for distance from CBD, which suggests that CTs located farther from the CBD will report lower transit use. Household size, however, is suggesting that CTs with large size households will report a slightly higher transit ridership: a result contrary to my initial assumption. Figure 8.19 plots the forecasted transit trips from the estimated model against the observed transit trips.

The same grouped logit model can be readily estimated in SPSS and R. The syntax and output from R is presented in Figure 8.20. Notice that the estimated coefficients are slightly different between R and Stata. This is because R uses the Maximum Likelihood Estimation (MLE) technique rather than the weighted least squares method.

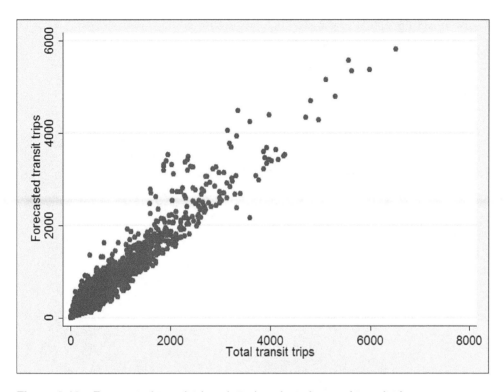

Figure 8.19 Forecasted transit trips plotted against observed transit trips

```
> summary(mod1 <- glm(cbind( n.transit, non.transit) ~ hh.autos + hh.size + d.cbd,
+ data = ny_grouped,family = binomial(),trace=T))
Deviance = 249880.9 Iterations - 1
Deviance = 246322.9 Iterations - 2
Deviance = 246320 Iterations - 3
Deviance = 246320 Iterations - 4

Call:
glm(formula = cbind(n.transit, non.transit) ~ hh.autos + hh.size +
    d.cbd, family = binomial(), data = ny_grouped, trace = T)

Deviance Residuals:
    Min      1Q   Median      3Q      Max
-44.678   -5.119   0.958    6.060   42.500

Coefficients:
              Estimate Std. Error z value Pr(>|z|)
(Intercept)  0.9737575  0.0051384  189.50   <2e-16 ***
hh.autos    -1.6928359  0.0030702 -551.38   <2e-16 ***
hh.size      0.0904690  0.0020433   44.28   <2e-16 ***
d.cbd       -0.0061976  0.0002263  -27.39   <2e-16 ***
---
Signif. codes:  0 '***' 0.001 '**' 0.01 '*' 0.05 '.' 0.1 ' ' 1

(Dispersion parameter for binomial family taken to be 1)

    Null deviance: 813569  on 2706  degrees of freedom
Residual deviance: 246320  on 2703  degrees of freedom
  (36 observations deleted due to missingness)
AIC: 266035
```

Figure 8.20 Grouped logit estimation using R

Stata also offers the option to use the MLE method for grouped logit using the `blogit` command. See the following syntax and the results in Table 8.17.

```
blogit n_transit n_trips hh_autos hh_size d_cbd
```

Table 8.17   Grouped Logit Estimation Using MLE in Stata

Variables	(1) Grouped Logit using blogit n_transit n_trips
Average autos per household	−1.693*** (0.00307)
Average persons per household	0.0905*** (0.00204)
Distance from CBD	−0.00620*** (0.000226)
Constant	0.974*** (0.00514)
Observations	4,109,296
Pseudo R-squared	0.100

Standard errors in parentheses

*** p<0.01, ** p<0.05, * p<0.1

Using SPSS to Explore the Smoking Data Set

SPSS continues to claim the dominant market share among those who are new to data science and statistical analysis. I am reproducing some analysis in the SPSS format for the readers who may be inclined to use SPSS for their projects.

After you open the data in SPSS, you will see the traditional tabular view of the data. Also available in SPSS is the variable view that allows you to see variable names, their types, and a brief description under the Label column. Figure 8.21 shows the variable view for the smoking data set.

For descriptive statistics you can use the **Summarize Cases** options in SPSS (see Figure 8.22). In the first dialog box you can select variables for the descriptive statistics you seek. Afterward you can click on **Statistics** to open another dialog box to select the statistics you want to estimate; for example, mean, median, standard deviation, and so on.

	Name	Type	Width	Decimals	Label
1	educ	Numeric	9	2	education in years
2	age	Numeric	8	0	age in years
3	income	Numeric	8	0	household income in dollars
4	pcigs79	Numeric	9	2	price of a pack in cents
5	ageeduc	Numeric	9	2	interaction between age and education
6	smoker	Numeric	8	0	1 if smokes, 0 otherwise
7	educincome	Numeric	12	0	interaction between education and income
8	qrt_age	Numeric	8	0	4 quantiles of age
9	inc_10k	Numeric	9	2	hhld income/ 10,000
10	fcast_reg	Numeric	9	2	OLS forecast
11	fcast_logit	Numeric	9	2	logit forecast
12	fcast_prob	Numeric	9	2	probit forecast
13	qrt_edu	Numeric	8	0	4 quantiles of educ
14	qrt_inc	Numeric	8	0	4 quantiles of income
15	qrt_price	Numeric	8	0	4 quantiles of pcigs79

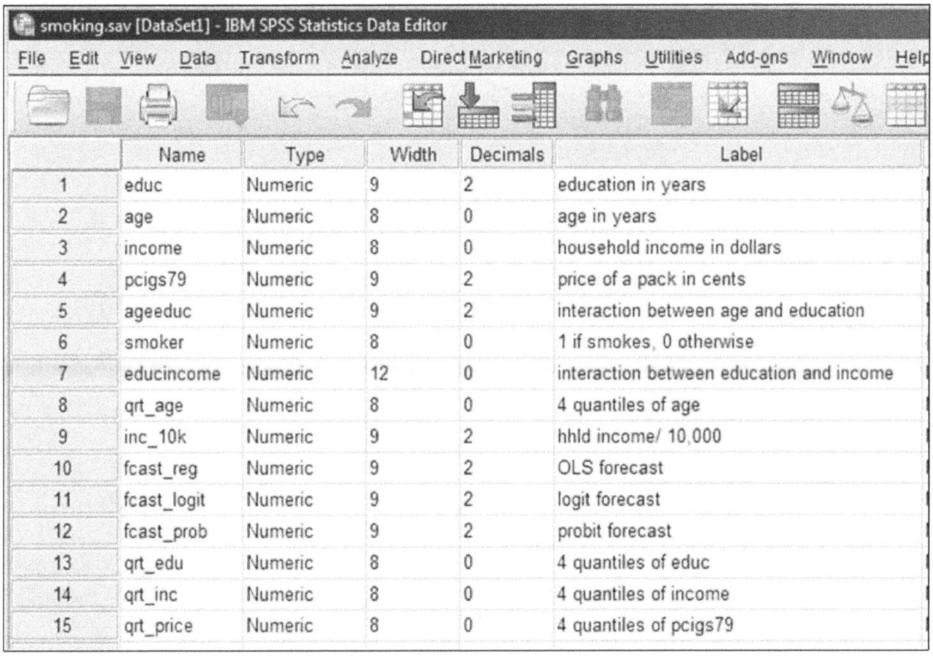

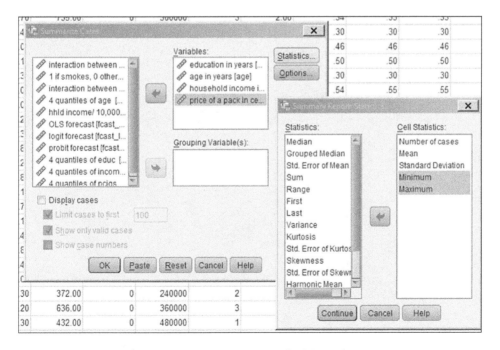

Figure 8.21 Variable view of smoking data set in SPSS

Figure 8.22 Summary statistics dialog boxes in SPSS

Figure 8.23 shows the resulting descriptive statistics. To produce summary statistics by groups, such as male versus female, you can enter the grouping variable in the dialog box presented in Figure 8.22. The resulting summary statistics will be broken down by groups.

Case Summaries

	N	Mean	Std. Deviation	Minimum	Maximum
education in years	1122	12.1912	3.29595	.00	18.00
age in years	1122	41.88	17.081	17	88
household income in dollars	1122	19359.18	9052.516	500	30000
price of a pack in cents	1122	60.9719	4.85213	46.30	69.80

Figure 8.23   Summary statistics in SPSS

SPSS is equipped with a powerful graphing engine that offers an interactive environment to generate plots. SPSS is more conducive for a point-and-click usage where you make the choices in the dialog boxes. The added advantage of SPSS, like Stata and SAS, is that it automatically generates the code that you can manipulate later to make changes to the output without having to use the dialog boxes. Figure 8.24 shows the dialog box to draw a histogram for the age variable.

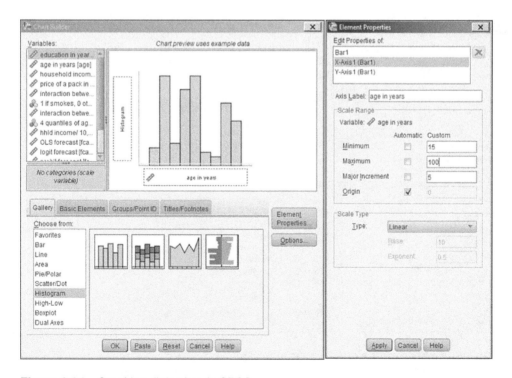

Figure 8.24   Graphing dialog box in SPSS

Figure 8.25 presents the resulting histogram for the age variable, drawn separately for smokers and non-smokers. The histogram illustrates that smokers belong to younger cohorts than do non-smokers.

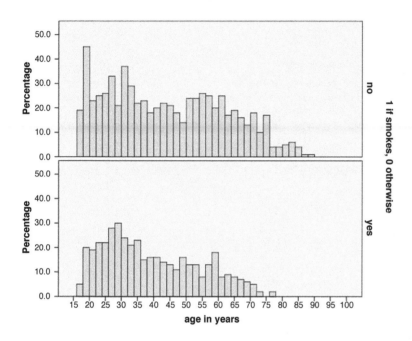

Figure 8.25   Histogram of age drawn separately for smokers and non-smokers

Regression Analysis in SPSS

SPSS provides a rich interface for econometric modeling. Figure 8.26 shows the dialog box for linear regression analysis. You can enter the dependent variable smoker under **Dependent**; the explanatory variables are listed under **Independent(s)**. The dialog box presents several other options that can help further refine the model. After you specify the model, select OK in the dialog box to run the model. The dialog box generates the output while executing the following syntax in the background.

```
REGRESSION
  /MISSING LISTWISE
  /STATISTICS COEFF OUTS R ANOVA
  /CRITERIA=PIN(.05) POUT(.10)
  /NOORIGIN
  /DEPENDENT smoker
  /METHOD=ENTER age educ income pcigs79.
```

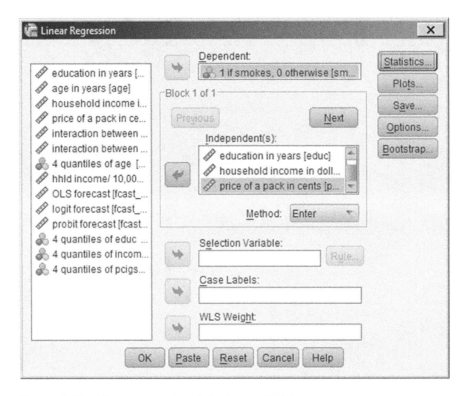

Figure 8.26   Linear regression dialog box in SPSS

Figure 8.27 shows the resulting output. Notice that the output (especially estimated coefficients and standard errors) is identical to that reported in Table 8.7 (Model 1), which presents the output for the estimated OLS models using Stata. The results are interpreted the same way as before for Table 8.7.

Coefficients^a

Model	Understandardized Coefficients		Standardized Coefficients		
	B	Std. Error	Beta	t	Sig.
1 (Constant)	1.181	.194		6.078	.000
age in years	-.005	.001	-.161	-5.357	.000
education in years	-.020	.005	-.133	-4.141	.000
household income in dollars	7.948E-7	.000	.015	.468	.640
price of a pack in cents	-.006	.003	-.063	-2.143	.032

a. Dependent Variable: 1 if smokes,0 otherwise

Figure 8.27   OLS output in SPSS

Estimating Logit and Probit Models in SPSS

Similar to its Linear Regression Model dialog box, SPSS also offers dialog boxes to estimate logit models (see Figure 8.28). In the SPSS parlance logit models are referred to as `logistic regression`. The dependent variable, `smoker`, is populated in the window beneath the `Dependent` option. You introduce the explanatory variables under the `Covariates` option. After populating the dialog box, as shown in Figure 8.28, click OK. SPSS executes the following syntax and produces the output presented in Figure 8.29.

```
LOGISTIC REGRESSION VARIABLES smoker
  /METHOD=ENTER age educ inc_10k pcigs79
  /CLASSPLOT
  /CRITERIA=PIN(0.05) POUT(0.10) ITERATE(20) CUT(0.5).
```

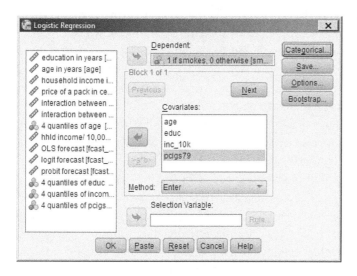

Figure 8.28   Logit model dialog box in SPSS

Notice that the estimated coefficients and standard errors presented in Figure 8.29 are similar to the logit model output reported in Table 8.9, which I generated using Stata. Note the difference in the income variable. In Stata output, I have used the raw `income` variable and in SPSS output, I have used the transformed `income` variable.

SPSS by default outputs the exponentiated coefficients for the logit and probit models. Compare the `Exp(B)` column in Figure 8.29 with the model labeled (2) in Table 8.10. You will see that the exponentiated coefficients are identical in Table 8.10 and Figure 8.29. The output in Figure 8.29 lists variable names and not variable labels, which can easily be altered by providing variable names in the data set.

Variables in the Equation

		B	Std. Error	Wald	df	Sig.	Exp(B)
Step 1[a]	age	-020	.004	27.557	1	.000	.980
	educ	-.087	.021	16.741	1	.000	.917
	inc_10k	.037	.075	.249	1	.618	1.038
	pcigs79	-.027	.013	4.536	1	.033	.973
	Constant	2.993	.855	12.241	1	.000	19.937

a. Variables(s) entered on step 1: age, educ, inc_10k, pcigs79.

Figure 8.29   Logit model output obtained from SPSS

You can interpret the SPSS output the same way I interpreted earlier the results listed in Table 8.10. SPSS also reports additional output for a classification table (not shown here), which is essentially a cross-tabulation between observed and predicted counts for smokers. I have restricted the output to estimated coefficients for brevity. Also note that whereas Stata reported the Z-values for each coefficient, SPSS reports Wald Chi-square test, which is the square of respective Z-values for each coefficient in Stata's output.

SPSS also offers the generic Generalized Linear Models dialog box to estimate a variety of models including logit and probit models (see Figure 8.30). We can readily estimate the probit model from the dialog box listed in Figure 8.30.

The resulting output from the probit model presented in Figure 8.31 is similar to the one reported in Figure 8.9 such that the estimated coefficients and standard errors are identical. However, SPSS reports a Wald test whereas the output from R reports Z-values. The choice between Z-values and the Wald test does not affect the interpretation of results from probit models. Notice that the significance values reported under the **Sig.** column in Figure 8.31 and the ones reported under **Pr(>|z|)** using R in Figure 8.9 are identical.

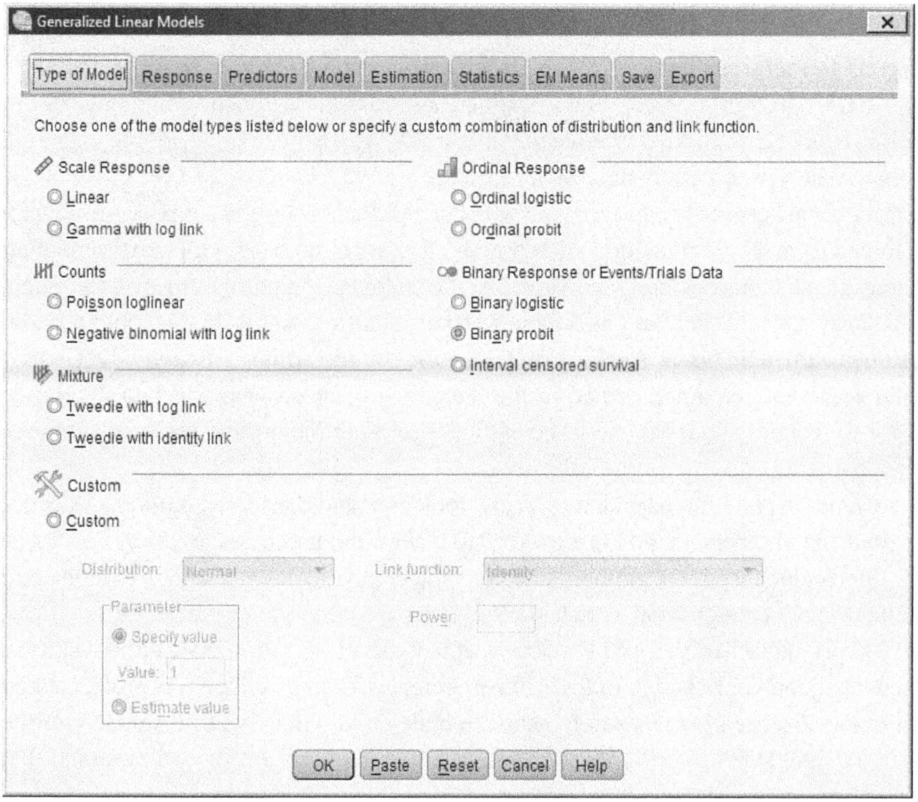

Figure 8.30 Generalized Linear Models dialog box in SPSS

Parameter Estimates

Parameter	B	Std. Error	95% Wald Confidence Interval		Hypothesis Test			Exp(B)
			Lower	Upper	Wald Chi-Square	Sf	Sig.	
(Intercept)	1.852	.5259	.821	2.882	12.398	1	.000	6.371
Age	-.013	.0024	-.017	-.008	28.290	1	.000	.988
Educ	-.054	.0130	-.079	-.028	17.103	1	.000	.948
pcigs79	-.017	.0079	-.032	-.001	4.529	1	.033	.983
inc_10k	.021	.0458	-.068	.111	.221	1	.639	1.022
(Scale)	1ª							

Dependent Variable: 1 if smokes, 0 otherwise
Model: (Intercept), age, educ, pcigs79, inc_10k

a. Fixed at the displayed value.

Figure 8.31 Probit model output from SPSS

Summary

"There are secrets beyond imagination. There are memories time cannot erase."[16] In the 1982 classic, *Sophie's Choice*, Meryl Streep plays Sophie Zawistowski, a Polish immigrant who in 1947 lived in Brooklyn, New York. Unknown to those around her, Sophie lived her life under the shadow of a choice she was forced to make years earlier.

In a flashback, viewers see Sophie arriving with her children, a boy and a girl, at Auschwitz. There she is forced to make an unimaginable choice. To prevent both her children from being condemned to death, she chooses her son to live. As the soldiers snatch the girl from Sophie's hands and walk away, the child screams as Sophie watches in horror, while clinging onto her son.

Meryl Streep earned an Oscar and Golden Globe for her performance in *Sophie's Choice*. Years later, the scene has remained etched in the memories of those who watched the movie as they continue to wonder about Sophie's secret choice and her memories that even centuries would have failed to erase.

Sophie's Choice is of a time when hate and evil took over and consumed millions. Decades later, we may think that mothers are no longer forced to make similar choices. But they do. Not as extreme as the one Sophie faced, yet mothers suffering abject poverty have to choose which child will eat when there is not enough food to be had.

In a 2013 paper, Jayachandran and Pande reveal that preference for a male child results in female children being malnourished in India.[17] The preference for male children is predicated on the belief that in the absence of social safety nets, the male child will serve as insurance for the parents in their old age. When faced with food insecurity, parents resort to food rationing that ultimately favors boys over girls.

This chapter began with a discussion about choices. I conclude this chapter with the focus on making choices. As Aristotle famously said, "Choice is deliberate desire." I focused on developing an improved understanding of the determinants of humans' deliberate desires. While the chapter looked at a rather mundane choice, to smoke or not to smoke, I want the readers to recognize that even with the tremendous wealth generated from inspiring innovations, individuals are being forced to make choices that leave them and the global society worse off.

I introduced in this chapter the tools needed to analyze binary or dichotomous variables. I showed that the OLS models are not ideally suited to model binary dependent variables. I introduced two alternatives: logit and probit models. Based on the ease in interpreting the model, I recommended logit over probit models.

I also demonstrated the use of grouped logit models using sample Census data on public transit ridership in and around New York City.

I showed how to interpret logit and probit models using marginal effects and graphics. Lastly, I illustrated the estimation and interpretation in R, SPSS, and Stata. The book's website offers complete code for all examples in the chapter in the three software tools listed earlier and SAS.

Given that the data sets and the code for the illustrated examples in this chapter are readily available from the book's website, I hope that you will make the right choice and test-drive the models.

Endnotes

1. http://www.cdc.gov/tobacco/data_statistics/fact_sheets/fast_facts/

2. http://www.cdc.gov/tobacco/data_statistics/state_data/data_highlights/2006/sections/index.htm

3. http://eml.berkeley.edu/~mcfadden/

4. https://heckman.uchicago.edu/

5. http://www.socsci.uci.edu/~rdluce/bio/pre1990/1977/Luce_JMP_1977a.pdf

6. https://sites.google.com/site/econometriks/3-chapters/8-binary

7. http://www.stata.com/manuals13/rregresspostestimationdiagnosticplots.pdf

8. http://www.ats.ucla.edu/stat/stata/faq/oratio.htm

9. "SPost: Postestimation Analysis with Stata," Scott Long and Jeremy Freese. http://www.indiana.edu/~jslsoc/spost.htm

10. http://www.r-project.org/

11. http://socserv.mcmaster.ca/jfox/Misc/Rcmdr/

12. http://gking.harvard.edu/zelig

13. Scott Long, J. and Freese, J. (2006). *Regression Models for Categorical Dependent Variables Using Stata*, Second Edition. Stata Press.

14. Imai, K., King, G., and Lau, O. 2007. *Zelig: Everyone's Statistical Software*. http://GKing.harvard.edu/zelig.

15. Imai, K., King, G., and Lau, O. (2008). "Toward A Common Framework for Statistical Analysis and Development." *Journal of Computational and Graphical Statistics*. Vol. 17, No. 4 (December), pp. 892–913.

16. Pakula, A. J., Barish, K., Gerrity, W. C., and Starger, M. (Producers), and Pakula, Alan J., (Director). (1982). *Sophie's Choice* [Motion Picture]. United States: Universal Pictures.

17. Jayachandran, S. and Pande, R. (2013). *Why Are Indian Children Shorter Than African Children*? Department of Economics, Northwestern. Retrieved from http://citeseerx.ist.psu.edu/viewdoc/download?doi=10.1.1.404.4791&rep=rep1&type=pdf.

CHAPTER 9

Categorically Speaking About Categorical Data

How I Met Your Mother is a popular sitcom with a cult-like following. Like several other popular sitcoms, it is also set in Manhattan, which happens to be one of the largest markets for relationships. A very large number of young men and women either live or work in Manhattan. Consequently, many form short- or long-term romantic relationships.

Romantic norms are evolving fast in the Internet age. The advances in Communication and Information Technologies (CITs) have altered all facets of our personal and professional lives. The social networking sites have changed the way we interact with each other and continue to stay in touch with friends and family.

Although the technological advances have changed the way the individuals and businesses interact, most individuals still meet their significant others offline. Nevertheless, if one were to answer, "How I met your mother," the following options might apply:

- At work, school, gym, place of worship, or a similar place

- Via family or mutual friends

- Online through social networking or matchmaking sites

The preceding is an example of a scenario with more than two options. This chapter builds on the last chapter, which focused on binary choices or outcomes. The focus now is on multinomial (several) choices. For instance, those interested in using matchmaking services can pick from Match.com, eHarmony, Plenty of Fish, OK Cupid, Christian Mingle, and others. Alternatively, consider the smart phone market that is dominated by iPhone, Android phones, and Blackberry, suggesting at least three choices. In the case of intercity travel, one can think of four alternatives, namely planes, trains, automobiles (recall John Hughes' hit comedy starring Steve Martin and John Candy), and buses.

The types of variables that represent these discrete choices are broadly known as *categorical* variables. When the variables are in no particular order, we can think of them as multinomial (for example, planes, trains, and automobiles). However, a categorical variable following a particular order, such as the number of cars owned by a household, is known as an *ordinal* variable.

In this chapter, I demonstrate how to analyze categorical variables (both binomial and multinomial), building on the discussion from the last chapter on binary outcomes (for example, to smoke or not to smoke). However, in this chapter I introduce the mathematical formulations behind the models so that I can generalize the discussion from binary to multinomial outcomes.

This chapter presents a variety of econometric models to provide a broader coverage of the topics under the larger umbrella of the categorical data analysis. I demonstrate estimating binary logit and multinomial logit models with a focus on their mathematical specification. A specific variant of the multinomial logit model is the discrete choice model that uses characteristics of the decision-maker and the attributes of choice to capture the behavioral underpinnings of the underlying decision-making. I demonstrate the estimation of discrete choice models with a special focus on how to structure the data set prior to estimating the model.

Several of this chapter's examples show how you may estimate models for categorical dependent variables. I demonstrate binary logit models with a data set on women's participation in the labor force, and capture the impact of the presence of young children on a woman's propensity to work.

I use a subset of a 2013 survey on online dating and the use of CITs. The survey was conducted by Pew Research Center, which interviewed more than 2,200 random respondents from across the U.S. Using a binary logit model, I explore the determinants for online dating and test several hypothesis, including:

- Are residents of urban areas more likely to have met their significant others online?

- Are individuals predisposed to flirting more likely to have met their significant others online?

- Does marital status explain one's likelihood of meeting the significant other online?

For multinomial logit models, I explore what influences one's choice of the matchmaking website. For instance, do suburban dwellers prefer Match.com to OK Cupid? I also explore the determinants of phone type choice—how individuals chose between various types of cellphones. For instance, are the people in the Midwest more or less likely to use iPhones than respondents elsewhere? Does having children in the household influence one's choice of a particular brand of cellphone?

I use another data set to determine whether women workers without access to their spouse's employer-provided health insurance are more likely to work full-time than do those who are insured by their spouse's health insurance.

The discrete choice model examples show how to estimate a travel mode choice model for intercity travel where the choices are automobile, bus, train, and airplane.

Let me first formally introduce categorical data.

What Is Categorical Data?

Categorical data deals with situations where the outcome of an experiment or a process is categorized into a finite number of mutually exclusive classes or categories. For instance, a survey of labor force participation records the status of an adult active in the labor force as either employed or unemployed. Thus the individual's status can be expressed as a dichotomous variable (1/0) where 1 denotes the outcome of being employed and 0 denotes the outcome of being unemployed.

Other examples of categorical data include making a choice among the make of automobiles. Consider the situation where the national make of automobiles is being researched. Automobile executives are interested in learning about the determinants of consumer choice. In this case, the choice could again be represented as a dichotomous variable with the value 1 if the consumer chooses an American make, and 0 otherwise. Similarly, if the choice were between American, European, or Japanese car manufacturers, the categorical variable representing the choice would have three categories: 1 (American), 2 (European), and 3 (Japanese). A categorical variable that represents more than two outcomes is called a *multinomial* variable.

The aforementioned examples are of unordered outcomes. In the previous example, I could have coded American as 2, Japanese as 1, and European as 3. The change in the order does not have an impact on the analysis because the order of alternatives is rather arbitrary.

However, scenarios exist where the ordering of outcomes matters. Consider, for instance, a study of automobile ownership where households are coded as shown in Table 9.1:

Table 9.1 Coding of Ordinal Variables

Categories	Description
0	Household without cars
1	Household owning 1 car
2	Household owning 2 cars
3	Household owning 3 cars
4 or more	Household owning 4 or more cars

In Table 9.1, there is a natural ordering, which suggests that households categorized as 2 own more cars than the households categorized as 1 or 0. In this particular case, you cannot arbitrarily change the order. Such data, where the order of outcomes is not arbitrary, but rather systematic, is called *ordered* data, which is also a type of categorical data.

The use of categorical variable as an explanatory variable, such as gender, is common in regression models. As an explanatory variable, a categorical variable captures the systematic differences latent in data that cannot be accounted for by other variables in the model. For instance, if a systematic difference exists between the wages of men and women in a particular profession, the gender variable can capture the gender-based wage differentials. However, when the dependent variable in an econometric model is categorical, rather than continuous, the use of the conventional regression (OLS) technique is no longer appropriate. The OLS models are therefore modified to account for the categorical dependent variables. Such modified models are called discrete choice, categorical, limited dependent variables, or qualitative response models.

The following section provides a discussion on analyzing binomial variables, multinomial variables, and estimating discrete choice models. This chapter also explains the theory and estimation of binomial, multinomial, and conditional logit models.

Analyzing Categorical Data

A wide variety of statistical techniques, methods, and models are available to analyze categorical data. Simple cross tabulations are commonly used to analyze categorical variables. To illustrate this point, I use a data set from a study of labor force participation of women (Mroz, 1987).[1] The data contains information on 753 white, married women between the ages of 30 and 60 years. The dependent variable, lfp, reports on women's status as employed (1), or otherwise (0). The description of other variables is listed in Table 9.2. Readers can download the data from the book's companion website (www.ibmpressbooks.com/title/9780133991024). Also provided is the syntax to reproduce the analysis in R, SPSS, Stata, and SAS.

Table 9.2   Description of Variables in the Labor Force Study

Variable	Description
lfp	Paid Labor Force: 1=yes 0=no
k5	Number of children less than 6 years old
k618	Children between 6 and 18 years of age
age	Wife's age in years
wc	Wife College: 1=yes 0=no
hc	Husband College: 1=yes 0=no
lwg	Log of wife's estimated wages
inc	Family income excluding wife's in thousands

Table 9.3 shows that 325 women (43%) in the sample were unemployed, whereas the remaining 57% were employed. I want to determine the relationship between the educational attainment of both husband and wife on a women's status in the labor force. I want to test the following hypothesis: If a woman has received college education, will she be more likely to be in the labor force? For this, I perform a cross-tabulation and conduct the chi-square test. Throughout this chapter, I have reproduced the R script used to generate the results. I provide the script (code) for other software on the accompanying website.

```
t1=table(lfp);t2=t1/sum(t1)*100
t3=rbind("In labor force (N)"=t1,"In labor force (%)"=round(t2,1))
htmlTable(txtRound(t3,0), rowlabel = "Labor Force Participation")
```

Table 9.3 Simple Tabulations of the Labor Force Data

Labor Force Participation	No	Yes
In labor force (N)	325	428
In labor force (%)	43	57

Table 9.4 suggests that 68% of college-educated women were employed against 52% of women who did not attend college. To find out whether the association between the wife's education and participation in labor force has any statistical significance, I use the chi-square statistics:

```
chitest=xtabs(~ lfp+wc); print(xtable(chitest, digits=0), type="html")
chisq.test(chitest)
t4<-prop.table(chitest,2)*100
t5<- cbind(chitest, t4)
rownames(t5)<- c( "Did not participate in labor force", "Participated
in labor force")
colnames(t5)<-c("Wife Didn't Attend College (N)", "Wife Attended
College (N)", "Wife Didn't Attend College (%)", "Wife Attended College
(%)")
htmlTable(txtRound(t5,0), rowlabel = "Labor Force Participation")
```

Table 9.4 Cross-Tabulation of Labor Force Participation and Women's Education

Labor Force Participation	Wife Didn't Attended College (N)	Wife Attended College (N)	Wife Didn't Attend College (%)	Wife Attended College (%)
Did not participate in labor force	257	68	48	32
Participated in labor force	284	144	52	68

X-squared = 14.16, df = 1, p-value = 0.0001681

A significance (p) value of 0.05 or less suggests a statistically significant relationship between two variables. The significance value of .0002 (refer to Table 9.4) suggests that a statistically significant relationship exists between women's education and their participation in the labor force. Another cross-tab, presented in Table 9.5, suggests that 60% of the women whose husbands received a college education were employed against 55% of the women whose husbands did not attend college. The significance of the chi-square test returned a value of 0.1835, which shows lack of statistical significance between the husband's education attainment and the wife's participation in labor force.

```
chitest=xtabs(~ lfp+hc); print(xtable(chitest, digits=0), type="html")
chisq.test(chitest)
rownames(chitest)<- c( "Did not participate in labor force",
"Participated in labor force")
colnames(chitest)<-c("Husband Didn't Attend College (%)", "Husband
Attended College (%)")
htmlTable(txtRound(chitest,0), rowlabel = "Wife's Labor Force
Participation")
```

Table 9.5   Chi-square Test for the Association Between Husband's Education and Employment Status

Wife's Labor Force Participation	Husband Didn't Attend College (%)	Husband Attended College (%)
Did not participate in labor force	45	40
Participated in labor force	55	60

X-squared = 1.7689, df = 1, p-value = 0.1835

Econometric Models of Binomial Data

For this section, readers have a choice. If you want to avoid the mathematical details and focus on the application of logit models, you can skip the next couple of pages and go to the section "Interpreting Binary Logit Models." Others may continue reading.

I derive the binary logit model as a latent variable model following Long and Freese (2005).[2] Assume a latent variable y^* that ranges from $-\infty$ to ∞. The latent variable y^* is related to the observed independent variables as per Equation 9.1:

$$y^* = \beta x_i + \in_i \quad \textbf{Equation 9.1}$$

Here i represents the observation and $\in$ the random error. Equation 9.1 is similar to the OLS model; however, the dependent variable is unobserved. Equation 9.2 links the latent variable y^* with the observed variable y.

$$y_i = \begin{cases} 1 \text{ if } y_i^* > 0 \\ 0 \text{ if } y_i^* \leq 0 \end{cases} \quad \textbf{Equation 9.2}$$

Now returning to the example of labor force survey of married women, I set $y = 1$ if the woman is in the labor force and $y = 0$ if she is unemployed. The independent variables include number of children, wife's education, and expected income. Now consider that a woman might be about to leave her job whereas another woman is steadfast in her career. Regardless of their intentions, in both instances one only observes $y = 1$. Now consider that an "underlying propensity to work" exists that manifests itself as being employed $y = 1$ or unemployed $y = 0$. We are not able to observe directly the propensity; however, at some point a change in y^* results in a change in y from 1 to 0 or from 0 to 1.

Thus, I can express the model as follows:

$$Pr(y = 1|x) = Pr(y^* > 0|x) \quad \textbf{Equation 9.3}$$

Substituting the structural model in the preceding equation gets Equation 9.4:

$$Pr(y = 1|x) = Pr(\beta x_i + \in_i > 0|x) = Pr(\in_i > -\beta x_i|x) \quad \textbf{Equation 9.4}$$

Assuming that $\in$ is distributed logistically with variance $\frac{\pi^2}{3}$ the Logit model can be expressed as shown in Equation 9.5:

$$Pr(y = 1|x) = \frac{\exp(\beta x_i)}{1 + \exp(\beta x_i)} \quad \textbf{Equation 9.5}$$

Unlike the OLS model, where the variance can be estimated because the dependent variable is observed, the variance of the binary logit model is assumed because the dependent variable, y^*, is latent.

One can argue that an OLS method can be used to estimate the binary logit model. However, this leads to serious estimation problems. The first and foremost problem is the heteroskedastic error terms. Because $\beta x_i + \in_i$ can only be 0 or 1, therefore (see Equation 9.6):

$$\beta x_i + \in_i = 0 \text{ or } \beta x_i + \in_i = 1 \quad \textbf{Equation 9.6}$$

This leaves $\in_i$ is equal to either $-x_i\beta$ or $1 - x_i\beta$. In such a case, variance is given by (Greene (1995), p.874)[3] in Equation 9.7:

$$Var(\in_i|x) = \beta x_i(1 - \beta x_i) \quad \textbf{Equation 9.7}$$

The preceding equation suggests that as x increases, so does the variance of $\in_i$. In addition, $x_i\beta$ cannot be constrained to the [0,1] interval.

Estimation of Binary Logit Models

To identify the binary logit model, you always set one category or alternative as the base case. The estimated coefficients are then interpreted as a comparison with the base case. Using the labor force example, the probability of being employed is given by Equation 9.8:

$$Pr(Work) = \frac{exp^{V_w}}{exp^{V_w} + exp^{V_u}} \quad \textbf{Equation 9.8}$$

V_w in Equation 9.8 represents the utility function for working and V_u represents the utility function for not working (i.e., unemployed). The utility functions are similar to the OLS equations, discussed earlier in Chapter 7, "Why Tall Parents Don't Have Even Taller Children."

Equation 9.9 gives the probability of being unemployed:

$$\Pr(unemp) = 1 - \Pr(work) \quad \textbf{Equation 9.9}$$

In this particular case, I set the coefficients for being unemployed to 0. This implies that

$$V_u = 0 = \beta_0 + \beta_1 X_1 + \dots + \beta_n X_n$$

Therefore,

$$\Pr(work) = \frac{exp^{V_w}}{exp^{V_w} + 1} \text{ because } \exp(0) = 1.$$

If you divide both the numerator and the denominator by exp^{Vw}, you have Equation 9.10 and 9.11:

$$\Pr(work) = \frac{1}{1 + \dfrac{1}{exp^{V_w}}} = \frac{1}{1 + exp^{-V_w}} \qquad \textbf{Equation 9.10}$$

$$\Pr(unemp) = 1 - \Pr(work) = 1 - \frac{1}{1 + exp^{-V_w}}$$

$$\Pr(unemp) = \frac{exp^{-V_w}}{1 + exp^{-V_w}} \qquad \textbf{Equation 9.11}$$

Odds Ratio

You may recall the discussion about odds ratios from Chapter 8, "To Be or Not to Be." Briefly, the odds ratio between the two outcomes is expressed as shown in Equation 9.12:

$$\frac{\Pr(work)}{\Pr(unemp)} = \frac{\dfrac{1}{1 + exp^{-V_w}}}{\dfrac{exp^{-V_w}}{1 + exp^{-V_w}}} = \frac{1}{exp^{-V_w}} = \exp(V_w)$$

$$\textbf{Equation 9.12}$$

Note that in the multinomial case, the correct term to use is the relative risk ratio (RRR), which is what the Stata uses for the exponentiated coefficients.

Log of Odds Ratio

Finally, the log of odds ratio, often refer to as log of odds, is expressed as

$$\ln\left(\frac{\Pr(work)}{\Pr(unemp)}\right) = \ln\left(\exp(V_w)\right) = V_w \text{ which is equal to } \beta x_i.$$

Let us revisit the labor force participation data set for married women and estimate a binary logit model of their participation in the labor force using income, children, and education of women and that of their husband's as explanatory variables.

Interpreting Binary Logit Models

If you skipped the mathematical details, you may rejoin the discussion here. We are interested in the determinants of women's participation in labor force. The explanatory variables and their expected relationship with the dependent variable is outlined in Table 9.6. One can argue that having children reduces the odds of a women working. I hypothesize that the odds of working increase for women with age, but only up to a certain limit (that is, the retirement age, where the odds would start to decline). If the wife or her husband is college educated, the wife's odds of working will be higher. Similarly, if a woman earns higher wages, there is a greater utility in her pursuing a career and hence her odds of continuing to work will be higher. On the other hand, higher family income (minus wife's wages) suggests that husband's income may be sufficient to support the household, which in turn will lower the odds of a woman working. I reproduce the list of variables and their description in Table 9.6.

Table 9.6 Description of Variables in the Labor Force Study

Variable	Description	Expected Outcome/Hypotheses
lfp	Paid Labor Force: 1=yes 0=no	Dependent variable
k5	Number of children less than 6 years old	Negative correlation
k618	Children between 6 and 18 years of age	Negative correlation
age	Wife's age in years	Positive correlation
wc	Wife College: 1=yes 0=no	Positive correlation
hc	Husband College: 1=yes 0=no	Positive correlation
lwg	Log of wife's estimated wages	Positive correlation
inc	Family income excluding wife's in thousands	Negative correlation

A good starting point will be to report descriptive statistics for the selected explanatory variables as they inform the dependent variable; that is, women's labor force participation. You can see from Table 9.7 that the percentage of women working declines with the number of young children. Working women are slightly younger than those who are not working. This is different from what I had hypothesized. I also see a larger percentage of college educated women, and those whose husbands attended college, work.

Table 9.7 reveals household income (net of wife's wages) of women who did not work was higher than those who worked. With this information in hand, I am ready to model the determinants of women's participation in the labor force to determine what determinants are statistically significant:

```
t1<- xtabs(~ k5 + lfp); t1; t.k5 = prop.table(t1,1)*100
t1<- xtabs(~ k618 + lfp); t1; t.k618 = prop.table(t1,1)*100
t.age<- tapply(age, lfp,mean)
t1<- xtabs(~ wc + lfp); t1; t.wc = prop.table(t1,1)*100
t1<- xtabs(~ hc + lfp); t1; t.hc = prop.table(t1,1)*100
t.wifelogwage<- tapply(lwg, lfp,mean)
t.faminc<- tapply(inc, lfp,mean)
t5<-rbind(t.k5, t.k618, t.age, t.wc, t.hc, t.wifelogwage, t.faminc)
t5<-round(t5,2)
colnames(t5)<- c("not working", "working")
rownames(t5)<-paste(c("no child", "1 child", paste0(2:3, " children"),
"no child", "1 child", paste0(2:8, " children"),
                    "wife's age", "college educated",
                    "did not attend college",
                    "college educated",
                    "did not attend college",
                    "log of wife's wages",
                    "family income excluding wife's"))
htmlTable( txtRound(t5,0, excl.rows = c(14,19,20)),
          rgroup=c("children under 6 (%)",
                  "children 6-18 years (%)",
          "wife's age in years", "wife's education (%)",
          "husband's education (%)", "wife's income",
          "family income ('000s)"),
          n.rgroup = c(4,9,1,2,2,1,1),
          cgroup = c("Wife's labor force participation"),
          n.cgroup = c(2))
```

Table 9.7   Descriptive Statistics of Explanatory Variables by Women's Working Status

Demographic Attributes	Wife's Labor Force Participation	
	Not Working	Working
Children under 6 (%)		
No child	38	62
1 child	61	39
2 children	73	27
3 children	100	0

Demographic Attributes	Wife's Labor Force Participation	
	Not Working	Working
Children 6–18 years (%)		
No child	42	58
1 child	46	54
2 children	40	60
3 children	44	56
4 children	43	57
5 children	42	58
6 children	100	0
7 children	100	0
8 children	0	100
Wife age in years		
Wife's age	43.28	41.97
Wife's education (%)		
College educated	48	52
Did not attend college	32	68
Husband's education (%)		
College educated	45	55
Did not attend college	40	60
Wife's income		
Log of wife's wages	0.97	1.19
Family income ('000s)		
Family income excluding wife's	21.7	18.94

Table 9.8 lists the coefficients of the binary logit model that estimates the probability of being employed for married, white women. The coefficients and their standard errors (in parentheses) are presented in the table. The asterisks inform the statistical significance of the estimated coefficients.

The negative coefficient for kids under 5 and kids under 6 to 18 suggest that the likelihood of a woman working declines with the presence of young children. The impact of children under 5 is statistically significant, as is evidenced by the three asterisks. As I explained earlier in Chapter 7, the asterisks serve as proxies for statistical significance. One asterisk suggests the coefficient is statistically significant at 10% level, two asterisks suggest significance at 5% level and three at 1%. Wife's age and family income, excluding that of the wife, are negatively correlated (statistically significant) with the likelihood of working. Wife's wage is positively (statistically significant) correlated with her likelihood of being employed. As for wife's education, the likelihood of working increases with wife's education.

```
lab.for <- glm(lfp ~ k5 + k618 + age+ wc + hc + lwg +inc, data=Mroz,
    family = binomial(link = "logit"))
    stargazer(lab.for, type="html", align=TRUE, no.space=TRUE,
    dep.var.labels=c("Labor Force Participation"),
    covariate.labels = c("Kids under 6", "Kids 6 to 18",
    "wife's age", "wife attended college", "Husband attended
    college", "log of wife's estimated wages", "family income
    excluding wife's"))
```

Table 9.8   Estimation of Binary Logit Model of Labor Force Participation

	Dependent Variable Labor Force Participation
Kids under 6	-1.463^{***}
	(0.197)
Kids 6 to 18	-0.065
	(0.068)
Wife's age	-0.063^{***}
	(0.013)
Wife attended college	0.807^{***}
	(0.230)
Husband attended college	0.112
	(0.206)

	Dependent Variable Labor Force Participation
Log of wife's estimated wages	0.605***
	(0.151)
Family income excluding wife's	−0.034***
	(0.008)
Constant	3.182***
	(0.644)
Observations	753
Log Likelihood	−452.600
Akaike Inf. Crit.	921.300

* p<0.1; ** p<0.05; *** p<0.01

Now I interpret the coefficients to communicate the results to those who do not live in a world of standard errors and t-statistics. It is preferable to use the odds ratio rather than the actual coefficients to interpret the model because the odds ratio lends itself to an interpretation using everyday language. The variable representing kids under 6 years of age represents the number of young children under the age of 6 in a household. The estimated coefficient (β) is equal to −1.463, and the odds are expressed as $\exp(−1.463) = 0.232$. Relying on the earlier discussion about odds ratio in Chapter 8, you can see that each additional young child decreases the odds of the mother's being employed by a factor of 0.23, all else being equal. Similarly, the odds of college-educated women being employed are 2.242 ($e^{.807}$) times higher than the women who did not receive college education.

You can also interpret the results as a percentage change in odds using the formula: $100(\exp(\beta_k\delta) − 1$. Again, each additional young child decreases the odds of being employed by 77% ($100(\exp(−1.4629) − 1) = −76.8\%$).

The impact of age could be interpreted as follows: with an increase in the age by one year, the odds for being employed decline by a factor of 0.94 ($e^{−.063}$). However, what if you were interested in determining the impact of being 10 years older, rather than being just one year older? The actual formula for odds is $e^{\beta*\delta}$ where δ is the change in the units. For a 10-year increase in age, the odds of working decline by a factor of $\exp(−0.063 * 10) = 0.53$. That is, the odds decline by almost 50% for a 10-year increase in age than by just 6% for a one-year increase in age. To determine the odds of not working, you can simply take the inverse of $\exp(\beta)$. Thus, each additional young child increases the odds of being unemployed by a factor of

$$\frac{1}{0.232} = 4.31.$$

Statistical Inference of Binary Logit Models

Logit models are interpreted similar to the OLS models. Instead of the `t-stat` (or `z-statistics`) to evaluate the statistical significance of the model, SPSS uses Wald statistics, which is expressed as

$\left(\dfrac{Coefficient}{SE} \right)^2$. Most software report the significance level for Wald statistics.

Another more informative and reliable method is the likelihood ratio test. The log-likelihood test returns a change in the value of –2 * log-likelihood (–2LL) if the effect is removed from the final model. The difference in –2LL for the model with only an intercept and –2LL for the final model has a `chi-square` distribution. The significance level for the `chi-square` can thus be used to evaluate the relative significance of the effect. The overall fit can also be evaluated from –2LL for the model. Equation 9.13 gives the model's chi-square:

$$\chi^2 = -2LL_{intercept} - (-2LL_{final}) \quad \textbf{Equation 9.13}$$

If the observed significance level is small for χ^2, you can reject the null hypothesis that coefficients for variables in the final model are equal to 0. The interpretation of this statistic is similar to the interpretation of `F-statistics` in the OLS tradition.

Other measures of goodness-of-fit statistics include McFadden's R-Square, expressed as shown in Equation 9.14:

$$R^2{}_{McFadden} = \frac{l(0)-l(B)}{l(0)} = 1 - \frac{l(B)}{l(0)} \quad \textbf{Equation 9.14}$$

Where $l(0)$ is the kernel of the log-likelihood of the intercept-only model (sample shares are the only information in the model), whereas $l(B)$ is the kernel of the log-likelihood of the final model. This formulation of McFadden's R-Square has been adopted in the logistic regression estimation techniques in some software—for example SPSS, which automatically generates this and other goodness-of-fit statistics.

For logit models, even small values of McFadden's R-square suggest a good fit. In fact, Louviere et al (2000)[4] have argued that small values of 0.2 to 0.4 are "considered to be indicative of extremely good model fits." They have cited a simulation experiment by Domencich and McFadden (1975) who have "equivalenced this range to 0.7 to 0.9 for a linear function."[5] The McFadden's R-Square for the women labor force model is 0.121.

Thus in R, the following code computes the McFadden's R-Square for the labor force model.

```
ll0 <- glm(lfp ~ 1 , data=Mroz, family = binomial(link = "logit"))
x2<-as.numeric(logLik(ll0)); x1<-as.numeric(logLik(lab.for))
McFaddenR<-1-(x1/x2)
McFaddenR
```

How I Met Your Mother? Analyzing Survey Data

The advances in Communication and Information Technologies (CITs) define our times. Emails, instant messaging, Voice over IP calls, Skyping, Twitter, Facebook, and several other communication platforms have taken over the way we communicate today. Most people cannot remember the last time they wrote a letter by hand and sent it by regular (snail) mail. People today spend as much leisure time online as they spend offline.

With such massive intervention in the social dimensions of our lives, we would expect CITs to play a much larger role in getting people together. More specifically, you may assume that a large number of people are getting romantically involved through first encounters online. This, however, is not the case. A survey of more than 2,000 American adults revealed that only a very small number of American adults, fewer than 6%, met their partner or spouse online. The rest met through more traditional offline interventions. This does not imply that CITs are not helping romantically involved individuals stay in touch with their love interests. What it suggests is that the first chance or planned encounter takes place online only in a tiny minority of the cases.

A 2013 report by the Pew Research Center titled, "Online dating and relationships" reported that only 5% American adults met their love interests online.[6] The rest met offline. The attitudes toward online dating have become favorable over the years. In 2013, 55% of all Internet users believed that "online dating is a good way to meet people." As recently as in 2005, only 44% agreed with the same statement. Why, then, have more individuals not turned to the Internet to find love?

One possible reason could be that individuals portray a rather exaggerated online image of themselves. No fewer than 54% online daters in the Pew data set found others to have misrepresented themselves in their profiles. Perhaps, men have been tempted to post pre-balding images while women may have posted rather dated, but younger-looking, images. However, given that 54% online daters felt that way, some of those individuals may have been guilty of the same.

However, the Internet and social networking sites (SNSs) such as Facebook have proven useful in maintaining romantic relationships. Consider that 31% of the SNS users between the ages of 18 and 29 posted online pictures or details from a date. Thus, SNSs have become the preferred platform for kiss-and-tell for young American adults.

At the same time, having an online presence opens one up to unwanted advances. The Pew survey reported that a large number of SNS users either "unfriended" (Facebook jargon) or blocked (Twitter jargon) someone who made them feel uncomfortable online.

The American social norms, just like technology, are fast evolving. Marriage is on a decline in the United States. According to the Pew report, in 1960, an overwhelming majority of American adults, 72%, were married. That number declined to 51% by 2013. Thus, a larger number of adult Americans are now involved in relationships that never consummate to marriage. This does not mean that marriage has lost its appeal altogether. A large number of those who never married (61%) still have hopes to be married someday.

The Pew report presents revealing statistics about the presence of a large number of inert adults. These are the adults who are single, but are not looking for a romantic partner. In fact, 28% of American adults are single, and yet are not looking for love. Another 28% have been with a significant other (married or otherwise) for 10 years or less. Almost 38% of the adults have been in a relationship with a partner for more than 10 years. This leaves only 7% of the adults who are both single and looking for a romantic partner.

Have you ever wondered why the electronic media is so obsessed with the 7% of the adult population that is single and looking for partners? Sitcoms like *Friends*, *Seinfeld*, and *How I Met Your Mother* are focused on a small segment of the demographics. In addition, why is it that a much larger segment of the population—that is, singles who are not looking for a partner,—is hardly mentioned in print and broadcast media, even when it is 28% of the adult demographics? You could argue that such demographics make boring TV. This may be true, but what is also true is that this demographic would have a very high potential for discretionary spending.

While the attitude toward online dating may have been changing, few admit to using it themselves. At the same time, a larger proportion of the population today reports that it knows of others who use online dating: 44% of the adult women and 41% of the adult men reported that they knew of others who have used online dating sites or apps. The uptake of online dating is much higher among Whites than the rest. In addition, as is true for any kind of new technology, younger adults are more aware of the prevalence of online dating than their older counterparts.

The real advantage of online dating is in helping people find significant others who are their mirror, or near mirror, images. It is easier to search online for someone with shared interests than offline, which is why 60% of those active in online dating preferred it for meeting others with similar interests or hobbies. If you are looking for someone who likes playing rugby, reads Confucius, and prefers Italian cuisine, the Internet is a much better place to run such searches than offline.

Approximately 5% of those who are married, living with a partner, or in a committed relationship met their partner/spouse online. A higher percentage of younger cohorts between the ages of 18 and 29 (8%) reported to have met their significant other online. Similarly, a higher percentage of those in shorter duration partnerships of up to 5 years, compared to those in longer duration partnerships, reported to have met their partner online.

Some basic human traits help both online and offline. Those with a predisposition to flirt can meet new people and form relationships easier than others do. The medium might have some influence on behavior. The Internet provides anonymity to some extent, allowing even the introverts to flirt. Almost 24% of the Internet users reported to have flirted online. The gender differences in flirting, or at least admitting to have flirted online, are large. More men (27%) than women (21%) who use the Internet reported to have flirted online. Could the difference be because men are more willing to brag about such things than women are?

Flirting, however, remains more of an urban phenomenon. Twenty-eight percent of urban dwellers, 23% of suburban dwellers, and only 18% of the rural residents reported to have flirted online. Almost half of those who are single and looking for partners reported to have flirted online compared to only 39% of those who are single, but not looking for love.

Even with the CIT-enabled changes in lifestyles, attitudes, approaches, and demeanors, some traditions have persisted on- and offline. Men are still more likely to have asked someone out for a first date. Of the Internet users, 23% of the male and 16% of the female Internet users asked someone out on a first date online.

Similar gender differences persist in other aspects of relationships. Men (52%) are more likely to be in a shorter duration relationship (10 years or less) than women (48%). At the same time, women (53%) are more likely than men (47%) to be in longer duration relationships (lasting for more than 10 years). Again, a larger proportion of single men (66%) are actively searching for a partner than are women (34%). On the other hand, a much larger proportion of single women (59%) are not searching for a partner than are men (41%).

I try to generate similar results from a subset of the Pew data set on online dating in the following section.

A Blind Date with the Pew Online Dating Data Set

Let us bring our data science skills to bear on the Pew data set for online dating. I demonstrate the empirical results and the code scripts in R, and provide similar scripts (on the website) for other software so that you can generate the results in a software of your choice.

I first report a series of descriptive statistics followed by estimating a binary logit model to determine what influences a person to meet a romantic partner online. I report frequencies as percentages for categorical variables. Using percentages and not the raw numbers is preferred primarily because we are accustomed to appreciating a distribution of some values that some up to 100%. If a category reports a share of more than 50%, we right away know that it represents the majority share. For continuous variables, I will report mean and standard deviations.

Readers can download the data set from the book's website. The results generated in this section used several packages in R that need to be loaded prior to their use as you can see in the R script.

```
load("dating.RData")
library(xtable)
library(psych)
```

Demographics of Affection

I present a detailed commentary from tabulations performed on the data set. However, for the sake of brevity, I reproduce results from a select few tabulations. The script provided on the book's website carries the entire code for all tabulations.

The survey respondents hailed from all across the United States. Table 9.9 shows their spatial breakdown. Most respondents were from the South followed by those in the Midwest.

```
x=cregion
x1=table(x);x2=x1/sum(x1)*100
tab=xtable(cbind( region  =x2))
htmlTable(txtRound(tab,0), rowlabel = "Region", header ="Percentage of
Respondents")
```

Table 9.9   Regional Distribution of Survey Respondents

Region	Percentage of Respondents
Northeast	17
Midwest	23
South	39
West	22

Most respondents were from suburban areas, followed by those residing in urban areas. Only one in five respondents reported living in the rural areas.

Women were more frequent in the sample than men, which may have influenced some gender-specific responses (see Table 9.10). One in four respondents lived alone, whereas 54% of households were comprised of two adults. One in four respondents was a parent whose young children lived with him or her. Forty-five percent of the households had at least one child in the household under the age of 6, 47% of the households had at least one child between the ages of 6 and 11, and 46% of the households had a child between the ages of 12 and 17.

```
x=sex
x1=table(x);x2=x1/sum(x1)*100
tab=xtable(cbind( gender  =x2))
htmlTable(txtRound(tab,0), rowlabel = "Gender", header ="Percentage of
Respondents")
```

Table 9.10   A Breakdown of Survey Respondents by Gender

Gender	Percentage of Respondents
Male	46
Female	54

Table 9.11 shows the education attainment breakdown. Individuals with high school diplomas and some university/college level training are the most frequent in the sample. At least 42% of the respondents are fulltime employed and another 11% are employed part time. Another large cohort is that of the retirees. Interestingly, 13% of the respondents are employed without pay.

```
x=educ2
x1=table(x);x2=x1/sum(x1)*100
tab=xtable(cbind( " education "  =x2))
htmlTable(txtRound(tab,0), rowlabel = "Educational Attainment",
        header ="Percentage of Respondents")
```

Table 9.11 Educational Attainment of Respondents

Educational Attainment	Percentage of Respondents
Less than high school (Grades 1–8 or no formal schooling)	2
High school incomplete (Grades 9–11 or Grade 12 with NO diploma)	5
High school graduate (Grade 12 with diploma or GED certificate)	28
Some college, no degree (includes some community college)	17
Two-year associate degree from a college or university	10
Four-year college or university degree/Bachelor's degree	21
Some postgraduate or professional schooling, no postgraduate degree	1
Postgraduate or professional degree, including master's, doctorate, medical, or law degree	15

Most respondents (89%) were non-Hispanics. Almost 78% of respondents identified themselves as White and 13% as Black or African American. Asians accounted for only 2% of the respondents. Approximately 96% identified themselves as heterosexual.

Surveys often ask questions to determine the state-of-mind of the respondents. The Pew online dating survey asked respondents to report their self-assessed quality of life (see Table 9.12). Most respondents appeared upbeat about their quality of life. Only 5% of the respondents reported a poor quality of life.

```
x=lifequal
x1=table(x);x2=x1/sum(x1)*100
tab=xtable(cbind( "quality of life"  =x2))
htmlTable(txtRound(tab,0), rowlabel = "Life Quality Indicator",
          header ="Percentage of Respondents")
```

Table 9.12 Respondents' Self-Assessed Quality of Life

Life Quality Indicator	Percentage of Respondents
Excellent	18
Very good	28
Good	34
Fair	15
Poor	5

High-Techies

The survey indicates that a large segment of the adult population (83%) in the United States reported using the Internet. Similarly, three in four respondents reported using email. A vast majority (92%) reported the use of mobile phones. These numbers reflect the level of penetration of digital technologies in the United States. Those left untouched by the advances in communication technologies constitute only a small minority in the United States. It is reasonable to assume that the technological advances will touch all aspects of our social behaviors, including the desire to seek relationships.

The advent of smart phones, tablets, and mini laptops have further extended the reach of the communication technologies as consumers discovered even more ways to interact online. Despite the affordability concerns, 34% of the respondents owned a smart tablet. Smart phones were even more prevalent with more than half of the respondents reporting owning one. The fact that at least 44% of the respondents did not own a smart phone may come as a surprise to some. Given the ubiquitous use of smart phones by the youth in cities, one may be forgiven to assume that such trends are common elsewhere and among all age cohorts.

The battle for smart phone consumers has resulted in tremendous innovation in product and services. The Canada-based Blackberry invented the market niche. However, the recent years have seen iPhones and other Android-based products, primarily developed by Samsung, steal the market share from Blackberry, which now holds only 4% of the market share. iPhones with 26% of the market and Android-based phones with 26% of the market are dominating the smart phone market. Again, 44% of respondents revealed that they still relied on basic mobile phones.

Smart phones and tablets are now increasingly being used to access the Internet. Almost 60% of the respondents reported accessing the Internet using such devices. The Internet is being increasingly used to perform activities that have been performed offline in the past. Consider banking chores, which in the past required one to visit a bank branch. Today, these tasks are being accomplished online. A large number of consumers, 59% in the U.S., perform banking online.

Not all innovations in CITs resulted in utilitarian uses. The emergence of Facebook revolutionized the way the Internet-enabled cohorts maintained and updated their social networks. With families and friends scattered across the planet, the geographically distributed generation needed tools to stay in touch with friends and family. Facebook and scores of other services opened the way to be in touch with friends and family in a 24/7 world. The result of these innovations is that 69% of the Internet users reported using Facebook or other social networking services.

Romancing the Internet

From a utilitarian use of the Internet, let's move the discussion to the pursuit of higher purposes, such as finding love. Does the Internet play a role in searching for love? The emergence of online dating services and the resulting bombardment of their online ads gives the impression that such practices are very common. This, however, is not the case.

This section explores how Americans cope with relationships, love, and nuptials. The Internet can be an indispensable tool for helping introverts and those who find it difficult to meet others and make new friendships to search for relationships. The relative anonymity afforded by the Internet reduces the fear of rejection that prohibits many from approaching others.

The Pew sample of adults reported 49% of the respondents to be married. As noted earlier, marriage has experienced a precipitous decline in the U.S. and other western countries since the seventies when 70% of the adults were married. Another 5% of the respondents reported living with a partner. Almost 12% were divorced, 11% were widowed, and 3% separated. Interestingly, one in five respondents has never been married.

Of those who were neither married nor living with a partner, 22% were in a committed romantic relationship. Conversely, a large number of those not married or living with a partner (78%) are not in a romantic relationship that involves some degree of commitment. It is hard to say if the respondents were reflecting on a romantic relationship or committed relationship when they responded to the question.

Almost 29% of those who have never been married in the past reported being in a committed romantic relationship (see Table 9.13). They were followed by the divorced (24%), separated (15%), and widowed (7%).

```
x1=xtabs(~ mar +romantic)
x2 = prop.table(x1,1)*100
tab=xtable(cbind( " xtab between married and romantic "  =x2))
htmlTable(txtRound(tab,0), rowlabel = "Marital Status",
          header=c("Yes (%)", "No (%)"),
          cgroup = c("In A Romantic Relationship"),
          n.cgroup= c(2))
```

Table 9.13 Romancing the Unhitched

Marital Status	In a Romantic Relationship	
	Yes (%)	No (%)
Divorced	24	76
Separated	15	85
Widowed	7	93
Never been married	29	71

Of those who were neither married nor in a romantic relationship, only 18% were looking for romantic interludes. The rest (82%) were not in the market. Of those who were looking for love, almost half found it easy to meet new people. Interestingly enough, men and women strikingly differ in their perception of meeting new people. Whereas the majority of men (59%) found it easy to meet people, an even larger share of women (63%) found it difficult to meet new people (see Table 9.14).

```
x1=xtabs(~ meet + sex)
x2 = prop.table(x1,2)*100
tab=xtable(cbind( " xtab between gender and meeting others "
htmlTable(txtRound(tab,0), rowlabel = "Meeting Others",
          header=c("Male (%)","Female (%)"),
          cgroup = c("Gender"),
          n.cgroup= c(2))=x2))
```

Table 9.14   Do Women Find It Harder to Meet New People?

	Gender	
Meeting Others	**Male (%)**	**Female (%)**
Easy to meet people	59	37
Difficult to meet people	41	63

Given the tremendous influence of the CITs on the way we communicate, socialize, and work, one would have imagined a large number of individuals making their first romantic introduction online. This seems not to be the case. Fewer than 5% respondents in the sample indicated that they had met their significant other online. The vast majority—that is, 95% of the sample—found their paramours the usual offline way. Of those who first met online, 61% of the respondents used a dating service, such as Match.com.

The online dating services realize the potential for their business because they are aware that a large number of adults are neither involved with someone nor are looking for a relationship. Such services are aggressively marketing online. Match.com is the industry leader as is evidenced by the 41% market share in the sample (see Table 9.15). eHarmony at 18% is the distant second.

Whereas most online dating services are generic, some specialize by ethnicity and others by religion. Christian Mingle is a well-known online dating service that caters to religiously oriented individuals, which happens to be a small segment in our data set (2%).

Note that 8% of the respondents when asked about using online dating services recorded their answer as "Don't know." The data provider coded another 1% of the respondents as "99," which is usually used to represent missing information. If we were to use this variable for further analysis, we would have to exclude the Don't knows and 99 from consideration.

```
x=datingbrand
x1=table(x);x2=x1/sum(x1)*100
tab=xtable(cbind( " dating site "   =x2))
print(tab, type="html")
```

Table 9.15 Market Share of Online Dating Services

Online Dating Services	Respondents (%)
Match.com	41
eHarmony	18
OK Cupid	11
Plenty of Fish	9
Christian Mingle	2
Zoosk	1
J Date	1
Adult Friend Finder	1
Other	10
Don't know	8
99	1

Whereas a very small percentage of people first met online (4.5%), a relatively larger percentage of people (16%) broke off their relationships online.

As our online lives have started to take shape, regular aspects of our lives—that is, work, life, and, yes, flirting—have also started to take on their online versions. One in five respondents reported to have flirted online. Interestingly, a majority of those who flirted online (57%) found it easy to meet other people. At the same time, the majority of those who did not flirt online (58%) found it hard to meet other people. In addition, women are less likely to flirt online (17%) than men (25%) are, using the unweighted data set. This suggests that our online demeanors often resemble our offline personalities.

Almost one in four respondents reported being in a long-distance relationship. This is a reflection of very mobile lifestyles, which take people away for business and school. An approximately equal share of men and women reported being in long-distance relationships.

Dating Models

Let's restate the focus of the inquiry: How are individuals romantically introduced? In particular, what determines the odds of meeting the significant other for the first time online? Table 9.16 summarizes the descriptive statistics for variables I intend to use as explanatory variables to model how people, who are now romantically involved, were first introduced.

I have initially hypothesized that because men are more attracted to technology, they are more likely to meet their significant others online. Similarly, those who are married, divorced, or separated are less likely to have used the online modes because of older age, whereas online technologies are essentially a recent phenomenon. Thus, those who are living with a partner, and not a spouse, are likely to be in a recently formed relationship at a time when the Internet technologies became widely available. I also believe that those who use the Internet-based communication technologies, such as email, are more likely to have met their love interests online.

I also hypothesize that individuals who are comfortable with flirting online are also more likely to have met significant others online. In addition, because the Internet-based communication technologies are ubiquitous in the urban areas, it is likely that individuals in urban areas would have met their love interests online. The summary statistics, presented in Table 9.16, largely agree with my assumptions.

```
dating$flirtonline <-factor(dating$flirtonline, labels = c("Flirts
Online", "Does Not Flirt Online"))
dating$email <-factor(dating$email, labels = c("Emails", "Does Not
Email"))
t1=xtabs(~ sex + metonline);gender=round(prop.table(t1,1)*100,2)
t1=xtabs(~ mar + metonline);mar2=round(prop.table(t1,1)*100,2)
t1=xtabs(~ email + metonline);email2=round(prop.table(t1,1)*100, 2)
t1=xtabs(~ flirtonline +
metonline);flirt2=round(prop.table(t1,1)*100,2)
t1=xtabs(~ community + metonline);comm2=round(prop.table(t1,1)*100,2)
tab=rbind(gender, mar2, email2, flirt2, comm2)
c1<-rbind("Sex","" , "Marital Status","","","","","","Email","",
"Flirting", "", "Urban/Rural","","" )
colnames(c1) <- "Categorical Variables"
tab1=  cbind(c1,"categories"=rownames(tab), tab)
tab2 <-xtable(tab1, digits=2)
print(tab2, type="html", include.rownames=FALSE, floating=FALSE)
```

Table 9.16 Summary Statistics for Variables to Model How Individuals First Met

Categorical Variables	Categories	Met Online (%)	Met Offline (%)
Sex	Male	4.79	95.21
	Female	4.12	95.88
Marital Status	Married	2.58	97.42
	Living with a partner	13.56	86.44
	Divorced	11.67	88.33
	Separated	0	100
	Widowed	0	100
	Never been married	9.45	90.55

Categorical Variables	Categories	Met Online (%)	Met Offline (%)
Email	Emails	5.29	94.71
	Does not email	0.84	99.16
Flirt Online	Flirts online	17.65	82.35
	Does not flirt online	2.13	97.87
Urban/Rural	Rural	3.14	96.86
	Suburban	3.86	96.14
	Urban	6.17	93.83

Before I proceed any further, a caveat is in order. Notice that only a small number of respondents (63) in our data set reported that they met their significant others online (see Table 9.17). The rest met offline in more traditional ways. Thus, drawing any meaningful and substantial conclusions with this sample about online dating may not be prudent. This is even more relevant when we realize that any finer dissection of the data may further reduce the observations.

```
dating$metonline <- factor(dating$metonline, levels = c("Met offline",
"Met online"))
htmlTable(txtRound(tab,0), rowlabel = "Did You Meet Online?",
         header=c("Number of respondents"))
```

Table 9.17 Breakdown of Those Who Met Online or Offline

Did You Meet Online?	Number of Respondents
Met online	63
Met offline	1354

I illustrate the results of the binomial or binary logit model in three separate tables. The first table presents the results without replacing the default variable names with descriptive names (see Table 9.18). I address this issue in the second table and replace the default variable names with descriptive names (see Table 9.19). In the third and final table of the series, I replace the estimated parameters with exponentiated coefficients for easy interpretation (see Table 9.20).

```
mod.0 <- multinom(metonline ~ sex + cregion + mar + email +flirtonline
+ age +community, data=dating)
stargazer(mod.0, type="html", no.space=TRUE)
```

Table 9.18 The Binomial Logit Model Exploring How Individuals Met Their Partners with Standard Variable Names

	Dependent Variable
	metonline
sexFemale	−0.045
	(0.402)
cregionMidwest	−0.152
	(0.654)
cregionSouth	−0.047
	(0.546)
cregionWest	0.258
	(0.580)
marLiving with a partner	1.312**
	(0.526)
marDivorced	0.923
	(0.712)
marSeparated	−7.706***
	(0.00002)
marWidowed	−6.603***
	(0.00003)
marNever been married	0.427
	(0.627)
emaildoes not email	−0.925
	(1.053)
flirtonlinedoes not flirt online	−1.745***
	(0.452)
age	0.006
	(0.016)
communitysuburban	0.307
	(0.609)

	Dependent Variable
communityurban	0.306
	(0.616)
Constant	−2.587**
	(1.079)
Akaike Inf. Crit.	245.800

Standard errors in parentheses: * p<0.1; ** p<0.05; *** p<0.01

Table 9.18 reveals that gender and regional location returned statistically insignificant coefficients. This implies that there exists no evidence for gender and location-based differences in how people met their significant others for the first time. Similarly, I did not find a statistically significant relationship for the use of email or for the respondent's location in urban or suburban regions. I also find age to be a statistically insignificant variable in presence of other proxies in the model. I do, however, find a statistically significant and positive correlation for those who are living with a partner, and a negative correlation for those who are separated or widowed. I also find a statistically significant and negative correlation between the dependent variable and those who reported to have not flirted online.

```
stargazer(mod.0, type="html", no.space=TRUE,
        covariate.labels=c("Female", "midwest","south", "west",
        "living with a partner", "divorced", "separated",
        "widowed", "never been married", "does not
        email", does not flirt online", "age in years",
        "suburban", "urban"))
```

Table 9.19   The Binomial Logit Model Exploring How Individuals Met Their Partners with Descriptive Variable Names

	Dependent Variable
	metonline
Female	−0.045
	(0.402)
midwest	−0.152
	(0.654)
south	−0.047
	(0.546)

	Dependent Variable
west	0.258
	(0.580)
living with a partner	1.312**
	(0.526)
divorced	0.923
	(0.712)
separated	−7.706***
	(0.00002)
widowed	−6.603***
	(0.00003)
never been married	0.427
	(0.627)
does not email	−0.925
	(1.053)
does not flirt online	−1.745***
	(0.452)
age in years	0.006
	(0.016)
suburban	0.307
	(0.609)
urban	0.306
	(0.616)
Constant	−2.587**
	(1.079)
Akaike Inf. Crit.	245.800

Standard error in parentheses: * p<0.1; ** p<0.05; *** p<0.01

A more effective way of interpreting the model is to use the odds ratio. For this, I first exponentiate the coefficient by multiplying it by a hundred after subtracting one from it. The results are presented in Table 9.20.

Consider that those who live with a partner are 271% more likely to have met their significant other online than someone who is married. Similarly, someone who is widowed is 100% less likely to have had an online rendezvous than someone who is currently married. In addition, someone who does not flirt online is 82% less likely to have met his or her significant other online than someone who does flirt online, all else being equal.

```
exponentiate <- function(x) (exp(x)-1)*100
stargazer(mod.0, type="html", no.space=TRUE, apply.coef= exponentiate,
se = list(NA), dep.var.labels=c("odds (%)"),
          covariate.labels=c("Female", "midwest","south", "west",
"living with a partner", "divorced", "separated", "widowed", "never
been married", "does not email", "does not flirt online", "age in
years", suburban", "urban"))
```

Table 9.20   The Binomial Logit Model of How Individuals Met Their Partners with Exponentiated Coefficients

	Dependent Variable
	Odds (%)
Female	−4.444
midwest	−14.110
south	−4.636
west	29.410
living with a partner	271.300
divorced	151.800
separated	−99.950
widowed	−99.860
never been married	53.230
does not email	−60.340
does not flirt online	−82.530
age in years	0.630
suburban	35.990
urban	35.850
Constant	−92.480
Akaike Inf. Crit.	245.800

* p<0.1; ** p<0.05; *** p<0.01

Despite the limitations in our sample, I am ready to make some concluding remarks. First, because the Internet-based communication technologies are a recent phenomenon, the models suggest that those who have formed their relationships in the recent past are more likely to have met online than those who formed their relationships some time ago. Thus, those who are married, separated, or widowed are less likely to have met online than those who currently live with a partner.

As expected, the use of the technology is a good indicator of one's likelihood to have met the significant other online. Still, some variables are more contributory in such outcomes than others are. For instance, I did not find a statistically significant relationship for the use of email in explaining the variance in the dependent variable. However, those who reported to have flirted online returned a statistically significant relationship with the dependent variable. Therefore, I can conclude that the use of technology and the age of the relationship are good determinants of one's likelihood of finding a significant other online.

Multinomial Logit Models

The preceding discussion leads us into the workings of the multinomial logit model. Those readers not interested in the mathematical details of the model may skip to the next section "Interpreting Multinomial Logit Models."

Consider the options to travel by different modes where an individual may commute to work by automobile, public transit, or non-motorized mode, such as bike or walk. I can code the choice set as 1, 2, 3. The model is represented in Equation 9.15:

$$Prob\left(Y_i = j\right) = \frac{e^{\beta'_j x_i}}{\sum_{k=1}^{3} e^{\beta'_k x_i}} \quad \textbf{Equation 9.15}$$

In this equation, β'_j is the coefficient for variable x_i when $Y_i = j$. The subscript i on x suggests that it varies across the decision-makers (i) and the subscript j on β suggests that it varies across choices (j). The preceding model will return a set of probabilities for J alternatives for the decision-maker with characteristics x_i. It will also return $J-1$ non-redundant baseline logits. As mentioned earlier, one normalizes the multinomial logit model by assuming that one set of parameters is equal to 0, that is, $\beta_1 = 0$; therefore $e^0 = 1$. The choice for the base category, whose coefficients are set to 0, is completely arbitrary. The probabilities are therefore expressed as follows in Equations 9.16 and 9.17:

$$Prob\left(Y = j\right) = \frac{e^{\beta'_j x_i}}{1 + \sum_{k=1}^{J} e^{\beta'_k x_i}} \text{ for j = 1,2, ..., J,} \quad \textbf{Equation 9.16}$$

$$Prob\left(Y = 1\right) = \frac{1}{1 + \sum_{k=1}^{J} e^{\beta'_k x_i}} \quad \textbf{Equation 9.17}$$

Remember that we arbitrarily set the coefficients of alternative 1 as 0.

For the multinomial case, assume we have three modes: 1) automobile, 2) transit, and 3) walk. We will have two logits; that is, two sets of parameters for two choices, while the third choice will serve as the reference category. Let's put walk as the reference category in the following example (see Equations 9.18 through 9.23).

$$g_1 = \ln\left(\frac{P(auto)}{P(walk)}\right) = \beta_{a0} + \beta_{a1}X_1 + \ldots + \beta_{ak}X_k \qquad \text{Equation 9.18}$$

$$g_2 = \ln\left(\frac{P(transit)}{P(walk)}\right) = \beta_{t0} + \beta_{t1}X_1 + \ldots + \beta_{tk}X_k \qquad \text{Equation 9.19}$$

$$g_3 = 0 \qquad \text{Equation 9.20}$$

$$P(auto) = \frac{\exp(g_1)}{\exp(g_1) + \exp(g_2) + \exp(g_3)} = \frac{\exp(g_1)}{1 + \exp(g_1) + \exp(g_2)} \qquad \text{Equation 9.21}$$

$$P(transit) = \frac{\exp(g_2)}{1 + \exp(g_1) + \exp(g_2)} \qquad \text{Equation 9.22}$$

$$P(walk) = \frac{1}{1 + \exp(g_1) + \exp(g_2)} \qquad \text{Equation 9.23}$$

Interpreting Multinomial Logit Models

The interpretation of coefficients in a multinomial logit model is slightly complicated. It is possible to have a decline in P_{ij} with an explanatory variable x_{ij}, which returns a positive coefficient β_{ij}. A model should therefore be interpreted in terms of odds ratio. Using the odds ratio ($\ln\left[\frac{P_{ij}}{P_{i0}}\right] = \beta'x_i$), a positive coefficient for a continuous explanatory variable suggests that odds of registering an observation in category j are larger than registering that observation in the reference category with the increase in that particular variable. Similarly, a negative coefficient for the explanatory variable suggests that the chances of a baseline outcome are higher than the outcome for category j.

I will use three examples to explain the estimation and interpretation of multinomial logit models. In the first example, I model the choice of an online dating service for those respondents in the Pew data set who reported using dating services. In the second example, I use the same data set to develop a model to determine what factors influence a consumer's choice for a mobile phone as they choose between iPhone, BlackBerry, Android, and regular phones. The third example analyzes the career choices for married women who may or may not be covered under their husbands' employer sponsored health insurance. I demonstrate using a data set of

22,272 married women from 1993 that the odds of a woman working fulltime are higher for those who lack health coverage from their husband's employer. Thus, the odds of working fulltime against not working or working part time are higher for women who do not receive health insurance coverage from their husbands. This example illustrates that the labor force participation decision for women is affected by a large number of factors including presence of young children at home and access to health insurance.

Choosing an Online Dating Service

The first example for multinomial logit models involves modeling the choice of online dating service by those respondents in the Pew data set who have reported using any kind of dating service in the past. First, I subset the data to include only the four major online dating services. I do this because only the four large online dating services recorded enough responses in the data set to be considered a viable alternative. Table 9.21 presents the summary statistics.

```
newdata <- subset(dating, datingbrand == "Match.com" |
                  datingbrand == "eHarmony" |
                  datingbrand == "OK Cupid" |
                  datingbrand == "Plenty of Fish")
newdata$datingbrand <- droplevels(newdata$datingbrand)
attach(newdata)
t1=xtabs(~ sex + datingbrand);gender=round(prop.table(t1,1)*100,2)
t1=xtabs(~community+datingbrand);
community2=round(prop.table(t1,1)*100,2)
t1=xtabs(~ par + datingbrand);parent2=round(prop.table(t1,1)*100,2)
t1=xtabs(~ email + datingbrand);email2=round(prop.table(t1,1)*100, 2)
t1=xtabs(~ intmob + datingbrand);intmob2=round(prop.table(t1,1)*100, 2)
t1=xtabs(~ teletype + datingbrand);
teletype2=round(prop.table(t1,1)*100, 2)

tab=rbind(gender, community2, parent2, email2, intmob2, teletype2)
c1<-rbind("Sex","","Community Type", "","","Parental
Status","","Email",""， "Mobile Internet", "",  "Telephone Type","" )
colnames(c1) <- "Categorical Variables"
tab1=  cbind(c1,"categories"=rownames(tab), tab)
tab2 <-xtable(tab1, digits=2)
print(tab2, type="html", include.rownames=FALSE, floating=FALSE)
```

Table 9.21 Individual Attributes as They Relate to the Choice of Dating Service. Responses Are in Percentages

Categorical Variables	Categories	Match. com	eHarmony	OK Cupid	Plenty of Fish
Sex	Male	60.81	17.57	10.81	10.81
	Female	44.44	27.16	16.05	12.35

Categorical Variables	Categories	Match.com	eHarmony	OK Cupid	Plenty of Fish
Community Type	Rural	61.11	22.22	5.56	11.11
	Suburban	56	24	10.67	9.33
	Urban	45.16	20.97	19.35	14.52
Parental Status	Parent	61.9	19.05	9.52	9.52
	Not parent	48.67	23.89	15.04	12.39
Email	Emails	54.02	20.69	11.49	13.79
	Does not email	50	0	50	0
Mobile Internet	Uses mobile Internet	52.94	21.01	13.45	12.61
	Does not use mobile Internet	50	27.78	13.89	8.33
Telephone Type	Landline	56.36	25.45	5.45	12.73
	Cell	50	21	18	11

The descriptive statistics revealed that Match.com has been the most dominant in the online dating market. Both men (60.8%) and women (44.4%) have chosen Match.com over other services. The choice of online dating services is largely similar across the urban, suburban, and rural markets. However, in rural areas, Match.com captures a much larger market share than it does in suburban and urban locations. Respondents with children reported much higher preference for Match.com than the respondents without children. I explore these correlations further in the multinomial logit model presented in Table 9.22.

```
mod.3 <- multinom(datingbrand ~ sex  + community + par + email +intmob
+teletype,
                data=dating,
                subset=datingbrand == "Match.com" |
                datingbrand == "eHarmony" |
                datingbrand == "OK Cupid" |
                datingbrand == "Plenty of Fish")
stargazer(mod.3, type="html", no.space=TRUE)
```

Table 9.22 Multinomial Logit Model with Choice of Dating Website

	Dependent Variable		
	eHarmony (1)	OK Cupid (2)	Plenty of Fish (3)
sexFemale	0.078 (0.607)	1.073 (0.804)	0.038 (0.699)

| | Dependent Variable | | |
	eHarmony (1)	OK Cupid (2)	Plenty of Fish (3)
communitysuburban	0.342	0.401	0.018
	(0.923)	(1.545)	(0.954)
communityurban	0.344	2.425	−0.036
	(0.959)	(1.513)	(1.000)
parNo	1.083	1.653	1.233
	(0.729)	(1.154)	(0.847)
emaildoes not email	−13.860***	2.283	−13.510***
	(0.00000)	(1.683)	(0.00000)
intmobNo	0.596	−0.134	−0.599
	(0.623)	(0.879)	(0.869)
teletypeCell	−0.481	1.771	−0.060
	(0.625)	(1.193)	(0.755)
Akaike Inf. Crit.	234.500	234.500	234.500

Standard errors in parentheses: * $p<0.1$; ** $p<0.05$; *** $p<0.01$

The first difference you will notice is that instead of just one set of coefficients, the multinomial logit model generates three sets of coefficients. In this example, I have put Match.com as the base reference case. The coefficients are interpreted with reference to Match.com. Note that only one variable, which captures the use of email, ended up being a statistically significant predictor of the choice of online dating service. Respondents who do not use email are less likely to prefer other options to Match.com. Stated differently, those who do not use email are more likely to prefer Match.com to other online dating services.

Also note that in Table 9.22, coefficients are hard to read and they mix the variable name and the response categories. I fix this in later models where you will see its impact on improved readability.

Pew Phone Type Model

In this section, I model the choice of a particular phone type using the Pew Research Center data on dating and Internet use. Over the past few years, smart phones have risen fast to claim huge chunks of market share in mobile communications. Before the advent of iPhones, Blackberry enjoyed a monopoly in the smart phone market. Still, Blackberry captured only a small fraction of the market share in mobile communications. iPhones, however, rapidly changed the landscape for mobile communications. Within a short span of a few years, iPhones commanded huge market share, leaving Blackberry and others behind.

The recent arrivals on the mobile communication scene included both hardware and software providers. The Android computing platform became the operating system of choice for smart phone manufacturers who competed with Apple's iPhones. In this exercise, I want to determine what sociodemographic factors influence the choice of a telephone type from a choice set that includes iPhones, Blackberry, Android Phone, and basic telephone.

I first perform cross-tabulations between the type of phone owned by individual consumers and their socio-demographics. I then estimate multinomial logit models to determine statistically significant determinants of the phone choice.

Before I conduct empirical analysis, some housekeeping is in order for data. Some explanatory variables that I intend to use in this analysis are coded as yes or no. I first replace these responses with adequate labels to avoid any confusion with tabulations or model outputs. Consider that the variable `intuse` captures an individual's use of the Internet. For those who use the Internet, the response is coded as *yes*, and those who do not, the response is coded as *no*. I change these labels to present a more adequate description of the choices being made as "uses Internet" and "does not use Internet." Similarly, I change the labels for the variables representing the parenting status and the use of mobile phones for Internet. I present the R code to assign appropriate labels.

```
dating$intuse <-factor(dating$intuse,
    labels = c("Uses Internet", "Does Not Use Internet"))
dating$par <-factor(dating$par,
    labels = c("Parent", "Not Parent"))
dating$intmob <-factor(dating$intmob,
labels = c("Uses Mobile Internet", "Does Not Use Mobile Internet"))
```

A breakdown by gender suggests that men are more likely to acquire Android phones whereas women are more likely to own basic cellphones (see Table 9.23). A regional background suggests that iPhone patronage is lower in the Midwest where basic phones are more popular. Similarly, divorced individuals are also less likely to own iPhones and are more likely to use regular phones. The widowed individuals are also much more likely to use regular phones than any type of smart phones. Parents are more likely to use iPhones and non-parents are more likely to own regular mobile phones. At the same time, those who do not use the Internet and/or email are more likely to use regular phones than smart phones. Those who access the Internet through mobile devices are more likely to use smart phones and those who do not access the Internet by mobile phones are more likely to use regular phones.

In the next phase, I develop a multinomial logit model to determine the factors that exert a statistically significance impact on the choice of phones.

```
t1=xtabs(~ sex + fonebrand);gender=round(prop.table(t1,1)*100,2)
t1=xtabs(~ cregion + fonebrand);region2=round(prop.table(t1,1)*100,2)
t1=xtabs(~ mar + fonebrand);mar2=round(prop.table(t1,1)*100,2)
t1=xtabs(~ par + fonebrand);parent2=round(prop.table(t1,1)*100,2)
t1=xtabs(~ intuse + fonebrand);intuse2=round(prop.table(t1,1)*100, 2)
t1=xtabs(~ email + fonebrand);email2=round(prop.table(t1,1)*100, 2)
t1=xtabs(~ intmob + fonebrand);intmob2=round(prop.table(t1,1)*100, 2)
t1=xtabs(~ teletype + fonebrand);teletype2=round(prop.table(t1,1)*100,
2)
tab=rbind(gender, region2, mar2, parent2, intuse2, email2, intmob2,
teletype2)
c1<-rbind("Sex","","Region", "","","",  "Marital","","","","","",
          "Parental Status","","Internet Use","","Email","",
          "Mobile Internet", "",  "Telephone Type","" )
colnames(c1) <- "Categorial Variable"
tab1=  cbind(c1,"categories"=rownames(tab), tab)
tab2 <-xtable(tab1, digits=2)
print(tab2, type="html", include.rownames=FALSE, floating=FALSE)
```

Table 9.23   Cross-Tabulations Between Explanatory Variables and the Dependent Variable: Choice of Phone Type (Responses Are in Percentages.)

Categorical Variable	Categories	iPhone	Blackberry	Android	Basic Cell Phone—Unspecified
Sex	Male	25.3	4.34	29.64	40.72
	Female	25.68	3.31	23.54	47.47
Region	Northeast	27.9	5.33	25.71	41.07
	Midwest	18.81	2.43	26.55	52.21
	South	28.1	3.83	25.59	42.48
	West	26.19	4.05	28.33	41.43
Marital	Married	28.29	4.09	25.03	42.59
	Living with a partner	26.85	2.78	32.41	37.96
	Divorced	18.47	3.15	23.42	54.95
	Separated	20.41	6.12	24.49	48.98
	Widowed	13.84	2.52	9.43	74.21

Categorical Variable	Categories	iPhone	Blackberry	Android	Basic Cell Phone—Unspecified
	Never Been Married	27.91	3.88	37.38	30.83
Parental Status	Parent	33.72	3.49	37.4	25.39
	Not Parent	22.54	3.93	22.47	51.05
Internet Use	Uses Internet	28.3	3.74	28.19	39.77
	Does not Use Internet	4.24	3.39	11.02	81.36
Email	Emails	28.98	3.73	28.98	38.31
	Does not Email	8.19	3.51	12.87	75.44
Mobile Internet	Uses Mobile Internet	37.01	4.3	37.87	20.81
	Does not Use Mobile Internet	3.59	2.84	4.63	88.94
Telephone Type	Landline	21.33	4.36	18.92	55.39
	Cell	28.88	3.34	32.5	35.28

Table 9.24 presents the results of the multinomial logit model. The coefficients are reported for the three choices: Blackberry, Android, basic cellphone. I have kept iPhones as the base category and hence the results are reported in relation to the base category; that is, the iPhones. Later, I make basic phone as the reference category and present the model results accordingly.

A quick look at the results reveals that with the exception of a couple of variables, the rest were not statistically significant in explaining consumers' choice for mobile phones. It turns out that females are more likely to prefer regular phones to smart phones ($p < 0.1$). Similarly, consumers in the Midwest are more likely to opt for regular phones ($p < .01$) as are those located in the West ($p < 0.1$). The use of email and the Internet were also statistically significant predictors of the mobile phone choice. Those who did not use the Internet preferred Android phones to the iPhone. Those who did not use email preferred Blackberry and regular phones to iPhones. This is rather counterintuitive because the Blackberry's claim to fame has been its ironclad email system. Furthermore, those who did not use mobile devices to access the Internet were likely to use regular mobile phones.

Note also that the coefficient names in Table 9.24 are generated automatically. I have transformed variable names to be more illustrative in Table 9.25.

```
mod.1 <- multinom(fonebrand ~ sex + cregion + mar + par + intuse +
email +intmob +teletype  , data=dating)
stargazer(mod.1, type="html", no.space=TRUE)
```

Table 9.24   Multinomial Logit Model of the Choice of Phone

	Dependent Variable		
	Blackberry (1)	Android (2)	Basic Cell Phone—Unspecified (3)
sexFemale	−0.628	−0.167	0.352*
	(0.384)	(0.186)	(0.208)
cregionMidwest	−0.293	0.457	1.045***
	(0.570)	(0.295)	(0.331)
cregionSouth	−0.496	0.105	0.448
	(0.489)	(0.262)	(0.304)
cregionWest	−0.175	0.320	0.613*
	(0.532)	(0.289)	(0.335)
marLiving with a partner	−0.675	0.476	0.010
	(1.076)	(0.387)	(0.452)
marDivorced	−0.479	0.535*	0.231
	(0.798)	(0.320)	(0.349)
marSeparated	0.899	−0.419	−0.077
	(0.908)	(0.748)	(0.680)
marWidowed	−1.141	−0.745	−0.098
	(1.099)	(0.532)	(0.440)
marNever been married	−0.257	0.299	−0.253
	(0.480)	(0.232)	(0.265)
parNo	0.204	−0.294	0.350
	(0.430)	(0.204)	(0.234)

	Dependent Variable		
	Blackberry (1)	Android (2)	Basic Cell Phone—Unspecified (3)
intuseNo	0.431	1.083*	0.613
	(0.945)	(0.617)	(0.593)
emaildoes not email	1.119*	0.128	0.759*
	(0.652)	(0.412)	(0.406)
intmobNo	1.036*	0.072	3.395***
	(0.565)	(0.409)	(0.318)
teletypeCell	−0.892**	0.150	−0.294
	(0.389)	(0.197)	(0.210)
Constant	−1.191**	−0.181	−1.413***
	(0.515)	(0.292)	(0.350)
Akaike Inf. Crit.	1,822.000	1,822.000	1,822.000

Standard errors in parentheses: * p<0.1; ** p<0.05; *** p<0.01

The next model differs from the one before because I have replaced the reference category to regular phones. This way, the model will allow us to interpret the log of odds between each smart phone and the basic mobile phone. The code to recast the variable is presented along with the model in Table 9.25.

I can focus on the iPhones to interpret the model. I notice that the coefficient for Female is statistically significant and negative, thus suggesting that women are less likely to prefer iPhones to regular mobile phones, all else being equal. Similarly, consumers in the Midwest are less likely to prefer iPhones to regular mobile phones, all else being equal. At the same time, consumers who do not use the Internet by mobile devices are less likely to prefer any type of smart phone to the basic mobile phone.

```
dating$brand2 <-dating$fonebrand
dating$brand2 <-factor(dating$brand2, levels = c("(VOL.) Basic cell
phone - unspecified", "iPhone", "Blackberry", "Android"),
labels = c("basic cell phone", "iPhone", "Blackberry", "Android"))
mod.1 <- multinom(brand2 ~ sex + cregion + mar + par + intuse + email
+intmob +teletype  , data=dating)
stargazer(mod.1, type="html", no.space=TRUE,
covariate.labels=c("Female", "Midwest","South", "West", "Living With A
Partner", "Divorced", "Separated", "Widowed", "Never Been Married", "No
Children", "Does Not Use Internet", "No Email", "No Internet On Mobile
Phone", "Respondent Reached On Cellular"))
```

Table 9.25   Multinomial Logit Model for the Choice of Phone with Basic Phone as the Reference Category

	Dependent Variable		
	iPhone (1)	**Blackberry (2)**	**Android (3)**
Female	−0.352*	−0.980**	−0.519**
	(0.208)	(0.386)	(0.206)
Midwest	−1.044***	−1.337**	−0.587*
	(0.331)	(0.571)	(0.331)
South	−0.447	−0.943*	−0.342
	(0.304)	(0.501)	(0.314)
West	−0.612*	−0.788	−0.292
	(0.335)	(0.545)	(0.340)
Living with A Partner	−0.010	−0.686	0.466
	(0.452)	(1.076)	(0.423)
Divorced	−0.231	−0.710	0.304
	(0.349)	(0.783)	(0.321)
Separated	0.077	0.977	−0.342
	(0.680)	(0.872)	(0.759)
Widowed	0.099	−1.045	−0.646
	(0.440)	(1.075)	(0.527)
Never Been Married	0.253	−0.005	0.552**
	(0.265)	(0.486)	(0.262)
No Children	−0.350	−0.146	−0.644***
	(0.234)	(0.437)	(0.230)
Does not Use Internet	−0.613	−0.183	0.471
	(0.593)	(0.819)	(0.480)
No Email	−0.760*	0.359	−0.632*
	(0.406)	(0.612)	(0.374)
No Internet on Mobile Phone	−3.395***	−2.358***	−3.323***
	(0.318)	(0.502)	(0.310)

	Dependent Variable		
	iPhone (1)	Blackberry (2)	Android (3)
Respondent Reached on Cellular	0.294	–0.599	0.444[**]
	(0.210)	(0.391)	(0.210)
Constant	1.413[***]	0.223	1.231[***]
	(0.350)	(0.542)	(0.354)
Akaike Inf. Crit.	1,822.000	1,822.000	1,822.000

Standard errors in parentheses: * $p<0.1$; ** $p<0.05$; *** $p<0.01$

Why Some Women Work Full-Time and Others Don't

In this section, I return to the women's participation in the labor force, but with a different data set and a new twist. Earlier in this chapter, I illustrated how the presence of young children in the household is negatively correlated with the women's decision to work. Now let me broaden this discussion and see what other factors influence a woman's decision to work. This time, I determine the impact of employer-provided health insurance on a woman's decision to work full-time.

Millions of working-age Americans are without access to quality healthcare. In the absence of a publically funded healthcare program for working adults, employer-provided health insurance has been the primary mechanism for working-age Americans to have health insurance. Since employers usually restrict health insurance to full-time employees, a large number of part-time workers have remained without health insurance, which restricts their access to expensive healthcare.

During his second term, U.S. President Barack Obama made a concerted effort to expand healthcare coverage to those who had remained uninsured in the past. However, the matter became quite controversial between the Democratic president and the Republican-controlled Congress.

The dispute between the Republicans and Democrats went all the way to the Supreme Court, which sided with the presidential initiative. This resulted in the Patient Protection and Affordable Care Act, also known as Obamacare, which was signed into law on March 23, 2010. The provisions in the Act intend to lower healthcare costs, improve quality and affordability of health insurance, and reduce the number of uninsured by instituting subsidies and public and private insurance exchanges.

The Act resulted in expanding coverage to 9.9 million people through the federal and state insurance exchanges. Earlier estimates by the Congressional Budget Office revealed that insurance exchanges would enroll 21 million individuals by 2016. Those estimates, however, have been significantly scaled down. Earlier published research also estimated 20 million Americans gaining coverage because of the mechanisms made possible by the Act.[7] Later estimates range between 7.0 and 16.4 million insured under the Act.[8]

The changes in the healthcare system caused discomfort to a considerable number of individuals who unexpectedly lost their health insurance. At the same time, the government website designed to enroll millions initially crashed and left many struggling to log in to the system. Eventually, these matters were resolved, but they provided fodder to those not enthused by the provisions in the Act.

Irrespective of the inconsistent estimates of the expanded healthcare, Blumenthal et. al. (2015) conducted a follow-up analyses and concluded that the Act "has brought about considerable improvements in access to affordable health insurance in the United States." Furthermore, since the Act has been enacted, the rate of increase in healthcare spending has slowed down.

I included details about the Act to provide the background needed to understand the next example, which illustrates how women lacking access to health insurance provided by their spouse's employer are more likely to work full-time than those who are insured under their spouse's employer-provided health insurance.

Professor Craig A. Olson published an influential paper studying the motivation for full-time work for women. Using a data set of 22,272 married couples, he analyzed married women's decision to not work, work part-time, or work full-time.[9] He relied on 1993 data from the U.S. Current Population Survey (CPS). The CPS data for 1995 reported that 84.6% of the U.S. population received either public or private insurance, of which employer-provided health insurance was the most common one. Furthermore, 61% of the total population received "health insurance benefits through a family member that received these benefits from a current or former employer."

Professor Olson further mentioned that in 1992, employers extended health insurance to only 23% of the employees who worked for fewer than 34 hours per week. However, 70% of the full-time employees working for more than 34 hours per week received employer-provided health insurance.

From this emerges the interesting question: Would women without spousal coverage be more likely to work full-time to receive employer-provided health insurance than the women who received health coverage through their spouses? Fortunately for us, we have access to the same data Professor Olson used. You can download it from the book's website under Chapter 9.

The data set is restricted to households where the wife is less than 65 years of age, and her work status (employed versus unemployed) in 1992 was the same as in 1993.

First I generate basic descriptive statistics about work status as it relates to factors that might influence wives' work status. I present the basic tabulations in Table 9.26. I also present the script in R to generate Table 9.26.

The first thing to note in Table 9.26 is that women without spousal coverage are much more likely to work full-time (60%) than are those with spousal coverage (44%). Also note that highly educated women with 16 years or more of schooling are more likely to work full-time

(73%) than those with 12 years of education (50%). In fact, I see a clear trend where an increase in wives' education is positively correlated with their educational attainment.

As with the previous example of women's participation in the labor force, I see that women working full-time on average have fewer children under the age of 6 (0.27 children per full-time working mother) than those who do not work (0.47 children per unemployed mother).

I see some interesting comparisons between full-time and part-time workers. Wives who work part-time on average have a higher number of children between the ages of 6 and 18 than those who work full-time. Similarly, spouses of part-time women workers earn more than the spouses of full-time women workers.

```
library (xtable)
library(htmlTable)
t1<- xtabs(~ hhi + lfp); insx= round(prop.table(t1,1)*100,2)
t1<- xtabs(~ edu2 + lfp); edux= round(prop.table(t1,1)*100,2)
t1<- xtabs(~ race2 + lfp); racex= round(prop.table(t1,1)*100,2)
exper.years<- round(tapply(experience, lfp,mean),2)
kids.under.6<- round(tapply(kidslt6, lfp,mean),2)
kids.6.to.18<- round(tapply(kids618, lfp,mean),2)
husb.inc<- round(tapply(husby, lfp,mean),2)
t1<- xtabs(~ region + lfp); regionx= round(prop.table(t1,1)*100,2)

tab<- rbind(insx, edux, racex, exper.years, kids.under.6, kids.6.to.18,
husb.inc, regionx)
tab1<-xtable(tab)
print(tab1, type="html")

htmlTable(txtRound(tab1,0, excl.rows = c(13,14)),
        rgroup=c("Husband's insurance covers wife (%)",
                "Education status (%)",
                "Race (%)",
                "Experience in years",
                "Children less than 6 years old",
                "Children between 6 and 18 years old",
                "Husband's income",
                "Region of origin (%)"),
        n.rgroup = c(2,6,3,1,1,1,1,4),
        cgroup = c("Wives' Work Status"),
        n.cgroup = c(3),
        rowlabel="Demographic Attributes")
```

Table 9.26　Descriptive Statistics of the Key Variables for Wives

	Wives' Work Status		
Demographic Attributes	**Unemployed**	**Part-Time**	**Full-Time**
Husband's insurance covers wife (%)			
no	26	14	60
yes	34	22	44
Education status (%)			
LT 9 years	65	9	26
9-11 years	52	14	34
12 years	32	19	50
13-15 years	24	21	56
16 years	20	18	62
GT 16 years	12	15	73
Race (%)			
Whites	30	18	51
African Americans	24	11	65
Other race	39	10	51
Experience in years			
exper.years	27	22	21
Children less than 6 years old			
kids.under.6	0.47	0.37	0.27
Children between 6 and 18 years old			
kids.6.to.18	0.67	0.85	0.65
Husband's income			
Husb.inc	26	30	27
Region of origin (%)			
other	29	21	50
northcentral	27	21	52
south	32	13	55
west	32	18	50

I estimate a multinomial logit model from the same data set. The dependent variable is the wife's work status, which is captured as unemployed, part-time worker, full-time worker. The estimated coefficients from the multinomial logit model are presented in Table 9.27. I also present the R code used to generate the results.

```
library(stargazer)
library(nnet)

mod.2<- multinom(lfp ~ hhi + factor(edu2) + race2 +
    factor(hispanic)+ experience + exp2 +exp3 +kidslt6 +
    kids618 + husby +factor(region), weight=mean_wt, data=HI)

stargazer(mod.2, type="html", no.space=TRUE,
    covariate.labels = c("Wife covered by husband's insurance",
    "9-11 years education", "12 years education",
    "13-15 years education", "16 years education",
    "GT 16 years education", "African-American",
    "Other race", "Hispanic",
    "Years of potential work experience", "Potential LF exp2/100",
    "Potential LF exp3/100"  ,"No. of children < 6 years old",
    "No. of children 6±18 years old",
    "Husband's income in thousands",
    "North Central Region", "South Region", "West Region"))
```

I have used "unemployed" as the base category. The two set of coefficients—that is, working full-time and part-time—are interpreted in comparison to the base category. Thus, one set of coefficients estimates the odds of working part-time against unemployed, and the other set of coefficients measures the odds of working full-time against being unemployed. Note that the output in Table 9.27 presents the actual coefficients, whereas the output in Table 9.28 presents the exponentiated coefficients.

I see a statistically significant and negative coefficient (−0.701) for women working full-time with access to spouse's health coverage. The estimated coefficient (−0.701) is measuring the change in log-odds (LN(Prob:Work full-time/Prob:Unemployed)) when the variable Spousal health coverage is increased by one unit; that is, from 0 to 1. Whereas $e^{-.701} = 0.49$ presents the ratio of odds (Prob:Work full-time/Prob:Unemployed) for working full-time against not working when Spouse's health insurance status equals 1.

The odds of wives covered by the spouse's health insurance working full-time (against not working) are $e^{-.701} = 0.49$ times than that for the wives who are not covered by their spouse's health insurance. Stated differently, the odds of wives not covered by spouse's health insurance working full-time are $1/.49 = 2.0$ times higher than do those covered under their spouse's health insurance. Even when I control for other important factors that could influence a woman's decision to work, the employer provided health insurance ends up being a significant determinant of a woman's decision to work.

Similarly, as seen from Table 9.28, which presents the exponentiated coefficients, the odds for a woman with 16 years of education working full-time are 4 times higher than that of a woman with less than 9 years of education, which is the reference category in the model. A single year increase in work experience increases the odds of working full-time for a woman by 1.11 times against not working. Notice in Table 9.27 the negative coefficient on the transformed variable (Potential LF exp2/100), which essentially squares the work experience and divides it by 100. The negative coefficient suggests that the increase in work experience increases the odds of working full-time, but at a declining rate. That is, for significantly higher work experience, which correlates with higher age, the odds of working full-time will start to slow or decline.

The presence of an additional young child under the age of six years increases the odds of not working full-time by 3 times ($\frac{1}{e^{-1.114}}$) than working full-time. An additional child between the ages of 6 and 18 years increases the odds of not working by 1.5 times ($\frac{1}{e^{-.39}}$) against working full-time.

Table 9.27   Output from the Multinomial Logit Model

	Dependent Variable	
	Part-Time (1)	**Full-Time (2)**
Wife covered by husband's insurance	0.064	-0.701***
	(0.047)	(0.038)
9-11 years education	0.219	0.166
	(0.140)	(0.105)
12 years education	0.839***	0.928***
	(0.124)	(0.093)
13-15 years education	1.119***	1.164***
	(0.129)	(0.097)
16 years education	1.121***	1.388***
	(0.136)	(0.103)
GT 16 years education	1.370***	1.897***
	(0.160)	(0.125)
African American	-0.172*	0.542***
	(0.101)	(0.072)
Other race	-0.534***	-0.179
	(0.081)	(0.190)

	Dependent Variable	
	Part-Time (1)	Full-Time (2)
Hispanic	-0.456***	-0.336***
	(0.108)	(0.082)
Years of potential work experience	0.007	0.106***
	(0.023)	(0.019)
Potential LF exp2/100	-0.058	-0.472***
	(0.103)	(0.086)
Potential LF exp3/100	-0.001	0.002**
	(0.001)	(0.001)
No. of children < 6 years old	-0.594***	-1.114***
	(0.038)	(0.033)
No. of children 6-18 years old	-0.049**	-0.390***
	(0.024)	(0.021)
Husband's income in thousands	-0.004***	-0.005***
	(0.001)	(0.001)
North Central Region	0.032	0.115**
	(0.061)	(0.053)
South Region	-0.510***	-0.081*
	(0.059)	(0.049)
West Region	-0.235***	-0.164***
	(0.064)	(0.055)
Constant	-0.252	0.952***
	(0.203)	(0.163)
Akaike Inf. Crit.	39,544.130	39,544.130

Standard errors in parentheses: * p<0.1; ** p<0.05; *** p<0.01

The following script and Table 9.28 present the increase in odds, which I have obtained by exponentiating the coefficients. The R script that I used to generate to Table 9.28 is presented here:

```
exponentiate <- function(x) exp(x)
stargazer(mod.2, type="html", no.space=TRUE, apply.coef= exponentiate,
     se= list(NA),
     covariate.labels = c("Wife covered by husband's insurance",
     "9-11 years education", "12 years education",
     "13-15 years education", "16 years education",
     "GT 16 years education", "African-American",
     "Other race", "Hispanic",
     "Years of potential work experience", "Potential LF exp2/100",
     "Potential LF exp3/100"  ,"No. of children < 6 years old",
     "No. of children 6±18 years old",
     "Husband's income in thousands",
     "North Central Region", "South Region", "West Region"))
```

Table 9.28 Output from a Multinomial Logit Model with Exponentiated Coefficients

	Dependent Variable	
	Part-Time (1)	Full-Time (2)
Wife covered by husband's insurance	1.067	0.496
9-11 years education	1.244	1.180
12 years education	2.314	2.531
13-15 years education	3.063	3.202
16 years education	3.067	4.006
GT 16 years education	3.934	6.669
African American	0.842	1.719
Other race	0.586	0.836
Hispanic	0.634	0.715
Years of potential work experience	1.007	1.112
Potential LF exp2/100	0.943	0.624
Potential LF exp3/100	0.999	1.002
No. of children < 6 years old	0.552	0.328
No. of children 6-18 years old	0.953	0.677
Husband's income in thousands	0.996	0.995
North Central Region	1.033	1.122
South Region	0.601	0.923
West Region	0.791	0.848
Constant	0.778	2.591

Although Table 9.28 presents the exponentiated coefficients, the coefficients are easier to interpret if they are converted to a percentage change notation, which are shown in Table 9.29. Here, I first exponentiate the coefficient and then subtract one from it. Afterward, I multiply the difference by 100 to obtain a percentage change interpretation. Thus, I see that if the wife is covered by her spouse's health insurance, the odds of her working full-time are 50.3% lower than being unemployed. I present the R script used to generate Table 9.29.

```
percentx <- function(x) (exp(x)-1)*100
stargazer(mod.2, type="html", no.space=TRUE, apply.coef= percentx,
     se= list(NA),
     covariate.labels = c("Wife covered by husband's insurance",
     "9-11 years education", "12 years education",
     "13-15 years education", "16 years education",
     "GT 16 years education", "African-American",
     "Other race", "Hispanic",
     "Years of potential work experience", "Potential LF exp2/100",
     "Potential LF exp3/100","No. of children < 6 years old",
     "No. of children 6±18 years old",
     "Husband's income in thousands",
     "North Central Region", "South Region", "West Region"))
```

Table 9.29 Converting Logit Coefficients to Percentage Change Interpretation

	Dependent Variable	
	Part-Time (1)	Full-Time (2)
Wife covered by husband's insurance	6.660	-50.385
9-11 years education	24.430	18.001
12 years education	131.402	153.065
13-15 years education	206.293	220.190
16 years education	206.689	300.579
GT 16 years education	293.446	566.864
African American	-15.761	71.947
Other race	-41.391	-16.390
Hispanic	-36.646	-28.508
Years of potential work experience	0.737	11.228
Potential LF exp2/100	-5.679	-37.613
Potential LF exp3/100	-0.110	0.245
No. of children < 6 years old	-44.762	-67.172

	Dependent Variable	
	Part-Time (1)	Full-Time (2)
No. of children 6-18 years old	-4.739	-32.300
Husband's income in thousands	-0.442	-0.505
North Central Region	3.293	12.193
South Region	-39.939	-7.735
West Region	-20.937	-15.161
Constant	-22.245	159.071

Conditional Logit Models

So far, the discussion has focused on models where the decision maker's characteristics, such as age, income, and the like, have been used as the regressors. However, you also encounter situations where the attributes of the choice may also have an impact on the outcome. Recall the modeling of the choice of various phone brands; that is, iPhone, Blackberry, and Android-based alternatives. We know that the choice of a phone is equally affected by the price of these phones. The binary and multinomial logit models described earlier cannot deal with situations where the outcome is also impacted by the attributes of choice. We would need to estimate a conditional logit model instead. I explain the model using travel choices as an example.

Consider the travel mode choices for a commuter. The characteristics of the decision-maker, that is, the commuter, and the attributes of choice, such as travel time and cost, which differ by mode, also affect the outcome. To deal with this challenge, Professor Daniel McFadden, the 2000 recipient of the The Sveriges Riksbank Prize in Economics, developed the conditional or McFadden logit model.[10] The conditional logit model has been widely applied in modeling choices in diverse fields such as market research, economics, psychology, and travel demand analysis.

Let's assume that some cast members of the popular TV show *Suits* are in Toronto (where the show is usually filmed) and are interested in shopping. They are staying at the different hotels. Rick Hoffman, who plays Louis Litt, is staying at a hotel near the airport. Gabriel Macht (the lead character, Harvey Specter) is staying at a hotel in downtown Toronto. Let's also assume that Meghan Markle (Rachel Zane) is staying at a hotel in suburban Toronto to be close to friends whom she would also like to visit.

The three would like to visit a large shopping center. I have shortlisted their choices to three large malls, one downtown, one near the airport, and one in the suburb. Their choices and attributes (including fake annual incomes) are reported in Table 9.30.

The three actors, decision-makers, are faced with three choices each for shopping destinations. The regressors are number of stores at each location, distance to the shopping center, and individual's income. It is obvious from the table that income does not change over alternatives for each decision-maker and hence if added as a regressor in the model, income will fall out of the probability equation.

Table 9.30 Data Sample for Conditional Logit Models

Shopper ID	Name	Malls	Stores	Distance (km)	Income ('000)	Choice
1	Rick Hoffman (Louis Litt)	Square One	360	4	325	1
1	Rick Hoffman	Eaton Centre	330	23	325	0
1	Rick Hoffman	Yorkdale	250	15	325	0
2	Gabriel Macht (Harvey Specter)	Square One	360	20	375	0
2	Gabriel Macht	Eaton Centre	330	1	375	1
2	Gabriel Macht	Yorkdale	250	15	375	0
3	Meghan Markle (Rachel Zane)	Square One	360	18	345	0
3	Meghan Markle	Eaton Centre	330	14	345	0
3	Meghan Markle	Yorkdale	250	8	345	1

The way to accommodate income as a regressor is to introduce alternative-specific dummy variables and multiply them with the common characteristics of the individual decision-maker. To create individual-specific effects, Greene (1995) suggests that a set of dummy variables could be created for the choices, which can then be multiplied with the individual-specific characteristics.[11] This method is analogous to the creation of interaction terms in OLS models. I can use the attributes of shopping centers as regressors along with the characteristics of the shoppers while modeling the choice of a shopping center. The assumption is that a shopper is likely to choose the destination that helps minimize his or her shopping trip distance and offers the most diverse shopping experience (number of stores). Note that for each trip maker, the number of shops and the distance from the shopper's point of origin to the shopping center are different. However, the characteristics of the trip-maker are the same for all alternatives.

The income variable is thus introduced in the model as an *alternative-specific variable*. For example, the variable *Inc – Eaton* in Table 9.31 captures the impact of income on the utility of shopping at Eaton Centre, whereas the variable *Inc – Yorkdale* captures the impact of income on shopping at the Yorkdale Mall. You can see that by interacting the characteristics of the decision-maker with the alternative-specific dummies, I have created new variables that vary across alternatives for each decision-maker. Also, remember not to include all interacted income variables in the utility function because if you add them together, they will again reproduce the original income variable and hence will fall out of the regression equation during estimation. In the preceding example, I will include income as an explanatory variable for any two out of the three alternatives.

Table 9.31   Example of Alternative-Specific Income Variable for Conditional Logit Models

Shopper ID	Name	Malls	Stores	Inc-Square One	Inc-Eaton	Inc-Yorkdale
1	Rick Hoffman	Square One	360	325	0	0
1	Rick Hoffman	Eaton Centre	330	0	325	0
1	Rick Hoffman	Yorkdale	250	0	0	325
2	Gabriel Macht	Square One	360	375	0	0
2	Gabriel Macht	Eaton Centre	330	0	375	0
2	Gabriel Macht	Yorkdale	250	0	0	375
3	Meghan Markle	Square One	360	345	0	0
3	Meghan Markle	Eaton Centre	330	0	345	0
3	Meghan Markle	Yorkdale	250	0	0	345

Random Utility Model

Readers who are not particularly interested in the mathematical details of the conditional logit models can skip ahead to the section titled, "Interpretation of Conditional Logit Models." Others are welcome to read along.

The conditional logit model can be derived from the Random Utility theory. Let's assume that a decision-maker is faced with two choices, a and b. Let U^a represent the utility of alternative a and U^b represent the utility of alternative b. The rational decision-maker will opt for the alternative that supposedly maximizes his or her utility. In addition, the utility can be divided into two components, the observed and unobserved part. The linear random utility model can be expressed as:

$$U^a = \beta'_a X + \epsilon_a \text{ and } U^b = \beta'_b X + \epsilon_b$$

If $Y = 1$ denotes the consumer's choice for alternative a, then the probability to choose alternative a is given by Equation 9.24.

$$Prob\left[y = 1|x\right] = Prob\left[U^a > U^b\right] = Prob\left[\beta'_a x + \epsilon_a - \beta'_b x - \epsilon_b > 0|x\right]$$

$$Prob\left[y = 1|x\right] = Prob\left[\left(\beta'_a - \beta'_b\right)x + \epsilon_a - \epsilon_b > 0|x\right]$$

$$Prob\left[y = 1 \| x\right] = Prob[\beta'x + \epsilon > 0 | x]$$ **Equation 9.24**

If Y is assumed to be a random variable, it can be shown in Equation 9.25 that

$$Prob\left(Y_i = j\right) = \frac{e^{\beta'z_{ij}}}{\sum_{j=1}^{J} e^{\beta'z_{ij}}}$$ **Equation 9.25**

For the conditional logit model, $z_{i\,j} = [x_{ij}, w_i]$. If x_{ij} represents the attributes of the choices, the subscript "ij" on x suggests that the x varies across the decision-makers (i) and choices (j), whereas wi represents the characteristics of the decision-maker (i) and hence it does not vary across alternatives. I can rewrite Equation 9.25 as shown in Equation 9.26:

$$Prob\left(Y_i = j\right) = \frac{e^{\beta'x_{ij} + \alpha'w_i}}{\sum_{j=1}^{J} e^{\beta'x_{ij} + \alpha'w_i}} = \frac{e^{\beta'x_{ij}} e^{\alpha'w_i}}{\sum_{j=1}^{J} e^{\beta'x_{ij}} e^{\alpha'w_i}}$$ **Equation 9.26**

It is useful to note that terms that do not vary across alternatives—that is, those specific to the individual—fall out of the probability formulation. Therefore, the Equation 9.26 can be simplified as shown in Equation 9.27:

$$Prob\left(Y_i = j\right) = \frac{e^{\beta'x_{ij}}}{\sum_{j=1}^{J} e^{\beta'x_{ij}}}$$ **Equation 9.27**

Unlike the multinomial logit model, the conditional logit model returns a single set of parameters, regardless of the number of alternatives. However, the data set has to be conditioned so that each decision-maker is repeated in the data set for the number of available alternatives, which is evident from the previous two tables. Therefore, the total number of rows in the data set is equal to the number of decision-makers (i) times the available alternatives (j). This is only true if all decision-makers are presented with the same choice set. The conditional logit model allows the analyst to restrict the number of alternatives available to a decision-maker. Consider the example of travel mode choice where the individual commuter can drive, walk, or take transit. The choice set for a trip-maker without a valid driver's license excludes the drive mode.

The marginal effects for any variable x_k can be computed by differentiating the logit model with respect to the variable x_k. Therefore, marginal effects are given by Equation 9.28:

$$\delta_{jk} = \frac{\partial P_j}{\partial x_k} = \left[P_j\left(1(j = k) - P_k\right)\right]\beta$$ **Equation 9.28**

The elasticities of probabilities are shown in Equation 9.29:

$$\frac{\partial lnP_j}{\partial lnx_{km}} = x_{km}\left[\left(1(j = k) - P_k\right)\beta_k = x_{km}\left(1 - P_k\right)\beta_k\right.$$ **Equation 9.29**

The preceding equation is referred to as *direct elasticity* where m indexes the regressor (attribute) variable and j, k index the alternatives. Consider the following example for determining the direct elasticity of the auto-drive mode with respect to the cost of driving. Direct elasticity calculations require the following inputs:

x_{km} is the cost of driving, P_k is the probability of auto-drive, and β_k is the estimated coefficient for the cost variable.

Cross elasticity is computed as shown in Equation 9.30:

$$\frac{\partial lnP_j}{\partial lnx_{km}} = -x_{jm}P_k\beta_k \text{ where, } k \neq j \quad \textbf{Equation 9.30}$$

The cross elasticity estimation for a change in the auto-drive mode with respect to changes in transit costs requires the following inputs:

x_{jm} is the cost of transit, P_k is the probability of auto-drive, and β_k is the estimated coefficient for the cost variable.

In estimating conditional logit models, you are not restricted by the number of choices. Here the "size of the estimation problem is independent of the number of choices" (Greene, 1995, p. 920). Greene further argues that the number of choices should be restricted to 100. The fact remains that even with 100 choices, interpretation of the model becomes a major concern. From the behavioral perspective, a decision-maker seldom undertakes simultaneous evaluation of 100 choices. To assume that a rational decision-maker can simultaneously evaluate 100 choices is debatable at best.

The conditional logit model does not contain a constant term (β_0 in the OLS tradition). Instead, the conditional logit model reports J-1 alternative-specific constants. In the travel mode choice example involving three alternatives,—that is, drive, walk, and transit—the model reports alternative-specific constants for two alternatives, which are interpreted against the omitted category.

The conditional logit models, unlike the multinomial logit models discussed earlier, do not set the systematic utility of any category to 0. I first present a binary choice between automobile and transit as conditional logit model where V^a represents the systematic utility of auto drive and V^t represents that of transit. Equation 9.31 shows this mathematically:

$$P(auto) = \frac{exp^{V_a}}{exp^{V_a} + exp^{V_t}} \quad \textbf{Equation 9.31}$$

If I divide both the numerator and the denominator by exp^{V_a}, I have Equation 9.32.

$$P(auto) = \frac{1}{1 + \dfrac{exp^{V_t}}{exp^{V_a}}} = \frac{1}{1 + exp^{V_t - V_a}} \quad \textbf{Equation 9.32}$$

The preceding equations present an interesting property of conditional logit models; that is, we do not observe the actual utility for a choice, but the difference in the utility of two choices, as shown in Equation 9.33.

$$P(transit) = 1 - \frac{1}{1 + exp^{V_t - V_a}} = \frac{exp^{V_t - V_a}}{1 + exp^{V_t - V_a}} \qquad \textbf{Equation 9.33}$$

The odds ratio for conditional logit is therefore given by Equation 9.34.

$$\frac{P(auto)}{P(transit)} = \frac{\dfrac{1}{1 + exp^{V_t - V_a}}}{\dfrac{exp^{V_t - V_a}}{1 + exp^{V_t - V_a}}} = exp^{V_a - V_t} \qquad \textbf{Equation 9.34}$$

Equation 9.35 gives the log of odds:

$$\ln\left(\frac{P(auto)}{P(transit)}\right) = \ln\left(exp^{(V_a - V_t)}\right) = V_a - V_t \qquad \textbf{Equation 9.35}$$

If I include a third choice, that is, walk, with the utility function expressed as V^w, the probabilities are expressed as:

$$P(auto) = \frac{exp^{V_a}}{exp^{V_a} + exp^{V_t} + exp^{V_w}}$$

$$P(transit) = \frac{exp^{V_t}}{exp^{V_a} + exp^{V_t} + exp^{V_w}}$$

$$P(walk) = \frac{exp^{V_w}}{exp^{V_a} + exp^{V_t} + exp^{V_w}}$$

Notice the probability function carefully where I am still dealing with the difference in utilities. Let's divide both the denominator and the numerator with $exp(Va)$ in $P(auto)$ as shown in Equation 9.36:

$$P(auto) = \frac{1}{1 + \dfrac{exp^{V_t}}{exp^{V_a}} + \dfrac{exp^{V_w}}{exp^{V_a}}} = \frac{1}{1 + exp^{V_t - V_a} + exp^{V_w - V_a}} \qquad \textbf{Equation 9.36}$$

Let us define the following two probabilities for event j and j' as shown in Equations 9.37 and 9.38:

$$P_{ij} = \frac{e^{\beta' x_{ij}}}{\sum_{j=1}^{J} e^{\beta' x_{ij}}} \qquad \textbf{Equation 9.37}$$

$$P_{ij'} = \frac{e^{\beta' x_{ij'}}}{\sum_{j=1}^{J} e^{\beta' x_{ij}}} \qquad \textbf{Equation 9.38}$$

Therefore, the odds of opting j over j' are given by Equation 9.39:

$$\frac{P_{ij}}{P_{ij'}} = \frac{e^{\beta' x_{ij}}}{e^{\beta' x_{ij'}}} = \exp\left(\beta'\left(x_{ij} - x_{ij'}\right)\right) \qquad \textbf{Equation 9.39}$$

Whereas the Logit is expressed in Equation 9.40:

$$\ln\left(\frac{P_{ij}}{P_{ij'}}\right) = \ln\left(\exp\left(\beta'\left(x_{ij} - x_{ij'}\right)\right)\right) = \beta'\left(x_{ij} - x_{ij'}\right) \qquad \textbf{Equation 9.40}$$

Independence From Irrelevant Alternatives

Recall from the previous section that the odds ratio $\left(\frac{P_j}{P_{k_i}}\right)$ for any two alternatives is independent of the other alternatives. This property of logit models is termed as the *Independence from Irrelevant Alternatives* (IIA). This property is rooted in the earlier assumption that error terms are independent and homoscedastic. From the estimation point of view, this is a highly desired property of the logit models. The IIA assumption, though, results in strong restrictions on consumer behavior.

Problems resulting from this assumption are highlighted in the literature as the red bus/blue bus problem (McFadden [1974])[12] cited in Powers and Xie [2000]).[13] Let's assume that a commuter's choice set consists of four modes: red bus, blue bus, car, and train. Let's also assume that commuters are equally likely to take any mode and hence the mode share for any particular mode is 25%. The odds between any two alternatives are 1. Let's also assume that the red bus and the blue bus are perfect substitutes for each other. Hence, if the blue bus is removed from the service (one can simply paint the blue buses red), the blue-bus riders will shift to the red bus with an increase in the red bus's mode share to 50% from 25%. This is because the two bus alternatives are substitutes of each other. The mode shares for train and car remain at 25%. However, this is not the case with logit models. IIA dictates that with the exclusion of blue bus, the mode share for red bus, car, and train will all be equal to 33.33%, thus maintaining the odds between any two alternatives at 1.

You can eliminate a subset of choices from the universal choice set, assuming that the subset "truly is irrelevant" (Greene [2003], p. 724).[14] The elimination of the subset of choices will not "change parameter estimates systematically." However, if the odd ratios of the remaining alternatives are not completely independent, the exclusion of the subset of choice set will return inconsistent parameter estimates. Hausman's specification test checks for independence and is presented in Equation 9.41:

$$\chi^2 = \left(\hat{\beta}_s - \hat{\beta}_f\right)' \left[\widehat{V_s} - \widehat{V_f}\right]^{-1} \left(\hat{\beta}_s - \hat{\beta}_f\right) \quad \textbf{Equation 9.41}$$

Where s represents the estimators obtained for the subset of the choice set and f represents estimators obtained for the complete choice set. $\widehat{V_s}$ and $\widehat{V_f}$ represent the estimates of the asymptotic covariance matrices. It has been proven that the test statistic is asymptotically distributed as chi-squared with K-degrees of freedom. If the aforementioned test suggests violations of the IIA assumption, one can either estimate a Nested Logit model or a Probit model instead.

Recall from Chapter 8 the discussion about Probit models, which assumes the error terms to be Normally distributed. The Probit equivalent of the conditional logit model is available in Stata, R, and other software. In Stata, the algorithm is referred to as the Alternative-Specific Multinomial Probit regression.[15] Whereas in R, the same model can be estimated using the `mlogit` package with `probit=TRUE` option.[16]

Interpretation of Conditional Logit Models

In this section, I explain the conditional logit model using the choice of travel modes for an intercity trip. Let's assume that commuters possess valid driver's licenses and that the distances between the origin and destination city pairs are suitable for the most common modes of travel; that is, the distances are neither too short to make travel by air impractical nor too long to render travel by road infeasible. Under such circumstances, one can travel from one city to another by car, bus, rail, and airplane.

The choice of travel mode is likely to be influenced by travel time, travel cost, and personal attributes of the commuter, such as gender, income, and the size of the traveling party. It is safe to assume that if the costs were the same, a commuter will choose the mode with shorter travel time. Similarly, if other considerations do not matter, a commuter will choose the cheaper travel alternative. Furthermore, a high-income commuter would be less sensitive to travel cost than the low-income commuter would. Similarly, a high-income commuter will be more sensitive to travel time than a low-income commuter. In addition, the probability of traveling by car is likely to increase with the number of commuters traveling together.

I test these assumptions using a data set on intercity travel in Australia. I estimate a conditional logit model to capture the travel mode choices. The data set comprises 210 respondents. The model consists of four choices: air, bus, car, and train. Variables included in the data set are described in Table 9.32. You can download the data set and the associated scripts from the book's website.

Table 9.32   Names and Description of Variables Used in the Conditional Logit Model

Variable	Description
Id	Person id
Alt	Alternatives
Chair	Air mode constant
Hinc	Household income ('000)
Psize	Party size
aasc	Air alternative-specific constant
tasc	Train alternative-specific constant
basc	Bus alternative-specific constant
casc	Car alternative-specific constant
psizea	Party size – air mode
mode	Chosen mode
twait	Terminal wait time
invc	In-vehicle cost
invt	In-vehicle time
gc	Generalized cost
mc	Binary choice
hinca	Income-air
hincb	Income-bus
hinct	Income-train
psizeb	Party size-bus
psizet	Party size-train
t	Dummy t
Choice	Numeric choice

I first determine the travel mode shares as they have been reported by the survey respondents: 27.6% respondents reported traveling by air, 14.3% reported traveling by bus, 28% reported traveling by car, and 30% reported traveling by train (see Table 9.33). Note that the mode shares are computed after I have subsetted the data set to include only those observations that represent the chosen alternative for each respondent. Recall that each respondent in the data set is repeated four times, one time for each available alternative. However, each respondent used one out of the four alternatives to make his or her intercity trip. This is the reason why I subsetted the data to include only those alternatives that were actually chosen by the respondent.

```
h09a <- h09[ which(mc== "yes"),]
tab1<-table(h09a$alt); tab2<-tab1/sum(tab1)*100
tab3=xtable(cbind(tab2))
htmlTable(txtRound(tab3,2), rowlabel = "Mode of Travel",
          header ="Percentage of Respondents")
```

Table 9.33 Percentage of Trips Made by Each Mode

Mode of Travel	Percentage of Respondents
Air	27.62
Bus	14.29
Car	28.10
Train	30.00

The summary statistics for key variables are presented in Table 9.34. Note that I report the summary statistics for each mode separately. The average terminal wait time (twait) is 46.53 minutes for air, 25.20 minutes for bus, 28.52 minutes for train, and 0 minutes for car.

```
attach(h09a)
library(psych)
tab3<-describeBy(cbind(twait, invc, invt, hinc, psize), alt, mat=TRUE ,
range=F, skew=F)
print(xtable(tab3, digits=c(0,0,0,0,0,2,2,2)), type="html")
```

Table 9.34 Descriptive Statistics of Variables Used in Estimating the Conditional Logit Models

	item	group1	vars	n	mean	sd	se
twait1	1	air	1	58	46.53	24.39	3.20
twait2	2	bus	1	30	25.20	14.92	2.72
twait3	3	car	1	59	0.00	0.00	0.00
twait4	4	train	1	63	28.52	19.35	2.44
invc1	5	air	2	58	97.57	31.73	4.17
invc2	6	bus	2	30	33.73	11.02	2.01
invc3	7	car	2	59	15.64	9.63	1.25

	item	group1	vars	n	mean	sd	se
invc4	8	train	2	63	37.46	20.68	2.60
invt1	9	air	3	58	124.83	50.29	6.60
invt2	10	bus	3	30	618.83	273.61	49.95
invt3	11	car	3	59	527.37	301.13	39.20
invt4	12	train	3	63	532.67	249.36	31.42
hinc1	13	air	4	58	41.72	19.12	2.51
hinc2	14	bus	4	30	29.70	16.85	3.08
hinc3	15	car	4	59	42.22	17.69	2.30
hinc4	16	train	4	63	23.06	17.29	2.18
psize1	17	air	5	58	1.57	0.82	0.11
psize2	18	bus	5	30	1.33	0.66	0.12
psize3	19	car	5	59	2.20	1.27	0.17
psize4	20	train	5	63	1.67	0.90	0.11

Before I estimate the model, let's briefly revisit the necessary theoretical underpinnings of the conditional logit model. When the attributes of choice as well as the characteristics of the decision-maker explain the utility of the alternatives, the model can contain alternative-specific variables as well as individual-specific covariates, which I obtain by multiplying individual-specific covariates with alternative-specific dummies.

The model is shown in Equation 9.42:

$$Prob(Y_i = j) = \frac{e^{\beta' x_{ij} + \alpha'_j w_i}}{\sum_{j=1}^{J} e^{\beta' x_{ij} + \alpha'_j w_i}} = \frac{e^{\beta' x_{ij}} e^{\alpha'_j w_i}}{\sum_{j=1}^{J} e^{\beta' x_{ij}} e^{\alpha'_j w_i}} \qquad \textbf{Equation 9.42}$$

where x_{ij} are the alternative-specific covariates, whereas w_i are individual-specific attributes. One can include as a regressor an individual-specific variable, household income (HINC), which does not vary across alternatives, by multiplying HINC with the alternative-specific dummies. In the models reported here, I have included household income as a regressor influencing only the air mode.

I report two parametrizations of the model. In the first case, I use automobile or car as the reference category. In the second case, I use air as the reference category. The results are presented in Table 9.35.

In the column labeled (1) in Table 9.35, you may find an intercept each for the air, bus, and train modes. These intercepts are analogous to the constant in the ordinary least squares regression model. The conditional logit model reports one less intercept than the number of available alternatives. In this particular case, I have chosen car as the reference case, therefore I obtained intercepts for air, bus, and train. Column (2) in Table 9.35 presents the output for the model in which air is chosen as the reference category. Thus, the model reports one intercept each for bus, car, and train.

I have used generalized cost, which is a combination of out-of-pocket travel cost and travel time, as a regressor. The statistically significant negative coefficient suggests that an increase in the generalized cost results in lower odds for a mode being chosen. Similarly, the terminal wait times also result in lowering the odds for a particular mode. Stated differently, an increase in terminal wait times will result in a lower likelihood for a mode being chosen. I find household income to be a statistically insignificant predictor of travel mode choice.

The McFadden R-Square for the model is 0.298, which suggests a good fit.

```
data1 <- mlogit.data (h09,choice="mc",shape="long",id.var="id",
        alt.var= "alt")

mod.1<-mlogit(mc~ gc + twait +hinca   ,data1,reflevel="car")
mod.2<-mlogit(mc~ gc + twait +hinca   ,data1,reflevel="air")
fit1<-fitted(mod.2,outcome=F)
library(stargazer)
stargazer(mod.1, mod.2,  type="html", no.space=TRUE,
          dep.var.labels = c("Travel Mode Choice"),
          title="Discrete Choice Models", covariate.labels =
            c("Air Intercept","Bus Intercept", "Car Intercept",
            "Train Intercept", "Generalized Cost",
            "Terminal Wait Times", "Household Income (Air Only)"))
```

Table 9.35 Estimates from a Conditional Logit Model with Alternative-Specific Attributes

Discrete Choice Models	Dependent Variable	
	Travel Mode Choice	
	(1)	(2)
Air Intercept	5.207***	
	(0.779)	
Bus Intercept	3.163***	−2.044***
	(0.450)	(0.555)
Car Intercept		−5.207***
		(0.779)
Train Intercept	3.869***	−1.338**
	(0.443)	(0.543)

Discrete Choice Models	Dependent Variable	
Generalized Cost	-0.016^{***}	-0.016^{***}
	(0.004)	(0.004)
Terminal Wait Times	-0.096^{***}	-0.096^{***}
	(0.010)	(0.010)
Household Income (Air Only)	0.013	0.013
	(0.010)	(0.010)
Observations	210	210
R^2	0.298	0.298
Log Likelihood	-199.100	-199.100
LR Test (df = 6)	169.300^{***}	169.300^{***}

Standard errors in parentheses: * $p<0.1$; ** $p<0.05$; *** $p<0.01$

The model could be used to forecast market shares for each travel mode. Table 9.36 presents the estimated mode shares from the model. The model forecasts 28% market share for air, 14% for bus, 28% for car, and 30% for train.

```
tab1<-describe(fit1, skew=F, range=F)
print(xtable(tab1, digits=c(0,0,0,2,2,2)), type="html")
```

Table 9.36   Forecasted Mode Share from the Conditional Logit Model

Modes	vars	n	mean	sd	se
air	1	210	0.28	0.28	0.02
bus	2	210	0.14	0.19	0.01
car	3	210	0.28	0.18	0.01
train	4	210	0.30	0.27	0.02

Estimating Logit Models in SPSS

Estimating multinomial logit models in SPSS is rather straightforward. The command **NOMREG** estimates the multinomial logit model, which in fact can also be used to estimate the binary logit model. The dependent variable could be a dichotomous variable taking the values 1/0, or it could be a polytomous variable taking values, such as 1, 2, and 3 as was the case in consumer's choice for smart phones. Remember that the estimated model will return $J - 1$ set of estimated coefficients, where J is the total number of alternatives.

The conditional logit model is not directly available within SPSS. However, one can trick the Cox Proportional Hazard model in SPSS to estimate a conditional logit model. The likelihood function of the Cox Proportional Hazard model is the same as the conditional logit model. The mechanics and theory of Hazard models are not explained here. I only offer necessary definitions required to restructure data to run the Cox Proportional Hazard model in SPSS.

The Cox Proportional Hazard model estimation requires three additional variables: `status`, `failure time`, and `strata`. Remember that the choice variable assumes the value 1 for the chosen alternative and 0 for non-chosen alternatives. I use the choice variable as the status variable in the Cox Proportional Hazard model. Make sure that you identify 1 as the single value event in the option "`Define Event`" for the status variable.

For the failure time variable in SPSS, the preferred choice (that is, the chosen mode) should occur at *time* = 1, while other modes (choices) should occur at *time* > 1. Therefore, the time (failure time) variable should assume the value 1 for the chosen alternative and 2 for other alternatives for every individual. This can be achieved by creating a new variable `t` as shown in Equation 9.43:

$$t = 2 - choice\ variable \quad \text{Equation 9.43}$$

Lastly, I need a variable to control for stratification in the Cox Proportional Hazard model. The `strata` variable identifies individual decision-makers. Because each decision-maker is represented by multiple observations, the strata variable has a unique ID for each individual and thus acts as a grouping variable. The SPSS code for conditional logit is as follows:

```
Coxreg t with aasc casc tasc gc twait hinca /status=mode(1)
/strata=subject.
```

Summary

Making choices is hard, and modeling them is even harder. In this chapter, I illustrated the use of statistical models for response or dependent variables that have more than two categories. I built on the discussion from the last chapter that focused on modeling binary outcomes.

This chapter began with a brief refresher on binary logit models. I then introduced the unordered categorical variables, referred to as the multinomial variables. The bulk of the discussion focused on how to develop statistical models to explain multinomial variables.

I did introduce the calculus behind these models. However, I structured the chapter in a way that readers could skip over the mathematical details so that they may remain focused on the applied aspects of these models. A key feature of this chapter is the use of multiple data sets to estimate a variety of multinomial logit models. Given my preference to work with data that captures human behavior, the chosen data sets are indicative of the everyday choices we make.

I demonstrated how to estimate and interpret the binary logit model using a data set on women's participation in the labor force. Although women's participation in the workforce is similar to that of men's in the western world, still middle-class women in numerous countries in

Asia and Middle East are battling societal taboos that restrict their chances to work, or be educated in the first place. I used a data set from the 1980s to illustrate how the presence of young children, education attainment of women and their husbands, and workers' age explained the likelihood of a woman working. A not-so-surprising finding was that women who attended college were more likely to work than women who did not attend college.

Bringing the discourse to present times, I used a data set on the use of smart phones and online dating to illustrate analyzing multinomial data and estimating multinomial logit models. I started by setting up the context and offered a brief summary of the key social trends captured by the data set. I offered examples of tabulations with the associated script. Although the discussion relies on several other tables that I have not shown in the text, the reader may readily download the script from the book's website to run the additional tabulations.

I first estimated a binomial logit model to explore what factors influence one's decision to find love interests online. The emergence of online dating services offers an alternative to meeting people. Even though the data set reveals only a small minority of individuals reporting to have found their significant others online, the societal taboos about online dating services are fast eroding.

I estimated a multinomial logit model to analyze the market of the four leading online dating services. Such models could be tricky to report given a large number of coefficients reported. I illustrated the use of specialized routines that helped format the results that are legible and easy on the eyes.

I then estimated another model to capture the consumers' choices for four types of phones, namely iPhone, Blackberry, Android, and regular phones. This application is a typical use of multinomial logit models in marketing and consumer behavior research. The models reveal that women are less likely to use smart phones than men are, all else being equal. Interestingly, those who have never been married favor Android phones more than their married counterparts do. Not so surprisingly, those who do not surf the Internet on their mobile phones are more likely to use regular phones. This is an example of a finding from a professor who teaches at the Department of Obvious Conclusions.

Access to affordable healthcare has generated significant debate and introspection in the United States. Unlike in Canada and many European countries, a publicly funded healthcare program does not exist in the U.S. that covers the working age Americans, who increasing rely on their employers for health insurance. Often, the spouse's health insurance covers the rest of the family. An interesting question emerges about women's participation in the labor force when they are not covered by their spouse's health insurance. Would women lacking spousal coverage be more likely to work full-time than do those with coverage?

I estimated a multinomial logit model to determine what factors influence women's labor force participation status in a multinomial case with three alternatives: unemployed, part-time work, and full-time work. The model illustrates that women with access to spousal coverage are much less likely to work full-time than do those without access to healthcare. I illustrated different ways to interpret and report results from the multinomial logit models.

Finally, I illustrated how to estimate the conditional logit models that are capable of using the attributes of choice and the characteristics of the decision-maker as explanatory variables. Note that the choice of a particular brand of smart phones is predicated on an individual's taste (characteristics of decision-makers) and availability/price of the brand (attributes of choice). The typical multinomial logit model can handle only the characteristics of the decision-maker and not the attributes of choice. This limitation is addressed in the conditional logit model.

I used an intercity travel choice data set to estimate the conditional logit model to show how terminal wait times, in-vehicle travel time, travel costs, and income may influence one's decision to choose from the four alternatives: air, bus, car, and train.

Endnotes

1. Mroz, T.A. (1987). "The sensitivity of an empirical model of married women's hours of work to economic and statistical assumptions." *Econometrica, 55*(4) 765–799.

2. Long, J. Scott and Freese, Jeremy. (2005). *Regression models for categorical dependent variables using Stata*. Stata Press. Texas.

3. Greene, William H. (1995). *Econometric Analysis*. 3rd edition. Prentice Hall.

4. Louviere, J.J., Hensher, D.A., Swait, J. (2000). *Stated Choice Methods: Analysis and Application*. Cambridge University Press, Cambridge.

5. Domencich, T.A. and McFadden, D. (1975). *Urban Travel Demand: A Behavioral Analysis*. North Holland Publishing, Amsterdam.

6. Smith, A. and Duggan, M. (2013). Online dating & relationships. *Pew Internet & American Life Project*. Retrieved from http://www.pewinternet.org/files/old-media/Files/Reports/2013/PIP_Online%20Dating%202013.pdf.

7. Hamel, M.B., Blumenthal, D., Collins, S.R. (2014). Health care coverage under the Affordable Care Act—a progress report. *The New England Journal of Medicine, 371*(3), 275–281.

8. Blumenthal, D., Abrams, M., Nuzum, R. (2015). The Affordable Care Act at 5 Years. *The New England Journal of Medicine, 372*(25), 2451–2458.

9. Olson, Craig A. (1998). "A Comparison of Parametric and Semiparametric Estimates of the Effect of Spousal Health Insurance Coverage on Weekly Hours Worked by Wives," *Journal of Applied Econometrics. 13*(5), September–October, 543–565.

10. McFadden, D. (1974). "The measurement of urban travel demand." *Journal of Public Economics, 3*(4) 303–328.

11. Greene. *"Econometric Analysis."*

12. McFadden, D.L. (1974). "Conditional logit analysis of qualitative choice behavior." In *Frontiers in Econometrics*, ed. P. Zarembka, 105-142. New York: Academic Press.

13. Powers and Xie. "Statistical Methods for Categorical Data Analysis."

14. Greene, William H. (2003). *Econometric Analysis*. 5th edition. Prentice Hall.

15. http://www.stata.com/manuals13/rasmprobit.pdf

16. https://cran.r-project.org/web/packages/mlogit/vignettes/mlogit.pdf

CHAPTER 10

Spatial Data Analytics

The housing market collapse in 2007–08 was brought about by mortgage defaults when a substantially large number of borrowers failed to meet their debt obligations, which resulted in foreclosures. The households forced out of their homes faced severe hardships and, most likely, mental anguish and stress. As for their neighbors, whose homes were not foreclosed, the stress of falling housing prices in general, and distressed housing in their neighborhood in particular, would have also caused grief and stress. But why did the foreclosures trigger the spread of West Nile virus in the foreclosed communities?

A distant disease spread by mosquitos landing at your doorstep in California, Florida, or Nevada is an unlikely event under normal circumstances. Not so much when the economy stalls and homeowners are pushed out of their homes. Subsequent to the foreclosure crisis in 2007, the vector control departments across California and Florida reported an alarming increase in the spread of West Nile virus.

For epidemiologists, the sudden spread of West Nile was a mystery. It would not have been a mystery had they relied on Geographic Information Systems (GIS), a computerized database system that tracks spatial attributes of data in addition to the relational attributes. The epidemiologists could have mapped the spread of disease to uncover its spatial correlation with foreclosed homes to discover the mosquitos that spread West Nile virus hovering over the algae-infested unattended swimming pools in foreclosed homes.

This chapter focuses on the oft-neglected aspect of data science; that is, the spatial data, which not only captures the relational attributes of the underlying data set, but also keeps track of its locational attributes. For the foreclosed homes, a geo-referenced database would have mapped the homes with swimming pools that had been foreclosed or were vacant for another reason. Another geo-referenced database capturing the spread of West Nile would have exposed the spatial correlation between foreclosed homes and incidence of West Nile.

The vector control departments across the United States that experienced substantial foreclosures relied on aerial observations to finally clue into the reasons behind the spread of West Nile virus. Had GIS been part of the analytics, West Nile would not have been a mystery for long.

If space is the final frontier, data science has certainly skipped it. To date, almost all discourse on data science and analytics is largely concentrated on large relational databases. Data scientists are busy debating *to SQL or not to SQL*. Given that spatial attributes also influence individuals' behaviors, ignoring them will result in the loss of relevant and essential information, which could have improved the predictive capabilities of statistical models and helped generate maps to illustrate spatially varying behaviors.

West Nile virus was first discovered in 2003 in Antelope Valley in California.[1] Initially, the virus affected birds and horses. Later, human deaths were recorded as well. In 2006, six human deaths were recorded followed by two more up until July 2007.

The Record in July 2007 first reported of the West Nile cases being correlated with foreclosures in San Joaquin County in California.[2] One of the cases affecting human beings was reported in San Joaquin County whereas another eight were reported in Kern county. In California, 30 out of 58 counties reported the presence of West Nile virus. As the housing crisis deepened in 2008, the number of foreclosed homes increased consequently. In states like California and Florida, where temperature during summer months is usually very high, often homes are equipped with swimming pools. As the number of abandoned or foreclosed homes increased, the number of unattended pools increased as well. In Maricopa County, the vector control department received 2,069 complaints for algae-laden pools by May 2008. In contrast, they received only 597 complaints up until May 2007.[3] In Phoenix, Arizona, the number of unattended and neglected pools increased from 6000 in 2007 to more than 9,000 in 2009.[4]

While the Feds were busy cleaning up the housing mess, the vector control departments deployed Gambusia Affinis, also known as the mosquito fish, to prevent mosquito populations from going out of control. The mosquito fish feeds on mosquito larva, thus limiting the growth of the very source of the West Nile virus.

In the Turlock Abatement District near Modesto, California, authorities used airplanes to spot swimming pools infested with algae.[5] Let us imagine for a second that the municipal authorities had access to satellite imagery, a GIS-enabled database of housing units that also contained information about foreclosures, and a database of known incidents of West Nile virus affecting human beings and animals. Equipped with a geospatial database, municipal authorities would have easily identified the culprit; that is, the mosquitoes breeding at the algae-infested pools left unattended in the foreclosed homes.

Geographic information systems, or GIS, have been instrumental in providing location-enabled analytics for smart decision-making. The emergence of big data has further enhanced the capacity and capabilities of GIS, which can now analyze hundreds of millions of records to unearth spatial dependencies inherent in large data sets, which the traditional relational databases fail to disclose.

In this chapter, I cover the fundamentals of GIS and then introduce the use of GIS and spatial analysis in business and marketing research. This is followed by examples of GIS-enabled analysis of urban and transport planning as well its use for analyzing electoral outcomes. I then present a hands-on introduction to spatial analysis of the U.S. census data using a freeware called Geoda.

Fundamentals of GIS

GISs are a combination of hardware, software, algorithms, data, and skilled labor that help collect, store, manipulate, analyze, and present spatial data. GISs are being used increasingly in different fields. For example, the Italian grape farmers use aerial photography and satellite imagery to monitor crops and merge the images with GIS to improve vineyard management and ultimately the wine quality. FedEx, a leader in global supply chain management, employs a GIS-enabled business directory in the UK to reduce its telemarketing costs and improve its ability to target prospects. CB Richard Ellis, a real estate industry leader, uses GIS and geo-demographics to analyze prospective sites for locating new shopping centers. The Insurance Services Office uses GIS to improve its marketing and underwriting.

At its core, GIS software is a database management system capable of explicitly managing and recognizing the spatial interdependencies inherent in data sets. Present-day computer systems are sufficiently powerful to run most off-the-shelf GIS software, which can, for example, shortlist consumers within a given distance from a store for target marketing or determine the trade areas around a store or a restaurant where the likelihood of patronage may be the strongest. Because an estimated 80% of all business data contain some spatial dimensions, can businesses and data scientists afford to remain oblivious to GIS?

Figure 10.1 illustrates the visualization and analytic capabilities of GIS. Figure 10.1 shows a map of housing prices in Toronto, Canada. The peaks and troughs highlight areas of high and low housing prices, respectively.

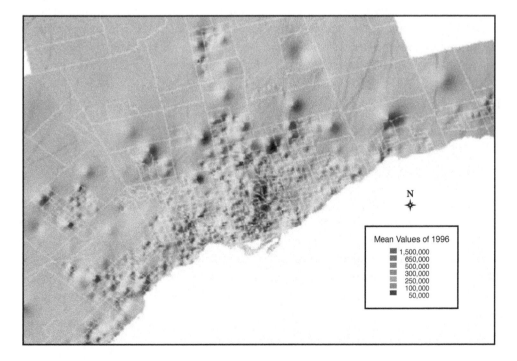

Figure 10.1 Spatial distribution of housing prices in Toronto, Canada

GIS data is available in different formats. An example of GIS data is the aggregated U.S. Census data, which are disbursed in a variety of formats, including census tracts (CTs), which are neighborhoods of approximately 4,000 individuals. CTs are mutually exclusive and collectively exhaustive neighborhoods that constitute, among others, local municipalities, counties and Census Metropolitan Statistical Areas (CMSA).

Similarly, in travel behavior research, data is often captured in point format for trip origins and destinations. The demographically homogenous spatial clusters of consumers can also be delineated as zones or polygons.

Whereas census is an important data source for business analytics, numerous other sources of spatial data further enhance the analytical capabilities with GIS. Clustering algorithms within GIS can classify census tracts or Zip codes into various homogenous groups highlighting the dominant characteristics of the residents within that zone. Such analysis generates homogenous population blocks, which consist of individuals who share similar demographic traits and consumer behavior. By classifying the market into distinct lifestyle groups, analysts can search for a profitable and loyal customer base by maximizing product and merchandising mix.

Although the data may be in point, polygon, or line formats, GIS can transfer or integrate data from one format to another. This allows aggregating point data, which is more disaggregate, to zonal levels. Thus, one can aggregate the total number of trip origins or destinations to the zonal level and correlate aggregated data with other sociodemographic data available at the zonal level.

The strength of GIS is ultimately tied to the underlying geo-referenced data. Spatially disaggregated data on consumer behavior is necessary for robust spatial analysis. Similar to the aggregation bias in statistical analysis, spatial analysis also loses its power when data are aggregated in space. For this very reason, spatially disaggregated data are preferred over aggregated data because the former would allow more extensive spatial analysis.

GIS Platforms

The advent of GIS opened up new possibilities for spatial research. GIS advances the state-of-practice in data collection, data management, data analysis, and spatial modeling. Fortunately, data analysts now have access to numerous GIS platforms that can incorporate spatial context in data analysis.

ESRI (www.esri.com) leads the GIS software vendors in market size. ArcGIS, which is also known as the enterprise GIS, is more suited for large databases that contain hundreds of millions of records. ArcInfo, initially available only for UNIX®, was later made available for Windows® under the name ArcView. The Windows version initially had relatively limited spatial database management and analysis capabilities compared to the larger enterprise version. Still, Windows-based ArcView is easier to learn and is sufficient for most projects requiring spatial data analysis.

MapInfo (www.mapinfo.com) was a late arrival, but it quickly gained market share in Windows-based GIS. In fact, MapInfo's popularity in the Windows environment could have been instrumental in convincing ESRI and others to embrace the Windows platform. Now marketed by Pitney Bowes, which is transforming into a data and analytics-driven enterprise, MapInfo is expected to evolve and improve in the future.

Caliper Corporation's Maptitude (www.maptitude.com) is another commercially available GIS that offers the biggest bang for the buck. It is priced significantly lower than ArcView and MapInfo, but offers significantly more features. For starters, unlike MapInfo, Maptitude is sensitive to topology that helps the software to identify neighbors in a GIS layer. It offers one of the fastest spatial computation engines.

GIS has its roots in academia. Jack and Laura Dangermond founded ESRI in 1969. In 1986, Professor Sean O'Sullivan at the Rennselaer Polytechnic Institute in Troy, New York, founded MapInfo, which in fact developed out of a class assignment. Dr. Howard Slavin, who specializes in transport of goods and urban spatial structure, founded Caliper Corporation in 1983. Caliper Corporation produces Maptitude, a general purpose GIS, and a specialized transport GIS, TransCAD.

Despite being developed in similar academic settings, these firms have evolved differently. ESRI continues to lead the GIS software vendors in market share. Esri's ArcView and ArcGIS are modular in nature. The base system offers advanced spatial database capabilities as well as some spatial analytical algorithms. Additional modules serve special purposes. For instance, ESRI's Business Analyst module offers sophisticated tools for market/business research. It can perform customer or store prospecting, market penetration analyses, and even gravity models for forecasting sales at the proposed new locations. Thus, one can acquire the base GIS engine for basic GIS functionality. Additional capabilities have to be acquired as add-ins, which cost more.

Firms and businesses that require GIS capabilities often wonder what platform to adopt. Because ESRI has been in the business longer than others have, there are more ESRI users out in the market; those who already are proficient with ESRI products recommend ESRI to new users. MapInfo is popular in universities and hence fresh graduates of GIS programs recommend MapInfo to their employers. For those concerned with ease of learning and price, MapInfo and Maptitude are the preferred alternatives.

Maptitude offers a diverse array of analytical tools at an affordable price. It is a comprehensive and the most affordable GIS software available on the market. Maptitude is a standalone product and comes fully loaded. Apart from the standard analytical tools, Maptitude offers extensive capabilities for analyzing competing businesses in a particular neighborhood using adjacency tools. It also performs route analysis to determine driving directions or delivery routes that minimize logistics costs. It offers almost all functionality available in the standard versions of MapInfo and ArcView. Maptitude has a stable database engine that can read and write data from most commercially available software. In fact, Maptitude can read GIS maps developed in MapInfo and ArcView proprietary formats without the need to first convert those maps into Maptitude format.

For the U.S., Maptitude is shipped with gigabytes of demographic data, a digital street net-work representing addresses for most of the U.S., and other data sets from the rest of the world. The demographic data has been organized at the census tract, county, and state level for liter-ally hundreds of variables from the 2000 and 2010 census. For instance, generating a household income map for any city or state takes less than a minute in Maptitude.

MapInfo and Pitney Bowes also offer an extensive and comprehensive suite of demo-graphic and location-aware databases that could be readily deployed for spatial analytics.

Freeware GIS

In the Vector GIS domain, QGIS is popular among the freeware GIS community.[6] It offers largely the same functionality offered by the desktop versions of the commercially available soft-ware. It supports creating and manipulating GIS maps from scratch. It also offers a strong map-ping engine.

I, however, found QGIS to be slow. The same task that a commercially available software takes less than a second to perform often takes significantly longer in QGIS. However, as a free-ware tool, it is stable and extremely useful.

Later in this chapter, I illustrate the use of Geoda, a freeware option for advanced spatial econometrics.

GIS Data Structure

Unlike most statistical software, GIS uses several unique files to contain the information neces-sary to display a map and conduct spatial analysis. ESRI's "shape format" stores the tabular data corresponding to the spatial elements as DBF files. The spatial details are stored in files that have the extensions *.shp and *.shx. As data becomes more advanced, the GIS software creates addi-tional files accordingly.

GIS Applications in Business Research

Market researchers have used GIS to profile and segment customers, analyze their purchasing behavior, and reach the intended customers using target marketing. After customer location is added to the spatial database, GIS can perform complex analysis, which is not possible using standard statistical analysis tools. For instance, GIS can readily evaluate customer density as a function of the distance from a particular business. Data generated by GIS can be later used in statistical analysis. For instance, GIS can generate the distance to various malls from the custom-ers' home locations, which could then be used to model the probability of a consumer shopping at a particular mall.

The relevance of GIS to retailing is obvious to most business analysts. The brick and mor-tar retailing, by definition, is place dependent. Demarcating trade areas is a direct application of GIS. Similarly, GIS applications in marketing can easily be extended to include many other areas such as tourism and health.

Retail Research

GIS are simple and effective tools to determine trade areas. Let us consider a restaurant chain that wants to develop trade areas around its franchises located in Manhattan for target marketing purposes. This implies that marketing material within a trade area should refer to the restaurant that lies within the trade area. Figure 10.2 (panel A) shows multiple locations of a restaurant chain in Manhattan. Figure 10.2 (panel B) presents the trade areas automatically generated by a GIS. We see that Central Park in Manhattan has also been included in trade areas of neighboring restaurants. Restaurant owners can also generate revised trade areas that exclude Central Park if so desired. The resulting trade areas are presented in Figure 10.2 (panel C), which show that Central Park is no longer part of the trade areas. With trade areas in place, one can easily target the promotional materials to households residing in specific trade areas.

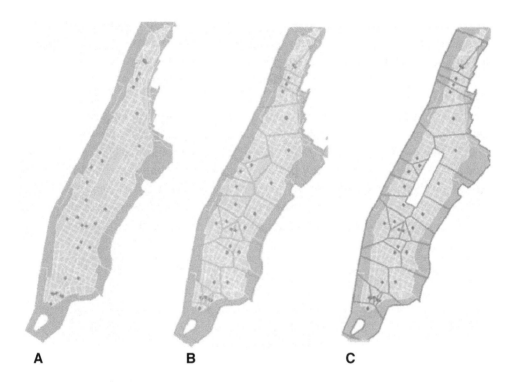

A   **B**   **C**

Figure 10.2 Trade area delineation in Manhattan

GIS can also help businesses find appropriate locations for new franchises. Facility location analysis used to require high-level programming and expertise in subjects, such as Operations Research. With GIS and appropriate geo-referenced data, facility location analysis can be done in a matter of minutes. Advanced GIS offers built-in algorithms to identify optimized locations for new outlets or franchises. After the database of existing outlets and current or potential customers is imported into a GIS, a click of a button can determine the locations of new outlets subject to the constraints specified by the analyst.

Hospitality and Tourism Research

GIS is an effective tool to capture, generate, and analyze consumer data to uncover spatial dependencies latent in the spatial preferences of the tourists. In tourism studies, analysts often collect data on tourist trips to develop insights about intercity and international movements. However, we know very little about how tourists move around after they have reached their destination city. Understanding the travel behavior and destination choices of tourists in the destination city can have significant implications for retail and hospitality industry. For instance, using GIS you can determine whether tourists frequent retail outlets and tourist attractions near their hotels, or their shopping destination choices are independent of their hotel's location. Similarly, you can determine whether first-time visitors to a city visit locations different from repeat visitors.

Answers to such questions can be found using GIS as is illustrated by the following case. Using GIS, researchers from the Hong Kong Polytechnic University studied tourists' movements in Hong Kong.[7] Independent travelers, that is, tourists not part of a large tourist group, who were traveling for pleasure, were surveyed for the study. Some 94 respondents provided approximately 400 trip diaries, which included information about trip origins, destinations, time spent at the location, and the mode of travel. The data collected in trip diaries was stored in a spatial database using GIS software.

The analysis of the spatial database generated maps of tourists' trip destinations in Hong Kong, which helped reveal trends that would have remained hidden in typical non-spatial marketing research. The researchers found significant differences in locations visited by repeat visitors and first-time visitors on the first day of their visit to Hong Kong. The first-time visitors concentrated on locations (tourist-oriented destinations and retail outlets) in close proximity of their hotels. However, the repeat visitors, even on the first day of their visit, ventured to remote destinations, which suggests their familiarity with the place (see Figure 10.3).

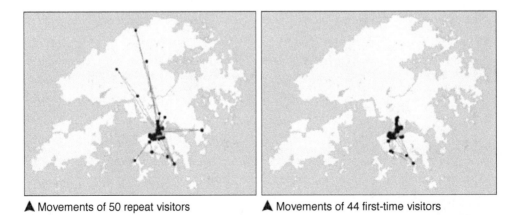

▲ Movements of 50 repeat visitors   ▲ Movements of 44 first-time visitors

Figure 10.3   Tourist destinations mapped by GIS mapped by Lau and McKercher (2006)

The spatial analysis also revealed differences in travel patterns on different days of the visit. Using a subsample of the tourists who stayed for six days, researchers found that tourists visited the locations near their hotels on the first day of their visit. However, on days 2, 3 and 4, tourists went in all different directions, producing a scattered trip pattern. As the date of departure approached, that is, around day 5 or 6, tourists again confined their trips to locations near their hotels.

The findings from the tourism case can be used to plan the locations of hotels and tourist-oriented retail in their vicinity. The difference in trip patterns of first-time and repeat visitors, and difference in trip patterns on different days of the visit suggests that tourists will frequent different locations depending upon their familiarity with the place, which is both a function of the length of their stay as well as experiences from their previous visits.

Lifestyle Data: Consumer Health Profiling

Lifestyle data sets and GIS can also be used to save lives. From customer to consumer health profiling, GIS has been used to identify at-risk populations for various diseases, including breast cancer.[8]

The National Cancer Institute (NCI) working in Alameda County in California wanted to extend breast cancer screening services to low-income neighborhoods with poor access to health care services. NCI provided Alameda County with consumer health profiles at the block group level where each block comprised 250 to 350 households. The NCI data included lifestyle information merged with data on accessibility to health care services by individual users. Using GIS, the County successfully identified at-risk populations that consisted of older African-American women with low mammography screening history. The results from the GIS-based analysis helped to develop a mammography screenings outreach program, which was tailored to meet the communication and other needs of the target groups. The resulting campaign was successful in reaching out to the at-risk populations, which did not access screening services in the past.

Competitor Location Analysis

GIS is also proficient for competitor location analysis. Commercially available data sets can be used to overlay competitors' locations along with the underlying demographics to understand their location strategies. For instance, a bank might want to learn about the location strategy of a competitor financial institution, determine the average household income near its competitors' new branches, or compare the average household income near its own branches. Such an analysis can be conducted in a matter of minutes with GIS, given ready access to location and demographics data.

Market Segmentation

Traditional market segmentation analysis identifies the potential consumers to pursue, but does not help in locating them. An imaginative combination of GIS with marketing research data can fill the gap. David Feldman offers an example of this approach by suggesting a method for consumer market segmentation combined with commercial market segmentation using spatial data.[9]

Spatial Analysis of Urban Challenges

Urban issues, such as urban politics or transport planning, are inherently spatial in nature. The challenges and conflicts arising in the urban context are also spatial. I illustrate the use of GIS and spatial analysis to generate analytics-driven commentary to frame the larger issues that occupy us. I begin with the discussion of public transit use in North America. The following piece is in fact a response to an op-ed in a leading Canadian newspaper.

The Hard Truths About Public Transit in North America

Published on June 30, 2014, in the Huffington Post.[10]

The first casualty of war, and the debate on public transit, is truth. Well-meaning environmentalists and transit enthusiasts routinely overstate the benefits of public transit and its capabilities. At the same time, the news media promote such misrepresentations that could hurt the discourse on public transit.

The latest in this series is an op-ed by David Suzuki and Faisal Moola in the *Globe and Mail* in which they make unsubstantiated claims about public transit's benefits and then urge Ontario's premier, Kathleen Wynne, to expedite spending $29 billion on public transit.[11] Messrs. Suzuki and Moola argue that transit-oriented communities "benefit from reduced congestion with shorter commuting times." The reverse is true for Canada where transit trips are 81% longer in duration than those by car.[12] The experience in the U.S. is no different.

The news media often promotes opinions that misrepresent the public transit's reality, such as the myth that more public transit will reduce congestion or travel times. Neither increasing public transit nor adding freeways will reduce traffic congestion or travel times. In fact, average trip times will increase for cities where a large number of commuters switch from cars to public transit.

Suzuki and Moola argue that transit-oriented communities benefit from shorter commute times. Instead, communities in urban Canada and in the U.S. with high transit ridership report longer commute durations. In July 2013, I exposed this myth in the *Globe and Mail* using data from Statistics Canada's 2011 National Household Survey (NHS). "Consider the example of Vancouver and Montreal, where travel to work by car takes on average 26.5 minutes. At the same time, commuting by public transit takes on average 42 minutes," I wrote.

The 2011 National Household Survey and the 2010 U.S. Census offer a treasure trove of information on commute times and modes of travel at the neighborhood level (census tracts) for large cities. A simple tabulation for work trips in the Toronto Census Metropolitan Area (CMA), an urban center of six million people, reveals that communities with higher transit use report longer, and not shorter, commuting times (see Figure 10.4).

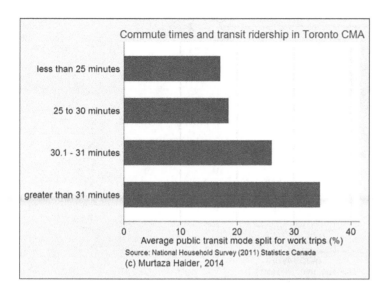

Figure 10.4   Commute times and transit ridership in Toronto

Some transit experts argue that commute times by high-speed rail transit are shorter. It is true for the individual trips, but not for the entire communities. Commuters in transit-dependent communities, with ready access to subways, can take faster transit to their destinations; however only those whose trip lengths are shorter enjoy shorter duration trips. Longer public transit trip lengths complemented by access, egress, and wait times negate the gains made by the fast traveling subways.

This point is illustrated with a map of Toronto neighborhoods that depicts the median commute times for each neighborhood (see Figure 10.5). The neighborhoods are color coded to represent the median commuting duration.[13] Blue-colored neighborhoods represent shorter commute duration, whereas dark pink-colored neighborhoods represent longer duration. The dark-blue colored dots represent the location of subway stations. Notice that neighborhoods located near Toronto's downtown report shorter commute durations whereas those located farther away, especially in the East, report longer commute durations, even when a subway station is located within or near the neighborhood.

NOTE

Full-color versions of the maps are available on the book's website at www.ibmpressbooks. com/title/9780133991024.

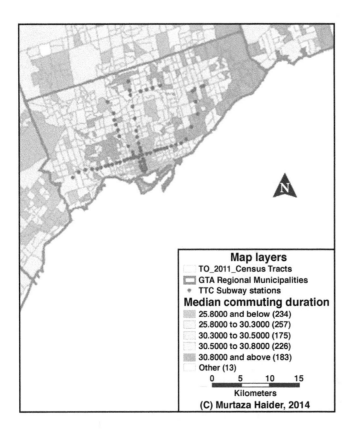

Figure 10.5   Spatial distribution of commute times in Toronto

Figure 10.5 shows that shorter duration commutes are as much a function of travel mode choice as they are of location. Neighborhoods located near Toronto's downtown report shorter commute durations than those located farther away. Remotely located neighborhoods, such as those in the East or in the North of the City of Toronto, with a large proportion of workers employed in or near Toronto's downtown, have longer duration commutes even by rapid transit because of the greater distances between suburban trip origins and trip destinations in or near downtown.

If remote locations relative to downtown imply longer commutes then why do we observe shorter commutes for ex-urban communities in Brampton, Mississauga, and Oakville? Figure 10.6 provides a partial answer to that riddle.

The ex-urban communities in the West, which report shorter commutes, benefit from the regional rail transit service, that is, GO Transit, to and from Union Station in downtown Toronto. The white collar workers living in the expensive neighborhoods along the GO Transit lines drive in the morning to GO Transit stations, park their cars for free, and hop onto the fast trains to downtown Toronto. This transit nirvana is made possible by the transit riders' ability to afford premium housing prices, free parking for cars at GO stations, the downtown location of the workers' employment, and the frequent GO Transit service throughout the day.

In Figure 10.6, I have added the red dashed lines depicting the GO Transit's Lakeshore route and other routes for Milton and Mississauga. Also, note that the thicker dark gray color lines represent the boundaries for the regional municipalities of Halton and Peel (to the west of Toronto), Toronto in the middle, York (to the north of Toronto), and Durham (to the east of Toronto).

As I mentioned earlier, the suburban communities to the west report shorter average commute times. However, why is the same not true for the eastern suburbs of Scarborough and exurban eastern suburbs in the Durham region where communities along the GO Transit line report longer trip durations (see Figure 10.6)? There are two plausible explanations. First, since GO rapid transit service efficiently serves trip ends in and near downtown Toronto, it fails to offer the same commuting advantage to workers whose employment destination is not in the downtown core. Thus, the commuters who may be living near the GO station in the eastern suburbs cannot benefit from it if their work destination is not in or near downtown Toronto. Second, the GO Transit service may not have as frequent and strategically located stations with abundant free parking in the East of Toronto than what it offers in the West of Toronto.

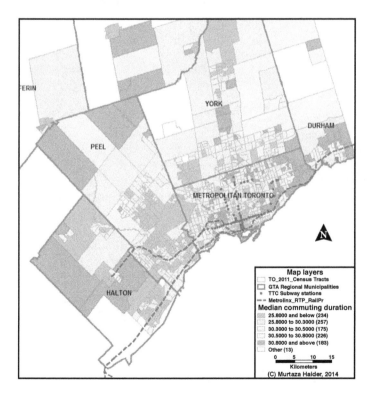

Figure 10.6 Commute times in the greater Toronto region

New York Is No Different

Some transit enthusiasts can object to the Toronto-centric analysis presented here. They may point to transit success cities, such as New York or Paris. Given that Canadian cities have more in common with North American cities, let us see if the transit-oriented communities in New York, which benefit from much more frequent and intensive rapid transit service than any Canadian city, report shorter commutes.

I use the 2000 U.S. Census to plot the relationship between transit ridership intensity in a community (Census Tract) and average commute duration. I categorize communities by distance to the downtown in Manhattan to account for the dissimilarities among communities in Bronx, Brooklyn, Manhattan, Queens, and Staten Island. The communities are, therefore, labeled as nearest, nearer, medium near, medium far, farther, and farthest to account for distance from downtown Manhattan. Because New York is known for extreme income disparities between the very rich and the rest, I also divided communities into low, middle, and high incomes.

Figure 10.7 presents the results, which highlights that average commute times increase with transit ridership irrespective of how far or near the community is from downtown Manhattan. In addition, low-income communities nearest to the downtown have longer commute times than mid- or high-income communities. This relationship reverses with distances from downtown Manhattan where high-income communities in remotely located suburbs report longer commute times than the low-income communities.

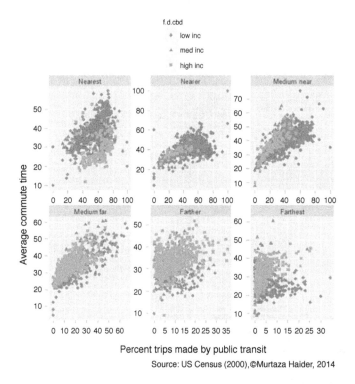

Source: US Census (2000),©Murtaza Haider, 2014

Figure 10.7   Commute times and transit ridership in Manhattan

What does not change, however, is the fact that transit-oriented communities in New York report higher commute times than other communities with lesser transit ridership.

With $29 billion in transport infrastructure spending already earmarked for Ontario, the decision-makers will receive tons of unsolicited advice, including this op-ed. They should, however, base their investment decisions on sound analysis rather than conjecture.

Toronto Is a City Divided into the Haves, Will Haves, and Have Nots

Published on October 30, 2014, after the mayoral elections in Toronto.

It's a tale of two cities: Toronto the rich, and Toronto the poor.[14] The city's rich have elected a mayor, John Tory, who has won with a convincing margin over his rivals. However, Mr. Tory's support is concentrated in the high-income, central parts of the city. He failed to attract voters in the economically deprived neighborhoods in the suburbs where the transport and other socio-economic challenges prevail.

In comparison, the runner-up, Doug Ford, out-polled his rivals in the high-immigrant, low-income, and transit-deprived parts of the former suburbs of Scarborough in the East and Etobicoke in the North. In fact, if Toronto were not amalgamated into one large municipality, Mr. Ford would have been the mayor of Scarborough and Etobicoke.

The income polarization in Toronto is now reflected in the political choices of its residents (see Figure 10.8). Mr. Tory captured the imagination and the votes of the Toronto's Haves, but not of the City's Have-Nots, who have been pushed to the physical and economic boundaries of the city (see Figure 10.9).

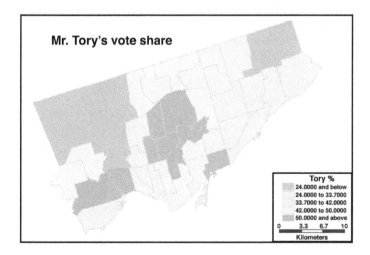

Figure 10.8 Mr. Tory's vote share by electoral wards

Data Source: City of Toronto. Map drawn by © Murtaza Haider, 2014.

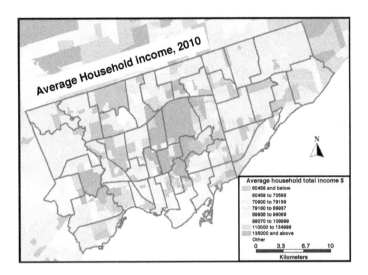

Figure 10.9 Income distribution in Toronto (2010)

Data Source: Statistics Canada and the City of Toronto. Map drawn by © Murtaza Haider, 2014.

Mr. Tory polled 394,775 votes capturing 40% of the total votes. His two main rivals, Doug Ford and Olivia Chow, received 57% of the votes. Stated differently, more voted for his rivals than for Mr. Tory. This comparison is not to diminish his victory. It is to point out that of the 44 wards comprising the City of Toronto, Mr. Tory secured the majority votes (50% or more) in only nine wards. Mr. Ford did better by obtaining the majority votes in 12 wards (see Figure 10.10).

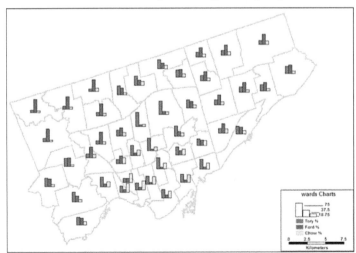

Figure 10.10 Vote share for the three leading candidates by wards

Data Source: City of Toronto. Map drawn by © Murtaza Haider, 2014.

The polarization poses yet another dimension of the spatial mismatch problem. The parts of the city that needed help with public transit and employment opportunities for the immigrants have not voted for Mr. Tory. In fact, a plot of commute times against the respective vote shares for the three leading candidates shows that Mr. Tory's vote share declines with an increase in the neighborhood's median commute times. At the same time, Mr. Ford's vote share grows with an increase in commute times (see Figure 10.11). This is a reflection of Mr. Ford's support base in parts of Scarborough in the East and Etobicoke in the Northwest, which have remained under-served by public transit.

Despite the fact that the administrative boundaries for these municipalities vanished with amalgamation, the deep-rooted political psyches, nurtured by the years of perceived and actual municipal neglect, have survived.

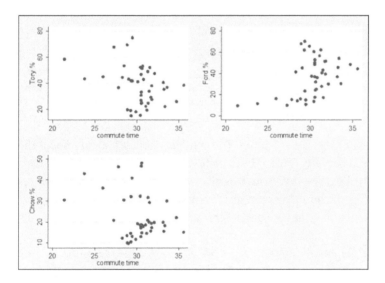

Figure 10.11   Vote shares for candidates plotted against commute times

Data Source: Statistics Canada and the City of Toronto. Graph drawn by © Murtaza Haider, 2014.

Another dimension of increasing polarization, which could have a spatial (urban/suburban manifestation), is the way immigrants have voted in the elections. The urban (especially high-income) wards had lower concentration of immigrants. These wards voted for Mr. Tory. The suburban (usually relatively low-income) wards voted increasingly for Ms. Chow and Mr. Tory. Thus, Mr. Tory's vote share declines with an increase in the immigrant population (see Figure 10.12). The reverse is true for Mr. Ford whose support increases with the immigrant concentration.

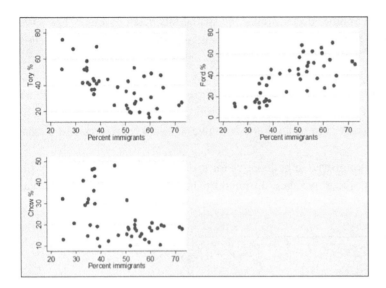

Figure 10.12 Vote shares for candidates plotted against immigrant concentration

Data Source: Statistics Canada and the City of Toronto. Graph drawn by © Murtaza Haider, 2014.

Professor David Hulchanski of the University of Toronto has warned the City about the growing income polarization. He called it the Three Cities comprising the Haves, the Will Haves, and the Have-Nots (see Figure 10.13). The Haves in Toronto are the residents of the neighborhoods (wards) that experienced significant increase in their incomes since 1970. The Haves live in the central parts of the City and along the Yonge-University subway line. They have overwhelmingly voted for Mr. Tory.

The Will Haves live in the neighborhoods that have not experienced any relative income growth since 1970, but are hopeful for a better future. They have voted mostly for Mr. Tory and sparingly for Ms. Chow. The Have-Nots are those who live in the neighborhoods where the incomes, since 1970, have fallen relative to the regional income levels. They have voted overwhelmingly for Mr. Ford.

Income polarization and inequality, and not just public transit, should have been the focus of the mayoral campaign. Instead, the media and the candidates made public transit the key issue. The mayoral hopefuls tried their best to outdo the others in promising the biggest, the fastest, and the smartest transit solutions.

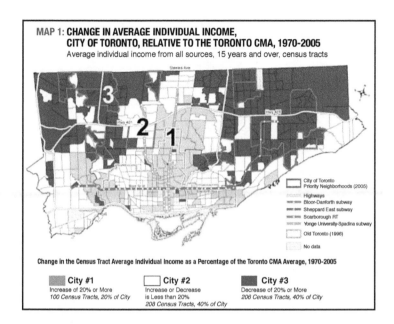

Figure 10.13   Toronto: a city divided

Source: http://www.urbancentre.utoronto.ca/pdfs/curp/tnrn/Three-Cities-Within-Toronto-2010-Final.pdf

The election results should serve as a wake-up call to the city elders and the politicians. Toronto is a divided city where income polarization is now manifesting in political outcomes and choices. The Haves have a Mayor and his name is John Tory. The Have-Nots are without a mayor.

It will take some effort on Mr. Tory's part to earn the trust and support of the city's marginalized. He will have to invest time and energy in Scarborough and Etobicoke to improve the lives of those left at the city's (and prosperity's) margins. Given his skills, dedication, and commitment, Mr. Tory should be able to win over those who did not choose him.

The voter turnout offers some insights for Mr. Tory. Mr. Ford has done well in those wards where the voter turnout has been low (see Figure 10.14). This suggests an opportunity. The lower turnout is indicative of the electorate's disengagement. As Mayor of the City of Toronto, Mr. Tory should engage not just his base, but also the rest of the city that lies at the margins. Real development, real dialogue, and real actions will mobilize those who saw no value in the political process.

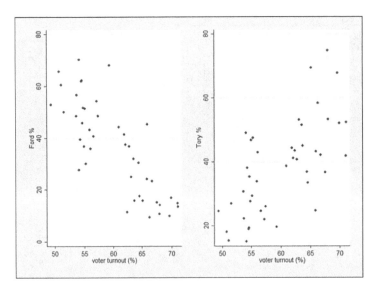

Figure 10.14   Voter turnout and vote share for Mr. Ford and Mr. Tory

When the disenfranchised groups observe positive change, they will mobilize and become part of the solution. They will also form the expanded base for the mayor if he is committed to an equitable and just Toronto.

Income Disparities in Urban Canada

When Robert Schiller, the Yale University economist who received the 2013 Nobel Memorial Prize in Economic Sciences, spoke publically after the Nobel announcement, he declared income inequality to be one of the greatest threats to the U.S. socio-economic well-being. While the reporters and others gathered at the press conference thought that Professor Schiller might pick asset prices, interest rates, or any other macro-economic concern such as trade deficit, he instead spoke of the rising income inequalities between the rich and the poor in the United States.

The income inequalities are not necessarily an American problem. A report released in early 2015 by Oxfam suggests that it is indeed a global phenomenon. At the Davos meeting of the World Economic Forum, the Oxfam report attracted a great deal of attention. The report mentioned that soon the world's richest 1% would control more than 50% of the world's wealth.[15] The Davos meeting is usually attended by the elite 1% group, which might have felt embarrassed by the brazen exposure of their unabated exploits.

What follows this preamble is an account of rising urban inequality in a major North American urban center: Toronto. With more than six million inhabitants, Toronto is among the top 10 most populous cities in North America. For years, researchers have been alarmed by the growing income disparities in Canada's large cities. Professor David Hulchanski at the University of Toronto put these concerns at the forefront of the public policy debate. He used census data and GIS to highlight the income polarization, which when mapped, were impossible to ignore.

In the following section, I reproduce a blog contributed earlier in which I used GIS and spatial analysis to understand the determinants of income polarization in Toronto. The slightly modified version reproduced here illustrates the utility of GIS and spatial analysis. I conducted a spatial analysis of the data to determine the deep-rooted phenomenon that explains, to some extent, the rising income disparities in urban centers.

The use of GIS allows the discovery of the main argument in this debate. I argue that urban boundaries are a function of political expediency and not necessarily a result of urban morphology or demographics. If I were to draw the urban boundaries differently, that is, expanding those to include the suburbs where the urban middleclass has relocated in search of affordable housing, we can observe lower incidence of income inequalities than the ones reported by Professor Hulchanski and others. I start the discussion with a review of Professor Hulchanski's report and my analysis, which are both based on spatial analysis and GIS.

Where Is Toronto's Missing Middle Class? It Has Suburbanized Out of Toronto

Published as a blog on Friday, December 17, 2010[16]

A recent study by the University of Toronto's (U of T) urban researchers has raised alarms about the increase in income polarization in the City of Toronto where the numbers of very rich and the very poor have multiplied and the middle class has shrunk over the years (see Figure 10.15).[17] The study raises concerns about the implications of the rising income inequalities in the City of Toronto.

The report is indeed an important contribution to the ongoing dialogue on how to create socially just societies and thus serves as a scorecard on how the City performs on income inequality. The report also mentioned that the growing number of the very poor in the City of Toronto are immigrants and visible minorities.

While I agree with the general findings of the report, and consider it a must read for those interested in cities, I have though some concerns about the methodology and some implied, yet unstated, conclusions. First the methodology. The authors have focused on the City of Toronto and have only tangentially mentioned the possibility that the middle class may have migrated to the outer suburbs. I call this phenomenon of suburbanizing middle classes "the brown flight," since immigrants from South and Southeast Asia constitute a large number of the new middle class, which has settled in Toronto's outer suburbs.

Second is the implied assumption that growing income inequality by default is at odds with social cohesion and long-term economic and social viability of the region. This assumes that the social safety nets, which are predominantly supported by the taxes imposed on high and very-high income earners, are incapable of providing short- and long-term services for the very poor in the City. Furthermore, the breakdown of neighborhoods by income also gives the impression that there may be a socially optimum breakdown of neighborhoods by income categories.

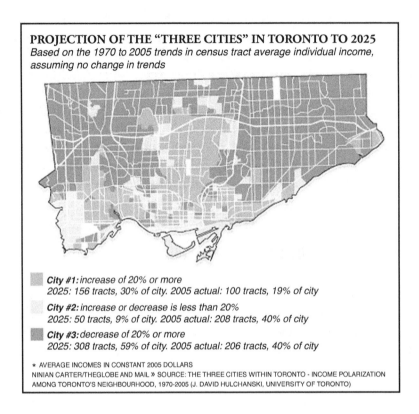

Figure 10.15   Income polarization in Toronto

Source: http://www.urbancentre.utoronto.ca/pdfs/curp/tnrn/Three-Cities-Within-Toronto-2010-Final.pdf

I repeat the U of T study with two differences. Instead of using individual income, I analyze household incomes. This does not fundamentally change the distribution of income profiles mentioned in the U of T study; however, it is theoretically more consistent because income manifests at the household level differently than it does at the individual level. For instance, a household with endowments can sustain a family member whose income is low. Thus, the individual may be categorized as low-income, but not the household. Conversely, a poor household is unlikely to have both poor and not poor members. The pooling of income within a household can help the household deal with poverty better than a single-person, single-income household. Earlier research on household dynamics also suggests that single-person households are more vulnerable to poverty than multiperson households because of lack of monetary support from other household members. Thus using household income as a metric to study income polarization is preferred to individual income.

The City of Toronto is part of a larger urban system or conurbation known as the Greater Toronto Area. Statistics Canada defines Toronto's conurbation as the Toronto Census Metropolitan Area (population 6 million, Census 2011) and includes the City of Toronto (population approximately 2.7 million) and the neighboring suburban municipalities, which are part of regional municipalities, namely Halton, Peel, York, and Durham (see Figure 10.16). Durham, Halton, and York are truncated in Figure 10.16 for space constraints.

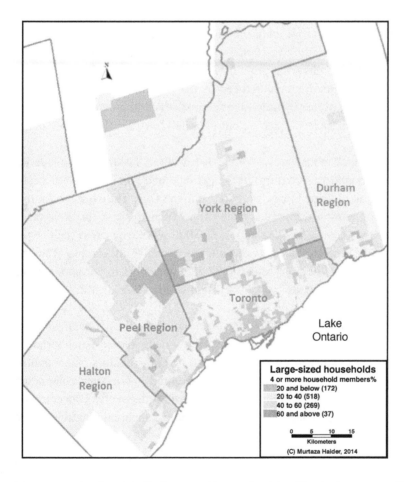

Figure 10.16   Spatial distribution of large-sized families in the greater Toronto region

Source: Statistics Canada, Census 2006. Map drawn by the author.

I argue that Toronto's middle class has migrated out of the City of Toronto and has settled in the outer suburbs of Toronto in Durham, Peel, York, and Halton. The reason for outward migration of the middle class is rooted in demographics and affordable housing. The middle class comprises growing families with children who need more shelter space at affordable prices, which is abundantly available in the outer suburbs. Furthermore, financially stable immigrant households, which are often multigenerational, abandon Toronto at an increasing rate than non-immigrants because immigrant households crave affordable shelter space more than non-immigrants do. This creates *the spatial mismatch* between the shelter needs of the middle class and the small-sized, yet prohibitively expensive, housing stock available in the City of Toronto.

Figure 10.16 shows the percentage of households with four or more persons. The brown and red-colored census tracts in the suburbs act as proof for the claim that the growing households have left for the suburbs. Similarly, the blue-colored census tracts within the City of Toronto along the waterfront and in areas of higher income suggest small-sized households comprising either young professionals or empty nesters have outbid households with children for shelter space in the choice neighborhoods.

I argue that income polarization in the City of Toronto is a result of the arbitrary boundaries used to define Toronto. These boundaries conform to the political and administrative necessities, but not to the housing and employment markets observed in the City. The evidence for this argument lies in the commuting patterns observed in the City. My analysis of the 2006 place of work data from Statistics Canada suggests that almost 600,000 work trips cross the City of Toronto's boundary every day. These are the individuals who either live in Toronto (186,555 trips) and work in the outer suburbs, or the suburbanites (407,535) who work in Toronto, but live elsewhere. This cohort of 0.6 million traverse the City's administrative boundary at least twice every working day.

Figure 10.17 depicts municipal boundaries in gray. Also shown are the pre-amalgamation boundaries of the City of Toronto's former inner suburbs. The green-colored neighborhoods in the map depict the middle class, which is primarily concentrated in Toronto's outer suburbs in Durham, Peel, and York regional municipalities. The blue-colored low-income cohorts are increasingly concentrated in the City of Toronto making a U-shaped poverty concentration around the high-income neighborhoods concentrated along Toronto's main arterial, the Yonge Street.

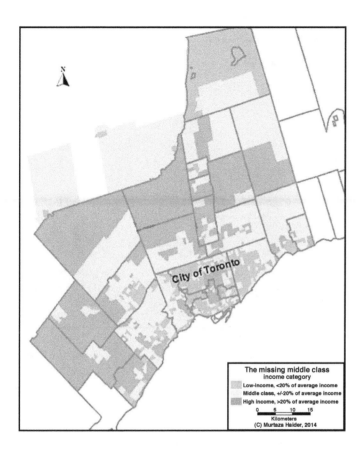

Figure 10.17   Spatial distribution of income polarization in Toronto

Data Source: Statistics Canada, Census 2006. Map drawn by the author.

The Egalitarian Suburbs

Toronto's outer suburbs are far more egalitarian than the City of Toronto. Consider first the histogram of household income (see Figure 10.18) that illustrates more than 60% of residents in the City of Toronto (2.5 million in 2006) earn at least 20% less than the average household income ($91,579 for 2005) observed for the Toronto CMA (5.1 million people in 2006).

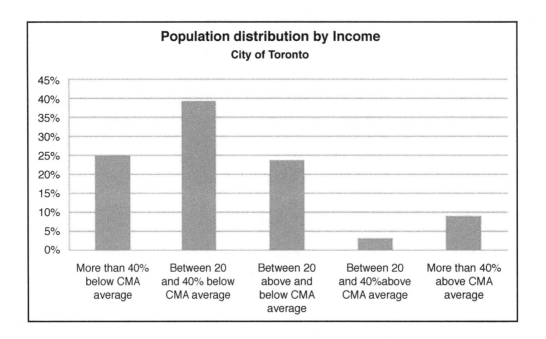

Figure 10.18   Household income distribution, the haves and have-nots

Data Source: Statistics Canada, Census 2006. Calculations by the author.

Figure 10.18 also shows that almost 8% of the population lives in census tracts (approximate population 4,000) where the average household income is more than 40% of the average household income in the Toronto CMA. The numbers presented here are slightly different from what is reported in the U of T study because the U of T study computed the percentage of the census tracts (that is, land area) and not the percent of population, which I have presented in Figure 10.18. I argue that the proportion of population in each income category and not the land area of the neighborhood is of consequence. For comparison, see Figure 10.19, which is based on the data presented in Map 3 on Page 5 of the U of T study.[18]

U of T data	CTS	CT %
More than 40% above CMA average	76	15%
Between 20% and 40% above CMA	21	4%
Between 20% above and below CMA	152	29%
Between 20 and 40% below CMA	206	39%
LT 40% average	67	13%

Figure 10.19   Income distribution as a function of land area instead of population

The Middle Class Discovered in Suburbia

The most interesting finding emerges when one plots the income distribution for the outer sub-urbs of the Toronto CMA; that is, after excluding the City of Toronto from the data set. The resulting histogram is presented in Figure 10.20, which is computed for the 2.6 million suburban-ites who live in the Durham, Halton, Peel, and York regions.

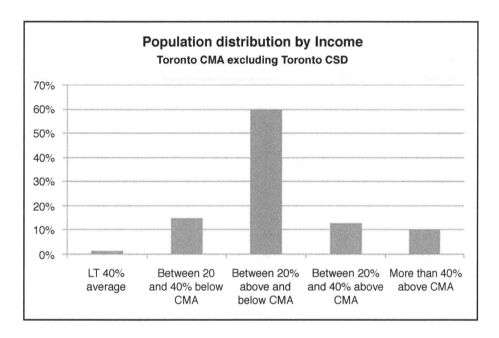

Figure 10.20   Income distribution in ex-urban communities in Toronto

Data Source: Statistics Canada, Census 2006. Calculations by the author.

Toronto's missing middle class is right in the middle of Figure 10.20 where 60% of the suburbanites live in neighborhoods where the average household income is within the +/− 20% of the average household income for the Toronto CMA. The symmetrical distribution presented in the Figure 10.20 suggests that the extreme income disparities seen in the City of Toronto (refer to Figure 10.18) do not exist in the outer suburbs of the Toronto CMA.

The U of T study highlights income polarization by pointing to a small number of very high-income neighborhoods. Figure 10.21 confirms the existence of the problem where a small number of census tracts report very high incomes in the range of $250,000 and $800,000.

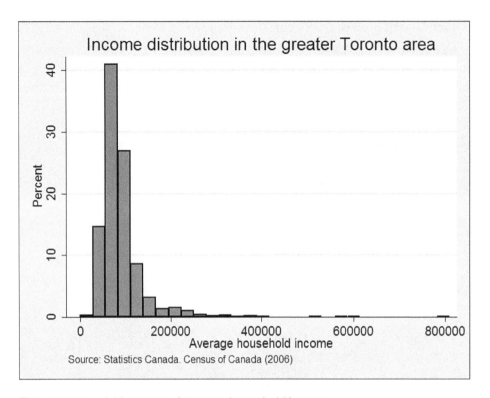

Figure 10.21   A histogram of average household incomes

Data Source: Statistics Canada, Census 2006. Calculations by the author.

Let us compare the income distribution in other municipalities that are part of the Toronto CMA. The municipalities exhibit a greater heterogeneity in the income distributions within the region. I have plotted income distributions for the nine main municipalities, which are home to 4.6 million of the 5.1 million residents of the Toronto CMA. I have ignored census tracts reporting household incomes of $250,000 or more because I believe them to be outliers. Figure 10.22 points out the peak incomes observed for the suburban municipalities, which are concentrated around the average household income observed in the region ($91,579). I also observe the skewed household income distribution for Toronto with a large number of low-income neighborhoods and a small number of very high-income neighborhoods..

Another way of looking at this issue is to examine the share of population for each income category distributed among the select nine local municipalities, including Toronto. Figure 10.23 illustrates the concept. Notice that 95% of those whose incomes are at least 40% less than the regional average and 76% of those whose incomes are at least 20% less than the regional average reside in the City of Toronto. Similarly, 53% of those whose incomes are more than 40% above the regional average also reside in the City of Toronto. This confirms the findings of income equality in the U of T study.

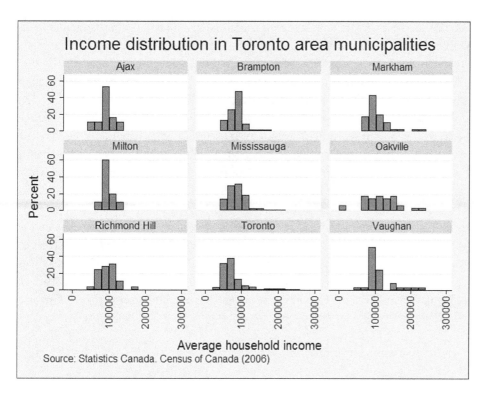

Figure 10.22 A breakdown by municipalities for histograms of average household incomes

Data Source: Statistics Canada, Census 2006. Calculations by the author

Population % of income range	More than 40% below CMA average	Between 20 and 40% below CMA average	Between 20% above and below CMA average	Between 20% and 40% above CMA average	More than 40% above CMA average
Ajax	1%	0%	4%	4%	
Brampton	2%	6%	17%	4%	2%
Markham	0%	1%	9%	19%	4%
Milton	0%	0%	2%	1%	1%
Mississauga	3%	14%	20%	12%	11%
Oakville	0%	0%	3%	16%	14%
Richmond Hill	0%	1%	5%	13%	4%
Toronto	95%	76%	32%	23%	53%
Vaughan	0%	1%	9%	8%	10%

Figure 10.23 Income distribution profiles of select municipalities

Data Source: Statistics Canada, Census 2006. Calculations by the author

However, even more interesting results are reported for the middle-income categories. Sixty-eight percent of those whose income falls within +/– 20% of the regional average income, that is, the middle class, live in Toronto's external suburbs. Furthermore, 77% of the slightly well off households whose incomes are 20% to 40% higher than the regional average also reside in the outer suburbs.

Also, note that the very low-income category is non-existent in local suburban municipalities, such as Markham, Milton, Oakville, Richmond Hill, and Vaughan.

Lastly, one can use Lorenz curves to determine the differences in income distribution between the City of Toronto and its surrounding suburbs. A Lorenz curve is essentially a chart representing the cumulative distribution function of the probability of wealth or income. The Lorenz curve plots the proportion of population, sorted by 0% to 100%, on the x-axis and the y-axis plots the corresponding proportion of wealth for those households. A straight-line Lorenz curve represents perfectly equal income distribution, which will allow us to make statements such as "the bottom 20% of the population have 20% of the total income." Any departure from perfect equality will be depicted in the Lorenz curve as the departure from the straight (perfect equality) line.

Consider the Lorenz curves for the City of Toronto (left panel in Figure 10.24) and the suburban municipalities (right panel in Figure 10.24). The Lorenz curve for the City of Toronto confirms signs of inequality where a small number of households earn very large incomes. This can be inferred from the sharp increase in slope of the line in the left panel for the top 10% of the population. On the other hand, the Lorenz curve for the outer suburbs suggests mild income inequality.

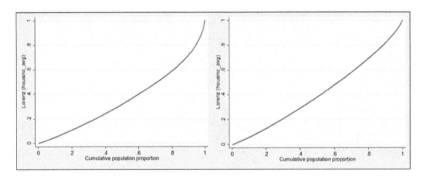

Figure 10.24   Lorenz curves for income distribution for Toronto and its suburbs

Data Source: Statistics Canada, Census 2006. Calculations by the author.

Adding Spatial Analytics to Data Science

Let's take out GIS for a quick spin. I illustrate spatial analytics using freeware, Geoda, which is developed by a team of researchers led by Professor Luc Anselin. Geoda is not a replacement for GIS software. Though it boasts powerful analytics, it lacks basic GIS capabilities, such as creating or editing a GIS map from scratch or performing other spatial tasks, such as buffering, overlaying and the like. Geoda complements a regular GIS, such as ArcView, MapInfo, Maptitude, or the freeware QGIS.

I picked Geoda for two reasons. First, it is freely available. Second, the census data used for the analysis here is available as "shape files," which is ESRI's proprietary file format that Geoda reads from and writes to. The analysis presented here is intended to serve as a teaser for the data analyst community, which is yet to embrace spatial as the new frontier!

I demonstrate spatial analytics using the 2000 census data for Chicago CMSA (see Figure 10.25). I have uploaded on the book's website data in ESRI's shape file format.

Figure 10.25 Chicago Census Metropolitan Statistical Area

Chicago CMSA comprises 2067 CTs or neighborhoods and 13 counties. Almost 9.16 million lived in Chicago CMSA in 2000. Chicago CMSA includes the Chicago City and extends far beyond the suburbs of Chicago. In fact, the farthest CT is located 106 km from Chicago's Central Business District (CBD) or downtown. It is quite likely that the residents of Chicago City may not consider the remote neighborhoods situated over a 100 km from the downtown as part of their City. Chicago City has a population of 2.7 million people and an area of 234 square miles.

CMSAs are administrative boundaries that often have little or no overlap with the spatial extents defined by the citizens. For analytic purposes, one must be concerned about the stark demographic differences between urban and suburban communities, and any naïve generalization that aggregates the two cohorts may lead to erroneous conclusions. For instance, Figure 10.26 shows the lower incidence of rental housing units in remotely located neighborhoods. From a high of 69.7% in neighborhoods within 5 km of the CBD, the rental units' market share collapses to 24.6% or less for neighborhood situated more than 20 kilometers away from the CBD.

f_d_cbd	mean
less than 5 km	69.72686
between 5 and 10 km	63.44869
between 10 and 20 km	43.35377
between 20 and 40 km	24.64542
between 40 and 60 km	24.22836
greater than 60 km	24.37141
Total	38.88224

Figure 10.26   The share of rental housing units declines with distance from downtown

Table 10.1 lists the variables and their description.

Table 10.1   Variables and Their Descriptions in the Chicago Data Set

Variable	Description
id	Record ID
area	Area of Census Tracts (CT) in square kilometer
tract	Census Tract ID
county	County ID
state	State ID
cmsa	Census Metropolitan Statistical Area
population	CT population
hh_autos	Average automobiles per household
m_hhinc	Median household income
subway_1	1 if CT contains or near a subway station, 0 otherwise
ct_dens	Population density
bachelors	Persons with a bachelor's (college degree), %
p_noveh	Percent of households with no automobile
d_cbd	CT's distance from downtown (CBD)
p_workers	Percent of adults working

Variable	Description
p_singmom	Percent of single-mother households
res_value	Average self-reported house price
p_rental	Percent of rental units
p_vacant	Percent of vacant units
p_poverty	Percent of households below the poverty line
p_black	Percent of African American households
p_white	Percent of non-visible minority households
p_asian	Percent of Asian households
p_hispanic	Percent of Hispanic households
p_unempl	Percent of unemployed adults
p_children	Percent of households with children
m_rent	Median rent
hh_size	Average persons per household
p_transit	Percent of commuters travelling to work by public transit
p_auto	Percent of commuters driving to work
p_walk	Percent of commuters walking to work
m_commtime	Median commute time to work
p_apmt	Percent of apartment units
p_singdet	Percent of single family detached units

Using GIS, I analyze the spatial underpinnings of socio-economic outcomes in Chicago. In particular, I illustrate how poverty and commute times are spatially correlated.

Race and Space in Chicago

Despite the riches and wealth generated in the U.S., racial minorities, especially African Americans, have benefitted to a much lesser extent than Whites and Hispanics. A disproportionately large number of the African-American youth are imprisoned and convicted of crimes, thus disenfranchising them by default. The sporadic breakout of violent protests against the police's alleged mistreatment of the black youth is indicative of unhealed racial wounds.

The increasing income polarization in the U.S., which I have referred to earlier in the chapter, has left many racialized communities at the margins of prosperity. Some unjust economic outcomes are a function of inherent systematic barriers that prevent the economically disadvantaged communities to break the cycle of intergenerational poverty. The spatial structure of the city, which confines the poor in undesirable urban ghettos and facilitates the affluent to develop suburban-gated communities, restricts interactions between the haves and have-nots. The lack of flow of ideas and information about opportunities restrict the opportunity space for the racialized poor in urban America.

Developing Research Questions

In this section, I explore questions about race, poverty, and opportunity using commuting to work as a proxy for opportunity. I want to determine answers for the following questions:

- Do African Americans, Whites, and Hispanics live in the same or separate communities in Chicago?
- Are African-American communities more poverty-stricken than other communities in general?
- Do the income profiles of White and African American communities differ?
- Do communities near subway stations enjoy shorter commute times?
- Are African-American communities likely to be poor and have longer commutes?
- Does public transit ridership increase with population density regardless of the income profiles of the community?

Figure 10.27 displays the distribution of African-American neighborhoods in the Chicago CMSA. The lighter shades indicate low concentration of African-American households and vice versa. One can see from the figure that African-American households are concentrated near the center of Chicago. As one moves away from the center of the city, the concentration of African-American households declines accordingly.

Figure 10.28, depicting concentration of White households, presents the near opposite image of the previous figure. The White households are concentrated primarily in the suburbs and they sparsely populate the neighborhoods located near the city center. Put together the last two figures expose the racial divide in Chicago where Whites and African Americans are mostly concentrated in different neighborhoods, which suggests a lack of neighborly interaction between the two communities.

A unique feature of Geoda is its built-in capabilities for spatial statistics. These include, among other features, measures of spatial autocorrelation (similar in concept to temporal autocorrelation) and spatially auto-regressive error models that enhance the capabilities of the traditional regression models by explicitly addressing the spatial autocorrelation in the dependent variable.

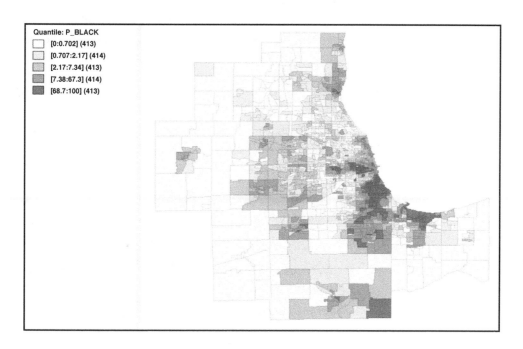

Figure 10.27 Spatial distribution of African-American households in Chicago CMSA

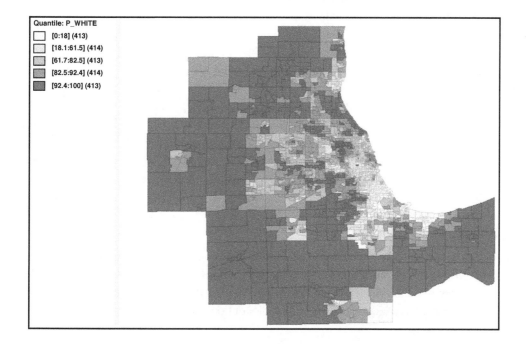

Figure 10.28 Spatial distribution of White households in Chicago

The preceding two figures show that racial communities are concentrated over space indicating the presence of spatial autocorrelation. Let us test the spatial autocorrelation, or the lack of it, between racial communities in the Chicago CMSA. Moran's I is a well-known measure of spatial autocorrelation. I test the presence of spatial autocorrelation between the share of White and African-American households in a CT using the local (instead of the global) version of Moran's I.

Let us think a 2×2 matrix representing high and low concentrations of White and African-American households in a CT or neighborhood (see Table 10.2). I want to determine how many neighborhoods have a high concentration of both races; a high concentration of one, but not the other; and a low concentration of both.

Table 10.2   Tabular Depiction of Association Between Two Variables

		White households	
		High White %	Low White %
African-American households	High African American %		
	Low African American %		

Using Moran's I, I can estimate the statistically significant high-high, high-low, low-high, and low-low correlations. The algorithm also identifies the neighborhoods where it fails to estimate a statistically significant correlation. The results are reported in Figure 10.29.

Note that the figure has color-coded the five categories mentioned previously. Also note that the algorithm did not find a statistically significant correlation in the gray-colored 734 CTs.[19] The algorithm identified only eight neighborhoods with a high concentration of Whites and African Americans. Otherwise, higher concentration of one was associated with the lower concentration of the other.

I repeat the same analysis to determine the spatial correlation between African-American and Hispanic households at the neighborhood level (see Figure 10.30). I obtain slightly better results where I observe a positive correlation for high concentration of African-American and Hispanic households in at least 73 neighborhoods. The color-coded version of Figure 10.30 that can be downloaded from the book's companion website clearly identifies the African-American- and Hispanic-dominated neighborhoods.

Race, Space, and Poverty

Now that we understand the spatial distribution of racialized communities in the Chicago CMSA, let us examine how poverty affects these communities. Specifically, we want to determine the concentration of low-income households, while controlling for the racial composition of the individual neighborhoods. I have used the Conditional plot option in Geoda to generate Figure 10.31, which answers the question.

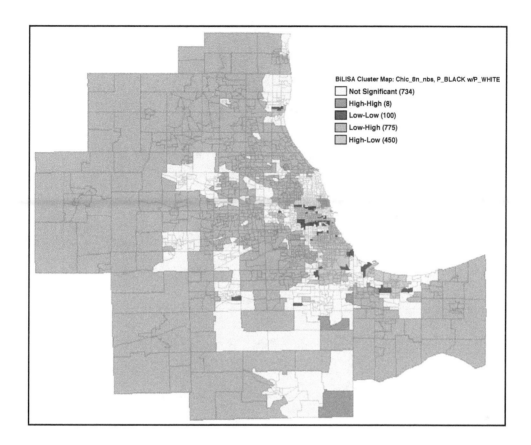

Figure 10.29 Plotting spatial autocorrelation between African American and White demographics using local Moran's I

Note that Figure 10.31 presents not one but nine maps of the Chicago CMSA. Moving from left to right, the neighborhoods are classified for low, medium, and high concentration of African-American households. Similarly, moving from bottom to top, the neighborhoods are classified for low, medium, and high concentration of White households. Thus, the top left map represents the map for neighborhoods that reported the highest concentration of White households and the lowest concentration of African-American households. Similarly, the bottom-right map represents the neighborhoods reporting the highest concentration of African-American households and the lowest concentration of White households. Also, note that the neighborhoods or CTs presented in each of the nine maps are mutually exclusive.

Lastly, the neighborhoods are color coded for the concentration of poverty. Dark pink represents a very high concentration of low-income households in a neighborhood and light blue represents a low concentration of low-income households such that no more than one in four households is categorized as low income.

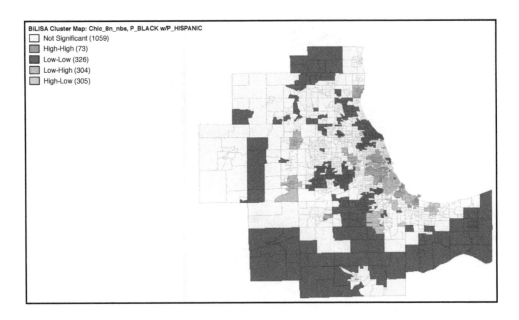

Figure 10.30   Plotting spatial autocorrelation between African-American and Hispanic demographics using local Moran's I

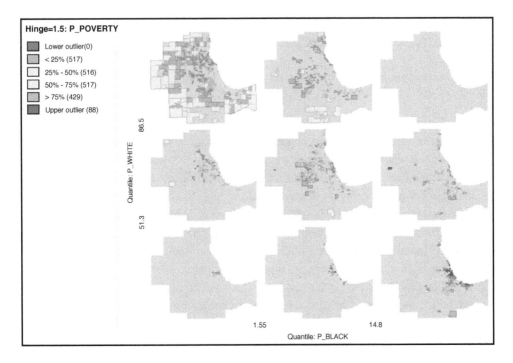

Figure 10.31   Spatial autocorrelation between race and poverty

The empty map reported in the top-right corner of Figure 10.31 is merely an outcome of demographics. The top row represents neighborhoods where White households account for 86.5% of more of the neighborhood. The rightmost column represents the neighborhoods where African-American households account for 14.8% or more of the neighborhood. It is not arithmetically possible to have the racial breakdown of a neighborhood where one race accounts for 87% of the population and the other 15%.

Note that the African-American concentrated neighborhoods (bottom-right map in Figure 10.31) are also the ones with an extremely high concentration of poverty. Similarly, the White majority neighborhoods (top-left map in Figure 10.31) exhibit low incidence of poverty. The map in the middle (second row, second column in Figure 10.31) accounts for White-majority neighborhoods with an average concentration of the African-American households. Again, we see that White-dominated neighborhoods depict low levels of poverty and African-American neighborhoods depict higher levels of poverty.

It is obvious from Figure 10.31 that the African-American neighborhoods depict a much higher incidence of poverty than the White neighborhoods do. This fact is further reinforced in Figure 10.32 that reports histograms for median household income where the neighborhoods are categorized the same way as in Figure 10.31. We see that the household income distribution in White-dominated neighborhoods suggest frequent incidence of higher income than the neighborhoods with high concentration of African-American households.

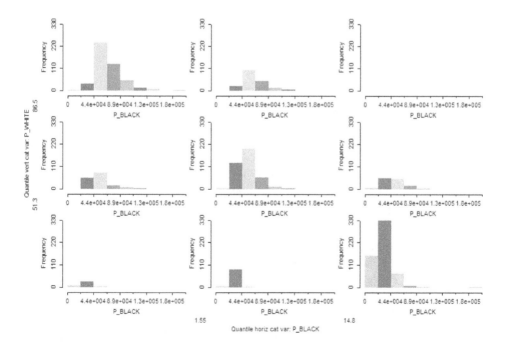

Figure 10.32 Histograms of income for varying levels of racial heterogeneity at the neighborhood level

The incidence of lower household income bears a positive correlation with higher incidence of rental housing units. This is depicted in Figure 10.33, which shows that the neighborhoods with high concentration of African-American households report a higher incidence of rental housing units. At the same time, suburban neighborhoods dominated by White households report much lower incidence of rental housing units.

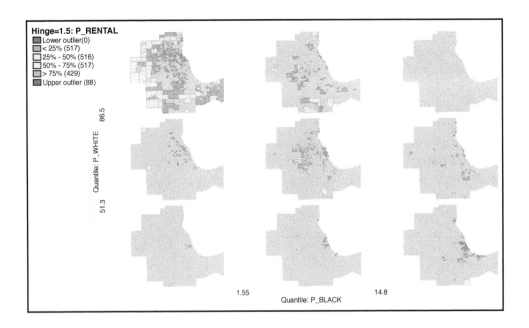

Figure 10.33   Spatial distribution of rental housing units for varying levels of racial heterogeneity

Race, Space, and Commuting

Traveling to and from work, also known as commuting, is a major part of workers' life in North America. In large cities, commuting can easily consume one to two hours every day. It contributes to stress and eats into productive and/or recreational time.

Commuting has another dimension of "how the other half travels." In the U.S., with the exception of large and high-density cities, low-income households, often immigrants or racial minorities, commute by public transit. We would like to know whether commuting patterns differ by race and income in Chicago. In addition, do communities located near subway stations in Chicago report lower commute times?

Let's begin with the subway question. Ideally, we want to see the impact of proximity to subway stations on public transit mode share and commute times. We can think of a three-by-two matrix of maps where the two columns represent neighborhoods near subway stations or otherwise. The three rows determine transit mode share increasing from bottom row to higher rows.

Figure 10.34 presents these six maps. The left column represents the neighborhoods lacking proximity to subway stations and the right column represents neighborhoods located near subway stations. The bottom-left map shows the largely suburban census tracts with low transit use and lacking proximity to subway stations. The large number of blue color census tracts indicate lower commute times in the suburbs suggest that transit proximity may not be a prerequisite for lower commute times. The two maps in the top row representing high transit use reveal that irrespective of the accessibility to subway stations, neighborhoods reporting higher public transit use also reported much higher commute times.

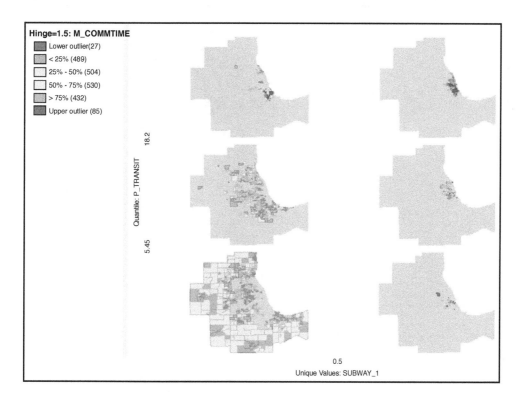

Figure 10.34 Commute times mapped after controlling for transit mode share and proximity to subway stations

If you remember the coverage of the regression models in Chapter 7, you know that the inferences drawn here are limited in their ability to draw conclusions. The impact of proximity to subway stations can be estimated only when controlling for other variables, such as distance from downtown, income, racial mix of the neighborhood, and transit ridership in the neighborhood. I report the results for the OLS and spatial auto-regressive models later in this chapter.

First, I return to map-based analysis. So far, we have looked at the entire CMSA. Now let's focus on those CTs that are within 10 km of the Chicago's downtown. The smaller data set allows us to focus on the urban parts of Chicago.

Figure 10.35 presents the spatial distribution of public transit ridership in neighborhoods within 10 km of Chicago's downtown. Neighborhoods in the Northeast and Southeast have high public transit ridership, which is evident from the darker shades. I can further explore if the high transit ridership clusters are similar or different in their demographic makeup.

Figure 10.35   Spatial distribution of transit mode share in neighborhoods within 10 km of Chicago's downtown

Figure 10.36 presents the matrix of maps for the subset of neighborhoods that fall within 10 km of the CBD. The average household income increases from left-to-right and the concentration of African-American households increases from bottom-to-top. The color-coded neighborhoods represent public transit ridership. The map in the top left represents neighborhoods depicting low-income and high African-American concentration. You can spot the concentration of high public transit use in the southeast of the map. On the other extreme is the map in the bottom-right corner that lists neighborhoods with high-income and low concentration of African-American households. This map shows high public transit use in the neighborhoods in the northeast. Both clusters of neighborhoods demonstrate high public transit mode share, but one cluster belongs to low-income racial minorities and the other belongs to mainstream affluent households.

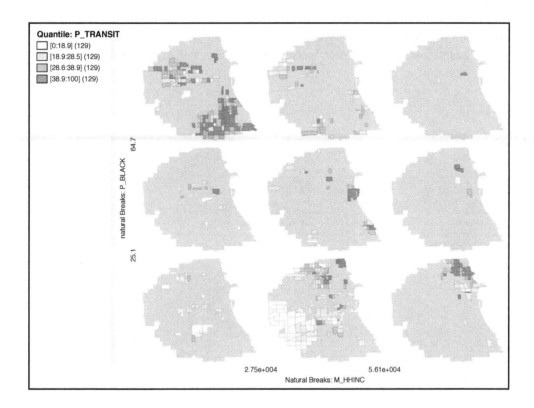

Figure 10.36   Spatial distribution of transit ridership after controlling for income and racial concentration

Regression with Spatial Lags

In this section, I demonstrate the application of an OLS regression model and its two variants that account for spatial autocorrelation. Spatial econometrics is fast gaining traction in academia and industry, such as real estate, where spatially correlated variables may be predicted better using appropriate tools.

I estimate the following model:

Commute time

$= \beta 0 + \beta 1 * hhld\ income + \beta 2 * subway\ proximity + \beta 3$

$* distance\ from\ downtown + \beta 4 * transit\ ridership + \beta 6$

$* African\ American(\%)$

Figure 10.37 shows the resulting OLS model. With the exception of distance from downtown, all other variables are statistically significant. The variable of interest is the proximity to subway. If I were to control for the aforementioned variables, proximity to subway stations results in a reduced commute time of 3.2 minutes. This finding is at odds with what I found earlier by mapping the variables. The model also shows that all else being equal, commute times increase with an increase in African American concentration as well as with an increase in public transit mode share.

```
SUMMARY OF OUTPUT: ORDINARY LEAST SQUARES ESTIMATION
Data set             :    esri_Ch_CT
Dependent Variable   :    M_COMMTIME   Number of Observations: 2067
Mean dependent var   :        31.672   Number of Variables   :       6
S.D. dependent var   :        8.3717   Degrees of Freedom    :    2061

R-squared            :      0.340083   F-statistic           :      212.424
Adjusted R-squared   :      0.338482   Prob(F-statistic)     :            0
Sum squared residual :         95600   Log likelihood        :     -6895.46
Sigma-square         :       46.3852   Akaike info criterion :      13802.9
S.E. of regression   :       6.81067   Schwarz criterion     :      13836.7
Sigma-square ML      :       46.2506
S.E of regression ML :       6.80078
```

Variable	Coefficient	Std.Error	t-Statistic	Probability
CONSTANT	25.02789	0.6307087	39.68216	0.00000
M_HHINC	3.706883e-005	7.402103e-006	5.007879	0.00000
SUBWAY_1	-3.263912	0.4744318	-6.879625	0.00000
D_CBD	-0.008493162	0.009336689	-0.9096546	0.36312
P_BLACK	0.06090177	0.00530083	11.4891	0.00000
P_TRANSIT	0.3092781	0.01634611	18.9206	0.00000

```
REGRESSION DIAGNOSTICS
MULTICOLLINEARITY CONDITION NUMBER     9.743224
TEST ON NORMALITY OF ERRORS
TEST                     DF            VALUE            PROB
Jarque-Bera               2        797241.5065          0.00000

DIAGNOSTICS FOR HETEROSKEDASTICITY
RANDOM COEFFICIENTS
TEST                     DF            VALUE            PROB
Breusch-Pagan test        5         11319.1916          0.00000
Koenker-Bassett test      5           231.5017          0.00000
========================= END OF REPORT =============================
```

Figure 10.37   The OLS model for commute times

The OLS model does not account for spatial autocorrelation inherent in commute times. Geoda allows one to estimate two variants of models that account for spatial auto-correlation. I will not describe the formulation of these models, which is beyond the scope of this book. I instead recommend the reader to consult excellent publications from Professor Luc Anselin and illustrate the models.[20] In fact, I strongly recommend *Modern Spatial Econometrics in Practice: A Guide to GeoDa, GeoDaSpace and PySAL* by Professor Anselin.

One modeling approach allows you to account for the impact of neighboring values by introducing them as an explanatory variable in the model. The results of the spatial lag model are presented in Figure 10.38. Note that the first coefficient reported in the figure is W_M_ COMMTIME, which is statistically significant and controls for the impact of neighboring values that are influential on the explanatory variable. Note that other coefficients have slightly changed, but the conclusions drawn from the spatial lag model will be statistically more robust.

```
SUMMARY OF OUTPUT: SPATIAL LAG MODEL - MAXIMUM LIKELIHOOD ESTIMATION
Data set              : esri_Ch_CT
Spatial Weight        : Chic_rook_order1.gal
Dependent Variable    :   M_COMMTIME  Number of Observations: 2067
Mean dependent var    :       31.672  Number of Variables   :    7
S.D. dependent var    :       8.3717  Degrees of Freedom    : 2060
Lag coeff.   (Rho)    :      0.360324

R-squared             :     0.415843  Log likelihood        :     -6798.17
Sq. Correlation       : -            Akaike info criterion :      13610.3
Sigma-square          :      40.9409  Schwarz criterion     :      13649.8
S.E of regression     :      6.39851

-----------------------------------------------------------------------------
      Variable    Coefficient     Std.Error       z-value      Probability
-----------------------------------------------------------------------------
W_M_COMMTIME       0.3603242      0.02647984      13.60749       0.00000
    CONSTANT        14.53466      0.9147228       15.88969       0.00000
      M_HHINC   2.904616e-005   7.016381e-006     4.139763       0.00003
     SUBWAY_1      -3.033617      0.4467554       -6.790331      0.00000
        D_CBD    0.009021629    0.008791242       1.026206       0.30479
      P_BLACK     0.03811099     0.00522513       7.293787       0.00000
     P_TRANSIT     0.2739875     0.01630682       16.80202       0.00000
-----------------------------------------------------------------------------

REGRESSION DIAGNOSTICS
DIAGNOSTICS FOR HETEROSKEDASTICITY
RANDOM COEFFICIENTS
TEST                                      DF      VALUE         PROB
Breusch-Pagan test                         5    16787.2622     0.00000

DIAGNOSTICS FOR SPATIAL DEPENDENCE
SPATIAL LAG DEPENDENCE FOR WEIGHT MATRIX : Chic_rook_order1.gal
TEST                                      DF      VALUE         PROB
Likelihood Ratio Test                      1     194.5913      0.00000
======================== END OF REPORT ================================
```

Figure 10.38   A spatial lag model for commute times

The other approach to model spatial auto-correlation is the spatial error model, shown in Figure 10.39. Instead of the spatially weighted coefficient of commute time, a new coefficient, lambda, is reported in the model. The results are indeed similar to the ones seen for OLS and the spatial lag model.

```
SUMMARY OF OUTPUT: SPATIAL ERROR MODEL - MAXIMUM LIKELIHOOD ESTIMATION
Data set              : esri_Ch_CT
Spatial Weight        : Chic_rook_order1.gal
Dependent Variable    :  M_COMMTIME   Number of Observations: 2067
Mean dependent var    :    31.672037  Number of Variables   :    6
S.D. dependent var    :     8.371705  Degrees of Freedom    : 2061
Lag coeff. (Lambda)   :     0.479729

R-squared             :     0.458969  R-squared (BUSE)      : -
Sq. Correlation       : -            Log likelihood        :-6743.513517
Sigma-square          :    37.9184    Akaike info criterion :       13499
S.E of regression     :     6.15779   Schwarz criterion     :     13532.8

-------------------------------------------------------------------------
    Variable      Coefficient     Std.Error       z-value     Probability
-------------------------------------------------------------------------
    CONSTANT         22.8135       0.8603135      26.51766      0.00000
     M_HHINC   4.823872e-005   8.79735e-006       5.483323     0.00000
    SUBWAY_1      -2.838986       0.6190556      -4.585995      0.00000
       D_CBD       0.01390986     0.0146914       0.9468031     0.34374
     P_BLACK       0.05567272     0.007029866     7.919456      0.00000
   P_TRANSIT       0.3738055      0.01792883     20.84941       0.00000
      LAMBDA       0.4797286      0.02651901     18.08999       0.00000
-------------------------------------------------------------------------

REGRESSION DIAGNOSTICS
DIAGNOSTICS FOR HETEROSKEDASTICITY
RANDOM COEFFICIENTS
TEST                                   DF       VALUE          PROB
Breusch-Pagan test                      5    17306.8607       0.00000

DIAGNOSTICS FOR SPATIAL DEPENDENCE
SPATIAL ERROR DEPENDENCE FOR WEIGHT MATRIX : Chic_rook_order1.gal
TEST                                   DF       VALUE          PROB
Likelihood Ratio Test                   1      303.8965       0.00000
========================= END OF REPORT =================================
```

Figure 10.39   A spatial error model for commute times

Summary

GIS are the missing component of the data science world. The marriage between the GIS software and demographic/spatial data could significantly improve current market research and data science practice. Now with web-based analytics in play, one can conduct spatial analysis using the Internet without needing to acquire either GIS data or software.

However, when working with personal proprietary data sets, web-based solutions may be limited in their capacity. With highly sophisticated algorithms and tools packaged in affordable software packages, data scientists can add spatial analytical capabilities to their portfolio, and include colorful maps in their reports to communicate findings to their clients.

Endnotes

1. Maeshiro, K. (2007, July 30). Tips offered to prevent West Nile Virus standing water in pools can be a source. *Los Angeles Daily News*.

2. Spence, B. (2007, July 18). Vacant pools have new residents: County officials battle mosquito breeding ground. *The Record*.

3. Associated Press Newswires. (2008, May 27). Foreclosed Phoenix homes become havens for mosquitoes.

4. McConnaughey, J. (2009, April 22). Pools become nasty mosquito havens in foreclosure. Associated Press Newswires.

5. Corkery, M. (2008, May 9). For mortgages underwater, help swims In -- Tiny fish clean pools of foreclosed homes; Eating up mosquitos. *The Wall Street Journal*.

6. http://www.qgis.org/en/site/

7. Lau, G. and McKercher, B. (2006). "Understanding tourist movement patterns in a destination: a GIS approach." *Tourism and Hospitality Research*. Volume 7, Issue 1, pp. 39–49.

8. Lubenow, A. and Tolson, K. (2001). "GIS technology helps pinpoint patients." *Health Management Technology*. Volume 22, Issue 1, pp. 54–55.

9. Felman, D. (2006). "Segmentation Building Blocks." *Marketing Research*. Summer 2006.

10. Haider, M. (2014, June 30). "The hard truths about public transit in Canada." *The Huffington Post*.

11. David Suzuki, F. M. (2014, June 27). Wynne's victory sent a message: It's time to get moving on transit. *The Globe and Mail*.

12. Haider, M. (2013, July 2). Public transit is better, but cars are faster. *The Globe and Mail*.

13. Color maps are available from the book's website: www.ibmpressbooks.com/title/9780133991024.

14. Haider, M. (2014, December 30). Toronto is a city divided into the Haves, Will Haves, and Have Nots. *The Huffington Post*.

15. http://www.oxfam.org/en/pressroom/pressreleases/2015-01-19/richest-1-will-own-more-all-rest-2016

16. http://ekonometrics.blogspot.com/2010/12/locating-torontos-missing-middle-class.html

17. http://beta.images.theglobeandmail.com/archive/01069/Read_The_Three_Cit_1069461a.pdf

18. http://beta.images.theglobeandmail.com/archive/01069/Read_The_Three_Cit_1069461a.pdf

19. For color maps, please consult the book's website.

20. https://geodacenter.asu.edu/biblio/author/232

CHAPTER 11

Doing Serious Time with Time Series

Time series data is a ubiquitous form of economic, environmental, and social data that intersects our lives on a daily basis. News media routinely discuss time series data and present time series charts, such as unemployment rate over the years. If you have read a news article about housing prices that carries a chart depicting the rise and fall in housing prices over time, you are already familiar with time series data.

The primary purpose of this chapter is to illustrate how one might analyze time series data. I first illustrate graphical methods to plot time series data. I then demonstrate using the familiar Ordinary Least Squares (OLS) model and its extensions to analyze time series data. This is followed by a detailed review of theoretical concepts in time series analytics.

Because the new housing construction (housing starts) is tracked diligently in both Canada and the United States, I use this data to illustrate time series concepts. I also demonstrate time series concepts for housing price dynamics.

As I mentioned earlier, this chapter uses two distinct approaches to demonstrate time series data analysis. The first approach is a slight modification of the OLS method. The second approach offers an introduction to the theory and application of specific time series methods, also known as time series econometrics.

Because the intended readers of this book are budding data scientists and practitioners, my preference therefore is to illustrate methods that practitioners could readily adopt. Thus, I focus on those extensions of the OLS model that could help practitioners gain valuable insights by using familiar tools. Also, I use Stata in the text to illustrate Time Series concepts. The book's website (www.ibmpressbooks.com/title/9780133991024) provides code and data in other software formats including R, SAS, and SPSS.

Introducing Time Series Data and How to Visualize It

A time series data set comprises repeated observations over time on some phenomenon, such as housing prices or temperature. A graphical depiction of time series data usually involves a line chart with time plotted on the *x*-axis and the data on the *y*-axis. Consider the following graph (see Figure 11.1) of median housing prices in the United States. Also presented is the code in Stata.

```
twoway (tsline med_home_price),
scheme(s2mono)
```

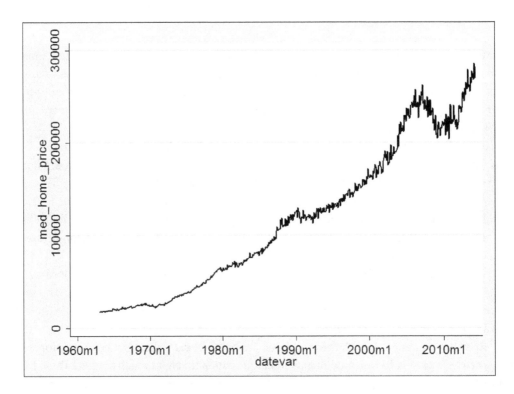

Figure 11.1   Median housing prices in the United States

Notice a few aspects of Figure 11.1. First, the data set begins in the early sixties and continues after 2010. The representation of the time variable as 1970m1 is conventional and depicts the first month in 1970. Housing prices appear to be rising over time. However, we see a decline in housing prices around 2007/08 and then a resumption of the upward trend after 2010.

The housing price data obviously depicts an upward trend, which is one of the characteristics, and a limiting factor for analysis, of many time series data sets. The time series analysis requires one to account for the trend in the data set.

I have purposefully left out some important elements in Figure 11.1 to reinforce the points about creating illustrative graphics, which I discussed earlier in Chapter 5, "Graphic Details." For instance, Figure 11.1 needs a descriptive title, some additional descriptions about the underlying data, and the source of data. Figure 11.2 presents the additional elements. The Stata code used to generate Figure 11.2 is also presented.

```
twoway (tsline med_home_price),  scheme(s2mono) ///
 ttitle(Months) ///
 title(Median housing prices in the United States) ///
 subtitle(Prices are in nominal dollars) ///
 ytitle(median house prices (nominal))  ///
 ytitle(, alignment(default)) ///
 note(Data obtained from Federal Reserve Economic Data)
```

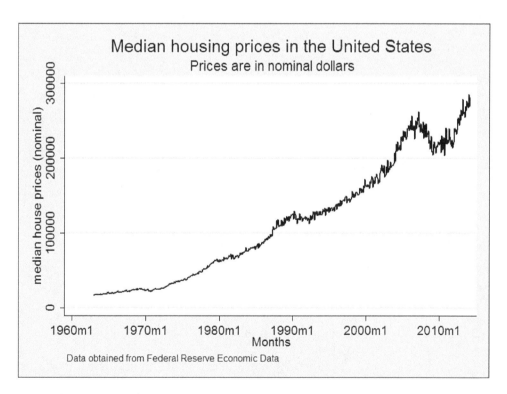

Figure 11.2 Adequately labeled chart of median house prices in the United States

The title explains that the figure depicts data for median housing prices in the United States. The subtitle informs the reader that prices are in nominal dollars and have not been corrected for inflation. A caption at the bottom reveals the source for the data set. Lastly, an appropriate caption for the *x*-axis replaces the name of the date variable.

In addition to trend, another important aspect of time series data is seasonality. News media often report of retail sales peaking in December. The time series modeling techniques should account for seasonality, which in some instances could be achieved by introducing seasonal dummies in the model. If seasonality is removed from a time series, the resulting series is called *the seasonally adjusted time series.*

I illustrate seasonality with another key economic variable, housing starts, which reports the number of new housing units on which construction began in a particular month. Housing starts are one of the most watched economic indicators because they are considered a "leading" indicator of changes in economic production. Housing starts decline in advance of a recession, and rise before post-recession economic recovery ensues.

Figure 11.3 shows seasonality in housing starts (not seasonally adjusted) in the United States from January 2003 to December 2006. Also listed is the Stata code.

```
twoway (tsline raw_starts) if tin(2003m1, 2006m12), ///
 ttitle(Months) ///
 title(Monthly Housing Starts in the United States) ///
 subtitle(Starts are in thousands) ///
 ytitle(housing starts in thousands) ///
 note(Data obtained from Federal Reserve Economic Data) ///
  scheme(s2mono)
```

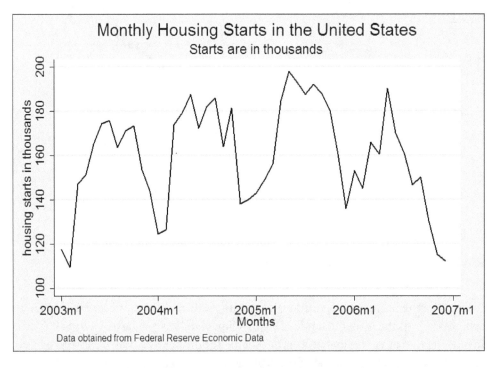

Figure 11.3   Monthly housing starts in the United States (2003–2006)

The housing starts data explicitly depicts seasonality. Note that housing construction picks up during summer months and falls during winter months. At its peak in the summer of 2005, work started on almost 200,000 houses. At its lowest point during the winter of 2003, the number of housing starts declined to less than 120,000 units. Again, robust empirical analysis should account for both the trend and seasonality in the underlying time series. As I mentioned earlier, time series are often adjusted to iron out seasonality, and the resulting transformed time series is a seasonally adjusted time series. I am not particularly a big fan of seasonally adjusted data, but will return to this later in the chapter.

Time series data are best appreciated when plotted. You can plot multiple time series in the same figure to see how two or more data sets are related over time. For instance, let's examine the relationship between housing prices and unemployment. One would assume that a rise in unemployment should correlate with lower housing prices. Let's see whether this assumption is borne out by the data set. Figure 11.4 presents both time series in the same figure. I also present the Stata code to generate the two time series.

```
twoway (tsline unemp_rate) (tsline med_home_price,  ///
yaxis(2)) ///
 if tin(2007m1, 2014m5) , ///
 ytitle(unemployment rate in percent) ///
 ytitle(, alignment(default)) ///
 ytitle(Median home prices for new housing ($), axis(2)) ttitle(Months)
///
 title(Unemployment rate and Median home prices in the US,
size(medium)) ///
 note(Data obtained from Federal Reserve Economic Data) ///
 scheme(s2mono)
```

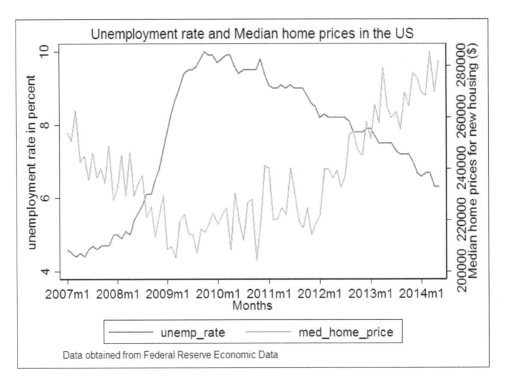

Figure 11.4   U.S. median house prices and unemployment rate (2007.01–2014.05)

The unemployment rate is depicted by the dark-colored line and housing prices are repre-sented by the gray-colored line. Housing prices correspond to the appropriately labeled *y*-axis on the right, and the unemployment rate is represented by the *y*-axis on the left. The figure explic-itly illustrates that the median house price declines with an increase in the unemployment rate, revealing the negative correlation between the two time series. Also note that unemployment in the U.S. peaked at around 10% in 2009 when housing prices were at their lowest levels. Further-more, the unemployment rate reached its lowest post-recession level in 2014 when the median housing price also climbed to its highest post-recession level.

How Is Time Series Data Different?

A quick look at the figures presented earlier shows that values at any time *t* are very similar to the values observed in the last time period, *t–1*. For instance, the median housing price in May 2014 was $282,000, and $269,700 in April 2014 (refer to Figure 11.4). Comparatively, median housing price in May 2013 was $263,700, suggesting that housing prices closer in time are more similar than those occurring at greater time intervals between them. In other words, housing prices are correlated to each other over time, or in the time series parlance, there is autocorrelation in housing prices.

In the following section, I first apply an OLS model to the time series data. I identify the challenges with time series data, and then proceed to the specialized time series concepts and their applications to housing starts data in the United States and Canada.

A recurring theme in this book is to deploy the OLS model as a first step for statistical analysis. As I have shown earlier, I recommend Regression even for the comparison of means test (the `t-test`). Similarly, I recommend deploying the OLS model as a first step for time series data.

Given the nature of time series data, a few time series–specific constructs first need to be introduced. I use the U.S. housing price data, which you can download from the book's website (www.ibmpressbooks.com/title/9780133991024), as an example. Let's begin with the *trend variable*. If a time series depicts a trend, you can capture the trend in an OLS regression by introducing a trend variable that accounts for the increase in time since the beginning of the time series. This variable is created by coding the first observation as *one* and adding *one* to every subsequent observation. Thus, the variable trend is 1 for the first observation and T for the last observation, where T is the length of the time series (see Column 2 in Table 11.1).

Time series often include data expressed as years, months, days, hours, and even seconds. Sometimes, the data depict seasonal fluctuations that need to be accounted for in the model. Consider the higher retail sales during December as an obvious sign of seasonality. If there are other month-specific deviations observable in the time series, this could be accounted for by introducing new binary (dummy) variables that will assume the value of 1 if true, 0 otherwise. Thus, "January" (see Column 10 in Table 11.1) assumes the value 1, if the month is January, and 0 otherwise. You can account for similar seasonal effects by creating binary variables for all, but one, seasonal effects.

Time series data also involves lags and leads. Remember earlier I mentioned that often, the observation at time period t is correlated with the observation at $t–1$. Thus, to estimate a model for a time series, y_t, you can use the observation in the last time period (y_{t-1}) as an explanatory variable. To implement this model, I will have to create a new lagged variable that puts the observation for y_{t-1} in the same row as y_t. This is explained in Table 11.1 for house price data.

Table 11.1 Sample Time Series Data on Housing Prices Covering the Period 2013.05 to 2014.05

Column 1	Column 2	Column 3	Column 4	Column 5	Column 6	Column 7	Column 8	Column 9	Column 10
Date	Trend	Month	Year	Median House Price (Y_t)	Lagged House Price (Y_{t-1})	Leading House Price (Y_{t+1})	First Differenced House Price (DY_t)	Second Differenced House Price (D_2Y_t)	January
May-13	1	5	2013	263700		259800			0
Jun-13	2	6	2013	259800	263700	262200	−3900		0
Jul-13	3	7	2013	262200	259800	255300	2400	6300	0
Aug-13	4	8	2013	255300	262200	269800	−6900	−9300	0
Sep-13	5	9	2013	269800	255300	264300	14500	21400	0
Oct-13	6	10	2013	264300	269800	277100	−5500	−20000	0
Nov-13	7	11	2013	277100	264300	275500	12800	18300	0
Dec-13	8	12	2013	275500	277100	269800	−1600	−14400	0
Jan-14	9	1	2014	269800	275500	268400	−5700	−4100	1
Feb-14	10	2	2014	268400	269800	285400	−1400	4300	0
Mar-14	11	3	2014	285400	268400	269700	17000	18400	0
Apr-14	12	4	2014	269700	285400	282000	−15700	−32700	0
May-14	13	5	2014	282000	269700		12300	28000	0

Notice in Table 11.1 that the month and year are jointly listed under *Date* in Column 1. The trend variable is listed in Column 2. The month variable in Column 3 represents each month numerically. May being the fifth month is labeled as 5, and June as 6. Column 4 controls for year and changes only when the year changes. Median house price is listed in Column 5.

Lagged values for median housing prices are presented in Column 6. Notice that the row for May 2013 has a missing value for lagged housing price. This is always the case for the lagged variable, which returns a missing value for each lag. For June 2013, the lagged variable reports $263,700, which is originally the value for May 2013. Thus, if I were to regress contemporaneous house prices against lagged house prices, the lagged variable will serve as an explanatory variable.

Column 7 presents leading housing prices, which is the opposite of the lagged variable, where the observation from $t+1$ is replaced for time period t.

Differenced variables are another useful way of working with time series data. Put simply, the differenced or integrated variable (in time series parlance) is created by subtracting the previous time period's value y_{t-1} from current value of time series, y_t. Thus, the first differenced variable is expressed as shown in Equation 11.1:

$$\Delta y_t = y_t - y_{t-1} \quad \textbf{Equation 11.1}$$

The second differenced variable is expressed as shown in Equation 11.2:

$$\Delta_2 y_t = \left(y_t - y_{t-1} \right) - \left(y_{t-1} - y_{t-2} \right) \quad \textbf{Equation 11.2}$$

First and second differenced variables are presented in Columns 8 and 9, respectively. Modern econometrics software, such as LimDep, R, Stata, SPSS, Eviews, and SAS have built-in functions that generate these variables on the fly and eliminate the need to create new lagged, differenced, or seasonal variables.

Starting with Basic Regression Models

Let's begin with a simple model of median housing prices using data for the period 1963.01 to 2014.05. We can estimate a model by regressing housing prices as a function of their own lagged values. Mathematically, if y_t represents housing prices then (see Equation 11.3):

$$y_t = \beta_0 + \beta_1 y_{t-1} + \epsilon_t \quad \textbf{Equation 11.3}$$

Figure 11.2 suggests a trend in median house prices. When the underlying time series displays a long-term trend, that is, the variable increases or decreases with time t, you can introduce trend as an explanatory variable, as shown in Equation 11.4.

$$y_t = \beta_0 + \beta_1 t + \beta_2 t^2 \quad \textbf{Equation 11.4}$$

Where $t = 2,1,...T$. The preceding equation is capable of capturing not only the long-term trend, but also the non-linearities; for example, a U-shaped trend in the time series data. The non-linearity in trend is often linearized by taking the logarithm of the variable captured as levels. Such a linearized trend is often referred to as an *exponential* or *log-linear* trend, which is expressed as shown in Equation 11.5:

$$y_t = \beta_0 e^{\beta_1 t} \quad \textbf{Equation 11.5}$$

To linearize the trend, especially when the data represents an exponential trend, you can take the logarithm of the preceding equation, resulting in Equation 11.6:

$$\ln(y_t) = \ln\left(\beta_0 e^{\beta_1 t}\right) = \ln(\beta_0) + \beta_1 t + \epsilon_t \quad \textbf{Equation 11.6}$$

Regression models can account for seasonality using dummy or binary variables. If the seasonality is quarterly, four quarterly dummies can be used in the model to capture the seasonal effects. If the model contains the intercept, the number of seasonal dummies used is always one less than the underlying seasonality. Thus, for quarterly dummies, at most three seasonal dummies could be used. The fourth season serves as the base case. This is necessary because the sum of all seasonal dummies returns a unit vector, which will result in perfect multicollinearity with the intercept in the model. A quarterly time series with seasonal effects and a trend is shown in Equation 11.7.

$$y_t = \beta_0 + \beta_1 t + \gamma_1 s_1 + \gamma_2 s_2 + \gamma_3 s_3 + \epsilon_t \quad \textbf{Equation 11.7}$$

Diebold (2001, p. 109) demonstrates seasonal impacts on housing starts.[1] A common practice in time series analytics is to estimate the model on a subset of the data and then use that model to forecast values for all observations. This allows you to test the out-of-sample forecasting capabilities of the model. Diebold used data for the period 1946.01 to 1993.12 to estimate the model, and used data from 1994.01 to 1994.11 to test the out-of-sample forecast. The model is expressed as shown in Equation 11.8:

$$y_t = \Sigma_{i=1}^{12}\left(\gamma_i D_{it}\right) + \epsilon_t \quad \textbf{Equation 11.8}$$

D_{it} represents the 12 seasonal dummies. The model explained 38% of the variance in housing starts. The seasonal model returned smaller residuals during recessions and larger residuals during boom cycles. Diebold further suggests that log transformations in the seasonal model can be used to stabilize variance.

What Is Wrong with Using OLS Models for Time Series Data?

If you were to estimate an Ordinary Least Squares (OLS) regression model on a time series that is autocorrelated and depicts a trend and seasonality, the resulting residuals will also be correlated in time and the variance of these residuals will not be constant over time. Thus, heteroskedasticity (inconstant variance) and autocorrelation require either addressing these limitations while applying the OLS model or adopting alternative methods more suited for the time series data.

Furthermore, the OLS tools that test the validity and robustness of the models might no longer be effective. This is because biased lower-bound standard errors could return inflated `t-statistics`, resulting in spurious correlations.

Despite this, and even in the presence of correlated residuals, estimated coefficients are unbiased. However, OLS models in such cases are likely to return smaller standard errors and inflated `t-statistics`. It is recommended to check for the presence of autocorrelation in a time series. The `Durbin-Watson` (DW) test is frequently used to test whether residuals are correlated. DW test is expressed as shown in Equation 11.9:

$$d = \frac{\sum_{t=2}^{n} \left(\epsilon_t - \epsilon_{t-1} \right)^2}{\sum_{t=2}^{n} \epsilon_t^2} \quad \textbf{Equation 11.9}$$

The DW statistic tests the null hypothesis, H_o: No residual correlation, against the alternative, H_a: Positive residual correlation. The DW statistic can only capture the first-order serial correlations; that is, the correlation between a variable and its first lagged value. The following are the critical values for the DW statistic:

Uncorrelated residuals	DW = 2
Positive correlation	0 < DW < 2
Negative correlation	2 < DW < 4

Newey–West Standard Errors

Fortunately, you do have a solution when confronted with serial autocorrelation and heteroskedasticity. The Newey–West (1987) variance estimator produces consistent estimates even in the presence of autocorrelation and heteroskedasticity.[2] You need to specify the number of lags in the model with Newey–West standard errors. The estimator assumes that at greater lags than the one specified for the model, autocorrelation might be ignored. Note that the point estimates in a Newey–West variance estimator are identical to the one obtained from an identically specified regression model. The only difference is in the standard errors, which are robust to the presence of autocorrelation and heteroskedasticity.

Regressing Prices with Robust Standard Errors

With this knowledge in hand, I can now model median housing prices first as a function of the lagged values of prices, followed by a model with two additional variables; that is, trend and seasons (monthly dummies), and a third model with only the trend and seasonal variables. Mathematically, the model with all explanatory variables included (Column 4 in Table 11.2) is expressed as shown in Equation 11.10:

$$y_t = \beta_0 + \beta_1 y_{t-1} + \beta_2 t + \Sigma_{i=2}^{12}\left(\gamma_i D_{it}\right) + \epsilon_t \quad \text{Equation 11.10}$$

The results are presented in Table 11.2. The first column presents the variable names and the details about model's fit. The second column presents the regression model that includes lagged housing prices as the only explanatory variable. The model was represented earlier by Equation 11.3. Note that the coefficient for the lagged value equals 1, suggesting that the price in the current time period is likely to be the same as in the last time period. The model reports an adjusted R-squared of 99.4%, which suggests that lagged housing prices are good determinants of current housing prices.

In the second model, I include the trend and 11 seasonal dummies for each month except January, which serves as the base case for comparison. Note that the lagged housing price suggests that a dollar increase in housing price in the last month correlates with a $0.93 increase in price in the current month. The trend variable, which is statistically significant, suggests that the median housing price increases by $30 each month. Only two monthly dummies are statistically significant. The inclusion of 11 seasonal dummies and the trend variable did not improve the adjusted R-squared, which suggests that these additional variables did not add to the explanatory power.

The Newey–West estimates are reported in the last column in Table 11.2. The first thing you will note is that the point estimates obtained from Newey and the ones from the identical OLS specification are indeed the same. The only difference is in the level of significance such that OLS model reports the trend variable (t) to be significant at $p<0.001$; the Newey–West estimator reports it to be significant at $p<0.01$. This is because the estimated standard errors are larger for the Newey–West estimator than those obtained from the OLS estimators.

Here is the Stata code to reproduce the results reported in Table 11.2.

```
reg med L.med
est store Reg_1
predict f_price_reg1
estat dwatson
```

```
** With trend and seasonality
reg med L.med t i.month
est store Reg_2
predict f_price_reg2
estat dwatson

reg med t i.month
est store Reg_3
predict f_price_reg3
estat dwatson

** Newey West **

newey med L.med t i.month, lag(48)
est store Newey

est table Reg_1 Reg_2 Reg_3 Newey, star b(%7.3f) stats(N r2_a)
```

Table 11.2 Regression Models to Forecast Median House Prices

Variables	Model with lagged variable	Lagged variable + trend + seasonality	Trend and seasonality alone	Newey–West: Lagged variable + trend + seasonality
Lagged housing price	1.000***	0.932***		0.932***
Trend		30.007***	425.156***	30.007**
February		2858.187*	1784.459	2858.187**
March		38.305	628.534	38.305
April		2325.829*	1839.916	2325.829**
May		−13.858	630.144	−13.858
June		1174.273	45.858	1174.273
July		19.409	−1.00E+03	19.409
August		863.909	−1.20E+03	863.909
September		931.7	−1.20E+03	931.7
October		1234.245	−970.454	1234.245

Variables	Model with lagged variable	Lagged variable + trend + seasonality	Trend and seasonality alone	Newey–West: Lagged variable + trend + seasonality
November		1810.7	–164.238	1810.7
December		1680.255	457.665	1680.255
Constant	481.266	–2.1e+03*	–1.6e+04***	–2.1e+03
Observations	616	616	617	616
Adjusted R Square	0.994	0.994	0.958	
Durbin-Watson Statistic	3.04	2.93	0.136	

* $p < 0.05$; ** $p < 0.01$; *** $p < 0.001$

The third model excludes the lagged variable and includes the trend variable as well as the 11 seasonal dummies. The statistically significant trend variable suggests that house prices increase each month by \$425. Seasonal dummies were again not statistically significant. The adjusted R-squared for this model at 95.8% might erroneously suggest that this model is as good in forecasting as the other specifications with lagged housing prices as the explanatory variable. This assumption would be a huge mistake because the model with trend and seasonal dummies will underpredict the earlier part of the time series by a huge margin. This is illustrated Figures 11.5 and 11.6. Also presented along with the figures is the Stata code.

```
twoway (tsline med_home_price) (tsline f_price_reg3)  ///
if tin(1963m1, 1982m12) , ttitle(Months) ///
 ytitle(Actual and predicted house prices) ///
 yline(0 22300)  scheme(s2mono)

twoway (tsline med_home_price) (tsline f_price_reg1)  ///
if tin(1963m1, 1982m12) , ttitle(Months) ///
 ytitle(Actual and predicted house prices)  scheme(s2mono)
```

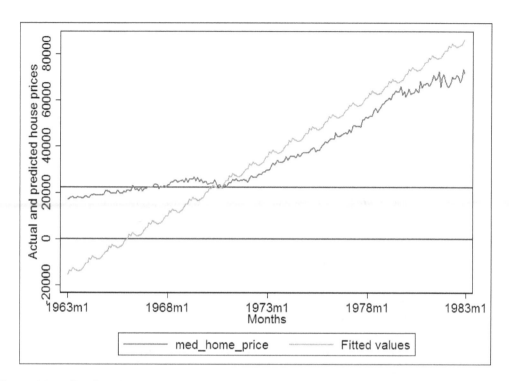

Figure 11.5   Predicted and actual (median) house prices using trend and seasonal dummies (1963.01 – 1982.12)

Notice that the model with trend and seasonal dummies underestimates the house prices from 1963 to the early 1970s (Figure 11.5). In fact, the model estimates negative house prices for the first few years, suggesting that the adjusted R-squared is a poor proxy for the model fit as it hides instances where the model systematically under- and/or overpredicts.

On the other hand, the model with the lagged variable consistently offers a better fit as shown in Figure 11.6.

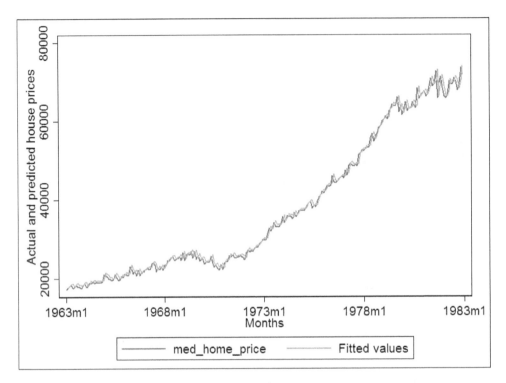

Figure 11.6   Predicted and actual (median) house prices using a lagged variable (1963.01 –
1982.12)

The last row in Table 11.2 presents the values for DW statistics for the three models. The
models with the lagged dependent variable exhibit a negative correlation among residuals, and
the model without the lagged variable exhibits positive correlation.

Time Series Econometrics

In this section, I present a formal introduction to the concepts related to time series econometrics,
first with a discussion of the concepts and definitions and later showing application of time series
methods.

Those readers interested in the applications of the time series methods might want to skip
the theoretical details to a later section in the chapter, *Application of Time Series Concepts to
Housing Starts Data*, where I illustrate the concepts in practice.

A *time series* is defined as a collection of data obtained by observing a response variable
at different points in time, such as monthly housing starts. Time series econometrics became
popular with the seminal work of Box and Jenkins (1970).[3] They proposed a new forecasting
approach that relied solely on the past behavior of the dependent variable. The traditional econometric approach was to use explanatory variables to forecast a time series. A common ground

was reached between the two approaches by using the Box and Jenkins approach for estimation with the inclusion of covariates.

Stationary Time Series

Theoretically, a time series realization begins in the infinite past and continues into the infinite future. To forecast a time series, the minimum requirements are that the mean and the covariance structure (the covariance between the current and past values) should be stable over time and finite. Such data are referred to as *covariance stationary*. A stationary time series model for regression residuals, therefore, "is one that has mean 0, constant variance, and autocorrelations that depend only on the distance between time points" (Mendenhall and Sincich, 1996).[4] The distance between time points is also called *displacement*.

The expected mean should be stable over time. This implies, as shown in Equation 11.11, that

$$E\left(y_t\right) = \mu_t = \mu \quad \textbf{Equation 11.11}$$

Because the mean is stable over time, I have dropped the subscript from μ. The autocovariance and autocorrelation functions are used to check whether the series is covariance stationary. The autocovariance function is expressed as shown in Equation 11.12:

$$\gamma\left(t,\tau\right) = cov\left(y_t, y_{t-\tau}\right) = E\left(y_t - \mu\right)\left(y_{t-\tau} - \mu\right) \quad \textbf{Equation 11.12}$$

For a covariance stationary time series, the autocovariance depends on displacement (τ) and not t. This implies that the autocovariance does not change over time, but it changes only with displacement: observations closer in time are more correlated than those further apart. In addition, the autocovariance function is symmetric; that is, the direction of displacement (forward or backward) does not influence the autocovariance function, that is, $\gamma(\tau) = \gamma(-\tau)$.

Trends and seasonality constitute violations of covariance stationarity; that is, either the mean increases with time or attains different values in different seasons. Often it has been observed that if the series violates covariance stationarity in levels, the same series is stable in growth rates. In other words, if y_t is not stable (covariance stationary), the first difference ($y_{tg} = y_t - y_{t-1}$) often ends up being stable.

Autocorrelation Function (ACF)

The covariance stationarity assumption is tested using the *Autocorrelation Function* (ACF). Statisticians prefer ACF over the autocovariance function because ACF is normalized by the standard deviations of the underlying variables and its value falls in the interval [−1, 1]. A plot of ACF against displacements is called a *correlogram*. To understand the autocovariance function, let's first revisit correlation and covariance functions. The correlation between two random variables (x and y) is expressed as shown in Equation 11.13:

$$\rho(x,y) = \frac{cov(x,y)}{\sigma_x \sigma_y} \qquad \text{Equation 11.13}$$

Where covariance is expressed as shown in Equation 11.14:

$$cov(x,y) = \frac{\sum_{i=1}^{n}(x_i - \mu_x)(y_i - \mu_y)}{n} \qquad \text{Equation 11.14}$$

Where σ_x and σ_y represent the standard deviations of the two random variables. The correlation, $\rho(x,y)$ always falls between -1 and 1.

The autocorrelation function is expressed as shown in Equation 11.15:

$$\rho(\tau) = \frac{\gamma(\tau)}{\gamma(0)} = \frac{cov(y_t, y_{t-\tau})}{\sigma(y_t)\sigma(y_{t-\tau})} \qquad \text{Equation 11.15}$$

$\gamma(\tau)$ is the covariance between y_t and y_{t-1}, whereas $\gamma(0)$ represents the product of σ_t and σ_{t-1}. The covariance stationarity assumption necessitates that σ_t and σ_{t-1} are both equal to the standard deviation of y_t, which is expressed as $\sqrt{\gamma(0)}$.

The ACF of a covariance stationary time series should decay with displacement and approach 0. The sample ACF is presented as shown in Equation 11.16:

$$\rho_{s(\tau)} = \frac{\sum_{t=\tau+1}^{T} \dfrac{(y_t - \mu_y)(y_{t-\tau} - \mu_y)}{T}}{\sum_{t=1}^{T} \dfrac{(y_t - \mu_y)^2}{T}} \qquad \text{Equation 11.16}$$

Bartlett (1946), quoted in Gujarati (1995, p. 717), has established that for purely random processes, ρ_τ is approximately normally distributed with zero mean and a variance equaling $1/T$, where T is the sample size.[5] For a standard normal distribution, a 95% confidence interval for the autocorrelation function is given by $+/-1.96\left(\dfrac{1}{\sqrt{T}}\right)$.

Partial Autocorrelation Function (PCF)

The *Partial Autocorrelation Function* (PCF) is merely the coefficient on $y_{t-\tau}$ in a population linear regression of y_t on $y_{t-\tau}$. The underlying assumption in the population linear regression is that the regression coefficients are estimated using an infinite sample of data. The PCF or ρ_τ is primarily an autoregressive model where a variable is regressed over its lagged values. Similarly, the sample PCF is computed from the sample rather than the population. Whereas the ACF captures the simple correlation between y_t and $y_{t-\tau}$, the PCF measures the association (partial correlation) between y_t and $y_{t-\tau}$ after controlling for other lagged values. I plot ACF (see Figure 11.7) and PCF (see Figure 11.8) with displacements represented on the x-axis. The Bartlett bands, two times the standard error, $(\frac{2}{\sqrt{T}})$, are also shown on the plots.

An oft-cited measure for lags of the correlogram is suggested to be 1/3 of the sample size (Gujarati [1995], p. 716). When coefficients fall outside of the Bartlett bands, we conclude that they are significantly different from 0 and suggest presence of autocorrelation, which must be addressed in the model specification. The ACF and PCF are presented along with the Stata code used to generate these.

```
ac med_home_price, scheme(s2mono) xlabel(#20)  ///
  ytitle (Autocorrelation of US Starts)
pac med_home_price, scheme(s2mono) xlabel(#20) ///
  ytitle (Partial autocorrelation of US Starts)
```

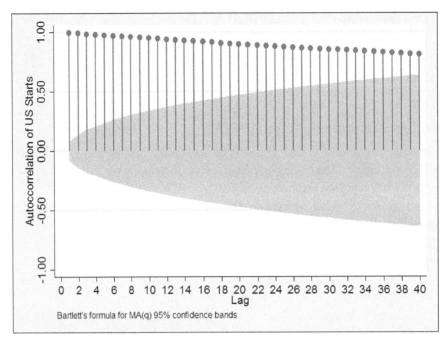

Figure 11.7   ACF for median house prices

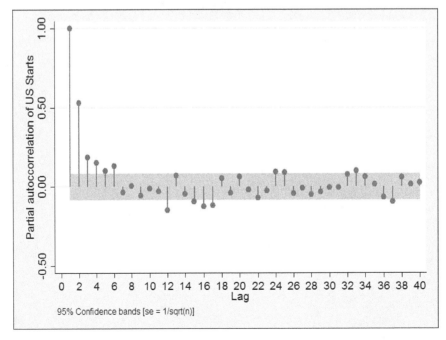

Figure 11.8   PCF for median house prices

White Noise Tests

A process with mean 0, constant variance, and no serial correlation is called White Noise. If y is the observed time series and is serially independent, then y_t is independent White Noise. We assume that $y_t = \epsilon_t$, where $\epsilon_t \sim (0, \sigma^2)$.

The shock (ϵ_t) is uncorrelated over time and is also expressed as $\epsilon_t \sim WN(0, \sigma^2)$. Hence, $y_t \sim_{iid} WN(0, \sigma^2)$, which implies that y_t is independently and identically distributed with 0 mean and constant variance. You should know that when someone refers to 0 mean, she is in fact referring to deviations from the mean of the time series; that is, $y_t - \mu$ and not just y_t. If y_t is normally distributed and serially uncorrelated, then y_t is Normal White Noise or Gaussian White Noise.

It has been suggested that one-step-ahead forecast errors should be White Noise.

You can use the *Box-Ljung Statistic* (1978) to test the hypothesis for whether the time series is White Noise.[6] The Box-Ljung (BL) statistic is estimated as shown in Equation 11.17:

$$BL = T(T+2) \sum_{\tau=1}^{m} \frac{\rho_\tau^2}{T-\tau} \sim \chi_m^2 \quad \text{Equation 11.17}$$

If the p-value of the BL statistic is indistinguishable from 0, you can reject the null hypothesis and conclude that the time series is not White Noise. On the other hand, when the p-value of the BL statistic is different from 0, you cannot reject the null hypothesis, and hence conclude that the underlying time series is White Noise.

Bartlett's periodogram-based test is also widely used to determine whether the estimated residuals from a model are White Noise. The null hypothesis is that the time series (residuals) lacks serial autocorrelation. If the p-value of the test is less than 5%, you can reject the null hypothesis and conclude that the time series is significantly different from White Noise. Conversely, if the p-value > 5%, you fail to find evidence against time series being White Noise.

The ACF of White Noise is constant at $\tau = 0$ and zero at $\tau \geq 1$, whereas the PCF for White Noise equals 1 at $\tau = 0$ and zero at $\tau \geq 1$.

Augmented Dickey Fuller Test

Another method of testing for stationarity is the *Augmented Dickey Fuller Test* (ADF). By regressing the differenced time series on trend, the first lag of the dependent variable, and the lag of differenced values of the dependent variable, you can test the null hypothesis that the coefficient for the lagged regressor equals zero. ADF is estimated using the model specification shown in Equation 11.18

$$y_t = \alpha + \rho y_{t-1} + \delta t + \mu_t \quad \text{Equation 11.18}$$

where μ_t is an independently and identically distributed zero mean error term. Subtracting y_{t-1} from both sides of the preceding equation yields:

$$y_t - y_{t-1} = \alpha + \rho y_{t-1} - y_{t-1} + \delta t + \mu_t$$

This becomes

$$\Delta y_t = \alpha + y_{t-1}(\rho - 1) + \delta t + \mu_t$$

Substituting $\beta = \rho - 1$ in the preceding equation returns the following:

$$\Delta y_t = \alpha + \beta y_{t-1} + \delta t + \mu_t$$

The modified version of the ADF test is shown in Equation 11.19:

$$\Delta y_t = \alpha + \beta y_{t-1} + \delta t + \gamma_1 \Delta y_{t-1} + \gamma_2 \Delta y_{t-2} + \ldots + \gamma_k \Delta y_{t-k} + \epsilon_t \qquad \textbf{Equation 11.19}$$

The null hypothesis states that $\beta = 0$. If the absolute value of the test statistic is smaller than the critical value of the τ statistic for β, you do not reject the null hypothesis that $\beta = 0$.

Econometric Models for Time Series Data

Autoregressive Moving Average (ARMA) models are one of the most frequently used time series methods. An ARMA representation is one where a time series is regressed as a function of lagged values of itself, the autoregressive (AR) part, as well as shocks (random errors), which I will describe later. The impact of lagged values of a time series is captured by the autoregressive part of the model, whereas the shocks are captured by the Moving Average part of the model.

Diebold (2001, p. 147) describes the difference between MA and AR processes. "An autoregressive representation has a current shock and lagged observed values of the series on the right, whereas a moving average representation has a current shock and lagged unobserved shocks on the right."

Mathematically, the MA model, as is described by Diebold, is expressed as shown in Equation 11.20:

$$y_t = \epsilon_t + \theta \epsilon_{t-1} \qquad \textbf{Equation 11.20}$$

Again, you assume that $\epsilon_t \sim WN(0, \sigma 2)$. A moving average model of qth order is presented in Equation 11.21:

$$y_t = \epsilon_t + \sum_{i=1}^{q} \theta_i \epsilon_{t-i} \qquad \textbf{Equation 11.21}$$

Thus, in a typical moving-average model (MA) model, we explain the current value of a time series as a function of current and lagged shocks (random shocks), whereas the Autoregressive (AR) model is expressed as shown in Equation 11.22:

$$y_t = \rho y_{t-1} + \epsilon_t \qquad \textbf{Equation 11.22}$$

Correlation Diagnostics

So how do you select the order for an ARMA model? The answer lies, at least partially, with the ACF. Here are some tips. If the ACF for a series does not damp gradually, the series might be non-stationary. Diebold (2001, p.121) argues that all covariance stationary processes have the autocorrelation and partial autocorrelation functions approach zero at large displacements.

Kennedy (1996, p. 260–61) offers some advice on diagnostics.[7] If $\rho(1)$ for the ACF is significantly different from zero, while autocorrelations at higher lags are not significantly different from zero, this indicates an MA(1) process. Similarly if $\rho(1)$ and $\rho(2)$ of the ACF are significantly different from zero, while autocorrelations at higher lags are not significantly different from zero, this suggests an MA(2) process.

The ACF that declines geometrically suggests an AR(1) process, though it could also be an AR(2) process. The ACF that declines geometrically, but reverses sign at each displacement, suggests an AR(1) process with a negative coefficient. If $\rho(1)$ for the ACF is significantly different from zero, but does not display a geometrically declining pattern, it might suggest an ARMA(1,1) process. A significant $\rho(\tau)$ at every twelfth displacement suggests seasonality.

I want to introduce two additional terms: random walk and unit roots. *Random walk*, a concept used widely in finance, is a time series that follows an AR(1) process where the coefficient for AR(1) is not less than 1. Random walk is not covariance stationary. However, if differenced once, that is subtracting the current value from the one observed in the last time period, random walk could be made to comply with stationarity.

The presence of *unit root* is an indicator of non-stationarity. If $\rho = 1$ in Equation 11.22, it suggests the presence of unit roots and an indication of non-stationarity.

You must realize that the ACF of a time series with unit roots will damp extremely slowly. The ACF will return large autocorrelations even at large displacements. On the other hand, the PCF will be close to 1 at displacement 1, and will decay very rapidly for higher displacements.

The ACF for MA(1) should experience a sudden cut-off at $\tau > 1$. By extension therefore, autocorrelations of an MA(q) process are 0 beyond displacement q. If the absolute value of θ is less than 1, the MA (1) process is considered *invertible*, implying that the current value of the series could be expressed in terms of a current shock and a lagged value of the time series. The finite order MA(q) process is similar to MA(1) process in the sense it is covariance stationary for any value of its parameters.

A good starting point therefore is the MA model, which could offer insights for future modeling directions. In other words, if $|\theta| < 1$, we know that the series could be expressed as an AR representation.

Invertible Time Series and Lag Operators

A finite order moving average process is always covariance stationary. However, an AR(1) process is covariance stationary if $|\rho| < 1$. In addition, for a true AR(1) process, the PCF is 0 at displacement greater than 1. The ACF for an AR(1) process might not damp to 0, but it should display a "damped monotonic display" when $\rho > 0$.

The MA(q) process is invertible if the inverses of all the roots are within the unit circle. Unlike MA processes, the AR processes, on the other hand, are always invertible. An AR(p) process is *covariance stationary* only if the "inverses of all roots of the autoregressive lag operator polynomial ... are inside the unit circle" Diebold (2001, p. 158) or as Greene (1997, pp. 829) suggests, the AR process is stationary if roots of the characteristics equation "lie outside the unit circle."[8] We may also check for covariance stationarity if the condition in Equation 11.23 is satisfied:

$$\sum_{i=1}^{p} \rho_i < 1 \quad \textbf{Equation 11.23}$$

The AR(p) process might or might not be stationary if the preceding condition is satisfied; however, it is definitely not stationary if the condition is violated.

For an AR(2) process, the absolute value of ρ_2 should be less than 1. The ACF of an AR(p) process also decays gradually with displacement. Unlike the ACF for an AR(1) process, the ACF for an AR(p) process could have damped oscillations. This is due to the complex roots of the autoregressive polynomial. For AR(1), ACF oscillates only when the coefficient for $\rho < 0$. In addition, the PCF of an AR(p) process declines sharply at displacement p. The PCF of AR(1) process is ρ at $\tau = 1$ and 0 at $\tau > 0$.

To understand how the roots of a lag operator polynomial are calculated, let's look at an alternative lag operator notation for the MA and AR models. A simple MA model is expressed as follows:

$$y_t = \epsilon_t + \theta \epsilon_{t-1}$$

Equation 11.24 shows the lag operator definition.

$$y_t = \left(1 + \theta L\right) \epsilon_t \quad \textbf{Equation 11.24}$$

Here $\theta L \epsilon_t$ is the same as $\theta \epsilon_{t-1}$. Thus (see Equation 11.25),

$$\epsilon_t = \frac{y_t}{1 + \theta L} \quad \textbf{Equation 11.25}$$

Using the lag operator notation, we can redefine the invertibility condition. "The inverse of the root of the moving average lag operator polynomial $(1 + \theta L)$ must be less than 1 in absolute value." The root of the polynomial can be obtained by solving $1 + \theta L = 0$. The root is therefore $L = -\frac{1}{\theta}$, whose inverse is $-\theta$. Thus, if $|\theta| < 1$, we satisfy the invertibility condition.

The MA(q) is invertible only if the inverses of all roots are inside the unit circle. The qth order MA process in lag notation is expressed as follows:

$$y_t = 1 + \sum_{i=1}^{q} \theta_q L^q + \epsilon_t$$

Remember that the AR process is expressed as $y_t = \rho y_{t-1} + \epsilon_t$. Therefore, $\epsilon_t = y_t - \rho y_{t-1}$. The lag notation of the AR process is expressed as shown in Equation 11.26:

$$\epsilon_t = y_t \left(1 - \rho L\right) \quad \text{Equation 11.26}$$

Thus, $y_t = \dfrac{\epsilon_t}{1 - \rho L}$. Conversely, $\rho L y_t = y_t - \epsilon_t$.

The ARMA Model

The AR and MA processes are often combined such that they result in an autoregressive moving-average model, ARMA (p,q). A simple ARMA(1,1) process is expressed as shown in Equation 11.27:

$$y_t = \rho y_{t-1} + \theta \epsilon_{t-1} + \epsilon_t \quad \text{Equation 11.27}$$

Where $\epsilon_t \sim WN(0,\sigma^2)$. Equation 11.28 shows a lag operator polynomial representation of the ARMA (1,1) process:

$$\left(1 - \rho L\right) y_t = \left(1 + \theta L\right) \epsilon_t \quad \text{Equation 11.28}$$

Again, for stationarity, $|\rho| < 1$ should be satisfied, while $|\theta| < 1$ should be satisfied for invertibility. The stationarity of an ARMA process is determined by the AR part of the model. The ACF and PCF of ARMA processes do not cut off at any particular displacement. These functions instead damp gradually.

Autoregressive techniques are preferred because they improve the overall fit of the model and also reduce the mean square error, thus offering a better fit. The estimated coefficients return almost the same values by both OLS and AR techniques. However, the AR model returns higher standard errors for estimators, thus returning lower t-values. As I have demonstrated earlier under the discussion of the Newey–West estimator, using OLS to model a time series with autocorrelation might result in the inclusion of insignificant variables, because such variables will return inflated t-statistics. This limitation is also referred to as Spurious Correlation.

ARIMA Models

If an ARMA (p,q) process has a unit root, the time series needs further massaging before it can be subject to ARMA models. Often, differencing a time series results in satisfying stationarity requirements. This implies that if y_t is not stationary, Δy_t might end up being stationary, where $\Delta y_t = y_t - y_{t-1}$. The differenced time series, when modeled as an ARMA(p,q) process, is known as the Autoregressive Integrated Moving Average (ARIMA) process.

By differencing, the stochastic trend is removed and then a stationary model is fitted to the difference. When the series is differenced once, it is integrated of the order 1 or $I(1)$. If the series requires d differences, it is integrated of the order $I(d)$. The number of unit roots determines the order of integration. Most common difference orders are $I(0)$ and $I(1)$. Hence, random walk is an example of an $I(1)$ process, while White Noise is the simplest $I(0)$ process.

A word about the model notation is in order. ARMA or ARIMA models are often expressed as ARIMA(p,d,q), where p denotes the auto-regressive component, d stands for the order of differencing, and q represents the moving averages. ARIMA(1,0,0) is essentially an AR(1) or an autoregressive model with one lag. Similarly, ARIMA (1,0,1) represents a model for a non-differenced time series (d=0) with one lag each for the autoregressive and the moving average components. ARIMA (1,0,1) can also be expressed as ARMA(1,1). Similarly, ARIMA (1,1,1) represents a model with one lag each for the moving average and autoregressive components, estimated on a differenced time series.

An Autoregressive Integrated Moving Average, ARIMA (p,1,q) is a stationary and invertible process in first differences. In other words, ARIMA (p,d,q) is a stationary and invertible ARMA (p,q) process with d differences. If $d = 0$, it implies that y is covariance stationary or $I(0)$, which implies that the time series is stationary at 1(0).

Because economic time series could be made stationary by differencing, you may model the differenced series as a function of its past differenced values along with current and past errors (shocks).

An ARIMA model with no differencing is an ARMA model. An AR model is also an ARMA model with $q = 0$, while a MA model is an ARMA model with $p = 0$.

Distributed Lag and VAR Models

When a time series is modeled as a function of distributed lags of the explanatory variable, the specification is known as the distributed lag model. Mathematically (see Equation 11.29),

$$y_t = \beta_0 + \sum_{i=0}^{N_x} \delta_i x_{t-i} + \epsilon_t \quad \textbf{Equation 11.29}$$

Note that y_t is a function of distributed lags of past values of x. The coefficients on lagged x's are called Lagged Weights whereas their pattern is called the Lag Distribution. The preceding equation is estimated as an OLS model where lagged values of the dependent variable are not used as regressors. Distributed Lag models may, however, include both contemporaneous and earlier values of regressors (Greene, 1997, p. 781). Diebold (2001, p. 249) argues that "lagged dependent variables absorb residual serial correlation and can dramatically enhance forecasting performance." If you introduce lagged dependent variables in the aforementioned model, you obtain the model shown in Equation 11.30:

$$y_t = \beta_0 + \sum_{i=1}^{N_y} \alpha_i y_{t-i} + \sum_{i=1}^{N_x} \delta_i x_{t-i} + \epsilon_t \quad \textbf{Equation 11.30}$$

Another common multivariate methodology, using the OLS estimation techniques, is *Vector Autoregression* (VAR). The VAR involves a series of equations where a VAR of order *p* involves regressing the left-hand side variables on *p* lags of the dependent variable, and *p* lags of every other explanatory variable(s). The correct number of lags in VAR estimation involves a more in-depth process. Consider the bivariate VAR model (see Equations 11.31 and 11.32):

$$y_{1,t} = \rho_{11} y_{1,t-1} + \rho_{12} y_{2,t-1} + \epsilon_{(1,t)} \quad \textbf{Equation 11.31}$$

$$y_{2,t} = \rho_{21} y_{1,t-1} + \rho_{22} y_{2,t-1} + \epsilon_{(2,t)} \quad \textbf{Equation 11.32}$$

Where $\epsilon_{1,t} \sim WN(0, \sigma_1^2)$ and $\epsilon_{2,t} \sim WN(0, \sigma_2^2)$ and $cov(\epsilon_{1,t}, \epsilon_{2,t}) = \sigma_{12}$

VAR models permit *cross-variable dynamics*. That is, "each variable is related not only to its own past, but also to the past of all other variables in the system" (Diebold, 2001, p. 252). VAR models are also useful in determining causality. Often the causality test (F-Statistics) are used to determine whether the lags of the explanatory variable alone can determine (cause) the independent variable. For example, Diebold (2001) observed that a VAR model of housing starts, using lagged values of housing completions and housing starts (four lags of each) returned insignificant coefficients for housing completions. Another explanation is that completions do not cause starts.

Akaike and Schwartz Information Criteria (AIC and SIC) are the tools used to select appropriate models. These tools are more comprehensive than an ordinary measure of fit, such as R^2. When models are being compared, we select the model that returns the lowest AIC and SIC values. When AIC and SIC do not pick the same model, it has been argued by econometricians that SIC should be used to pick the best model.

The strength of a good model relies on its ability to offer prudent out-of-sample forecasts. While evaluating the out-of-sample forecasts, the key criterion is to see whether the realizations fall within the 95% confidence interval. If the realizations fall within the interval, or better, if the forecast and realizations return similar values, the forecasts are considered reasonably accurate.

Table 11.3 summarizes the key tests used in time series and their interpretation. Also presented are the key terms to be used as a reference in the following section.

Table 11.3   Time Series Tests and Their Interpretation

Type	Test Value	Interpretation
Dickey Fuller test H_0 = the series has a unit root (not stationary). H_1 = the series does not possess a unit root. — Lag specification is a challenge. Some practitioners suggest using the same number of lags as the frequency of the time series; thus four lags for quarterly time series.	`p-value` of `Z(t)` < 0.05	Reject the null hypothesis of a unit root and conclude that the Time Series (TS) is stationary if the value of the Test Statistics is greater than the critical values for Dickey Fuller test. Example: `Z(t)` = `.4065`, we fail to reject the null hypothesis that the unit root exists. TS is NOT stationary. Some researchers mention that the null hypothesis in ADF and PP test is that the TS is I(1). If we fail to reject the null, then we conclude that the time series is I(1).
DFGLS H_0 = the series has a unit root (not stationary). H_1 = the series does not possess a unit root.	τ	The null hypothesis of the test is that TS is a random walk, possibly with drift, I(1). If τ of the DFGLS > the critical value, the null hypothesis of a unit root is rejected. If the computed test statistic is less than the critical value, we fail to reject the null of a unit root and conclude that the TS is I(1).
Phillips-Perron test: H_0 = the series has a unit root (not stationary) H_1 = the series does not possess a unit root	`Z(rho)` or `Z(t)`	The null is that the TS is I(1). If the values of the test statistics (`Z(rho)` or `Z(t)`) are greater than the interpolated Dickey Fuller Test values, reject the null hypothesis of a unit root.
WNtestb, Bartlett's B statistic H_0 = there is no serial correlation H_1 = there is a trend of serial correlation	P > 0.05	We conclude that the process is not different from White Noise.
WNtestq is the same as WNtestb	P < 0.05	We reject the null hypothesis of White Noise and conclude that the TS is significantly different from WN.

Type	Test Value	Interpretation
Autocorrelation Function (ACF)		Helps specifies MA() or q in the p,d,q specification.
		When $\rho(\tau)$ coefficients fall outside of the Bartlett bands, we conclude that $\rho(\tau)$ are significantly different from 0.
		If $\rho(1)$ is significantly different from 0, but others are not, it suggests MA(1). If $\rho(1)$ and $\rho(2)$ are both significantly different from 0, it suggests an MA(2) process.
		If ACF declines geometrically, it suggests AR(1).
		If the ACF declines geometrically, but reverses sign at each displacement, it suggests an AR(1) process with a negative coefficient.
		If $\rho(1)$ is significantly different from zero, but does not display a geometrically declining pattern, it might suggest an ARMA(1,1) process. A significant $\rho(\tau)$ at every twelfth displacement suggests seasonality.
Partial Autocorrelation Function (PCF)		Helps specify AR() or p in p,d,q.
		The PCF of an AR(2) process will have only $\rho(1)$ and $\rho(2)$ different from 0.
		The PCF of MA(2) process will have only $\rho(1)$ and $\rho(2)$ different from 0 with $\rho(2)$ being negative.
Box Ljung	p-value	If the p-value of BL statistics is indistinguishable from 0, it implies that we reject the null hypothesis and conclude that the time series is not White Noise. On the other hand, when the p-value of BL statistics is different from 0, we cannot reject the null hypothesis, and hence conclude that the underlying time series is White Noise.
White Noise		ACF of White Noise is constant at $\tau = 0$, and 0 at $\tau \geq 1$.
		PCF for White Noise is 1 at $\tau = 0$, and 0 at $\tau \geq 1$.
Durbin-Watson		Uncorrelated residuals: $d = 2$
		Positive correlation: $0 < d < 2$
		Negative correlation: $2 < d < 4$

Applying Time Series Tools to Housing Construction

This section illustrates time series concepts using data from my past research on housing and other macroeconomic variables to forecast housing starts for Toronto, Canada's most populous city. Housing starts is the term used to define the start of construction of new housing. When the demand for housing is expected to increase in the future, a sign of a strong economy, the work begins on the construction of new homes (housing starts) months in advance.

The following analysis is based on monthly time series from 1987.03 to 2001.05. Notice that housing starts in Toronto declined in the late eighties and early nineties, only to recover starting in 1996 (see Figure 11.9). The time series therefore has two distinct trends, one declining and the other increasing. I present the Stata code used to generate these graphics.

```
twoway (tsline to_st_to), ytitle(Housing Starts in Toronto) ///
  ttitle(Months) scheme(s2mono)
```

Often, time series data are correlated in time; that is, the value of a variable at time t is correlated with its value at $t-1$. The correlogram (a plot of ACF against displacements) presented in Figure 11.10 reveals that ACF gradually declines at higher displacements, suggesting that the underlying time series could be an auto-regressive process.

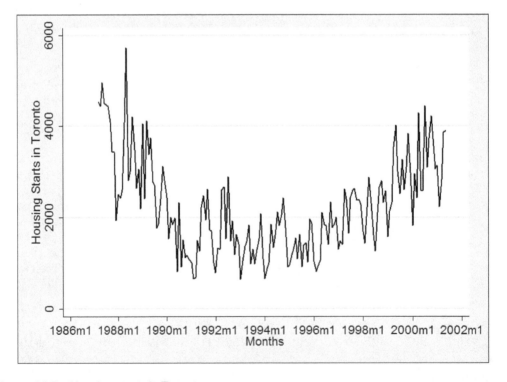

Figure 11.9   Housing starts in Toronto

The PCF plot of housing starts suggests that housing starts are an AR(2) process, as the coefficients of PCF are insignificant at $\tau > 2$ (see Figure 11.11). Interestingly, PCF at $\tau = 13$ and $\tau = 15$ are significantly different from 0, indicating potential annual seasonality in the underlying time series. The ACF in Figure 11.10 also suggests seasonality at $\tau = 12$.

```
ac to_st_to, scheme(s2mono) xlabel(#20) ///
 ytitle(Autocorrelations of Toronto Starts)
pac to_st_to, scheme(s2mono) xlabel(#20) ///
ytitle (Partial autocorrelation of Toronto Starts)
```

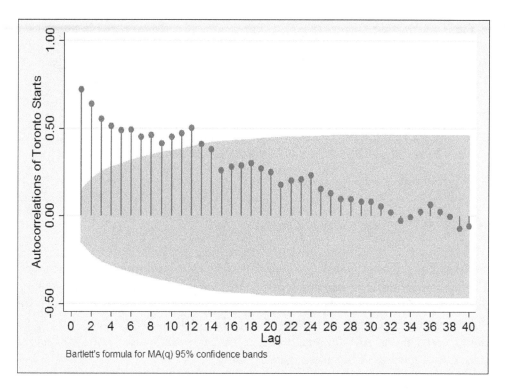

Figure 11.10 ACF of Toronto's housing starts

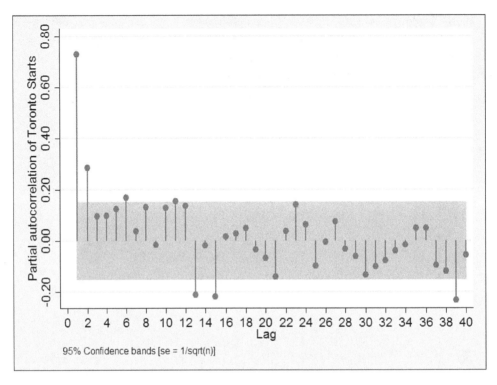

Figure 11.11   PCF of Toronto's housing starts

A breakdown of starts by structural type of housing reveals systematic differences between the correlograms for different housing types—for example, single-family detached and semi-detached housing. Consider that the ACF for the single-detached housing starts declines sharply only to reverse trends at $\tau = 9$ (see Figure 11.12). The ACF peaks again at $\tau = 12$ and again reverses its direction. The ACF for semi-detached starts, however, presents a different picture, in which the starts decline gradually (see Figure 11.13).

```
ac to_st_si, scheme(s2mono) xlabel(#20) ///
ytitle("Autocorrelations of single-family detached" "housing starts")
ac to_st_se, scheme(s2mono) xlabel(#20) ///
ytitle (Autocorrelations of semi-detached housing starts)
```

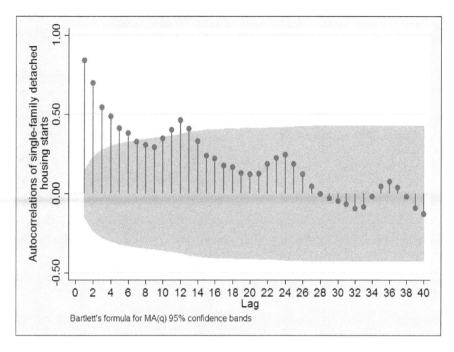

Figure 11.12 ACF of single-family detached housing starts

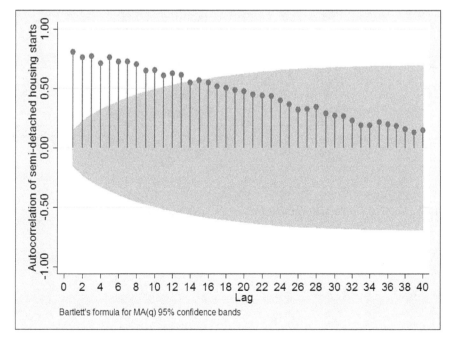

Figure 11.13 ACF of semi-detached housing starts

Related to housing starts is the concept of housing completions, which is the number of new housing units that have been certified to be completed. Housing completions lag by a year or so behind housing starts. The autocorrelation structure of housing completions for detached and semi-detached housing is very similar and these are presented in Figure 11.14 and Figure 11.15, respectively, preceded by the Stata code used to generate these graphics.

```
ac to_com_s, scheme(s2mono) xlabel(#20) ///
ytitle("Autocorrelations of single-family" "detached housing
completions")
ac v30, scheme(s2mono) xlabel(#20) ///
ytitle ("Autocorrelation of semi-detached" "housing completions")
```

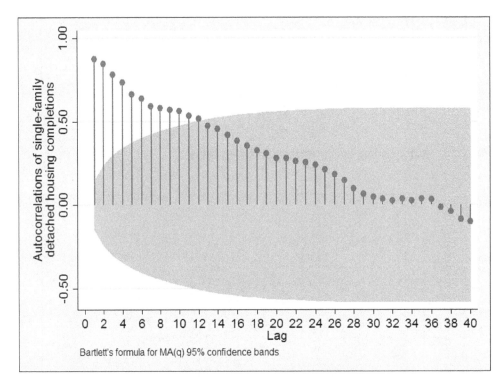

Figure 11.14   ACF of single-family detached housing completions

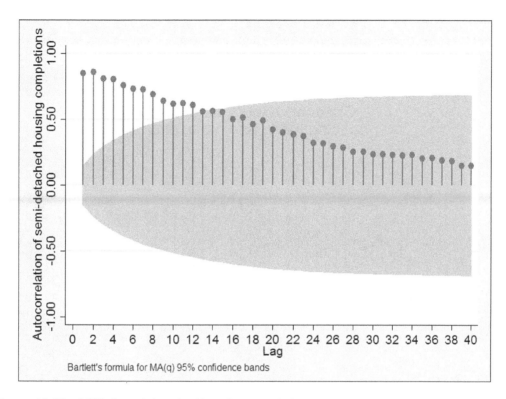

Figure 11.15 ACF of semi-detached housing completions

I used the cross-correlation function to determine the lags at which housing starts and completions are most correlated in the Toronto CMA. Diebold (2001, pp. 260-65) found that housing starts and completions returned high correlations at all lags. However, the contemporaneous correlation at $\tau = 0$, as well as correlations at lags 6 to 9, were very high. This correlation structure suggested that in Diebold's data for the U.S. housing markets, on average, the construction of a single housing unit took 6 to 9 months to complete.

Toronto CMA data return similar results for cross-correlations. Significant positive correlation between housing starts and completions can be observed in Figure 11.16, preceded by the Stata code used to generate it. However, the cross-correlation between starts and completions is most pronounced at $\tau = 0$, and at lags 2 and 3. The cross-correlations indicate that housing starts have the strongest correlations at the three-month lag. The cross-correlations decline for the next few lags and increase again at $\tau = 8$ and 9. This implies that, on average, it takes three to six months to complete the construction of new housing in Toronto. The higher values for cross-correlations at lags 8 and 9 suggest that for some housing types construction takes, on average, 8 to 9 months to complete. Figure 11.16 suggests that completion time in the Toronto housing market is lower than in the U.S. housing market.

```
xcorr to_st_to to_com_t, scheme(s2mono) xlabel(#20) ///
title("Cross-correlogram between" "housing starts and completions") ///
ytitle("Cross correlation")
```

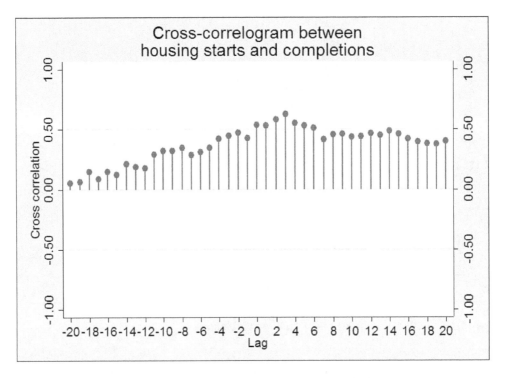

Figure 11.16   Cross-correlation between housing starts and completions

Macro-Economic and Socio-Demographic Variables Influencing Housing Starts

Let us examine the impact of macroeconomic variables on housing starts. Interest and mortgage rates, to name a few, are expected to influence the construction decision of builders. Interest rates represent the cost of borrowing for real estate developers. I can hypothesize that an increase in the interest rates results in fewer starts. The correlogram between interest rates and housing starts, presented in Figure 11.17, suggests a negative correlation between the Bank of Canada rate and housing starts. However, the correlation is small at lower displacements ($\tau < 13$). This implies that changes in the Bank of Canada rate (interest rate) would not have a large impact on contemporaneous housing starts. Similarly, the five-year mortgage rate also suggests small correlation for shorter displacements (see Figure 11.18). The following Stata code generated Figures 11.17 and 11.18.

```
xcorr boc_rate to_st_to, scheme(s2mono) xlabel(#20) ///
title("Cross-correlogram between" "Interest rate and housing starts")
ytitle("Cross correlation")

xcorr v15 to_st_to, scheme(s2mono) xlabel(#20) ///
title("Cross-correlogram between" "5-year mortgage rate and housing
starts") ///
ytitle("Cross correlation")
```

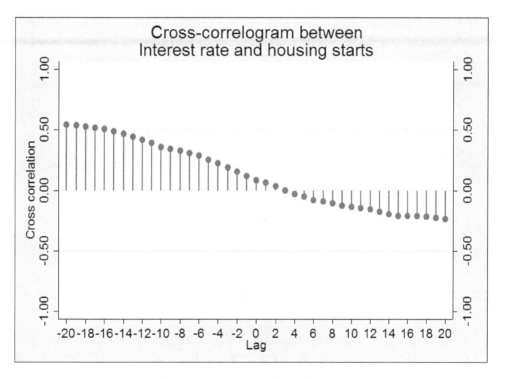

Figure 11.17   Cross-correlation between Bank of Canada rate and housing starts

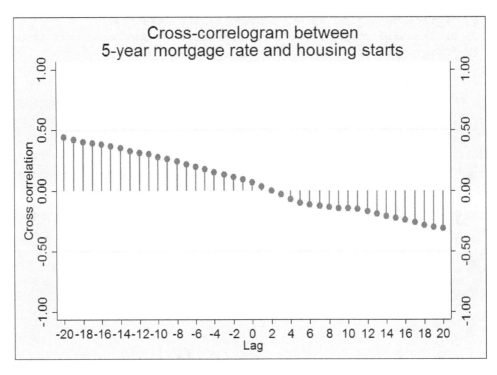

Figure 11.18   Cross-correlation between 5-year mortgage rate and housing starts

Estimating Time Series Models to Forecast New Housing Construction

Here, I apply the knowledge accumulated about time series econometrics in the previous sections. I am interested in forecasting housing starts and will use a time series data set of housing starts from Canada's most populous city, Toronto, for the period 1987.03 to 2001.05. I have other macroeconomic variables for Canada for the same time period. The data sets are available from the website accompanying this book; you can download them in the SPSS, Stata, R, and SAS formats.

Because housing starts are a leading indicator, that is shifts in housing starts are indicative of the forthcoming changes in the larger economy, I am interested in determining trends in housing starts to see whether it is possible to develop foresight into overall macroeconomic activity. Getting the forecast for housing starts right implies that I will be able to approximate upcoming economic trends.

I first employ a series of OLS regression models, and then estimate VAR and distributed lag models. Finally, I estimate the ARIMA and ARMAX models.

OLS Models

The simplest regression model of a time series involves regressing the time series on its lagged values. Thus, I model the housing starts as a function of their first lagged values. In the second model specification, I include yearly dummies for each year starting 1988. In the third model, I include the monthly dummies as well, with the exception of January, which serves as the base case.

Readers can recall the earlier discussion regarding Newey–West estimator to address the issues with autocorrelation and heteroskedasticity. I am reporting the OLS results here and encourage the readers to re-estimate the same model with the Newey–West robust standard errors.

Table 11.4 presents the results.

The first model labeled *reg1* indicates that each start in the last time period results in 0.73 starts in the current time period. The model explains 54% variance in the starts. The second model (*reg2*) includes two lags of housing starts and yearly dummies. Only the first lag is statistically significant. Some yearly dummies are statistically significant while others are not. The model fit (R-squared) increases to 60.7%. The third model (*reg3*) includes monthly dummies as well, which improves the R-squared to 69.3%. The model suggests that compared to January, starts in all other months are higher and in many instances, the monthly coefficients are statistically significant. The following Stata code generated the output reported in Table 11.4.

```
reg to_st_to L1.to_st_to
 est store reg1
 reg to_st_to L1.to_st_to L2.to_st_to i.year_
 est store reg2
 reg to_st_to L1.to_st_to L2.to_st_to i.year_ i.month_
 est store reg3
 est table reg1 reg2 reg3, star stat(N r2_a)
```

Table 11.4 Regression Models of Housing Starts with Lagged Starts and Yearly and Seasonal Dummies

Variable	reg1	reg2	reg3
L1.	.72930382***	.27762999***	.20639668*
L2.		0.06432784	0.16418729
Years			
1988		−325.82666	−231.45337
1989		−510.9544	−403.58581

Variable	reg1	reg2	reg3
1990		−1492.2344***	−1367.9401***
1991		−1425.7143***	−1277.0166***
1992		−1308.0398**	−1167.931**
1993		−1607.7579***	−1452.6248***
1994		−1454.1878***	−1311.8674***
1995		−1534.9041***	−1380.6211***
1996		−1413.5909***	−1270.1691***
1997		−1045.2838**	−911.87381**
1998		−1029.5584**	−901.85243**
1999		−524.70878	−405.10692
2000		−319.25404	−223.60815
2001		−297.66837	−196.62147
Months			
February			53.043864
March			397.56995
April			1067.7549***
May			947.55745***
June			217.75643
July			694.91793**
August			485.64111*
September			674.79926**
October			495.67504*
November			662.26041**

Variable	reg1	reg2	reg3
December			168.82763
Constant	600.4596***	2458.5015***	1780.3458***
N	170	169	169
Adjusted R2	53.6%	60.7%	69.3%

* p<0.05; ** p<0.01; *** p<0.001

Based on the results, I pick the model with the best fit (*reg3*) for further scrutiny. I estimate the residuals from the chosen model and conduct White Noise tests on residuals. Bartlett's periodogram-based test for White Noise returned the `p-value` of 0.3884, which suggests that I fail to find evidence against the hypothesis that residuals are different from White Noise. The other two tests are the variations of the Dickey Fuller test. The Augmented Dickey Fuller test with 12 lags returned the `p-value` of 0.00, suggesting that the residuals are free of a unit root (see Figure 11.19). Similarly, the Generalized Least Squares version of the DF test also suggests that for lags up to 7, the null hypothesis of a unit root is rejected (see Figure 11.20). Thus, the residuals reveal no sign of serial correlation, suggesting that the model used to generate the residuals meets the restrictions for serial correlation.

```
Augmented Dickey-Fuller test for unit root        Number of obs   =      156

                                 ------- Interpolated Dickey-Fuller -------
                    Test         1% Critical      5% Critical      10% Critical
                 Statistic          Value            Value            Value

 Z(t)             -5.051           -3.491           -2.886           -2.576

MacKinnon approximate p-value for Z(t) = 0.0000
```

Figure 11.19 Augmented Dickey Fuller test of unit root for OLS residuals

```
DF-GLS for resmod3                                      Number of obs =    155
Maxlag = 13 chosen by Schwert criterion

              DF-GLS tau      1% Critical      5% Critical     10% Critical
  [lags]    Test Statistic      Value            Value           Value

    13         -1.559          -3.497           -2.798          -2.522
    12         -1.725          -3.497           -2.814          -2.537
    11         -1.719          -3.497           -2.830          -2.551
    10         -1.905          -3.497           -2.845          -2.565
     9         -2.184          -3.497           -2.860          -2.579
     8         -2.578          -3.497           -2.874          -2.592
     7         -2.905          -3.497           -2.888          -2.604
     6         -3.801          -3.497           -2.901          -2.616
     5         -4.170          -3.497           -2.913          -2.628
     4         -4.773          -3.497           -2.925          -2.638
     3         -5.182          -3.497           -2.936          -2.648
     2         -5.826          -3.497           -2.946          -2.657
     1         -7.594          -3.497           -2.955          -2.666

Opt Lag (Ng-Perron seq t) = 13 with RMSE   474.0175
Min SC   =  12.60961 at lag  1 with RMSE   529.6759
Min MAIC =  12.69581 at lag 13 with RMSE   474.0175
```

Figure 11.20   GLS version of Dickey Fuller test of unit root for OLS residuals

The ultimate utility of a regression model is judged from the forecasts generated by the model. The best way to judge this in a time series model is to generate a forecast from the model (reg3) and then plot the forecast along with the actual time series, which I have presented in Figure 11.21. A quick glance suggests that the model is successful in capturing the non-linear nature of the data, such that the initial decline in housing starts from 1988 to 1996 and the subsequent increase are reflected in the forecasted data. Even more interesting is the model's ability to replicate monthly fluctuations. The following Stata code generated Figure 11.21.

```
twoway (tsline to_st_to) (tsline regmod3) , scheme(s2mono) ///
  title("Comparing actual housing starts" ///
  "and forecasted housing starts") ///
  ytitle("Toronto housing starts")
```

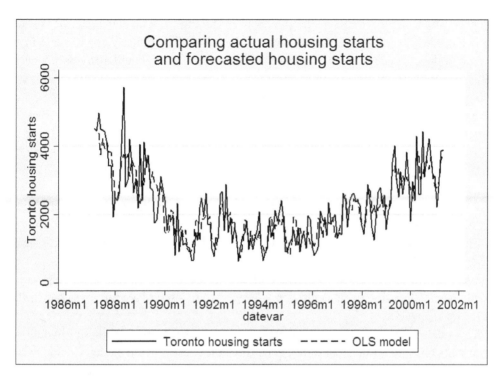

Figure 11.21 Plot of actual and forecasted housing starts

The model fit, statistical significance of coefficients, and the resulting forecasts suggest that the OLS model is quite capable of capturing the non-linear trends in housing starts. The very high R-squared in such models, however, is rather misleading. It has been argued in the literature that when data are detrended and regressed, the resulting R-squared, which is often lower than that for the regular data, is a more realistic depiction of the model fit.

Distributed Lag Model

Now I will model the housing starts as a function of lagged starts and lags of other explanatory variables that are expected theoretically to impact housing starts. Table 11.5 presents the results for three versions of the Distributed Lag models. In the first version (*regmod4*), I model starts as a function of three lagged values of starts. That is, housing starts are being modeled as a function of the number of starts one month earlier, two months earlier, and three months earlier. The underlying assumption is that housing starts are correlated over time and thus starts in earlier periods might influence the starts in the current period.

The same logic is applied to the lagged values of other variables. That is, lagged values of other explanatory variables, such as interest rates, could affect the starts in the current time period. For instance, recent increases in interest rates should increase the cost of borrowing for developers, which might deter some developers from starting work on new projects. This would result in a negative correlation between starts and interest rates. Similarly, the increase in mortgage rates, a direct result of the increase in the base interest rate, should also return a negative correlation with housing starts. Finally, recent returns on the stock exchange in Toronto should also have a negative correlation with starts because increases in stock returns suggest a competitive productive use of capital that might restrict the flow of funds to developers. I test these hypotheses in the following models.

The first model (*regmod4*) in Table 11.5 regresses starts on lagged values of housing starts. Each start in the last month is correlated with 0.47 starts in the current month; starts two month earlier are correlated with 0.23 starts in the current month. The first two lagged variables are statistically significant, while the third lag returned a statistically insignificant coefficient. The model returned an R-squared of 55%.

The second model (*regmod5*) adds three lags each for starts, interest rates, mortgage rates, and average monthly values for the Toronto Stock Exchange index. The first two lags of housing starts returned statistically significant coefficients, whereas all other remaining variables returned statistically insignificant coefficients. The model fit also did not improve upon the fit we observed for *regmod4*.

This model suggests that the explanatory variables that I had hypothesized could affect housing starts failed to do so, at least for the lag structure I tested in the model. Could the lagged housing starts in the model be responsible for the lack of statistical significance of other explanatory variables? It might be possible that the complex dynamics between macroeconomic variables and housing starts are captured by the lagged values of housing starts, thus depriving other explanatory variables of statistical significance. To test this hypothesis, I estimate yet another model (*regmod6*), in which I exclude lagged starts as explanatory variables.

The resulting model reveals that the macroeconomic variables fail to return statistically significant coefficients even when the lagged starts are excluded. Thus, I conclude that *regmod4* represents a better model. I ran the White Noise tests on residuals from the model and failed to find evidence for a unit root. The following Stata code generated the output reported in Table 11.5.

```
reg to_st_to L(1/3).to_st_to
est store regmod4
reg to_st_to L(1/3).to_st_to L(1/3).boc_rate  L(1/3).tse_300
L(1/3).v15
est store regmod5
predict resmod5, residuals
wntestb resmod5, table // p>.05, residuals not different from white
noise
reg to_st_to  L(1/3).boc_rate  L(1/3).tse_300  L(1/3).v15
est store regmod6
est table regmod4 regmod5 regmod6, star stat(N r2_a)
```

Table 11.5   Distributed Lag Models of Housing Starts with Macroeconomic Models

Variable	regmod4	regmod5	regmod6
Starts			
L1.	.47618054***	.43287876***	
L2.	.22755652**	.2103499*	
L3.	0.09672182	0.0726366	
BOC interest rate			
L1.		76.605352	147.72442
L2.		79.041977	91.369272
L3.		−168.23262	−317.1766
TSE 300 index			
L1.		0.03373573	0.14453628
L2.		0.06939732	0.07622826
L3.		−0.01402613	0.11706068
5-year mortgage rate			
L1.		50.514088	296.6055
L2.		−17.338812	78.011558
L3.		18.767477	−52.502231
Constant	431.54661**	−225.64853	−1968.3407*
N	168	168	168
Adjusted R2	54.9%	54.7%	22.2%

* $p<0.05$; ** $p<0.01$; *** $p<0.001$

Out-of-Sample Forecasting with Vector Autoregressive Models

Let me now introduce another concept: out-of-sample forecasting (OOF). I illustrate OOF using the Vector Autoregressive Models (VAR). OOF can be implemented with any regression-type model. The main idea behind OOF is to determine the forecasting capability of the model. Remember, we are interested in making forecasts about future, and not necessarily replicating the results of the past.

Here I use two time series, that is, housing starts and housing completions. I use three lags of both housing starts and housing completions in the model. Housing starts are modeled as a function of three lags each for both housing starts and housing completions. Similarly, housing completions are modeled as a function of three lags each for both starts and completions.

I restrict the estimation of the model to the period starting in 1987.03 and ending in 2000.05. I exclude the last 12 months in the time series data set from estimation. After estimating the model, I will use it to forecast housing starts for the final 12 months, which I did not use to estimate the model.

The resulting model is presented in Table 11.6. Note that the model returns two separate equations, one each for housing starts and completions. The equation for housing starts returned the first and second lag for housing starts as having statistically significant coefficients. Meanwhile, lagged values for housing completions did not return statistically significant coefficients in the housing starts equation. Simply put, the model suggests that housing starts are a function of two lags of housing starts and that housing completions do not affect housing starts.

The equation for housing completions suggests that only two coefficients, that is, the third lag for starts and the third lag for completions, returned statistically significant coefficients. Thus, we see housing completions being influenced by lagged housing starts as well as lagged housing completions, but housing starts did not show any correlation with the lagged values of housing completions.

You can generate forecasts from the VAR model. The results are presented in Figure 11.22. Also plotted in the figure are the actual starts and the forecast from the OLS model. You can see that the actual time series and the OLS forecast stop at 2001.05. However, the forecast from the VAR model offers the OOF forecast. There is, however, a small problem. The VAR forecast does not appear to be terribly accurate, as it slopes down and misses the mark for the time for which data was available. Needless to say, there remains room for improvement. The following Stata code generated the output in Table 11.6.

```
varsoc to_st_to to_com_t
var to_st_to to_com_t if tin(1987m3, 2000m5 )   , lags(1/3)
est store varmod1
est table varmod1, star stat(N aic)

predict resvar1, residuals
 wntestb resvar1, table // p>.05, residuals not different from white
noise
fcast compute f_, step(18)
```

Table 11.6 VAR Model of Housing Starts and Housing Completions

Variable	varmod1
Starts equation	
Starts	
L1.	.46705771***
L2.	.24440427**
L3.	−0.01916128
Completions	
L1.	−0.09210856
L2.	0.1545498
L3.	0.11234812
Constant	265.09043
Completions equation	
Starts	
L1.	0.065623
L2.	0.15784773
L3.	.18210304*
Completions	
L1.	0.13070722
L2.	0.01619801
L3.	.25513056***
Constant	410.91343**
Statistics	
N	156
AIC	4915.3062

The following Stata code generated Figure 11.22.

```
twoway (tsline to_st_to) (tsline regmod3) ///
  (tsline f_to_st_to) if tin(2000m5,), ///
  title("Toronto Starts, Regression, and VAR forecasts") ///
  ytitle("Toronto housing starts")  scheme(s2mono)
```

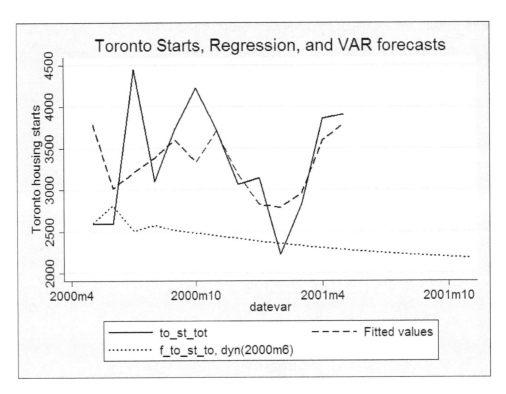

Figure 11.22   Actual starts, OLS and VAR forecasts

ARIMA Models

I finally turn to estimating ARIMA models. The first step involves reviewing the stationarity assumptions for housing starts, by plotting the ACF and PCF for Toronto's housing starts followed by looking at the stationarity tests. I have plotted the ACF and PCF in Figure 11.10 and Figure 11.11, respectively. The ACF declines and approaches 0 at large displacements. The increase in ACF at the twelfth lag suggests seasonality. The PCF returns significant values for the first and second lag only. Based on the correlation diagnostics reviewed earlier, I can assume that the housing starts could be an ARIMA(1,0,1) process because the ACF does not depict a geometrically declining pattern. Because the autocorrelation and partial autocorrelation functions of covariance stationary processes approach zero at large displacements, I can also assume that the starts time series is covariance stationary. The time series might also be an AR(2) process because only $\rho(1)$ and $\rho(2)$ of the PCF are different from 0.

   A good starting point is to estimate ARIMA(1,0,0), ARIMA (1,0,1), ARIMA (2,0,0), and ARIMA (2,0,1) models for the non-differenced starts. Table 11.7 lists the results of these models.

Note that the autoregressive coefficient in the AR(1) model is statistically significant and similar in magnitude (0.74) to the one observed in the OLS model. The estimated standard deviation of the White Noise disturbance is 707. Also included in the table are the AIC and BIC statistics, which are helpful in comparing goodness-of-fit in alternative model specifications. The second model, ARMA(1,1), returns a statistically significant autoregressive coefficient and moving average disturbance. The third model, AR(2), again returns statistically significant coefficients for the autoregressive lags. Finally, the fourth model with two autoregressive lags and one moving average disturbance returns statistically significant coefficients.

To determine a better model of the four presented in Table 11.7, you can compare values of AIC and BIC across the four models such that the model with the lowest values is deemed the best. Based on AIC, I can pick model four, ARMA(2,1) as the one that offers the best fit. Note that the model reports a slightly higher BIC than the one for ARMA(1,1). This suggests that if I were to base my decision on BIC, I could have easily picked ARMA(1,1) as the preferred model.

The following Stata code generated the output reported in Table 11.7.

```
arima to_st_to, arima(1,0,0)
est store ar100
predict ar100, y
label variable ar100 "arima(1,0,0)"

arima to_st_to, arima(1,0,1)
est store ar101
predict ar101, y
label variable ar101 "arima(1,0,1)"

predict resar101, res
wntestb resar101, table // p>.05, residuals not different from white
noise

arima to_st_to, arima(2,0,0)
est store ar200
predict ar200, y
label variable ar200 "arima(2,0,0)"

arima to_st_to, arima(2,0,1)
est store ar201
predict ar201, y
label variable ar201 "arima(2,0,1)"

predict resar201, res
wntestb resar201, table // p>.05, residuals not different from white
noise

est table ar100 ar101 ar200 ar201, star stat(N aic bic ll)
```

Table 11.7   ARMA Models of Non-Differenced Housing Starts

Variable	arima(1,0,0)	arima(1,0,1)	arima(2,0,0)	arima(2,0,1)
Starts				
_cons	2307.3675***	2654.1051***	2382.9915***	2955.633***
ARMA				
Ar				
L1.	.74644501***	.96420344***	.53641651***	1.2551161***
L2.			.29441484***	−.26489241***
Ma				
L1.		−.57393185***		−.80418013***
Sigma				
_cons	707.20792***	664.68014***	676.55837***	654.26761***
Statistics				
N	171	171	171	171
aic	2736.066	2717.4837	2723.1439	2714.3871
bic	2745.491	2730.0504	2735.7106	2730.0954
ll	−1365.033	−1354.7419	−1357.572	−1352.1936

* $p<0.05$; ** $p<0.01$; *** $p<0.001$

The White Noise tests on residuals obtained from both ARMA(1,1) and ARMA(2,1) revealed that they were no different from White Noise.

The next step involves forecasting housing starts from each of the four models and comparing them against the actual time series. This is illustrated using two figures. First, I plot the entire time series starting in March 1987. Later, I take a closer look at the forecast for the last 17 months starting January of 2000 to see how forecasts from each of the four models behave.

Figure 11.23 shows that the forecasts generated by the four models resemble fluctuations in housing starts. The decline in housing starts from 1987 to 1992, the flat starts between 1992 and 1996, and the increase in housing starts starting in 1996 with monthly fluctuations have been captured by all four models. Figure 11.24 zooms into data from January 2000 to May 2001. Again, note that all models capture the time series well. However, you may notice that there remains a lag between the peaks in the actual time series and the peaks generated by the forecasts. Also note that the forecasts generated by the two chosen models, that is, ARMA(1,1) and ARMA(2,1), are very similar, suggesting that you can choose the simpler model, ARMA(1,1), without any loss in prediction capability.

The following Stata code generated Figures 11.23 and 11.24.

```
twoway  (tsline to_st_to) (tsline ar100) (tsline ar101) ///
 (tsline ar200) (tsline ar201), ///
  title("Toronto Starts, ARIMA models") ///
  ytitle("Toronto housing starts")  scheme(s2mono)

twoway  (tsline to_st_to) (tsline ar100) (tsline ar101) ///
 (tsline ar200)  ///
 (tsline ar201) if tin(2000m1, 2001m5), scheme(s2mono) ///
  title("Toronto Starts, ARIMA models") ///
  ytitle("Toronto housing starts")
```

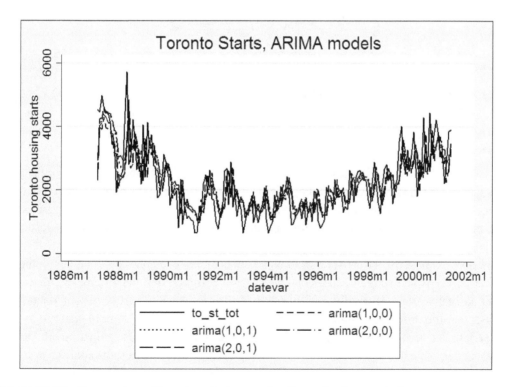

Figure 11.23 Forecasts and housing starts covering the entire time period

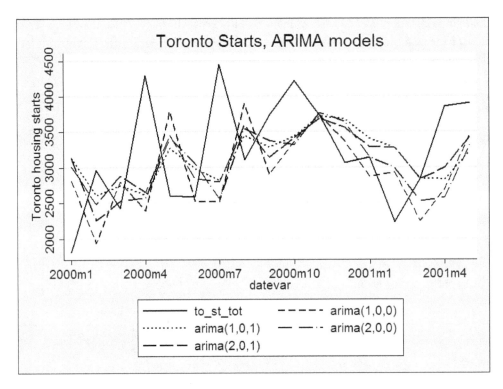

Figure 11.24   Forecasts and housing starts covering the period starting January 2000

Differenced Time Series

The Augmented Dickey Fuller test, as well as the generalized least squares version of the same test, suggests that the housing starts time series is I(1). I fail to reject the null hypothesis of a unit root for both tests, and conclude that the underlying time series is I(1). As a result, I estimate the same models for the differenced time series as I did for the non-differenced series. The results are presented in Table 11.8.

I first estimate the ARIMA(1,1,0), which contains only one autoregressive lag on the differenced series. Note that unlike the actual housing starts time series, the differenced time series returns a negative, yet statistically significant coefficient for the autoregressive component. This suggests that the differenced starts are negatively related with the differenced starts in the last time series. The second model adds a moving average component, thus estimating an ARIMA (1,1,1) model. Note that when I include the moving average disturbances, the coefficient for the autoregressive component returns a positive, yet statistically significant coefficient. The ARIMA (2,1,0) model with two autoregressive coefficients returned both negative, yet statistically significant coefficients, such that the first lag of the differenced time series had a much stronger negative impact (–0.444) than the second lag (–0.15). The final model, ARIMA (2,1,1), included two autoregressive lags and one moving average disturbance. Only the first autoregressive coefficient (positive) was statistically significant, as was the moving average coefficient (negative).

Both AIC and BIC picked ARIMA (1,1,1) as the best fit model. I ran the White Noise test on the residuals from ARIMA(1,1,1), which suggested that the residuals were not different from White Noise.

The following Stata code generated the output reported in Table 11.8.

```
arima to_st_to, arima(1,1,0)
est store ar110
predict ar110, y
label variable ar110 "arima(1,1,0)"

arima to_st_to, arima(1,1,1)
est store ar111
predict ar111, y
label variable ar111 "arima(1,1,1)"

predict resar111, res
wntestb resar111, table // p>.05, residuals not different from white
noise

arima to_st_to, arima(2,1,0)
est store ar210
predict ar210, y
label variable ar210 "arima(2,1,0)"

arima to_st_to, arima(2,1,1)
est store ar211
predict ar211, y
label variable ar211 "arima(2,0,1)"

predict resar211, res
wntestb resar211, table // p>.05, residuals not different from white
noise

est table ar110 ar111 ar210 ar211, star stat(N aic bic ll)
```

Table 11.8 ARIMA Models of Differenced Housing Starts

Variable	arima(1,1,0)	arima(1,1,1)	arima(2,1,0)	arima(2,1,1)
Starts				
_cons	−3.6891899	−5.0714183	−4.583172	−4.7216976
ARMA				
Ar				

Variable	arima(1,1,0)	arima(1,1,1)	arima(2,1,0)	arima(2,1,1)
L1.	−.38258485***	.26899425***	−.44432756***	.27751189***
L2.			−.15964957*	0.07574863
Ma				
L1.		−.81180308***		−.83610947***
Sigma				
_cons	695.79008***	656.4199***	686.77558***	654.96933***
Statistics				
N	170	170	170	170
Aic	2713.9146	2696.6024	2711.5439	2697.8382
Bic	2723.322	2709.1456	2724.0871	2713.5172
Ll	−1353.9573	−1344.3012	−1351.7719	−1343.9191

* $p<0.05$; ** $p<0.01$; *** $p<0.001$

I plot the forecasts from the differenced time series in Figure 11.25 and Figure 11.26. Notice that the models are able to capture long-term trends as well as short-term fluctuations. Figure 11.26 focuses on the last 17 months of the time series and reveals that there is not much marked difference between forecasts obtained from the four models, especially between ARIMA(1,1,1) and ARIMA (2,1,1). At the same time, notice that there is not much difference in the forecasts generated by differenced and non-differenced time series. Because I tested for stationarity in the time series, I favor the use of the differenced time series in the analysis.

The following Stata code generated Figures 11.25 and 11.26.

```
twoway  (tsline to_st_to) (tsline ar110) (tsline ar111) ///
 (tsline ar210) (tsline ar211), scheme (s2mono) ///
  title("Toronto Starts, ARIMA models" "with differenced time series")
///
  ytitle("Toronto housing starts")
```

```
twoway  (tsline to_st_to) (tsline ar110) ///
 (tsline ar111) (tsline ar210)  ///
(tsline ar211) if tin(2000m1, 2001m5), scheme (s2mono) ///
  title("Toronto Starts, ARIMA models" "with differenced time series")
///
  ytitle("Toronto housing starts")
```

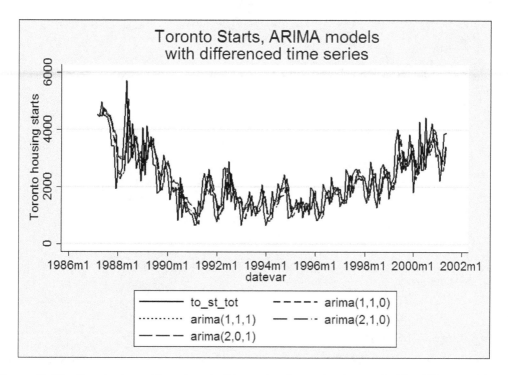

Figure 11.25 Forecasts and housing starts covering the entire time period for differenced time series

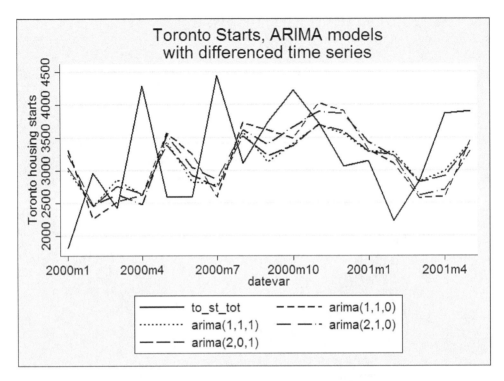

Figure 11.26   Forecasts and housing starts covering the period starting in January 2000 for differenced time series

ARIMA versus OLS Model

Once again, I compare the ARIMA forecasts with the ones obtained from the OLS model. The results are plotted in Figure 11.27. The OLS forecasts are listed as "Fitted values" in the figure. Note that compared to the ARIMA model, the OLS forecasts follow the trends in the time series slightly better. Even though I acknowledge that the ARIMA model is theoretically sounder than the OLS model, you can see here that the forecasts obtained from the two models are quite similar. The Stata code used to generate Figure 11.27 is presented below.

```
twoway  (tsline to_st_to) (tsline regmod3) (tsline ar111)   ///
if tin(2000m1, 2001m5), scheme (s2mono) ///
  title("OLS & ARIMA models" "with differenced time series") ///
  ytitle("Toronto housing starts")
```

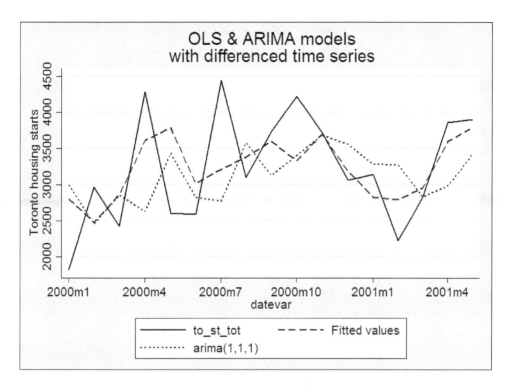

Figure 11.27   Comparing forecasts from the ARIMA(1,1,1) and OLS models

Out-of-Sample Forecasts with ARIMA and OLS Models

In this section, I estimate out-of-sample forecasts for ARIMA and OLS models. For both models, I restrict the estimation to time series starting in March 1987 and ending in May 2000. I exclude the data corresponding to June 2000 through May 2001 from estimation. After I estimate the model, I generate forecasts for the entire time starting in March 1987 and ending in May 2001. The purpose of this exercise is to evaluate the out-of-sample forecasting ability of the model. Figure 11.28 shows the results.

First, note that I have placed a vertical line at May 2000 to indicate the end of the estimation period. Starting in June 2000, the forecasts are for the out-of-sample data. Note again that both ARIMA and the OLS models generate similar forecasts for the period starting in June 2000. In fact, the OLS model offers a better fit for the last few months by following the actual time series much more closely than the forecast generated by the ARIMA model.

I must caution against overfitting in the out-of-sample forecasts. It might happen that the model, instead of describing the underling relationships, describes random noise. This happens when there are numerous explanatory variables and the model is selected based on its performance on the training data, rather than how well it performs for out-of-sample forecasting. The models presented here are rather simple and when they are used to make the out-of-sample forecasts, they have done reasonably well.

The following Stata code generated forecasts that have been plotted in Figure 11.28.

```
arima to_st_to if tin(, 2000m5), arima(1,1,1)
est store arima111_oos
predict arima111_oos, y
label variable arima111_oos "arima(1,1,1) out of sample"

reg to_st_to L1.to_st_to L2.to_st_to i.year_ i.month_ ///
if tin(, 2000m5)
 est store reg3oos
 predict regmod3_oos
 label variable regmod3_oos "Out of sample-OLS"

twoway  (tsline to_st_to) (tsline regmod3_oos) ///
 (tsline arima111_oos)  ///
  if tin(2000m1,), scheme (s2mono) tline(2000m6) ///
  title("OLS & ARIMA models" "with differenced time series" ///
  "out of sample forecasts") ///
  ytitle("Toronto housing starts")
```

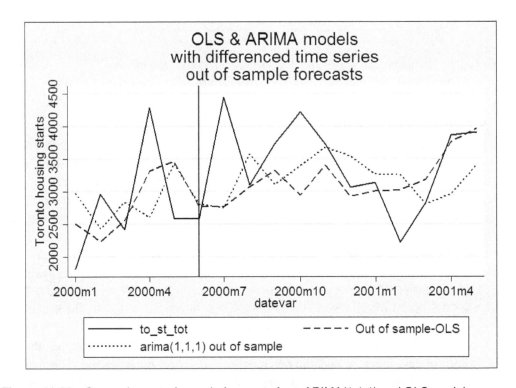

Figure 11.28 Comparing out-of-sample forecasts from ARIMA(1,1,1) and OLS models

ARMAX Model

In this final section of the chapter, I estimate an ARIMA model with exogenous variables. Such models are often referred to as ARMAX models. The exogenous variable chosen is the new housing price index. It is argued that an increase in housing prices in the recent past suggests an increase in demand for new housing, thus encouraging housing builders to start work on additional units, resulting in higher housing starts.

I have estimated three models. The first one is a typical ARIMA(1,1,1) model without any exogenous variables. This is the same model presented earlier in Table 11.8. The second model specification adds six lags of the house price index to the ARIMA(1,1,1) model. The third model adds only one lag of the house price index to the ARIMA(1,1,1) model. The results are presented in Table 11.9.

The ARIMA(1,1,1) model with six lags of the housing price index returned statistically significant coefficients for the autoregressive and moving average components. However, the model returned a statistically significant coefficient for only the first lag of the house price index. I find a positive correlation between the new house price index in the last month and the contemporaneous values for the difference in housing starts. Because the higher order lags of the housing price index are not statistically significant, I exclude them from the estimation in the third model, which results in a statistically insignificant coefficient for the first lag of the housing price index.

Based on the values obtained for AIC and BIC, I pick the model with six lags of the house price index because the lowest AIC and BIC values.

The following Stata code generated the output reported in Table 11.9.

```
arima to_st_to, arima(1,1,1)
est store ar111
arima to_st_to L(1/6).house_in  , arima(1,1,1)
est store arimax111
arima to_st_to L.house_in  , arima(1,1,1)
est store arimax111a
est table  ar111 arimax111 arimax111a, star stat(N aic bic ll)
```

Table 11.9 ARMAX Models of Differenced Housing Starts

Variable	arima(1,1,1)	arimax(1,1,1)	arimax(1,1,1)
Starts			
_cons	–5.0714183	1.1469271	–5.0414985
House price index			
LD.		157.52664***	12.214138
L2D.		–115.9588	

Variable	arima(1,1,1)	arimax(1,1,1)	arimax(1,1,1)
L3D.		–36.935855	
L4D.		101.35863	
L5D.		–74.215428	
L6D.		–29.344328	
ARMA			
Ar			
L1.	.26899425***	.20078623*	.26900895**
Ma			
L1.	–.81180308***	–.86285203***	–.81394685***
Sigma			
_cons	656.4199***	620.73621***	656.87507***
Statistics			
N	170	164	169
Aic	2696.6024	2595.756	2683.0343
Bic	2709.1456	2626.7547	2698.6838
Ll	–1344.3012	–1287.878	–1336.5172

* p<0.05; ** p<0.01; *** p<0.001

Summary

Losing a job during a recession poses great hardships on individuals and their families. Economic recovery, from the unemployed person's perspective, could not come any sooner. Apart from the financial stress, economic hardships take a toll on one's physical health and emotional well-being. When one loses one's livelihood, the recession seems to be the worst ever.

However, economic downturns differ in their magnitude and the aspects of economy they affect the most. Whereas the recession in 2008 is termed the "Great Recession" for the scale and scope of economic devastation it caused, it still did not result in the highest increase in the unemployment rate in the U.S. That distinction belongs to the economic recession in the early eighties when the unemployment rate hit 10.8%. The two recessions that followed were brief and caused fewer job losses.

Figure 11.29 demonstrates the power and utility of the time series analysis. The graphical depiction of time series data allows you to see how the behavior or phenomenon has changed over time. The civilian unemployment rate, shown in Figure 11.29, shows increases during recessions and declines afterward.

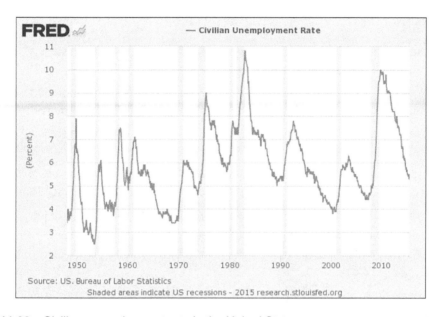

Figure 11.29   Civilian unemployment rate in the United States

This chapter presented discussion on the theory and application of time series analysis. The chapter first discussed the types of time series data and their graphic depiction, and introduced the main distinctive features of time series data: trend, seasonality, autocorrelation, lead, and lags.

In this book, I have recommended the OLS regression as the starting point for empirical analysis. I do the same here and demonstrate the use of OLS model for time series data. The presence of heteroskedasticity and autocorrelation could render the OLS estimate of limited use because of spurious correlation. I demonstrated estimating Newey–West variance estimators that are robust to autocorrelation and heteroskedasticity.

The chapter then presented a detailed description of the theoretical constructs whose understanding is a prerequisite for applying time series econometrics. I introduced White Noise, and stationarity and its tests including Dickey Fuller, ACF, and PCF.

The remaining sections in the chapter concentrated on estimating ARIMA, VAR, and distributed lag models of housing starts in Canada. I presented several parameterizations for the same model and used graphical displays of out-of-sample forecasts, and not merely the goodness-of-fit statistics, such as R-squared or AIC, to select the preferred model.

Mastering time series analysis offers unique advantage to data scientists who will be able to analyze business, economic, environmental, and other data. Given that time series data is reported at regular intervals, as frequently as daily or hourly, data scientists can be instrumental in turning live data feeds into insights.

Endnotes

1. Diebold Francis, X. (2001). *Elements of Forecasting*. South-Western, a division of Thomson Learning, United States of America.

2. Newey, W.K. and K.D. West. (1987). "A simple, positive semi-definite, heteroskedasticity and autocorrelation consistent covariance matrix." *Econometrica 55*: 703–708.

3. Box, George and Jenkins, Gwilym (1970). *Time series analysis: Forecasting and control*. San Francisco: Holden-Day.

4. Mendenhall, W., Sincich, T., and Boudreau, N.S. (1996). *A second course in statistics: regression analysis* (Vol. 5). Upper Saddle River, New Jersey: Prentice Hall.

5. Gujarati, D.N. (1995). *Basic Econometrics,* New York: McGraw-Hill. Inc.

   Bartlett, M.S. (1946). "On the Theoretical Specification and Sampling Properties of Autocorrelated Time-Series." Supplement to the *Journal of the Royal Statistical Society, 8*(1), 27–41.

6. Ljung, G.M. and Box, G.E.P. (1978). "On a Measure of a Lack of Fit in Time Series Models." *Biometrika 65* (2): 297–303.

7. Kennedy, P. (1996). *A Guide to Econometrics*. MIT Press.

8. Greene, W.H. (1997). *Econometric Analysis*. 5th. ed. Upper Saddle River, New Jersey.

CHAPTER 12

Data Mining for Gold

Does an extramarital affair lead to heartbreak? A brief answer is yes. A detailed response hints at more than one heartbreak. Typically, the faithful spouse is the one with the broken heart when an affair is discovered. However, the cheating spouse must also brace for a heart break, literally. New research shows that the cheating spouse faces a higher risk of heart-related ailments than the faithful spouse does, and this is not all. The sexual prowess of the paramour (the third leg in the relationship stool) determines largely the extent of the cardiac discomfort to the cheating spouse. Research shows that the odds for a cheating spouse facing a Major Adverse Cardiovascular Event (MACE) are high when the paramour depicts a strong sexual desire. Some, perhaps many, would still consider an affair worth the risk; the heart wants what the heart wants.

Ray C. Fair in 1978 published the seminal work on the economics of extramarital affairs.[1] Since then, several studies have tried to determine why spouses have an affair or, more importantly, how prevalent affairs are among the married cohorts. Research in economics, sociology, and, as of late, in epidemiology has explored the dynamics of extramarital affairs. Of course, religious texts in the Abrahamic traditions have something to contribute on this matter. *Thou shalt not covet thy neighbor's wife* has been a part of the religious doctrine. Sexual transgressions have been looked on unfavorably by the religious establishment of all persuasions. In some religions, the consequences could be more drastic. For instance, under the strictest interpretation of the Islamic jurisprudence, a married Muslim man found guilty of fornication could be sentenced to death by stoning. The risks indeed are not just to the heart, but also to life!

This chapter focuses on *data mining*, which is a term to describe a collection of statistical and machine-learning algorithms for discovering trends and patterns in data. Machine-learning algorithms are unique in that they analyze data while learning from data, and in the process modify the algorithm for improved analysis. I subject data from Professor Fair's research to data mining algorithms to determine what traits correlate with extramarital affairs (Fair, 1978). In particular, I would like to determine the impact of individuals' religious beliefs on their propensity to engage in extramarital affairs. We already know that the Abrahamic traditions abhor a little extra indulgence. In this chapter, you will learn to determine:

- Whether those who take the gospel seriously are less or more likely to indulge in an extramarital affair
- Whether individuals satisfied with their marriage are less likely to have an affair
- Whether the duration of marriage or presence of young children influence the likelihood of one having an extramarital affair
- Whether men and women differ in the propensity to have an extramarital affair

Can Cheating on Your Spouse Kill You?

Extramarital affairs are as old as the institution of marriage. However, the narrative around affairs has been contextualized in religious interpretations. As a result, the nomenclature of extramarital affairs includes terms such as *cheating, unfaithful, heartbreak,* and *sin.* If that was not enough, the epidemiologists joined the fray by suggesting higher risks of heart ailments for unfaithful spouses.

The fact remains that most, if not all, societies attach a great premium to fidelity. Marriage is no exception. However, in spite of almost universal support for fidelity, we know that affairs do happen. What we do not know with certainty is the prevalence of affairs. The low estimates put the number below 5%. In an unpublished paper, Michael and others (1993),[2] cited in Smith (2006), estimated that in a given year, 3%–4% of the currently married people had sex with a partner beside their spouse. They further estimated that about 15% to 18% of ever-married people have had a sexual partner other than their spouse while married."[3]

Anderson (2006) reviewed 67 studies on paternity conflicts to conclude that approximately 1.9% of the men who were highly confident of being the father were not the biological father of the child.[4] These men were ignorant of the fine details related to the paternity of the children they were raising as their own.

While the religious discourse on extramarital affairs has existed for several millennia, the literature on the cardiac well-being of those who cheat is recent. Fisher and others (2011) found a deleterious effect of extramarital affairs on the cardiovascular system. More than 8% of the respondents (married men) in their survey reported a stable secondary relationship. A follow up a few years later revealed 95 incidences of Major Adverse Cardiovascular Events (MACE), of which eight were fatal. They found that men whose paramours did not experience a lack or absence of sexual desire were more likely to experience MACE. Put differently, "infidelity induces not only heart trouble in the betrayed partners, but seems to be also able to increase the betrayer's heart-related events," noted Fisher and others.

Are Cheating Men Alpha Males?

Some research suggests that the men who cheat are psycho-biologically inclined to do so. The cheating males report significantly higher "testosterone levels and testis volume," a lower prevalence of lack of sexual desire and erectile dysfunction (Fisher et. al., 2012).[5] In fact, some research suggests that the characteristics common among cheating males are similar to those that qualify one as an alpha male. "As unfaithful subject seems to be an alpha male, a sort of super hero, with a better hormonal milieu and better vascular function." Should women then be concerned about the fidelity of their alpha male partners?

When we dig deep into data, we realize that those who cheated on their spouses were in fact more likely to suffer from cardiovascular disease (CVD). At the beginning of the study, Fisher and others observed that the married men who reported a secondary stable relationship were about two times more likely to be suffering from a CVD. Could it be true that the men engaging in extramarital affairs were predisposed to CVD, and the causal effect of extramarital affair on CVD might not hold true?

UnFair Comments: New Evidence Critiques Fair's Research

Since the publication of Fair's analysis, some researchers, equipped with advanced statistical methods, have revisited the study. In particular, they question Fair's findings about the effect of duration of marriage on the likelihood of having an extramarital affair. Fair found that the likelihood of an extramarital affair increases with the duration of marriage. Li and Racine (2004), using a different statistical method, concluded that the duration of marriage, in the presence of other covariates, was not a statistical predictor for individuals' likelihood of engaging in extramarital affairs.[6]

Fair (1978) used two data sets that produced slightly different results. Of particular interest is the finding that the likelihood of an extramarital affair was higher for professionals than it was for blue-collar workers. At the same time, the likelihood was found to decline with education. Because both education and professional status are essentially proxies for income, the two variables returned counterintuitive results. This prompted Ian Smith (2012) to revisit the question with new data sets.[7] He concluded that higher socioeconomic status resulted in a greater likelihood for extramarital affairs. At the same time, college education was found to be negatively correlated with extramarital affairs when the occupation status was held constant.

Before applying the data mining algorithms to Fair's data set, I offer a brief introduction of select data mining concepts and apply them to Fair's data set and another data set on precipitation/weather.

Data Mining: An Introduction

Data mining applications have become increasingly numerous with the advent of big data, inexpensive computing, and efficient data storage platforms. Both the struggling and thriving retailers have turned to data mining to learn more about their customers' habits and preferences to expand sales and minimize costs. Advanced algorithms can do a good job of predicting consumer needs.

Banks and financial institutions use data mining algorithms to identify fraudulent transactions. If you own a major credit card, you might have, at some point in the past, received a call from the financial institution inquiring about your recent transactions, which were flagged by their data mining algorithms as purchases unlikely to have been made by you. Even before you realized that your credit card had been fraudulently used by others, your financial institution intervened to prevent further losses from taking place.

At times, the analytics might venture too far afield such that individuals may feel their privacy is being breached. The infamous incident at a Target store in Minneapolis serves as a good example. Andrew Pole, a statistician working for the retail chain, developed a maternity prediction model by analyzing the recent purchases made by women. A year after the model was in operation, an angry father walked into the Target store in Minneapolis and showed manager coupons and clippings about baby formula, cribs, and pregnancy clothes the retail chain had sent to his teenage daughter. He was furious with the retailer whom he thought was trying to encourage his teenage daughter to become pregnant. A few weeks later, though, the father became aware of his daughter's pregnancy, which had been kept from him. What the father didn't know, Target did.[8]

The question then emerges about how much of predictive analytics is of benefit to society. Using the same data mining tools, insurance companies can refuse to enroll individuals who might be predisposed to diseases that could require expensive treatments. Even if one were ignorant of one's likelihood of becoming ill, advanced algorithms can predict the likelihood of one's future well-being from purchases and genetic predispositions. Such advanced analytics could serve to benefit individuals and societies by alerting those predisposed to future illnesses. For instance, Angelina Jolie, a leading Hollywood actress, has undergone proactive surgeries to remove tissues that could have caused cancer in the future.[9] She did so because her genetic makeup predicted the likelihood of her becoming ill in the future. Yet, low-income individuals, who often have no or inadequate health insurance, could be denied health insurance later because analytics might predict their odds for higher insurance claims.

There is, though, a limit to what data mining could reveal. Despite the advances being made in statistical analysis and algorithms, predictive analytics is still far from being a perfect science. While Target could identify a pregnant teenager, much sooner than her father did, it still did not prevent the same retailer from losing billions of dollars in Canada. In January 2015, the giant retailer suddenly disclosed several billion dollars in losses after operating in Canada for less than two years. Target could not be profitable for another six years and thus decided to close the 133 stores in Canada.[10]

What went wrong at Target? A lot. However, the most important thing to remember is that no amount of analytics and predictive modeling can come even close to replacing sound business management and execution. Generating insights from analytics and data mining is one thing; executing the plan efficiently is completely another.

Let's begin with the discussion of what is meant by *data mining*. There are two divergent approaches to data mining. One is the traditionalist approach of considering data mining synonymous to statistical analysis. The other group insists that it differs from the traditional statistical analysis approach and leans toward unsupervised, machine-learning algorithms. I consider both approaches correct. The debate is somewhat superficial because it focuses on methods rather than the objectives. Data mining should be taken at its face value: an attempt to explore hitherto unknown trends and insights by subjecting data to analysis. The search for the "models" hidden in the data should not be restricted to certain methods.

Statistical methods rely on probability distributions whereas machine-learning methods are based on algorithms. Ultimately, the two approaches help us learn new facts about the phenomenon we study. The methods used should be flexible enough for us to discover not only what we are searching for, but also trends and facts that might not be on our radar. The known unknowns are rather easier to find than the unknown unknowns. Data mining should be equally good for both.

Seven Steps Down the Data Mine

Ultimately, we analyze data to gain insights that could help us with smart decision-making. Fong and others (2002) offer a seven-step approach to data mining to support smart decisions.[11] These are the following:

1. Establish data mining goals
2. Select data
3. Preprocess data
4. Transform data
5. Store data
6. Mine data
7. Evaluate data mining results

The sections that follow describe the seven steps in more detail.

Establishing Data Mining Goals

The first step in data mining requires you to set up goals for the exercise. Obviously, you must identify the key questions that need to be answered. However, going beyond identifying the key questions are the concerns about the costs and benefits of the exercise. Furthermore, you must determine, in advance, the expected level of accuracy and usefulness of the results obtained from data mining. If money were no object, you could throw as many funds as necessary to get the answers required. However, the cost benefit trade-off is always instrumental in determining the goals and scope of the data mining exercise. The level of the accuracy expected from the results also influences the costs. High levels of accuracy from data mining would cost more and vice versa. Furthermore, beyond a certain level of accuracy, you do not gain much from the exercise, given the diminishing returns. Thus, the cost benefit trade-offs for the desired level of accuracy are important considerations for data mining goals.

Selecting Data

The output of a data mining exercise largely depends upon the quality of data being used. At times, data are readily available for further processing. For instance, retailers often possess large databases of customer purchases and demographics. On the other hand, data may not be readily available for data mining. In such cases, you must identify other sources of data or even plan new data collection initiatives, including surveys. The type of data, its size, and frequency of collection have a direct bearing on the cost of data mining exercise. Therefore, identifying the right kind of data needed for data mining that could answer the questions at reasonable costs is critical.

Preprocessing Data

Preprocessing data is an important step in data mining. Often raw data are messy, containing erroneous or irrelevant data. In addition, even with relevant data, information is sometimes missing. In the preprocessing stage, you identify the irrelevant attributes of data and expunge such attributes from further consideration. At the same time, identifying the erroneous aspects of the data set and flagging them as such is necessary. For instance, human error might lead to inadvertent merging or incorrect parsing of information between columns. Data should be subject to checks to ensure integrity. Lastly, you must develop a formal method of dealing with missing data and determine whether the data are missing randomly or systematically.

If the data were missing randomly, a simple set of solutions would suffice. However, when data are missing in a systematic way, you must determine the impact of missing data on the results. For instance, a particular subset of individuals in a large data set may have refused to disclose their income. Findings relying on an individual's income as an input would exclude details of those individuals whose income was not reported. This would lead to systematic biases in the analysis. Therefore, you must consider in advance if observations or variables containing missing data be excluded from the entire analysis or parts of it.

Transforming Data

After the relevant attributes of data have been retained, the next step is to determine the appropriate format in which data must be stored. An important consideration in data mining is to reduce the number of attributes needed to explain the phenomena. This may require transforming data. Data reduction algorithms, such as Principal Component Analysis (demonstrated and explained later in the chapter), can reduce the number of attributes without a significant loss in information. In addition, variables may need to be transformed to help explain the phenomenon being studied. For instance, an individual's income may be recorded in the data set as wage income; income from other sources, such as rental properties; support payments from the government, and the like. Aggregating income from all sources will develop a representative indicator for the individual income.

Often you need to transform variables from one type to another. It may be prudent to transform the continuous variable for income into a categorical variable where each record in the database is identified as low, medium, and high-income individual. This could help capture the non-linearities in the underlying behaviors.

Storing Data

The transformed data must be stored in a format that makes it conducive for data mining. The data must be stored in a format that gives unrestricted and immediate read/write privileges to the data scientist. During data mining, new variables are created, which are written back to the original database, which is why the data storage scheme should facilitate efficiently reading from and writing to the database. It is also important to store data on servers or storage media that keeps the data secure and also prevents the data mining algorithm from unnecessarily searching for pieces of data scattered on different servers or storage media. Data safety and privacy should be a prime concern for storing data.

Mining Data

After data is appropriately processed, transformed, and stored, it is subject to data mining. This step covers data analysis methods, including parametric and non-parametric methods, and machine-learning algorithms. A good starting point for data mining is data visualization. Multi-dimensional views of the data using the advanced graphing capabilities of data mining software are very helpful in developing a preliminary understanding of the trends hidden in the data set.

Later sections in this chapter detail data mining algorithms and methods.

Evaluating Mining Results

After results have been extracted from data mining, you do a formal evaluation of the results. Formal evaluation could include testing the predictive capabilities of the models on observed data to see how effective and efficient the algorithms have been in reproducing data. This is known as an *in-sample forecast*. In addition, the results are shared with the key stakeholders for feedback, which is then incorporated in the later iterations of data mining to improve the process.

Data mining and evaluating the results becomes an iterative process such that the analysts use better and improved algorithms to improve the quality of results generated in light of the feedback received from the key stakeholders.

Rattle Your Data

In this section, I illustrate data mining concepts using a specialized Graphical User Interface (GUI) for data mining, Rattle, that runs the algorithms programmed in R. This chapter differs from others in the book because here I rely on the point-and-click functionality of the GUI, whereas in other chapters I displayed the command line interface for R and other software.

Graham Williams is the programmer behind Rattle. He has authored a book, *Data Mining with Rattle and R: The Art of Excavating Data for Knowledge Discovery*, which explains the functionality of Rattle.[12] I strongly recommend the text for those interested in applied data mining. Rattle can be installed free from within R. Details on installation and other supporting materials are available from the Graham Williams at http://www.togaware.com/.

Rattle has been designed with data mining in mind. After the GUI is up and running, a series of tabs laid out in sequence from left to right appears (see Figure 12.1). Note that the first tab, **Data**, offers options to import data in Rattle from a variety of data formats. Other options available from the **Data** tab include partitioning the data for estimation and testing purposes. Partitioning of data allows analysts to estimate the model using a subset of the data and then apply the model to the unused part of the data to test how well the model performs for "out-of-sample" forecasting. The same tab displays a data dictionary offering details about variable names and type (continuous or numeric versus categorical) and options for identifying the dependent variable as "Target," and excluding variables using the "Ignore" option. The tab identifies how many unique values are in a particular variable. You can also change the type of the Target variable.

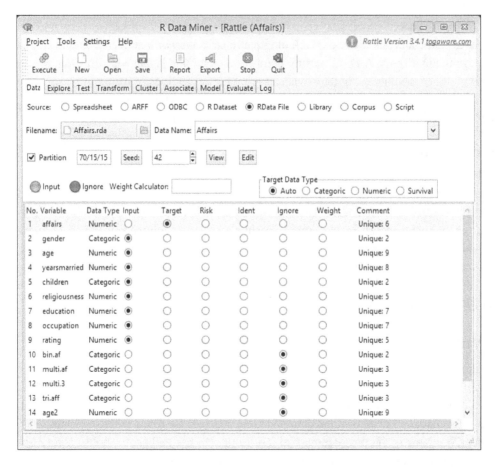

Figure 12.1   Rattle graphical user interface displaying data attributes for the affairs data set

Rattle follows a logical order to data mining. After the data has been imported into Rattle and converted to R's native format, the next step involves exploring the data set using the `Explore` tab. This could entail reporting summary statistics and generating insightful charts. Afterward, the analyst may want to test the relationship between variables using statistical tests, which are available from the `Test` tab. At this stage, the data scientist might want to transform variables to see whether different types of tests could be conducted. Data transformation options are available under the `Transform` tab. The following three tabs, `Cluster`, `Associate`, and `Model`, offer functionality for advanced data mining methods. The last tab, `Log`, maintains a sequential log of the commands executed in the session. You can download the log file to edit it for reproducing the work later.

To launch Rattle, I first launch R and type:

```
library(rattle)
rattle()
```

As mentioned earlier, Rattle launches in the `Data` tab. If I were to click the `Execute` button, Rattle would offer the option to launch the practice data set. Otherwise, you can opt to select your own data. I illustrate the data mining concepts using the Affairs data set, which you can download from the book's website at www.ibmpressbooks.com/title/9780133991024.[13]

Also note that in the case where Rattle requires a particular package that does not exist in your R library, it will offer the option and instructions to download the package and then proceed with installation and subsequently the analysis.

What Does Religiosity Have to Do with Extramarital Affairs?

In this section, I illustrate the use of data mining techniques using one of the data sets analyzed by Ray C. Fair in 1978. Remember, you can download the data from the course's website from the material listed under Chapter 12. Table 12.1 describes the data set.

Table 12.1 Affairs Data Set

Variable	Description	Values
affairs	How often have you engaged in extramarital sexual intercourse during the past year?	0=none, 1 = once, 2 = twice, 3 = three times, 7 = 4 to 10 times, 12 = more than 10 times
gender	Sex of the respondent	0 = female, 1 = male
age	Age of the respondent	17.5 = under 20, 22.0 = 20–24, 27.0 = 25–29, 32.0 = 30–34, 37.0 = 35–39, 42.0 = 40–44, 47.0 = 45–49, 52.0 = 50–54, 57.0 = 55 or over

Variable	Description	Values
yearsmarried	No. of years married	0.125 = 3 months or less, 0.417 = 4–6 months, 0.75 = 6 months–1 year, 1.5 = 1–2 years, 4.0 = 3–5 years, 7.0 = 6–8 years, 10.0 = 9–11 years, 15 = 12 years or more
children	Presence of children, categorical	0 = no, 1 = yes
religiousness	How religious are you?	5 = very, 4 = somewhat, 3 = slightly, 2 = not at all, 1 = anti-religion
education	Level of education	9.0 = grade school, 12.0 = high school graduate, 14.0 =some college, 16.0 = college graduate, 17.0 = some graduate work, 18.0 = master's degree, 20.0 = Ph.D., M.D., or other advanced degree
occupation	Occupation	1–7, according to Hollingshead classification (reverse numbering)
rating	How do you rate your marriage?	5 = very happy, 4 = happier than average, 3 = average, 2 = somewhat unhappy, 1 = very unhappy
bin.af	Binary indicator of affairs	0 = none, 1 = at least once

You move from the **Data** tab to the **Explore** tab to compute summary statistics for the selected variables by selecting the **Summary** radio button, again checking the **Summary** box in the options listed, and clicking the **Execute** button to run the command. Figure 12.2 shows the results. These results are similar to the one obtained by R's Summary command. Note that frequency tabulation is presented for categorical variables (gender) and mean and other distributional statistics are presented for continuous variables. Also, note that the data set treats education, occupation, rating, religiousness, yearsmarried, and affairs as continuous variables. However, these could also be treated as factor or discrete variables.

Figure 12.2 Summary statistics using the `Explore` tab

Cross-tabulations are also available under **Summary**. Running a cross tabulation between gender and affairs produces the output shown in Figure 12.3. Note that the output presents the count, the expected count, the chi-square contribution, and values presented as a percent of the row, column, and table total. Thus, you can see that 77% of the females compared to 72.7% of the males reported having no affair. At the same time, the same proportion of males and females (6.3%) reported having more than 10 affairs in the past 12 months. I can also report from Figure 12.3 that 53.9% of those who did not report an affair were women in the sample.

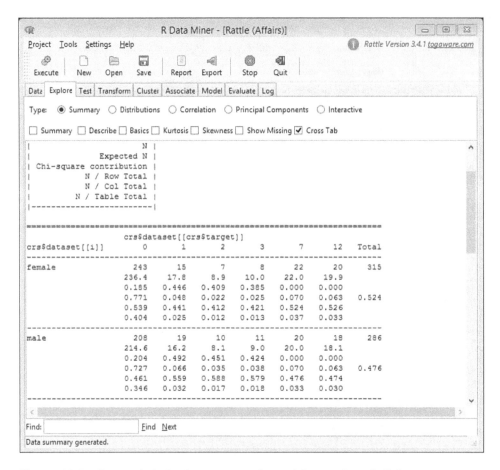

Figure 12.3   Cross tabulation between gender and the number of affair

The **Explore** tab offers comprehensive functionality for presenting results as graphics. To activate graphing capabilities you click on the **Distributions** radio button. You can select the number of plots to be presented on the same page. A different set of plots are available for continuous and categorical variables. Figure 12.4 shows selections for four plots per page and four variables for histograms. Figure 12.5 shows the resulting histograms.

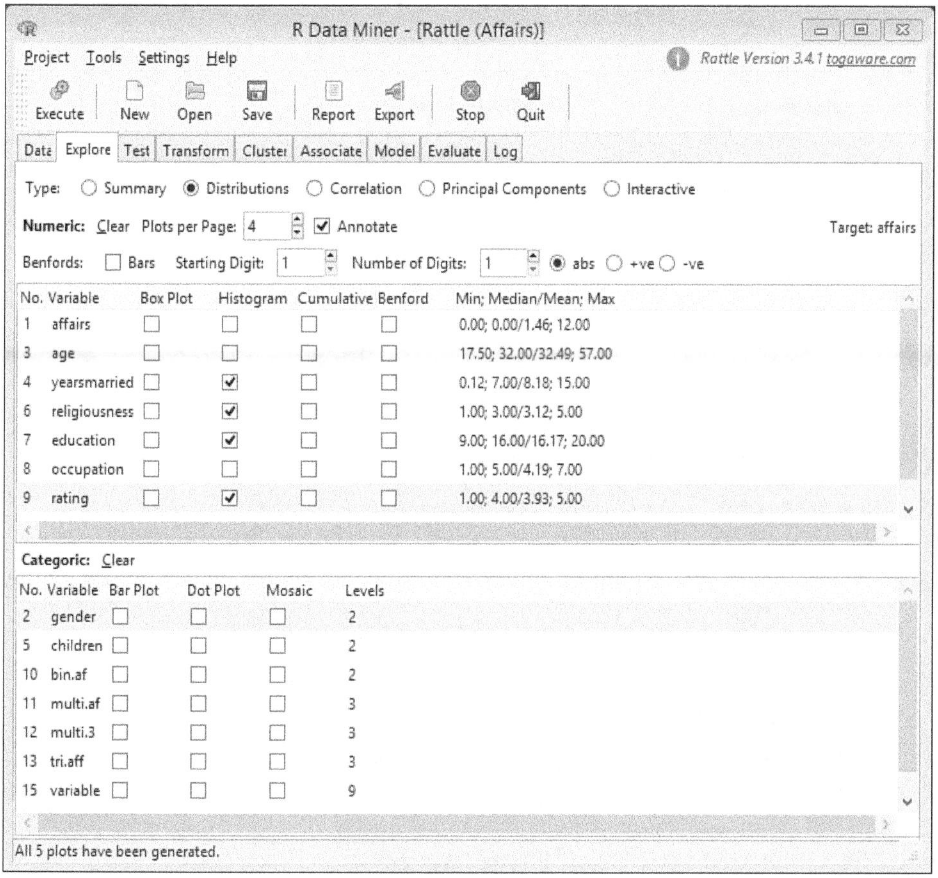

Figure 12.4   Dialog box for generating graphics

The histogram in the top-left corner presents the distribution of yearsmarried. The most frequently occurring cohort comprises those married for 12 years or more. The histogram for religiousness indicates that anti-religion individuals constituted a small minority in the data set. Most respondents report to be either somewhat or very religious. The distribution of education variable suggests that "some college education" was the most frequent response. At the same time, a majority of the respondents reported at least a college degree. Lastly, most respondents were happy or very happy with their marriage, as is evident from the histogram in the bottom-right quadrant in Figure 12.5.

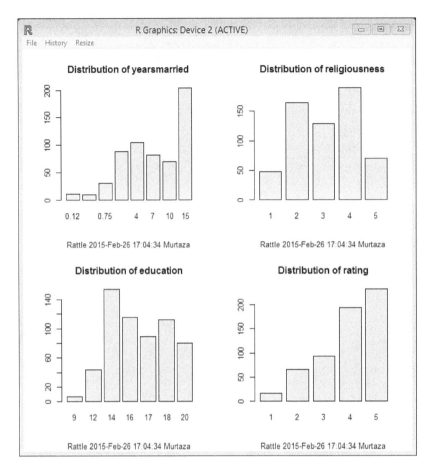

Figure 12.5   Histograms plotted for four continuous variables

R's unique graphing capabilities are also available with Rattle. The traditional approach to explore correlation between variables is to generate a correlation matrix depicting the Pearson correlation statistics. R and Rattle can do better. The correlation matrix can instead be presented as a graphic. Figure 12.6 shows the correlation matrix for select variables. The upward sloping lines running along the diagonal represent the perfect correlation between the variable with itself. The white circles and ovals represent weak or no correlation between variables. The downward sloping, gray shaded ovals represent negative correlation. The shades become darker and the shapes become narrower corresponding to the strength of correlation. Positive correlation is represented by upward sloping gray shaded ovals. R by default differentiates negative and positive correlations with different colors.

A negative and strong correlation exists between `affairs` and marriage satisfaction `rating`, which is represented by a downward sloping, dark shaded oval. The lighter shade and wider shapes for the correlation between `affairs` and `religiousness/education` implies that a relatively weaker correlation exists between these variables. Occupation type, `age`, and the duration of marriage do not report strong correlation with affairs. At the same time, a strong positive correlation exists between age and years of marriage. Similarly, a negative correlation exists between duration of marriage and satisfaction with the respondents' marriage.

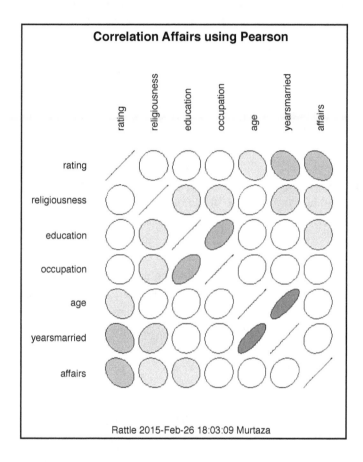

Figure 12.6   A graphical distribution of the correlation matrix

The Principal Components of an Extramarital Affair

Working with a data set with not only a very large number of records, but also a large number of attributes or variables is quite common now. Furthermore, it may happen that several variables may serve as proxies for a phenomenon that could not be readily measured, such as aptitude. Such situations might require two interventions: reducing the number of variables being used in the analysis and computing one or more new variables from the existing variables that essentially serve as proxies for the hard-to-measure variable. Data scientists can turn to Principal Component Analysis (PCA) for this task.

Essentially, PCA generates a new set of variables called *principal components* or eigenvectors that explain almost all variance explained by the original variables. The first eigenvector is the one that explains the most variance in the data set. This implies that no possible combination of original variables will be able to explain more of the total variance. The subsequent eigenvectors are in descending order of their ability to explain the total variance. Each eigenvector is a linear function that resembles a regression model, minus the intercept.

Assume that we perform PCA on 10 variables, which were normalized to mean = 0, and variance =1. Let's assume that the total variance explained by the first eigenvector is 4.0. Because the total number of variables is 10, we can calculate $\frac{4}{10}$ * 100 to conclude that the first eigenvector explains 40% of the variance in the data set. Stated otherwise, the first eigenvector explained as much variance as the four original variables in the data set did.

The amount of the total variance explained by an eigenvector is known as *eigenvalue*. The subsequent eigenvectors maximize the amount of remaining variance. This implies that the variance explained by the second or subsequent eigenvectors is independent of, or uncorrelated with, the first eigenvector. This allows us to add the variance of the eigenvectors to determine how much variance is explained cumulatively by the eigenvectors. We can also say that eigenvectors are orthogonal to each other. The number of eigenvectors required to explain the total variance is called *rank*.

Because PCA is considered a data reduction technique, having an idea about how many eigenvectors to use might be useful. Replacing the variables with as many eigenvectors will defeat the very purpose of using data reduction strategies. Data scientists might want to use as many eigenvectors as are needed to satisfy an arbitrary threshold for explaining variance, such as 75%.

Interpreting the eigenvectors may at times be difficult. You can try interpreting them by reviewing the *factor loading coefficients*, which are similar to the coefficients estimated by the regression models for the corresponding variables. The coefficients report the correlation between a given eigenvector and the corresponding variable. The correlation could be either positive or negative. The informal general rule is to consider a factor loading of 0.3 or more as substantial. A factor loading of 0.3 suggests that the variable and the eigenvector share 9% (0.3^2 * 100) of their variance.

For additional details on PCA, consult Jolliffe (2014).[14]

Will It Rain Tomorrow? Using PCA For Weather Forecasting

Because PCA is suited for continuous variables, let's now turn to the weather data set that comes bundled with the Rattle GUI. Recall that most variables in the affairs data set are categorical and hence not suited for PCA. This example shows running PCA on 14 variables that report atmospheric conditions, such as temperature, humidity, wind speed, evaporation, sunshine, and the like. The data set is readily available from within the R environment. You can learn more about the data set from within R and Rattle. I have made it available from the book's website in other software formats. Figure 12.7 presents the first 10 eigenvectors and the factor loadings corresponding to the 14 variables.

```
Standard deviations:
 [1] 2.32370291 1.71664235 1.45924716 0.95749026 0.88578420 0.69076645
 [7] 0.62745524 0.57667520 0.53588625 0.46020102 0.26482728 0.16654962
[13] 0.13129391 0.07251371

Rotation:
                    PC1          PC2          PC3          PC4          PC5
MinTemp       0.35308104 -0.028357602  0.30967084 -0.24390336  0.07055162
MaxTemp       0.37469699  0.238590201  0.11790366  0.02604696 -0.00972905
Rainfall      0.02053868 -0.246898869  0.28301079  0.31613763  0.81319923
Evaporation   0.35371388  0.060823527  0.02998295 -0.18767793 -0.03192073
Sunshine      0.18538724  0.232662107 -0.38473909  0.42823065  0.23560624
WindGustSpeed 0.19569293 -0.354868628 -0.26797247 -0.03812817 -0.08834745
WindSpeed9am  0.09559703 -0.398784400 -0.19249157 -0.37376528  0.28167411
WindSpeed3pm  0.07608490 -0.360757785 -0.39502423  0.04530430 -0.08035079
Humidity9am  -0.23000433 -0.009884399  0.42183352  0.31082248 -0.17140780
Humidity3pm  -0.19610442 -0.316882263  0.38048582 -0.25218282 -0.07591668
Pressure9am  -0.25809858  0.372252977 -0.12574676 -0.33322377  0.21837523
Pressure3pm  -0.27710236  0.313141305 -0.12582767 -0.38999438  0.31314539
Temp9am       0.38928834  0.045404145  0.17773561 -0.23068134  0.04969064
Temp3pm       0.36810840  0.263002037  0.10163804  0.03903992 -0.01195254
                    PC6          PC7          PC8          PC9         PC10
MinTemp      -0.02767775  0.18454209 -0.05571908 -0.150570334  0.15045378
MaxTemp      -0.15705116  0.16971008 -0.09814325  0.059161317 -0.07670736
Rainfall     -0.18568315 -0.20530279  0.00208020  0.038057391 -0.12700600
Evaporation  -0.04304457 -0.51939590  0.65102234 -0.256536430  0.21980492
Sunshine      0.19841179  0.20053991 -0.03337688 -0.034484202  0.66073977
WindGustSpeed -0.48127016  0.13509898  0.23659480  0.651996752  0.11102937
WindSpeed9am  0.42717780  0.48531308  0.25282575 -0.126533563 -0.11000160
WindSpeed3pm -0.47649487 -0.01984322 -0.27262915 -0.625771998 -0.01364947
Humidity9am  -0.27631440  0.51901760  0.42316075 -0.253982915  0.08967124
Humidity3pm  -0.01719493 -0.09179942 -0.27166294  0.072813073  0.63712246
Pressure9am  -0.30811086  0.09156320  0.01196196  0.006728314  0.04763456
Pressure3pm  -0.24942886  0.08055238  0.07151669 -0.050541878  0.10892989
Temp9am      -0.05686402  0.08589532 -0.32522436 -0.006442928  0.01205378
Temp3pm      -0.14385923  0.17542498 -0.06477545  0.015120171 -0.13265621
```

Figure 12.7 Output from PCA, factor loadings

What is more interesting is the proportion of variance explained by each eigenvector. Figure 12.8 shows the results. Note the first eigenvector explains 38.5% of the variance. Together, the first six eigenvectors, PC1 to PC6 represent 90.3% variance that was explained by the 14 original variables. You can substitute these eigenvectors instead of the original variables. The added advantage is that these eigenvectors are not correlated, which implies that by using the eigenvectors as explanatory variables in a regression model, you would not need to be concerned with issues related with multicollinearity.

```
Importance of components:
                          PC1     PC2     PC3     PC4     PC5     PC6     PC7
Standard deviation     2.3237  1.7166  1.4592 0.95749 0.88578 0.69077 0.62746
Proportion of Variance 0.3857  0.2105  0.1521 0.06548 0.05604 0.03408 0.02812
Cumulative Proportion  0.3857  0.5962  0.7483 0.81376 0.86980 0.90389 0.93201
                          PC8     PC9    PC10    PC11    PC12    PC13    PC14
Standard deviation     0.57668 0.53589 0.46020 0.26483 0.16655 0.13129 0.07251
Proportion of Variance 0.02375 0.02051 0.01513 0.00501 0.00198 0.00123 0.00038
Cumulative Proportion  0.95576 0.97627 0.99140 0.99641 0.99839 0.99962 1.00000
```

Figure 12.8 Proportion of variance explained by eigenvectors

Do Men Have More Affairs Than Females?

The `Test` tab provides options to conduct several statistical tests. Assuming that the `affairs` variable is continuous, in this example I conduct a `t-test` to determine whether men on average have more affairs than women do. Figure 12.9 presents the results, where x represents women and y represents men. The t-statistics of -0.2873 suggests that the average number of affairs do not differ statistically between men and women. The output presents results for equal and unequal variances. In addition, the `p-value` for the three possible outcomes, namely equal, less than, and greater than, are also reported.

```
Test Results:
  PARAMETER:
    x Observations: 315
    y Observations: 286
   mu: 0
  SAMPLE ESTIMATES:
    Mean of x: 1.419
    Mean of y: 1.4965
    Var  of x: 10.9512
    Var  of y: 10.8403
  STATISTIC:
                 T: -0.2873
    T | Equal Var: -0.2873
  P VALUE:
    Alternative Two-Sided: 0.774
    Alternative      Less: 0.387
    Alternative   Greater: 0.613
    Alternative Two-Sided | Equal Var: 0.774
    Alternative      Less | Equal Var: 0.387
    Alternative   Greater | Equal Var: 0.613
  CONFIDENCE INTERVAL:
    Two-Sided: -0.6069, 0.452
         Less: -Inf, 0.3666
      Greater: -0.5216, Inf
    Two-Sided | Equal Var: -0.607, 0.4521
         Less | Equal Var: -Inf, 0.3667
      Greater | Equal Var: -0.5217, Inf
```

Figure 12.9   `t-test` to test whether men on average have more affairs than women do

Two Kinds of People: Those Who Have Affairs, and Those Who Don't

Robert Benchley, an American humorist once said, "There are two kinds of people in the world, those who believe there are two kinds of people in the world, and those who don't." I also believe that the universe of married individuals can be divided into two groups: those who have extra-marital affairs and those who do not. The challenge is to determine how to divide the married populations into two or more groups.

The reality is that when it comes to marital infidelity, there are more than two groups or clusters of people. Fortunately, data mining offers several options to cluster observations into homogenous groups. One such technique, and not necessarily the best, is the K-means clustering. For additional details, see Everitt & Hothorn (2011, page 175).[15] The clustering options are available under the `Cluster` tab in Rattle.

To illustrate the clustering example, I select a subset of variables from the **Cluster** tab. I want to know what kind of demographic and other attributes are correlated with the propensity to have affairs. Using the options available in the dialog box, I select five clusters so that each observation in the data set belongs to one of the five clusters. Figure 12.10 presents the results.

```
Cluster sizes:

[1] "82 27 95 75 141"

Data means:

      affairs           age  yearsmarried religiousness     education
   1.338095238  32.752380952    8.305559524   3.133333333  16.154761905
    occupation          rating
   4.252380952    3.921428571

Cluster centers:

         affairs          age yearsmarried religiousness    education   occupation
1 0.6707317073 21.89024390   1.931414634     2.817073171  15.07317073  3.890243902
2 9.9629629630 38.29629630  14.259259259     2.814814815  16.85185185  4.666666667
3 0.3894736842 35.21052632  12.038157895     3.389473684  16.44210526  4.315789474
4 0.8400000000 48.33333333  14.786666667     3.653333333  16.09333333  4.573333333
5 0.9787234043 28.06382979   4.910170213     2.929078014  16.48936170  4.170212766
        rating
1 4.439024390
2 3.148148148
3 3.831578947
4 3.706666667
5 3.943262411

Within cluster sum of squares:

[1] 1308.606409 1162.666667 3311.358882 4080.560000 3864.717512
```

Figure 12.10   K-mean clustering of affairs data

The output is structured as follows. Cluster sizes report the number of observations belonging to each cluster. The largest cluster contains 141 observations, and the smallest 27 observations. The output also produces the average values for each variable such that the average number of affairs is 1.3 and the average age is 32.75. The third set of output reports the average statistics for each cluster. The second cluster reports the highest average value of affairs at 9.96. Individuals falling in the affair-happy category have an average age of 38.3 years, average marriage duration of 14.3 years, and average religiosity of 2.81. At the same time, individuals belonging to this cluster rate their marriages much lower than respondents belonging to other clusters.

Cluster 3 reports the lowest average value for affairs at 0.39. Note that the average religiousness for these individuals is 3.38, which is also the second highest average value for religiousness for any cluster. Thus, we can see that individuals clustered together depicting the lowest propensity for affairs also report a higher degree of religiousness.

To view the output from the clustering algorithm as a graphic, see Figure 12.11, which shows the five clusters scattered in a two-dimensional space. You can see that observations belonging to a particular cluster are bunched together.

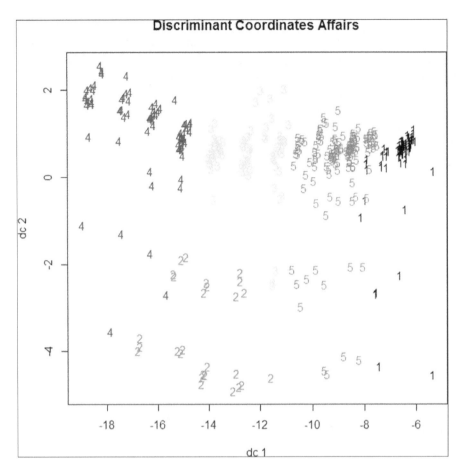

Figure 12.11   Graphical display of clusters

Models to Mine Data with Rattle

Rattle offers a variety of modeling alternatives under the **Model** tab (see Figure 12.12). This section covers two commonly used data mining algorithms, namely Decision Trees and Neural Networks.

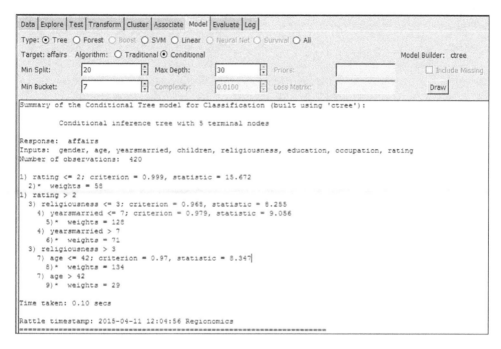

Figure 12.12 Modeling options available with Rattle

Applying Decision Trees to the Affairs Data

Rattle fits Decision Trees using binary recursive partitioning. The data are successively partitioned for explanatory variables such that two groups emerge around a certain threshold for the variable. One group contains observations below the threshold and the other above the threshold. The splitting continues until a variable is unable to partition data given the homogeneity in the remaining observations. For additional details on decision trees, you can review Quinlan (1986).[16]

I apply the Decision Trees model to the Affairs data. The dependent variable is `affairs`. I use the Conditional option for Decision Trees. The output in Rattle identifies the dependent and explanatory variables along with the empirical output for the nodes in the estimated Decision Tree (see Figure 12.13). Clicking **Draw** presents the results graphically.

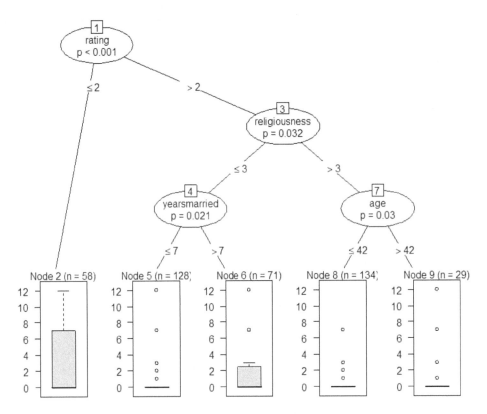

Figure 12.13   Decision Tree output for the Affairs data set

The first node in Figure 12.13 splits the data along the `rating` variable such that those who were not satisfied with their marriage and rated it less than or equal to two fall under one category and those who were satisfied with their marriage and rated it greater than two fall in a separate category. Those who are unsatisfied with their marriage are not further categorized by other variables. For them the results are presented in Node 2 that contains 58 respondents with the average number of affairs reported above six. Thus, we can see that satisfaction with one's marriage is an important determinant of extramarital affairs.

Those who rank their marriage for two or more see another split along `religiousness`. Those who are less religious and ranked religiosity to be less than or equal to three fall into one group and the rest in the other. Those who are more religious are further subdivided along `age` into two groups; that is, less than 42 years old and greater than 42 years old. The two nodes under age do not appear to differ much. However, there is greater dispersion in the number of affairs under Node 9 than under Node 8.

Those respondents who are less religious are further split along the duration of marriage. Those with a the marriage duration of more than 7 years have relatively higher value for reported affairs than those whose marriage duration was less than 7 years.

From the Decision Tree in Figure 12.13, you can conclude the following. The most important determinant for having an affair is how one rates one's marriage. Those who are less satisfied with their marriage are more likely to have extramarital affairs than those satisfied with their marriage. Also, those who are more religious are less likely to have an extramarital affair. Furthermore, those who are less religious and have been married for more than seven years are also likely to have extramarital affairs.

Neural Networks of Extramarital Affairs

Neural Networks are also a very popular data-mining tool. These are commonly regarded as a black box tool because you can specify the inputs and evaluate the outputs from the model, yet be limited in appreciating the inner workings of the model. Still, Neural Networks have gained a greater acceptance as a data-mining tool in the recent past. For additional details on Neural Networks I recommend Rojas (2013).[17]

This example uses the binary variable bin.af as the dependent variable and other sociodemographic characteristics as explanatory variables. Figure 12.14 shows the output from the Neural Network model.

How well is the Neural Network model performing? It is hard to tell from the output in Figure 12.14. The output does not report any goodness of fit statistics for you to know how good the model fits or what explanatory variables are good predictors of the dependent variable.

```
Summary of the Neural Net model (built using nnet):

A 8-10-1 network with 109 weights.
Inputs: gender[T.male], age, yearsmarried, children[T.yes], religiousness,
Output: as.factor(bin.af).
Sum of Squares Residuals: 57.5511.

Neural Network build options: skip-layer connections; entropy fitting.

In the following table:
   b   represents the bias associated with a node
   h1  represents hidden layer node 1
   i1  represents input node 1 (i.e., input variable 1)
   o   represents the output node

Weights for node h1:
  b->h1   i1->h1  i2->h1  i3->h1  i4->h1  i5->h1  i6->h1  i7->h1  i8->h1
 -92.70 -108.47   17.45  -87.00   -2.86    4.81   37.08   85.93  -49.65

Weights for node h2:
  b->h2   i1->h2  i2->h2  i3->h2  i4->h2  i5->h2  i6->h2  i7->h2  i8->h2
  95.89    43.51   48.07  -36.07  -88.23   31.11  -72.19   43.05 -165.40

Weights for node h3:
  b->h3   i1->h3  i2->h3  i3->h3  i4->h3  i5->h3  i6->h3  i7->h3  i8->h3
  -0.55     0.24   -1.12   -0.19   -0.09   -0.26    0.09   -0.12   -0.09
```

Figure 12.14   Output from the Neural Network model

The preferred way of evaluating the performance of a Neural Networks model is to see how accurately it has predicted the outcome. At the same time, I also estimate a binary logit model with the same inputs for comparing the outputs from the two modeling approaches. Figure 12.15 shows the output from the binary logit model.

Figure 12.15 shows that three statistically significant variables are duration of marriage, respondent's religiousness, and marriage satisfaction. The output shows that the odds for an affair increase with the duration of marriage, but decline with religiousness and marital bliss. Also, the overall model fit, presented as the pseudo R-square, is 0.27. Please consult Chapter 8 for details on how to interpret a binary logit model.

```
Summary of the Logistic Regression model (built using glm):

Call:
glm(formula = bin.af ~ ., family = binomial(link = "logit"),
    data = crs$dataset[crs$train, c(crs$input, crs$target)])

Deviance Residuals:
      Min        1Q      Median         3Q        Max
-1.3941916  -0.7440647  -0.5710893  -0.3774581   2.3643077

Coefficients:
                  Estimate  Std. Error  z value  Pr(>|z|)
(Intercept)     0.35434324  1.08376605  0.32696  0.7437016
gender[T.male]  0.22229082  0.29007103  0.76633  0.4434786
age            -0.02780817  0.02148740 -1.29416  0.1956095
yearsmarried    0.08436824  0.04054208  2.08100  0.0374335 *
children[T.yes] 0.28532584  0.36801239  0.77532  0.4381530
religiousness  -0.29771249  0.10663703 -2.79183  0.0052411 **
education       0.04333895  0.06113238  0.70894  0.4783642
occupation     -0.03175150  0.08639606 -0.36751  0.7132379
rating         -0.35938284  0.11003579 -3.26605  0.0010906 **
---
Signif. codes:  0 '***' 0.001 '**' 0.01 '*' 0.05 '.' 0.1 ' ' 1

(Dispersion parameter for binomial family taken to be 1)

    Null deviance: 453.95663  on 419  degrees of freedom
Residual deviance: 422.41722  on 411  degrees of freedom
AIC: 440.41722

Number of Fisher Scoring iterations: 4

Log likelihood: -211.209 (9 df)
Null/Residual deviance difference: 31.539 (8 df)
Chi-square p-value: 0.00004630
Pseudo R-Square (optimistic): 0.27184724
```

Figure 12.15   Output from a binary logit model for the dichotomous variable, `bin.af`

The `Evaluate` tab in Rattle offers the functionality to test how good the model has fitted to the data and is able to predict incorporating the unused segment of the data set that was set aside for validation purposes. Figure 12.16 presents the results.

```
Error matrix for the Linear model on Affairs [validate] (counts):

        Predicted
Actual  0  1
    0  64  0
    1  22  4

Error matrix for the Linear model on Affairs [validate] (proportions):

        Predicted
Actual    0    1 Error
    0  0.71 0.00  0.00
    1  0.24 0.04  0.85

Overall error: 0.2444444444, Averaged class error: 0.1279069767

Rattle timestamp: 2015-04-11 09:04:04 Regionomics
=================================================================
Error matrix for the Neural Net model on Affairs [validate] (counts):

        Predicted
Actual  0  1
    0  55  9
    1  23  3

Error matrix for the Neural Net model on Affairs [validate] (proportion

        Predicted
Actual    0    1 Error
    0  0.61 0.10  0.14
    1  0.26 0.03  0.88

Overall error: 0.3555555556, Averaged class error: 0.5224358974

Rattle timestamp: 2015-04-11 09:04:04 Regionomics
=================================================================
```

Figure 12.16   Error matrix for Neural Network and binary logit models

The first set of results in Figure 12.16 corresponds to the binary logit model where a 2×2 matrix of actual and predicted observations is presented. The binary logit model has done a good job of correctly categorizing all respondents who did not have an affair. However, the binary logit model erroneously categorized 22 out of the 26 respondents who had an affair as ones who did not have an affair. The overall error is reported as 0.244.

The output from the Neural Networks model is shown in the bottom part of Figure 12.16. The Neural Networks model wrongly categorizes 9 out of 64 respondents who did not have an affair. The neutral network model was equally poor as the binary logit model in categorizing those who had an affair. The overall error reported for the neural network model is higher than that for the binary logit model.

This comparison shows that machine-learning algorithms might not necessarily outperform the traditional parametric models. At the same time, the added advantage of using parametric models is that you can learn from the inner workings of the model, which is not possible with the black box approaches.

Summary

The discourse in this chapter is intended only to be an introduction to the rich and rapidly evolving field of data mining. The topics covered constitute a very small subset of techniques and models being used for data mining purposes today.

Over the next few years, data mining algorithms are likely to experience a revolution. The availability of large data sets, inexpensive data storage capabilities, and advances in computing platforms are all set to change the way we go about data analysis. It is quite possible that the contents of this chapter will be dated in the next few years, or perhaps months. Such a rapid pace of development and innovation holds great promise for data scientists. The advances in computing and storage are also making analytics less expensive and the open source platforms are democratizing the landscape such that talented individuals scattered across the globe will have the opportunity to put their talents to work using the open source tools.

I am confident that with big and small data, advances in computing, and open source platforms, the analytics community will break new ground in finding cures for diseases and devising strategies to achieve a more equitable world where resources and riches are shared among all.

Endnotes

1. Fair, R. C. (1978). "A theory of extramarital affairs." *The Journal of Political Economy*, 45–61.

2. Michael, R. T., Laumann, E. O., and Gagnon, J. H. (1993). *The Number of Sexual Partners in the U.S.*

3. Smith, T. W. (2006). *American Sexual Behavior: Trends, Socio-Demographic Differences, and Risk Behavior.* GSS Topical Report No. 25. National Opinion Research Center, University of Chicago.

4. Anderson, K. G. (2006). How Well Does Paternity Confidence Match Actual Paternity? Evidence from Worldwide Nonpaternity Rates. *Current Anthropology*, *47*(3), 513–520.

5. Fisher, A. D., Bandini, E., Corona, G., and Monami, M. (2012). Stable extramarital affairs are breaking the heart. *International Journal of Andrology*, *35*(1), 11–17.

6. Li, Q. I. and Racine, J. (2004). "Predictor relevance and extramarital affairs." *Journal of Applied Economics*, *19*(4), 533–535.

7. Smith, I. (2012). "Reinterpreting the economics of extramarital affairs." *Review of Economics of the Household*, *10*(3), 319–343.

8. Duhigg, C. (2012, February 16). How Companies Learn Your Secrets. *The New York Times*. Retrieved from http://www.nytimes.com/2012/02/19/magazine/shopping-habits.html.

9. Pitt, A. J. (2015, March 24). Angelina Jolie Pitt: Diary of a Surgery. *The New York Times*. Retrieved from http://www.nytimes.com/2015/03/24/opinion/angelina-jolie-pitt-diary-of-a-surgery.html.

10. Shaw, H. (2015, January 15). Target Corp to exit Canada after racking up billions in losses. *The Financial Post*. Retrieved from http://business.financialpost.com/news/retail-marketing/target-corp-calls-it-quits-in-canada-plans-fair-and-orderly-exit.

11. Fong, A. C. M., Hui, S. C., and Jha, G. (2002). "Data mining for decision support." *IT Professional, 4*(2), 9–17. http://doi.org/10.1109/MITP.2002.1000455

12. Williams, G. (2011). *Data mining with Rattle and R: the art of excavating data for knowledge discovery*. Springer Science & Business Media.

13. https://sites.google.com/site/econometriks/

14. Jolliffe, I. (2014). "Principal Component Analysis." In *Wiley Stats Ref: Statistics Reference Online*. John Wiley & Sons, Ltd.

15. Everitt, B. and Hothorn, T. (2011). *An introduction to applied multivariate analysis with R*. Springer Science & Business Media.

16. Quinlan, J. R. (1986). "Induction of Decision Trees." *Machine Learning, 1*(1), 81–106.

17. Rojas, R. (2013). *Neural networks: a systematic introduction*. Springer Science & Business Media.

Index

CPSIA information can be obtained
at www.ICGtesting.com
Printed in the USA
LVHW040755180219
607863LV00015B/542/P